QUICKBOOKS® 2013: A COMPLETE COURSE

QUICKBOOKS® 2013: A COMPLETE COURSE

Janet Horne, M.S.
Los Angeles Pierce College

PEARSON

Boston Columbus Indianapolis New York San Francisco Upper Saddle River

Amsterdam Cape Town Dubai London Madrid Milan Munich Paris Montreal Toronto

Delhi Mexico City Sao Paulo Sydney Hong Kong Seoul Singapore Taipei Tokyo

Editor in Chief: *Donna Battista*	Senior Operations Specialist: *Carol Melville*
Acquisitions Editor: *Victoria Warneck*	Media Procurement Specialist: *Ginny Michaud*
Editorial Project Manager: *Melissa Pellerano*	Cover Designer: *Anthony Gemmellaro*
Editorial Assistant: *Jane Avery*	Cover Photo: *Shutterstock/Vladitto*
Director of Marketing: *Maggie Moylan Leen*	Media Project Manager: *John Cassar*
Marketing Manager: *Alison Haskins*	Full-Service Project Management: *GEX Publishing Services*
Marketing Assistant: *Kimberly Lovato*	Printer/Binder: *R. R. Donnelley/Menasha*
Managing Editor: *Jeffrey Holcomb*	Cover Printer: *Lehigh-Phoenix Color/Hagerstown*
Production Project Manager: *Karen Carter*	Text Font: *Calibri*

Credits and acknowledgments borrowed from other sources and reproduced, with permission, in this textbook appear on the appropriate page within text.

Screen shots © Intuit Inc. All rights reserved.

Microsoft and/or its respective suppliers make no representations about the suitability of the information contained in the documents and related graphics published as part of the services for any purpose. All such documents and related graphics are provided "as is" without warranty of any kind. Microsoft and/or its respective suppliers hereby disclaim all warranties and conditions with regard to this information, including all warranties and conditions of merchantability, whether express, implied or statutory, fitness for a particular purpose, title and non-infringement. In no event shall Microsoft and/or its respective suppliers be liable for any special, indirect or consequential damages or any damages whatsoever resulting from loss of use, data or profits, whether in an action of contract, negligence or other tortious action, arising out of or in connection with the use or performance of information available from the services.

The documents and related graphics contained herein could include technical inaccuracies or typographical errors. Changes are periodically added to the information herein. Microsoft and/or its respective suppliers may make improvements and/or changes in the product(s) and/or the program(s) described herein at any time. Partial screen shots may be viewed in full within the software version specified.

Microsoft® and Windows® are registered trademarks of the Microsoft Corporation in the U.S.A. and other countries. This book is not sponsored or endorsed by or affiliated with the Microsoft Corporation.

Library of Congress Cataloging-in-Publication Data

Horne, Janet.
  QuickBooks 2013 : a complete course / Janet Horne, M.S., Los Angeles Pierce College.
    pages cm
  Includes index.
  ISBN-13: 978-0-13-302335-0
  ISBN-10: 0-13-302335-4
  1. QuickBooks. 2. Small business—Accounting—Computer programs. 3. Small business—Finance—Computer programs. I. Title.
  HF5679.H6638 2013
  657'.9042028553—dc23
                          2013008565

2 3 4 5 6 7 8 9 10 V064 18 17 16 15 14

ISBN 10: 0-13-302335-4
ISBN 13: 978-0-13-302335-0

To my family

BRIEF TABLE OF CONTENTS

TABLE OF CONTENTS

Preface

Chapter 3—Payables and Purchases: Service Business

Chapter 4—General Accounting and End-of-Period Procedures: Service Business

Chapter 6—Payables and Purchases: Merchandising Business

Chapter 7—General Accounting and End-of-Period Procedures: Merchandising Business

Your Name's Ultimate Golf Practice Set: Merchandising Business

Chapter 8—Payroll

Chapter 9—Creating a Company in QuickBooks®

PREFACE

QuickBooks® 2013: A Complete Course is a comprehensive instructional learning resource. The text provides training using the *QuickBooks® Premier Accountant 2013* accounting program (for simplicity, the program is referred to as *QuickBooks 2013* throughout the text). Even though the text was written using the 2013 Accountants version of QuickBooks Premier, it may be used with the Pro version of the program as well. (Because of the many differences between the Windows and Mac versions of QuickBooks, this text should not be used for training using QuickBooks for the Mac.)

ORGANIZATIONAL FEATURES

QuickBooks® 2013: A Complete Course is designed to present accounting concepts and their relationship to *QuickBooks® 2013.* Within each chapter, students learn the underlying accounting concepts and receive hands-on training on how to implement them in QuickBooks 2013. This is accomplished by using a variety of fictitious companies when analyzing and recording transactions for service and merchandising businesses. A single company is used within the chapters for a full business cycle. At the end of each chapter, a reinforcement application problem is completed using a different company. The same end-of-chapter company is used for the entire business cycle. In addition, at the end of every chapter, the concepts and applications learned are reinforced by the completion of true/false, multiple-choice, fill-in, and essay questions. There are three practice sets in the text. The first two include all the major concepts and transactions presented within an area of study. The third practice set is comprehensive and includes all the major concepts and transactions presented within the entire textbook.

The text introduces students to QuickBooks accounting for a service business, a merchandising business, payroll, and a company setup for QuickBooks. The appendices include information regarding QuickBooks Program Integration using Word, Excel, Outlook, and Apps; QuickBooks Features such as Calendar, QuickBooks Notes, Time Tracking, Job Costing and Tracking, Sending Merchandise using QuickBooks Shipping Manager, Price Levels, Batch Invoicing, Collections Center, Document Center, Attached Documents, Client Data Review, Customizing the Icon Bar, Classes, and QuickBooks Statement Writer; QuickBooks Online Features such as Intuit and the Internet, Internet Connection, Access QuickBooks' Online Features, Online Banking and Payments, Billing Solutions, Merchant Services and Intuit Payment Solutions, Direct Deposit, Online Backup Services, and Other Marketing Tools.

DISTINGUISHING FEATURES

Throughout the text, emphasis has been placed on the use of QuickBooks' innovative approach to recording accounting transactions based on a business form rather than using the traditional journal format. This approach, however, has been correlated to traditional accounting through adjusting entries, end-of-period procedures, and use of the "behind the scenes" journal.

Unlike many other computerized accounting programs, QuickBooks is user-friendly when corrections and adjustments are required. The ease of corrections and the ramifications as a result of this ease are explored thoroughly. With thorough exploration of the program in the text, students should be able to transition from training to using *QuickBooks® 2013* in an actual business.

Accounting concepts and the use of *QuickBooks® 2013* are reinforced throughout the text with the use of screen shots that show QuickBooks screens, completed transactions, and reports. Some reports are shown completely while others, due to space limitations, are only shown in part. However, instructor materials show all of the reports in full. To provide a real-world experience within the text, students are required to print many business forms and reports. However, instructors are free to customize printing requirements for their students.

Students develop confidence in recording business transactions using an up-to-date commercial software program designed for and used by businesses and accountants. The text uses a tutorial-style training method to guide the students in the use of QuickBooks in a step-by-step manner. In addition, there is extensive assignment material in the form of tutorials, end-of-chapter questions (true/false, multiple-choice, fill-in, and essay), and practice sets. The practice sets at the end of each section, provide reinforcement of the concepts learned and require students to analyze and record transactions without specific instructions on how to do something.

Students will explore and use many of the features of QuickBooks as it pertains to a service business and to a merchandising business, including recording transactions ranging from simple to complex, preparing a multitude of reports, closing an accounting period, compiling charts and graphs, creating a company, and preparing the payroll. Students also learn ways in which QuickBooks can be customized to fit the needs of an individual company.

If you need assistance with QuickBooks, go to www.QuickBooks.Com/Support and click on one of the Resource Centers for help. The Resource Centers include Install, Payroll Year End, Online Backup, Account, Connection Diagnostic Tool, and New User Resource. For specific information when installing the trial version of the software, please go to the Intuit Install Center at http://support.quickbooks.intuit.com/Support/InstallCenter/default.aspx

---

WHAT'S NEW TO THIS EDITION

Each version of QuickBooks comes with changes, enhancements, and new features. Many of these changes are incorporated into the text, while others may or may not be mentioned. Some of the features are only available on a subscription basis. Since the companies in the text are fictitious, the dates used are not current, and the subscriptions are not free; those areas are not explored in the greatest detail.

That being said, some of the new features and changes in the 2013 text include the following:

- ❖ Providing more explicit directions for installation and registration of the QuickBooks® 2013 Educational Trial Version of the program
- ❖ Addressing and using the "new look" for QuickBooks
- ❖ Customizing the placement of the Icon Bar
- ❖ Using updated pricing, tax rates, and payroll deductions
- ❖ Customizing additional forms including the Sales Order Invoice
- ❖ Viewing applied credits
- ❖ Re-calculating discounts based on the actual amounts owed after applying credits rather than always accepting QuickBooks' calculations.
- ❖ Restructuring the instruction, discussion, and printing of end-of-period reports
- ❖ Adding shipping addresses
- ❖ Viewing quantity available when processing invoices, sales receipts, and sales orders
- ❖ Using the History feature on invoices, sales receipts, and bills
- ❖ Exploring the Apps Center and some of the Apps available for integration with QuickBooks

COURSES

QuickBooks® 2013: A Complete Course is designed for a one-term course in microcomputer accounting. This text covers using QuickBooks in a service business, a merchandising business, a sole proprietorship, and a partnership. Preparing payroll and creating a new company are also included. When using the text, students should be familiar with the accounting cycle and how it is related to a business. No prior knowledge of or experience with computers, Windows, or QuickBooks is required; however, an understanding of accounting is essential to successful completion of the coursework.

SUPPLEMENTS FOR THE INSTRUCTOR

Pearson Education maintains a Web site where student and instructor materials may be downloaded for classroom use at **www.pearsonhighered.com/horne**. The *Instructor's Resource Center* contains the following:

- Data & Solution Files that include the following:
  - o Backup company files for each chapter that may be restored to a QuickBooks company file. These will be downloaded in several batches.
  - o Master data files for all the companies in the text. These are the same as the Student company files and will be downloaded in two groups: Chapters 1–4 and Chapters 5–8.
- Instructor Resource Manual (IM) materials including:
  - o An online appendix with instructions to install and register QuickBooks, download company files, open a company file, backup and restore company files
  - o Answers to the end-of-chapter questions
  - o Excel files for all the reports prepared in the text
  - o Lectures for each chapter designed for a hands-on demonstration lecture

- o Instructor's Manual Materials, which include:
  - Assignment Sheets for full- and short-term courses
  - IM Preface for instructors
  - IM Table of Contents listing all the files available for download
  - Teaching suggestions
- o Transmittal sheets that include the totals of reports and documents
- o Textbook errata, which is posted as errors are discovered
- PowerPoint Presentation containing lectures with notes for each chapter in the text including a separate lecture for installing and registering the QuickBooks Trial Version
- Solutions Manual containing Adobe.pdf files for all the printouts prepared in the text. (The Solutions Manual is also available in print.) In the chapters of the text, some reports that are printed are shown in a partial display due to space limitations. The full copies of the printed reports are included in this folder. While instructors may customize the printing required by students, everything that students are asked to print within the text are included in this folder.
- Test Bank contains four folders:
  - o Written Exams containing exams and keys for each area of study and a written final exam
  - o Folders for each practice set that contains a computer exam and an answer key for the practice set exam

ERRATA AND INSTRUCTOR COMMENTS

While I strive to write an error-free textbook, it is inevitable that some errors will occur. As I become aware of any errors, they will be added to an errata sheet that is posted in the Instructor's Resource Center on the Pearson Web site at **www.pearsonhighered.com/horne**. Once an errata is posted, instructors should feel free to share that information with their students and to check back periodically to see if any new items have been added. If you or your students discover an error, or have suggestions and/or concerns, I would appreciate it if you would contact me and let me know what they are. My email address for instructors is also shown in the Instructor's Resource Center.

ACKNOWLEDGMENTS

I wish to thank my colleagues for testing and reviewing the manuscript, the professors who use the text and share their thoughts and suggestions with me, and my students for providing me with a special insight into problems encountered in training. All of your comments and suggestions are greatly appreciated. A special thank you goes to Cheryl Bartlett for her proofreading and comments. In addition, I would like to thank Donna Battista, Victoria Warneck, Melissa Pellerano, and the production team at Pearson Education for their editorial support and assistance.

INTRODUCTION TO QUICKBOOKS® 2013 AND COMPANY FILES

LEARNING OBJECTIVES

At the completion of this chapter, you will be able to:

1. Identify QuickBooks desktop features, be familiar with the QuickBooks Centers, and understand the QuickBooks Home Page.
2. Recognize menu commands and use some keyboard shortcuts.
3. Recognize QuickBooks forms and understand the use of lists and registers in QuickBooks.
4. Access QuickBooks' reports and be familiar with QuickZoom.
5. Open and close QuickBooks
6. Copy a company file and open a company
7. Add your name to a company name
8. Access QuickBooks reports and be familiar with QuickZoom.
9. Prepare QuickBooks graphs and use QuickReport within graphs.
10. Use QuickMath and the Windows Calculator.
11. Download a company file
12. Back up a company
13. Restore a company from a backup file
14. Close a company

MANUAL AND COMPUTERIZED ACCOUNTING

The work performed to keep the books for a business is the same whether you use a manual or a computerized accounting system. Transactions need to be analyzed, recorded in a journal, and posted to a ledger. Business documents such as invoices, checks, bank deposits, and credit/debit memos need to be prepared and distributed. Reports to management and owners for information and decision-making purposes need to be prepared. Records for one business period need to be closed before recording transactions for the next business period.

In a manual system, each transaction that is analyzed must be entered by hand into the appropriate journal (the book of original entry where all transactions are recorded) and posted to the appropriate ledger (the book of final entry that contains records for all of the accounts used in the business). A separate business document such as an invoice or a check must be prepared and distributed. In order to prepare a report, the accountant or bookkeeper must go through the journal or ledger and look for the appropriate amounts to include in the report. Closing the books must be done item by item via closing entries, which are recorded in the journal and posted to the appropriate ledger accounts. After the closing entries are recorded, the ledger accounts must be ruled and balance sheet accounts must be reopened with Brought Forward Balances being entered. All of this is extremely time consuming.

When using a computerized system and a program such as QuickBooks, the transactions must still be analyzed and recorded. QuickBooks operates from a business document point of view. As a transaction occurs, the necessary business document (an invoice or a check, for example) is prepared. Based on the information given on the business document, QuickBooks records the necessary debits and credits behind the scenes in the Journal. If an error is made when entering a transaction, QuickBooks allows the user to return to the business document and make the correction. QuickBooks will automatically record the changes in the debits and credits in the Journal. If you want to see or make a correction using the actual debit/credit entries, QuickBooks allows you to view the transaction register and make corrections directly in the register or use the traditional General Journal. Reports and graphs are prepared by simply clicking "Report" on the menu bar.

VERSIONS OF QUICKBOOKS®

While this text focuses on training using QuickBooks® Premier Accountant 2013 (for simplicity in the text, the program is referred to as QuickBooks® 2013). The text may also be used with QuickBooks Pro and the industry specific versions of Premier. The Premier version of the program may be toggled to QuickBooks Pro and the following industry editions: General Business, Professional Bookkeeper, Contractor, Manufacturing & Wholesale, Nonprofit, and Professional Services. The Premier version offers some additional enhancements not available in the Pro version but the mechanics of using the programs are the same.

In addition to QuickBooks Premier, there is also QuickBooks Enterprise Solutions, which is designed for larger businesses that want a great deal of customization and have more complex accounting requirements.

There are several Online Editions of QuickBooks—Simple Start, Essentials, Plus, Essentials with Payroll, and Plus with Payroll--that are available online for a monthly fee. However, the functions available are limited and many features of QuickBooks cannot be utilized.

There is even a QuickBooks program for Macs that has many of the same functions as QuickBooks for Windows. (Because of the many differences between the Windows and Mac versions of QuickBooks, this text should not be used for training using QuickBooks for the Mac.)

For a comparison of features available among the different versions of the QuickBooks programs, access Intuit's Web site at www.quickbooks.intuit.com.

BEGIN COMPUTER TRAINING

 When you see this arrow, it means you will be performing a computer task. Sometimes the computer task will have several steps. Continue until all steps listed are completed.

INSTALL TRIAL VERSION OF QUICKBOOKS® PREMIER 2013 (OPTIONAL)

If you use your school's computers to complete the training in the text, you may omit this step. However, if the textbook containing the trial version of QuickBooks 2013 was ordered, you may install the software on your home computer. The school should have a site license for QuickBooks for classroom use.

If you already have any version of QuickBooks 2013 on your home computer, you may not install the Trial Version for 2013. For example, if you currently have QuickBooks Pro 2013, you may not install QuickBooks Premier Accountant 2013 on the same computer. Installing QuickBooks 2013 has no effect on earlier versions of QuickBooks that are currently installed on your home computer.

The free trial of the QuickBooks 2013 program may be installed on your computer and used for 160 days. However, you must register it within 30 days of installation. Without registration it's only good for 30 days.

If you run into difficulties with the installation, go to the Intuit Install Center at http://support.quickbooks.intuit.com/Support/InstallCenter/InstallCenter.aspx or www.quickbooks.com/support to find help on how to install QuickBooks.

 Install the Trial Version of QuickBooks® 2013

Insert the CD into your CD/DVD drive, wait for a period of approximately one minute, then follow the screens to install the software.
- If you get an AutoPlay screen, click **Run setup.exe** in the section for Install or run program from your media
- Depending on your Internet security system, you may get a screen after clicking Run asking you to allow Intuit to make changes to your computer. Anytime you get this type of message during the program installation, click Yes or OK.

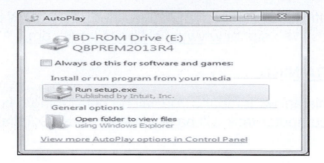

OR: If it the QuickBooks screen does not appear after several seconds,
   Click the **Start** button
   In the **Search programs and files** text box enter the location of your CD/DVD
      drive (**E:** in this example)
   Click **Setup**

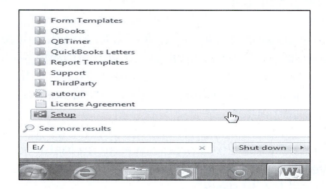

You should see the QuickBooks Premier 2013 screen
- As QuickBooks is updated by Intuit, the screens you see may change. If they do, simply follow the prompts given by QuickBooks to complete the installation.

After waiting for up to one minute, you should see the Intuit QuickBooks® Installer screen saying Welcome to QuickBooks

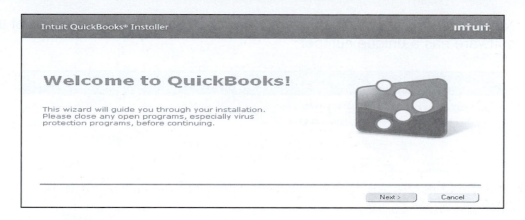

Click **Next**
Scroll through and read the License Agreement. After reading, click the checkbox for
    "I accept the terms of the license agreement"
Click **Next**

Use the **Express** installation; and then, click **Next**

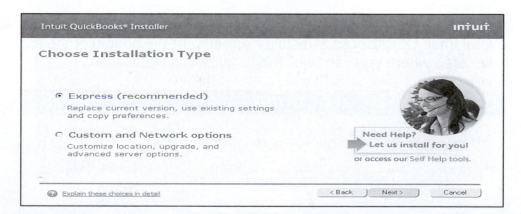

Enter the **License Number** and **Product Number** that appear on the CD cover,
- You will not need to enter any hyphens or tab between sections. QuickBooks
  automatically jumps from the License Number to the Product Number as well.

- No license or product numbers are shown below because each copy of the software has a unique number.

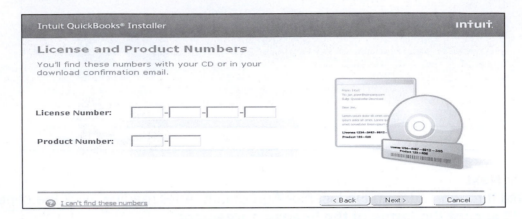

Click **Next**

Your license number, product number, and program location will be shown, click
   Install

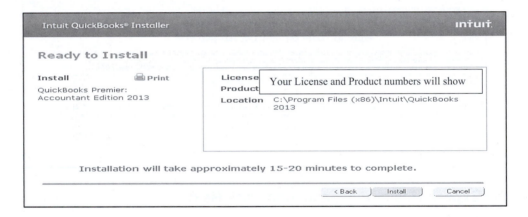

- During the program installation, which may take up to 20 minutes, you will get several Intuit QuickBooks ® Installer screens. At the bottom of the screen, is a status area where you can track the QuickBooks installation.

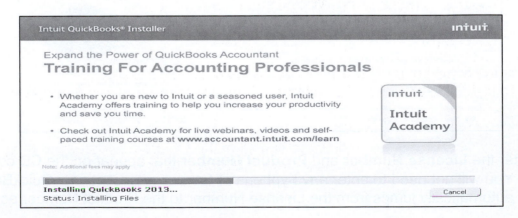

After a successful installation, you will get a congratulations screen

- If the Open QuickBooks and Help me get started are selected, click them to remove the check marks.

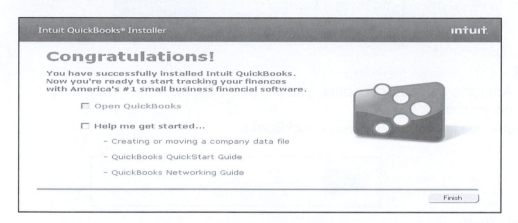

Click the **Finish** button to complete the installation
If you get a screen telling you to Reboot, click **Yes**

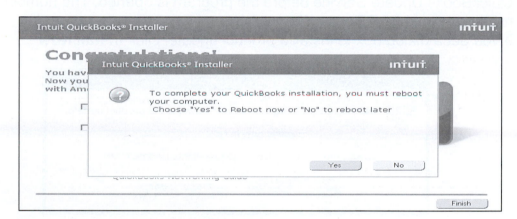

OPEN AND UPDATE QUICKBOOKS®

Once you are in Windows, opening QuickBooks is as easy as point and click. Note: instructions illustrate screens using Windows 7.

 Open QuickBooks

Click the **Start** button in the lower-left of the desktop
Point to **All Programs** and scroll through the list of programs and program
    folders
Click the **QuickBooks** folder
- You may have to scroll down to see all of the folders on your computer.
Click **QuickBooks Premier-Accountant Edition 2013**

OR

- After the computer reboots, you will see a QuickBooks Premier icon on your desk top

Double-click the icon to open QuickBooks

- QuickBooks is frequently updated. When you install your software, depending on the manufacture date of your program, you may get a message regarding QuickBooks Update Service before the program is opened. The number in the message could be R5 or another number.
- If you get a dialog box to install a product update, click **Install Now**

You will a see a QuickBooks Update screen while the update is being installed

When the update is complete, click **OK**

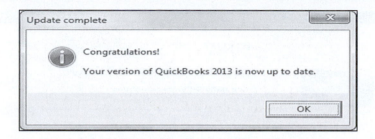

When QuickBooks is open you will see the title bar

- If you run into difficulties with the installation, go to the Intuit Install Center at http://support.quickbooks.intuit.com/Support/InstallCenter/default.aspx or www.quickbooks.com/support to find help on how to install QuickBooks.

REGISTER QUICKBOOKS® TRIAL VERSION

You may use QuickBooks for 30 days without registering the program. To use the Trial Version for 160 days, you must Register QuickBooks. Register QuickBooks is available on the Help menu only if you have not yet registered your copy of QuickBooks. You can verify that your copy of QuickBooks is registered by pressing the F2 key when QuickBooks is open. The Product Information window displays either REGISTERED or UNREGISTERED based on the registration status. Make sure to have your License Number and Product Number available.

 Register QuickBooks

If a Register QuickBooks Premier: Accountant Edition 2013 screen does not automatically appear, click the **Help** menu and click **Register QuickBooks**
- As QuickBooks is updated by Intuit, the screens you see may change. Most of the registration information required is the same. So, if the screens you see are different from the ones displayed in the text, complete the information in the order presented by QuickBooks.

Click **Register** on the Register QuickBooks screen

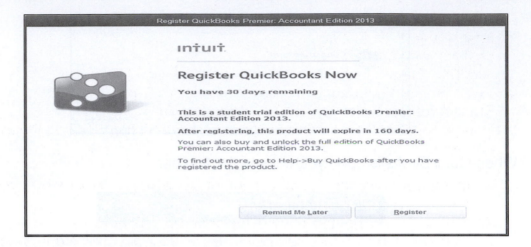

If you are online, you will be instructed to setup an Intuit Account

Click **Don't have an account** on the first screen

You will get a screen to Register QuickBooks and Create your Account

Enter your email address, enter a password, and then enter your password a second time

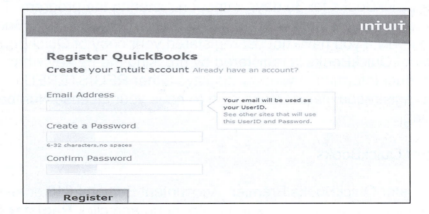

Click **Register**

Complete the information to Review your Customer Account

* If the order sequencing or the questions change from the list below, answer everything that appears with your actual information.

Enter the information for the fields with an asterisk as follows:

Company Information:

    Country: **United States**

    Company name: **Student**

    Industry: **Other**

    Address 1: Enter your actual address

    City: Enter your city

    State: Enter your state

    Zip/Postal Code: Enter your Zip or Postal Code

    Business Phone: Enter your phone number

Primary Contact:
  First Name: Your first name
  Last Name: Your last name
  Job Title: Other
  Work Phone: Your phone number
  Email Address: Enter your email address again
In the next section, click the drop-down list arrow and then click on the appropriate answer:
  Tell us about your company Contacts:
  1. Is this your company's first version of QuickBooks: **Yes** (unless you own a previous version of the program)
  2. Where did you get this copy of QuickBooks?: **Other**
  3. Number of full & part-time employees on your payroll?: **None, just myself**
  4. Does your company
     a. Accept credit cards? **No**
     b. Print checks? **Yes**
     c. Use a payroll service or payroll software? **No**
  For Accountants, Intuit ProAdvisors, and Intuit Solution Providers
     Are you an Accountant, Intuit ProAdvisor, or Intuit Solution Provider? **No**
Click **Next**
On the QuickBooks Registration – Confirmation screen, click **Start Using QuickBooks Now** under your Product Code or click **No Thanks, Start QuickBooks** at the bottom of the screen

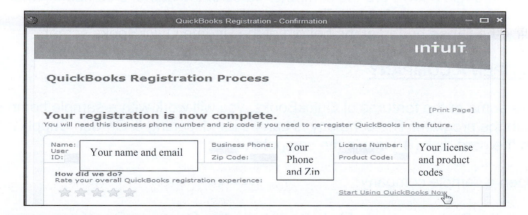

UPDATE QUICKBOOKS (OPTIONAL)

QuickBooks is setup to automatically update the program whenever Intuit releases new features, maintenance files, or other enhancements to the program. You may also update the program manually. This is especially important to do if you install a trial version of the software.

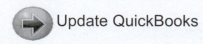 Update QuickBooks

- If you get a dialog box to install a product update, click **Install Now** (This is shown in the Open QuickBooks section.) When the update is complete, you will get a message box to restart your computer, click **Yes**.
Click the **Help** menu and click **Update QuickBooks…**
Click the **Update Now** tab
Click **Get Updates**

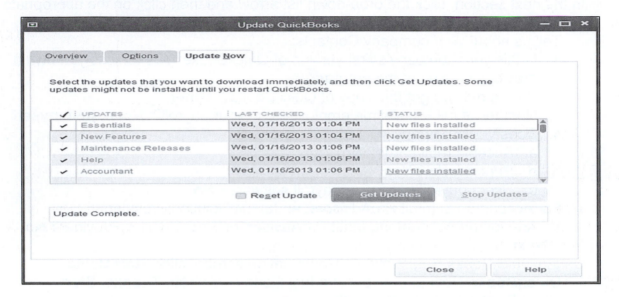

- The dates shown are the computer dates of the author's computer when different updates were performed. The dates will not match your dates
Click the **Close** button at the bottom of the Update QuickBooks screen

HOW TO OPEN A COMPANY

To explore some of the features of QuickBooks, you will work with a sample company that comes with the program. The company is Larry's Landscaping & Garden Supply and is stored on the hard disk (C:) inside the computer.

 Open a sample company

Click the **Open a sample file** button on the "No Company Open" screen
Click **Sample service-based business**

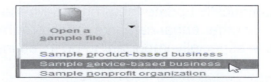

- If you get a Warning message box regarding the number of days left to use the Sample Company, click **OK**.

- When using the sample company for training, a warning screen will appear. This is to remind you NOT to enter the transactions for your business in the sample company. It will show a date that is several years into the future.

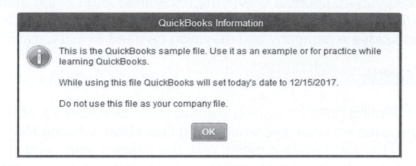

Click **OK** to accept the sample company data for use

VERIFY AN OPEN COMPANY

It is important to make sure you have opened the data for the correct company. Always verify the company name in the title bar. The title bar is located at the top of the screen and will tell you the name of the company and the program.

 Verify an open company

Check the **title bar** at the top of the QuickBooks screen to make sure it includes the company name. The title bar should show:

- If your title bar shows QuickBooks Premier Accountant 2013, that is fine. There is no difference in the program since QuickBooks Accountant is part of the Premier version of QuickBooks.
- Remember, throughout the text the program is referred to as QuickBooks 2013 rather than QuickBooks Premier or QuickBooks Accountant, etc.

QUICKBOOKS® DESKTOP FEATURES

Once you have opened a company, and the title bar displays the **Company Name - QuickBooks 2013.** (The following example shows: Sample Larry's Landscaping & Garden Supply – QuickBooks Accountant 2013.) Beneath the Title Bar, you will see the Menu Bar. There are Menu Commands that may be used to issue commands to QuickBooks.

Title Bar with Colored Flag and Menu Bar

MENU BAR

The first line displayed beneath the title bar is the **Menu Bar**. By pointing and clicking on a menu or using the keyboard shortcut of Alt+ the underlined letter in the menu item you will give QuickBooks the command to display the drop-down menu. For example, the File menu is used to open and close a company and may also be used to exit QuickBooks.

QUICKBOOKS MENUS

Menus can be the starting point for issuing commands in QuickBooks. Many commands will be the same as the ones you can give when using QuickBooks Home Page, which will be detailed later in the chapter. To use a menu, click the desired menu and click on the command you want to use. Notice that available keyboard shortcuts are listed next to the menu item. Click outside the menu to close it.

 Access each of the menus by clicking or pointing to each menu item

File menu is used to access company files and perform several other functions—New Company, New Company from an Existing Company File, Open or Restore Company, Open Previous Company, Open a Second Company, Back up Company, Create Copy, Close Company, Switch to Multi-user Mode, Utilities, Set Up Intuit Sync Manager, Accountant's Copy, Print, Save as PDF, Print Forms, Printer Setup, Send Forms, Shipping, Update Web Services, Toggle to Another Edition, and Exit.

Edit menu is used to make changes such as: Undo, Revert, Cut, Copy, Paste, Use Register, Use Calculator, Find, Search, and Preferences.

View menu is used to select the use of an Open Window List, Top Icon Bar, Left Icon Bar, Hide Icon Bar, Search Box, Customize Icon Bar, Add "Home" to Icon Bar, Favorites Menu, and One, or Multiple Windows.

Lists menu is used to show lists used by QuickBooks. These lists include: Chart of Accounts (the General Ledger), Item List, Fixed Asset Item List, Price Level List, Billing Rate Level List, Sales Tax Code List, Payroll Item List, Class List, Workers Comp List, Other Names List, Customer & Vendor Profile Lists, Templates, Memorized Transaction List, and Add/Edit Multiple List Entries.

Favorites menu is used to place your favorite or most frequently used commands on this list. It is customized with your selected commands.

Accountant menu is used to access the Accountant Center, the Chart of Accounts, and the Fixed Asset Item List. It is also used to Batch Enter Transactions, perform a Client Data Review, Make General Journal Entries, Send General Journal Entries, Reconcile (an account), prepare a Working Trial Balance, Set Closing Date, Condense Data, Remote Access to clients QuickBooks files, Manage Fixed Assets,

QuickBooks File Manager, use the QuickBooks Statement Manager, participate in the ProAdvisor Program, and use the Online Accountant Resources.

Company menu is used to access the Home Page, the Company Snapshot, the Calendar, Documents, and Lead Center. It is also used to change Company Information, Advanced Service Administration, Set Up Users and Passwords, Customer Credit Card Protection, Set Closing Date, Planning & Budgeting, access the To Do List, access Reminders, use the Alerts Manager, display the Chart of Accounts, Make General Journal Entries, Manage Currency, Enter Vehicle Mileage, and Prepare Letters with Envelopes.

Customers menu is used to access the Customer Center, Create Sales Orders, prepare Sales Order Fulfillment Worksheet, Create Invoices, Create Batch Invoices, Enter Sales Receipts, Enter Statement Charges, Create Statements, Assess Finance Charges, Receive Payments, Create Credit Memos/Refunds, and access the Lead Center. In addition, you may Add Credit Card Processing, Add Electronic Check Processing, Link Payment Service to Company File, and Intuit Payment Network. It is also used to access the Item List and to Change Item Prices.

Vendors menu is used to access the Vendor Center and the Item List. In addition, this menu is used to enter transactions to Enter Bills, Pay Bills, Sales Tax, Create Purchase Orders, Receive Items and Enter Bill, Receive Items, Enter Bill for Received Items, Inventory Activities, and Print/E-file 1099s.

Employees menu is used to access the Employee Center, the Payroll Center and the Billing Rate Level List; Pay Employees; prepare After-the-Fact Payroll, Add or Edit Payroll Schedules; Edit/Void Paychecks; process Payroll Taxes and Liabilities; access Payroll Tax Forms & W-2s; offer Labor Law Posters, access Workers Compensation; offer Intuit Health Benefits, perform My Payroll Service activities; Pay with Direct Deposit, Pay with Pay Card, Payroll Setup; Manage Payroll Items; and Get Payroll Updates.

Banking menu is used to Write Checks, Order Checks & Envelopes, Enter Credit Card Charges, Use Register, Make Deposits, Transfer Funds, Reconcile accounts, access Online Banking, use the Loan Manager, and access the Other Names List.

Reports menu is used to access the Report Center, access Memorized Reports, display the Company Snapshot, Process Multiple Reports, and use the QuickBooks Statement Writer. In addition, it is used to prepare reports in the following categories: Company & Financial; Customers & Receivables; Sales; Jobs, Time & Mileage; Vendors & Payables; Purchases; Inventory; Employees & Payroll; Banking; Accountant & Taxes; Budgets & Forecasts; List, and Industry Specific. You may also create Contributed Reports, Custom Reports; QuickReports, Transaction History; and a Transaction Journal.

Window menu is used to arrange icons, close all windows, to switch between windows that have been opened, and to tile or cascade open windows.

Help menu is used to access QuickBooks Help, Ask Intuit, find out What's New, access the Quick Start Center, Find Training, Learning Center Tutorials, Support, Find a Local QuickBooks Expert, and Send Feedback Online. The Help menu includes topics such as: Internet Connection Setup, Year-End Guide, Add QuickBooks Services, App Center: Find More Business Solutions, Update QuickBooks, Manage My License, Manage Data Sync, QuickBooks Privacy Statement, About Automatic Update, and About QuickBooks 2013. If QuickBooks has not been registered, you will also see the task Register QuickBooks.

ICON BAR

An icon bar contains small picture symbols called icons that may be clicked to give commands to QuickBooks. By default, QuickBooks® 2013 comes with a Left Icon Bar (shown below).

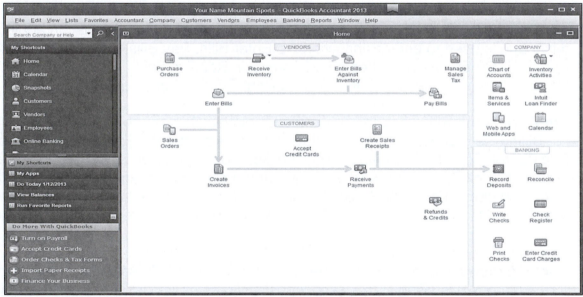

Home Page and Left Icon Bar

However, Left Icon bar has been changed to a Top Icon Bar that is used throughout the text. This is done to save screen space and to focus on tasks rather than shortcuts and Do More With QuickBooks. Once the Top Icon bar is selected, it will appear below the Menu bar and the Left Icon bar will not be seen. The Top Icon bar may be customized. The standard icon bar is divided into four specific areas: Home and Calendar, Snapshots and Command Centers, Command Icons, and Search. Depending on the screen size of your computer, not all of the icons may be displayed. This will be discussed later in the text.

 To change to the top-icon bar, Click the **View Menu**, and click **Top Icon Bar**

- If you already have the Top Icon Bar showing, there is no need to change it.

First Section of the Top Icon Bar:

QuickBooks Home is the first icon shown below the Menu bar and is used to go to the Navigator screen.

QuickBooks Calendar is used to maintain a monthly calendar and contains information for the To Do List, Upcoming: Next 7 days, and Due: Past 60 days.

Second Section of the Top Icon Bar:

QuickBooks Snapshots is next to the Calendar icon. When you click this icon, you may click on one of three tabs to get information about the Company, Payments, and Customer. The information displayed on each tab may be customized by selecting a variety of options.

QuickBooks Command Centers Next to the Company Snapshot icon there are icons for Centers. Each center goes to a specific list within the program. The centers are: Customers, Vendors, Employees, Online Banking, Docs, Reports, Statement Writer, and App Center.

Third Section of the Top Icon Bar:

Command Icons are used to give commands to QuickBooks by pointing to a picture and clicking the primary mouse button. Depending on the size of your monitor, you may or may not see the command icons. If they do not appear, click the ⟫ to show them.

Fourth Section of the Top Icon Bar:

QuickBooks Search is used to search through QuickBooks Help for information or the Company file for various transactions, accounts, items, customers, vendors, employees, etc.

QUICKBOOKS® COMPANY SNAPSHOTS AND CENTERS

As shown in the screenshot above, QuickBooks 2013 has buttons that allow access to the Company Snapshot and QuickBooks Centers. The snapshot and the centers focus on providing detailed information.

 Access the snapshots and each of the centers by clicking the appropriate icon beneath the menu bar and close each Snapshot or Center before opening the next one.

Snapshots provides three tabs used to display information about the company, payments, and customers. You may customize the Company Snapshot by clicking Add Content and selecting from among different options to determine what you want displayed.

To see how your business is doing, click the Company tab. When you click Add Content, there are 12 different items that may be displayed for the company. These options include listings or graphs for Account Balances, Previous Year Income Comparison, Income Breakdown, Previous Year Expense Comparison, Expense Breakdown, Income and Expense Trend, Top Customers by Sales, Best-Selling Items, Customers Who Owe Money, Top Vendors by Expense, Vendors to Pay, and Reminders; but may not be shown in the same order listed in this paragraph.

When you click the Payments tab, you may select from among seven options to display information about your company revenue. These include Recent Transactions, Receivables Reports, A/R by Aging Period, Invoice Payment Status, Customers Who Owe Money, QuickLinks, and Payment Reminders. These selections may be shown in an different order than described in this paragraph.

To view information regarding individual customers, click the Customer tab to select from among four items to display. These are Recent Invoices, Recent Payments, Sales History, and Best-Selling Items.

Customers Center shows a Customers & Jobs tab and a Transactions tab. The Customers & Jobs tab displays a list of customers and their balances, customer information and transactions for a selected customer. This is the default tab. Clicking the Transactions tab displays transaction categories and allows you to get information about transaction groups; such as, estimates, sales orders, invoices, statement charges, sales receipts, credit memos, and refunds.

In addition to information displayed on tabs, icons at the top of the Customers Center may be used to add New Customer & Job, enter New Transactions, and

Print. You may print Customer & Job List, Customer & Job Information, and Customer & Job Transaction List. Clicking the Excel button allows you to Export Customer List, Export Transactions, Import from Excel, and Paste from Excel. Clicking the Word button allows you prepare a letter to the customer whose information is displayed, Prepare Customer Letters, Prepare Collection Letters, and Customize Letter Templates. The Collections Center may be accessed to see which customers have Overdue and Almost Due balances.

Vendors Center has a Vendors tab and a Transactions tab. The Vendors tab allows you to display a list of vendors and their balances, vendor information and transactions for a selected vendor. This is the default tab. Clicking the Transactions tab displays transaction categories and allows you to get information about transaction groups; such as, purchase orders, item receipts, bills, bill payments, checks, credit card activities, and sales tax payments.

In addition to the information displayed on tabs, icons at the top of the Vendors Center may be used to add New Vendors and enter New Transactions. When the Print icon is clicked, the Vendor List, Vendor Information, and Vendor Transaction List may be printed. When the Excel icon is clicked; Vendor List and Vendor Transactions may be exported to or imported or pasted from Excel. When the Word icon is clicked, a variety of letters applicable to vendors may be prepared and letter templates may be customized.

Employees Center has an Employees tab, a Transactions tab, and a Payroll tab. The Employees tab allows you to display a list of employees, employee information and payroll transactions for a selected employee and is the default tab. Clicking the Transactions tab displays transaction categories and allows you to get information about transaction groups; such as, paychecks, liability checks, liability adjustments, year-to-date adjustments, and non-payroll transactions. The Payroll tab provides information regarding payroll dates, payroll taxes, and payroll forms.

In addition to the information displayed on the three tabs, each tab has a set of icons that may be used. On the Employees tab, you may add New Employees and Manage Employee Information. Paychecks may be printed and paystubs may be printed or emailed. The Employee List, Employee Information, and the Employee Transaction List may be printed. The Employee List, Transactions, Client-Ready Payroll Reports and Summarized Payroll Data may be exported to Excel. Word may be used to prepare letters applicable to employees. The Transactions tab has icons to add a New Employee, Manage Employee Information, Print a Transaction Report, and export information to Excel. The Payroll tab allows printing of Paychecks and Paystubs. Client-Ready Payroll Reports may be prepared if you subscribe to Enhanced Payroll for Accountants, information may be obtained regarding My Payroll Service, and Learning Resources for the Payroll Learning Center, a Payroll How To Guide, Payroll News and Updates, Payroll User Community, Tax Tools and

Resources, Support, Customer Service, and Internal Revenue Service may be accessed.

Online Banking Center allows you to perform online banking transactions through the center. You select whether information will be displayed in a Side-by-Side Mode or in a Register Mode.

Docs Center keeps track of documents you use with QuickBooks. It allows you to Add a Document to the Doc Center from your computer or scanner. You may attach documents, view and add document details, search for documents, detach documents, and remove documents from the Doc Center. Documents may be items such as receipts, spreadsheets, bills, invoices, etc.

Reports Center accesses the Reports available in QuickBooks and allows all of them to be prepared. These include specific reports, such as, Profit & Loss, Balance Sheet, Tax Reports, Transaction Detail Reports, Journal, General Ledger, Trial Balance, Income Tax Summary, Income Tax Detail, and an Audit Trail. Reports specific to payroll, customers, vendors, inventory, purchases, banking, and taxes may be prepared. Memorized, Favorites, Recent, and Contributed reports are available. The Report Center lists reports by category. The categories are: Company & Financial; Customers & Receivables; Sales; Jobs, Time & Mileage; Vendors & Payables; Purchases; Inventory; Employees & Payroll; Banking; Accountant & Taxes; Budgets & Forecasts; List, Contractor, Mfg & Wholesale, Professional Services, Retail, and Nonprofit. The available reports in each category may be displayed in a carousel view, a list view, or a grid view.

Statement Writer is a feature that is installed separately and provides a "live link" between QuickBooks Accountant and Microsoft Office. Once this feature is installed, it enables you to set preferences and formats for your reports, design new financial reports, open an existing financial report, and create a new financial report from an existing one. There are one button updates that make creating new statements faster than ever and you are able to compile documents and statements into PDF format to present professional reports

App Center is a link to Intuit apps for Mobile, Billing and Invoicing, Customer Management (CRM), Collaboration, Expense Management, and more. Some Apps are free and others require a subscription service.

COMMAND ICON BAR

In addition to giving commands via QuickBooks Menus, they may be given by clicking command icons on the icon bar. The command section of the icon bar has a list of buttons

(icons) that may be clicked in order to access activities, lists, or reports. The icon bar may be turned on or off and it may be customized. If there is a double >> at the edge of the icon bar, that means that there are more icons available for use.

QUICKBOOKS® ACCOUNTANT CENTER

If the company has selected to "Show Accountant Center when opening a company file," the Accountant Center will appear whenever the company is opened. It if doesn't open automatically, simply click the Accountant menu and then click Accountant Center. The Accountant Center has Tools that may be customized and used for: Lists, Accountant, Company, Customers, Vendors, Employees, and Banking. Within each category, many QuickBooks tasks can be selected as Tools. In the Accountant Center you may select an account for reconciliation, select memorized reports, and get accountant updates.

QUICKBOOKS® HOME PAGE

The QuickBooks Home Page allows you to give commands to QuickBooks according to the type of transaction being entered. The Home Page tasks are organized into logical groups (Vendors, Customers, Employees, Company, and Banking). Each of these areas on the Home Page is used to enter different types of transactions. When appropriate, the Home Page shows a flow chart with icons indicating the major activities performed. The icons are arranged in the order in which transactions usually occur. Depending on the type of company in use, the icons on the Home Page may change.

Information regarding Getting Started, Account Balances, Do More with QuickBooks, Backup Status, and Reminders & Alerts is displayed on the right side of the Home Page and may be expanded or minimized.

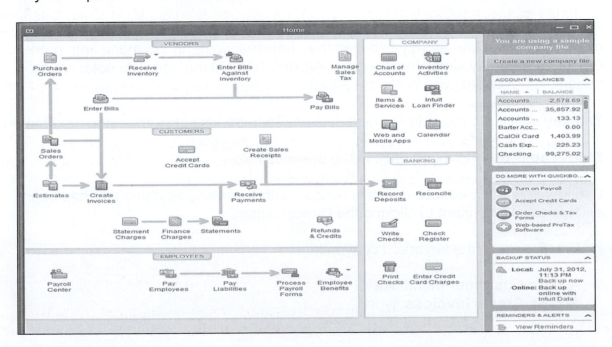

View each of the areas on the Home Page:

Vendors allows service and merchandising businesses to enter bills and to record the payment of bills. Companies with inventory can create purchase orders, receive inventory items, enter bills against inventory, and manage sales tax.

Customers allows you to record transactions associated with cash sales, credit sales, cash receipts, refunds and credits. If you create estimates, accept sales orders, issue statements, or charge finance charges, these are entered in this section as well.

Employees allows access to the Payroll Center, paychecks to be created, payroll liabilities to be paid, payroll forms to be processed, and employee benefits to be accessed.

Company allows you to display information about your company. There are graphic icons used to display the Chart of Accounts, Inventory Activities, Items & Services, Intuit Loan Finder, Web and Mobile Apps, and Calendar.

Banking allows you to Record Deposits, Write Checks, Print Checks, Reconcile Balance Sheet Accounts, Access the Check Register, and Enter Credit Card Charges.

KEYBOARD CONVENTIONS

When using Windows, there are some standard keyboard conventions for the use of certain keys. These keyboard conventions also apply to QuickBooks and include:

Alt key is used to access the drop-down menus on the menu bar. Rather than click on a menu item, press the Alt key and type the underlined letter in the menu item name. Close the menu by simply pressing the Alt key. *Note*: Menu items do not have an underlined letter until you press the Alt key.

Tab key is used to move to the next field or, if a button is selected, to the next button.

Shift+Tab is used to move back to the previous field.

Esc key is used to cancel an active window without saving anything that has been entered. It is equivalent to clicking the Cancel button.

 Practice using the keyboard conventions:

Access **Customer** menu: **Alt+U**
Access **Create Invoices**: type **I**

- Note: Ctrl + I is shown on the menu. This is a keyboard shortcut that may be used to open an invoice without using the Customer menu.
  Press **Tab** key to move forward through the invoice, press **Shift+Tab** to move back through the invoice, press **Esc** to close the invoice

ON-SCREEN HELP

QuickBooks has on-screen help, which is similar to having the QuickBooks reference manual available on the computer screen. Help can give assistance with a particular function you are performing. QuickBooks Help also gives you information about the program using an on-screen index. Help may be accessed to obtain information on a variety of topics, and it may be accessed in different ways:

To find out about the window in which you are working, press F1, click on the list of relevant topics displayed and read the information given; or enter the topic you wish to view, and then click the Start Search button .

To learn about the new features available in QuickBooks, click QuickBooks Help on the Help Menu, type "New Features" in the "Have a Question?" textbox, click the Start Search button.

When the topic for Help has been located, a list of results will be shown. Click on the result you want information about. The information is provided in the Help Article. If there is more information than can be shown on the screen, scroll bars will appear on the right side of the Help screen. A scroll bar is used to show or go through information. As you scroll through Help, information at the top of the Help screen disappears from view while new information appears at the bottom of the screen.

Sometimes words appear in blue in the QuickBooks Help screen. Clicking on the blue word(s) will give you more information or will take you to other topics.

Often, the onscreen help provides links to an external Web site. To visit these links, you must have an Internet connection and be online. The Have a Question? Screen will show Ask Community.

If you want to see a different topic, you may type in different key words at the top of the Have a Question? Screen and then click the Search button. Information will be provided on the new topic.

If you want to print a copy of the QuickBooks Help screen, click the Printer icon at the top of the Help Article. You may close a QuickBooks Help Article or Have a Question? by clicking the Close button ⊠ in the upper right corner of the screen.

To get additional information on how to use QuickBooks or to enter a question and get immediate answers drawn from the QuickBooks Help system and the technical support database, click the Help menu and click Support.

PRACTICE USING HELP SEARCH TO FIND KEYBOARD SHORTCUTS

Frequently, it is faster to use a keyboard shortcut to give QuickBooks a command than it is to point and click the mouse through several layers of menus or icons. The list of common keyboard shortcuts may be obtained by using Help.

Use Help
    Click **Help** on the Menu bar
Click **QuickBooks Help**
Type **keyboard shortcuts** in the textbox
Click the **Search** button
Look at the list of topics provided

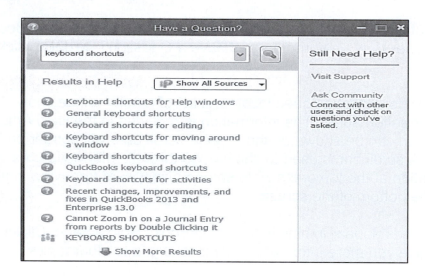

    Click **QuickBooks keyboard shortcuts** and view the results

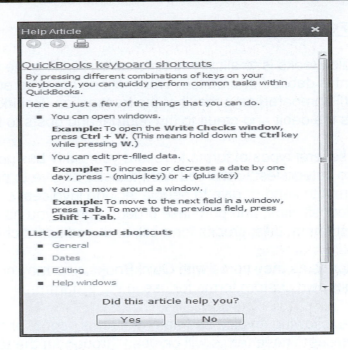

Click **General** in the list of keyboard shortcuts to see the General keyboard shortcuts

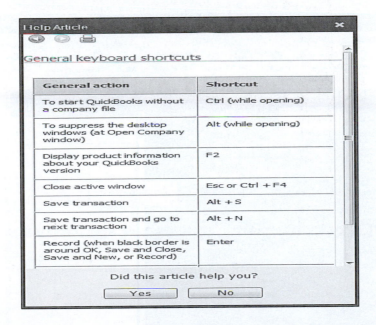

- As an option, if you wish to let Intuit know if the article helped you, click either Yes or No.

Click the **Close** button in the upper right corner of the Help Article and Have a Question? screens

QUICKBOOKS® FORMS

The premise of QuickBooks is to allow you to focus on running the business, not deciding whether an account is debited or credited. Transactions are entered directly onto the business form that is prepared as a result of the transaction. Behind the scenes, QuickBooks enters the debit and credit to the Journal and posts to the individual accounts.

QuickBooks uses several types of forms to record your daily business transactions. They are divided into two categories: forms you want to send or give to people and forms you have received. Forms to send or give to people include invoices, sales receipts, credit memos, checks, deposit slips, and purchase orders. Forms you have received include payments from customers, bills, credits for a bill, and credit card charge receipts.

You may use the forms as they come with QuickBooks, you may change or modify them, or you may create your own custom forms for use in the program.

 Examine the following invoice and note the terms, icons, and buttons listed as they apply to invoices. These terms will be used throughout the text when giving instructions for entries.

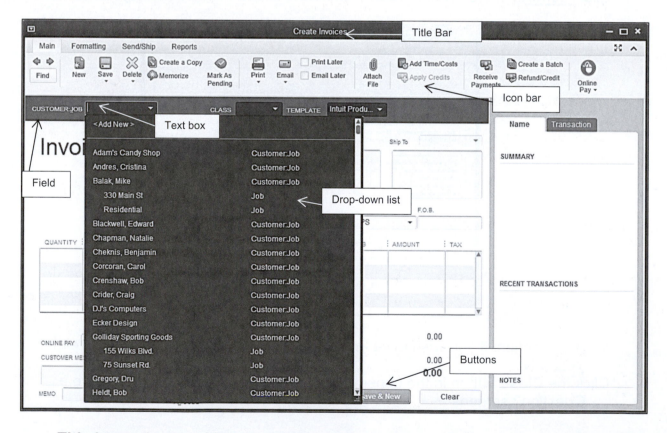

Title bar at the top of form indicates what you are completing. In this case, it says **Create Invoices**. The title bar also contains some buttons. They include:

Minimize button ☐ clicking this will remove the form from the screen but still leave it open. You may click the form on the Taskbar to re-display it.

Maximize ☐ **or restore button** ☐ enlarges the form to fill the screen or restores the form to its previous size

Close button ☒ closes the current screen.

- Depending on the size of your screen, the task for Create Invoices may be shown on the QuickBooks title bar. (See below) If this happens, the buttons on the title bar are applicable to the program. Clicking on the Close button on the title bar will close QuickBooks, which could result in the loss of data. Clicking on the separate Close button located on the menu bar just below the one for QuickBooks will close the invoice.

Field is an area on a form requiring information. Customer:Job is a field.
Text box is the area within a field where information may be typed or inserted. The area to be filled in to identify the Customer:Job is a text box.

Drop-down list arrow appears next to a field when there is a list of options available. On the invoice for Larry's Landscaping & Garden Supply, clicking the drop-down list arrow for Customer:Job will display the names of all customers who have accounts with the company. Clicking a customer's name will insert the name into the text box for the field.

Buttons on the bottom of the invoice are used to give commands to QuickBooks.

Save & Close   Save & New   Clear

Save & Close button is clicked when all information has been entered for the invoice and you are ready for QuickBooks to save the invoice and exit the Create Invoices screen.

Save & New button is clicked when all information has been entered for the invoice and you are ready to complete a new invoice.

Clear button is clicked if you want to clear the information entered on the current invoice.

Icon bar is at the top of the invoice just below the title bar. It has four tabs containing icons that are used to give commands to QuickBooks or to get information regarding linked or related transactions. If an icon has an arrow at the bottom, it means that there is a variety of choices/commands that may be selected.

Main Tab Icons include:

Previous is clicked to go back to the previous invoice. This is used when you want to view, print, or correct the previous invoice. Each time the Previous icon is clicked, you go back one invoice. You may click the Previous icon until you go all the way back to invoices with opening balances.

Next is clicked to go to the next invoice after the one you entered. If the invoice on the screen has not been saved, this saves the invoice and goes to the next invoice. The next invoice may be one that has already been created and saved or it may be a blank invoice.

Find is used to find invoices previously prepared.

New is clicked to create a new invoice

Save is clicked to save the invoice and leave it on the screen. The arrow at the bottom of the Save icon means you can save it in more than one way. An invoice may be saved as a QuickBooks invoice and as a PDF file.

Delete will delete the invoice. To void the invoice, click the arrow at the bottom and then click Void.

Create a Copy allows you to make a copy of the invoice using a new number. This invoice may be edited and saved.

Memorize allows QuickBooks to save an invoice as a template for future use.

Mark As Pending saves the invoice but doesn't record the accounting behind the scenes. Later, the invoice may be marked as Final to record the accounting.

Print is used to print the invoice. The arrow at the bottom of the icon may be clicked so you can preview an invoice. Other choices include printing an invoice, a batch of invoices, packing slips, shipping labels, and envelopes. You may also save the invoice as PDF file. There is a checkbox that may be clicked so the invoice may be printed later.

Email is used to e-mail an invoice or a batch of invoices. It, too, has a checkbox that may be clicked so the invoice is emailed later.

Attach File attaches a file or a scanned document to this invoice.

Add Time/Costs adds any costs you marked as billable to this Customer:Job.

Apply Credits is used to apply an existing credit for this Customer:Job to this invoice. A credit for a return or overpayment is recorded as a Credit Memo.

Receive Payments is used to record the receipt of payment for this invoice.

Create a Batch creates one invoice to send to multiple customers.

Refund/Credit enables you to create a Credit Memo using the items and prices on this invoice. It may be edited and saved and is an alternate method to preparing a Credit Memo in Refunds & Credits.

Online Pay is used to accept customer invoice payments on line. This is a fee for service feature and requires a subscription.

Formatting Tab Icons include:

Preview allows you to see how the printed invoice will look

Manage Templates allows you to view a list of standard forms available in QuickBooks. These may be copied, edited, and customized.

Download Templates allows you to download preformatted forms that are customized.

Customize Data Layout allows you to customize the information that appears and where it appears on the form your customer sees.

Spelling is used to check the spelling in the item descriptions.

Insert Line will insert a blank line above the selected item so additional text may be added, extra space may be created, or a new line item may be inserted.

Delete Line is used to delete a selected line item.

Customize Design allows online form customization and requires an online Intuit account so you can save your designs.

Send/Ship Tab Icons include:

Email is used to email the current invoice, invoices marked to email, and batch invoices.

FedEx, UPS, and **USPS** allow you to send/ship packages, find drop off locations, schedule pickups, and track packages; as well as, setup accounts for shipping.

Mail Invoice uses QuickBooks Billing Solution to mail invoices.

Prepare Letter uses Microsoft ® Word to create letters and envelopes for customers using templates provided by QuickBooks. These templates may be edited and/or customized.

Reports Tab Icons include:

QuickReport is used to display transactions for the Customer:Job on this invoice.

Transaction History is a report that lists all transactions that are linked to this invoice.

Transaction Journal displays a report showing the journal entry that QuickBooks makes behind the scenes for this invoice.

QUICKBOOKS® LISTS

In order to expedite entering transactions, QuickBooks uses lists as an integral part of the program. Customers, vendors, sales items, and accounts are organized as lists. In fact, the chart of accounts is considered to be a list in QuickBooks. Frequently, information can be entered on a form by clicking on a list item.

Most lists have a maximum. However, it's unlikely that you'll run out of room on your lists. With so many entries available, there is room to add list items "on the fly" as you work. The vendors, customers, and employees lists are all provided in the related Centers. If you open the Customer Center, the Customer List will appear on the left side of the Center as follows:

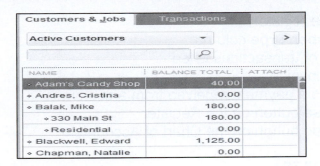

 Examine several lists:

Click the **Customers** icon on the Top Icon Bar to view the list of customers (in accounting concepts this is referred to as the Accounts Receivable Subsidiary Ledger), click the **Close** button to exit

Click the **Lists** menu, click **Chart of Accounts** to view the Chart of Accounts, click the **Close** button to exit

Click the **Vendors** icon on the Top Icon Bar to view the list of vendors (in accounting concepts this is referred to as the Accounts Payable Subsidiary Ledger)

Click the **Close** button to exit

QUICKBOOKS® REGISTERS

QuickBooks prepares a register for every balance sheet account. An account register contains records of all activity for the account. Registers provide an excellent means of looking at transactions within an account. For example, the Accounts Receivable register maintains a record of every invoice, credit memo, and payment that has been recorded for credit customers (in accounting concepts this is the Accounts Receivable account).

 Examine the Accounts Receivable Register

Click **Chart of Accounts** in the Company section of the Home Page
Click **Accounts Receivable**
Click the **Activities** button at the bottom of the screen
Click **Use Register**

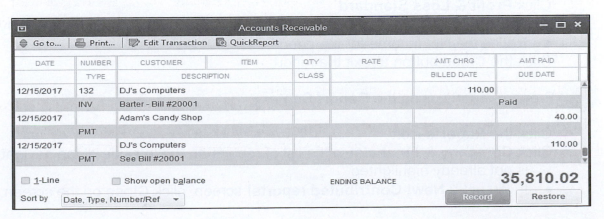

Scroll through the register
Look at the **Number/Type** column
Notice the types of transactions listed:

      INV is for an invoice
      PMT indicates a payment received from a customer
      Click the **Close** button on the Register
      Click the **Close** button on the Chart of Accounts

QUICKBOOKS® REPORTS

Reports are an integral part of a business. Reports enable owners and managers to determine how the business is doing and to make decisions affecting the future of the company. Reports can be prepared showing the profit and loss for the period, the status of the Balance Sheet (assets equal liabilities plus owner's equity), information regarding accounts receivable and accounts payable, and the amount of sales for each item. QuickBooks has a wide range of reports and reporting options available. Reports may be customized to better reflect the information needs of a company. Reports may be generated in a variety of ways.

Reports menu includes a complete listing of the reports available in QuickBooks and is used to prepare reports including: company and financial reports such as profit and loss (income statement), balance sheet; accounts receivable reports; sales reports; accounts payable reports; budget reports; banking reports; transaction detail reports; payroll reports; budget and forecast reports; list reports; industry specific reports; custom reports; graphs showing graphical analysis of business operations; and several other classifications of reports.

Reports Center includes a complete listing of the reports available in QuickBooks. Reports may be shown in a Carousel view, a Grid view, and a List view.

 Prepare reports from the **Reports** menu

    Click **Reports** on the menu bar
    Point to **Company & Financial**
    Click **Profit & Loss Standard**
    Scroll the Profit and Loss Statement for Larry's Landscaping & Garden Supply
    •   Notice the Net Income for the period.
    Click the **Close** button to exit the report

 Prepare reports using the **Report Center**

    Click the **Reports** icon
    Click **Company & Financial** in the list of reports on the left side of the navigator if it
        is not already highlighted
    •   If you get a **New! Contributed reports!** screen, click **Close** on the screen.

Explore the report list view options by clicking the following buttons in the upper-right corner of the Report Center:

Click the button for **Carousel View**
- Sample reports revolve when clicked and are shown in the correct format.

Click the button for **Grid View**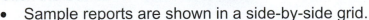
- Sample reports are shown in a side-by-side grid.

Click the button for **List View**
- Reports and a brief description are listed.

Scroll through the list of reports available until you see Balance Sheet Standard
Click **Balance Sheet Standard**

Balance Sheet Standard

What is the value of my company (its assets, liabilities, and equity), showing me the individual balances for each account?

| Run | Info | Fave | Help | Dates: This Fiscal Year-to-date ▾ | 10/1/2017 | 12/15/2017 |

Click the green **Run** button to display the report
Scroll through the report
- Notice that Total Assets equal Total Liabilities & Equity.

Do not close the report

QUICKZOOM

QuickZoom allows you to view transactions that contribute to the data on reports or graphs.

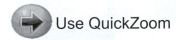 Use QuickZoom

Scroll through the Balance Sheet on the screen until you see the fixed asset Truck
Position the mouse pointer over the amount for **Total Truck**

- The mouse pointer turns into 🔍.

Double-click the mouse to see the transaction detail for the Total Truck
Click the **Close** button to close the **Transactions by Account** report
Click the **Close** button to close the **Balance Sheet**
Do <u>not</u> close the Report Center

QUICKBOOKS® GRAPHS

Using bar charts and pie charts, QuickBooks gives you an instant visual analysis of different elements of your business. You may obtain information in a graphical form for Income & Expenses, Sales, Accounts Receivable, Accounts Payable, Net Worth, and Budget vs. Actual. For example, using the Report Center and Company & Financial as the type of report, double-clicking Net Worth Graph allows you to see an owner's net worth in relationship to assets and liabilities. This is displayed on a bar chart according to the month. To obtain information about liabilities for a given month, you may zoom in on the liabilities portion of the bar, double-click, and see the liabilities for the month displayed in a pie chart.

 View a Graph

> Report Center should be on the screen
> **Company & Financial** is the **Type of Report**
>
> Click the **Carousel View** button
> As you use the bottom scroll bar to scroll through the reports, you will see samples displayed
> Scroll through the list of reports, click **Net Worth Graph**,

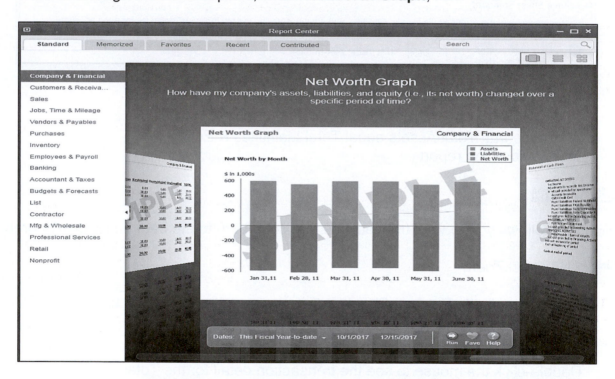

Click **Run** and then view the Net Worth Graph

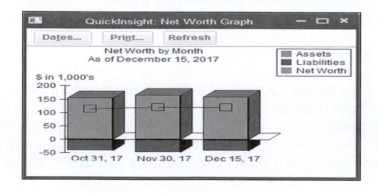

Zoom in on the Liabilities for October by pointing to the liabilities portion of the graph and double-clicking

View the pie chart for October's liabilities

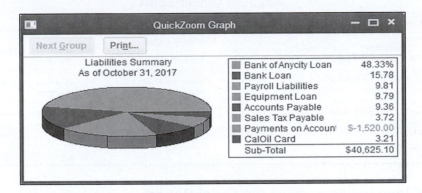

Click the **Close** button to close the pie chart
Zoom in on the **Net Worth** for **December** and double-click
View the pie chart for **December's Net Worth Summary**
Use the keyboard shortcut **Ctrl+F4** to close the pie chart
Click the **Close** button to close the Net Worth graph
Close the **Report Center**

QUICKREPORT

QuickReports are reports that give you detailed information about items you are viewing. They look just like standard reports that you prepare but are considered "quick" because you don't have to go through the Reports menu or Reports Center to create them. For example, when you are viewing the Employee List, you can obtain information about an individual employee simply by clicking the employee's name in the list, clicking the Reports button, and selecting QuickReports from the menu.

 View a QuickReport

Click **Lists** on the menu bar
Click **Chart of Accounts**
Click **Prepaid Insurance**
Click **Reports** button at the bottom of the Chart of Accounts List
Click **QuickReport: Prepaid Insurance**

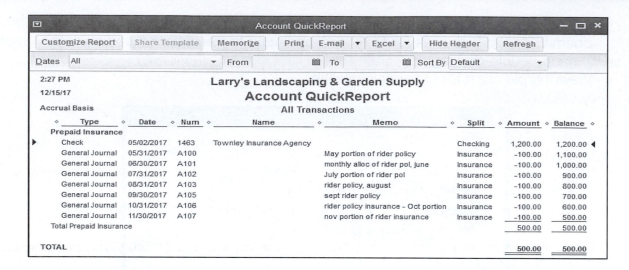

Click the **Close** button to close the **QuickReport**
Click the **Close** button to close the **Chart of Accounts**

HOW TO USE QUICKMATH

QuickMath is available for use whenever you are in a field where a calculation is to be made. Frequently, QuickBooks will make calculations for you automatically; however, there may be instances when you need to perform the calculation. For example, on an invoice, QuickBooks will calculate an amount based on the quantity and the rate given for a sales item. If for some reason you do not have a rate for a sales item, you may use QuickMath to calculate the amount. To do this, you tab to the amount column, type an **=** or a number and the **+**. QuickBooks will show an adding machine tape on the screen. You may then add, subtract, multiply, or divide to obtain a total or a subtotal. Pressing the enter key inserts the amount into the column.

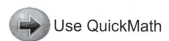 Use QuickMath

Click the **Create Invoices** icon on the Home Page
Click in the **Amount** column on the Invoice

Enter the numbers: **123+**
456+
789

	123.00
+	456.00
+	789

Press **Enter**
The total **1,368** is inserted into the Amount column
Click the **Clear** button to remove the total amount of **1,368**, do not close the invoice

HOW TO USE WINDOWS® CALCULATOR

Windows includes accessory programs that may be used to complete tasks while you are working in QuickBooks. One of these accessory programs is Calculator. Using this program gives you an on-screen calculator. To use the Calculator in Windows, click Start, click All Programs, click the Accessories folder, click Calculator. A calculator appears on your screen. The Windows calculator is also accessible through QuickBooks.

 Access Windows Calculator through QuickBooks

Click **Edit** on the menu bar
Click **Use Calculator**
Change from a standard calculator to a scientific calculator: click the **View** menu on the Calculator menu bar, click **Scientific**
- In addition to standard and scientific, you may also select programmer or statistics
Change back to a standard calculator: click the **View** menu on the Calculator menu bar, click **Standard**
Numbers may be entered by:
Clicking the number on the calculator
Keying the number using the numeric keypad
Typing the keyboard numbers
Enter the numbers: **123+**
456+
789+
The amount is subtotaled after each entry
After typing 789+, the answer 1368 appears automatically

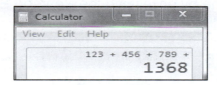

- Note: Using the Windows Calculator does not insert the amount into a QuickBooks form.
To clear the answer, click the **C** button on the calculator
Enter: **55*6**
Press **Enter** or click **=** to get the answer 330
- Again, note that answer is not inserted into the invoice.
Click **Control menu icon** (the picture of the Calculator on the left side of the calculator title bar), click **Close** to close the **Calculator**
Click the **Close** button on the Invoice to close the invoice without saving

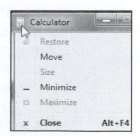

HOW TO CLOSE A COMPANY

The sample company—Larry's Landscaping & Garden Supply—will appear as the open company whenever you open QuickBooks. In order to discontinue the use of the sample company, you must close the company. In a classroom environment, you should always back up your work and close the company you are using at the end of a work session. If you use different computers when training, not closing a company at the end of each work session may cause your files to become corrupt, your disk to fail, or leave unwanted .qbi (QuickBooks In Use) files on your data disk.

 Close a company

>   Click **File** menu, click **Close Company**
>   Close **QuickBooks**
>   If you get a message regarding Exiting QuickBooks, click the check box for **"Do not display this message in the future,"** and then click **Yes**

COMPANY FILES

When working in QuickBooks, you will use files that contain data for companies that are in the text. Before beginning to use the program, you need to get a working copy of the company files. This may be done by accessing the Pearson Education Web Site. Instructions follow for downloading and extracting files.

DOWNLOAD COMPANY FILES

The company files for the text are available on the Prentice Hall web site http://www.pearsonhighered.com/horne/.

 Download company files

>   Insert your USB drive into your computer or ask you professor for specific directions to be used at your school
>   Open **Internet Explorer** or whatever browser you use
>   Enter the address **http://www.pearsonhighered.com/horne/**
>   • Sometimes it is difficult to read "horne" so, remember the name is HORNE.
>   • Note: At the time of writing, a temporary cover image was posted. The actual cover will change when the site is finalized.
>   • When completing the following steps, be sure to use the section for the QuickBooks 2013 edition of the text.
>   • Check with your instructor to determine if you will use a different procedure.
>   Click **Company Master Files** Chapters 1-4 (Student Data Files) next to the QuickBooks 2013 cover image

You will download the files for Chapters 1, 2, 3, 4, and the Service practice set at this time. When you get to Chapter 5, you will download the remaining company files from Company Master Files Chapters 5-8 (Student Data Files).

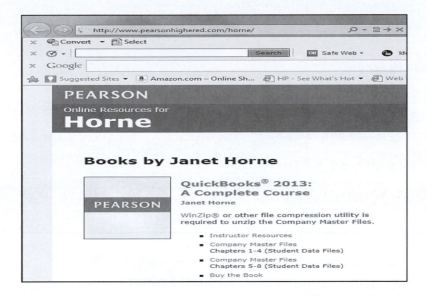

- Depending on your version of Windows and Internet Explorer, your screens may be different from the examples shown.

On the Windows Internet Explorer screen, click **Save as**

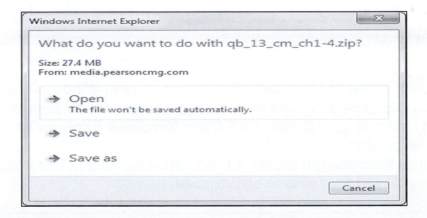

When the **Save As** screen appears, scroll through the listing on the left side of the Save As screen; and then click on the drive location for your USB drive
- In the example, the drive location is K:. Your USB location may show a different letter, accept what you are shown.

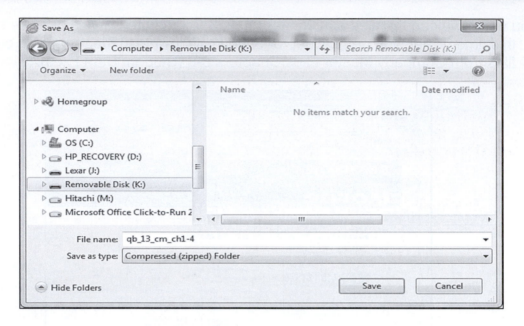

Accept the file name given **qb_13_cm_ch1-4**
Save as type: **Compressed (zipped) Folder**
Click the **Save** button
- It could take several minutes for the download to finish
- Internet Explorer will show a message at the bottom of the screen while the download is being completed.

The folder saved on your USB drive should show in Windows Explorer
- If you don't get this, right-click the **Start** button on the Task Bar in the lower-left corner of your screen, click **Open Windows Explorer** and click your USB drive location
- Notice the zipper on the qb_13_cm_ch1-4.zip folder. This means the compressed file needs to be unzipped.

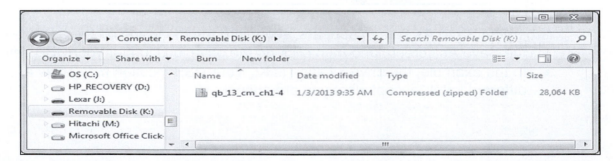

- The Internet Explorer message will show that the download has completed and will allow you to Open the Folder

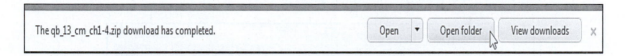

Click **Open Folder** on the Internet Explorer message
Double-click the **qb_13_cm_ch1-4.zip** folder
Click **Extract all files**

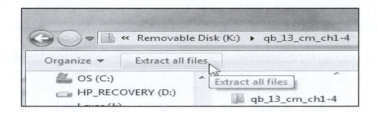

You will get the following screen (your USB may show a different letter):

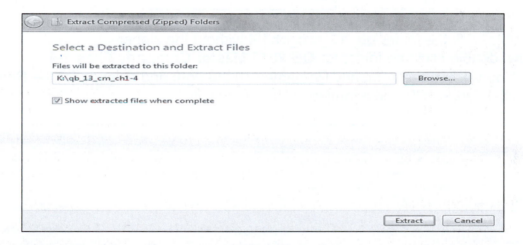

Backspace until you only see the letter of your USB drive as the folder (**K:** in this example):

- Make sure **Show extracted files when complete** is checked. If it is not marked, click to insert the check mark.

Click the **Extract** button

While the files are being extracted, you will see:

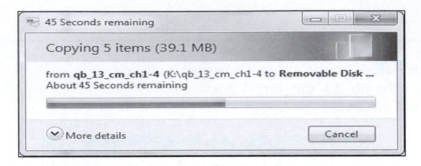

When the files have been extracted, you will see two folders with the same name

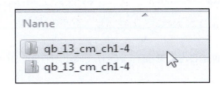

Double-click the folder **qb_13_cm_ch1-4** without the zipper
Now, double-click the folder for **QB 2013 Master Company Files 1-4**
- You will see the company file names on the right and a listing for the Removable Disk (your USB, the example is **K:**) on the left

- It is possible that the company file will be marked as "Read Only" and/or "Archive."
- In addition to removing the properties at this point, as you work through the chapters and switch from one company to the next; i.e., Computer to Landscape and then back to Computer, QuickBooks might mark your company file as read only. If this happens, refer to the following steps on how to change the file Properties from Read Only.

Right-click the file **Computer**
Click **Properties**

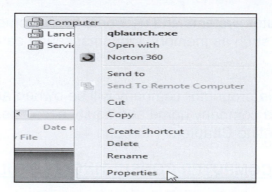

If there is a check mark next to **Read Only** and/or **Archive**, click the check box to remove the mark
- Your Properties for Computer may show a different storage location and different dates. This should not be of any concern.

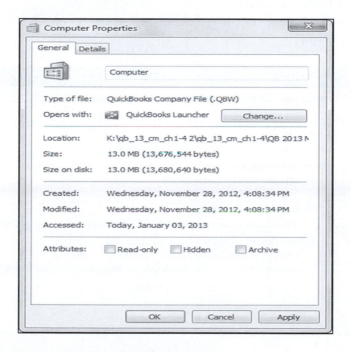

Click the **Apply** button, and then click **OK**
- The file is now ready for use.

Repeat for all of the companies to make those files ready for use

Close **Internet Explorer**

Close all screens

COMPUTER CONSULTING BY STUDENT'S NAME—COMPANY DESCRIPTION

In the text you will be recording transactions for a fictional company that specializes in computer consulting. The company provides program installation, training, and technical support for today's business software as well as helping clients learn how to go online and giving instruction in the use of the Internet. In addition, Computer Consulting by Student's

Name will set up computer systems and networks for customers and will install basic computer components, such as memory, modems, sound cards, hard drives, and CD/DVD drives.

This fictitious, small, sole proprietor company will be owned and run by you. You will be adding your name to the company name and equity accounts. This company will be used for training while completing Chapters 1 through 4.

OPEN A COMPANY—COMPUTER CONSULTING BY STUDENT'S NAME

 Open a company

> Open QuickBooks as previously instructed
> Click **Open or restore an existing company** button at the bottom of the No Company Open screen
> The Open or Restore Company screen appears, click **Open a company file**; and then, click **Next**

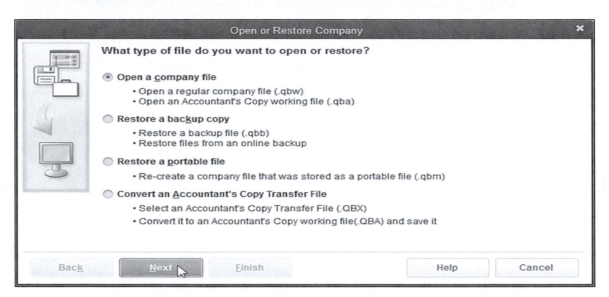

> Click the drop-down list arrow for **Look in**
> Click **Removable Disk (USB Drive Letter:)**
> Locate **Computer** (in the list of file names that appear in the dialog box)
> - Your company file may have an extension of **.qbw.** This is the file extension for your "QuickBooks Working" file. This is the company file that may be opened and used.
> Click **Computer** and click **Open**
> - It is possible to open a company file by double-clicking the company file name. However, if you use this method to open a company, QuickBooks will sometimes give you an error message.

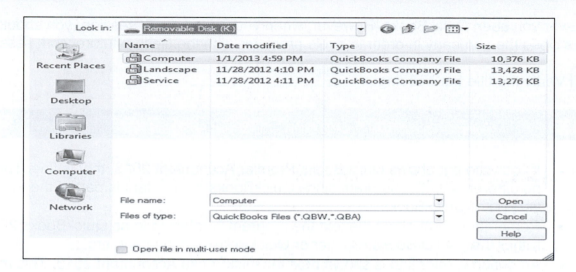

If you get a screen to update your company file, click **Yes**

QUICKBOOKS OPENING SCREENS

Sometimes company files open with screens such as Update Company File, QuickBooks Products and Services, QuickBooks Alerts, Set Up an External Accountant User and others. These screens provide information and/or instructions on how to use QuickBooks, how to subscribe to optional services, or give information regarding reminder alerts. In addition, QuickBooks may open business forms with wizards, questions, or tutorials regarding options, methods of work, and other items.

 If you receive any opening screens, read them and select an appropriate answer. For example, you would always update your company file, but you would not enter passwords or create an external user. If you receive an alert, simply click Mark as Done

VERIFYING AN OPEN COMPANY

Unless you tell QuickBooks to create a new company, open a different company, or close the company, Computer Consulting by Student's Name will appear as the open company whenever you open QuickBooks. However, when you finish a work session, you should always close the company in order to avoid problems with the file in a future work session.

 Verify the title bar heading:

| Company Name | Program Name | Color Flag |

Computer Consulting by Student's Name - QuickBooks Accountant 2013

- If your title bar shows QuickBooks Premier Accountant 2013, that is fine. There is no difference in the program since QuickBooks Accountant is part of the Premier version of QuickBooks.
- Remember, throughout the text the program is referred to as QuickBooks 2013 rather than QuickBooks Premier or QuickBooks Accountant, etc.
- An optional color flag is shown next to QuickBooks Accountant 2013. This may be used to color code different company files. The color chosen for Computer Consulting by Student's Name is yellow.

ADD YOUR NAME TO THE COMPANY NAME

Because each student in the course will be working for the same companies and printing the same documents, personalizing the company name to include your name will help identify your work.

 Add your name to the company name and legal name

Click **Company** on the menu bar
Click **Company Information...**
Click to the right of **Computer Consulting by**
Replace the words **Student's Name** with your real name by holding down the left mouse button and dragging through the "Student's Name" to highlight
   OR
Click in front of the S in Student's Name; press the **Delete** key to delete one letter at a time
Type your actual name, *not* the words *Your Name* as is shown in the text. For example, Janet Horne would type **Janet Horne**
Repeat the steps to change the legal name to **Computer Consulting by Your Name** (Remember your actual name—not the words "Your Name")

Click **OK**

- The title bar now shows **Computer Consulting by Your Name – QuickBooks Accountant 2013**

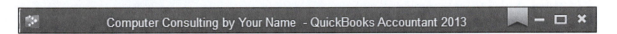

- Remember your actual name is now part of the company name and will be on the title bar. In the text, however, the title bar will show the words **Your Name**.
- If your title bar shows QuickBooks Premier Accountant 2013, that is fine. There is no difference in the program since QuickBooks Accountant is part of the Premier version of QuickBooks.
- No distinction will be made regarding Premier or Accountant from this point forward in the text. The text will use QuickBooks 2013 rather than QuickBooks Premier or QuickBooks Accountant, etc.

HOW TO CREATE A COMPANY BACKUP FILE

As you work with a company and record transactions, it is important to back up your work. This allows you to keep the information for a particular period separate from current information. A backup also allows you to restore information in case your data disk becomes damaged. QuickBooks has a feature to make a backup copy of your company file. A condensed file is created by QuickBooks. The file contains the essential transaction and account information. This file has a **.qbb** extension and is <u>not</u> usable unless it is restored to a company file that has a **.qbw** extension. This can be an existing company file or a new company file.

In this text, you will make a backup file at the end of each chapter. It will contain all of the transactions entered up until the time you made the backup. At the end of each chapter, you will be instructed to make a backup file for the chapter. *Future transactions will not be part of the backup file unless you make a new backup file.* For example, Chapter 1 backup will not contain any transactions entered in Chapter 2. However, Chapter 2 backup will contain all the transactions for both Chapters 1 and 2. Chapter 3 backup will contain all the transactions for Chapters 1, 2, and 3, and so on.

In many classroom configurations, you will be storing your backup files onto the same USB drive that you use for the company file. In actual business practice, you should save the backup to a different location. Most likely, you will store your company file on the hard disk of the computer and the backup file will be stored on a USB drive, a network drive, or some other remote location. Check with your instructor to see if there are any other backup file locations you should use in your training.

 Make a QuickBooks backup of the company data for Computer Consulting by Your Name.

Click **File** on the Menu Bar
Click **Back Up Company**
Click **Create Local Backup**
• Make sure the Create Backup screen has Local backup selected. If not, click **Local backup** to select.

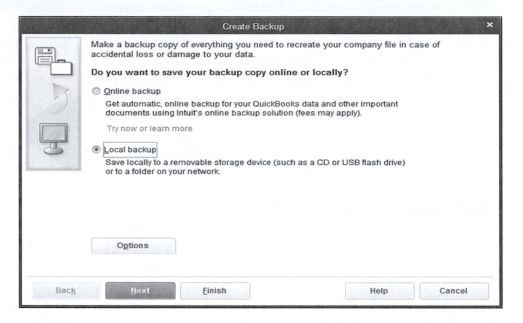

Click the **Next** button
• If you get a screen with Backup Options, complete the following. If not, continue with the information that says "Resume with the following:"

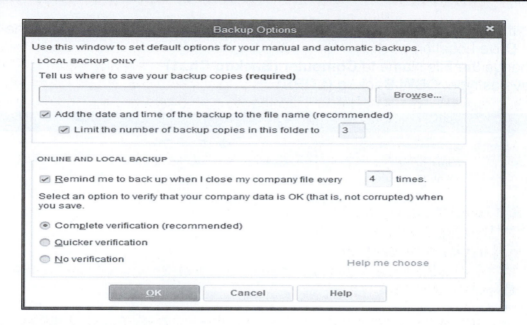

Click the **Browse** button next to "Tell us where to save your backup copies (required)"

Scroll through the list of folders, click the location of your USB drive (or designated storage area)

- The text uses (K:\)

Click **OK**

Click the checkboxes for **Add the date and time of the backup to the file name** and **Remind me to back up when I close my company file** to remove the check marks

Keep **Complete verification**

Click **OK**

If you are saving the backup file to the same USB drive that you are using to store the company file, you will get the following screen

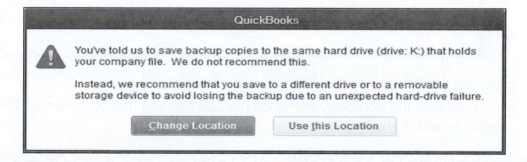

Click **Use this Location**

To complete the **Create Backup** screen, make sure **Save it now** is selected, then click the **Next** button

On the Save Backup Copy screen, **Save in:** should be **USB Drive Location**

- If necessary, click the drop-down list arrow next to Save in: and click the USB Drive Location

Change the File Name to **Computer (Backup Ch. 1)**

Save as type: **QBW Backup (*.QBB)**

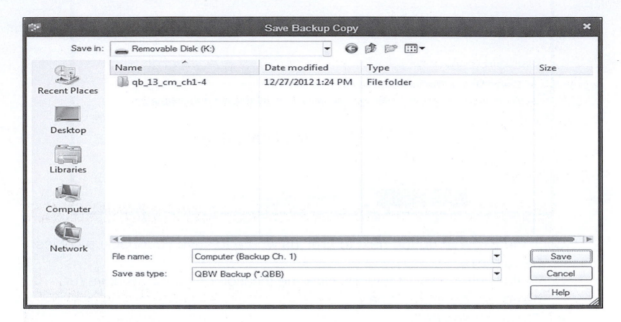

Click the **Save** button

- QuickBooks will back up the information for Computer Consulting by Your Name on the USB disk

When the backup is complete, you will see

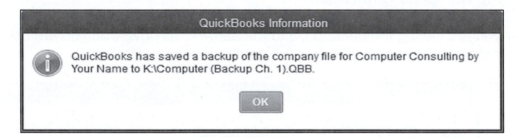

Click **OK**

- Notice that the company name on the title bar still has your name. This change was saved in the backup.

CHANGE THE NAME OF AN EXISTING ACCOUNT IN THE CHART OF ACCOUNTS

QuickBooks makes it easy to set up a company using the Easy Step Interview. You will learn how to create a company in Chapter 9 of the text. When creating a company using QuickBooks' Easy Step Interview, account names are assigned automatically. They might need to be changed to names more appropriate to the individual company. Even if an account has been used to record transactions or has a balance, the name can still be changed.

Change account names

> To access the **Chart of Accounts**, click **Lists** on the menu bar, and click **Chart of Accounts**
> Scroll through accounts until you see Student's Name, Capital
> Click **Student's Name, Capital**
> Click the **Account** button at the bottom of the Chart of Accounts
> Click **Edit Account**
> On the **Edit Account** screen, highlight **Student's Name**
> Enter *your actual first and last name*
> Click the **Save & Close** button

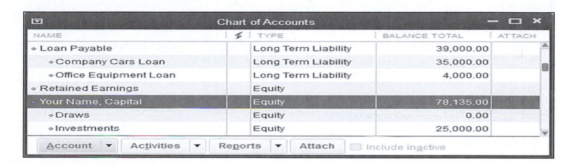

- Remember the text shows Your Name, Capital instead of an actual student's name.
  Close the **Chart of Accounts**

VIEW A REPORT

To see the change in the capital account name in use, you may view a report.

Open the Report Center and view a Trial Balance for January 1, 2013

> Click **Reports** on the icon bar to open the Report Center
>
> Click the icon for **List View**
> Click **Accountant & Taxes** on the left side of the screen
> Scroll through the reports
> Click **Trial Balance** in the Account Activity section

Click **Run**

At the top of the screen, Dates should show Last Month

- Since your computer will show a different date than the example in the text you will need to insert the date used for the report.

Press the **Tab** key to highlight the **From** date

Key in the date **01/01/2013**

Press the **Tab** key to highlight the **To** date

When the **To** date is highlighted, enter **01/01/2013**

Press **Tab** two times to generate the Trial Balance for January 1, 2013

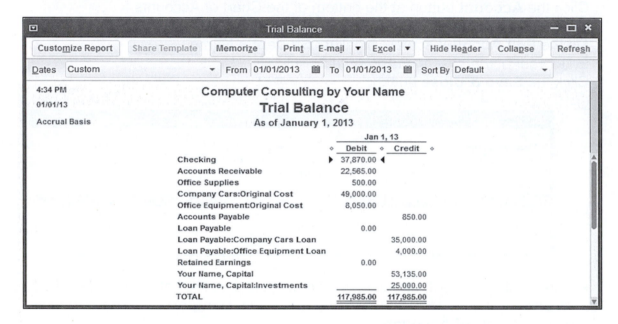

- In the upper-left corner of the report you will see the time and date the report was prepared along with the report basis. Since the date and time of your computer is current, it will not match the dates shown above.
- Notice that the company name in the title of the report shows Computer Consulting by Your Name and the capital account in the report shows Your Name, Capital.
- These changes were made when working in Chapter 1 and show in this report.

Click the **Close** button to close the report

- If you get a Memorize Report screen, click **No**

Click the **Close** button to close the Report Center

RESTORE A COMPANY BACKUP FILE

If you make an error in your training, you may find it beneficial to restore your .qbb backup file. The only way in which a .qbb backup file may be used is by restoring it to a .qbw company file. Using QuickBooks' Open or Restore Company… command on the File menu restores a backup file.

IMPORTANT: A restored backup file replaces the current data in your company file with the data in the backup file so any transactions recorded after the backup was made will be erased. In this chapter, the backup was made after you added your name to the company name but before you changed the capital account name. After restoring the Computer (Backup Ch. 1.qbb) backup file to Computer.qbw, the name of the capital account will have Student's Name, Capital as the account name rather than Your Name, Capital; but the company name will still contain your name.

 Practice restoring a backup file after a change has been made in the company file

Click **File** on the menu bar
Click **Open or Restore Company…**
Click **Restore a backup copy**, then click the **Next** button

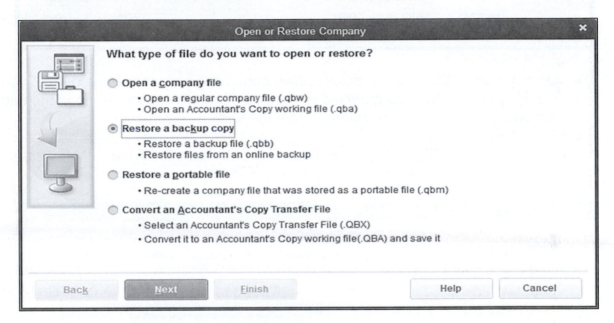

Click **Local backup**, then click the **Next** button
On the Open Backup Copy screen, make sure that Look in: shows the name of your **USB Drive** location
The File name: should be **Computer (Backup Ch. 1)**, if necessary, click the file name to insert it

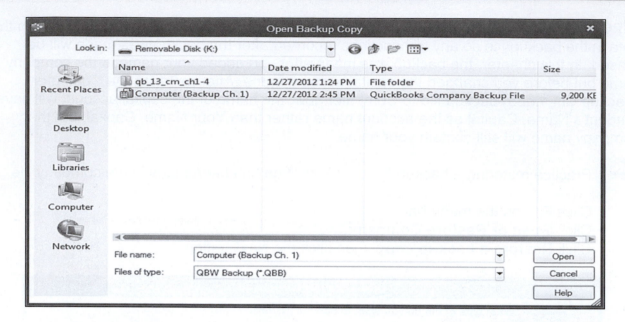

- Do not worry if the Date modified shown above does not match the date of your file. Remember the date modified is the date of your computer when you created the backup file and will be different from the text

Click the **Open** button

An Open or Restore Company screen appears to determine "Where do you want to restore the file?"

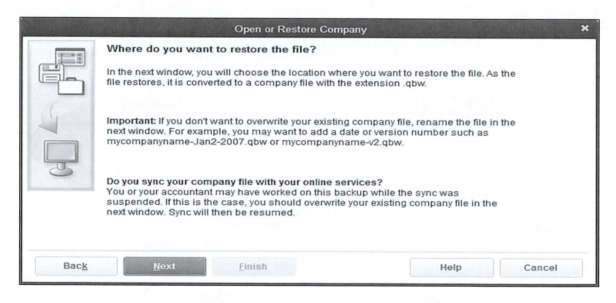

Click the **Next** button

Save in: should be your **USB Drive Location**

File name: should be **Computer**

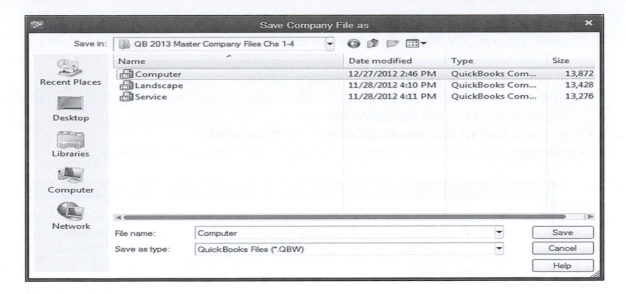

Click the **Save** button
Click **Yes** on the screen telling you the file already exists

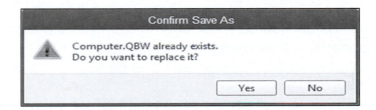

You will get a **Delete Entire File** warning screen
Enter the word **Yes** and click **OK**

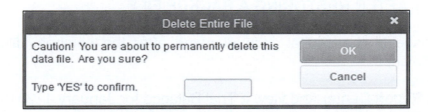

- When you restore a file to an existing company file, all the data contained in the company file will be replaced with the information in the backup file.
When the file has been restored, you will get the following

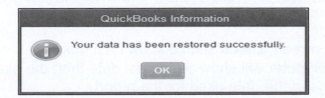

Press Enter or click **OK**

Verify that Computer Consulting by Your Name is still on the Title bar and that Student's Name, Capital is the account name for the Owner's Capital account.

Look at the Title bar to verify the company name
- The company name was changed before you made the backup. Thus, your name remains in the company name.

Open the **Chart of Accounts** as previously instructed

Scroll through the Chart of Accounts until you find Student's Name, Capital

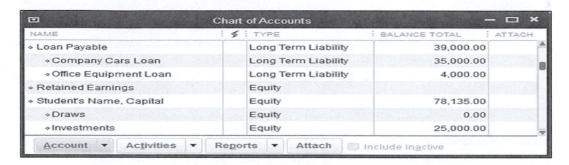

- Your Name, Capital no longer shows because the company information was restored from the backup file made prior to changing the account name.
- The account name will be changed to back your real name in Chapter 4. Check with your instructor to see if you should change the Capital account name now or wait until Chapter 4.
- If you change the account name now, be sure to use your First and Last Name, Capital as the account name.

Close the Chart of Accounts

VIEW A REPORT AFTER RESTORING A BACKUP FILE

To see the change in the capital account name after the company file was restored, prepare a Trial Balance.

Open the Report Center and view a Trial Balance for January 1, 2013

    Click **Reports** on the icon bar to open the Report Center
    Click the icon for **List View**
    Click **Accountant & Taxes** on the left side of the screen
    Scroll through the reports
    Click **Trial Balance** in the Account Activity section
    Click **Run**
    At the top of the screen, **Dates** should show Last Month
    - Since your computer will show a different date than the example in the text you will need to insert the date used for the report.
    Press the **Tab** key to highlight the **From** date
    Key in the date **01/01/13**

Press the **Tab** key to highlight the **To** date
When the **To** date is highlighted, enter **01/01/13**
Press **Tab** two times to generate the Trial Balance for January 1, 2013

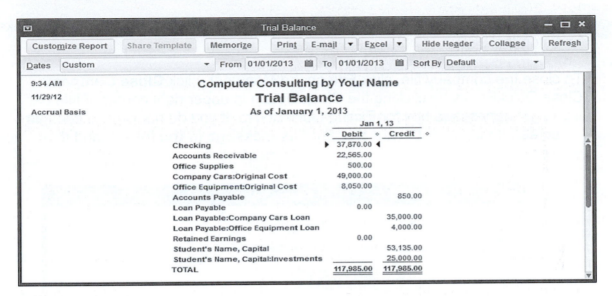

- Notice that the company name in the title of the report shows Computer Consulting by Your Name. This is because the company name was changed before you made your backup file.
- The capital account in the report shows Student's Name, Capital. This is because the account name was changed after the backup file was created. When the backup file was restored, it erased all the changes made after the backup was created. (If your instructor had you change the account name again after the backup was restored, you will see Your Name, Capital.)
Click the **Close** button to close the report
- If you get a Memorize Report screen, click **No**
Click the **Close** button to close the Report Center

CREATE A DUPLICATE USB DRIVE

In addition to making a backup of the company file, you should always have a duplicate of the USB drive you use for your work. Follow the instructions provided by your instructor to copy your files to another USB drive.

EXIT QUICKBOOKS® AND REMOVE YOUR USB DRIVE (CRITICAL!)

When you complete your work, you need to exit the QuickBooks program. If you are saving work on a separate data disk or USB drive, you must <u>not</u> remove your disk until you exit the program. Once QuickBooks has been closed, your USB drive must be removed properly. Following the appropriate steps to close and exit a program and to remove a USB drive is extremely important. There are program and data files that must be closed in order to leave the program and company data so that they are ready to be used again. If a USB drive is simply removed from the computer, damage to the drive and its files may occur. It is common for a beginning computer user to turn off the computer without exiting a program. This can cause corrupt program and data files and can make a disk or program unusable.

 Close the company file for Computer Consulting by Your Name, close QuickBooks, and stop the USB

To close the company file, click **File** on the Menu bar, click **Close Company**
Close QuickBooks by clicking the **Close** button in upper right corner of title bar
If you get a message box for Exiting QuickBooks, If you do not wish to see this
   screen again, click **Do not display this message in the future**, and then, click
   Yes

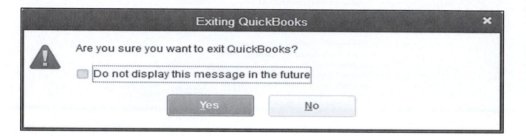

Click the icon for the USB drive in the lower right portion of the Taskbar
Click on the drive location where you have your USB drive

- Your Open Devices and Printers will be different from the example above. Make
   sure to click on the location for your USB.
When you get the message that it is safe to remove hardware or when the light goes
   out on your USB drive, remove your USB

SUMMARY

Chapter 1 provides general information regarding QuickBooks. In this chapter, various QuickBooks features were examined. A company file was opened, your name was added to the company name, and an account name was changed. QuickBooks backup files were made and restored. Companies were closed, QuickBooks was closed, and USB drives were removed.

END-OF-CHAPTER QUESTIONS

TRUE/FALSE

ANSWER THE FOLLOWING QUESTIONS IN THE SPACE PROVIDED BEFORE THE QUESTION NUMBER.

_____   1. There are various methods of giving QuickBooks commands, including use of QuickBooks Home Page, icon bar, menu bar, and keyboard shortcuts.

_____   2. A company file with a .qbw extension is used to record transactions.

_____   3. Once an account has been used, the name cannot be changed.

_____   4. If an error is made when entering a transaction, QuickBooks will not allow the user to return to the business document and make the correction.

_____   5. In a computerized accounting system, each transaction that is analyzed must be entered by hand into the appropriate journal and posted to the appropriate ledger.

_____   6. QuickBooks Home Page appears beneath the title bar and has a list of drop-down menus.

_____   7. When you use QuickBooks to make a company backup file, you are actually having QuickBooks create a condensed file that contains the essential transaction and account information.

_____   8. The Alt key + a letter are used to access the drop-down menus on the menu bar.

_____   9. When you end your work session, you must close your company, close QuickBooks, and remove your USB drive properly.

_____   10. Transactions entered today will be erased if a backup from an earlier date is restored.

MULTIPLE CHOICE

WRITE THE LETTER OF THE CORRECT ANSWER IN THE SPACE PROVIDED
BEFORE THE QUESTION NUMBER.

_____ 1. The extension for a company file that may be used to enter transactions is
      A. .qbi
      B. .qbb
      C. .qbw
      D. .qbc

_____ 2. A (n) ___ is considered to be a list in QuickBooks.
      A. Invoice
      B. Chart of Accounts
      C. Company
      D. none of the above

_____ 3. QuickBooks keyboard conventions ___.
      A. are not available
      B. use the mouse
      C. use certain keys in a manner consistent with Windows
      D. incorporate the use of QuickBooks Company Center

_____ 4. Buttons on the invoice icon bar and on the bottom of an invoice are used to ___.
      A. give commands to QuickBooks
      B. add Customers
      C. prepare reports
      D. show graphs of invoices prepared

_____ 5. QuickBooks' QuickMath displays ___.
      A. a calculator
      B. an adding machine tape
      C. a calculator with adding machine tape
      D. none of the above

_____ 6. QuickBooks Home Page ___.
      A. allows you to give commands to QuickBooks according to the type of transaction being entered
      B. are icons shown in a row beneath the menu bar
      C. appears above the menu bar
      D. appears at the bottom of the screen

_____ 7. An icon is ___.
   A. a document
   B. a picture
   C. a chart
   D. a type of software

_____ 8. A way to find out the keyboard shortcuts for various commands is to look them up using ___.
   A. the Internet
   B. Help
   C. the File menu
   D. a Keyboard icon

_____ 9. A .qbb extension on a file name means that the file is ___.
   A. open
   B. the working file
   C. a restored file
   D. a backup file

_____ 10. To verify the name of the open company, look at ___.
   A. the icon bar
   B. QuickBooks Home Page
   C. the menu bar
   D. the title bar

FILL-IN

IN THE SPACE PROVIDED, WRITE THE ANSWER THAT MOST APPROPRIATELY COMPLETES THE SENTENCE.

1. Whether you are using a manual or a computerized accounting system, transactions must still be _____, _____, and _____.

2. The _____ menu is used to open and close a company and may also be used to exit QuickBooks.

3. The Report Center has three different views available to display reports. They are _____ view, _____ view, and _____ view.

4. In QuickBooks you may change the company name by clicking Company Information on the _____ menu.

5. The _____ organizes tasks into logical groups (Vendors, Customers, Employees, Company, and Banking).

SHORT ESSAY

Describe the importance of making a backup of a company file and explain what will happen to transactions entered today if a backup from an earlier date is restored.

_____
_____
_____
_____
_____
_____
_____
_____
_____
_____
_____
_____
_____.

END-OF-CHAPTER PROBLEM

At the end of each chapter, you will work with a different company and enter transactions that are similar to the ones you competed in the text. Follow the instructions given for transaction entry and printing. You may refer to the chapter for assistance.

YOUR NAME LANDSCAPE & POOL SERVICE

Your Name Landscape and Pool Service is owned and operated by you. Laura Lewis and Lupe Gonzalez also work for the company. Laura manages the office and keeps the books for the business. Lupe provides lawn maintenance and supervises the lawn maintenance employees. You provide the pool maintenance. The company is located in Santa Barbara, California.

INSTRUCTIONS

► Download the company file for Student's Name Landscape and Pool Service, **Landscape.qbw**, as instructed in the chapter.
► Open the company.
► Add your name to the company name and the legal name. The company name will be **Your Name Landscape and Pool Service**. (Type your actual name, *not* the words *Your Name*. Do this whenever you are instructed to add *Your Name*.)
► Unless your instructor directs you to a different storage location for your backup file, create a Local backup of the Landscape.qbw file to **Landscape (Backup Ch. 1)** on the same USB drive where you have your company file.
► Change the name of Student's Name, Capital to **Your Name, Capital**
► Use the Report Center to prepare a Trial Balance
► Verify the capital account name change; then close the report and the Report Center
► Restore the **Landscape (Backup Ch 1)** file.
  o   Your Name, Capital no longer shows because the company information was restored from the backup file made prior to changing the account name.
  o   The account name will be changed to back your real name in Chapter 4. Check with your instructor to see if you should change the Capital account name now or wait until Chapter 4.
  o   If you change the account name now, be sure to use your First and Last Name, Capital as the account name.
► Use the Report Center to prepare a Trial Balance
► Verify that the capital account name change now shows Student's Name Landscape and Pool Service; then close the report and the Report Center

SALES AND RECEIVABLES: SERVICE BUSINESS

LEARNING OBJECTIVES

At the completion of this chapter, you will be able to:

1. Create invoices and record sales transactions on account.
2. Create sales receipts to record cash sales.
3. Edit, void, and delete invoices/sales receipts.
4. Create credit memos.
5. Add new customers and modify customer records.
6. Record cash receipts.
7. Enter partial cash payments.
8. Display and print invoices, sales receipts, and credit memos.
9. Display and print Quick Reports, Customer Balance Summary Reports, Customer Balance Detail Reports, and Transaction Reports by Customer.
10. Display and print Summary Sales by Item Reports and Itemized Sales by Item Reports.
11. Display and print Deposit Summary, Journal Reports, and Trial Balance.
12. Display Accounts Receivable Graphs and Sales Graphs.

ACCOUNTING FOR SALES AND RECEIVABLES

Rather than use a traditional Sales Journal to record sales on account using debits and credits and special columns, QuickBooks uses an invoice to record sales transactions for accounts receivable in the Accounts Receivable Register. Because cash sales do not involve accounts receivable and would be recorded in the Cash Receipts Journal in traditional accounting, the transactions are recorded on a Sales Receipt. However, all transactions, regardless of the activity, are placed in the General Journal behind the scenes.

QuickBooks puts the money received from a cash sale and from a customer's payment on account into the Undeposited Funds account. When a bank deposit is made the Undeposited Funds are placed in the Checking or Cash account.

A new customer can be added on the fly as transactions are entered. Unlike many computerized accounting programs, in QuickBooks, error correction is easy. A sales form may be edited, voided, or deleted in the same window where it was created. Customer information may be changed by editing the Customer in the Customer Center.

A multitude of reports are available when using QuickBooks. Accounts receivable reports include Customer Balance Summary and Customer Balance Detail reports. Sales reports provide information regarding the amount of sales by customer. Transaction Reports by Customer are available as well as the traditional accounting reports such as Trial Balance, Profit and Loss, and Balance Sheet. QuickBooks also has graphing capabilities so you can see and evaluate your accounts receivable and sales at the click of a button.

TRAINING TUTORIAL

The following tutorial is a step-by-step guide to recording sales (both cash and credit), customer payments, bank deposits, and other transactions for receivables for a fictitious company with fictional employees. This company was used in Chapter 1 and is called Computer Consulting by Your Name. In addition to recording transactions using QuickBooks, we will prepare several reports and graphs for the company. The tutorial for Computer Consulting by Your Name will continue in Chapters 3 and 4, where accounting for payables, customizing a chart of accounts, bank reconciliations, financial statement preparation, and closing an accounting period will be completed.

TRAINING PROCEDURES

To maximize the training benefits, you should:

1. Read the entire chapter *before* beginning the tutorial within the chapter.
2. Answer the end-of-chapter questions.
3. Be aware that transactions to be entered are given within a **MEMO**.
4. Complete all the steps listed for the Computer Consulting by Your Name tutorial in the chapter. (Indicated by: ➡)
5. When you have completed a section, put a check mark next to the final step completed.
6. If you do not complete a section, put the date in the margin next to the last step completed. This will make it easier to know where to begin when training is resumed.
7. You may not finish the entire chapter in one computer session. At the end of your work session, make a backup file that will contain all of the work you completed from Chapter 1 through the current day. Name this file **Computer (Daily Backup)**
8. In addition to the daily backup, always use QuickBooks to back up your work at the end of the chapter as described in Chapter 1. The name of the chapter backup for Chapter 2 is **Computer (Backup Ch 2)**. Make a duplicate copy of your USB drive as instructed by your professor.
9. As you complete your work, proofread carefully and check for accuracy. Double-check amounts of money and the accounts, items, and dates used.
10. If you find an error while preparing a transaction, correct it. If you find the error after the Invoice, Sales Form, Credit Memo, or Customer:Job List is complete, follow the steps indicated in this chapter to correct, void, or delete transactions.

11. Print as directed within the chapter. There is a transmittal sheet at the end of the chapter that lists everything that is printed when working through the chapter. (Check with your instructor to see if you should print everything listed or if there is printing that you may omit.)

12. When you complete your computer session, always close your company. If you try to use a computer and a previous student did not close the company, QuickBooks may freeze when you start to work. In addition, if you do not close the company as you leave, you may have problems with your company file, your USB drive may be damaged, and you may have unwanted .qbi (QuickBooks In Use) files that cause problems when using the company file.

DATES

Throughout the text, the year used for the screen shots is 2013, which is the same year as the version of the program. You may want to check with your instructor to see if you should use 2013 as the year for the transactions.

Always pay special attention to the dates when recording transactions. It is not unusual to forget to enter the date that appears in the text and to use the date of the computer for a transaction. This can cause errors in reports and other entries. There will be times when you can tell QuickBooks which date to use such as, business documents and some reports. There will be other instances when QuickBooks automatically inserts the date of the computer, and it cannot be changed. This will occur later in the chapter when you print the bank deposit summary. When this happens, accept QuickBooks' printed date.

PRINTING

Throughout the text, you will be instructed when to print business documents and reports. Everything that is to be printed within the chapter is listed on a transmittal sheet. The end-of- chapter problem also has everything to be printed listed on a transmittal sheet. In some instances, your instructor may direct you to change what you print. Always verify items to be printed with your instructor.

COMPANY FILE

In Chapter 1, you began using Computer Consulting by Student's Name. You changed the company name from Computer Consulting by Student's Name to Computer Consulting by Your Name (your real name). A backup of the file was made. An account name was changed. The backup file was restored and you learned that the account name change had been replaced by the original account name that was in the backup file. During Chapters 2-4, you will continue to use the Computer.qbw file originally used in Chapter 1 to record transactions. In Chapter 4, you will customize your chart of accounts and change the name of the capital account to Your Name, Capital.

If you did not complete the work in Chapter 1, you will need to download the company file from the Pearson Web site. Refer to Chapter 1 for step-by-step procedures to do this. You will also need to refer to Chapter 1 to add your name to the company name. If you plan to install the trial version of QuickBooks and want to use step-by-step instructions to install and register the program, refer to Chapter 1 or go to www.PearsonHigherEd.com/Horne. You should refer to the Web site periodically for updates, new material, and errata.

COMPANY PROFILE: COMPUTER CONSULTING BY YOUR NAME

As you learned in Chapter 1, Computer Consulting by Your Name is a company specializing in computer consulting. The company provides program installation, training, and technical support for today's business software as well as setting up company networks, and giving instruction in the use of the Internet and going online. In addition, Computer Consulting by Your Name will set up computer systems for customers and will install basic computer components, such as memory, modems, sound cards, disk drives, and DVD and CD-ROM drives.

Computer Consulting by Your Name is located in Southern California and is a sole proprietorship owned by you. You are involved in all aspects of the business and have the responsibility of obtaining clients. There are three employees: Jennifer Lockwood, who is responsible for software training; Rom Levy, who handles hardware and network installation and technical support; and Alhandra Cruz, whose duties include being office manager and bookkeeper and providing technical support.

Computer Consulting by Your Name bills by the hour for training, hardware and software installation, and network setup. Each of these items has a minimum charge of $95 for the first hour and $80 per hour thereafter. Clients with contracts for technical support are charged a monthly rate for service.

BEGIN TRAINING IN QUICKBOOKS®

As you continue this chapter, you will be instructed to enter transactions for Computer Consulting by Your Name. As you learned in Chapter 1, the first thing you must do in order to work is boot up or start your computer, open the program QuickBooks, and open the company.

 Refer to Chapter 1 to Open QuickBooks

OPEN A COMPANY—COMPUTER CONSULTING BY YOUR NAME

In Chapter 1, Computer Consulting by Your Name was opened and a backup of the company file was made using QuickBooks. Computer Consulting by Your Name should have been closed in Chapter 1. To open the company for this work session you may click the Open an Existing Company button on the No Company Open screen or by clicking on File menu and Open or Restore Company. Verify this by checking the title bar.

 Open **Computer Consulting by Your Name**

Click **Open or Restore an Existing Company** button at the bottom of the No
    Company Open screen
        <u>OR</u>

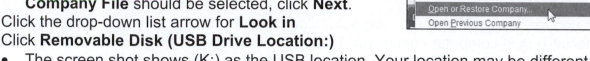

Click **File** on the Menu bar and click **Open or Restore
Company**
On the Open or Restore Company screen, **Open a
Company File** should be selected, click **Next**.
Click the drop-down list arrow for **Look in**
Click **Removable Disk (USB Drive Location:)**

- The screen shot shows (K:) as the USB location. Your location may be different.

Locate **Computer** (under the **Look in** text box)

- Your company file may have an extension of **.qbw.** This is the file extension for
your "QuickBooks Working" file. This is the company file that may be opened and
used. As you learned in Chapter 1, you may not use a .qbb (backup) file for direct
entry. A backup file must be restored to a .qbw (company) file.

- The files shown below are the company files for Chapters 1-4. If you downloaded
the files for Chapters 5-8 you will have additional company files on the USB
drive.

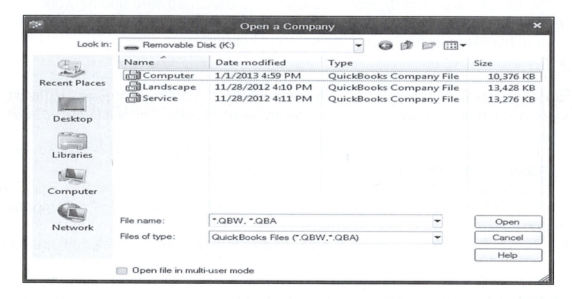

- Since this company was used in Chapter 1, when you see the Open a Company
screen, you may see other QuickBooks files and/or folders associated with that
company. QuickBooks will create them as you use a company file. Some of
these files may have extensions of QBW.ND or .QBW.TLG. Folders that say
QuickBooksAutoDataRecovery or Restored are common. For the most part, you
do not use or change any of these files or folders, simply click the company file
and click the Open button. (These are not shown above.)

Click **Computer** and click **Open**

- Remember, this is the same file you used in Chapter 1.

- It is possible to open a company file by double-clicking the company file name. However, if you use this method to open a company, QuickBooks will sometimes give you an error message.
- Sometimes, when switching from one company to the next; i.e., Computer to Landscape and then back to Computer, QuickBooks might mark your company file as read only. If this happens, refer to Chapter 1 for steps on how to change the file Properties from Read Only.

If QuickBooks has received an update from Intuit, you may need to update your file for use.

If you get a screen to Update Company, click **Yes**

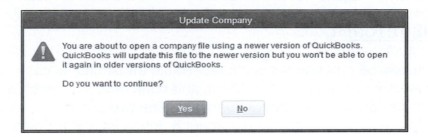

VERIFYING AN OPEN COMPANY

 Verify the title bar heading:

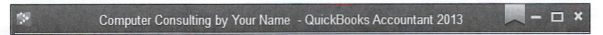

- The title bar should show **Computer Consulting by Your Name** as the company name. (Remember you will have your actual name in the title.)
- If your title bar shows QuickBooks Premier Accountant 2013, that is fine. There is no difference in the program since QuickBooks Accountant is part of the Premier version of QuickBooks.
- Remember, throughout the text the program is referred to as QuickBooks 2013 rather than QuickBooks Premier or QuickBooks Accountant, etc.
- Note: Unless you tell QuickBooks to create a new company, open a different company, or close the company, Computer Consulting by Your Name will appear as the open company whenever you open QuickBooks. However, when you finish a work session, you should always close the company in order to avoid problems with the file in a future work session.

QUICKBOOKS® HOME PAGE AND TOP ICON BAR

The QuickBooks Home Page allows you to give commands to QuickBooks according to the type of transaction being entered. The Home Page tasks are organized into logical groups (Vendors, Customers, Employees, Company, and Banking). Each of the areas on the Home Page is used to enter different types of transactions. When appropriate, the Home Page shows a flow chart with icons indicating the major activities performed. The icons are arranged in the order in which transactions usually occur and are clicked to access screens in order to enter information or transactions in QuickBooks.

You may also choose to use the menu bar, the icon bar, or the keyboard to give commands to QuickBooks. For more detailed information regarding the QuickBooks Home Page and the Top Icon Bar, refer to Chapter 1. Instructions in this text will be given primarily using the QuickBooks Home Page. However, the menu bar, the Top Icon bar, and/or keyboard methods will be used as well.

 If the Top Icon Bar is not showing, click the **View** menu, and then click **Top Icon** Bar; if the Home Page is not showing, click the **Home** icon to display it

BEGINNING THE TUTORIAL

In this chapter you will be entering accounts receivable transactions, cash sales transactions, receipts for payments on account, and bank deposits. Much of the organization of QuickBooks is dependent upon lists. The two primary types of lists you will use in the tutorial for receivables are a Customers & Jobs List and a Sales Item List. The names, addresses, telephone numbers, credit terms, credit limits, and balances for all established credit customers are contained in the Customer & Jobs List in the Customer Center. To conform with GAAP (Generally Accepted Accounting Principles), the Customer Center may also be referred to as the Accounts Receivable Ledger. QuickBooks does not use this term; however, the Customer Center does function as the Accounts Receivable Subsidiary Ledger. A transaction entry for an individual customer is posted to the customer's account in the Customer Center just as it would be posted to the customer's individual account in an Accounts Receivable Ledger.

The balance of the Customer & Jobs List in the Customer Center will be equal to the balance of the Accounts Receivable account in the Chart of Accounts. The Chart of Accounts would be referred to as the General Ledger when using GAAP standards. Invoices and accounts receivable transactions can also be related to specific jobs you are completing for customers. To see the balance of all customers, you would click the Transactions tab in the Customer Center.

You will be using the following Customers & Jobs List in the Customer Center for established credit customers.

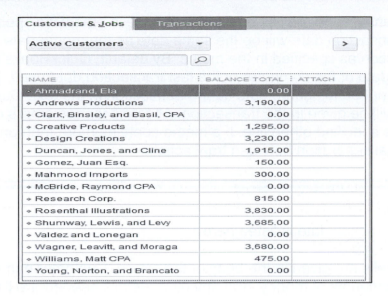

Note: When you display the Customers & Jobs list in the Customer Center, the customer names may not be displayed in full. The lists shown in the text have been formatted to show the names in full.

Sales are often made up of various types of income. In Computer Consulting by Your Name, there are several income accounts. In order to classify income regarding the type of sale, the sales account may have subaccounts. When recording a transaction for a sale, QuickBooks requires that a Sales Item be used. When the sales item is created, a sales account is required. When the sales item is used in a transaction, the income is credited to the appropriate sales/income account. For example, Training 1 is a sales item and uses the account Training Income, a subaccount of Sales, when a transaction is recorded.

In addition, there are categories within an income account. For example, Computer Consulting by Your Name uses Training Income to represent revenues earned by providing on-site training. The sales items used for Training Income are Training 1 for the first or initial hour of on-site training and Training 2 for all additional hours of on-site training. As you look at the Item List, you will observe that the rates for the two items are different. Using lists for sales items allows for flexibility in billing and a more accurate representation of the way in which income is earned. The following Item List for the various types of sales will be used for the company.

In the tutorial all transactions are listed on memos. Unless otherwise specified within the transaction, the transaction date will be the same date as the memo date. Always enter the date of the transaction as specified in the memo. By default, QuickBooks automatically enters the current date of the computer or the last transaction date used. In many instances, this will not be the same date as the transaction in the text. Customer names, when necessary, will be given in the transaction. All terms for customers on account are Net 30 days unless specified otherwise. If a memo contains more than one transaction, there will be a visual separation between transactions.

MEMO

DATE: The transaction date is listed here

Transaction details are given in the body of the memo. Customer names, the type of transaction, amounts of money, and any other details needed are listed here.

Even when you are given instructions on how to enter a transaction step by step, you should always refer to the memo for transaction details. Once a specific type of transaction has been entered in a step-by-step manner, additional transactions will be made without having instructions provided. Of course, you may always refer to instructions given for previous transactions for ideas or for the steps used to enter those transactions. Again, always double-check the date and the year used for the transaction. QuickBooks automatically inserts the computer's current date, which will probably be different from the date in the text. Using an incorrect date will cause reports to have different totals and contain different transactions than those shown in the text.

ENTER SALE ON ACCOUNT

Because QuickBooks operates on a business form premise, a sale on account is entered via an invoice. You prepare an invoice, and QuickBooks records the transaction in the Journal and automatically posts to the customer's account in the Customer Center.

MEMO:
DATE: January 2, 2013

Invoice 1: Juan Gomez has had several questions regarding his new computer system. He spoke with you about this and has signed up for 10 hours of technical support (Tech Sup 2) for January. Bill him for this and use <u>Thank you for your business.</u> as the message.

 Record the sale on account shown in the invoice above. This invoice is used to bill a customer for a sale using one sales item:

Click the **Create Invoices** icon on the Home Page

Create Invoices

- A blank invoice will show on the screen.

Click the drop-down list arrow next to **CUSTOMER:JOB**

Click **Gomez, Juan Esq.**

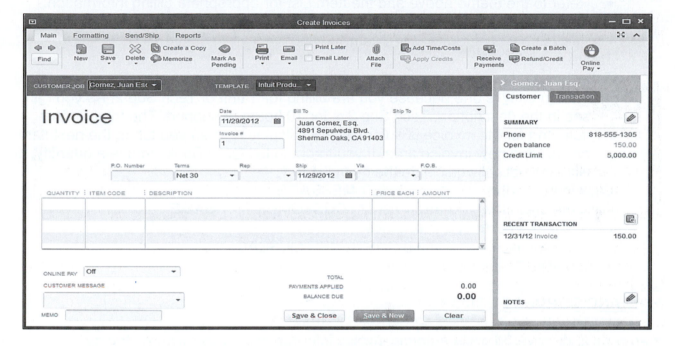

- His name is entered as CUSTOMER:JOB, and Bill To information is completed automatically.
- Notice the History section on the right side of the invoice. This will give you information about Juan Gomez. Including his Open balance, Credit Limit, and Recent Transactions.

To save space on your screen, click the **Hide history** button to close the History section

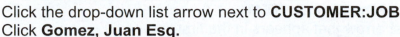

- If you wish to view the history later, simply click the Show History button

Show history

Click the drop-down list arrow for **TEMPLATE**, click **Intuit Service Invoice**

- Intuit Service Invoice is the appropriate invoice to use for this company since only services are sales items.

Press the **Tab** to tab to and highlight the date in the **Date** field

Type **01/02/13** as the date

- This should replace the date shown in the field. If you did not tab to the date, drag through the date to highlight and then type 01/02/13.

Invoice 1 should be showing in the **Invoice #.** box

- The Invoice #. should not have to be changed.

There is no PO No. (Purchase Order Number) to record

Terms should be indicated as **Net 30**
- If not, click the drop-down list arrow next to **Terms** and click **Net 30**.

Tab to or click in the first line beneath **ITEM**

Click the drop-down list arrow that appears in the first line
- Refer to the memo above and the Item List for appropriate billing information.

Click **Tech Sup 2** to bill for 10 hours of technical support
- Tech Sup 2 is entered as the Item.

Tab to or click **QTY**

Type **1**
- The quantity is one because you are billing for 1 unit of Tech Sup 2. As you can see in the description, Tech Sup 2 is for 10 hours of support. The total for the item and for the invoice is automatically calculated when you tab to the next item or click in a new invoice area. If you forget to tell QuickBooks to use a quantity, it will automatically calculate the quantity as 1.

Click in the textbox for **CUSTOMER MESSAGE**

Click the drop-down list arrow next to **CUSTOMER MESSAGE**

Click **Thank you for your business.**
- Message is inserted in the CUSTOMER MESSAGE box.
- ONLINE PAY should say Off.

EDIT AND CORRECT ERRORS

If an error is discovered while entering invoice information, it may be corrected by positioning the cursor in the field containing the error. You may do this by clicking in the field containing the error, tabbing to move forward through each field, or pressing Shift+Tab to move back to the field containing the error. If the error is highlighted, type the correction. If the error is not highlighted, you can correct the error by pressing the backspace or the delete key as many times as necessary to remove the error, and then typing the correction. (Alternate method: Point to the error, highlight by dragging the mouse through the error, then type the correction or press the Delete key to remove completely.)

 Practice editing and making corrections to Invoice 1

Click the drop-down list arrow next to **CUSTOMER:JOB**

Click **Williams, Matt CPA**
- Name is changed in CUSTOMER:JOB and Bill To information is also changed.

Click to the left of the first number in the **Date**—this is **0**

Hold down primary mouse button and drag through the date to highlight.

Type **10/24/13** as the date
- This removes the 01/02/2013 date originally entered.

Click to the right of the **1** in **QUANTITY**

Backspace and type a **2**

Press **Tab** to see how QuickBooks automatically calculates the new total

To eliminate the changes made to Invoice 1, click the drop-down list arrow next to
  Customer:Job

Click **Gomez, Juan, Esq.**
Tab to the Date textbox to highlight the date
Type **01/02/13**
Click to the right of the **2** in **QUANTITY**
Backspace and type a **1**
Press the **Tab** key

- This will cause QuickBooks to calculate the amount and the total for the invoice and will move the cursor to the Description field.
- Verify that Invoice 1 has been returned to the correct customer, date, and quantity. Compare the information you entered with the information provided in the memo.

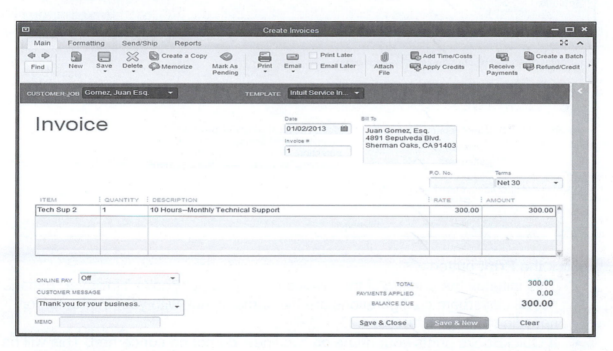

PRINT AN INVOICE

 With Invoice 1 on the screen, print the invoice immediately after entering information

Click the **Print** icon (looks like a printer) at the top of the **Create Invoices** screen
- If you click the drop-down list arrow for the Print button, you will get a list of printing options. Click the **Invoice** option.
Check the information on the **Print One Invoice Settings** tab:
Printer name (should identify the type of printer you are using):
- This may be different from the printer identified in this text.
Printer type: Page-oriented (Single sheets)
Print on: Blank paper
- The circle next to this should be filled. If it is not, click the circle to select.
Click **Do not print lines around each field** to insert a check mark in the check box
- If a check is not in the box, lines will print around each field.

- If there is a check in the box, lines will not print around each field.

Number of copies should be 1

- If a number other than 1 shows: click in the box, drag to highlight the number, and then type **1**

Collate may show a check mark

- Since the invoice is only one-page in length, you will not be using the collate feature.

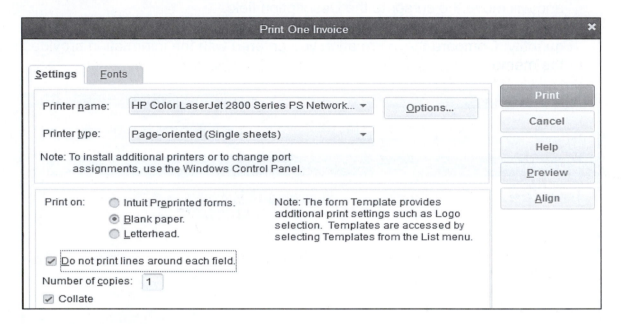

Click the **Print** button

- This initiates the printing of the invoice through QuickBooks. However, because not all classroom configurations are the same, check with your instructor for specific printing instructions.
- If QuickBooks prints your name on two lines, do not be concerned. This will be changed later.

Click the **Save & New** button to save Invoice 1 and go to a new invoice

ENTER TRANSACTIONS USING TWO SALES ITEMS

MEMO:

Date: January 3, 2013

Invoice 2: Matt Williams, CPA, spoke with you regarding the need for on-site training to help him get started using the Internet. Bill him for a 5-hour on-site training session with Jennifer Lockwood. Use <u>Thank you for your business.</u> as the message. (Remember to use Training 1 for the first hour of on-site training and Training 2 for the four additional hours of training.)

Record a transaction on account for a sale involving two sales items

On Invoice 2, click the drop-down list arrow next to **CUSTOMER:JOB**
Click **Williams, Matt, CPA**

- Name is entered as CUSTOMER:JOB. Bill To information is completed automatically.
- Make sure that <u>Intuit Service Invoice</u> is shown as the Template; if not, click the drop-down list arrow and select it.

Tab to or click **Date**
Delete the current date

- Refer to instructions for Invoice 1 or to editing practice if necessary.

Type **01/03/13** as the date
Make sure that **2** is showing in the **Invoice #** text box

- The Invoice #. should not have to be changed.

There is no PO No. to record
Terms should be indicated as **Net 30**
Tab to or click the first line beneath **ITEM**

- Refer to the Memo and to the Item List for appropriate billing information.
- *Note:* Services are recorded based on sales items and are not related to the employee who provides the service.

Click the drop-down list arrow next to **ITEM**
Click **Training 1**

- Training 1 is entered as the Item.

Tab to or click **QUANTITY**
Type **1**

- Amount will be calculated automatically and entered into the Amount Column when you go to the next line. Notice the amount is $95.00.

Tab to or click the second line for **ITEM**
Click the drop-down list arrow next to **ITEM**
Click **Training 2**
Tab to or click **QUANTITY**
Type **4**, press **Tab**

- The total amount of training time is five hours. Because the first hour is billed as Training 1, the remaining four hours are billed as Training 2 hours. The total amount due for the Training 2 hours and the total for the invoice are automatically calculated when you go to the CUSTOMER MESSAGE box.

Click **CUSTOMER MESSAGE**
Click the drop-down list arrow next to **CUSTOMER MESSAGE**
Click **Thank you for your business.**

- Message is inserted in the CUSTOMER MESSAGE box.
- ONLINE PAY should say Off.

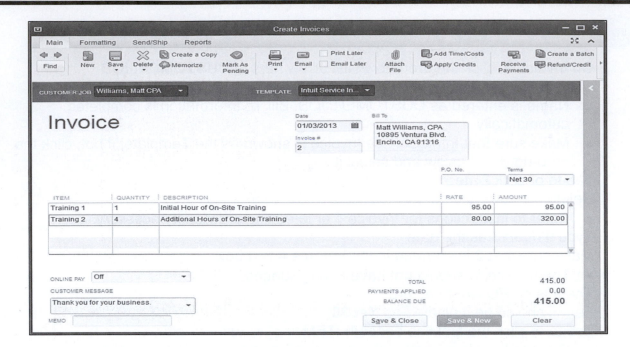

PRINT AN INVOICE

 With Invoice 2 on the screen, print the invoice immediately after entering invoice information

> Click **Print** button on the **Create Invoices** screen
> - If you click the drop-down list arrow for the Print button, you will get a list of printing options. Click the **Invoice** option.
> Check the information on the **Print One Invoice Settings** tab:
> > **Printer name** (should identify the type of printer you are using):
> > **Printer type**: Page-oriented (Single sheets)
> > **Print on:** Blank paper
> > **Do not print lines around each field** check box should have a check mark
> > Click the **Print** button
> After the invoice has printed, click the **Save & Close** button at the bottom of the
> > **Create Invoices** screen to record Invoice 2 and exit Create Invoices

ANALYZE TRANSACTIONS ENTERED INTO THE JOURNAL

Whenever a transaction is recorded on an invoice or any other business form, QuickBooks enters the transactions into the Journal in the traditional Debit/Credit format.

 View the Journal and verify the transaction entries

> Click **Reports** on the Menu bar
> Point to **Accountant & Taxes**
> Click **Journal**

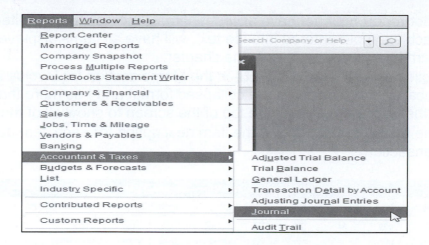

Click **OK** on the Collapsing and Expanding Transactions dialog box

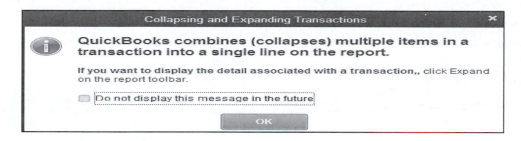

Tab to the **From** textbox
Enter the date **01/01/13**
Tab to the **To** textbox
Enter the date **01/03/13**
Press Tab twice to generate the report

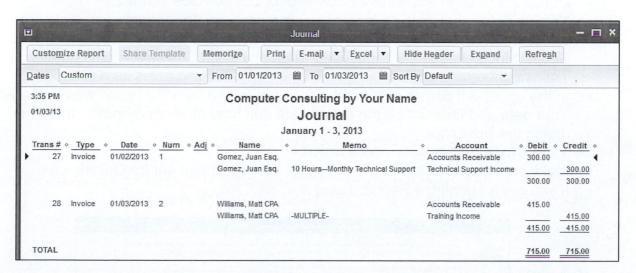

- Your report may not have account names, memos, or other items shown in full. Each example entered into the text, will have all items displayed in full. You will learn how to do this later in the chapter.
- Notice the word –MULTIPLE- in the Memo section for Invoice 2. This appears because the report is in the collapsed format and has more than one sales item.

Click the **Expand** button at the top of the screen to show all of the entries

- The Memo column shows the item description for each item used in the transaction

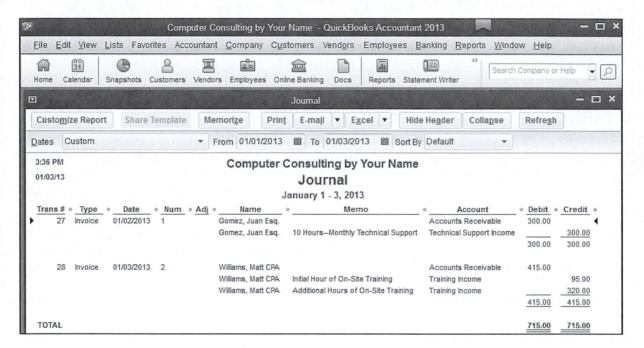

- Notice the debit to Accounts Receivable for both Invoice 1 and 2.
- The credit for each invoice is to an income account. The income accounts are different for each invoice because the sales items are different. Technical Support Income is the account used when any Tech Sup sales item is used. Training Income is the account used when any Training sales item is used.
- In the upper-left corner of the report is the date and time the report was prepared. Your date and time will be the actual date and time of your computer. It will not match the illustration.

Click the **Close** button to close the report

- Make sure you click the Close button for the report and not for QuickBooks.
- If you get a Memorize Report dialog box, click **No**.

PREPARE INVOICES WITHOUT STEP-BY-STEP INSTRUCTIONS

MEMO:

DATE: January 5, 2013

Invoice 3: Ela Ahmadrand needed to have telephone assistance to help her set up her Internet connection. Prepare an invoice as the bill for 10 hours of technical support for January. (Remember customers are listed by last name in the Customers & Jobs List. Refer to Item List to select the correct item for billing.)

Invoice 4: Valdez and Lonegan have several new employees that need to be trained in the use of the office computer system. Bill them for 40 hours of on-site training from Jennifer Lockwood. (Computer Consulting by Your Name does not record a transaction based on the employee who performs the service. It simply bills according to the service provided.)

Invoice 5: Clark, Binsley, and Basil, CPA, need to learn the basic features of QuickBooks, which is used by many of their customers. Bill them for 10 hours of on-site training and 15 hours of technical support for January so they may call and speak to Rom Levy regarding additional questions. (Note: You will use three sales items in this transaction.)

Invoice 6: Young, Norton, and Brancato has a new assistant office manager. Computer Consulting by Your Name is providing 40 hours of on-site training for Beverly Wilson. To obtain additional assistance, the company has signed up for 5 hours technical support for January.

 Enter the four transactions in the memo above. Refer to instructions given for the two previous transactions entered

- Remember, when billing for on-site training, the first hour is billed as Training 1, and the remaining hours are billed as Training 2.
- If you forget to enter the quantity, QuickBooks calculates the amount based on a quantity of 1.
- Always use the Item List to determine the appropriate sales items for billing.
- Use **Thank you for your business.** as the message for these invoices.
- ONLINE PAYMENT should say Off.
- If you make an error, correct it.
- Print each invoice immediately after you enter the information for it.
- To go from one invoice to the next, click the **Save & New** button.
- Click **Save & Close** after Invoice 6 has been entered and printed.

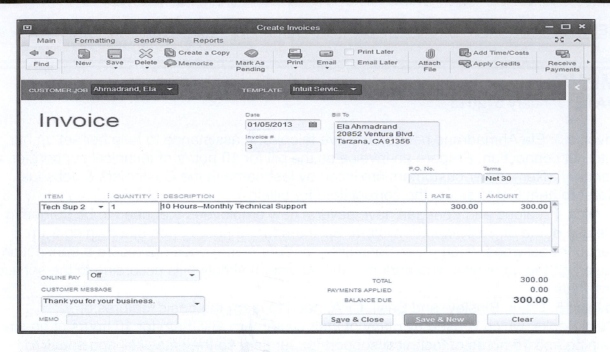

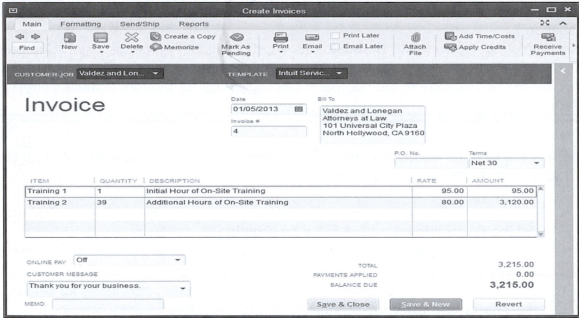

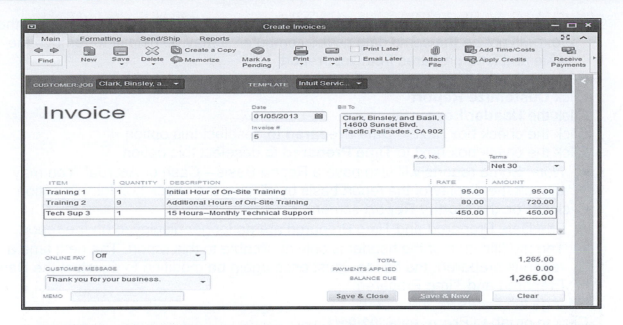

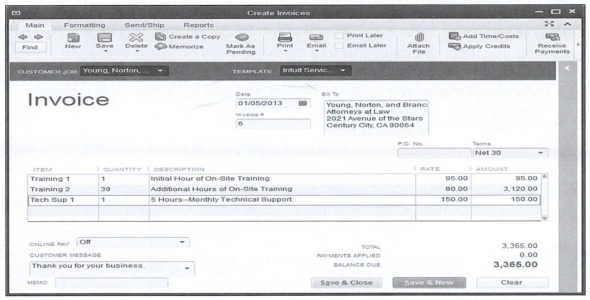

PRINT ACCOUNTS RECEIVABLE REPORTS

QuickBooks has several reports available for accounts receivable. One of the most useful is the Customer Balance Summary Report. It shows you the balances of all the customers on account.

 Print the Customer Balance Summary Report

Click **Reports** on the menu bar
Point to **Customers & Receivables**
Click **Customer Balance Summary**
- The report should appear on the screen.

- The current date and time will appear on the report. Since the dates given in the text will not be the same date as the computer, it may be helpful to remove the date and time prepared from your report.

Remove the date prepared and the time prepared from the report:

Click **Customize Report**

Click the **Header/Footer** tab

Click the check box next to **Date Prepared** to deselect this option

Click the check box next to **Time Prepared** to deselect this option

- *Note:* Some reports will also have a Report Basis—Cash or Accrual. You may turn off the display of the report basis by clicking the check box for this option.

Click **OK** on the **Modify Report** screen

- The Date Prepared and Time Prepared are no longer displayed on the report.
- The modification of the header is only applicable to this report. The next time a report is prepared, the header must once again be modified to deselect the Date Prepared and Time Prepared.

Change the Dates for the report:

Click in or tab to **From**, enter **01/01/13**

Tab to **To**, Enter **01/05/13**

Press the Tab key

- After you enter the date, pressing the tab key will generate the report.
- This report lists the names of all customers with balances on account. The amount column shows the total balance for each customer. This includes opening balances as well as current invoices.

```
Computer Consulting by Your Name
      Customer Balance Summary
           As of January 5, 2013
                               ◇ Jan 5, 13 ◇
  Ahmadrand, Ela              ▶     300.00 ◀
  Andrews Productions              3,190.00
  Clark, Binsley, and Basil, CPA   1,265.00
  Creative Products               1,295.00
  Design Creations                3,230.00
  Duncan, Jones, and Cline        1,915.00
  Gomez, Juan Esq.                  450.00
  Mahmood Imports                   300.00
  Research Corp.                    815.00
  Rosenthal Illustrations         3,830.00
  Shumway, Lewis, and Levy        3,685.00
  Valdez and Lonegan              3,215.00
  Wagner, Leavitt, and Moraga     3,680.00
  Williams, Matt CPA                890.00
  Young, Norton, and Brancato     3,365.00
  TOTAL                          31,425.00
```

Click the **Print** button at the top of the Customer Balance Summary Report

Complete the information on the **Print Reports Settings** tab:

Printer To: Printer (should identify the type of printer you are using):

- This may be different from the printer identified in this text.

Orientation: Should be Portrait. If it is not, click **Portrait** to select Portrait orientation for this report

- Portrait orientation prints in the traditional 8 ½- by 11-inch paper size.

Page Range: **All** should be selected; if it is not, click **All**
Page Breaks: Smart page breaks (widow/orphan control) should be selected
Number of copies should be **1**
Collate is not necessary on a one-page report, it may be left with or without the
   check mark
If necessary, click on **Fit report to 1 page(s) wide** to deselect this item
- When selected, the printer will print the report using a smaller font so it will be
   one page in width.
Leave **Print in color** without a check mark

Click **Print** on the **Print Reports** screen
Do not close the **Customer Balance Summary Report**

USE THE QUICKZOOM FEATURE

You ask the office manager, Alhandra Cruz, to obtain information regarding the balance of
the Valdez and Lonegan account. To get detailed information regarding an individual
customer's balance while in the Customer Balance Summary Report, use the QuickZoom
feature. With the individual customer's information on the screen, you can print a report for
that customer.

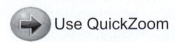 Use QuickZoom

Point to the balance for **Valdez and Lonegan**

- Notice that the mouse pointer turns into a magnifying glass with a **Z** in it.
Click once to mark the balance **3,215.00**
- Notice the marks on either side of the amount.

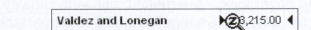

Double-click to **Zoom** in to see the details

The report dates used should be from **01/01/13** to **01/05/13**
Remove the Date Prepared and Time Prepared from the header
- Follow the instructions previously listed for removing the date and time prepared from the header for the Customer Balance Summary Report.

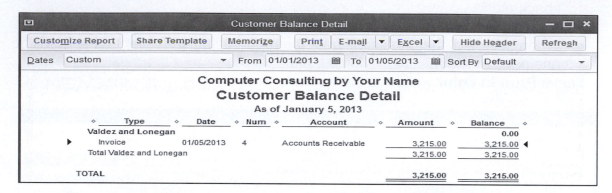

- Notice that Invoice 4 was recorded on 01/05/2013 for $3,215.
- To view Invoice 4, simply double-click on this transaction, and the invoice will be shown on the screen.

To exit Invoice 4 and return to the Customer Balance Detail Report, click the **Close** button on the title bar of the **Create Invoices** screen for Invoice 4.

Print the **Customer Balance Detail Report** for Valdez and Lonegan
- Follow the steps previously listed for printing the Customer Balance Summary Report.

Click **Close** to close **Customer Balance Detail Report**
- If you get a screen for Memorize Report, always click **No**

Click **Close** to close **Customer Balance Summary Report**
- If you get a screen for Memorize Report, always click **No**

CORRECT AN INVOICE AND PRINT THE CORRECTED FORM

Errors may be corrected very easily with QuickBooks. Because an invoice is prepared for sales on account, corrections may be made directly on the invoice or in the Accounts Receivable account register. We will access the invoice via the register for the Accounts Receivable account. The account register contains detailed information regarding each transaction that used the account. Therefore, anytime an invoice is recorded, it is posted to the Accounts Receivable register.

MEMO:

DATE: January 7, 2013

The actual amount of time spent for on-site training at Clark, Binsley, and Basil, CPA increased from 10 hours to 12 hours. Change Invoice 5 to correct the actual amount of training hours to show a total of 12 hours.

Correct an error in Invoice 5 using the Accounts Receivable Register and print the corrected invoice

Click the **Chart of Accounts** icon in the Company Section of the Home Page
In the Chart of Accounts, click **Accounts Receivable**

Chart of Accounts

Click the **Activities** button and click **Use Register**
    OR
Double-click **Accounts Receivable** in the Chart of Accounts
- The Accounts Receivable Register appears on the screen with information regarding each transaction entered into the account.
- *Note:* This is the same as the Accounts Receivable General Ledger Account
- Look at the **NUMBER/TYPE** column to identify the number of the invoice and the type of transaction.
- When the <u>NUMBER</u> line shows an <u>invoice number</u>, the <u>TYPE</u> line will show <u>INV</u>
- If the <u>NUMBER</u> line shows a <u>check number</u>, the <u>TYPE</u> line will show <u>PMT</u>. This indicates that a payment on account was received.

If necessary, scroll through the register until the transaction for **Invoice 5** is on the screen
- When scrolling through the register, you may see some beginning balances that are dated 12/31/2012.

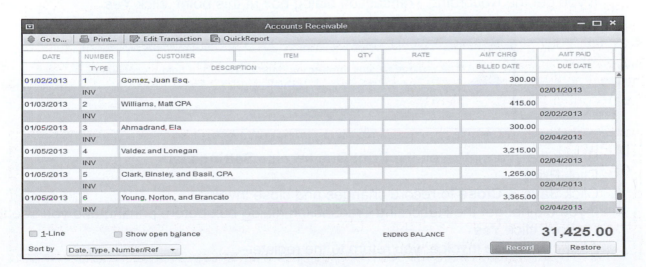

Click anywhere in the transaction for Invoice 5 to Clark, Binsley, and Basil, CPA
Click **Edit Transaction** at the top of the register
- Invoice 5 appears on the screen.

Click the line in the **QUANTITY** field that corresponds to the **Training 2** hours
Change the quantity from 9 hours to 11 hours
Position cursor in front of the 9
Press **Delete**
Type **11**
Press **Tab** to generate a new total

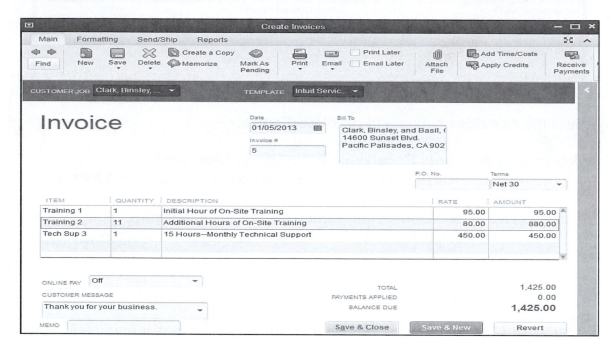

- Notice that the date remains 01/05/2013.

Click **Print** button on the **Create Invoices** screen to print a corrected invoice
If you get the Recording Transaction dialog box at this point, click **Yes**

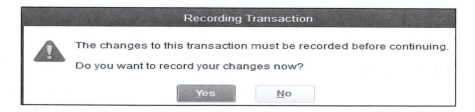

Check the information on the **Print One Invoice Settings** tab
Click **Print**
Click **Save & Close** to record changes and close invoice
If you did not get the Recording Transaction dialog box before printing and you see it now, click **Yes**
After closing the invoice, you return to the register.

VIEW A QUICKREPORT

After editing the invoice and returning to the register, you may get a detailed report regarding the customer's transactions by clicking the QuickReport button.

 View a QuickReport for Clark, Binsley, and Basil, CPA

Click the **QuickReport** button [QuickReport] at the top of the Register to view the **Clark, Binsley, and Basil** account
Verify the balance of the account. It should be **$1,425.00**
- *Note:* You will get the date prepared, time prepared, and the report basis in the heading of your QuickReport.

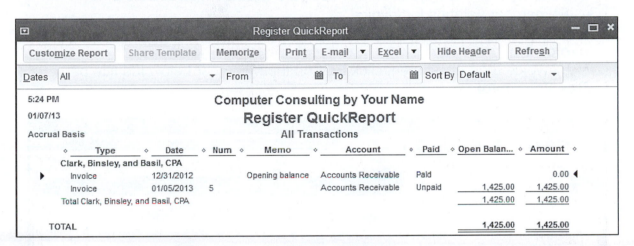

ANALYZE THE QUICKREPORT FOR CLARK, BINSLEY, AND BASIL

 Analyze the QuickReport

Notice that the total of Invoice 5 is $1,425.00
Close the **QuickReport** without printing
Close the **Accounts Receivable Register**
Close the **Chart of Accounts**

VOID AND DELETE SALES FORMS

Deleting an invoice or sales receipt permanently removes it from QuickBooks without leaving a trace. If you would like to correct your financial records for the invoice that you no longer want, it is more appropriate to void the invoice. When an invoice is voided, it remains in the QuickBooks system with a zero balance.

VOID AN INVOICE

> **MEMO:**
> **DATE:** January 7, 2013
>
> Ela Ahmadrand called to cancel the 10 hours of technical support for January. Since none of the technical support had been used, you decide to void Invoice 3.

 Void the invoice above by going directly to the original invoice:

Use the keyboard shortcut **Ctrl+I** to open the Create Invoices screen
- Remember I stands for Invoice

Click the **Previous** or **Back** arrow on the Invoice icon bar until you get to **Invoice 3**

With Invoice 3 on the screen, click **Edit** on the <u>Menu</u> bar below the title bar
Click **Void Invoice**

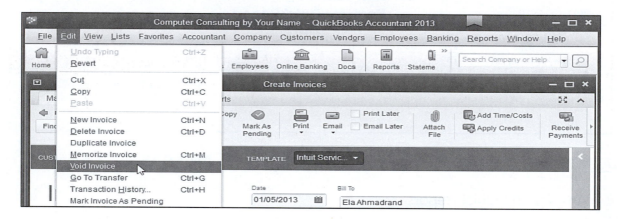

- Notice that the amount and total for the invoice are no longer 300. They are both **0.00**.
- Find the Memo text box at the bottom of the invoice and verify that **VOID:** appears as the memo.

Click **Save & Close** on the **Create Invoices** screen
Click **Yes** on the **Recording Transaction** dialog box
Click the **Reports** button on the Icon bar
Click **Customers & Receivables** as the Type of Report

- The report categories are displayed on the left side of the Report Center. To prepare a report, click the desired type of report.

Click the **List View** button to select the report list

- Remember there are three ways to view a report list—carousel view, list view, and graph view.

After selecting the List view, scroll through the list of reports, and click **Transaction List by Customer** in the Customer Balance section

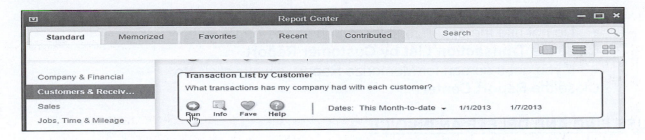

Click the **Run** button
Tab to or Click in **From**
Remove the current date; if it is not highlighted, and enter **010113**

- Using a **/** between the items in a date is optional.

Tab to or click in **To**
Remove the current date; if it is not highlighted, and enter **010713**, press **Tab**
Remove the date prepared and the time prepared from the report heading:

    Click **Customize Report**
    Click **Header/Footer** tab
    Click the check box next to **Date Prepared** and **Time Prepared** to deselect these options
    Click **OK**

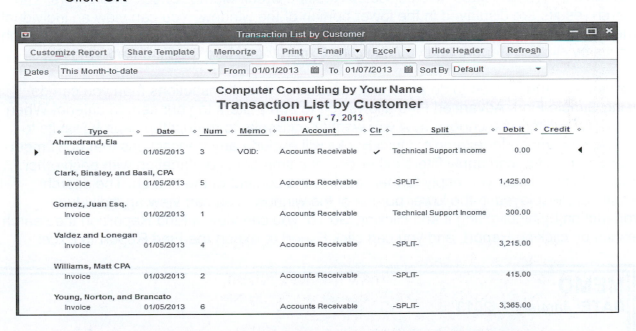

- This report gives the amount for each transaction with the customer.
- Notice that Invoice 3 is marked VOID in the Memo column and has a √ in the **Clr** (Cleared) column.
- The SPLIT column tells you which account was used to record the income. If the word **-SPLIT-** appears in the column, this means the transaction amount was split or divided among two or more accounts.

Print the **Transactions List by Customer Report** in Landscape orientation following printing instructions provided earlier in the chapter

Click **Landscape** to use Landscape Orientation (11 wide by 8 ½ long).
- Do not use the option to fit the report to one-page wide.

Close the **Transaction List by Customer Report**
- If you get a screen for Memorize Report, always click **No**

Close the **Report Center**

USE FIND AND DELETE AN INVOICE

When an invoice is deleted, it is permanently removed from QuickBooks. It will no longer be listed in any reports or shown as an invoice.

Find is useful when you have a large number of invoices and want to locate an invoice for a particular customer. Using Find will locate the invoice without requiring you to scroll through all the invoices for the company. For example, if customer Jimenez's transaction was on Invoice 3 and the invoice on the screen was Invoice 1,084, you would not have to scroll through 1,081 invoices because Find would locate Invoice 3 instantly. QuickBooks® 2013 has two methods for finding transactions: Simple Find and Advanced Find.

Simple Find allows you to do a quick search using the most common transaction types. Transaction Types include Invoice, Sales Receipt, Credit Memo, Check, and others. The search results are displayed in the lower portion of the window. You can view an individual transaction by highlighting it and clicking Go To, you can view a Find Report on the search results by clicking Report, and you can click Export the export the Find Report to Excel.

Advanced Find is used to do a more detailed search for transactions than you can do using Simple Find. Advanced Find allows you to apply filters to your search criteria. When you apply a filter, you choose how you want QuickBooks to restrict the search results to certain customers, for example. QuickBooks will exclude any transactions that don't meet your criteria. You can apply filters either one at a time or in combination with each other. Each additional filter you apply further restricts the content of the search. The search results are displayed in the lower portion of the window. You can view an individual transaction by highlighting it and clicking Go To, you can view a Find Report on the search results by clicking Report, and you can click Export to export the Find Report to Excel.

MEMO:

DATE: January 7, 2013

Because of the upcoming tax season, Matt Williams has had to reschedule his 5-hour training session with Jennifer Lockwood three times. He finally decided to cancel the training session and reschedule it after April 15. Delete Invoice 2.

 Delete Invoice 2 to Matt Williams, using Find to locate the invoice:

Use Simple Find by clicking **Edit** on the menu bar, clicking **Find** on the Edit menu
    and clicking the **Simple Find** tab
The Transaction Type should be **Invoice**.
- If it is not, click the drop-down list arrow for Transaction Type and click Invoice.

Click the drop-down list arrow for **Customer:Job**
Click **Williams, Matt CPA**
- This allows QuickBooks to find any invoices recorded for Matt Williams.

Click the **Find** button
Click the line for **Invoice 2**
- Make sure you have selected Invoice 2 and not the invoice containing the
  opening balance.

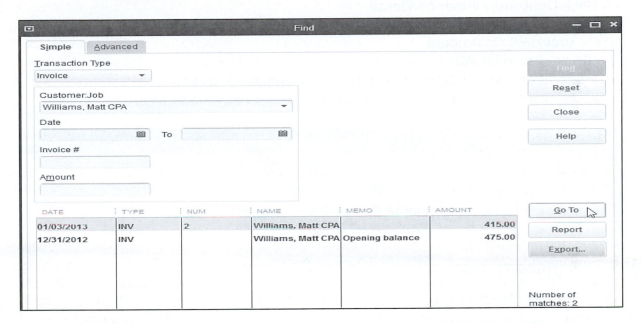

Click **Go To**
- Invoice 2 appears on the screen.

With the invoice on the screen, click **Edit** on the menu bar

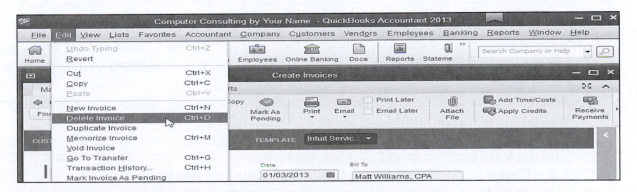

Click **Delete Invoice**
Click **OK** in the **Delete Transaction** dialog box

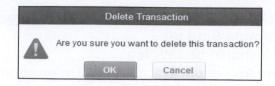

- Notice that the cursor is now positioned on Invoice 3

Click **Save & Close** button on the **Create Invoices** screen to close the invoice

- Notice that Invoice 2 no longer shows on **Find**.

Click the **Close** button to close **Find**

Click **Reports** on the menu bar

Point to **Customers & Receivables**

Click **Customer Balance Detail**

Remove the **Date Prepared** and **Time Prepared** from the report header as previously instructed

Dates should be **All**

Print the report in Portrait orientation as previously instructed

- In order to save space, only a partial report is displayed below.

Customize Report	Share Template	Memorize	Print	E-mail ▼	Excel ▼	Hide Header	Refresh

Dates All ▼   From [ ] 📅 To [ ] 📅 Sort By Default ▼

Computer Consulting by Your Name
Customer Balance Detail
All Transactions

Type	Date	Num	Account	Amount	Balance
Williams, Matt CPA					
Invoice	12/31/2012		Accounts Receivable	475.00	475.00
Total Williams, Matt CPA				475.00	475.00
Young, Norton, and Brancato					
Invoice	12/31/2012		Accounts Receivable	0.00	0.00
Invoice	01/05/2013	6	Accounts Receivable	3,365.00	3,365.00
Total Young, Norton, and Brancato				3,365.00	3,365.00
TOTAL				30,870.00	30,870.00

Partial Report

- Look at the account for Matt Williams. Notice that Invoice 2 does not show up in the account listing. When an invoice is deleted, there is no record of it anywhere in the report.
- Notice that the Customer Balance Detail Report does not include the information telling you which amounts are opening balances.
- The report does give information regarding the amount owed on each transaction plus the total amount owed by each customer.

Click the **Close** button to close the **Customer Balance Detail Report**

If you get the Memorize Report screen, click **Do not display this message in the future**; and then, click **No**

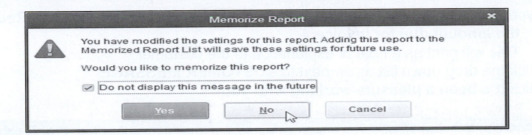

PREPARE A CREDIT MEMO

Credit memos are prepared to show a reduction to a transaction. If the invoice has already been sent to the customer, it is more appropriate and less confusing to make a change to a transaction by issuing a credit memo rather than voiding or deleting the invoice and issuing a new one. A credit memo notifies a customer that a change has been made to a transaction.

MEMO:
DATE: January 8, 2013

Credit Memo 7: Valdez and Lonegan did not need 5 hours of the training billed on Invoice 4. Issue a Credit Memo to reduce Training 2 by 5 hours.

 Prepare a Credit Memo

Click the **Refunds and Credits** icon in the Customers area of the Home Page
Click the down arrow for the drop-down list box next to **CUSTOMER:JOB**
Click **Valdez and Lonegan**
- Notice that the History for Valdez and Lonegan is shown on the right side of the invoice.
The **Template** textbox should say **Custom Credit Memo**.
- If not, click the drop-down list arrow and click **Custom Credit Memo**.
Tab to or click **Date**
Type in the date of the credit memo: **01/08/13**
The **Credit No.** field should show the number **7**
- Because credit memos are included in the numbering sequence for invoices, this number matches the number of the next blank invoice.
There is no PO No.
Tab to or click in **ITEM**
Click the drop-down list arrow in the Item column
Click **Training 2**
Tab to or click in **QUANTITY**
Type in **5**
Click the next blank line in the DESCRIPTION column

Type **Deduct 5 hours of additional training, which was not required. Reduce the amount due for Invoice 4.**

- This will print as a note or explanation to the customer.

Click the drop-down list arrow next to **CUSTOMER MESSAGE**

Click **It's been a pleasure working with you!**

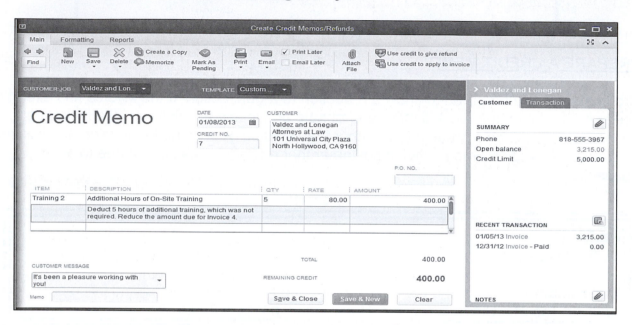

To apply the credit to an invoice, click **Use credit to apply to invoice** on the Icon bar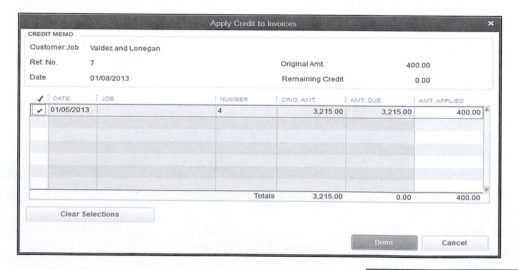

- Make sure there is a check mark for Invoice 4 on the Apply Credit to Invoices screen.

Click **Done**

- Notice the Recent Transactions section in the History pane. It includes the Credit Memo.

RECENT TRANSACTION	
01/08/13 Credit Memo	400.00
01/05/13 Invoice	3,215.00
12/31/12 Invoice – Paid	0.00

Click **Print** on **Create Credit Memos/Refunds**
Click **Print** on **Print One Credit Memo**
Click the **Save & Close** button

VIEW CUSTOMER BALANCE DETAIL REPORT

Periodically viewing reports allows you to verify the changes that have occurred to accounts. The Customer Balance Detail report shows all the transactions for each credit customer. Cash customers must be viewed through sales reports.

 View the Customer Balance Detail Report

Click the **Reports** button on the Icon bar
Click **Customers & Receivables** as the report type
In the Customer Balance section, click **Customer Balance Detail** on the list of
    reports displayed; and then, click the **Run** icon
Scroll through the report
- Notice that the account for Valdez and Lonegan shows Credit Memo 7 for $400.00. The total amount owed was reduced by $400 and is $2,815.00.
- In order to save space, only a partial report is displayed below.

10:50 AM
01/08/13

Computer Consulting by Your Name
Customer Balance Detail
All Transactions

Type	Date	Num	Account	Amount	Balance
Valdez and Lonegan					
Invoice	12/31/2012		Accounts Receivable	0.00	0.00
Invoice	01/05/2013	4	Accounts Receivable	3,215.00	3,215.00
Credit Memo	01/08/2013	7	Accounts Receivable	-400.00	2,815.00
Total Valdez and Lonegan				2,815.00	2,815.00
Wagner, Leavitt, and Moraga					
Invoice	12/31/2012		Accounts Receivable	3,680.00	3,680.00
Total Wagner, Leavitt, and Moraga				3,680.00	3,680.00
Williams, Matt CPA					
Invoice	12/31/2012		Accounts Receivable	475.00	475.00
Total Williams, Matt CPA				475.00	475.00
Young, Norton, and Brancato					
Invoice	12/31/2012		Accounts Receivable	0.00	0.00
Invoice	01/05/2013	6	Accounts Receivable	3,365.00	3,365.00
Total Young, Norton, and Brancato				3,365.00	3,365.00
TOTAL				30,470.00	30,470.00

Partial Report

Click the **Close** button to close the report without printing
Close the **Report Center**

ADD A NEW ACCOUNT TO THE CHART OF ACCOUNTS

Because account needs can change as a business is in operation, QuickBooks allows you to make changes to the chart of accounts at any time. Some changes to the chart of accounts require additional changes to lists.

You have determined that Computer Consulting by Your Name has received a lot of calls from customers for assistance with hardware and network installation. Even though Computer Consulting by Your Name does not record revenue according to the employee performing the service, it does assign primary areas of responsibility to some of the personnel. Rom Levy will be responsible for installing hardware and setting up networks for customers. As a result of this decision, you will be adding a third income account. It will be used when revenue from hardware or network installation is earned. In addition to adding the account, you will also have to add two new sales items to the Item list.

MEMO:

DATE: January 8, 2013

Add a new account, Installation Income. It is a subaccount of Income.

 Add a new income account for Hardware and Network Installation

Click the **Chart of Accounts** icon in the Company section of the Home Page
- Remember that the Chart of Accounts is also the General Ledger.

Click the **Account** button at the bottom of the Chart of Accounts screen

Click **New**

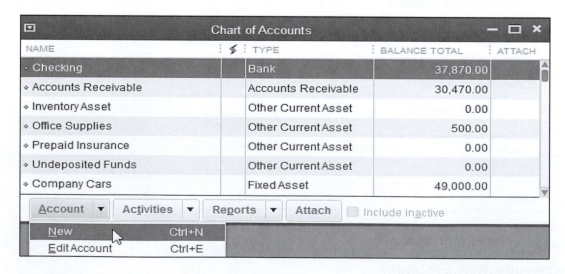

Click **Income** to choose one account type

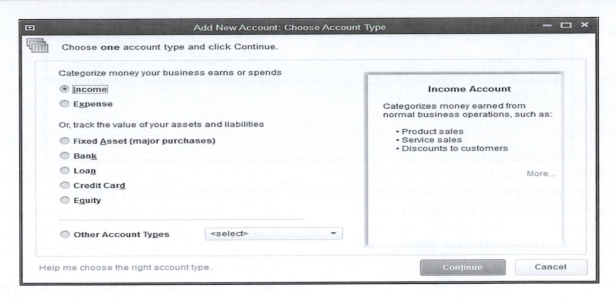

Click the **Continue** button.
If necessary, tab to or click in the text box for **Account Name**
Type **Installation Income**
Click the check box for **Subaccount of**
Click the drop-down list arrow for **Subaccount of**
Click **Income**
Tab to or click **Description**
Type **Hardware and Network Installation Income**

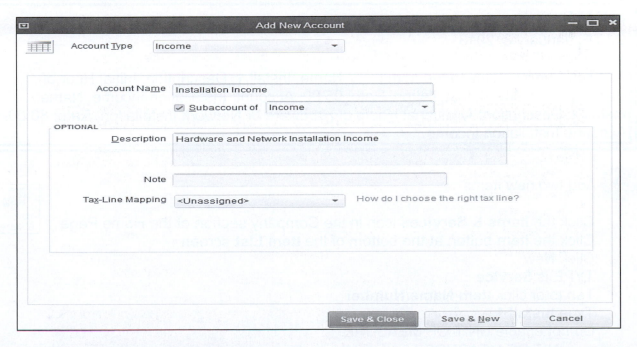

Click the **Save & Close** button
Scroll through the Chart of Accounts
Verify that Installation Income has been added under Income

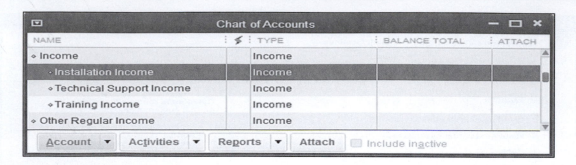

- Notice that the subaccounts are shown below Income and are indented .
Close **Chart of Accounts**

ADD NEW ITEMS TO THE ITEMS LIST

In order to accommodate the changing needs of a business, all QuickBooks lists allow you to make changes at any time. The Item List stores information about the services Computer Consulting by Your Name provides. Items are sometimes called Sales Items because an item is identified when recording a cash or credit sale.

In order to use the new Installation Income account, two new items need to be added to the Item List. When these items are used in a transaction, the amount of revenue earned in the transaction will be posted to the Installation Income account.

MEMO:

DATE: January 8, 2013

Add two Service items to the Item List—Name: Install 1, Description: Initial Hour of Hardware or Network Installation, Rate: 95.00, Account: Installation Income. Name: Install 2, Description: Additional Hours of Hardware or Network Installation, Rate: 80.00, Account: Installation Income.

 Add two new items

Click the **Items & Services** icon in the Company section of the Home Page
Click the **Item** button at the bottom of the **Item List** screen
Click **New**
TYPE is **Service**
Tab to or click **Item Name/Number**
Type **Install 1**
Do <u>not</u> enable UNIT OF MEASURE
- UNIT OF MEASURE (not available in Pro) is used to indicate what quantities, prices, rates, and costs are based on. For example, a quantity of 4 for installation

could mean four hours, four days, or four weeks. Setting the unit of measure allows clarification of this.

Tab to or click **Description**

Type **Initial Hour of Hardware/Network Installation**

Tab to or click **Rate**

Type **95**

To indicate the general ledger account to be used to record the sale of this item, click the drop-down list arrow for **Account**

Click **Installation Income**

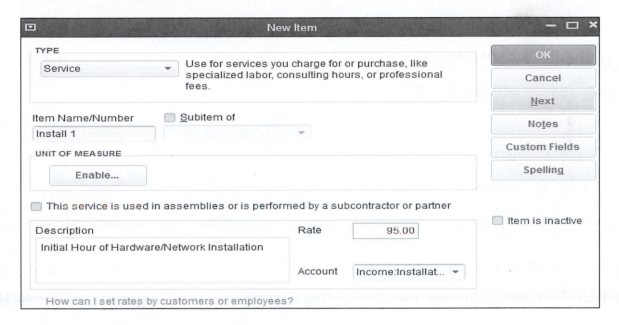

Click **Next** on the New Item dialog box

Repeat the steps above to add **Install 2**

The description is **Additional Hours of Hardware/Network Installation**

The rate is **80.00** per hour

The account is **Installation Income**

When finished adding Install 2, click **OK** to add new items and to close **New Item** screen

- Whenever hardware or network installation is provided for customers, the first hour will be billed as Install 1, and additional hours will be billed as Install 2.

Verify the addition of Install 1 and Install 2 on the Item List

- If you find an error, click on the item with the error, click the **Item** button, click **Edit**, and make corrections as needed.

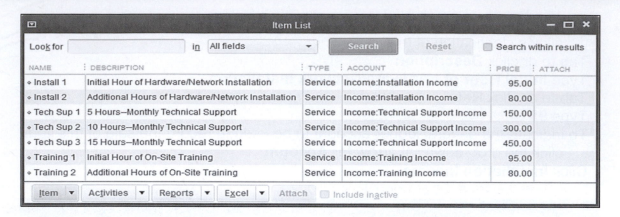

Close the **Item List**

ADD A NEW CUSTOMER

Because customers are the lifeblood of a business, QuickBooks allows customers to be added "on the fly" as you create an invoice or a sales receipt. You may choose between Quick Add (used to add only a customer's name) and Set Up (used to add complete information for a customer).

> **MEMO:**
>
> **DATE:** January 8, 2013
>
> Invoice 8: A new customer, Ken Collins, has purchased several upgrade items for his personal computer. He needs assistance with the installation. Rom Levy spent two hours installing this hardware. Bill Mr. Collins for 2 hours of hardware installation. His address is: 20985 Ventura Blvd., Woodland Hills, CA 91371. His telephone number is: 818-555-2058. His fax number is 808-555-8502. His E-mail is KCollins@123.com. His credit limit is $1,000; and the terms are Net 30.

 Add a new customer and record the above sale on account

    Click the **Create Invoices** icon on the Home Page
    In the Customer:Job dialog box, type **Collins, Ken**
    Press **Tab**
- You will see a message box for **Customer:Job Not Found** with buttons for three choices:
  - **Quick Add** (used to add only a customer's name)
  - **Set Up** (**used** to add complete information for a customer)
  - **Cance**l (used to cancel the **Customer:Job Not Found** message box)

    Click **Set Up**

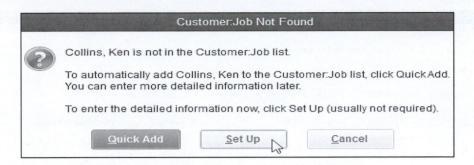

Complete the **New Customer** dialog box
- The name **Collins, Ken** is displayed in the CUSTOMER NAME field and as the first line of INVOICE/BILL TO in the ADDRESS DETAILS section on the Address Info tab.

There is no Opening Balance, so leave this field blank
- An opening balance may be given only when the customer's account is created. It is the amount the customer owes you at the time the account is created. It is not the amount of any transaction not yet recorded.

Complete the information for the **Address Info** tab

Tab to or click in the text box for **First** in the line for Full Name, type **Ken**

Tab to or click in text box for **Last** in the line for Full Name, type **Collins**

Tab to or click in text box for **Main Phone**

Type the phone number **818-555-2058**

Tab to or click in text box for **Main E-mail**, enter **KCollins@123.com**

Tab to or click in text box for **Fax**, enter **818-555-8502**

Tab to or click the first line for **INVOICE/BILL TO**

If necessary, highlight **Collins, Ken**

Type **Ken Collins**
- Entering the customer name in this manner allows for the Customer:Job List to be organized according to the last name, yet the bill will be printed with the first name, then the last name.

Press **Enter** or click the second line of the billing address

Type the address **20985 Ventura Blvd.**

Press **Enter** or click the third line of the billing address

Type **Woodland Hills, CA 91371**

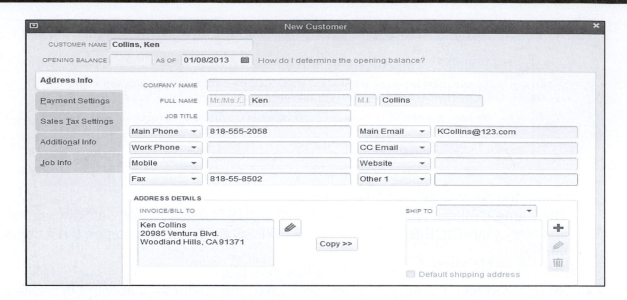

Click the **Payment Settings** tab on the left-side of the New Customer screen
Tab to or click **PAYMENT TERMS**
Click the drop-down list arrow
Click **Net 30**
Tab to or click **CREDIT LIMIT**
Type the amount **1000**, press **Tab**

- Do not use a dollar sign. QuickBooks will insert the comma and decimal point.

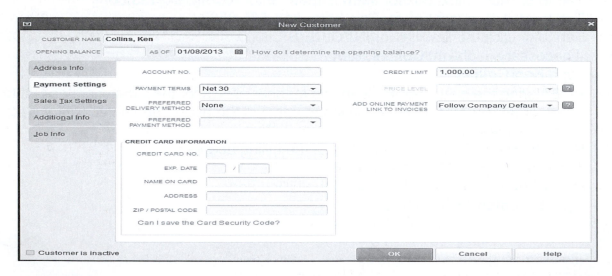

Click **OK** to return to the Invoice
Enter Invoice information as previously instructed
Date of the invoice is **01/08/13**
Invoice # is **8**
The bill is for 2 hours of hardware installation

- Remember to bill for the initial or first hour, then bill the other hour separately.

The message is **Thank you for your business.**

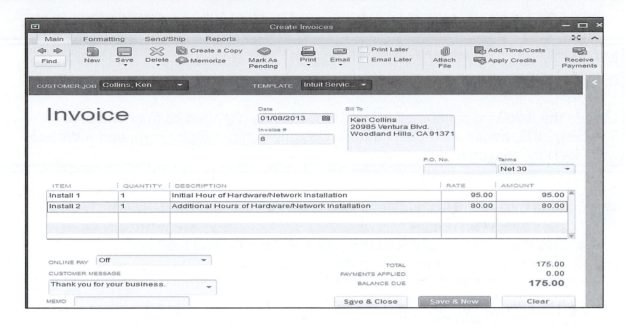

    Print the invoice as previously instructed
    Click **Save & Close** on the invoice to record and close the transaction

PREPARE A DAILY BACKUP

A backup file is prepared as a safe guard in case you make an error. After a number of transactions have been recorded, it is wise to prepare a backup file. In addition, a backup should be made at the end of every work session. The Daily Backup file is an appropriate file to create for saving your work as you progress through a chapter.

If you have created a daily backup file while you are working in a chapter and make an error later in your training and cannot figure out how to correct it, you may restore the backup file. Restoring your daily backup file will restore your work from the previous training session and eliminate the work completed in the current session. By creating the backup file now, it will contain your work for Chapter 1 and up through entering Invoice 8 in Chapter 2.

 Prepare the Computer (Daily Backup).qbb file

    Follow the steps presented in Chapter 1 for creating a backup file
    Name the file **Computer (Daily Backup)**
    The file type is **QBW Backup (* .QBB)**

MODIFY CUSTOMER RECORDS

Occasionally, information regarding a customer will change. QuickBooks allows you to modify customer accounts at any time by editing the Customer:Job List.

MEMO:

DATE: January 8, 2013

Update the following account: Design Creations has changed its fax number to 310-555-2109, added an e-mail address DesignCreations@abc.com, and a Website www.DesignCreations.

 Edit the customer Design Creations:

Access the Customer:Job List using one of the following methods:
- Click the **Customers** icon on the icon bar.
- Use the keyboard shortcut: **Ctrl+J**
- Click the **Customers** icon on the Home Page
- Click the **Customers** menu, click **Customer Center**
- When the Customer Center is opened, you may see abbreviated customer names .

Widen the **NAME** column by pointing to the dotted vertical line between **NAME** and **BALANCE TOTAL**

When you get a double arrow, hold down the primary mouse button and drag to the right until the full customer name appears for all the customers

Click **Design Creations** in the Customers & Jobs list in the Customer Center

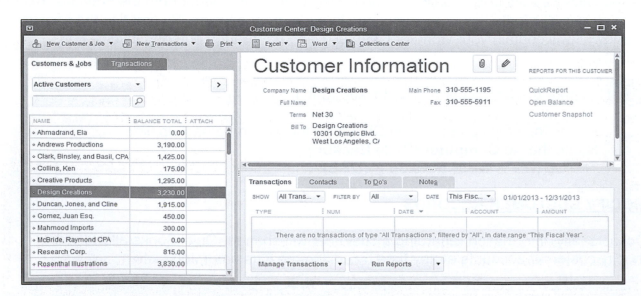

Edit the customer in one of three ways:
Click the **Edit** button
Use the keyboard shortcut **Ctrl+E**.
Double-click **Design Creations** on the **Customer:Job List**.
To change the fax number to **310-555-2109**: Click at the end of the fax number, backspace to delete **5911**, type **2109**
Tab to or click in the text box for **Main E-mail**, enter the e-mail address **DesignCreations@abc.com**
Tab to or click in the text box for **Website**, enter the Web address **www.DesignCreations**

Click **OK**
• Note the change to the Fax, Email, and Website.
Close the **Customer Center**

RECORD CASH SALES

Not all sales in a business are on account. In many instances, payment is made at the time the service is performed and is entered as a cash sale. When entering a cash sale, you prepare a sales receipt rather than an invoice. QuickBooks records the transaction in the Journal and places the amount of cash received in an account called Undeposited Funds. The funds received remain in Undeposited Funds until you record a deposit to your bank account.

MEMO:

DATE: January 10, 2013

Sales Receipt 1: You provided 5 hours of on-site training to Raymond McBride, CPA, and received Ray's Check 3287 for the full amount due. Prepare Sales Receipt 1 for this transaction. Use "It's been a pleasure working with you!" as the message.

Record a Cash Sale

Click the **Create Sales Receipts** icon in the Customers section of the Home Page

- Since Sales Receipts are used for cash sales, the customer history does not need to be displayed on the right side of the screen each time you create a Sales Receipt.

To remove the History, click the **Hide History** button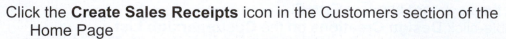

Resize the form by pointing to the right edge of the Sales Receipt

When your cursor turns into a double arrow ⬌, hold down the cursor and drag to the left to make the form smaller

- If the Sales Receipt is maximized, you will not be able to using the sizing handle (the double arrow) to resize the form. If that is the case, click the **Restore** button; and then resize as instructed above.

Click the drop-down list arrow next to **CUSTOMER:JOB**

Click **McBride, Raymond, CPA**

Tab to **TEMPLATE**

- This should have **Custom Cash Sale** as the template. If not, click the drop-down list arrow and click **Custom Cash Sale**.

Tab to or click **DATE**

Type **01/10/13**

- You may click on the calendar icon next to the date text box. Make sure the month is January and the year is 2013 then click **10**.

SALE NO. should be **1**

Tab to or click **CHECK NO.**

Type **3287**

Click the drop-down list arrow next to **PAYMENT METHOD**

Click **Check**

Tab to or click the first line for **ITEM**

Click the drop-down list arrow next to **ITEM**

Click **Training 1**

Tab to or click **QTY**

Type **1**

Tab to or click the second line for **ITEM**

Click the drop-down list arrow next to **ITEM**

Click **Training 2**

Tab to or click **QTY**

Type **4**

- The amount and total are automatically calculated when you go to the CUSTOMER MESSAGE or tab past QTY.

Click **CUSTOMER MESSAGE**

Click the drop-down list arrow for **CUSTOMER MESSAGE**

Click **It's been a pleasure working with you!**

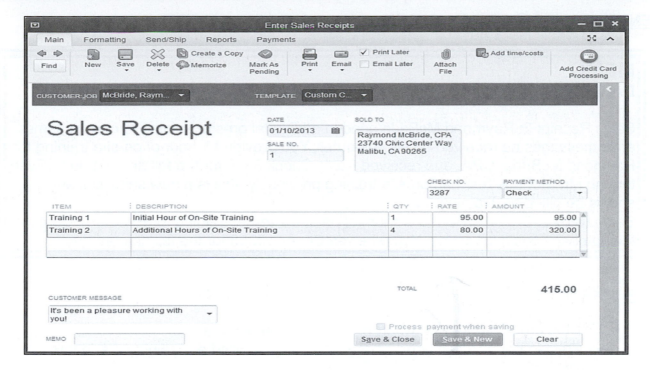

Do not close the Sales Receipt

PRINT SALES RECEIPT

 Print the sales receipt

Click **Print** button on the top of the **Enter Sales Receipts** screen
Check the information on the **Print One Sales Receipt Settings** tab:
Printer name (should identify the type of printer you are using):
Printer type: Page-oriented (Single sheets)
Print on: Blank paper
Do not print lines around each field check box should have a check mark
Number of copies should be **1**
Click **Print**
- This initiates the printing of the sales receipt through QuickBooks. However, since not all classroom configurations are the same, check with your instructor for specific printing instructions.
Once the Sales Receipt has been printed, click **Save & New** on the bottom of the **Enter Sales Receipts** screen
- If you get a Recording Transaction message, click **Yes**.

ENTER CASH SALES TRANSACTIONS WITHOUT STEP-BY-STEP INSTRUCTIONS

> **MEMO:**
> **DATE:** January 12, 2013
>
> Sales Receipt 2: Raymond McBride needed additional on-site training to correct some error messages he received on his computer. You provided 1 hour of on-site training for Raymond McBride, CPA, and received Ray's Check 3306 for the full amount due. (Even though Mr. McBride has had on-site training previously, this is a new sales call and should be billed as Training 1.)
>
> Sales Receipt 3: You provided 4 hours of on-site Internet training for Research Corp. so the company could be online. You received Check 10358 for the full amount due.

 Record the two January 12, 2013 transactions listed above

Use the procedures given when you entered Sales Receipt 1:
- Remember, the <u>first hour for on-site training</u> is billed as <u>Training 1</u> and the <u>remaining hours</u> are billed as <u>Training 2</u>.
- Always use the Item List to determine the appropriate sales items for billing.
- Use **Thank you for your business.** as the message for these sales receipts.
- **Print** each sales receipt immediately after entering the information for it.
- If you make an error, correct it.
- To go from one sales receipt to the next, click the **Save & New** button on the bottom of the **Enter Sales Receipts** screen.
- Click **Save & Close** after you have entered and printed Sales Receipt 3.

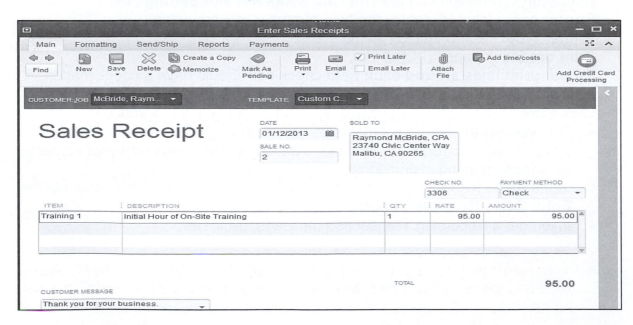

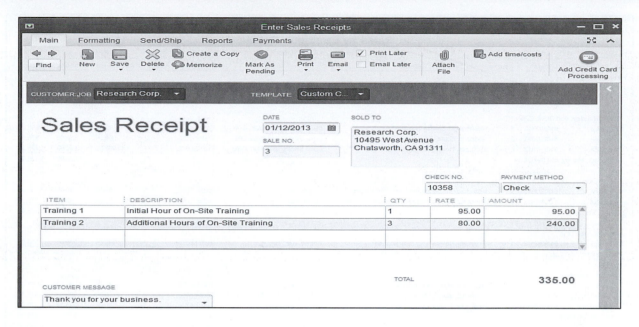

PRINT SALES BY CUSTOMER DETAIL REPORT

QuickBooks has reports available that enable you to obtain sales information about sales items or customers. To get information about the total amount of sales to each customer during a specific period, print a Sales by Customer Detail Report. The total shown represents both cash and/or credit sales.

 Prepare and print a Sales by Customer Detail Report

> Click **Reports** on the menu bar
> Point to **Sales**
> Click **Sales by Customer Detail**
> To remove the **Date Prepared**, **Time Prepared**, and **Report Basis** from the report, click the **Customize Report** button and follow the instructions given previously for deselecting the date prepared, time prepared, and report basis from the Header/Footer
> Change the dates to reflect the sales period from **01/01/13** to **01/12/13**
> Tab to generate the report
> - Notice that the report information includes the type of sales to each customer, the date of the sale, the sales item(s), the quantity for each item, the sales price, the amount, and the balance.
> - The report does not include information regarding opening or previous balances due.
> - The scope of this report is to focus on sales.
> - Your report may not show all of the information in the columns. The illustration shown in the text shows all of the information except the detail next to the Item name.

Computer Consulting by Your Name
Sales by Customer Detail
January 1 - 12, 2013

Type	Date	Num	Memo	Name	Item	Qty	Sales Price	Amount	Balance
Ahmadrand, Ela									
Invoice	01/05/2013	3	10 Hours—Monthly Technical Support	Ahmadrand, Ela	Tech Sup 2...	0	300.00	0.00	0.00
Total Ahmadrand, Ela						0		0.00	0.00
Clark, Binsley, and Basil, CPA									
Invoice	01/05/2013	5	Initial Hour of On-Site Training	Clark, Binsley, and Basil, CPA	Training 1 (...	1	95.00	95.00	95.00
Invoice	01/05/2013	5	Additional Hours of On-Site Training	Clark, Binsley, and Basil, CPA	Training 2 (...	11	80.00	880.00	975.00
Invoice	01/05/2013	5	15 Hours—Monthly Technical Support	Clark, Binsley, and Basil, CPA	Tech Sup 3...	1	450.00	450.00	1,425.00
Total Clark, Binsley, and Basil, CPA						13		1,425.00	1,425.00
Collins, Ken									
Invoice	01/08/2013	8	Initial Hour of Hardware/Network Installation	Collins, Ken	Install 1 (Init...	1	95.00	95.00	95.00
Invoice	01/08/2013	8	Additional Hours of Hardware/Network Installation	Collins, Ken	Install 2 (Ad...	1	80.00	80.00	175.00
Total Collins, Ken						2		175.00	175.00
Gomez, Juan Esq.									
Invoice	01/02/2013	1	10 Hours—Monthly Technical Support	Gomez, Juan Esq.	Tech Sup 2...	1	300.00	300.00	300.00
Total Gomez, Juan Esq.						1		300.00	300.00
McBride, Raymond CPA									
Sales Receipt	01/10/2013	1	Initial Hour of On-Site Training	McBride, Raymond CPA	Training 1 (...	1	95.00	95.00	95.00
Sales Receipt	01/10/2013	1	Additional Hours of On-Site Training	McBride, Raymond CPA	Training 2 (...	4	80.00	320.00	415.00
Sales Receipt	01/12/2013	2	Initial Hour of On-Site Training	McBride, Raymond CPA	Training 1 (...	1	95.00	95.00	510.00
Total McBride, Raymond CPA						6		510.00	510.00
Research Corp.									
Sales Receipt	01/12/2013	3	Initial Hour of On-Site Training	Research Corp.	Training 1 (...	1	95.00	95.00	95.00
Sales Receipt	01/12/2013	3	Additional Hours of On-Site Training	Research Corp.	Training 2 (...	3	80.00	240.00	335.00
Total Research Corp.						4		335.00	335.00
Valdez and Lonegan									
Invoice	01/05/2013	4	Initial Hour of On-Site Training	Valdez and Lonegan	Training 1 (...	1	95.00	95.00	95.00
Invoice	01/05/2013	4	Additional Hours of On-Site Training	Valdez and Lonegan	Training 2 (...	39	80.00	3,120.00	3,215.00
Credit Memo	01/08/2013	7	Additional Hours of On-Site Training	Valdez and Lonegan	Training 2 (...	-5	80.00	-400.00	2,815.00
Total Valdez and Lonegan						35		2,815.00	2,815.00
Young, Norton, and Brancato									
Invoice	01/05/2013	6	Initial Hour of On-Site Training	Young, Norton, and Brancato	Training 1 (...	1	95.00	95.00	95.00
Invoice	01/05/2013	6	Additional Hours of On-Site Training	Young, Norton, and Brancato	Training 2 (...	39	80.00	3,120.00	3,215.00
Invoice	01/05/2013	6	5 Hours—Monthly Technical Support	Young, Norton, and Brancato	Tech Sup 1...	1	150.00	150.00	3,365.00
Total Young, Norton, and Brancato						41		3,365.00	3,365.00
TOTAL						102		8,925.00	8,925.00

Click the **Print** button on the **Sales by Customer Detail** screen

On the **Print Report** screen, check the Settings tab to verify that **Print to**: Printer is selected and that the name of your printer is correct

If necessary, click **Landscape** to change the **Orientation** from Portrait

- Landscape changes the orientation of the paper so the report is printed 11-inches wide by 8½-inches long.

Verify that the **Page Range** is **All**

Make sure **Smart page breaks** have been selected

Do not select **Fit** report **to one page wide**. The printed report may require more than one page.

On the **Print Report** screen, click **Print**

Close the **Sales by Customer Detail Report**

- If you get a Memorize Transaction dialog box, click **No**.

CORRECT A SALES RECEIPT AND PRINT THE CORRECTED FORM

QuickBooks makes correcting errors user friendly. When an error is discovered in a transaction such as a cash sale, you can simply return to the form where the transaction was recorded and correct the error. Thus, to correct a sales receipt, you would open a Sales Receipt, click the Previous button until you found the appropriate sales receipt, and then correct the error. Because cash or checks received for cash sales are held in the Undeposited Funds account until the bank deposit is made, you can access the sales receipt through the Undeposited Funds account in the Chart of Accounts as well. Accessing the receipt in this manner allows you to see all the transactions entered in the account for Undeposited Funds.

When a correction for a sale is made, QuickBooks not only changes the form, it also changes all journal and account entries for the transaction to reflect the correction. QuickBooks then allows a corrected sales receipt to be printed.

MEMO:
DATE: January 14, 2013

After reviewing transaction information, you realize the date for the Sales Receipt 1 to Raymond McBride, CPA, was entered incorrectly. Change the date to 1/9/2013.

 Correct the error indicated in the memo, and print a corrected sales receipt

Click the **Chart of Accounts** icon on the Home Page
Click **Undeposited Funds**

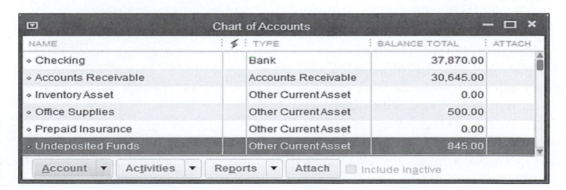

Click the **Activities** button
Click **Use Register**
- The register maintains a record of all the transactions recorded within the Undeposited Funds account.

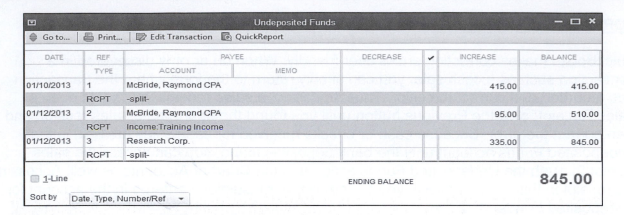

Click anywhere in the transaction for Sales Receipt 1 to Raymond McBride, CPA
- Look at the REF/TYPE column to see the type of transaction.
- The number in the REF line indicates the number of the sales receipt or the customer's check number.
- TYPE shows RCPT for a sales receipt.

Click the **Edit Transaction** button at the top of the register
- The sales receipt appears on the screen.

Tab to or click **DATE** field
Change the Date to **01/09/13**
Tab to enter the date

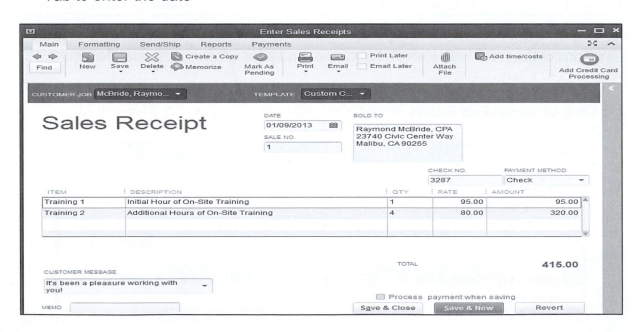

Print the Sales Receipt as previously instructed
Click **Yes** on the **Recording Transaction** dialog box
Click **Save & Close**
After closing the sales receipt, you are returned to the register for the Undeposited Funds account
Do not close the register

VIEW A QUICKREPORT

After editing the sales receipt and returning to the register, you may get a detailed report regarding the customer's transactions by clicking the QuickReport icon.

 Prepare a QuickReport for Raymond McBride

>   Click the **QuickReport** icon to display the Register QuickReport for Raymond
>   McBride, CPA

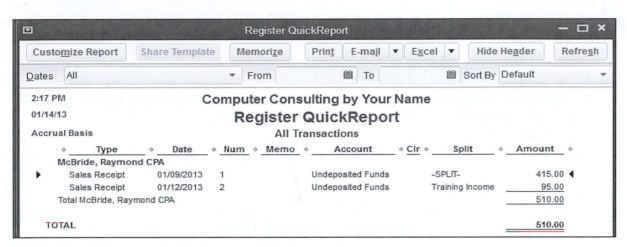

ANALYZE THE QUICKREPORT FOR RAYMOND MCBRIDE

 Analyze the QuickReport

>   Notice that the date for Sales Receipt 1 has been changed to **01/09/2013**
>   - You may need to use the horizontal scroll bar to view all the columns in the
>   report.
>   The account used is Undeposited Funds
>   The Split column contains the other accounts used in the transaction
>   - For Sales Receipt 2, the account used is **Training Income**.
>   - For Sales Receipt 1, you see the word **Split** rather than an account name.
>   - Split means that more than one sales item or account was used for this portion of
>   the transaction.
>   View the sales items or accounts used for the Split by using QuickZoom to view the
>   actual Sales Receipt
>   Use QuickZoom by double-clicking anywhere on the information for Sales Receipt 1
>   - You will see Sales Receipt 1.
>   - The sales items used are Training 1 and Training 2.
>   Close the **Sales Receipt**
>   Close the **Register QuickReport** without printing
>   Close the **Register for Undeposited Funds**
>   Close the **Chart of Accounts**

ANALYZE SALES

To obtain information regarding the amount of sales by item, you can print or view sales reports. Sales reports provide information regarding cash and credit sales. When information regarding the sales according to the Sales Item is needed, a Sales by Item Summary Report is the appropriate report to print or view. This report enables you to see how much revenue is being generated by each sales item. This provides important information for decision making and managing the business. For example, if a sales item is not generating much income, it might be wise to discontinue that sales item.

 Print a summarized list of sales by item

> Click the **Reports** icon
> Click **Sales** as the type of report
> Double-click **Sales by Item Summary** in the Sales by Item report list
> The dates of the report are from **01/01/13** to **01/14/13**
> Tab to generate the report
> Turn off the Date Prepared, Time Prepared, and Report Basis following instructions
>> given previously

Computer Consulting by Your Name
Sales by Item Summary
January 1 - 14, 2013

	Qty	Amount	% of Sales	Avg Price
Service				
Install 1 (Initial Hour of Hardware/Network Installation)	1	95.00	1.1%	95.00
Install 2 (Additional Hours of Hardware/Network Installation)	1	80.00	0.9%	80.00
Tech Sup 1 (5 Hours—Monthly Technical Support)	1	150.00	1.7%	150.00
Tech Sup 2 (10 Hours—Monthly Technical Support)	1	300.00	3.4%	300.00
Tech Sup 3 (15 Hours—Monthly Technical Support)	1	450.00	5%	450.00
Training 1 (Initial Hour of On-Site Training)	6	570.00	6.4%	95.00
Training 2 (Additional Hours of On-Site Training)	91	7,280.00	81.6%	80.00
Total Service	102	8,925.00	100.0%	87.50
TOTAL	102	8,925.00	100.0%	87.50

> - You may not see the item description in parentheses; this should be of no concern.
> Click **Print**
> The Orientation should be **Portrait**
> Click **Print** on **Print Reports** dialog box
> Close the report

 View a Sales by Item Detail report to obtain information regarding which transactions apply to each sales item

> Double-click **Sales by Item Detail** on the Sales by Item report list
> The dates of the report are from **01/01/13** to **01/14/13**
> Tab to generate the report

Scroll through the report to view the types of sales and the transactions that occurred within each category

- Notice how many transactions occurred in each sales item.

2:24 PM			Computer Consulting by Your Name					
01/14/13			**Sales by Item Detail**					
Accrual Basis			January 1 - 14, 2013					
◇ Type ◇	Date ◇	Num ◇	Memo	Name	◇ Qty ◇	Sales Price ◇	Amount ◇	Balance ◇
Service								
Install 1 (Initial Hour of Hardware/Network Installation)								
Invoice	01/08/2013	8	Initial Hour of Hardware/Network Installation	Collins, Ken	1	95.00	95.00	95.00
Total Install 1 (Initial Hour of Hardware/Network Installation)					1		95.00	95.00
Install 2 (Additional Hours of Hardware/Network Installation)								
Invoice	01/08/2013	8	Additional Hours of Hardware/Network Installation	Collins, Ken	1	80.00	80.00	80.00
Total Install 2 (Additional Hours of Hardware/Network Installation)					1		80.00	80.00
Tech Sup 1 (5 Hours--Monthly Technical Support)								
Invoice	01/05/2013	6	5 Hours--Monthly Technical Support	Young, Norton, and Brancato	1	150.00	150.00	150.00
Total Tech Sup 1 (5 Hours--Monthly Technical Support)					1		150.00	150.00
Tech Sup 2 (10 Hours--Monthly Technical Support)								
Invoice	01/02/2013	1	10 Hours--Monthly Technical Support	Gomez, Juan Esq.	1	300.00	300.00	300.00
Invoice	01/05/2013	3	10 Hours--Monthly Technical Support	Ahmadrand, Ela	0	300.00	0.00	300.00
Total Tech Sup 2 (10 Hours--Monthly Technical Support)					1		300.00	300.00
Tech Sup 3 (15 Hours--Monthly Technical Support)								
Invoice	01/05/2013	5	15 Hours--Monthly Technical Support	Clark, Binsley, and Basil, CPA	1	450.00	450.00	450.00
Total Tech Sup 3 (15 Hours--Monthly Technical Support)					1		450.00	450.00
Training 1 (Initial Hour of On-Site Training)								
Invoice	01/05/2013	4	Initial Hour of On-Site Training	Valdez and Lonegan	1	95.00	95.00	95.00
Invoice	01/05/2013	5	Initial Hour of On-Site Training	Clark, Binsley, and Basil, CPA	1	95.00	95.00	190.00
Invoice	01/05/2013	6	Initial Hour of On-Site Training	Young, Norton, and Brancato	1	95.00	95.00	285.00
Sales Receipt	01/09/2013	1	Initial Hour of On-Site Training	McBride, Raymond CPA	1	95.00	95.00	380.00
Sales Receipt	01/12/2013	2	Initial Hour of On-Site Training	McBride, Raymond CPA	1	95.00	95.00	475.00
Sales Receipt	01/12/2013	3	Initial Hour of On-Site Training	Research Corp.	1	95.00	95.00	570.00
Total Training 1 (Initial Hour of On-Site Training)					6		570.00	570.00
Training 2 (Additional Hours of On-Site Training)								
Invoice	01/05/2013	4	Additional Hours of On-Site Training	Valdez and Lonegan	39	80.00	3,120.00	3,120.00
Invoice	01/05/2013	5	Additional Hours of On-Site Training	Clark, Binsley, and Basil, CPA	11	80.00	880.00	4,000.00
Invoice	01/05/2013	6	Additional Hours of On-Site Training	Young, Norton, and Brancato	39	80.00	3,120.00	7,120.00
Credit Memo	01/08/2013	7	Additional Hours of On-Site Training	Valdez and Lonegan	-5	80.00	-400.00	6,720.00
Sales Receipt	01/09/2013	1	Additional Hours of On-Site Training	McBride, Raymond CPA	4	80.00	320.00	7,040.00
Sales Receipt	01/12/2013	3	Additional Hours of On-Site Training	Research Corp.	3	80.00	240.00	7,280.00
Total Training 2 (Additional Hours of On-Site Training)					91		7,280.00	7,280.00
Total Service					102		8,925.00	8,925.00
TOTAL					102		8,925.00	8,925.00

Close the report without printing
Close the **Report Center**

PREPARE A DAILY BACKUP

As you learned earlier in the chapter, creating a backup file saves your work up to that point. The daily backup prepared earlier contains all of Chapter 1 and the portion of Chapter 2 where invoices were entered. By creating the backup file now and using the same file name, it will contain your work for Chapter 1 and all the work completed through entering Sales Receipts in Chapter 2.

Prepare the Computer (Daily Backup).qbb file

Follow the steps presented in Chapter 1 for creating a backup file
Name the file **Computer (Daily Backup)**
The file type is **QBW Backup (* .QBB)**
- This backup is using the same backup file that you prepared earlier in the chapter.
- The daily backup will now contain all of Chapter 1 and Chapter 2 up through entering sales receipts.

RECORD CUSTOMER PAYMENTS ON ACCOUNT

Since a sale on account is originally recorded on an invoice, Receive Payments is used when a customer pays you what is owed on an invoice. Frequently, new users of QuickBooks will try to record a payment receipt using a Sales Receipt, which is used only for cash sales.

When you start to record a payment made by a customer who owes you money for an invoice, you see the customer's balance, any credits made to the account, and a complete list of outstanding invoices. QuickBooks automatically places a check in the check mark column for the invoice that has the same amount as the payment. If there isn't an invoice with the same amount, QuickBooks marks the oldest invoice and enters the payment amount in the Payment column for the invoice being paid. When customers make a full or partial payment of the amount they owe, QuickBooks places the money received in an account called Undeposited Funds. The money stays in the account until a bank deposit is made.

MEMO:
DATE: January 15, 2013

Record the following cash receipt: Received Check 684 for $815 from Research Corp. as payment on account.

 Record the receipt of a payment on account

Click the **Receive Payments** icon in the Customers section of the Home Page
- Notice the flow chart line from Create Invoices to Receive Payments. This icon is illustrated in this manner because recording a payment receipt is for a payment made on account. This is <u>not</u> a cash sale.

Click the drop-down list arrow for **RECEIVED FROM**
Click **Research Corp.**

- Notice that the current date or the last transaction date shows in the **DATE** column and the total amount owed appears as the balance.
- Also note that previous cash sales to Research Corp. are not listed. This is because a payment receipt is used only for payments on account.

Tab to or click **AMOUNT**

- If you click, you will need to delete the 0.00. If you tab, it will be deleted when you type in the amount.

Enter **815**

- QuickBooks will enter the **.00** when you tab to or click **DATE**
- When you press Tab, QuickBooks automatically places a check in the check mark column for the invoice that has the same amount as the payment. If there isn't an invoice with the same amount, QuickBooks marks the oldest invoice and enters the payment amount in the Payment column for the invoice being paid.

Tab to or click **DATE**

- If you click, you will need to delete the date. If you tab, the date will be replaced when you type 01/15/13.

Type date **01/15/13**

Click the drop-down list arrow for **PMT. METHOD**

Click **Check**

Tab to or click in the text box for **CHECK #**

Enter **684**

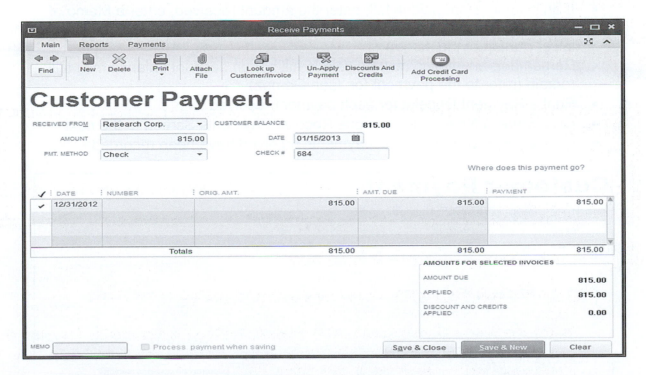

Click the **Print** button and print a copy of the Payment Receipt following steps presented earlier for printing other business forms

When the Payment Receipt has been printed, click **Save & New**

RECORD ADDITIONAL PAYMENTS ON ACCOUNT WITHOUT STEP-BY-STEP INSTRUCTIONS

MEMO:

DATE: January 15, 2013

Received Check 1952 from Wagner, Leavitt, and Moraga for $3,680.

Received Check 8925 for $2,000 from Rosenthal Illustrations in partial payment of account. This receipt requires a Memo notation of Partial Payment. Make sure "Leave as an underpayment" is selected in the lower portion of the Customer Payment.

Received Check 39251 from Matt Williams, CPA for $475.

Received Check 2051 for $2,190 from Andrews Productions as a partial payment. Record a Memo of Partial Payment for this receipt. Leave as an underpayment.

Received Check 5632 from Juan Gomez, Esq. for $150 for payment of his opening balance. Since this is payment in full for the opening balance, no memo is required.

Received Check 80195 from Shumway, Lewis, and Levy for $3,685.

 Enter the above payments on account; if necessary, refer to the previous steps listed

- If an invoice is not paid in full, enter the amount received, enter a Memo of **Partial Payment**, and make sure **Leave as an underpayment** is selected in the lower portion of the screen
- Remember, an invoice may be paid in full but an account balance may still remain (refer to the payment for Juan Gomez)
- Print a Payment Receipt for each payment received
- Click **Save & New** to go from one Receive Payments Screen to the next
- Click **Save & Close** after all payments received have been recorded

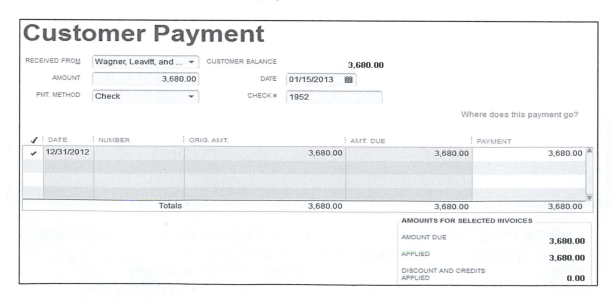

Customer Payment

RECEIVED FROM	Rosenthal Illustrations ▼	CUSTOMER BALANCE 3,830.00
AMOUNT	2,000.00	DATE 01/15/2013 📅
PMT. METHOD	Check ▼	CHECK # 8925

Where does this payment go?

✓	DATE	NUMBER	ORIG. AMT.	AMT. DUE	PAYMENT
✓	12/31/2012		3,830.00	3,830.00	2,000.00
	Totals		3,830.00	3,830.00	2,000.00

UNDERPAYMENT $ 1,830.00.

WHEN FINISHED:
- ⦿ LEAVE THIS AS AN UNDERPAYMENT
- ◯ WRITE OFF THE EXTRA AMOUNT

[VIEW CUSTOMER CONTACT INFORMATION]

AMOUNTS FOR SELECTED INVOICES

AMOUNT DUE	3,830.00
APPLIED	2,000.00
DISCOUNT AND CREDITS APPLIED	0.00

MEMO Partial Payment   ☐ Process payment when saving

[Save & Close] [Save & New] [Clear]

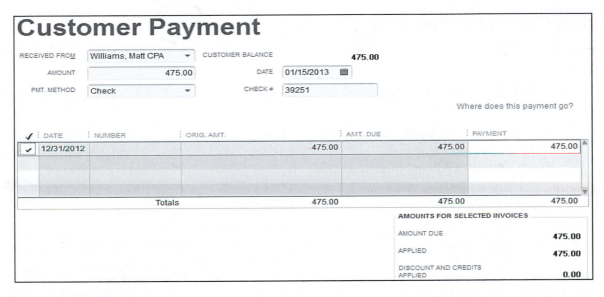

Customer Payment

RECEIVED FROM	Williams, Matt CPA ▼	CUSTOMER BALANCE 475.00
AMOUNT	475.00	DATE 01/15/2013 📅
PMT. METHOD	Check ▼	CHECK # 39251

Where does this payment go?

✓	DATE	NUMBER	ORIG. AMT.	AMT. DUE	PAYMENT
✓	12/31/2012		475.00	475.00	475.00
	Totals		475.00	475.00	475.00

AMOUNTS FOR SELECTED INVOICES

AMOUNT DUE	475.00
APPLIED	475.00
DISCOUNT AND CREDITS APPLIED	0.00

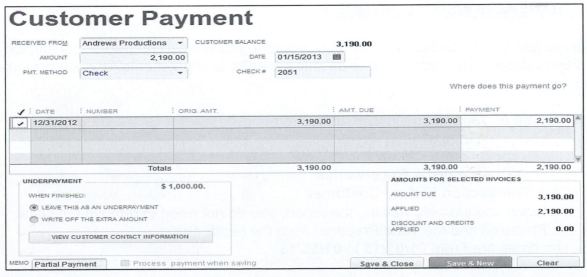

Customer Payment

RECEIVED FROM	Andrews Productions ▼	CUSTOMER BALANCE 3,190.00
AMOUNT	2,190.00	DATE 01/15/2013 📅
PMT. METHOD	Check ▼	CHECK # 2051

Where does this payment go?

✓	DATE	NUMBER	ORIG. AMT.	AMT. DUE	PAYMENT
✓	12/31/2012		3,190.00	3,190.00	2,190.00
	Totals		3,190.00	3,190.00	2,190.00

UNDERPAYMENT $ 1,000.00.

WHEN FINISHED:
- ⦿ LEAVE THIS AS AN UNDERPAYMENT
- ◯ WRITE OFF THE EXTRA AMOUNT

[VIEW CUSTOMER CONTACT INFORMATION]

AMOUNTS FOR SELECTED INVOICES

AMOUNT DUE	3,190.00
APPLIED	2,190.00
DISCOUNT AND CREDITS APPLIED	0.00

MEMO Partial Payment   ☐ Process payment when saving

[Save & Close] [Save & New] [Clear]

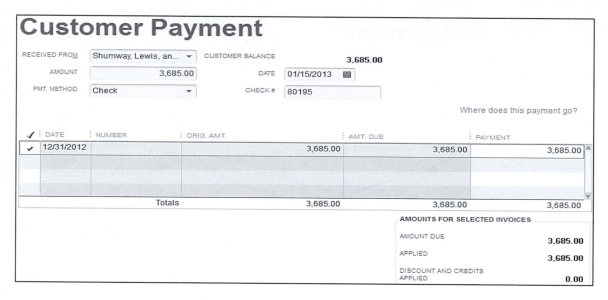

VIEW TRANSACTIONS BY CUSTOMER

In order to see the transactions for credit customers, you need to prepare a transaction report by customer. This report shows all sales, credits, and payments for each customer on account.

 Prepare a Transaction List by Customer report

Click **Reports** on the menu bar
Point to **Customers & Receivables**
Click **Transaction List by Customer**
- Since you are only viewing the report, you do not need to remove the Date Prepared and the Time Prepared from the header
The dates are From **01/01/13** to **01/15/13**

Tab to generate the report

Scroll through the report

- Notice that information is shown for the invoices, cash sales, credit memo, and payments made on the accounts.
- Notice that the **Num** column shows the invoice numbers, sales receipt numbers, credit memo numbers, and check numbers.

3:00 PM			**Computer Consulting by Your Name**				
01/15/13			**Transaction List by Customer**				
			January 1 - 15, 2013				

Type	Date	Num	Memo	Account	Clr	Split	Debit	Credit
Ahmadrand, Ela								
Invoice	01/05/2013	3	VOID:	Accounts Receivable	✓	Technical Support Income	0.00	
Andrews Productions								
Payment	01/15/2013	2051	Partial Payment	Undeposited Funds		Accounts Receivable	2,190.00	
Clark, Binsley, and Basil, CPA								
Invoice	01/05/2013	5		Accounts Receivable		-SPLIT-	1,425.00	
Collins, Ken								
Invoice	01/08/2013	8		Accounts Receivable		-SPLIT-	175.00	
Gomez, Juan Esq.								
Invoice	01/02/2013	1		Accounts Receivable		Technical Support Income	300.00	
Payment	01/15/2013	5632		Undeposited Funds		Accounts Receivable	150.00	
McBride, Raymond CPA								
Sales Receipt	01/09/2013	1		Undeposited Funds		-SPLIT-	415.00	
Sales Receipt	01/12/2013	2		Undeposited Funds		Training Income	95.00	
Research Corp.								
Sales Receipt	01/12/2013	3		Undeposited Funds		-SPLIT-	335.00	
Payment	01/15/2013	684		Undeposited Funds		Accounts Receivable	815.00	
Rosenthal Illustrations								
Payment	01/15/2013	8925	Partial Payment	Undeposited Funds		Accounts Receivable	2,000.00	
Shumway, Lewis, and Levy								
Payment	01/15/2013	80195		Undeposited Funds		Accounts Receivable	3,685.00	
Valdez and Lonegan								
Invoice	01/05/2013	4		Accounts Receivable		-SPLIT-	3,215.00	
Credit Memo	01/08/2013	7		Accounts Receivable		-SPLIT-		400.00
Wagner, Leavitt, and Moraga								
Payment	01/15/2013	1952		Undeposited Funds		Accounts Receivable	3,680.00	
Williams, Matt CPA								
Payment	01/15/2013	39251		Undeposited Funds		Accounts Receivable	475.00	
Young, Norton, and Brancato								
Invoice	01/05/2013	6		Accounts Receivable		-SPLIT-	3,365.00	

Click the **Close** button to exit the report without printing

DEPOSIT CHECKS RECEIVED FOR CASH SALES AND PAYMENTS ON ACCOUNT

When you record cash sales and the receipt of payments on accounts, QuickBooks places the money received in the Undeposited Funds account. Once the deposit has been made at the bank, it should be recorded. When the deposit is recorded, the funds are transferred from Undeposited Funds to the account selected when preparing the deposit.

MEMO:

DATE: January 15, 2013

Deposit all checks received for cash sales and payments on account.

 Deposit checks received

Click the **Record Deposits** icon in the Banking section of the Home Page
- **Payments to Deposit** window shows all amounts received for cash sales and payments on account that have not been deposited in the bank.
- The column for **TYPE** contains RCPT, which means the amount is for a Sales Receipt (Cash Sale), and PMT, which means the amount received is for a payment on account.
- Notice that the √ column to the left of the DATE column is empty.

Click the **Select All** button
- Notice the check marks in the √ column.

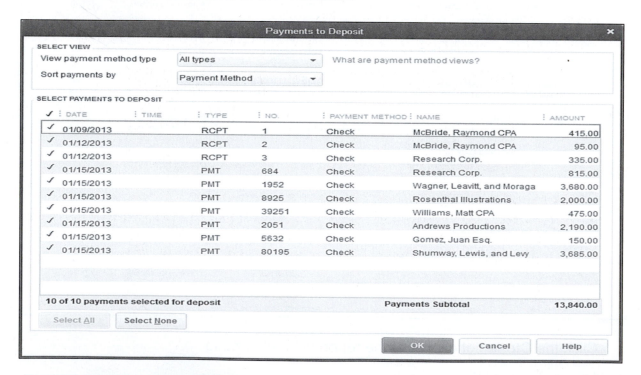

Click **OK** to close **Payments to Deposit** screen and open **Make Deposits** screen
On the **Make Deposits** screen, **Deposit To** should be **Checking**
Date should be **01/15/2013**
- Tab to date and change if not correct.

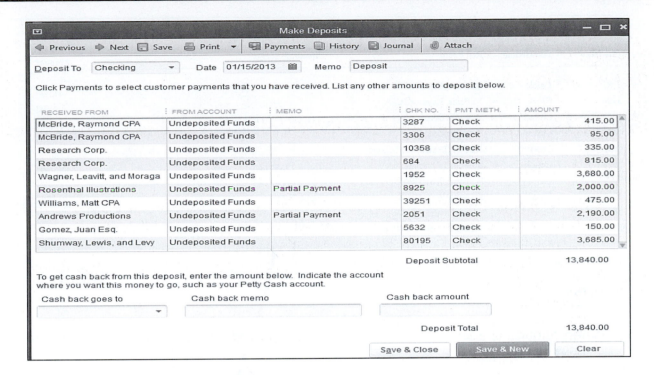

Click the **Print** button to print **Deposit Summary**
Select **Deposit summary only** on the **Print Deposit** dialog box, click **OK**

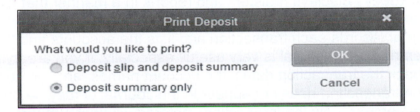

Check the **Settings** for **Print Lists**, click **Print**

- *Note:* QuickBooks automatically prints the date that the Deposit Summary was printed on the report. It is the current date of your computer and cannot be changed; therefore, it may not match the date shown in the answer key.

Deposit Summary				1/15/2013 3:13 PM

Summary of Deposits to Checking on 01/15/2013

Chk No.	PmtMethod	Rcd From	Memo	Amount
3287	Check	McBride, Raymond CPA		415.00
3306	Check	McBride, Raymond CPA		95.00
10358	Check	Research Corp.		335.00
684	Check	Research Corp.		815.00
1952	Check	Wagner, Leavitt, and Moraga		3,680.00
8925	Check	Rosenthal Illustrations	Partial Payment	2,000.00
39251	Check	Williams, Matt CPA		475.00
2051	Check	Andrews Productions	Partial Payment	2,190.00
5632	Check	Gomez, Juan Esq.		150.00
80195	Check	Shumway, Lewis, and Levy		3,685.00

Less Cash Back:

Deposit Total:				13,840.00

When printing is finished, click **Save & Close** on **Make Deposits** screen to record and close

PRINT JOURNAL

Even though QuickBooks displays registers and reports in a manner that focuses on the transaction—for example, entering a sale on account via an invoice—it still keeps a Journal. The Journal records each transaction and lists the accounts and the amounts for debit and credit entries. The Journal is very useful; especially, if you are trying to find errors. Always check the transaction dates, the account names, and the items listed in the Memo column. If a transaction does not appear in the Journal, it may be due to using an incorrect date. Remember, only the transactions entered within the report dates will be displayed. In many instances, going through the Journal entries will help you find errors in your transactions.

In your concepts course, you may have learned that the General Journal was where all entries were recorded in debit/credit format. In QuickBooks, you do record some non-recurring debit/credit transactions in the General Journal and then display all debit/credit entries no matter where the transactions were recorded in the Journal. (At times in the text Journal and General Journal are used synonymously to represent the report).

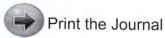 Print the Journal

Open the **Report Center** as previously instructed
Click **Accountant & Taxes** as the Report type
Double-click **Journal** and then click the **Display** icon
• If you get the Collapsing and Expanding Transactions dialog box, click **OK**
Click the **Expand** button
The dates are from **01/01/13** to **01/15/13**

Customize the Report to change the **Header/Footer** so the **Date Prepared** and
   Time Prepared are not selected, click **OK**
Scroll through the report to view the transactions
- You may find that your Trans # is not the same as shown. QuickBooks automatically numbers all transactions recorded. If you have deleted and re-entered transactions more than directed in the text, you may have different transaction numbers. Do not be concerned with this.
- Many of the columns do not display in full. In order to see important information; such as, the account used in the transactions, the columns need to be resized.
Resize the width of the Account column so the account names are displayed in full
Position the cursor on the sizing diamond between **Account** and **Debit**
- The cursor turns into a plus with arrows pointing left and right.

Hold down the primary (left) mouse button
Drag the cursor from the diamond between **Account** and **Debit** to the right until you
   have the account names displayed in full
- You will see a dotted vertical line while you are dragging the mouse and holding down the primary mouse button.
Look at the other columns, if any have … to represent information not shown, point
   to the sizing diamond and drag until the information is shown
- You may make columns smaller by pointing to the sizing diamond and dragging to the left.
Point to the sizing diamond between the **Debit** and **Credit** columns
Drag to the left to make the Debit column smaller
- If you make the column too small, the numbers that cannot be displayed will be shown as ******. If this happens, make the column larger.
Resize the remaining columns to eliminate extra space and to display names,
   memos, and accounts in full
Once the columns have been resized, click **Print**
Click **Preview**
- You will be able to see how the report will appear when it is printed. If the report prints two-pages wide, you may want to resize the columns until you can get it to print on one-page wide. If you need to hide a few words in the Memo column in order to do this, that is acceptable. For example, you may need to hide the word Installation for Initial Hour of Hardware/Network Installation in the Memo column.
Click **Close** to close the **Preview**
Once you have the column widths adjusted so the report is one-page wide, click
   Print
On the **Print Reports** screen, the settings will be the same used previously except:
   Click **Landscape** to select Landscape orientation

- If you cannot get the report to print on one-page even after resizing the columns, click on **Fit report to one page wide** to select this item
- The printer will print the Journal using a smaller font so the report will fit across the 11-inch width.

Click Print

- The Journal will be several pages in length so only a partial report is shown.

Computer Consulting by Your Name

Journal

January 1 - 15, 2013

Trans #	Type	Date	Num	Adj	Name	Memo	Account	Debit	Credit
44	Payment	01/15/2013	80195		Shumway, Lewis, and Levy		Undeposited Funds	3,685.00	
					Shumway, Lewis, and Levy		Accounts Receivable		3,685.00
								3,685.00	3,685.00
45	Deposit	01/15/2013				Deposit	Checking	13,840.00	
					McBride, Raymond CPA	Deposit	Undeposited Funds		415.00
					McBride, Raymond CPA	Deposit	Undeposited Funds		95.00
					Research Corp.	Deposit	Undeposited Funds		335.00
					Research Corp.	Deposit	Undeposited Funds		815.00
					Wagner, Leavitt, and Moraga	Deposit	Undeposited Funds		3,680.00
					Rosenthal Illustrations	Partial Payment	Undeposited Funds		2,000.00
					Williams, Matt CPA	Deposit	Undeposited Funds		475.00
					Andrews Productions	Partial Payment	Undeposited Funds		2,190.00
					Gomez, Juan Esq.	Deposit	Undeposited Funds		150.00
					Shumway, Lewis, and Levy	Deposit	Undeposited Funds		3,685.00
								13,840.00	13,840.00
TOTAL								36,560.00	36,560.00

Partial Report

Close the report, do <u>not</u> close the Report Center

PRINT THE TRIAL BALANCE

When all sales transactions have been entered, it is important to print the Trial Balance and verify that the total debits equal the total credits.

 Print the Trial Balance

Click **Trial Balance** on the Report Center list of Accountant & Taxes reports
Click the **Run** icon
Enter the dates from **010113** to **011513**
Click the **Customize Report** button and change **Header/Footer** so **Date Prepared**,
     Time Prepared, and **Report Basis** do not print
Print the report in **Portrait** orientation

- If necessary, click on **Fit report to one page wide** to deselect this item

Computer Consulting by Your Name
Trial Balance
As of January 15, 2013

| | Jan 15, 13 | |
	Debit	Credit
Checking	51,710.00	
Accounts Receivable	17,650.00	
Office Supplies	500.00	
Undeposited Funds	0.00	
Company Cars:Original Cost	49,000.00	
Office Equipment:Original Cost	8,050.00	
Accounts Payable		850.00
Loan Payable	0.00	
Loan Payable:Company Cars Loan		35,000.00
Loan Payable:Office Equipment Loan		4,000.00
Retained Earnings	0.00	
Student's Name, Capital		53,135.00
Student's Name, Capital:Investments		25,000.00
Income:Installation Income		175.00
Income:Technical Support Income		900.00
Income:Training Income		7,850.00
TOTAL	126,910.00	126,910.00

- If your instructor had you change the capital account back to your real first and last name, your actual name will show rather than "Student's Name."

Close the report

Do <u>not</u> close the Report Center

GRAPHS IN QUICKBOOKS®

Once transactions have been entered, transaction results can be visually represented in a graphic form. QuickBooks illustrates Accounts Receivable by Aging Period as a bar chart, and it illustrates Accounts Receivable by Customer as a pie chart. For further details, double-click on an individual section of the pie chart or chart legend to create a bar chart analyzing an individual customer. QuickBooks also prepares graphs based on sales and will show the results of sales by item and by customer.

PREPARE ACCOUNTS RECEIVABLE GRAPHS

Accounts Receivable graphs illustrate account information based on the age of the account and the percentage of accounts receivable owed by each customer.

 Create graphs for accounts receivable:

Click **Customers & Receivables** in the Report Center list to select the type of report
Scroll through the list of reports; and then, double-click **Accounts Receivable Graph** to select the report
Click **Dates** on the QuickInsight: Accounts Receivable Graph screen
On the **Change Graph Dates** change **Show Aging As of** to **01/15/13**

Click **OK**

- QuickBooks generates a bar chart illustrating Accounts Receivable by Aging Period and a pie chart illustrating Accounts Receivable by Customer

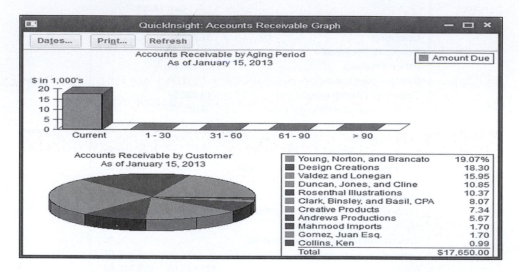

Printing is not required for this graph

- If you want a printed copy, click **Print** and print in Portrait mode

Click **Dates**

Enter **02/01/13** for the **Show Aging As of** date

Click **OK**

- Notice the difference in the aging of accounts.

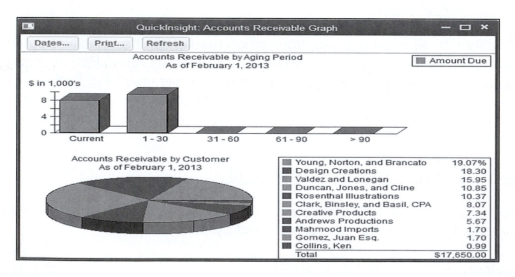

Click **Dates**

Enter **01/15/13**

Do not close the graph

USE QUICKZOOM FEATURE TO OBTAIN INDIVIDUAL CUSTOMER DETAILS

It is possible to get detailed information regarding the aging of transactions for an individual customer by using the QuickZoom feature of QuickBooks.

 Use QuickZoom to see information for Young, Norton, and Brancato

Double-click on the section of the pie chart for **Young, Norton, and Brancato**
- You get a bar chart aging the transactions of the customer.

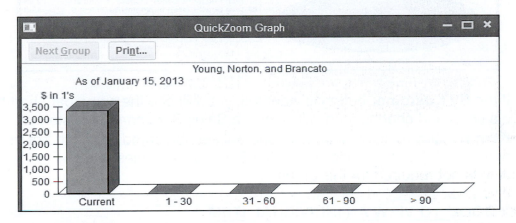

Printing is not required for this graph
Close the **QuickZoom Graph** for Young, Norton, and Brancato
Close the **Accounts Receivable Graph**

PREPARE SALES GRAPHS

Sales graphs illustrate the amount of cash and credit sales for a given period as well as the percentage of sales for each sales item.

 Prepare a Sales Graph

Click **Sales** in the Report Center
Double-click **Sales Graph**
Click the **Dates** button
Click in **From**
Enter **01/01/13**
Tab to **To**
Enter **01/15/13**
Click **OK**
The **By Item** button should be indented (depressed)
- You will see a bar chart representing Sales by Month and a pie chart displaying a Sales Summary by item.

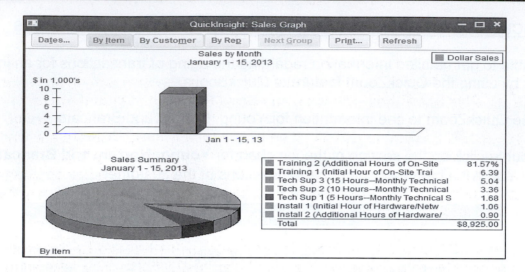

- If the **By Customer** button is indented, you will see the same bar chart but the pie chart and chart legend will display a Sales Summary by customer.
- If the **By Rep** button is indented, you will see the same bar chart but the pie chart and chart legend will display a Sales Summary by sales rep.

Printing is not required for this graph

USE QUICKZOOM TO VIEW AN INDIVIDUAL ITEM

It is possible to use QuickZoom to view details regarding an individual item's sales by month.

 Use QuickZoom to see information for Install 1

Since Install 1 is such a small area in the pie chart, double-click **Install 1** In the chart legend

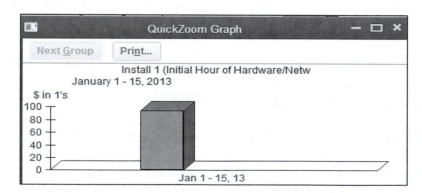

You will see the Sales by Month for Install 1
Close the **QuickZoom Graph** and the **Sales Graph** without printing
Close the **Report Center**

CREATE THE BACK UP FILE FOR THE CHAPTER

As you learned in Chapter 1, when you use QuickBooks to make a backup file, the program creates a condensed file that contains all the data for the entries made up to the time of the backup file. This file has a **.qbb** extension and cannot be used to record transactions. When new transactions are recorded, a new backup file must be made. In training, it is wise to make a daily backup as well as an end-of-chapter backup. If errors are made in training, the appropriate backup file can be restored. For example, if you back up Chapter 2 and make errors in Chapter 3, the Chapter 2 backup may be restored to a company file with the **.qbw** extension. The data entered for Chapter 3 will be erased and only the data from Chapters 1 and 2 will appear.

A duplicate copy of the file may be made using Windows. Instructions for this procedure should be provided by your professor. You may hear the duplicate copy referred to as a backup file. This is different from the QuickBooks backup file.

 Back up the company

Follow the instructions provided in Chapter 1 to make your backup
The name for the Chapter 2 backup file should be **Computer (Backup Ch. 2)**.
- Your Computer (Backup Ch. 1) file contains all of your work from Chapter 1
- Your Computer (Backup Ch. 2) file contains all your work from Chapters 1 and 2.
- The Computer (Backup Ch. 2) will not contain transactions from the work you do in Chapter 3.
- Keeping a separate backup file for each chapter is helpful for those times when you have made errors and cannot figure out how to correct them. Restoring your Chapter 2 back up file will restore your work from Chapters 1 and 2 and eliminate any work completed in Chapter 3. This will allow you to start over at the beginning of Chapter 3. If you do not have a backup file for Chapter 2, you would need to re-enter all the transactions for Chapter 2 before beginning Chapter 3.
- Your Daily Backup file will contain all of your work up to the point where you created the daily backup file. It does not need to be redone at this point since the Computer (Backup Ch. 2) contains all of the work for both Chapters 1 and 2.

EXIT QUICKBOOKS AND CLOSE THE COMPANY

 After the backup file has been made, close the Company and QuickBooks

Follow the procedures given in Chapter 1 to close a company and to close QuickBooks

SUMMARY

In this chapter, cash and credit sales were prepared for Computer Consulting by Your Name, a service business, using sales receipts and invoices. Credit memos were issued. Customer accounts were added and revised. Invoices and sales receipts were edited, deleted, and voided. Cash payments were received and bank deposits were made. All the transactions entered reinforced the QuickBooks concept of using the business form to record transactions rather than enter information in journals. However, QuickBooks does not disregard traditional accounting methods. Instead, it performs this function in the background. The Journal was accessed and printed. The fact that the Customer:Job List functions as the Accounts Receivable Ledger and that the Chart of Accounts is the General Ledger in QuickBooks was pointed out. The importance of reports for information and decision-making was illustrated. Exploration of the various sales and accounts receivable reports and graphs allowed information to be viewed from a sales standpoint and from an accounts receivable perspective. Sales reports emphasized both cash and credit sales according to the sales item generating the revenue. Accounts Receivable reports focused on amounts owed by credit customers. The traditional trial balance emphasizing the equality of debits and credits was prepared.

END-OF-CHAPTER QUESTIONS

TRUE/FALSE

ANSWER THE FOLLOWING QUESTIONS IN THE SPACE PROVIDED BEFORE THE QUESTION NUMBER.

_____ 1. A new customer can be added to a company's records on the fly.

_____ 2. In QuickBooks, error correction for a sale on account can be accomplished by editing the invoice.

_____ 3. An Item List stores information about products you purchase.

_____ 4. Once transactions have been entered, modifications to a customer's account may be made only at the end of the fiscal year.

_____ 5. In QuickBooks all transactions must be entered using the traditional debit/credit method.

_____ 6. Checks received for cash sales are held in the Undeposited Funds account until the bank deposit is made.

_____ 7. When a correction for a transaction is made, QuickBooks not only changes the form used to record the transaction, it also changes all journal and account entries for the transaction to reflect the correction.

_____ 8. QuickGraphs allow information to be viewed from both a sales standpoint and from an accounts receivable perspective.

_____ 9. QuickZoom allows you to print a report instantly.

_____10. A customer's payment on account is immediately recorded in the cash account.

MULTIPLE CHOICE

WRITE THE LETTER OF THE CORRECT ANSWER IN THE SPACE PROVIDED BEFORE THE QUESTION NUMBER.

_____ 1. To remove an invoice without a trace, it is ___.
     A. voided
     B. deleted
     C. blocked
     D. reversed

_____ 2. To enter a cash sale, ___ is completed.
A. a debit
B. an invoice
C. a sales receipt
D. receive payments

_____ 3. Two primary types of lists used in this chapter are ___.
A. receivables and payables
B. invoices and checks
C. registers and navigator
D. customers and item

_____ 4. When you enter an invoice, an error may be corrected by ___.
A. backspacing or deleting
B. tabbing and typing
C. dragging and typing
D. all of the above

_____ 5. While in the Customer Balance Summary Report, it is possible to get an individual customer's information by using ___.
A. QuickReport
B. QuickZoom
C. QuickGraph
D. QuickSummary

_____ 6. Undeposited Funds represents ___.
A. cash or checks received from customers but not yet deposited in the bank
B. all cash sales
C. the balance of the accounts receivable account
D. none of the above

_____ 7. QuickBooks uses graphs to illustrate information about ___.
A. the chart of accounts
B. sales
C. the cash account
D. supplies

_____ 8. Changes to the chart of accounts may be made ___.
A. at the beginning of a fiscal period
B. before the end of the fiscal year
C. at any time
D. once established, the chart of accounts may not be modified

_____ 9. To obtain information about sales by item, you can view ___.
A. the income statement
B. the trial balance
C. receivables reports
D. sales reports

_____10. When you add a customer using the Set Up method, you add ___.
A. complete information for a customer
B. only a customer's name
C. the customer's name, address, and telephone number
D. the customer's name and telephone number

FILL-IN

IN THE SPACE PROVIDED, WRITE THE ANSWER THAT MOST APPROPRIATELY COMPLETES THE SENTENCE.

1. The report used to view only the balances on account of each customer is the _____.

2. The form prepared to show a reduction to a sale on account is a(n) _____.

3. The report that proves that debits equal credits is the _____.

4. QuickBooks shows icons on the _____ and on the _____ that may be clicked to open the business documents used in recording transactions.

5. To verify the company being used in QuickBooks, you check the _____.

SHORT ESSAY

Explain how the method used to enter an Accounts Receivable transaction in QuickBooks is different from the method used to enter a transaction according to an accounting textbook.

_____

_____

_____

_____

_____

NAME_____

TRANSMITTAL

CHAPTER 2: COMPUTER CONSULTING BY YOUR NAME

Attach the following documents and reports:

Invoice 1: Juan Gomez, Esq.
Invoice 2: Matt Williams, CPA
Invoice 3: Ela Ahmadrand
Invoice 4: Valdez and Lonegan
Invoice 5: Clark, Binsley, and Basil
Invoice 6: Young, Norton, and Brancato
Customer Balance Summary, January 5, 2013
Customer Balance Detail, Valdez and Lonegan
Invoice 5 (corrected): Clark, Binsley, and Basil
Transaction List by Customer, January 1-7, 2013
Customer Balance Detail Report
Credit Memo 7: Valdez and Lonegan
Invoice 8: Ken Collins
Sales Receipt 1: Raymond McBride, CPA
Sales Receipt 2: Raymond McBride, CPA
Sales Receipt 3: Research Corp.
Sales by Customer Detail Report, January 1-12, 2013
Sales Receipt 1 (corrected): Raymond McBride, CPA
Sales by Item Summary, January 1-14, 2013
Payment Receipt: Research Corp.
Payment Receipt: Wagner, Leavitt, and Moraga
Payment Receipt: Rosenthal Illustrations
Payment Receipt: Matt Williams, CPA
Payment Receipt: Andrews Productions
Payment Receipt: Juan Gomez, Esq.
Payment Receipt: Shumway, Lewis, and Levy
Deposit Summary
Journal, January 1-15, 2013
Trial Balance, January 15, 2013

END-OF-CHAPTER PROBLEM

YOUR NAME LANDSCAPE AND POOL SERVICE

Chapter 2 continues with the entry of both cash and credit sales, receipt of payment by credit customers, credit memos, and bank deposits. In addition, reports focusing on sales and accounts receivable are prepared.

INSTRUCTIONS

Use the company file **Landscape.qbw** that you used for Chapter 1. The company name should be Your Name Landscape and Pool Service. (You changed the company name to include your real name in Chapter 1.) Since this company was used in Chapter 1, when you see the Open a Company screen, you may see other QuickBooks files and/or folders associated with that company. QuickBooks will create them as you use a company file. Some of these files may have extensions of QBW.ND or .QBW.TLG. Folders that say QuickBooksAutoDataRecovery or Restored are common. For the most part, you do not use or change any of these files or folders, simply click the company file and click the Open button. Sometimes, when switching from one company to the next; i.e., Computer to Landscape, QuickBooks might mark your company file as read only. If this happens, refer to Chapter 1 for steps on how to change the file Properties from Read Only.

The invoices and sales receipts are numbered consecutively. Invoice 25 is the first invoice number used in this problem. Sales Receipt 15 is the first sales receipt number used when recording cash sales in this problem. If you wish, you may hide the History for customers on the invoices and sales receipts. Each invoice recorded should be a Service Invoice and contain a message. When selecting a message, choose the one that you feel is most appropriate for the transaction. Print each invoice and sales receipt as it is completed and do not print lines around each field. Remember that payments received on account should be recorded as Receive Payments and not as a Sales Receipt.

When recording transactions, use the following Sales Item chart to determine the item(s) billed. If the transaction does not indicate the size of the pool or property, use the first category for the item; for example, LandCom 1 or LandRes 1 would be used for standard-size landscape service. Remember that SpaCom 1 and SpaRes 1 are services for spas—not pools. The appropriate billing for a standard-size pool would be PoolCom 1 or PoolRes 1. If you get a message regarding the spelling of Lg., click Ignore All.

When printing reports, always remove the Date Prepared, Time Prepared, and Report Basis from the Header/Footer and adjust the column size to display the information in full.

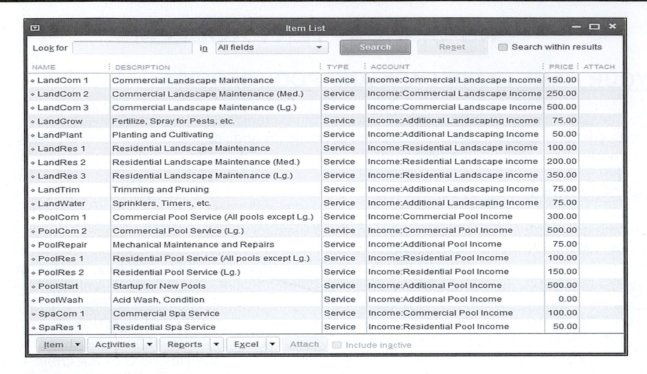

RECORD TRANSACTIONS

January 1

▶ Billed Ocean View Motel for monthly landscape services and monthly pool maintenance services, Invoice 25. (Use a Service Invoice. Use LandCom 1 to record the monthly landscape service fee and PoolCom 1 to record the monthly pool service fee. The quantity for each item is 1.) Terms are Net 15. If you get a message regarding the spelling of Lg., click Ignore All.

▶ Billed Dr. Sanchez for monthly landscape and pool services at his home. Both the pool and landscaping are standard size. The terms are Net 30.

▶ Billed Creations for You for 2 hours shrub trimming. Terms are Net 30.

▶ Received Check 381 for $500 from Deni Anderson for pool startup services at her home, Sales Receipt 15.

▶ Received Check 8642 from Hiroshi Chang for $150 as payment in full on his account. (Don't forget to print the Payment Receipt.)

January 15

▶ Billed a new customer: Eric Matthews (remember to enter the last name first for the customer name and change the billing name to first name first)—10824 Hope Ranch St., Santa Barbara, CA 93110, 805-555-9825, terms Net 30—for monthly service on his large pool and large residential landscape maintenance.

▶ Received Check 6758 from Ocean View Motel in full payment of Invoice 25.

▶ Received Check 987 from a new customer: Wayne Childers (a neighbor of Eric Matthews) for $75 for 1 hour of pool repairs. Even though this is a cash sale, do a complete customer setup: Main Phone 805-555-7175, Fax 805-555-5717, Main E-mail wchilders@abc.com, 10877 Hope Ranch St., Santa Barbara, CA 93110, Payment Terms Net 30.

▶ Billed Santa Barbara Beach Resorts for their large pool service and large landscaping maintenance. Also bill for 5 hours planting, 3 hours trimming, 2 hours spraying for pests, and 3 hours pool repair services. Terms are Net 15.

January 30
▶ Received Check 1247 for $525 as payment in full from Creations for You.
▶ Received Check 8865 from Doreen Collins for amount due.
▶ Billed Central Coast Resorts for large pool and large landscaping maintenance. Terms are Net 15.
▶ Billed Anacapa Apartments for standard-size commercial pool service and standard-size commercial landscape maintenance (LandCom1). Terms are Net 30.
▶ Deposit all cash receipts (this includes checks from both Sales Receipts and Payments on Account). Print the Deposit Summary.

PRINT REPORTS AND BACKUP

▶ Customer Balance Detail Report for all transactions. Remember to remove Date Prepared and Time Prepared from the report. Use Portrait orientation.
▶ Sales by Item Summary Report for 1/1/2013 through 1/30/2013. Portrait orientation.
▶ Journal for 1/1/2013 through 1/30/2013. Remember to Expand the transactions in the report. Print in Landscape orientation, fit to one page wide.
▶ Trial Balance for 1/1/2013 through 1/30/2013. Portrait orientation.
▶ Backup your work to **Landscape (Backup Ch 2)**

NAME _____

TRANSMITTAL

CHAPTER 2: YOUR NAME LANDSCAPE AND POOL SERVICE

Attach the following documents and reports:

Invoice 25: Ocean View Motel
Invoice 26: Dr. Alex Sanchez
Invoice 27: Creations for You
Sales Receipt 15: Deni Anderson
Payment Receipt: Hiroshi Chiang
Invoice 28: Eric Matthews
Payment Receipt: Ocean View Motel
Sales Receipt 16: Wayne Childers
Invoice 29: Santa Barbara Beach Resorts
Payment Receipt: Creations for You
Payment Receipt: Doreen Collins
Invoice 30: Central Coast Resorts
Invoice 31: Anacapa Apartments
Deposit Summary
Customer Balance Detail Report
Sales by Item Summary, January 1-30, 2013
Journal, January 1-30, 2013
Trial Balance, January 30, 2013

PAYABLES AND PURCHASES: SERVICE BUSINESS

LEARNING OBJECTIVES

At the completion of this chapter you will be able to:

1. Understand the concepts for computerized accounting for payables.
2. Enter, edit, correct, delete, and pay bills.
3. Add new vendors and modify vendor records.
4. View Accounts Payable transaction history from the Enter Bills window.
5. View and/or print QuickReports for vendors, Accounts Payable Register, etc.
6. Use the QuickZoom feature.
7. Record and edit transactions in the Accounts Payable Register.
8. Enter vendor credits.
9. Print, edit, void, and delete checks.
10. Pay for expenses using petty cash.
11. Add new accounts.
12. Display and print the Accounts Payable Aging Summary Report, an Unpaid Bills Detail Report, and a Vendor Balance Summary Report.
13. Display an Accounts Payable Graph by Aging Period.

ACCOUNTING FOR PAYABLES AND PURCHASES

In a service business, most of the accounting for purchases and payables is simply paying bills for expenses incurred in the operation of the business. Purchases are for things used in the operation of the business. Some transactions will be in the form of cash purchases, and others will be purchases on account. Bills can be paid when they are received or when they are due. Rather than use cumbersome journals, QuickBooks continues to focus on recording transactions based on the business document; therefore, you use the Enter Bills and Pay Bills features of the program to record the receipt and payment of bills. QuickBooks can remind you when payments are due and can calculate and apply discounts earned for paying bills early. Payments can be made by recording payments in the Pay Bills window or, if using the cash basis for accounting, by writing a check. A cash purchase can be recorded by writing a check or by using petty cash. Even though QuickBooks focuses on recording transactions on the business forms used, all transactions are recorded behind the scenes in the Journal. QuickBooks uses a Vendor List for all vendors with which the company has an account. QuickBooks does not refer to the Vendor List as the Accounts Payable Ledger; yet, that is exactly what it is. The total of the Vendor

List/Accounts Payable Ledger will match the total of the Accounts Payable account in the Chart of Accounts/General Ledger. The Vendor List may be accessed through the Vendor Center.

As in Chapter 2, corrections can be made directly on the business form or within the account. New accounts and vendors may be added on the fly as transactions are entered. Reports illustrating vendor balances, unpaid bills, accounts payable aging, transaction history, and accounts payable registers may be viewed and printed. Graphs analyzing the amount of accounts payable by aging period provide a visual illustration of the accounts payable.

TRAINING TUTORIAL AND PROCEDURES

The following tutorial will once again work with Computer Consulting by Your Name. As in Chapter 2, transactions will be recorded for this fictitious company. You should enter the transactions for Chapter 3 in the same company file that you used to record the Chapter 2 transactions. The tutorial for Computer Consulting by Your Name will continue in Chapter 4, where accounting for bank reconciliations, financial statement preparation, and closing an accounting period will be completed. To maximize training benefits, you should follow the Training Procedures given in Chapter 2.

DATES

As in the other chapters and throughout the text, the year used for the screen shots is 2013, which is the same year as the version of the program. You may want to check with your instructor to see if you should use 2013 as the year for the transactions. The year you used in Chapters 1 and 2 should be the same year you use in Chapters 3 and 4.

PRINTING

Throughout the text, you will be instructed when to print business documents and reports. Everything that is to be printed within the chapter is listed on a transmittal sheet. The end-of- chapter problem also has everything to be printed listed on a transmittal sheet. In some instances, your instructor may direct you to change what you print. Always verify items to be printed with your instructor.

BEGINNING THE TUTORIAL

In this chapter, you will be entering bills incurred by the company in the operation of the business. You will also be recording the payment of bills, purchases using checks, and purchases/payments using petty cash.

The Vendor List keeps information regarding the vendors with whom you do business and is the Accounts Payable Ledger. Vendor information includes the vendor names, addresses, telephone numbers, payment terms, credit limits, and account numbers. You will be using the following list for vendors with which Computer Consulting by Your Name has an account:

Active Vendors ▼		
🔍		
NAME	BALANCE TO...	ATTACH
Artistic Advertising	500.00	
Cal Water	0.00	
California Insurance Company	0.00	
California Realtors	0.00	
Communication Telephone Co.	0.00	
Computer Professionals Magazine	0.00	
Garcia Garage and Auto Services	0.00	
Southern CA Gas Co.	0.00	
Southern California Electric	0.00	
Speedy Delivery Service	0.00	
Supply Station	350.00	

As in the previous chapters, all transactions are listed on memos. The transaction date will be the same as the memo date unless specified otherwise within the transaction. Vendor names, when necessary, will be given in the transaction. Unless other terms are provided, the terms are Net 30. Once a specific type of transaction has been entered in a step-by-step manner, additional transactions of the same or a similar type will be made without having instructions provided. Of course, you may always refer to instructions given for previous transactions for ideas or for steps used to enter those transactions. To determine the account used in the transaction, refer to the Chart of Accounts. When you are entering account information on a bill, clicking on the drop-down list arrow will show a copy of the Chart of Accounts.

OPEN QUICKBOOKS® AND COMPUTER CONSULTING BY YOUR NAME

 Open QuickBooks and Computer Consulting by Your Name as instructed in Chapter 1 (the transactions for both Chapters 1 and 2 will be in this company file).

ENTER A BILL

QuickBooks provides accounts payable tracking. Entering bills as soon as they are received is an efficient way to record your liabilities. Once bills have been entered, QuickBooks will be able to provide up-to-date cash flow reports. A bill is divided into two sections: a <u>vendor-related section</u> (the upper part of the bill that looks similar to a check and has a memo text box under it) and a <u>detail section</u> (the area that is divided into columns for Account, Amount, and Memo). The vendor-related section of the bill is where information for the actual bill is entered, including a memo with information about the transaction. The detail section is where the expense accounts, expense account amounts, and transaction explanations are indicated.

MEMO
DATE: January 16, 2013

Record the bill: Artistic Advertising prepared and placed advertisements in local business publications announcing our new hardware and network installation service. Received Artistic's Invoice No. 9875 for $260 as a bill with terms of Net 30.

 Record a bill

Click the **Enter Bills** icon in the Vendors section of the Home Page
Verify that Bill and Bill Received are marked at the top of the form
Complete the Vendor-section of the bill:
    Click the drop-down list arrow next to **VENDOR**
    Click **Artistic Advertising**
- Name is entered as the vendor.

    Tab to **DATE**
- As with other business forms, when you tab to the date, it will be highlighted.
- When you type in the new date, the highlighted date will be deleted.

    Type **01/16/13** as the date
    Tab to **REF. NO.**
    Type the vendor's invoice number: **9875**
    Tab to **AMOUNT DUE**
    Type **260**
- QuickBooks will automatically insert the .00 after the amount.

    Tab to **TERMS**
    Click the drop-down list arrow next to **TERMS**
    Click **Net 15**
- QuickBooks automatically changes the Bill Due date to show 15 days from the transaction date.

    Click the drop-down list arrow for **TERMS**, and click **Net 30**
- QuickBooks automatically changes the Bill Due date to show 30 days from the transaction date.

    Tab to or click the first line in **MEMO** at the bottom of the Vendor section
    Enter the transaction explanation of **Ads for Hardware/Network Installation Services**
- The memo will appear as part of the transaction in the Accounts Payable account as well as all in any report that used the individual transaction information.

Complete the detail section of the bill using the **Expenses** tab
- Notice that the Expenses tab shows $260, the amount of the bill.
    Tab to or click in the column for **ACCOUNT**
    Click the drop-down list arrow next to **ACCOUNT**

Click **Advertising Expense**
- Based on the accrual method of accounting, Advertising Expense is selected as the account used in this transaction because this expense should be matched against the revenue of the period.

The **AMOUNT** column already shows **260.00**—no entry required

Copy the memo **Ads for Hardware/Network Installation Services** from the Memo text box in the Vendor section of the bill to the Memo column in the Detail section of the bill:

Click to the left of the letter **A** in Ads

Highlight the memo text—**Ads for Hardware/Network Installation Services** by holding down the primary mouse button and dragging through the memo text

Click **Edit** on the menu bar; and then, click **Copy**
- Notice that the keyboard shortcut **Ctrl+C** is listed. This shortcut could be used rather than using the Edit menu and the Copy command.
- This actually copies the text and places it in a temporary storage area of Windows called the Clipboard.

Click in the **MEMO** column on the Expenses tab

Click **Edit** on the menu bar; and then, click **Paste**
- Notice the keyboard shortcut **Ctrl+V**.
- This inserts a copy of the material in the Windows Clipboard into the Memo column
- This memo prints on all reports that include the transaction.

Click the **Save** icon at the top of the bill to save the transaction, leave it on the screen, and update the History
- If you get an Information Changed box for terms, click **No**
- The Recent Transaction section of the Vendor History has been updated to include this bill

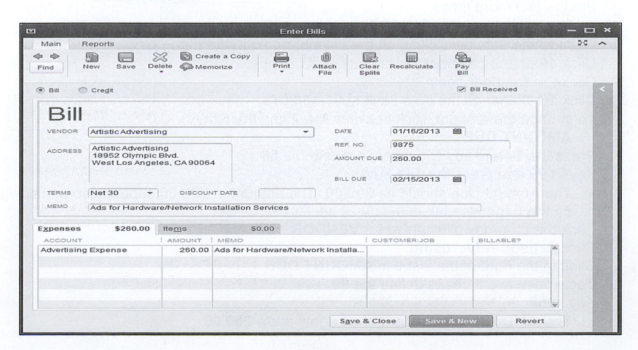

If you want to save screen space, hide the vendor history, click the tab for Hide history

Do <u>not</u> click Save & Close

EDIT AND CORRECT ERRORS

If an error is discovered while you are entering information, it may be corrected by positioning the cursor in the field containing the error. You may do this by tabbing to move forward through each field or pressing Shift+Tab to move back to the field containing the error. If the error is highlighted, type the correction. If the error is not highlighted, you can correct the error by pressing the backspace or the delete key as many times as necessary to remove the error, and then type the correction. (*Alternate method:* Point to the error, highlight it by dragging the mouse through the error, and then type the correction.)

 Practice editing and making corrections to the bill for Artistic Advertising

Click the drop-down list arrow for **Vendor**
Click **Communication Telephone Co.**
Tab to **DATE**
To increase the date by one day, press **+**
- You may press shift and the **=** key next to the backspace key, or you may press the **+** key on the numerical keypad.

Press **+** two more times
- The date should be **01/19/13**.

To decrease the date by one day, press **-**
- You may type a hyphen (**-**) next to the number **0**, or you may press the hyphen (**-**) key on the numerical keypad.

Press **-** two more times
- The date should be **01/16/13**.

Change the date by clicking on the calendar next to the date
Click **19** on the calendar for January 2013
Click the calendar again
Click **16** to change the date back to 01/16/2013
To change the amount, click between the **2** and the **6** in **AMOUNT DUE**
Press the **Delete** key two times to delete the **60**
Key in **99** and press the **Tab** key
- The Amount Due should be **299.00**. The amount of 299.00 should also be shown on the Expenses tab in the detail section of the bill.

Click the drop-down list arrow for **VENDOR**
Click **Artistic Advertising**
Click to the right of the last **9** in **AMOUNT DUE**
Backspace two times to delete the **99**
Key in **60**
- The **AMOUNT DUE** should once again show **260.00**

- If the terms do not show Net 30, click the **TERMS** drop-down list arrow
- Click **Net 30**

Refer back to the original bill from Artistic Advertising shown before Edit and Correct Errors to verify your entries

- Since you received the bill from the vendor, you do not print this entry unless your professor requests printing.

Click **Save & New** button to record the bill and go to the next bill

- If you get the Recording Transaction dialog box, click **Yes**

PREPARE A BILL USING MORE THAN ONE EXPENSE ACCOUNT

MEMO
DATE: January 18, 2013

On the recommendation of the office manager, Alhandra Cruz, the company is trying out several different models of fax machines on a monthly basis. Received a bill from Supply Station for one month's rental of a fax machine, $25, and for fax supplies, which were consumed during January, $20, Invoice No. 1035A, Terms Net 10.

 Record a bill using two expense accounts

Complete the vendor-related section of the bill
Click the drop-down list arrow next to **VENDOR**
Click **Supply Station**
Tab to or click **DATE**
- If you click in Date, you will have to delete the current date.
Enter **01/18/13**
Tab to or click **REF. NO.**
Key in the vendor's invoice number: **1035A**
Tab to or click **AMOUNT DUE**
Enter **45**
Tab to or click on the line for **TERMS**
Type **Net 10** on the line for Terms, press the **Tab** key
- You will get a **Terms Not Found** message box.
Click the **Set Up** button
Complete the information required in the **New Terms** dialog box:
    Net 10 should appear as the Terms
    Standard should be selected
    Change the **Net due** from 0 to **10** days
    Discount percentage should be **0%**
    Discount if paid within **0** days

Click **OK**

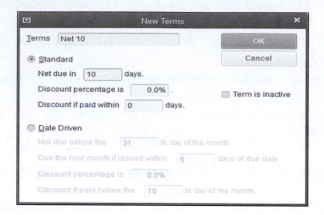

Tab to or click **MEMO** beneath the Terms

Enter **Fax Rental and Fax Supplies for the Month** as the transaction description

To complete the **DETAIL SECTION** of the bill, use the Expenses tab and click the first line for **ACCOUNT**

Click the drop-down list arrow next to **ACCOUNT**

Click **Equipment Rental**

- Because a portion of this transaction is for equipment that is being rented, Equipment Rental is the appropriate account to use.

AMOUNT column shows **45.00**

Change this to reflect the actual amount of the Equipment Rental

Tab to **AMOUNT** to highlight

Type **25**

Tab to **MEMO**

Enter **Fax Rental for the Month** as the transaction explanation

Tab to **ACCOUNT**

Click the drop-down list arrow next to **ACCOUNT**

Click **Office Supplies Expense**

- The transaction information indicates that the fax supplies will be used within the month of January. Using Office Supplies Expense account correctly charges the supplies expense against the period.
- If the transaction indicated that the fax supplies were purchased to have on hand, the appropriate account to use would be the asset Office Supplies.
- Remember the formula:
  - o Used within the month = Expense
  - o Have on hand = Asset

The **AMOUNT** column correctly shows **20.00** as the amount

Tab to or click **MEMO**

Enter **Fax Supplies for the Month** as the transaction explanation

Click **Save & Close** to close the bill

- If you get an Information Changed message regarding the change of Terms for Supply Station, click **Yes**. This will change the Terms to Net 10 for all transactions with Supply Station.

PRINT TRANSACTION LIST BY VENDOR REPORT

To obtain information regarding individual transactions grouped by vendor, you prepare a Transaction Report by Vendor. This allows you to view the vendors for which you have recorded transactions. The type of transaction is identified; for example, the word *Bill* appears when you have entered the transaction as a bill. The transaction date, any invoice numbers or memos entered when recording the transaction, the accounts used, and the transaction amount appear in the report.

 Prepare a **Transaction List by Vendor Report**

Click **Reports** on the Top Icon Bar
Click **Vendors & Payables** to select the type of report
Double-click **Transaction List by Vendor** in the Vendor Balances Section
Enter the Dates From **01/01/13** To **01/18/13**, press **Tab**
Once the report is displayed, click the **Customize Report** button
Click the **Header/Footer** tab
Click **Date Prepared** and **Time Prepared** to deselect these features
Click **OK**
Resize the width of the Memo column so the memos are displayed in full
      Position the cursor on the sizing diamond between **Memo** and **Account**

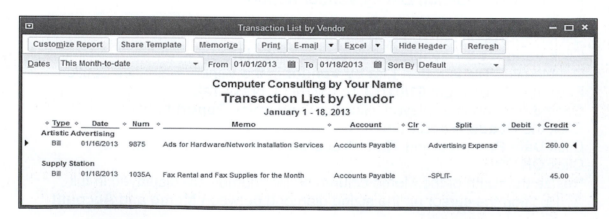

- The cursor turns into a plus with arrows pointing left and right.

Hold down the primary (left) mouse button

Drag the cursor from the diamond between **Memo** and **Account** to the right until you have the memo displayed in full

- You will see a dotted vertical line while you are dragging the mouse and holding down the primary mouse button.

Look at the other columns, if any have … to represent information not shown, point to the sizing diamond and drag until the information is shown

- You may make columns smaller by pointing to the sizing diamond and dragging to the left.

Once the columns have been resized, click the **Print** icon

Click **Landscape** for the orientation

Click **Preview**

- You will be able to see how the report will appear when it is printed. If the report prints two-pages wide, you may want to resize the columns until you can get it to print on one-page wide.

Click **Close** to close the **Preview**

Click **Cancel** to cancel printing

With the resized report on the screen, look at each vendor account

- Note the type of transaction in the Type column and the invoice numbers in the Num column
- The Memos shown are the ones entered in the Vendor (upper) section of the bill.
- The **Account** column shows **Accounts Payable** as the account.
- As in any traditional accounting transaction recording a purchase on account, the Accounts Payable account is credited.
- The **Split** column shows the other accounts used in the transaction.
- If the word **-SPLIT-** appears in this column, it indicates that more than one account was used.
- The transaction for Supply Station has -SPLIT- in the Split Column. This is because the transaction used two accounts: Equipment Rental and Office Supplies Expense for the debit portion of the transaction.

Print the report in Landscape orientation (11-inches wide by 8 ½ inches long) as instructed in Chapter 2, do <u>not</u> close the report

USE THE QUICKZOOM FEATURE

Alhandra Cruz wants more detailed information regarding the accounts used in the Split column of the report. Specifically, she wants to know what accounts were used for the transaction of January 18, 2013 for Supply Station. In order to see the account names, Alhandra will use the QuickZoom feature of QuickBooks.

 Use QuickZoom

Point to the word **-SPLIT-** in the Split column
- The mouse pointer turns into ⊕
Double-click to **Zoom** in to see the accounts used in the transaction
- This returns you to the *original bill* entered for Supply Station for the transaction of 01/18/2013.
- The Expense accounts used are Equipment Rental and Office Supplies Expense.
Click the **Close** button on the bill to return to the Transaction List by Vendor Report
To close the report, click the **Close** button
- If you get a Memorize Report dialog box, click **No**
Close the Report Center

EDIT A VENDOR

The Vendor Center contains a list of all the vendors with whom Computer Consulting by Your Name has an account. As information changes or errors in the vendor information are noted, the Vendor Information may be edited.

MEMO
DATE: January 19, 2013

It has been called to your attention that the address for Garcia Garage and Auto Services does not have a space between Garcia and Garage. Please correct this.

 Open the Vendor Center and correct the address for Garcia Garage and Auto Services

Click **Vendors** on the Top Icon Bar
Click **Garcia Garage and Auto Services** in the Vendor List, click the **Edit** icon
In the Address Details Billed From section, click between **Garcia** and **Garage**, press the **Space** bar

Click **OK**
View the corrected information as shown. Then, close the Vendor Center

ACCRUAL METHOD OF ACCOUNTING

The accrual method of accounting matches the expenses of a period against the revenue of the period. Frequently, when in training, there may be difficulty in determining whether something is recorded as an expense or as an asset (a prepaid expense). When you buy or pay for something in advance that will eventually be an expense for operating the business, it is recorded as an increase to an asset rather than an increase to an expense.

When you have an expense that is paid for in advance, such as insurance, it is called a prepaid expense. At the time the prepaid asset is used (such as using one month of the six months of insurance shown in the Prepaid Insurance account), an adjusting entry is made to account for the amount used during the period. This adjusting entry will be made in Chapter 4.

Unless otherwise instructed in a transaction, use the accrual basis of accounting when recording the following entries. (Notice the exception in the first transaction.)

PREPARE BILLS WITHOUT STEP-BY-STEP INSTRUCTIONS

MEMO:
DATE: January 19, 2013

Received a bill from Computer Professionals Magazine for a 6-month subscription, $74, Net 30 days, Invoice No. 1579-53. (Enter as a Dues and Subscriptions expense.) Memo: Six-Month Subscription

Alhandra Cruz received office supplies from Supply Station, Invoice No. 8950, $450, terms Net 10 days. These supplies will be used over a period of several months so record the entry in the <u>asset</u> account Office Supplies. (Note: After you enter the vendor's name, the information from the previous bill appears on the screen. As you enter the transaction, simply delete any unnecessary information. This may be done by tabbing to the information and pressing the delete key until the information is deleted. Or you may drag through the information to highlight, and press the Delete key. After the "old" information is deleted, enter the new information.) Memo: Supplies to have on hand

While Jennifer Lockwood was on her way to a training session at Valdez and Lonegan, the company car broke down. Garcia Garage and Auto Services towed and repaired the car for a total of $575, Net 30 days, Invoice No. 630, Memo: Auto Repairs.

Received a bill from California Insurance Company for the annual auto insurance premium, $2,850, terms Net 30, Invoice No. 3659, Memo: Annual Auto Insurance (This is a prepaid expense)

 Enter the four transactions in the memo

- Refer to the instructions given for the two previous transactions entered.
- When recording bills, you will need to determine the accounts used in the transaction. Refer to the Chart of Accounts/General Ledger for account names.
- If a memo is required for a bill, enter it in the vendor (top) section and in the detail (lower) section of the bill.
- To go from one bill to the next, click the **Save & New** button.
- Do not change terms for any of the vendors.
- After entering the fourth bill, click **Save & Close.**

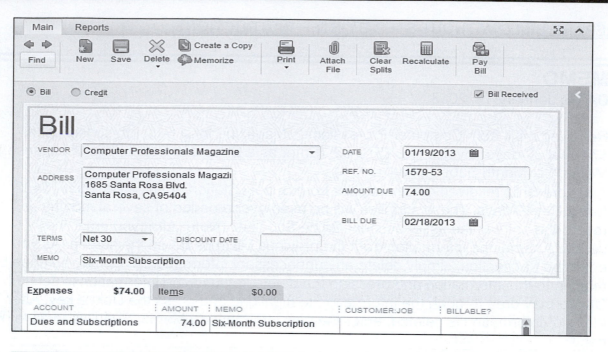

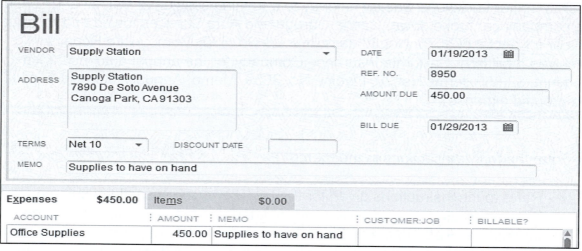

Bill

VENDOR	California Insurance Company	DATE	01/19/2013
		REF. NO.	3659
ADDRESS	California Insurance Company 7809A Oxnard Ave. Woodland Hills, CA 91367	AMOUNT DUE	2,850.00
		BILL DUE	02/18/2013
TERMS	Net 30 DISCOUNT DATE		
MEMO	Annual Auto Insurance		

Expenses	$2,850.00	Items	$0.00		
ACCOUNT	AMOUNT	MEMO		CUSTOMER:JOB	BILLABLE?
Prepaid Insurance	2,850.00	Annual Auto Insurance			

ENTER A BILL USING THE ACCOUNTS PAYABLE REGISTER

The Accounts Payable Register maintains a record of all the transactions recorded within the Accounts Payable account. Entering a bill directly into the Accounts Payable Register can be faster than filling out all of the information through Enter Bills. When entering a bill in the register, QuickBooks also completes a bill behind the scenes.

MEMO
DATE: January 19, 2013

Speedy Delivery Service provides all of our delivery service for training manuals delivered to customers. Received monthly bill for January deliveries from Speedy Delivery Service, $175, terms Net 10, Invoice No. 88764.

 Use the **Accounts Payable Register** to record the above transaction

Click the **Chart of Accounts** icon on the Home Page
  OR
Use the keyboard shortcut **Ctrl+A**
Click **Accounts Payable**

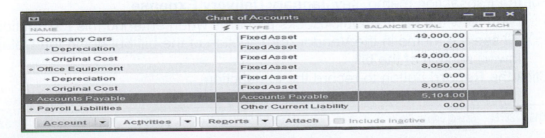

NAME		TYPE	BALANCE TOTAL	ATTACH
◦ Company Cars		Fixed Asset	49,000.00	
◦ Depreciation		Fixed Asset	0.00	
◦ Original Cost		Fixed Asset	49,000.00	
◦ Office Equipment		Fixed Asset	8,050.00	
◦ Depreciation		Fixed Asset	0.00	
◦ Original Cost		Fixed Asset	8,050.00	
◦ Accounts Payable		Accounts Payable	5,104.00	
◦ Payroll Liabilities		Other Current Liability	0.00	

Account ▼   Activities ▼   Reports ▼   Attach   ☐ Include inactive

Click the **Activities** button at the bottom of the Chart of Accounts
Click **Use Register**
• OR Use the keyboard shortcut **Ctrl+R**

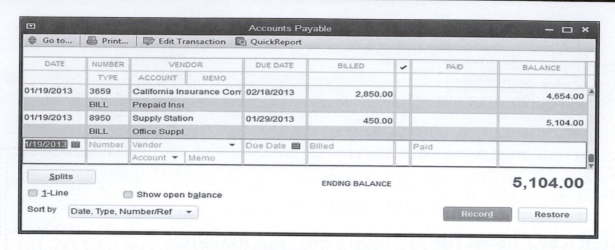

The transaction date of **01/19/2013** is highlighted in the blank entry at the end of the
    Accounts Payable Register
- If it is not, click in the date column in the blank entry and key in **01/19/13**.
The word *Number* is in the next column
Tab to or click **Number**
- The word *Number* disappears.
Enter the Invoice Number **88764**
Tab to or click **Vendor**
Click the drop-down list arrow for **Vendor**
Click **Speedy Delivery Service**
Tab to or click **Due Date**
Since the terms are Net 10, enter the due date of **01/29/2013**
Tab to or click **Billed**
Enter the amount **175**
Tab to or click **Account**
- Note that "Bill" is inserted into the Type field
Click the drop-down list arrow for **Account**
Determine the appropriate account to use for the delivery expense
- Scroll through the accounts until you find the one appropriate for this entry.
Click **Postage and Delivery**
Tab to or click **Memo**
For the transaction memo, key **January Delivery Expense**
- If you view the bill that QuickBooks prepares when entering this transaction, you
    will see the memo in the Vendor (top) section of the bill but not in the Detail
    (lower) section of the bill.
Click the **Record** button to record the transaction

01/19/2013	88764	Speedy Delivery Service		01/29/2013	175.00			5,279.00
	BILL	Postage and Delivery	January Delivery Expense					

Do <u>not</u> close the register

EDIT A TRANSACTION IN THE ACCOUNTS PAYABLE REGISTER

Because QuickBooks makes corrections extremely user friendly, a transaction can be edited or changed directly in the Accounts Payable Register as well as on the original bill. By eliminating the columns for Type and Memo, it is possible to change the register to show each transaction on one line. This can make the register easier to read.

MEMO

DATE: January 20, 2013

Upon examination of the invoices and the bills entered, Alhandra Cruz discovers two errors: The actual amount of the invoice for Speedy Delivery Services was $195. The amount recorded was $175. The amount of the Invoice for *Computer Professionals Magazine* was $79, not $74. Change the transaction amounts for these transactions.

 Correct the above transactions in the Accounts Payable Register

Click the check box for **1-line** to select
- Each Accounts Payable transaction will appear on one line.

Click the transaction for *Speedy Delivery Service*

Click between the **1** and **7** in the Billed column for the transaction

Press **Delete** to delete the 7, type **9**
- The amount should be **195.00**.

Scroll through the register until the transaction for *Computer Professionals Magazine* is visible

Click the transaction for *Computer Professionals Magazine*

The **Recording Transaction** dialog box appears on the screen

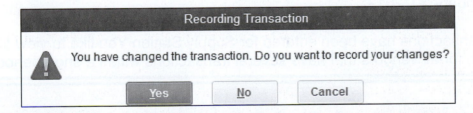

Click **Yes** to record the changes to the Speedy Delivery Service transaction
- The transaction for *Computer Professionals Magazine* will be the active transaction.

Click between the **4** and the **decimal point** in the Billed column

Press the **Backspace** key one time to delete the 4, type **9**
- The amount for the transaction should be **79.00**.

Click the **Record** button at the bottom of the register to record the change in the transaction

Click **Yes** on the Recording Transaction Dialog Box

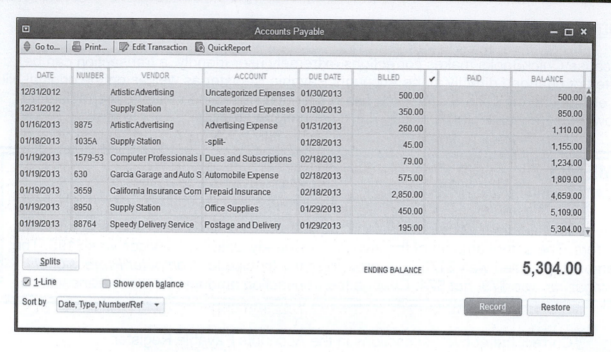

DATE	NUMBER	VENDOR	ACCOUNT	DUE DATE	BILLED	✓	PAID	BALANCE
12/31/2012		Artistic Advertising	Uncategorized Expenses	01/30/2013	500.00			500.00
12/31/2012		Supply Station	Uncategorized Expenses	01/30/2013	350.00			850.00
01/16/2013	9875	Artistic Advertising	Advertising Expense	01/31/2013	260.00			1,110.00
01/18/2013	1035A	Supply Station	-split-	01/28/2013	45.00			1,155.00
01/19/2013	1579-53	Computer Professionals I	Dues and Subscriptions	02/18/2013	79.00			1,234.00
01/19/2013	630	Garcia Garage and Auto S	Automobile Expense	02/18/2013	575.00			1,809.00
01/19/2013	3659	California Insurance Com	Prepaid Insurance	02/18/2013	2,850.00			4,659.00
01/19/2013	8950	Supply Station	Office Supplies	01/29/2013	450.00			5,109.00
01/19/2013	88764	Speedy Delivery Service	Postage and Delivery	01/29/2013	195.00			5,304.00

ENDING BALANCE **5,304.00**

Do <u>not</u> close the register

PREVIEW AND PRINT A QUICKREPORT
FROM THE ACCOUNTS PAYABLE REGISTER

After editing a transaction, you may want to view information about a specific vendor. This can be done quickly and efficiently by clicking the vendor's name within a transaction and then clicking the QuickReport button at the top of the Register.

MEMO

DATE: January 20, 2013

Several transactions have been entered for Supply Station You like to view transaction information for all vendors that have several transactions within a short period of time.

 Prepare a QuickReport for Supply Station

Click any field in any transaction for *Supply Station*
Click the **QuickReport** button at the top of the Register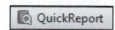
- The Register QuickReport for All Transactions for Supply Station appears on the screen.
Remove the **Date Prepared**, **Time Prepared**, and **Report Basis** as previously instructed
Resize any columns that are not fully displayed and make the Amount column smaller

Click **Print**
Select **Landscape** orientation
Click **Preview** to view the report before printing

				Computer Consulting by Your Name **Register QuickReport** All Transactions				
◇ Type ◇	Date ◇	Num ◇		Memo	◇ Account ◇	Paid ◇	Open Balance ◇	Amount ◇
Supply Station								
Bill	12/31/2012			Opening balance	Accounts Payable	Unpaid	350.00	350.00 ◀
Bill	01/18/2013	1035A		Fax Rental and Fax Supplies for the Month	Accounts Payable	Unpaid	45.00	45.00
Bill	01/19/2013	8950		Supplies to have on hand	Accounts Payable	Unpaid	450.00	450.00
Total Supply Station							845.00	845.00
TOTAL							845.00	845.00

- The report appears on the screen as a full page.
- Sometimes, a full-page report on the screen cannot be read.

To read the text in the report, click the **Zoom In** button at the top of the screen

- Use the scroll buttons and bars to view the report columns

Click **Zoom Out** to return to a full-page view of the report
When finished viewing the report, click **Close**

- You will return to the **Print Reports** screen.

After resizing, the report should fit on one page; if it doesn't keep resizing or click **Fit report to one page wide** to select
Click **Print** button on the **Print Reports** screen
Close the **Register QuickReport**, the **Accounts Payable Register**, and the **Chart of Accounts**

PREPARE UNPAID BILLS DETAIL REPORT

It is possible to get information regarding unpaid bills by simply preparing a report—no more digging through tickler files, recorded invoices, ledgers, or journals. QuickBooks prepares an Unpaid Bills Report listing each unpaid bill grouped and subtotaled by vendor.

MEMO
DATE: January 25, 2013

Alhandra Cruz prepares an Unpaid Bills Report for you each week. Even though Computer Consulting by Your Name is a small business, you like to have a firm control over cash flow so you determine which bills will be paid during the week.

 Prepare and print an Unpaid Bills Report

Click **Unpaid Bills Detail** in the **Vendors & Payables** list on the Reports Menu
   OR

Click **Reports** on the Top Icon Bar, click **Vendors & Payables**, and double-click **Unpaid Bills Detail** in the Vendor Balances section
Remove the Date Prepared and Time Prepared from the report header
Provide the report date by clicking in the text box for **Date**, dragging through the date to highlight, and typing **01/25/13**
Tab to generate the report

Computer Consulting by Your Name
Unpaid Bills Detail
As of January 25, 2013

Type	Date	Num	Due Date	Aging	Open Balance
Artistic Advertising					
Bill	12/31/2012		01/30/2013		500.00
Bill	01/16/2013	9875	02/15/2013		260.00 ◄
Total Artistic Advertising					760.00
California Insurance Company					
Bill	01/19/2013	3659	02/18/2013		2,850.00
Total California Insurance Company					2,850.00
Computer Professionals Magazine					
Bill	01/19/2013	1579-53	02/18/2013		79.00
Total Computer Professionals Magazine					79.00
Garcia Garage and Auto Services					
Bill	01/19/2013	630	02/18/2013		575.00
Total Garcia Garage and Auto Services					575.00
Speedy Delivery Service					
Bill	01/19/2013	88764	01/29/2013		195.00
Total Speedy Delivery Service					195.00
Supply Station					
Bill	01/18/2013	1035A	01/28/2013		45.00
Bill	01/19/2013	8950	01/29/2013		450.00
Bill	12/31/2012		01/30/2013		350.00
Total Supply Station					845.00
TOTAL					**5,304.00**

Adjust column widths as necessary and print in **Portrait** orientation
- Notice that the bills for each vendor are organized by Due Date rather than the date of the transaction.

Click **Close** to close the report
Click **No** if you get a Memorize Report dialog box
If necessary, click **Close** to close the **Report Center**

DELETE A BILL

QuickBooks makes it possible to delete any bill that has been recorded. No adjusting entries are required in order to do this. Simply access the bill or the go to the transaction in the Accounts Payable Register and delete the bill.

MEMO

DATE: January 26, 2013

After reviewing the Unpaid Bills Report, Alhandra realizes that the bill recorded for *Computer Professionals Magazine* should have been recorded for *Computer Technologies Magazine*.

Delete the bill recorded for Computer Professionals Magazine

> Access the Chart of Accounts:
>> Click the **Chart of Accounts** icon on the Home Page
>>> OR
>> Use the keyboard shortcut **Ctrl+A**
>>> OR
>> Use the menu bar, click **Lists**, and click **Chart of Accounts**
> With the Chart of Accounts showing on the screen, click **Accounts Payable**
> Open the Accounts Payable Register:
>> Use keyboard shortcut **Ctrl+R**
>>> OR
>> Click **Activities Button**, click **Use Register**
> Click on the bill for *Computer Professionals Magazine*
> To delete the bill:
>> Click **Edit** on the QuickBooks menu bar, click **Delete Bill**

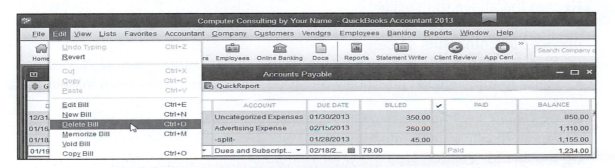

>> OR
> Use the keyboard shortcut **Ctrl+D**
> • The **Delete Transaction** dialog box appears on the screen.

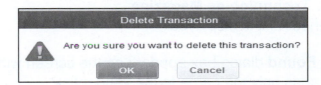

> Click **OK** to delete the bill
> • Notice that the transaction no longer appears in the Accounts Payable Register and that the Ending Balance of the account is 5,225.00 rather than 5,304.00.
> Close the **Accounts Payable Register**
> Close the **Chart of Accounts**

ADD A NEW VENDOR WHILE RECORDING A BILL

When you type the first letter(s) of a vendor name on the Vendor Line, QuickBooks tries to match the name to one in the Vendor List and enter it on the Vendor line. If the vendor is not in the Vendor List, a QuickBooks dialog box for Vendor Not Found appears with choices for a Quick Add—adding just the vendor name—or Set Up—adding the vendor name and all vendor account information. When the new vendor information is complete, QuickBooks fills in the blanks on the bill for the vendor, and you finish entering the rest of the transaction.

MEMO

DATE: January 26, 2013

Record the bill for a six-month subscription to *Computer Technologies Magazine*. The transaction date is 01/19/13, amount $79, Terms Net 30, Invoice No. 1579-53. This is recorded as an expense. The address and telephone for *Computer Technologies Magazine* is 12405 Menlo Park Drive, Menlo Park, CA 94025, 510-555-3829.

 Record the above transaction

Access the **Enter Bills** screen
- Step-by-step instructions will be provided only for entering a new vendor.
- Refer to transactions previously recorded for all other steps used in entering a bill.
- When you key the first few letters of a vendor name, QuickBooks will automatically enter a vendor name.

On the line for Vendor, type the **C** for *Computer Technologies Magazine*
- The vendor name **Cal Water** appears on the vendor line and is highlighted and the list of Vendor names that start with C is displayed.

Type **omp**
- The vendor name changes to **Computer Professionals Magazine**.

Finish typing **uter Technologies Magazine**
- The entire Vendor List is displayed

Press **Tab**

The **Vendor Not Found** dialog box appears on the screen with buttons for:
- **Quick Add**—adds only the name to the vendor list.
- **Set Up**—adds the name to the vendor list and allows all account information to be entered.
- **Cancel**—cancels the addition of a new vendor.

Click **Set Up**
- Computer Technologies Magazine is shown in the VENDOR NAME text box

If necessary, highlight the VENDOR NAME in the VENDOR NAME text box

Copy the name to the Company Name textbox by using the **Ctrl+C** keyboard shortcut for copy

Click in the COMPANY NAME textbox and use **Ctrl+V** to paste the name into the textbox
- Since this is a new vendor, notice that there is no OPENING BALANCE to enter.

Tab to or click in the text box for **Main Phone**

Enter the telephone number **510-555-3829**

Tab to or click the first line for **BILLED FROM** in the **ADDRESS DETAILS** section

- Computer Technologies Magazine appears as the first line in the address.

Position the cursor at the end of the name, press **Enter** or click the line beneath the company name (Do not tab)

Type the address listed in the Memo

Press **Enter** at the end of each line

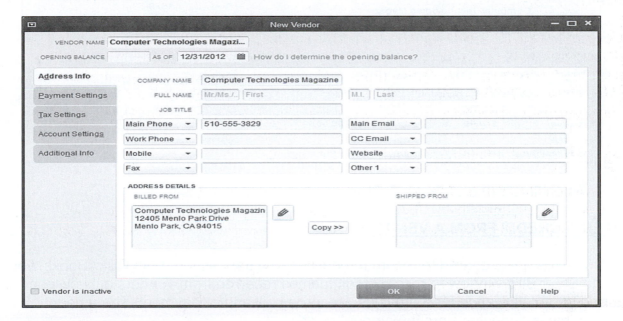

To enter the information for Terms, click the **Payment Settings** tab on the left side of the New Vendor screen

Click drop-down list arrow next to **PAYMENT TERMS**

Click **Net 30**

Make sure **PRINT NAME ON CHECK AS** shows **Computer Technologies Magazine**

- If not enter the name.

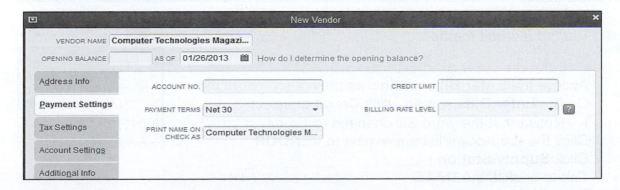

Click the **OK** button for **New Vendor** screen

- The information for Vendor, Terms, and the Dates is filled in on the Enter Bills screen.

If necessary, change the transaction date to **01/19/13**

Complete the bill using instructions previously provided for entering bills

Bill

VENDOR	Computer Technologies Magazine ▼		DATE	01/19/2013 📅
ADDRESS	Computer Technologies Magazin 12405 Menlo Park Drive Menlo Park, CA 94025		REF. NO.	1579-53
			AMOUNT DUE	79.00
			BILL DUE	02/18/2013 📅
TERMS	Net 30 ▼	DISCOUNT DATE		
MEMO	Six-Month Subscription			

Expenses	$79.00	Items	$0.00		
ACCOUNT	AMOUNT	MEMO	CUSTOMER:JOB	BILLABLE?	
Dues and Subscriptions	79.00	Six-Month Subscription			▲

When finished, click **Save & Close** to close the bill and exit

ENTER A CREDIT FROM A VENDOR

Credit memos are prepared to record a reduction to a transaction. With QuickBooks, you use the Enter Bills window to record credit memos received from vendors acknowledging a return of or an allowance for a previously recorded bill and/or payment. The amount of a credit memo is deducted from the amount owed.

MEMO

DATE: January 26, 2013

Received Credit Memo No. 789 for $5 from Supply Station for a return of fax paper that was damaged.

 Record a credit memo

Access the **Enter Bills** window as previously instructed
On the **Enter Bills** screen, click **Credit** to select
- Notice that the word *Bill* changes to *Credit*.
Click the drop-down list arrow next to **VENDOR**
Click **Supply Station**
Tab to or click the **DATE**
Type **01/26/13**
Tab to or click **REF. NO.**

Type **789**

Tab to or click **CREDIT AMOUNT**

Type **5**

Tab to or click in **MEMO** in the vendor (upper) section of the Credit

Enter **Returned Damaged Fax Paper**

Tab to or click the first line of **ACCOUNT**

Click the drop-down list arrow

Since the fax supplies were to be used within the month, this was entered originally as an expense, click the account **Office Supplies Expense**

- The AMOUNT column should show **5.00**; if not, enter **5**.

Copy the Memo to the **MEMO** column in the detail (lower) section of the Credit

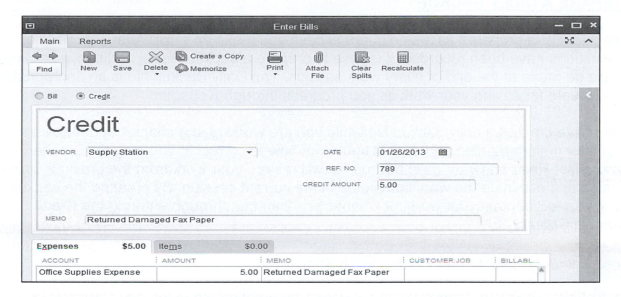

Click **Save & Close** to record the credit and exit **Enter Bills**

- QuickBooks records the credit in the Accounts Payable account and shows the transaction type as BILLCRED in the Accounts Payable Register.

VIEW CREDIT IN ACCOUNTS PAYABLE REGISTER

When recording the credit in the last transaction, QuickBooks listed the transaction type as BILLCRED in the Accounts Payable Register.

 Verify the credit from Supply Station

Follow steps previously provided to access the Accounts Payable Register

If a check mark shows in the **1-Line** check box, remove it by clicking the check box

- This changes the display in the Accounts Payable Register from 1-Line to multiple lines.

Look at the **Number/Type** column and verify the type **BILLCRED**

- Notice the balance of 5,299.00. The balance of Accounts Payable after the bill for Computer Technologies Magazine was entered was 5,304.00. The new balance of 5,299.00 is 5.00 less, which is the amount of the credit.

01/26/2013	789	Supply Station					5.00	5,299.00
	BILLCRE	Office Supplies Expense	Returned Damaged Fax Paper					

Close the **Accounts Payable Register**
Close the **Chart of Accounts**

PREPARE A DAILY BACKUP

A backup file is prepared as a safe guard in case you make an error. After a number of transactions have been recorded, it is wise to prepare a backup file. In addition, a backup should be made at the end of every work session. The Daily Backup file is an appropriate file to create for saving your work as you progress through a chapter.

If you have created a daily backup file while you are working in a chapter and make an error later in your training and cannot figure out how to correct it, you may restore the backup file. Restoring your daily backup file will restore your work from the previous training session and eliminate the work completed in the current session. By creating the backup file now, it will contain your work for Chapters 1, 2 and up through entering the Credit Memo in Chapter 3.

 Prepare the Computer (Daily Backup).qbb file

Follow the steps presented in Chapter 1 for creating a backup file
Name the file **Computer (Daily Backup)**
The file type is **QBW Backup (* .QBB)**
- This uses the same backup file that you prepared in Chapter 2.
- The daily backup file will now contain the work from Chapters 1 and 2 plus Chapter 3 up through entering the credit for a vendor.

PAYING BILLS

When using QuickBooks, you should pay any bills entered through "Enter Bills" directly from the pay bills command and let QuickBooks write your checks for you and mark the bills "Paid." If you have not entered a bill for an amount you owe, you will need to write the check yourself. If you have recorded a bill for a transaction and write the check for payment yourself, the bill will not be marked as being paid and will continue to show up as an amount due.

Using the Pay Bills window enables you to determine which bills to pay, the method of payment—check or credit card—and the appropriate account. When determining which bills to pay, QuickBooks allows you to display the bills by due date, discount date, vendor, or amount. All bills may be displayed, or only those bills that are due by a certain date may be displayed.

MEMO

DATE: January 26, 2013

Whenever possible, Alhandra pays the bills on a weekly basis. With the Pay Bills window showing the bills due for payment on or before 01/31/2013, Alhandra compares the bills shown with the Unpaid Bills Report previously prepared. The report has been marked by you to indicate which bills should be paid. Alhandra will select the bills for payment and record the bill payment for the week.

 Pay the bills for the week

Click the **Pay Bills** icon in the Vendors section of the Home Page to access the **Pay Bills** window

- The Pay Bills screen is comprised of three sections: SELECT BILLS TO BE PAID, DISCOUNT & CREDIT INFORMATION FOR HIGHLIGHTED BILL, and PAYMENT.

Complete the SELECT BILLS TO BE PAID section:

If necessary, click **Show All Bills** to select

Filter By should be **All Vendors**

Sort By should be **Due Date**

- If this is not showing, click the drop-down list arrow next to the **Sort By** text box, click **Due Date**.

Scroll through the list of bills

Click the drop-down list arrow next to the **Sort By** text box

Click **Vendor**

- This shows you how much you owe each vendor.

Again, click the drop-down list arrow next to the **Sort By** text box

Click **Amount Due**

- This shows you your bills from the highest amount owed to the lowest.

Click drop-down list arrow next to the **Sort By** text box, click **Due Date**

- The bills will be shown according to the date due.

Click **Due on or before** in the Select Bills to be Paid section to select this option

Click in the text box for the date

Drag through the date to highlight, enter **01/31/13** as the date, press **Tab**

- Since you pressed Tab after making a change to **Show Bills**, you must select **Filter By** or you will get a warning message. If this happens, click **OK**. Click the drop-down list arrow on **Filter By**. Select **All Vendors**.

Scroll through the list of bills due
Select the bills to be paid
- The bills shown on the screen are an exact match to the bills you marked to be paid when you reviewed the Unpaid Bills Report.

Click the **Select All Bills** button beneath the listing of bills
- The **Select All Bills** button changes to **Clear Selections** so bills can be unmarked and the bills to be paid may be selected again
- If you do not want to pay all of the bills shown, mark each bill to be paid by clicking on the individual bill or using the down-cursor key to select a bill and then press the space bar.

To apply the **$5** credit from **Supply Station**, click in the **VENDOR** column for the $45 transaction for Supply Station with a DUE DATE of **01/28/2013**
- This will highlight the bill and leave the check in the check box for selecting the bill. If you click the check box and remove the check mark, you will need to click the check box a second time to mark the bill as being selected.

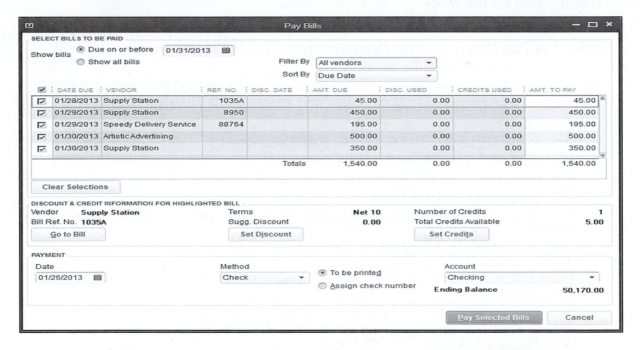

Complete the **DISCOUNT & CREDIT INFORMATION FOR HIGHLIGHTED BILL**:
In the **DISCOUNT & CREDIT INFORMATION FOR HIGHLIGHTED BILL** the
Vendor is **Supply Station**
The Number of **Credits** is **1**
Total Credits Available is **$5.00**.

DISCOUNT & CREDIT INFORMATION FOR HIGHLIGHTED BILL					
Vendor	**Supply Station**	Terms	**Net 10**	Number of Credits	1
Bill Ref. No. 1035A		Sugg. Discount	0.00	Total Credits Available	5.00
Go to Bill		Set Discount		Set Credits	

Click the **Set Credits** button

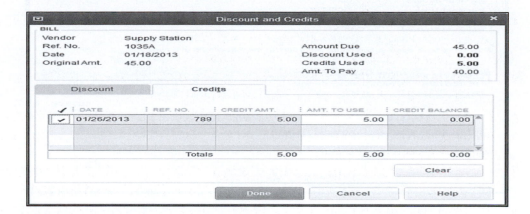

Make sure that there is a check mark √ in the √ column on the **Discounts and Credits** screen

Click **Done** on the **Discounts and Credits** screen

- Notice that the **CREDITS USED** column for the transaction displays **5.00** and the **AMT. TO PAY** for the bill is **40.00**.

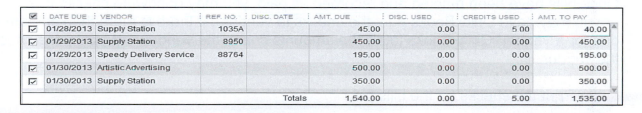

	DATE DUE	VENDOR	REF. NO.	DISC. DATE	AMT. DUE	DISC. USED	CREDITS USED	AMT. TO PAY
☑	01/28/2013	Supply Station	1035A		45.00	0.00	5 00	40.00
☑	01/29/2013	Supply Station	8950		450.00	0.00	0.00	450.00
☑	01/29/2013	Speedy Delivery Service	88764		195.00	0.00	0.00	195.00
☑	01/30/2013	Artistic Advertising			500.00	0.00	0.00	500.00
☑	01/30/2013	Supply Station			350.00	0.00	0.00	350.00
				Totals	1,540.00	0.00	5.00	1,535.00

- Make sure that Supply Station is marked along with the other bills to be paid

Complete the Select Bills to be Paid section

Tab to or click **Date** in the **PAYMENT** section of the screen

Enter the **Date** of **01/26/13**

Check should be selected as the **Method**

Make sure **To be printed** box has been selected

- If it is not selected, click in the circle to select

The **Account** should be **Checking**

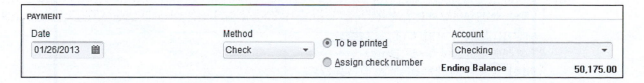

Click the **Pay Selected Bills** button to record your payments and close the **Pay Bills** window

After clicking Pay Selected Bills, you will see a Payment Summary screen.

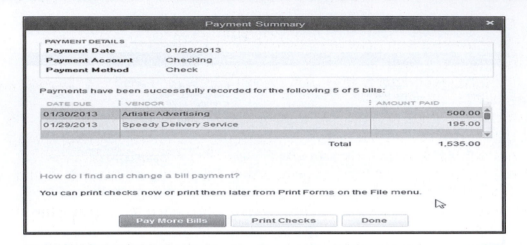

- Scroll through the Payment Summary and review the Vendors and Amounts Paid. Notice the three amounts for Supply Station of $40, $450, and $350.
Continue with the next section

PRINTING CHECKS FOR BILLS

Once bills have been marked and recorded as paid, you may handwrite checks to vendors, or you may have QuickBooks print the checks to vendors. If there is more than one amount due for a vendor, QuickBooks totals the amounts due to the vendor and prints one check to the vendor.

 Print the checks for the bills paid

Click **Print Checks** on the Payment Summary screen
Bank Account should be **Checking**
- If this is not showing, click the drop-down list arrow, click **Checking**.
The **First Check Number** should be **1**
- If not, delete the number showing, and key **1**.
In the √ column, the checks selected to be printed are marked with a check mark

- Notice that the three bills from Supply Station have been combined into one check for payment.
Click **OK** to print the checks

- The **Print Checks** screen appears.

Verify and if necessary change information on the **Settings** tab

Printer name: The name of your printer should show in the text box

- If the correct printer name is not showing, click the drop-down list arrow, click the correct printer name.

Printer type: Page-oriented (Single sheets) should be in the text box

- If this does not show or if you use Continuous (Perforated Edge) checks, click the drop-down list arrow, click the appropriate sheet style to select.

Check style: Three different types of check styles may be used: Standard, Voucher, or Wallet

If the radio button is not marking Standard as the check style, click **Standard** to select

Print Company Name and Address: If the box does not have a check mark, click to select

Use Logo should not be selected; if a check mark appears in the check box, click to deselect

Print Signature Image should not have a check mark

- Notice the Number of checks on first page is 3

Click **Print** to print the checks

- All three checks will print on one page.

Print Checks - Confirmation dialog box appears

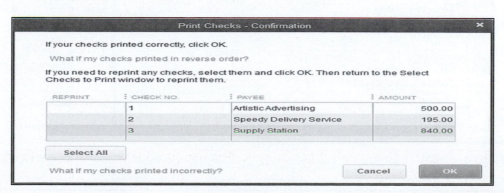

In addition to verifying the correct amount, payee, and payment date, review the checks for the following:

- The checks have the address for Computer Consulting by Your Name, the name and address of the company being paid, and the amount being paid.
- The actual checks will not have a check number printed because QuickBooks is set up to work with preprinted check forms containing check numbers.
- In the memo section of the check, any memo entered on the bill shows.
- If there was no memo entered for the bill, the vendor account number appears as the memo.
- If you cannot get the checks to print on one page, it is perfectly acceptable to access the checks by clicking the **Write Checks** icon in the Banking section of the Home Page, and printing them one at a time. This method is also useful if you need to correct a check and reprint it.

If checks **printed** correctly, click **OK**

- If the checks did not print correctly, click the checks that need to be reprinted to select, and then click **OK**. Return to the Select Checks to print window and reprint them.

If you get a message box regarding purchasing checks, click **No**

REVIEW BILLS THAT HAVE BEEN PAID

In order to avoid any confusion about the payment of a bill, QuickBooks marks the bill PAID. Scrolling through the recorded bills in the Enter Bills window, you will see the paid bills marked PAID.

 Scroll the **Enter Bills** window to view PAID bills

Click **Enter Bills** in the Vendors section of the Home Page
Click the **Previous** or back arrow on the Bills icon bar to go back through all of the bills recorded

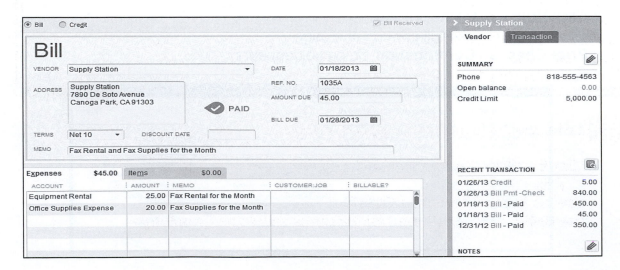

- Notice that the bills paid for Supply Station, Speedy Delivery Service, and Artistic Advertising are marked **PAID**.
- The Credit from Supply Station remains unmarked even though it has been used. Look at the History for Supply Station
- Notice the Open Balance is 0.00. In the Recent Transaction section, all the bills have been marked paid, the Bill Pmt – Check shows, and the $5 credit shows.

Click the **Close** button

PAY BILLS BY WRITING CHECKS

Although it is more efficient to record all bills in the Enter Bills window and pay all bills through the Pay Bills window, QuickBooks also allows bills to be paid by writing a check to record and pay bills. This may be more appropriate process for bills that you pay routinely every month. (Remember, though, if you record a bill in Enter Bills, you must use Pay Bills to write the bill payment check.) When you write a check, it is not entered as a bill in Enter Bills.

When writing a check to record a bill and its payment, you will note that the check window is divided into two main areas: the check face and the detail area. The check face includes information such as the date of the check, the payee's name, the check amount, the payee's address, and a line for a memo—just like a paper check. The detail area is used to indicate transaction accounts and amounts.

MEMO
DATE: January 30, 2013

Since these items were not previously recorded as bills, write checks to record and pay them

California Realtors, $1,500
Communication Telephone Co., $350
Southern California Electric, $250
Cal Water, $35
Southern CA Gas Co., $175

 Write checks to pay the bills listed above

Click the **Write Checks** icon in the Banking section of the Home Page
    OR
Use the keyboard shortcut **Ctrl+W**
The BANK ACCOUNT used for the check should be **Checking**.

- The ENDING BALANCE of the Checking account is shown. This lets you know how much money is in the account before your write the check. This will not change until the check is saved.
- NO. is where the check number will be entered

NO. should show **To Print**, which means that the check will be printed at a later.

- If 1 is showing for the check number, click the **Print Later** checkbox on the Write Checks - Checking Icon Bar.

Tab to or click **Date**

Enter **01/30/13**

To complete the <u>check face</u>, click the drop-down list arrow next to **PAY TO THE ORDER OF**

Click **California Realtors**

Tab to or click in the text box for **$**

Enter the amount of the rent

Tab to or click **MEMO**

- If you do not provide a memo on the check, QuickBooks will enter an account number, a telephone number, an address, or a description as the memo.
- The memo will print on the check, not on reports.

Use the **Expenses** tab to complete the <u>detail section</u> of the check

Tab to or click the first line of **ACCOUNT**

Click the drop-down list arrow for **ACCOUNT**

Click the Expense account **Rent**

- The total amount of the check is shown in AMOUNT column.
- If you want a transaction description to appear in reports, enter the description in the MEMO column in the detail section of the check. Because these are standard transactions, no memo is entered.

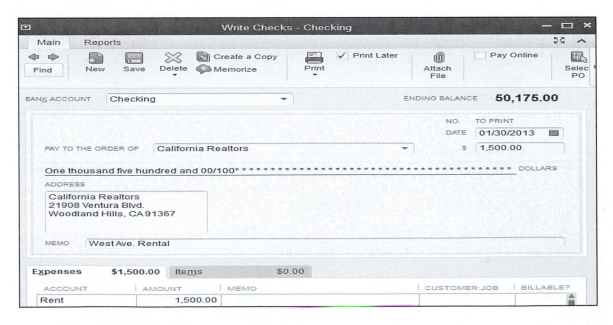

Do <u>not</u> print any of the checks being entered

Click the **Save & New** button or click **New** on the Check Icon Bar to record the check and advance to the next check

Repeat the steps indicated above to record payment of the telephone, electric, water, and gas bills

- While entering the bills, you may see a dialog box on the screen, indicating that QuickBooks allows you to do online banking. Online banking will not be used at this time. Click **OK** to close the dialog box.

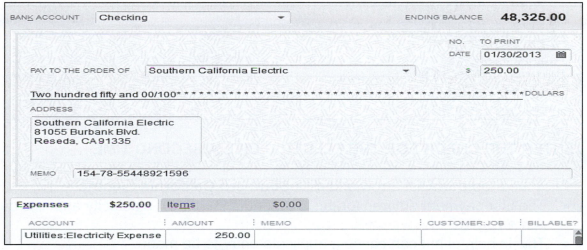

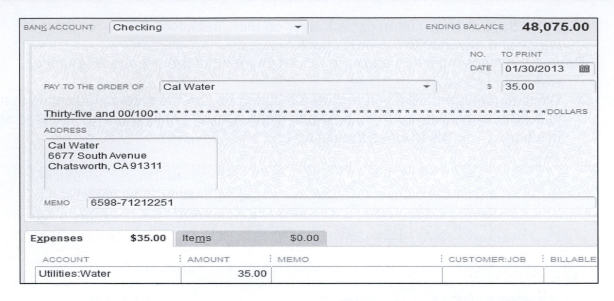

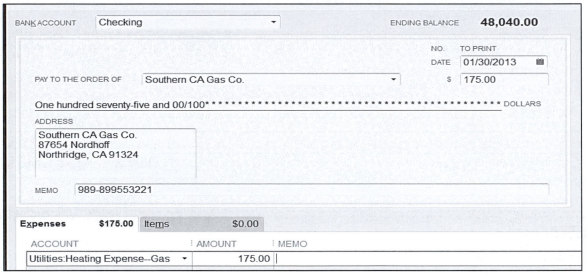

 ENTER THE CHECK FOR THE ELECTRIC BILL A SECOND TIME

Click the drop-down list arrow and click **Southern California Electric**
- The first payment entered for the payment of the bill for electricity appears on the screen.
- This is helpful but can cause a duplicate entry to be made.

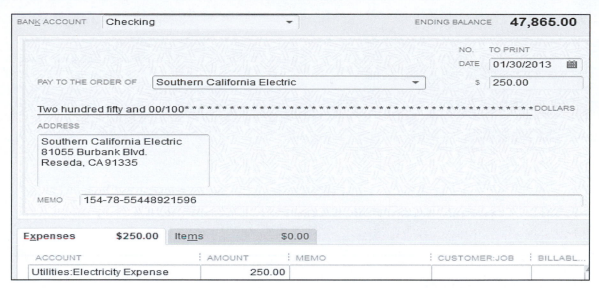

Duplicate Check

Click the **Save & Close** button or click **Save** on the Check Icon Bar and then click the Close button at the top of Write Checks-Checking to record the second payment for the electric bill and exit the **Write Checks** window

EDIT CHECKS

Mistakes can occur in business—even on a check. QuickBooks allows for checks to be edited at any time. You may use either the Check Register or the Write Checks window to edit checks.

MEMO

DATE: January 30, 2013

Once the check for the rent had been entered, Alhandra realized that it should have been for $1,600. Edit the check written to California Realtors.

 Revise the check written to pay the rent

> Open **Write Checks** as previously instructed
> Click **Previous** or back arrow until you reach the check for California Realtors
> Click between the **1** and the **5** in the **$** text box under the DATE
> Press **Delete** to delete the **5**
> Type **6**, press the **Tab** key

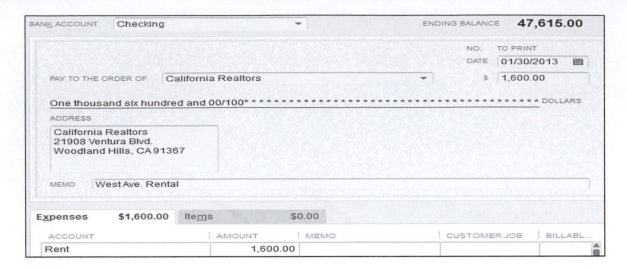

Do not print the check
Click **Save & Close**
Click **Yes** on the screen asking if you want to save the changed transaction

VOID CHECKS

QuickBooks allows checks to be voided. Rather than deleting the transaction, voiding a check changes the amount of the check to zero but keeps a record of the transaction. The check may be voided in the Checking account register or on the check. The following transaction will show you how to void a check in the Checking account register.

> **MEMO:**
>
> **DATE:** January 30, 2013
>
> The telephone bill should not have been paid until the first week of February. Void the check written for the telephone expense.

 Use the steps given previously to access the Register for the **Checking** account

Click the **Check Register** icon in the Banking section of the Home Page
Make sure **Checking** is shown for Select Account on the Use Register screen, click
     OK
Void the check written for the telephone expense
Click anywhere in the check to **Communication Telephone Co.**
Click **Edit** on the QuickBooks menu bar at the top of the screen—not the Edit
     Transaction button
Click **Void Check**
Click the **Record** button in the Checking Register
Click **Yes** on the Recording Transaction dialog box

Click **No, just void the check** on the QuickBooks dialog box

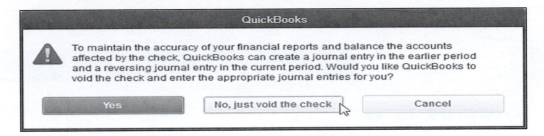

- The amount of the check is now 0.00. The memo shows VOID: Monthly Telephone Bill.

Do not close the register for checking

01/30/2013		Communication Telephone Co.		0.00	✔		50,175.00
	CHK	Telephone	VOID: 678-89-5812				
01/30/2013	To Print	Southern California Electric		250.00			49,925.00
	CHK	Utilities:Electricity Expensi 154-78-55448921596					
01/30/2013	To Print	Southern CA Gas Co.		175.00			49,750.00
	CHK	Utilities:Heating Expense- 989-899553221					
01/30/2013	To Print	Southern California Electric		250.00			49,500.00
	CHK	Utilities:Electricity Expensi 154-78-55448921596					
01/30/2013	To Print	California Realtors		1,600.00			47,900.00
	CHK	Rent	West Ave. Rental				
1/30/2013 📖	To Print	Cal Water	▼	35.00		Deposit	47,865.00
	CHK	Utilities:Water ▼	6598-71212251				

| Splits | | ENDING BALANCE | **47,865.00** |

DELETE CHECKS

Deleting a check completely removes it and any transaction information for the check from QuickBooks. Make sure you definitely want to remove the check before deleting it. Once it is deleted, a check cannot be recovered. It is often preferable to void a check than to delete it because a voided check is maintained in the company records; whereas, no record is kept in the active company records of a deleted check.

MEMO
DATE: January 30, 2013

In reviewing the register for the checking account, Alhandra Cruz discovered that two checks were written to pay the electric bill. Delete the second check.

 Delete the second entry for the electric bill

- Notice that there are two transactions showing for Southern California Electric. Click anywhere in the second entry to Southern California Electric

Click **Edit** on the QuickBooks menu bar at the top of the screen, click **Delete Check**

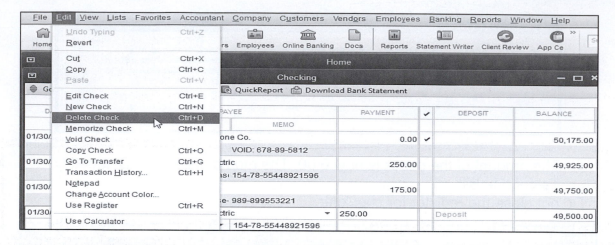

Click **OK** on the **Delete Transaction** dialog box
- After you have clicked the **OK** button, there is only one transaction in Checking for Southern California Electric.

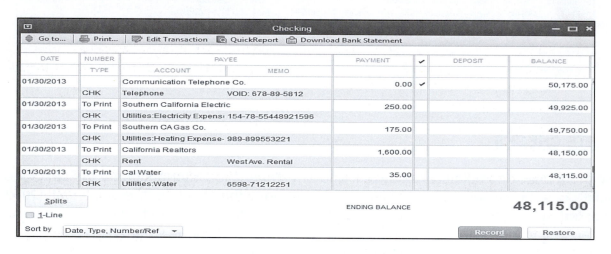

- Notice the change in the Checking account balance.

Close the **Check Register**

PRINT CHECKS

Checks may be printed as they are entered, or they may be printed at a later time. When checks are to be printed, QuickBooks inserts the words *To Print* rather than a check number in the Check Register. The appropriate check number is indicated during printing. Because QuickBooks is so flexible, a company must institute a system for cash control. For example, if the check for rent of $1,500 had been printed, QuickBooks would allow a second check for $1,600 to be printed. In order to avoid any impropriety, more than one person should be designated to review checks. As a matter of practice in a small business, the owner or a person other than the one writing checks should sign the checks. Prenumbered checks should be used, and any checks printed but not mailed should be submitted along with those for signature.

As a further safe guard, QuickBooks automatically tracks all the additions, deletions, and modifications made to transactions in your data file. This record of tracked changes is called an audit trail. The audit trail ensures that an accurate record of your data is maintained. QuickBooks' Audit Trail Report should be printed and viewed on a regular basis.

MEMO

DATE: January 30, 2013

Alhandra needs to print checks and obtain your signature so they can be mailed.

 Print the checks for rent and utility bills paid by writing checks

Click the **File** menu, point to **Print Forms**, click **Checks**
Bank Account should be **Checking**
- If this is not showing, click the drop-down list arrow, click **Checking**
Because Check Nos. 1, 2, and 3 were printed previously, **4** should be the number in the **First Check Number** text box
- If not, delete the number showing, and key **4**
In the √ column, the checks selected for printing are marked with a check mark
- If not, click the **Select All** button.

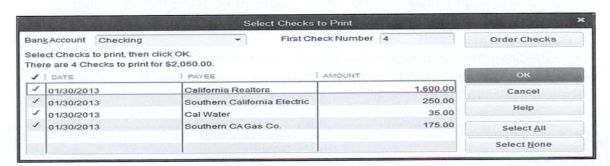

Click **OK** to print the checks
- The **Print Checks** screen appears.
Verify and, if necessary, change information on the **Settings** tab to use **Standard Checks** as previously shown in this chapter
Click **Print** to print the checks
- The checks have the address for Computer Consulting by Your Name, the name and address of the company being paid, and the amount being paid. There is no check number printed on the checks because QuickBooks is set up to use pre-numbered checks.

- If you run into difficulties or find you made an error and want to correct and/or print an individual check, you may do so by printing directly from the check.
Did check(s) print OK? dialog box appears
If the checks printed correctly, click **OK**

PREPARE CHECK DETAIL REPORT

Once checks have been printed, it is important to review information about checks. The Check Detail Report provides detailed information regarding each check, including the checks for 0.00 amounts. Information indicates the type of transaction, the date, the check number, the payee, the account used, the original amount, and the paid amount of the check.

MEMO

DATE: January 30, 2013

Now that the checks have been printed, Alhandra prints a Check Detail Report. She will give this to you to examine when you sign the printed checks.

 Print a Check Detail Report

Open the **Report Center**
The type of report should be **Banking**
Double-click **Check Detail** to select the report
Remove the **Date Prepared** and **Time Prepared** from the report header
The report is From **01/01/13** to **01/30/13**
Tab to **generate** report
- Checks prepared through Pay Bills show Bill Pmt-Check.
- The checks prepared through Write Checks show Check.
Resize the columns as previously instructed

Computer Consulting by Your Name
Check Detail
January 1 - 30, 2013

Type	Num	Date	Name	Item	Account	Paid Amount	Original Amount
Check		01/30/2013	Communication Telephone Co.		Checking		0.00
TOTAL						0.00	0.00
Bill Pmt -Check	1	01/26/2013	Artistic Advertising		Checking		-500.00
Bill		12/31/2012			Uncategorized Expenses	-500.00	500.00
TOTAL						-500.00	500.00
Bill Pmt -Check	2	01/26/2013	Speedy Delivery Service		Checking		-195.00
Bill	88764	01/19/2013			Postage and Delivery	-195.00	195.00
TOTAL						-195.00	195.00

Partial Report

Print the report in **Landscape** Orientation
Click **Close** to close the report
Do <u>not</u> close the Report Center

VIEW MISSING CHECKS REPORT

A Missing Checks Report lists the checks written for a bank account in order by check number. If there are any gaps between numbers or duplicate check numbers, this information is provided. The report indicates the type of transaction, Check or Bill Payment-Check, check date, check number, payee name, account used for the check, the split or additional accounts used, and the amount of the check. Check means that you wrote the check and Bill Payment-Check means the check was written when you used Pay Bills.

MEMO
DATE: January 30, 2013

To see a listing of all checks printed, view a Missing Checks Report for all dates.

 View a Missing Checks Report

Double-click **Missing Checks** in the Banking section to select the report being prepared
- If **Checking** appears as the account on the **Missing Checks Report** dialog box, click **OK**.
- If it does not appear, click the drop-down list arrow, click **Checking**, click **OK**.
Examine the report:

			Computer Consulting by Your Name				
1:01 PM			**Missing Checks**				
01/30/13			All Transactions				
Type	Date	Num	Name	Memo	Account	Split	Amount
Bill Pmt -Check	01/26/2013	1	Artistic Advertising	1-2567135-54	Checking	Accounts Payable	-500.00
Bill Pmt -Check	01/26/2013	2	Speedy Delivery Service	January Delivery Ex...	Checking	Accounts Payable	-195.00
Bill Pmt -Check	01/26/2013	3	Supply Station	456-45623	Checking	Accounts Payable	-840.00
Check	01/30/2013	4	California Realtors	West Ave. Rental	Checking	Rent	-1,600.00
Check	01/30/2013	5	Southern California Electric	154-78-55448921596	Checking	Electricity Expense	-250.00
Check	01/30/2013	6	Cal Water	6598-71212251	Checking	Water	-35.00
Check	01/30/2013	7	Southern CA Gas Co.	989-899553221	Checking	Heating Expense—Gas	-175.00

In a transaction that is decreasing cash, you would credit cash or checking and debit the expense or accounts payable account used in the transaction
The **Account** in all cases is **Checking**, which is the account credited
The **Split** column indicates which accounts in addition to checking have been used in the transaction. The Split accounts are the accounts debited.

Look at the **Type** column:

> The checks written through Pay Bills indicate the transaction type as **Bill Pmt-Check** and the Split account is **Accounts Payable**
> The bills paid by actually writing the checks show **Check** as the transaction type and indicates the other accounts used

Close the report without printing

VIEW THE VOIDED/DELETED TRANSACTION SUMMARY

QuickBooks has a report for all voided/deleted transactions. This report appears in the Accountant & Taxes section for reports. This report may be printed as a summary or in detail. It will show all the transactions that have been voided and/or deleted.

MEMO

DATE: January 30, 2013

In order to be informed more fully about the checks that have been written, you have Alhandra prepare the Voided/Deleted Transaction Summary Report for January.

 Prepare the Voided/Deleted Transaction Summary report

Click **Accountant & Taxes** in the Report Center
Double-click **Voided/Deleted Transaction Summary** in the Account Activity section
The report dates are **All**

1:07 PM
01/30/13

Computer Consulting by Your Name
Voided/Deleted Transactions Summary
Entered/Last Modified

Num	Action	Entered/Last Modified	Date	Name	Memo	Account	Split	Amount
Transactions entered or modified by Admin								
Bill 1579-53								
▶ 1579-53	Deleted Transaction	01/20/2013 16:38:06						0.00
1579-53	Changed Transaction	01/20/2013 16:13:03	01/19/2013	Computer Professionals Magazine		Accounts Payable	Dues and Subscriptions	-79.00
1579-53	Added Transaction	01/19/2013 15:49:19	01/19/2013	Computer Professionals Magazine		Accounts Payable	Dues and Subscriptions	-74.00
Check								
	Voided Transaction	01/30/2013 12:27:17	01/30/2013	Communication Telephone Co.	VOID: 678-89-5812	Checking	Telephone	0.00
	Added Transaction	01/30/2013 12:07:39	01/30/2013	Communication Telephone Co.	678-89-5812	Checking	Telephone	-350.00
Check								
	Deleted Transaction	01/30/2013 12:34:50						0.00
	Added Transaction	01/30/2013 12:13:43	01/30/2013	Southern California Electric	154-78-55448921596	Checking	Utilities:Electricity Expense	-250.00
Invoice 2								
2	Deleted Transaction	01/07/2013 10:18:18						0.00
2	Added Transaction	11/29/2012 14:49:48	01/03/2013	Williams, Matt CPA		Accounts Receivable	-SPLIT-	415.00
Invoice 3								
3	Voided Transaction	01/07/2013 10:01:21	01/05/2013	Ahmadrand, Ela	VOID:	Accounts Receivable	Income:Technical Support Income	0.00
3	Added Transaction	01/05/2013 16:51:06	01/05/2013	Ahmadrand, Ela		Accounts Receivable	Income:Technical Support Income	300.00

- The Entered Last Modified column shows the actual date and time that the entry was made. The report header shows your computer's current date and time. The dates and times shown will <u>not</u> match your date and time.
- In addition, your report may not match the one illustrated if you have voided or deleted anything else during your work session.

Close the report without printing, and close the Report Center

PETTY CASH

Frequently, a business will need to pay for small expenses with cash. These might include expenses such as postage, office supplies, and miscellaneous expenses. For example, rather than write a check for postage due of 75 cents, you would use money from petty cash. QuickBooks allows you to establish and use a petty cash account to track these small expenditures. Normally, a Petty Cash Voucher or Petty Cash Ticket is prepared; and, if available, the receipt(s) for the transaction is (are) stapled to it. In QuickBooks you can scan a receipt and attach it electronically to the transaction. (This will be discussed later in training.) It is important in a business to keep accurate records of the petty cash expenditures, and procedures for control of the Petty Cash fund need to be established to prohibit access to and unauthorized use of the cash. Periodically, the petty cash expenditures are recorded so that the records of the company accurately reflect all expenses incurred in the operation of the business.

ADD PETTY CASH ACCOUNT TO THE CHART OF ACCOUNTS

QuickBooks allows accounts to be added to the Chart of Accounts list at any time. Petty Cash is identified as a "Bank" account type so it will be placed at the top of the Chart of Accounts along with other checking and savings accounts.

MEMO
DATE: January 30, 2013

Occasionally, there are small items that should be paid for using cash. Alhandra Cruz needs to establish a petty cash account for $100

 Add Petty Cash to the **Chart of Accounts**

Access **Chart of Accounts** as previously instructed
Click the **Account** button at the bottom of the Chart of Accounts, click **New** or use the keyboard shortcut **Ctrl+N**
Click **Bank** on the Add New Account: Choose Account Type screen

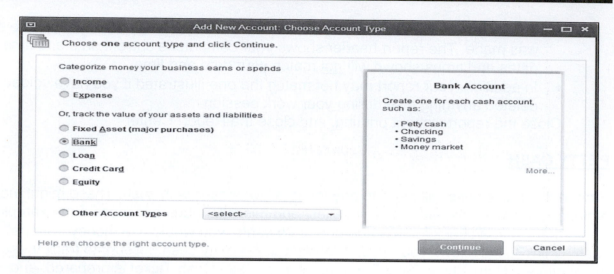

Click the **Continue** button
Enter **Petty Cast** in the **Account Name** text box
- Yes, it should be Cash and will be changed later. So enter Cast.

Leave the other items blank

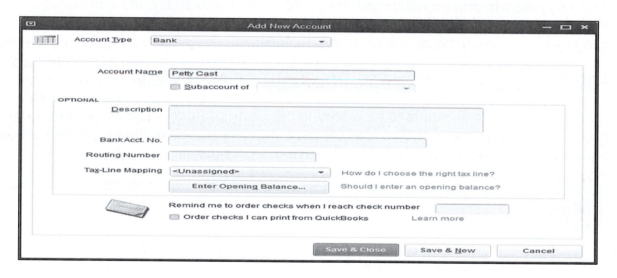

Click **Save & Close** to record the new account
If you get a message to "Set Up Online Services," click **No**
Look at the Chart of Accounts and see that you misspelled the name as Petty Cast
Click **Petty Cast**
Edit the account name by using the keyboard shortcut **Ctrl+E**
Change the account name to **Petty Cash**

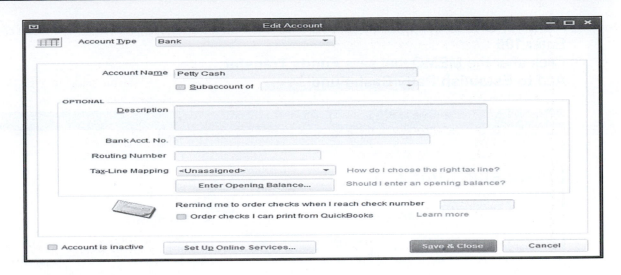

Click **Save & Close**
- If you get a dialog box, to Set up Online Services, click **No**

Do not close the **Chart of Accounts**

ESTABLISH PETTY CASH FUND

Once the account has been established, the petty cash fund must have money in order to pay for small expenses. Two alternate methods for obtaining the funds for Petty Cash are: make a withdrawal from the company checking account at the bank or write a check for cash and then cash it at the bank. If a check is used to obtain cash, the transaction is recorded when writing the check. If a withdrawal is made, it is either recorded directly in the Checking account register or by completing a Transfer Funds for Checking. Since you know how to write a check and how to record a transaction in an account register, completing the Transfer of Funds will be illustrated below.

 Record the Transfer of Funds from Checking to Petty Cash:

Open the **Chart of Accounts** as previously instructed, if necessary
Click the **Checking** account
Click the drop-down list arrow for **Activities**
Click **Transfer Funds**
- As discussed above, this method may be used when a withdrawal is made from the Checking account and the amount is made available for Petty Cash.
- If the cursor is not already in the DATE text box, click in it.
- The date should be highlighted; if it is not, drag through the date to highlight.

If the DATE is not 01/30/2013, enter **01/30/13**
TRANSFER FUNDS FROM should show **Checking**
- The **ACCOUNT BALANCE** for Checking should show **48,115.00**

Click the drop-down list arrow for **TRANSFER FUNDS TO**
Click **Petty Cash**
- The **ACCOUNT BALANCE** for Petty Cash should show **0.00**

Tab to or click in the textbox for **TRANSFER AMOUNT**
Enter **100**
Click after the **MEMO** that says **Funds Transfer**
Add **to Establish Petty Cash Fund**

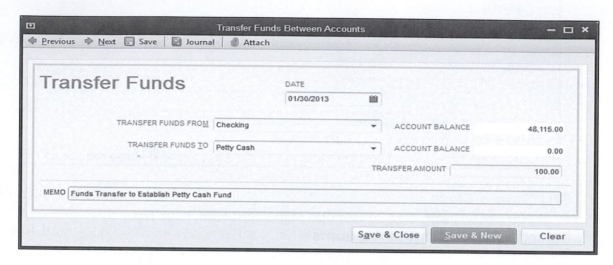

Click **Save & Close** button to record the withdrawal/transfer
View the results in the account balances in the Chart of Accounts

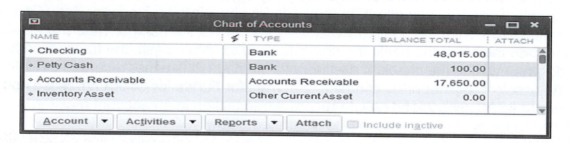

Do not close the **Chart of Accounts**

RECORD PAYMENT OF AN EXPENSE USING PETTY CASH

As petty cash is used to pay for small expenses in the business, these payments must be recorded. QuickBooks makes it a simple matter to record petty cash expenditures directly into the Petty Cash Register.

MEMO
DATE: January 30, 2013

Alhandra Cruz needs to record the petty cash expenditures made during the week: postage due, 34 cents; purchased staples and paperclips, $3.57 (this is an expense); reimbursed Jennifer Lockwood for gasoline purchased for company car, $13.88.

In the Petty Cash account, record a compound entry for the above expenditures

> In the **Chart of Accounts,** double-click **Petty Cash** to open the **Register**
> Click in the **DATE** column, highlight the date if necessary
> Type **01/30/13**
> Tab to Number, enter **1** for the number
> * This would be the number of the Petty Cash Voucher or Petty Cash Ticket that would be filled out and have the receipts stapled to it.
> * No entry is required for Payee.
> Tab to or click **Payment**
> Enter **17.79** (you must type the decimal point)
> Tab to or click in **Account** text box
> Since the total amount of the transaction will be split among three expense accounts, click **Splits** at the bottom of the screen
> You will get an area where you can record the different accounts and amounts used in this transaction.
> In the **ACCOUNT** column showing on the screen, click the drop-down list arrow
> Scroll until you see **Postage and Delivery**
> Click **Postage and Delivery**
> Tab to **AMOUNT** column
> * Using the Tab key will highlight **17.79**.
> Type **.34**
> * MEMO notations are not necessary because the transactions are self-explanatory.
> Tab to or click the next blank line in **ACCOUNT**
> Repeat the steps listed above to record **3.57** for **Office Supplies Expense** and **13.88** for **Automobile Expense**

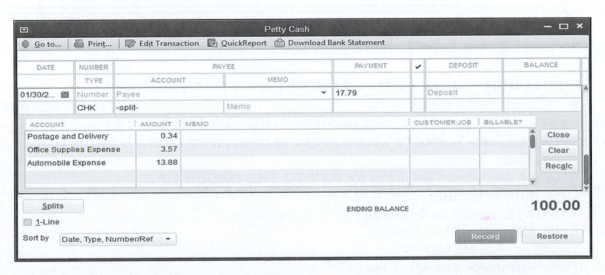

> Click the **Close** button for Splits when all expenses have been recorded
> Click **Record** to record the transaction

01/30/2013	1				17.79			-17.79
	CHK	-split-						
01/30/2013						100.00		82.21
	TRANSFI	Checking	Funds Transfer to Establish Petty Cash Fund					

- Since the transfer of funds and the recording of petty cash expenditures are shown on the same date, the expenditures show first.
- Notice that after the Record button has been clicked, the word "payee," the account name, and memo are removed from the transaction. Instead of showing the accounts used, **-split-** is shown.
- In the Num column, the transaction is marked as a CHK. This actually refers to the number of the Petty Cash Voucher or Ticket, but QuickBooks does not use an identifier of Voucher or Ticket.
- Verify the account Ending Balance of 82.21.

Close **Petty Cash** and the **Chart of Accounts**

PURCHASE AN ASSET WITH A COMPANY CHECK

Not all purchases will be transactions on account. If something is purchased and paid for with a check, a check is written and the purchase is recorded.

> **MEMO**
> **DATE:** January 30, 2013
>
> Having tried out several fax machines from Supply Station on a rental basis, you decide to purchase one from them. Because the fax machine is on sale if it is purchased for cash, you decide to buy it by writing a company check for the asset for $486.

 Record the check written for the purchase of a fax machine

Access **Write Checks - Checking** window as previously instructed
- You wrote the check by hand. It does not need printing. If there is a check mark in the **Print Later** box, click to deselect. **NO.** should show as **1**.

Because Check Numbers 1 through 7 have been printed, enter **8** for the check number

Click the drop-down list arrow for **PAY TO THE ORDER OF**

Click **Supply Station**

The **DATE** should be **01/30/2013**

Enter **486** in the **$** text box

Tab to or click **MEMO**

Enter **Purchase Fax Machine**

Tab to or click **ACCOUNT** on the **Expenses** tab

Click the drop-down list arrow, scroll to the top of the **Chart of Accounts**, and click

       Original Cost under **Office Equipment**

- **AMOUNT** column shows the transaction total of **486.00**. This does not need to be changed.

Click **MEMO**, enter **Purchase Fax Machine**

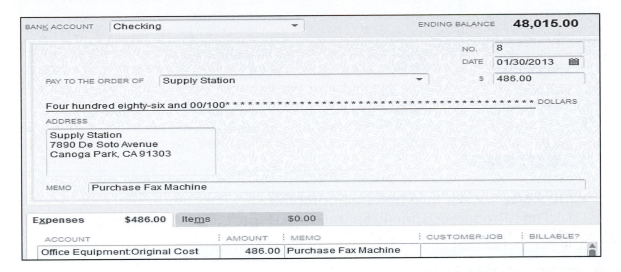

Click **Save & Close** to record the check and exit the **Write Checks - Checking** window without printing

CUSTOMIZE REPORT FORMAT

The report format used in one company may not be appropriate for all companies that use QuickBooks. In order to allow program users the maximum flexibility, QuickBooks makes it very easy to customize many of the user preferences of the program. For example, you may customize menus, reminder screens, and reports and graphs.

 Customize the report preferences to make permanent changes for all reports so reports are automatically refreshed, and the date prepared, time prepared, and report basis do not print on reports

Click the QuickBooks **Edit** menu, click **Preferences**
Scroll through the items listed on the left side of the screen until you get to Reports and Graphs
Click the **Reports and Graphs** icon   ▮▮▮   Reports & Graphs
- If **Refresh Automatically** on the **My Preferences** tab has not been selected, click it to select
Whenever data is changed and a report appears on the screen, QuickBooks will automatically update the report to reflect the changes.
Click the **Company Preferences** tab
Click the **Format** button

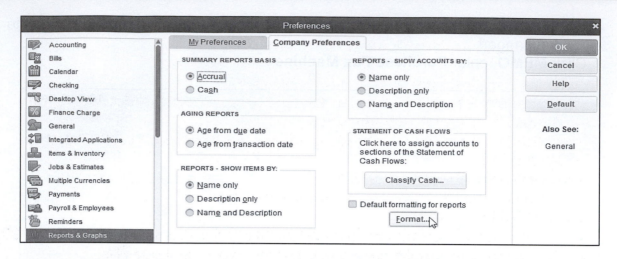

- If necessary, click the **Header/Footer** tab

Click **Date Prepared**, **Time Prepared**, and **Report Basis** to deselect

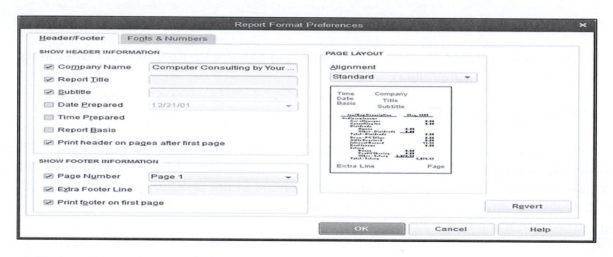

Click **OK** to save the change

Click **OK** to close **Preferences**

PRINT ACCOUNTS PAYABLE AGING SUMMARY

It is important in a business to maintain a good credit rating and to make sure that payments are made on time. In order to avoid overlooking a payment, the Accounts Payable Aging Summary lists the vendors to which the company owes money and shows how long the money has been owed.

MEMO

DATE: January 30, 2013

Prepare the Accounts Payable Aging Summary

Prepare an **Accounts Payable Aging Summary**

> Open the **Report Center** as previously instructed
> Click **Vendors & Payables** to select the type of report, double-click **A/P Aging Summary** in the **A/P Aging** section
> - Notice that the date and time prepared do not appear as part of the heading information.
> Tab to or click in the box for the **Date**
> - If it is not highlighted, highlight the current date.
> Enter **01/30/13**
> - Tab through but leave Interval (days) as 30 and Through (days past due) as 90.
> - The report will show the current bills as well as any past due bills.

Computer Consulting by Your Name
A/P Aging Summary
As of January 30, 2013

	Current	1 – 30	31 – 60	61 – 90	> 90	TOTAL
Artistic Advertising	260.00	0.00	0.00	0.00	0.00	260.00
California Insurance Company	2,850.00	0.00	0.00	0.00	0.00	2,850.00
Computer Technologies Magazine	79.00	0.00	0.00	0.00	0.00	79.00
Garcia Garage and Auto Services	575.00	0.00	0.00	0.00	0.00	575.00
TOTAL	3,764.00	0.00	0.00	0.00	0.00	3,764.00

> Follow instructions provided earlier to print the report in Portrait orientation
> Close the **A/P Aging Summary** screen
> Do not close the Report Center

PRINT UNPAID BILLS DETAIL REPORT

Another important report is the Unpaid Bills Detail Report. Even though it was already printed once during the month, it is always a good idea to print the report at the end of the month.

MEMO
DATE: January 30, 2013

At the end of every month, Alhandra Cruz prepares and prints an Unpaid Bills Detail Report for you.

 Prepare and print the report

> Follow instructions provided earlier in the chapter to prepare and print an **Unpaid Bills Detail Report** for **01/30/2013** in Portrait orientation

```
                    Computer Consulting by Your Name
                           Unpaid Bills Detail
                          As of January 30, 2013
       Type          ◇  Date    ◇  Num  ◇  Due Date  ◇ Aging ◇ Open Balance  ◇
  Artistic Advertising
       Bill             01/16/2013   9875    02/15/2013                 260.00  ◄
  Total Artistic Advertising                                           260.00

  California Insurance Company
       Bill             01/19/2013   3659    02/18/2013               2,850.00
  Total California Insurance Company                                 2,850.00

  Computer Technologies Magazine
       Bill             01/19/2013   1579-53  02/18/2013                 79.00
  Total Computer Technologies Magazine                                   79.00

  Garcia Garage and Auto Services
       Bill             01/19/2013   630     02/18/2013                 575.00
  Total Garcia Garage and Auto Services                                575.00

  TOTAL                                                              3,764.00
```

Close the report
- If you get a Memorize Report dialog box, remember to always click No.

Do not close the Report Center

PRINT VENDOR BALANCE SUMMARY

There are two Vendor Balance Reports available in QuickBooks. There is a Summary Report that shows unpaid balances for vendors and a Detail Report that lists each transaction for a vendor. In order to see how much is owed to each vendor, prepare a Vendor Balance Summary report.

MEMO

DATE: January 30, 2013

At the end of each month, Alhandra prepares and prints a Vendor Balance Summary Report to give to you so you can see how much is owed to each vendor. In addition, she will prepare an Accounts Payable Graph and will use QuickZoom to view graph details. Alhandra will also prepare a Journal and Trial Balance

---

 Prepare and print a **Vendor Balance Summary Report**

Double-click **Vendor Balance Summary** in the Vendor Balances section
- The report should show only the totals owed to each vendor on January 30, 2013.
- If it does not, tab to or click **From**, enter **01/01/13**. Then tab to or click **To**, enter **01/30/13**.

Computer Consulting by Your Name
Vendor Balance Summary
As of January 30, 2013

	◇ Jan 30, 13 ◇
Artistic Advertising	▶ 260.00 ◀
California Insurance Company	2,850.00
Computer Technologies Magazine	79.00
Garcia Garage and Auto Services	575.00
TOTAL	3,764.00

Follow steps listed previously to print the report in Portrait orientation
Close the report; do not close the **Report Center**

CREATE AN ACCOUNTS PAYABLE GRAPH BY AGING PERIOD

Graphs provide a visual representation of certain aspects of the business. It is sometimes easier to interpret data in a graphical format. For example, to determine if any payments are overdue for accounts payable accounts, use an Accounts Payable Graph to provide that information instantly on a bar chart. In addition, the Accounts Payable Graph feature of QuickBooks also displays a pie chart showing what percentage of the total amount payable is owed to each vendor.

 Prepare an Accounts Payable Graph

Double-click **Accounts Payable Graph** in the Vendors & Payables list of reports
Click the **Dates** button at the top of the report
Enter **01/30/13** for **Show Aging as of** in the **Change Graph Dates** text box

Click **OK**

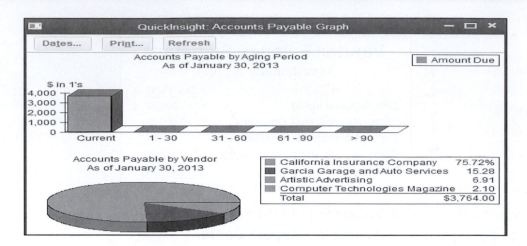

Click the **Dates** button again; enter **02/28/13** for the date
Click **OK**

- Notice that the bar moved from Current to 1-30. This means at the end of
  February the bills will be between 1 and 30 days overdue.

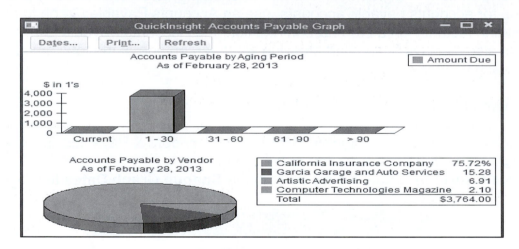

USE QUICKZOOM TO VIEW GRAPH DETAILS

To obtain detailed information from a graph, use the QuickZoom feature. For example, to
see the overdue category of an individual account, double-click on a vendor in the pie chart
or in the legend, and this information will appear in a separate bar chart.

 Use QuickZoom to see how many days overdue the California Insurance Company's
bill will be at the end of February

Point to the section of the pie chart for **California Insurance Company**
Double-click

- The bar chart shows the bill will be in the 1-30 day category at the end of
  February.

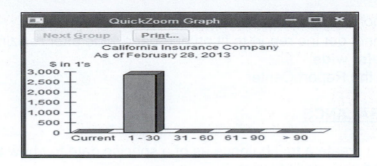

Close the QuickZoom Graph for California Insurance Company
Close the **QuickInsight: Accounts Payable Graph**

PRINT THE JOURNAL

It is always a good idea to review your transactions for appropriate amount, account and item usage. In tracing errors, the Journal is an invaluable tool. If you suspect an error, always check the transaction dates, amounts, accounts used, and items listed in the Memo column to verify the accuracy of your entry.

 Prepare the Journal as previously instructed

The report dates are From **01/01/13** To **01/30/13**
Click the **Expand** button to display each transaction in full

Computer Consulting by Your Name
Journal
January 1 - 30, 2013

Trans #	Type	Date	Num	Adj	Name	Memo	Account	Debit	Credit
64	Transfer	01/30/2013				Funds Transfer to Establish Petty Cash Fund	Checking		100.00
						Funds Transfer to Establish Petty Cash Fund	Petty Cash	100.00	
								100.00	100.00
65	Check	01/30/2013	1				Petty Cash		17.79
							Postage and Delivery	0.34	
							Office Supplies Expense	3.57	
							Automobile Expense	13.88	
								17.79	17.79
66	Check	01/30/2013	8		Supply Station	Purchase Fax Machine	Checking		486.00
					Supply Station	Purchase Fax Machine	Original Cost	486.00	
								486.00	486.00
TOTAL								45,217.79	45,217.79

Partial Report

Resize the columns as previously instructed so you can see the accounts in full and so the report may be printed on one-page in width
- Review the report and check the dates, amounts, accounts, and items used
- Scroll through the report. You will see all of the transactions entered for Chapters 2 and 3.

Print the Report in **Landscape** orientation
- If you cannot get the report to fit on one-page wide after resizing, click **Fit report to 1 page(s) wide**

Do <u>not</u> close the Report Center

VIEW THE TRIAL BALANCE

It is always helpful to create a trial balance as of a specific date to show the balance of each account in debit and credit format.

 Prepare a Trial Balance as previously instructed

The report dates are From **01/01/13** To **01/30/13**
Your account balances should match the following:

Computer Consulting by Your Name
Trial Balance
As of January 30, 2013

	Jan 30, 13	
	Debit	Credit
Checking	47,529.00	
Petty Cash	82.21	
Accounts Receivable	17,650.00	
Office Supplies	950.00	
Prepaid Insurance	2,850.00	
Undeposited Funds	0.00	
Company Cars:Original Cost	49,000.00	
Office Equipment:Original Cost	8,536.00	
Accounts Payable		3,764.00
Loan Payable	0.00	
Loan Payable:Company Cars Loan		35,000.00
Loan Payable:Office Equipment Loan		4,000.00
Retained Earnings	0.00	
Student's Name, Capital		53,135.00
Student's Name, Capital:Investments		25,000.00
Income:Installation Income		175.00
Income:Technical Support Income		900.00
Income:Training Income		7,850.00
Advertising Expense	260.00	
Automobile Expense	588.88	
Dues and Subscriptions	79.00	
Equipment Rental	25.00	
Office Supplies Expense	18.57	
Postage and Delivery	195.34	
Rent	1,600.00	
Telephone	0.00	
Utilities:Electricity Expense	250.00	
Utilities:Heating Expense—Gas	175.00	
Utilities:Water	35.00	
TOTAL	129,824.00	129,824.00

Close the report without printing
Close the Report Center

BACK UP COMPUTER CONSULTING BY YOUR NAME AND CLOSE COMPANY

Whenever an important work session is complete, you should always back up your data. If your data disk or company file is damaged or an error is discovered at a later time, the backup file (.qbb) may be restored to the same or a new company file and the information used for recording transactions. As in previous chapters, you should close the company at the end of each work session.

 Follow the instructions given in Chapters 1 and 2 to back up data for Computer Consulting by Your Name and to close the company. Refer to the instructions provided by your professor for making a duplicate disk

Name your back up file **Computer (Backup Ch. 3)**

SUMMARY

In this chapter, bills were recorded and paid, checks were written, and reports were prepared. The petty cash fund was established and used for payments of small expense items. Checks were voided, deleted, and corrected. Accounts were added and modified. QuickReports were accessed in various ways, and QuickZoom was used to obtain transaction detail while in various reports. Reports were prepared for Missing Checks and Check Details. Unpaid Bills and Vendor Balance Summary Reports provided information regarding bills that had not been paid. The graphing feature of QuickBooks allowed you to determine Accounts Payable by aging period and to see the percentage of Accounts Payable for each vendor.

END-OF-CHAPTER QUESTIONS

TRUE/FALSE

ANSWER THE FOLLOWING QUESTIONS IN THE SPACE PROVIDED BEFORE THE QUESTION NUMBER.

_____ 1. Credit Memos are prepared to record a reduction to a transaction.

_____ 2. When using QuickBooks, checks may not be written in a checkbook.

_____ 3. QuickZoom is a QuickBooks feature that allows detailed information to be displayed.

_____ 4. A cash purchase can be recorded by writing a check or by using petty cash.

_____ 5. Once a report format has been customized as a QuickBooks preference for a company, QuickBooks will automatically use the customized format.

_____ 6. In a service business, most of the accounting for purchases and payables is simply paying bills for expenses incurred in the operation of the business.

_____ 7. Report columns may not be resized and report formats may not be customized.

_____ 8. A Missing Check Report lists any duplicate check numbers or gaps between check numbers.

_____ 9. The Accounts Payable Register keeps track of all checks written in the business.

_____ 10. If a check has been edited, it cannot be printed.

MULTIPLE CHOICE

WRITE THE LETTER OF THE CORRECT ANSWER IN THE SPACE PROVIDED BEFORE THE QUESTION NUMBER.

_____ 1. When using QuickBooks' graphs, information regarding the percentage of accounts payable owed to each vendor is displayed as a ___.
A. pie chart
B. bar chart
C. line chart
D. both A and B

_____ 2. A check may be edited in ___.
   A. the Write Checks window
   B. the Check Register
   C. both A and B
   D. neither A nor B

_____ 3. When you enter a bill, typing the first letter(s) of a vendor's name on the Vendor line ___.
   A. enters the vendor's name on the line if the name is in the Vendor List
   B. displays a list of vendor names
   C. displays the Address Info tab for the vendor
   D. both A and B

_____ 4. To erase an incorrect amount in a bill, you may ___, then key the correction.
   A. drag through the amount to highlight
   B. position the cursor in front of the amount and press the delete key until the amount has been erased
   C. position the cursor after the amount and press the backspace key until the amount has been erased
   D. all of the above

_____ 5. When a document prints 11" wide by 8 ½" long, it is in ___ orientation.
   A. portrait
   B. landscape
   C. standard
   D. horizontal

_____ 6. A correction to a bill that has been recorded can be made on the bill or ___.
   A. not at all
   B. on the Accounts Payable Graph
   C. in the Accounts Payable Register
   D. none of the above

_____ 7. When a bill is deleted, ___.
   A. the amount is changed to 0.00
   B. the word _deleted_ appears as the Memo
   C. it is removed without a trace
   D. a bill cannot be deleted

_____ 8. To increase the date on a bill by one day, ___.
   A. press the + key
   B. press the - key
   C. tab
   D. press the # key

_____ 9. If a bill is recorded in the Enter Bills window, it is important to pay the bill by ___.
   A. writing a check
   B. using the Pay Bills window
   C. using petty cash
   D. allowing QuickBooks to generate the check automatically five days before the due date

_____ 10. When entering several bills at once on the Enter Bills screen, it is most efficient to ___ to go to the next blank screen.
   A. click Previous
   B. click Save & New
   C. click OK
   D. click Preview

FILL-IN

IN THE SPACE PROVIDED, WRITE THE ANSWER THAT MOST APPROPRIATELY COMPLETES THE SENTENCE.

1. The _____ section of a check is used to record the check date, payee, and amount for the actual check. The _____ area of a check is used to record the accounts used for the bill, the amount for each account used, and transaction explanations.

2. An Accounts Payable Graph by Aging Period shows a _____ chart detailing the amounts due by aging period and a _____ chart showing the percentage of the total amount payable owed to each vendor.

3. Three different check styles may be used in QuickBooks: _____, _____, or _____.

4. The keyboard shortcut to edit or modify an account in the Chart of Accounts is _____.

5. Petty Cash is identified as a _____ account type so it will be placed at the top of the Chart of Accounts along with checking and savings accounts.

SHORT ESSAY

When viewing a Transaction by Vendor Report that shows the entry of a bill for the purchase of office supplies and office equipment, you will see the term **-split-** displayed. Explain what the term **Split** means when used as a column heading and when used within the Split column for the bill indicated.

_____

_____

_____

_____

_____

_____

_____

NAME_____

TRANSMITTAL

CHAPTER 3: COMPUTER CONSULTING BY YOUR NAME

Attach the following documents and reports:

Transaction List by Vendor, January 1-18, 2013
Register QuickReport, Supply Station
Unpaid Bills Detail Report, January 25, 2013
Check No. 1: Artistic Advertising
Check No. 2: Speedy Delivery Service
Check No. 3: Supply Station
Check No. 4: California Realtors
Check No. 5: Southern California Electric
Check No. 6: Cal Water
Check No. 7: Southern CA Gas Co.
Check Detail Report, January 1-30, 2013
A/P Aging Summary, Current and Total
Unpaid Bills Detail Report, January 30, 2013
Vendor Balance Summary, January 30, 2013
Journal, January 1-30, 2013

END-OF-CHAPTER PROBLEM

YOUR NAME LANDSCAPE AND POOL SERVICE

Chapter 3 continues with the transactions for bills, bill payments, and purchases for Your Name Landscape and Pool Service. Cash control measures have been implemented. Laura prints the checks and any related reports; and you, the owner, sign the checks.

INSTRUCTIONS

Continue to use the company file that you used in Chapters 1 and 2 **Landscape.qbw**. Record the bills, bill payments, and purchases as instructed within the chapter. Always read the transactions carefully and review the Chart of Accounts when selecting transaction accounts. Print reports and graphs as indicated. Even though bills may be printed, it is not required. Check with your instructor to see if printing bills is assigned. If a bill is recorded on the Enter Bills screen, it should be paid on the Pay Bills screen—not by writing the check.

RECORD TRANSACTIONS

January 1
▶ Edit the vendor Communications Services. On the Payment Settings tab change the "Print Name on Check as" from Total Communications to Communications Services.
▶ Received a bill from Communications Services for cellular phone service, $485, Net 10, Invoice No. 1109, Memo: January Cell Phone Services.
▶ Received a bill from the Office Supply Store for the purchase of office supplies to have on hand, $275, Net 30, Invoice No. 58-9826. (This is a prepaid expense so an asset account is used.) No memo is necessary.
▶ Received a bill from Douglas Motors for truck service and repairs, $519, Net 10, Invoice No. 1-62, Memo: Truck Service and Repairs. (Use Automobile Expense as the account for this transaction. We will change the name to something more appropriate in Chapter 4.)
▶ Received a bill from State Street Gasoline for gasoline for the month, $375, Net 10, Invoice No. 853, Memo: Gasoline for the Month.
▶ Received a bill from Richard's Cooler/Heating for a repair of the office heater, $150, Net 30, Invoice No. 87626, Memo: Heater Repair. (The heater is part of the building.)

January 15
▶ Add a new expense account: Disposal Expense, Description: County Dump Charges.
▶ Received a bill from County Dump for disposing of lawn, tree, and shrub trimmings, $180, Net 30, Invoice No. 667, no memo necessary.
▶ Received a bill from Santa Barbara Water Company, $25, Net 10, Invoice No. 098-1, no memo necessary.

▶ Change the QuickBooks Company Preferences to customize the report format so that reports refresh automatically, and that the Date Prepared, the Time Prepared, and the Report Basis do not print as part of the header.

▶ Prepare an Unpaid Bills Detail Report for January 15, 2013, resize columns as needed, print in Portrait orientation.

▶ Pay all bills *due on or before January 15*, print the checks. (Use Pay Bills to pay bills that have been entered in the Enter Bills window.) Print the checks standard style.

▶ Record the receipt of a bill from Repairs Plus. Add this new vendor as you record the transaction. Additional information needed to do a complete Set Up is: 1234 State Street, Santa Barbara, CA 93110, 805-555-0770, Net 10. The bill was for the repair of the lawn mower (equipment), $75, Invoice No. 5-1256, Memo: Lawn Mower Repair.

▶ Change the telephone number for County Dump. The new number is 805-555-3798.

▶ Prepare, resize columns, and print the Vendor Balance Detail Report for all transactions.

January 30

▶ Received a $10 credit from Repairs Plus. The repair of the lawn mower wasn't as extensive as originally estimated.

▶ Add Petty Cash to the Chart of Accounts.

▶ After obtaining $50 as a cash withdrawal from the bank, complete a Transfer Funds form to transfer $50 from Checking to Petty Cash, Memo: Funds Transfer to Establish Petty Cash Fund.

▶ Record the use of Petty Cash to pay for postage due 64 cents, and office supplies, $1.59 (this is a current expense). Memo notations are not necessary.

▶ Write and print Check No. 5 to Repairs Plus to buy a lawn fertilizer spreader as a cash purchase of equipment, $349, Check Memo: Purchase Fertilizer Spreader. Print the check. (If you get a dialog box indicating that you currently owe money to Repairs Plus, Click **Continue Writing Check**. Remember, this is a purchase of equipment.)

▶ Prepare, resize columns and print an Unpaid Bills Detail Report for January 30.

▶ Pay all bills *due on or before January 30*; print the checks. (Note: There may be some bills that were due after January 15 but before January 30. Be sure to pay these bills now. If any vendor shows a credit and has a bill that is due, apply it to the bill prior to payment. You may need to click on each bill individually in order to determine whether or not there is a credit to be applied.) Print the checks using standard style.

▶ Prepare an Accounts Payable Graph as of 1/30/2013. Do not print.

▶ Prepare a QuickZoom Graph for County Dump as of 1/30/2013. Do not print.

▶ Prepare the Journal for January 1-30, 2013, expand the report, resize the columns, and then print the report in Landscape.

▶ Print a Trial Balance for January 1-30, 2013

▶ Back up your data and close the company.

NAME_____

TRANSMITTAL

CHAPTER 3: YOUR NAME LANDSCAPE AND POOL SERVICE

Attach the following documents and reports:

(Note: When paying bills and printing a batch of checks, your checks may be in a different order than shown below. As long as you print the checks to the correct vendors and have the correct amounts, do not be concerned if your check numbers are not an exact match.)

Unpaid Bills Detail Report, January 15, 2013
Check No. 1: Communications Services
Check No. 2: County Dump
Check No. 3: Douglas Motors
Check No. 4: State Street Gasoline
Vendor Balance Detail
Credit Memo: Repairs Plus
Check No. 5: Repairs Plus
Unpaid Bills Detail Report, January 30, 2013
Check No. 6: Repairs Plus
Check No. 7: Santa Barbara Water Co.
Journal, January 1-30, 2013
Trial Balance, January 1-30, 2013

GENERAL ACCOUNTING AND END-OF-PERIOD PROCEDURES: SERVICE BUSINESS

LEARNING OBJECTIVES

At the completion of this chapter, you will be able to:

1. Complete the end-of-period procedures.
2. Change account names, delete accounts, and make accounts inactive.
3. View an account name change and its effect on subaccounts.
4. Record depreciation and enter the adjusting entries required for accrual-basis accounting.
5. Record owner's equity transactions for a sole proprietor including capital investment and owner withdrawals.
6. Reconcile the bank statement, record bank service charges, automatic payments, and mark cleared transactions.
7. Print Trial Balance, Profit and Loss Statement, and Balance Sheet.
8. Export a report to Microsoft® Excel
9. Perform end-of-period backup and close the end of a period.

GENERAL ACCOUNTING AND END-OF-PERIOD PROCEDURES

As previously stated, QuickBooks operates from the standpoint of a business document rather than an accounting form, journal, or ledger. While QuickBooks does incorporate all of these items into the program, in many instances they operate behind the scenes. QuickBooks does not require special closing procedures at the end of a period. At the end of the fiscal year, QuickBooks transfers the net income into the Retained Earnings account and allows you to protect the data for the year by assigning a closing date to the period. All of the transaction detail is maintained and viewable, but it will not be changed unless OK is clicked on a warning screen.

Even though a formal closing does not have to be performed within QuickBooks, when you use accrual-basis accounting, several transactions must be recorded to reflect all expenses and income for the period. For example, bank statements must be reconciled and any charges or bank collections need to be recorded. During the business period, the accountant for the company will review things such as account names, adjusting entries, depreciation schedules, owner's equity adjustments, and so on. Sometimes the changes and adjustments will be made by the accountant in a separate file called the Accountant's Copy of the business files. This file is then imported into the company file that is used to record day-to-day business transactions, and all adjustments made by the accountant are added to the current company file. There are certain restrictions to the types of transactions that may be made on an Accountant's Copy of the business files.

Once necessary adjustments have been made, reports reflecting the end-of-period results of operations should be prepared. For archive purposes at the end of the fiscal year an additional backup disk is prepared and stored.

TRAINING TUTORIAL AND PROCEDURES

The following tutorial will once again work with Computer Consulting by Your Name. As in Chapters 2 and 3, transactions will be recorded for this fictitious company. To maximize training benefits, you should follow the steps illustrated in Chapter 2 and be sure to use the same file that you used to record transactions for Chapters 2 and 3.

OPEN QUICKBOOKS® AND COMPUTER CONSULTING BY YOUR NAME

 Open QuickBooks

Open Computer Consulting by Your Name as previously instructed
- This file should contain all the transactions that you recorded for Chapters 2 and 3.

Check the title bar to verify that Computer Consulting by Your Name is the open company
Prepare a Journal for 01/01/13 – 01/30/13
Verify that all transactions from Chapters 2 and 3 are shown.
- Hint: the last transaction should be the Check 8 written to Supply Station for the purchase of a Fax machine.

Close the Journal without printing

DATES

As in the other chapters in the text, the year used for the screen shots is 2013, which is the same year as the version of the program. You may want to check with your instructor to see if you should use 2013 as the year for the transactions. Be sure to use the same year for all the transactions in Chapters 2, 3, and 4.

PRINTING

Throughout the text, you will be instructed when to print business documents and reports. Everything that is to be printed within the chapter is listed on a transmittal sheet. The end-of- chapter problem also has everything to be printed listed on a transmittal sheet. As in the other chapters, check with your instructor for printing requirements.

BEGINNING THE TUTORIAL

In this chapter, you will be recording end-of-period adjustments, reconciling bank statements, changing account names, and preparing traditional end-of-period reports. Because QuickBooks does not perform a traditional "closing" of the books, you will learn how to assign a closing date to protect transactions and data recorded during previous accounting periods.

As in the earlier chapters, all transactions are listed on memos. The transaction date will be the same as the memo date unless otherwise specified within the transaction. Once a specific type of transaction has been entered in a step-by-step manner, additional transactions of the same or a similar type will be made without instructions being provided. Of course, you may always refer to instructions given for previous transactions for ideas or for steps used to enter those transactions. To determine the account used in the transaction, refer to the Chart of Accounts, which is also the General Ledger.

CHANGE THE NAME OF EXISTING ACCOUNTS IN THE CHART OF ACCOUNTS

Even though transactions have been recorded during the month of January, QuickBooks makes it a simple matter to change the name of an existing account. Once the name of an account has been changed, all transactions using the "old" name are updated and show the "new" account name.

MEMO

DATE: January 31, 2013

Upon the recommendation from the company's CPA, you decided to change the names of several accounts: Student's Name, Capital to Your Name, Capital (Use your actual name); Company Cars to Business Vehicles; Company Cars Loan to Business Vehicles Loan; Automobile Expense to Business Vehicles Expense; Auto Insurance Expense to Business Vehicles Insurance; Office Equipment Loan to Office Furniture/Equipment Loan; and Office Equipment to Office Furniture/Equipment

---

 Change the account names

> Access the **Chart of Accounts** using the keyboard shortcut Ctrl+A
> Scroll through accounts until you see **Student's Name, Capital**, click the account.
> - The account name was changed in Chapter 1 after the Computer (Backup Ch. 1).qbb file was created.
> - When the backup file was restored, the account name reverted back to the original name Student's Name, Capital.
> - If your instructor had you rename the account with your name in Chapter 2, you will not need to change the name of the capital account.

Click the **Account** button at the bottom of the Chart of Accounts, click **Edit Account**
  OR
Use the keyboard shortcut **Ctrl+E**
On the **Edit Account** screen, highlight **Student's Name**
Enter your name
- The name of the account should be **Your Name, Capital** (your real name!)
Click **Save & Close** to record the name change and close the **Edit Account** screen
- Notice that the name of the account appears as **Your Name, Capital** in the Chart of Accounts and that the balance of $78,135.00 shows.
- The balances of any subaccounts of Your Name, Capital will be reflected in the account total on the Chart of Accounts and in reports.
- While the subaccount names remain unchanged, the name of the account to which they are attached is changed.
Follow the steps above to change the names of:
  Company Cars to **Business Vehicles**
- If the subaccount included the name of Company Cars, the name would need to be changed. Changing the name of the master account does not change the name of a related subaccount.
  Company Cars Loan to **Business Vehicles Loan**
  Automobile Expense to **Business Vehicles Expense**
  Delete the Description by highlighting it and then pressing the **Delete** key
  Auto Insurance Expense to **Business Vehicles Insurance**
  Office Equipment Loan to **Office Furniture/Equipment Loan**
  - Due to exceeding the allotted number of characters in an account name, the symbol and spaces " & " were omitted and the "/" was used.
  Office Equipment to **Office Furniture/Equipment**
Do not close the **Chart of Accounts**

EFFECT OF AN ACCOUNT NAME CHANGE ON SUBACCOUNTS

Any account (even a subaccount) that uses Company Car (the master account) as part of the account name needs to be changed. When the account name of Company Car was changed to Business Vehicles, the subaccounts of Company Car automatically became subaccounts of Business Vehicles. Because the subaccount did not include "Business Vehicles" as part of the account name, the name did not change. If the subaccount included "Business Vehicles" as part of the account name, then the subaccount name would need to be changed.

 Examine the Depreciation and Original Cost accounts for Business Vehicles

Click **Depreciation** under Business Vehicles
Use the keyboard shortcut **Ctrl+E**
The text box for **Subaccount of** shows as **Business Vehicles**
- Remember you do not have to change the name of the Depreciation account. You are just verifying that Depreciation is a subaccount of Business Vehicles.

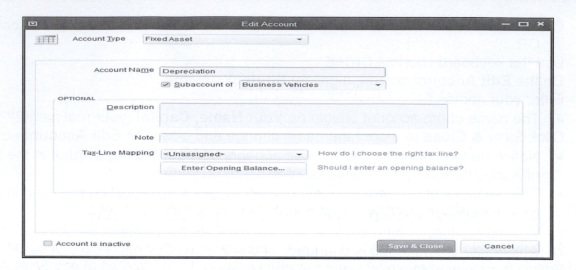

Click **Cancel**

- Repeat the above steps to examine the **Original Cost** account.
- Examine **Your Name, Capital** and **Office Furniture/Equipment** and their subaccounts.

Do not close the **Chart of Accounts**

MAKE AN ACCOUNT INACTIVE

If you are not using an account and do not have plans to use it in the near future, the account may be made inactive. The account remains available for use, yet it does not appear on your chart of accounts unless you check the Show All check box.

MEMO

DATE: January 31, 2013

At present, the company does not plan to purchase its own building. Make Interest Expense: Mortgage and Taxes: Property inactive.

 Make the accounts listed above inactive

Click **Mortgage** under Interest Expense
Click the **Account** button at the bottom of the **Chart of Accounts**
Click **Make Account Inactive**

- The account no longer appears in the Chart of Accounts.

To view all accounts including the inactive ones, click the **Include Inactive** check box at the bottom of the **Chart of Accounts** and all accounts will be displayed.

- Notice the icon next to Mortgage. It marks the account as inactive.

⋄Interest Expense		Expense
⋄Finance Charge		Expense
⋄Loan Interest		Expense
✖ ⋄Mortgage		Expense

Repeat the above to make **Taxes: Property** inactive

⋄Taxes		Expense
⋄Federal		Expense
⋄Local		Expense
✖ ⋄Property		Expense
⋄State		Expense

DELETE AN EXISTING ACCOUNT FROM THE CHART OF ACCOUNTS

If you do not want to make an account inactive because you have not used it and do not plan to use it at all, QuickBooks allows an unused account to be deleted at any time. As a safeguard, QuickBooks prevents the deletion of an account once it has been used even if it simply contains an opening or an existing balance.

MEMO

DATE: January 31, 2013

In addition to previous changes to account names, you find that you do not use nor will use the expense account: Cash Discounts. Delete this account from the Chart of Accounts. In addition, delete the accounts: Inventory Asset, Cost of Goods Sold, and Dues and Subscriptions account.

 Delete the **Cash Discounts** expense account

Scroll through accounts until you see Cash Discounts, click **Cash Discounts**
Click the **Account** button at the bottom of the Chart of Accounts, click **Delete Account** or use the keyboard shortcut **Ctrl+D**
Click **OK** on the **Delete Account** dialog box

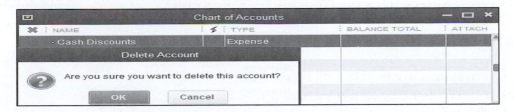

- The account has now been deleted.
Repeat the above steps for the deletion of **Inventory Asset**, **Cost of Goods Sold**, **Dues and Subscriptions**
- Since this Dues and Subscriptions account has been used, QuickBooks will not allow it to be deleted.

- As soon as you try to delete Dues and Subscriptions, a **QuickBooks Message** appears. It describes the problem (account has a balance or has been used) and offers a solution (make account inactive).

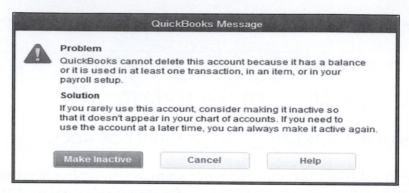

Click **Cancel**

- The account remains in the Chart of Accounts.

NAME	TYPE	BALANCE TOTAL	ATTACH
Checking	Bank	47,529.00	
Petty Cash	Bank	82.21	
Accounts Receivable	Accounts Receivable	17,650.00	
Office Supplies	Other Current Asset	950.00	
Prepaid Insurance	Other Current Asset	2,850.00	
Undeposited Funds	Other Current Asset	0.00	
Business Vehicles	Fixed Asset	49,000.00	
Depreciation	Fixed Asset	0.00	
Original Cost	Fixed Asset	49,000.00	
Office Furniture/Equipment	Fixed Asset	8,536.00	
Depreciation	Fixed Asset	0.00	
Original Cost	Fixed Asset	8,536.00	
Accounts Payable	Accounts Payable	3,764.00	
Payroll Liabilities	Other Current Liability	0.00	
Loan Payable	Long Term Liability	39,000.00	
Business Vehicles Loan	Long Term Liability	35,000.00	
Office Furniture/Equipm...	Long Term Liability	4,000.00	
Retained Earnings	Equity		
Your Name, Capital	Equity	78,135.00	
Draws	Equity	0.00	
Investments	Equity	25,000.00	
Income	Income		
Installation Income	Income		
Technical Support Income	Income		
Training Income	Income		
Other Regular Income	Income		
Reimbursed Expenses	Income		
Uncategorized Income	Income		
Advertising Expense	Expense		
Bank Service Charges	Expense		
Business Vehicles Expense	Expense		
Contributions	Expense		
Depreciation Expense	Expense		
Dues and Subscriptions	Expense		

Partial Chart of Accounts

Review the changes made, and then close the **Chart of Accounts**

To print the Chart of Accounts, click **Reports** on the menu bar, point to **List**, click
Account Listing (QuickBooks will insert the date of your computer as the report
date)

Resize the columns of the reports to show the columns in full.

To hide the column for **Tax Line**, drag the diamond on the right-side of **Tax Line** to
the diamond on the right-side of **Description**

Print in Landscape orientation and close the report

ADJUSTMENTS FOR ACCRUAL-BASIS ACCOUNTING

As previously stated, the accrual basis of accounting matches the income and the
expenses of a period in order to arrive at an accurate figure for net income or net loss.
Thus, the revenue is earned at the time the service is performed or the sale is made no
matter when the actual cash is received. The cash basis of accounting records income or
revenue at the time cash is received no matter when the sale was made or the service
performed. The same holds true when a business buys things or pays bills. In accrual-basis
accounting, the expense is recorded at the time the bill is received or the purchase is made
regardless of the actual payment date. In cash-basis accounting, the expense is not
recorded until it is paid. In QuickBooks, the Summary Report Basis for either Accrual or
Cash is selected as a Report Preference. The default setting is Accrual.

For example, to record $1,000 of sales on account and one year of insurance for $600 in
November: Using the accrual basis of accounting, you would record $1,000 as income or
revenue and $600 as a prepaid expense in an asset account—Prepaid Insurance. Month
by month, an adjusting entry for $50 would be made to record the amount of insurance
used for the month. In the accrual basis of accounting, when the $1,000 payment on
account is received, it will not affect income. It will be recorded as an increase in cash and
a decrease in accounts receivable. When using the cash basis of accounting, you would
have no income and $600 worth of insurance recorded as an expense for November with
nothing else recorded for insurance until the following November. The income of $1,000
would not be shown until the cash payment was received. A Statement of Profit and Loss
prepared in November would show:

November	Accrual		Cash	
Income		$1,000		$ 0
Insurance Expense	($600/12) =	-50		-600
Net Profit (Loss)	**Profit**	$950	Loss	-$600

When you are using the accrual basis of accounting, there are several internal transactions
that must be recorded. These entries are called adjusting entries. Some items used in a
business are purchased and or paid for in advance. When this occurs, they are recorded as
an asset. These are called prepaid expenses. As these are used, they become expenses of
the business. For example, insurance for the entire year would be used up month by month
and should, therefore, be a monthly expense. Commonly, the insurance is billed and paid
for the entire year. Until the insurance is used, it is an asset. Each month, the portion of the
insurance used becomes an expense for the month. (Refer to the chart above.) Another

example for adjusting entries is in regard to equipment. Since it does wear out and will eventually need to be replaced, rather than wait until replacement to record the use of the equipment, an adjusting entry is made to allocate the use of equipment as an expense for a period. This is called depreciation.

ADJUSTING ENTRIES—PREPAID EXPENSES

A prepaid expense is an item that is paid for in advance. Examples of prepaid expenses include: Insurance—policy is usually for six months or one year; Office Supplies—buy to have on hand and use as needed. (This is different from supplies that are purchased for immediate use.) A prepaid expense is an asset until it is used. As the insurance or supplies are used, the amount used becomes an expense for the period. In accrual basis accounting, an adjusting entry is made in the General Journal at the end of the period to allocate the amount of prepaid expenses (assets) used to expenses.

The transactions for these adjustments may be recorded in the register for the account by clicking on the prepaid expense (asset) in the Chart of Accounts, or they may be made in the General Journal.

MEMO

DATE: January 31, 2013

Alhandra, remember to record the monthly adjustment for Prepaid Insurance. The amount we paid for the year for business vehicles insurance was $2,850. Also, we used $350 worth of office supplies this month. Please adjust accordingly.

 Record the adjusting entries for office supplies expense and business vehicles insurance expense in the General Journal.

Access the General Journal:
Click **Company** on the menu bar, click **Make General Journal Entries…**
On the screen regarding Assigning Numbers to Journal Entries, click **Do not display this message in the future**; and then, click **OK**
The General Journal Entries screen appears
- Note the checkbox for Adjusting Entry
- A list of entries made Last Month is shown at the bottom of the screen
  - If the date of your computer does not match the text, you may not have anything shown in the List of Entries.
  - If you wish, you can change the time period to be displayed by clicking the drop-down list arrow for **List of Selected General Journal Entries** and selecting a time period or you may hide the list by clicking the **Hide List** icon on the Make General Journal Entries icon bar.

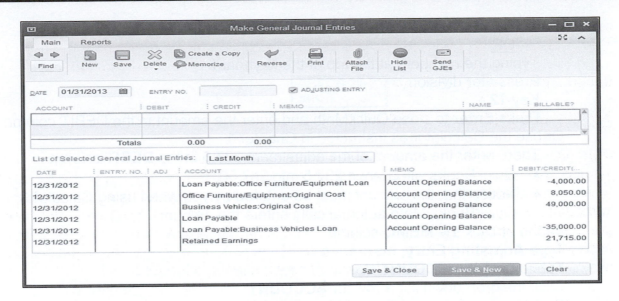

Record the adjusting entry for Prepaid Insurance

Enter **01/31/13** as the **DATE**

- QuickBooks will enter the year as 2013.
- **ENTRY NO.** is left blank unless you wish to record a specific number.
- Because all transactions entered for the month have been entered in the Journal as well as on an invoice or a bill, all transactions automatically have a Journal entry number.

Notice the check box for **ADJUSTING ENTRY** is marked.

- Adjusting journal entries are entered by accountants to make after-the-fact changes to specific accounts.
- Accountants make adjustments for a variety of reasons, including depreciation, prepaid income or expenses; adjusting sales tax payable; and entering bank or credit card fees or interest.
- The ADJUSTING ENTRY check box allows QuickBooks to indicate whether or not an entry is an adjustment.
- You can view a list of all adjusting journal entries in the Adjusting Journal Entries report.
- By default, this checkbox is selected for new transactions in the Accountant version but is not available in QuickBooks Pro.

Tab to or click the **ACCOUNT** column

Click the drop-down list arrow for **ACCOUNT**; click the expense account **Business Vehicles Insurance**

Tab to or click **DEBIT**

- The $2,850 given in the memo is the amount for the year; calculate the amount of the adjustment for the month by using QuickBooks QuickMath or the Calculator.

Use QuickBooks QuickMath

Enter **2850** by:

Keying the numbers on the **10-key pad** (preferred)

- Be sure Num Lock is on. If not, press Num Lock to activate.

  <u>OR</u>

Typing the numbers at the top of the keyboard

Press / for division

Key **12**

Press **Enter** to close QuickMath and enter the amount in the DEBIT column

Or use the Calculator as instructed in Chapter 1

Then, enter the amount of the adjustment **237.5** in the **DEBIT** column

- QuickBooks will change 237.5 into 237.50.
- Notice that the amount must be entered by you when using Calculator; QuickBooks Math automatically enters the amount.

Tab to or click the **MEMO** column

Type **Adjusting Entry, Insurance**

Tab to or click **ACCOUNT**

Click the drop-down list arrow for **ACCOUNT**

Click the asset account **Prepaid Insurance**

- The amount for the Credit column should be entered automatically. However, there are several reasons why an amount may not appear in the Credit column. If 237.50 does not appear, type it in the Credit column.
- If the memo does not appear automatically, tab to or click the **MEMO** column, and type **Adjusting Entry, Insurance**

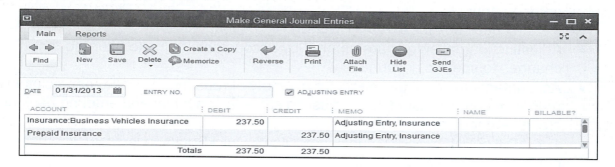

- Note the Totals for the Debit and Credit shown at the bottom of the screen.

Click **Save & New** to record the adjustment and advance to the next **Make General Journal Entries** screen

Repeat the above procedures to record the adjustment for the office supplies used

Use the Memo **Supplies Used**

- The amount given in the memo is the actual amount of the supplies used in January so you will not need to use QuickMath or the calculator.
- Remember, when supplies are purchased to have on hand, the original entry records an increase to the asset Office Supplies. Once the supplies are used, the adjustment correctly records the amount of supplies used as an expense.

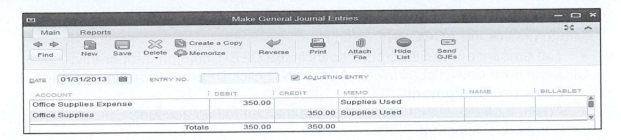

Click **Save & New**

ADJUSTING ENTRIES—DEPRECIATION

Equipment and other long-term assets lose value over their lifetime. Unlike supplies—where you can actually see, for example, the paper supply diminishing—it is very difficult to see how much of a computer has been "used up" during the month. To account for the fact that machines do wear out and need to be replaced, an adjustment is made for depreciation. This adjustment correctly matches the expenses of the period against the revenue of the period.

The adjusting entry for depreciation can be made in the account register for Depreciation, or it can be made in the General Journal.

MEMO:

DATE: January 15, 2013

Having received the necessary depreciation schedules, Alhandra records the adjusting entry for depreciation: Business Vehicles, $583 per month; Equipment, $142 per month.

 Record a compound adjusting entry for depreciation of the equipment and the business vehicles in the **General Journal**:

Continue to use **Make General Journal Entries**
- The **DATE** should show as **01/31/13** and **ADJUSTING ENTRY** should have a check. If not, enter the date and click ADJUSTING ENTRY to select.

ENTRY NO. is left blank
- Normally, the debit portion of a General Journal entry is entered first. However, in order to use the automatic calculation feature of QuickBooks, you will enter the **credit** entries first.

Tab to or click in the **ACCOUNT** column
Click the drop-down list arrow for **ACCOUNT**, click **Depreciation** under **Business Vehicles**
- Make sure that you do not click the controlling account, Business Vehicles

Tab to or click in the **CREDIT** column, enter **583**

Tab to or click in the **MEMO** column, enter **Adjusting Entry, January**
Tab to or click the **ACCOUNT** column

- The amount of the 583 credit shows in the DEBIT column temporarily.

Click the drop-down list arrow for **ACCOUNT**; click **Depreciation** under **Office Furniture/Equipment**

- Again, make sure that you do <u>not</u> use the controlling account, Office Furniture/Equipment.
- If the DEBIT column shows 583.00, do not worry about it.

Tab to or click in the **CREDIT** column, enter **142**

- The 583 in the DEBIT column is removed when you tab to or click **MEMO**.
- The adjusting entry **Adjusting Entry, January** should have been entered automatically. If not, enter it in the **MEMO** column

Tab to or click in the **ACCOUNT** column
Click the drop-down list arrow for **ACCOUNT**, click **Depreciation Expense**
DEBIT column should automatically show **725**

- If 725 does not appear, enter it in the DEBIT column. The MEMO **Adjusting Entry, January** should be entered automatically. If not, enter it.

ACCOUNT	DEBIT	CREDIT	MEMO	NAME	BILLABLE?
Business Vehicles:Depreciation		583.00	Adjusting Entry, January		
Office Furniture/Equipment:Depreciation		142.00	Adjusting Entry, January		
Depreciation Expense	725.00		Adjusting Entry, January		
Totals	725.00	725.00			

DATE 01/31/2013   ENTRY NO.   ☑ ADJUSTING ENTRY

Click the **Save** icon to record the adjustment

- If you get a message regarding Tracking Fixed Assets, click **Do not display this message in the future** and click **OK**.

Click the drop-down list arrow for **List of Selected General Journal Entries** shown below the Totals
Click **This Fiscal Year**

- If your computer does not have 2013 as the year, click **Last Fiscal Year**

View the entries recorded in 2013

- Note that only the first line/account used in a transaction appears.
- If you click on one of the transactions, it will take to you that transaction in the General Journal.

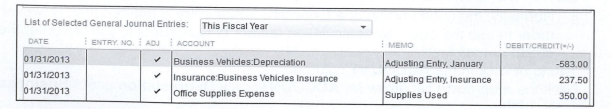

List of Selected General Journal Entries: This Fiscal Year

DATE	ENTRY. NO.	ADJ	ACCOUNT	MEMO	DEBIT/CREDIT(+/-)
01/31/2013		✔	Business Vehicles:Depreciation	Adjusting Entry, January	-583.00
01/31/2013		✔	Insurance:Business Vehicles Insurance	Adjusting Entry, Insurance	237.50
01/31/2013		✔	Office Supplies Expense	Supplies Used	350.00

Close **Make General Journal Entries**

VIEW JOURNAL

Once transactions have been entered in the General Journal, it is important to view them. QuickBooks refers to the General Journal as the location of a transaction entry and to the Journal as a report. Even with the special ways in which transactions are entered in QuickBooks through invoices, bills, checks, and account registers, the Journal is still the book of original entry. All transactions recorded for the company may be viewed in the Journal even if they were entered elsewhere. The Journal may be viewed or printed at any time.

 View the Journal for January

Click **Reports** on the menu bar, point to **Accountant & Taxes,** and click **Journal**
If you get the Collapsing and Expanding Transactions dialog box, click the **Do not display this message in the future**; and then, click **OK**
Always **Expand** your transactions even if not specifically instructed to do so
Enter the dates from **01/01/13** to **01/31/13**
Tab to generate the report
- Notice that the transactions do not begin with the adjustments entered directly into the Journal.
- The first transaction displayed is the entry for Invoice No. 1 to Juan Gomez.
- If corrections or changes are made to entries, the transaction numbers may differ from the key. Since QuickBooks assigns transaction numbers automatically, disregard any discrepancies in transaction numbers.

Scroll through the report to view all transactions recorded in the Journal
Verify the total Debit and Credit Columns of $46,530.29
- If your totals do not match, check for errors and make appropriate corrections.
- Since the adjusting entries were marked as adjustments when entered in the General Journal, the Adj column shows checks for these entries.

Computer Consulting by Your Name
Journal
January 2013

Trans #	Type	Date	Num	Adj	Name	Memo	Account	Debit	Credit
67	General Journal	01/31/2013		✓		Adjusting Entry, Insurance	Business Vehicles Insurance	237.50	
				✓		Adjusting Entry, Insurance	Prepaid Insurance		237.50
								237.50	237.50
68	General Journal	01/31/2013		✓		Supplies Used	Office Supplies Expense	350.00	
				✓		Supplies Used	Office Supplies		350.00
								350.00	350.00
69	General Journal	01/31/2013		✓		Adjusting Entry, January	Depreciation		583.00
				✓		Adjusting Entry, January	Depreciation		142.00
				✓		Adjusting Entry, January	Depreciation Expense	725.00	
								725.00	725.00
TOTAL								**46,530.29**	**46,530.29**

Partial Report

Close the Journal without printing

OWNER WITHDRAWALS

In a sole proprietorship an owner cannot receive a paycheck because he or she owns the business. An owner withdrawing money from a business—even to pay personal expenses—is similar to withdrawing money from a savings account. A withdrawal simply decreases the owner's capital. QuickBooks allows you to establish a separate account for owner withdrawals. If a separate account is not established, owner withdrawals may be subtracted directly from the owner's capital or investment account.

MEMO

DATE: January 31, 2013

Because you work in the business full time, you do not earn a paycheck. Prepare the check for your monthly withdrawal, $2,500.

 Write Check No. 9 to yourself for $2,500 withdrawal

Open the **Write Checks - Checking** window:
Click **Banking** on the menu bar, click **Write Checks**
    OR
Click the **Write Checks** icon in the Banking section of the Home Page
    OR
Use the keyboard shortcut **Ctrl+W**
NO. should be **TO PRINT**
- If not, click the check box **Print Later** on the Write Checks - Checking icon bar

DATE should be **01/31/13**
Enter **Your Name** (type your real name) on the **PAY TO THE ORDER OF** line
Press the **Tab** key
- Because your name was not added to any list when the company was created, the **Name Not Found** dialog box appears on the screen.

Click **Quick Add** to add your name to a list

The **Select Name Type** dialog box appears
Click **Other**

- Your name is added to a list of "Other" names, which are used for owners, partners, and other miscellaneous names.

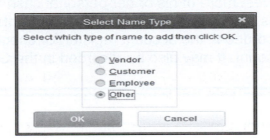

Click **OK**

Tab to or click in the area for the amount of the check

- If necessary, delete any numbers showing for the amount (0.00).

Enter **2500** in the text box for **$**

Tab to or click **MEMO** on the check face and enter **Monthly Withdrawal**

Tab to or click in the **ACCOUNT** column in the detail section at the bottom of the check

Click the drop-down list arrow, click the Equity account **Draws**

- This account is a subaccount of Your Name, Capital.
- The amount 2,500.00 should appear in the **AMOUNT** column.
- If it does not, tab to or click in the **AMOUNT** column and enter 2500.

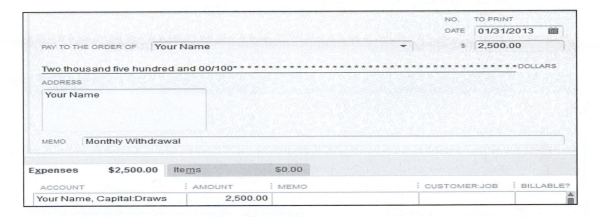

Click **Print** to print the check

The **Print Check** dialog box appears

Printed Check Number should be **9**

- If necessary, change the number to 9.

Click **OK**

Print the standard style check as previously instructed

Once the check has printed successfully, click **OK** on the **Print Checks - Confirmation** dialog box

Click **Save & Close** to record the check, close any reminder screens that may appear

ADDITIONAL CASH INVESTMENT BY OWNER

An owner may decide to invest more of his or her personal cash in the business at any time. The new investment is entered into the owner's investment account and into cash. The investment may be recorded in the account register for checking or in the register for the owner's investment account. It may also be recorded in the General Journal.

> # MEMO
> **DATE:** January 31, 2013
>
> You received money from a certificate of deposit. Rather than reinvest in another certificate of deposit, you have decided to invest an additional $5,000 in the company.

 Record the owner's additional cash investment in the Journal

    Access Make General Journal Entries as previously instructed
    The **DATE** should be **01/31/13**
- Nothing is needed for ENTRY No.

    This is <u>not</u> an adjusting entry, so click **ADJUSTING ENTRY** to remove the check
    DEBIT **Checking, $5,000**
    The MEMO for both entries should be **Cash Investment**
    CREDIT **Investments, $5,000**
- This account is listed as a subaccount of Your Name, Capital

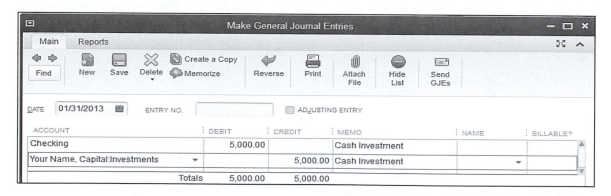

    Click **Save & New**

NON-CASH INVESTMENT BY OWNER

An owner may make investments in a business at any time. The investment may be cash; but it may also be something such as reference books, equipment, tools, buildings, and so on. Additional investments by an owner(s) are added to owner's equity. In the case of a sole proprietor, the investment is added to the Capital account for Investments.

> **MEMO**
>
> **DATE:** January 31, 2013
>
> Originally, you planned to have an office in your home as well as in the company and purchased new office furniture for your home. Since then, you decided the business environment would appear more professional if the new furniture were in the office rather than your home. You gave the new office furniture to the company as an additional owner investment. The value of the investment is $3,000.

 Record the non-cash investment in the Journal

> The **DATE** should be **01/31/13, ENTRY NO**. should be blank, **ADJUSTING ENTRY** should not be marked
> DEBIT **Original Cost** (the subaccount of **Office Furniture/Equipment**) $3,000
> The MEMO for both entries should be **Investment of Furniture**
> CREDIT **Investments** (the subaccount of **Your Name, Capital**) $3,000
> * When you select the account and press tab, the Memo should automatically appear. If it does not, copy the memo for the second entry rather than retype it, drag through the memo text to highlight; press Ctrl+C; position the cursor in the memo area for the second entry; press Ctrl+V.

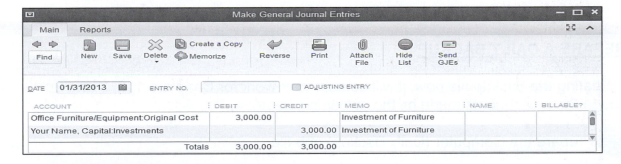

> Click **Save & Close** to record and exit
> * If you get a message regarding Tracking Fixed Assets, click **OK.**

VIEW BALANCE SHEET

Prior to writing the check for the monthly withdrawal, there had been no withdrawals by the owner, and the drawing account balance was zero. Once a withdrawal is made, that amount is carried forward in the owner's drawing account. Subsequent withdrawals are added to this account. When you view the Balance Sheet, notice the balance of the Drawing account after the check for the withdrawal was written. Also notice the Net Income account that appears in the equity section of the Balance Sheet. This account is automatically added by QuickBooks to track the net income for the year.

View a Standard Balance Sheet:

Click **Reports** on the menu bar, point to **Company & Financial**, and click **Balance Sheet Standard**
Tab to or click **As of**
Enter the date **01/31/13**
Tab to generate the report
Scroll through the report
- Notice the Equity section, especially Net Income.

- The ⌄ next to Equity and Your Name, Capital show that the report is expanded. If you click it, you will collapse the detail and only the heading **Equity** and the total equity amount of **$88,020.71** will show.

Computer Consulting by Your Name
Balance Sheet
As of January 31, 2013

	Jan 31, 13
⌄ **Equity**	
⌄ **Your Name, Capital**	
Draws	-2,500.00
Investments	33,000.00
Your Name, Capital – Other	53,135.00
Total Your Name, Capital	83,635.00
Net Income	4,385.71
Total Equity	88,020.71
TOTAL LIABILITIES & EQUITY	130,784.71

Partial Report

Close the report without printing

PREPARE A DAILY BACKUP

By creating the backup file now, it will contain your work for Chapters 1, 2, 3 and up through the investments made by the owner in Chapter 4.

 Prepare the Computer (Daily Backup).qbb file

Follow the steps presented in Chapter 1 for creating a backup file
Name the file **Computer (Daily Backup)**
The file type is **QBW Backup (* .QBB)**
On the Confirm Save As screen asking if you want to replace the backup file that already exists, click **Yes**

BANK RECONCILIATION

Each month, the checking account should be reconciled with the bank statement to make sure that the balances agree. The bank statement will rarely have an ending balance that matches the balance of the checking account. This is due to several factors: outstanding checks (written by the business but not paid by the bank), deposits in transit (deposits that were made too late to be included on the bank statement), bank service charges, interest earned on checking accounts, collections made by the bank, and errors made in recording checks and/or deposits by the company or by the bank.

In order to have an accurate amount listed as the balance in the checking account, it is important that the differences between the bank statement and the checking account be reconciled. If something such as a service charge or a collection made by the bank appears on the bank statement, it needs to be recorded in the checking account.

Reconciling a bank statement is an appropriate time to find any errors that may have been recorded in the checking account. The reconciliation may be out of balance because a transposition was made (recording $94 rather than $49), a transaction was recorded backwards, a transaction was recorded twice, or a transaction was not recorded at all. If a transposition was made, the error may be found by dividing the difference by 9. For example, if $94 was recorded and the actual transaction amount was $49, you would subtract 49 from 94 to get 45. The number 45 can be divided by 9, so your error was a transposition. If the error can be evenly divided by 2, the transaction may have been entered backwards. For example, if you were out of balance $200, look to see if you had any $100 transactions. Perhaps you recorded a $100 debit, and it should have been a credit (or vice versa).

BEGIN RECONCILIATION

To begin the reconciliation, you need to open the Reconcile - Checking window. Verify the information shown for the checking account. The Opening Balance should match the amount of the final balance on the last reconciliation, or it should match the starting account balance.

MEMO
DATE: January 31, 2013

Received the bank statement from Sunshine Bank. The bank statement is dated January 31, 2013. Alhandra Cruz needs to reconcile the bank statement and print a Detail Reconciliation Report for you.

 Reconcile the bank statement for January

> Click the **Reconcile** icon in the Banking section of the Home Page `Reconcile`
>   to open the **Begin Reconciliation** window and enter preliminary information
> The **Account** should be **Checking**
>   If not, click the drop-down list arrow, click **Checking**
> The **Statement Date** should be **01/31/2013**
> - The Statement Date is entered automatically by the computer. If the date is not shown as 01/31/2013, change it.

Beginning Balance should be **12,870**

- This is the same amount as the checking account starting balance.

ENTER BANK STATEMENT INFORMATION FOR BEGIN RECONCILIATION

Some information appearing on the bank statement is entered into the Begin Reconciliation window as the next step. This information includes the ending balance, bank service charges, and interest earned.

 Continue to reconcile the following bank statement with the checking account

SUNSHINE BANK
12345 West Colorado Avenue
Woodland Hills, CA 91377
(818) 555-3880

Computer Consulting by Your Name
2895 West Avenue
Woodland Hills, CA 91367

Acct. # 123-456-7890   January 2013

Beginning Balance 1/1/13			$12,870.00
01/02/13 Deposit	25,000.00		37,870.00
1/15/13 Deposit	13,840.00		51,710.00
1/26/13 Check 1		500.00	51,210.00
1/26/13 Check 2		195.00	51,015.00
1/26/13 Check 3		840.00	50,175.00
1/30/13 Cash Transfer		110.00	50,065.00
1/31/13 Business Vehicle Loan Pmt.: $467.19 Principal, $255.22 Interest		722.41	49,342.59
1/31/13 Office Furniture/Equipment Loan Pmt.: $29.17 Principal, $53.39 Interest		82.56	49,260.03
1/31/13 Service Chg.		8.00	49,252.03
1/31/13 Interest	66.43		49,318.46
Ending Balance 1/31/13			49,318.46

Enter the **Ending Balance** from the Bank Statement, **49,318.46**
Tab to or click **Service Charge**
Enter **8**
Tab to or click Service Charge **Date**; if necessary, change to **01/31/2013**

- Don't forget to check the date, especially the year. If you leave an incorrect date, you will have errors in your accounts and in your reports.

Click the drop-down list arrow for **Account**

- Shortcut: If you click the drop-down list arrow, you do not have to Tab to the account text box.

Click **Bank Service Charges**

Tab to or click **Interest Earned**, enter **66.43**

Tab to or click Interest Earned **Date**; if necessary, change to **01/31/2013**

Click the drop-down list arrow for **Account**

Scroll through the list of accounts, click **Interest Income**

Begin Reconciliation	✕

Select an account to reconcile, and then enter the ending balance from your account statement.

Account	Checking ▼	last reconciled on 12/31/2012.
Statement Date	01/31/2013 📷	
Beginning Balance	12,870.00	What if my beginning balance doesn't match my statement?
Ending Balance	49,318.46	

Enter any service charge or interest earned.

Service Charge	Date		Account	
8.00	01/31/2013 📷		Bank Service Charges ▼	
Interest Earned	Date		Account	
66.43	01/31/2013 📷		Interest Income ▼	

Locate Discrepancies	Undo Last Reconciliation	Continue	Cancel	Help

Click the **Continue** button

MARK CLEARED TRANSACTIONS FOR BANK RECONCILIATION

Once bank statement information for service charges and interest has been entered, compare the checks and deposits listed on the statement with the transactions for the checking account. Remember, the dates shown for the checks on the bank statement are the dates the checks were processed by the bank, not the dates the checks were written. If a deposit or a check is listed correctly on the bank statement and in the Reconcile - Checking window, it has cleared and should be marked. An item may be marked individually by positioning the cursor on the deposit or the check and clicking the primary mouse button. If all deposits and checks match, click the Mark All button. To remove all the checks, click the Unmark All button. To unmark an individual item, click the item to remove the check mark.

 Mark cleared checks and deposits

Compare the bank statement with the **Reconcile - Checking** window

Click the items that appear on both statements

- *Note*: The date next to the check or the deposit on the bank statement is the date the check or deposit cleared the bank, not the date the check was written or the deposit was made.
- If you are unable to complete the reconciliation in one session, click the **Leave** button to leave the reconciliation and return to it later.
- Under no circumstances should you click **Reconcile Now** until the reconciliation is complete.

Make sure that the **Highlight Marked** checkbox in the lower-left corner is checked

- This will change the background color of everything that you mark and make it easier to view the selections in the reconciliation.

For Deposits and Other Credits, include the Voided Check for **0.00** on **01/30/2013**

On the Checks and Payments side, include the transaction for **100.00** on **01/30/2013**

- This was the transfer from Checking to Petty Cash.

Once you have marked the transactions that appear on the bank statement and in the Reconcile-Checking screen, look at the bottom of screen

In the section labeled "**Items you have marked cleared**" should show the following:

    3 Deposits and Other Credits for 38,840.00

- This includes the voided check to Communication Telephone Co.

    4 Checks and Payments for 1,635.00

- This includes the $100 for petty cash.

On the right-side of the lower section next to the Modify button, the screen should show:

    The Service Charge is -8.00

    The Interest Earned is 66.43

    The Ending Balance is 49,318.46

    The Cleared Balance is 50,133.43

    There is a Difference of -814.97

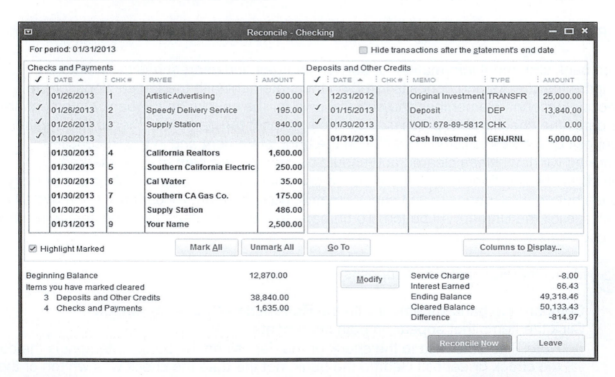

ADJUSTING AND CORRECTING ENTRIES—BANK RECONCILIATION

As you complete the reconciliation, you may find errors that need to be corrected or transactions that need to be recorded. Anything entered as a service charge or interest earned will be entered automatically when the reconciliation is complete and the Reconcile Now button is clicked. To correct an error such as a transposition or an incorrect amount, click on the entry, then click the Go To button. The original entry will appear on the screen. The correction can be made and will show in the Reconcile - Checking window. If there is a transaction, such as an automatic loan payment to the bank, you need to access the register for the account used in the transaction and enter the payment.

 Correct the error on the cash transfer into Petty Cash

In the section of the reconciliation for **Checks and Payments**, click the entry for **100.00** dated **01/30/2013**
  - This was actually the Cash transfer to Petty Cash from Checking.
Click the **Go To** button

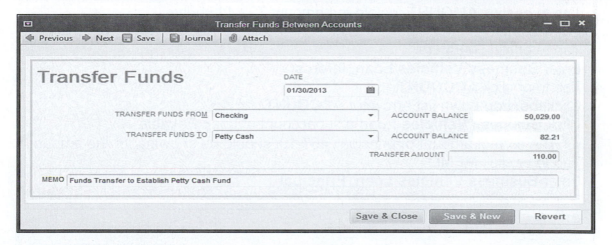

Change the amount on **Transfer Funds Between Accounts** from 100 to **110**

Click **Save & Close**
Click **Yes** on the **Recording Transaction** dialog box
  - Notice that the amount for the Petty Cash transaction now shows 110.
Click the cash transfer to Petty Cash transaction to mark it.
  - The amount shown at the bottom of the Reconcile window for the 4 Checks and Payments, shows 1,645.00

With the **Reconcile - Checking** window still showing, enter the automatic loan payments:

> To enter the automatic payments, access the Checking Account Register by using the keyboard shortcut **Ctrl+R**
>
> In the blank transaction at the bottom of the Checking register enter the **Date, 01/31/13**
>
> Tab to or click **Number**
>
> Enter **Transfer**
>
> Tab to or click **Payee**
>
> Enter **Sunshine Bank**
>
> Tab to or click the **Payment** column
>
> - Because Sunshine Bank does not appear on any list, you will get a **Name Not Found** dialog box when you move to another field.
>
> Click the **Quick Add** button to add the name of the bank to the Name list
>
> Click **Other**
>
> Click **OK**
>
> - Once the name of the bank has been added to the Other list, the cursor will be positioned in the **PAYMENT** column.
>
> Enter the amount of the Business Vehicles Loan payment of **722.41** in the **PAYMENT** column
>
> Since more than one account is used, click the **Splits** button at the bottom of the register
>
> Click the drop-down list arrow for **ACCOUNT**
>
> Click **Loan Interest** under Interest Expense
>
> Tab to or click **AMOUNT**, delete the amount 722.41 shown
>
> Enter **255.22** as the amount of interest
>
> Tab to or click **MEMO**
>
> Enter **Business Vehicles Loan, Interest**
>
> Tab to or click **ACCOUNT**
>
> Click the drop-down list arrow for **ACCOUNT**
>
> Click **Business Vehicles Loan** a subaccount of Loan Payable
>
> - The correct amount of principal, 467.19, should be showing for the amount.
>
> Tab to or click **MEMO**
>
> Enter **Business Vehicles Loan, Principal**

> Click the **Close** button in the Splits window
>
> - This closes the window for the information regarding the way the transaction is to be "split" between accounts.
>
> For the **Memo** in the Checking Register, record **Loan Pmt. Business Vehicles**

Click the **Record** button to record the transaction
- Because the **Register** organizes transactions according to date and the transaction type, you will notice that the loan payment will not appear as the last transaction in the Register. You may need to scroll through the Register to see the transaction since transfers are shown before other transactions entered on the same date.

01/31/2013	Transfer	Sunshine Bank		722.41		46,796.59
	CHK	-split-	Loan Pmt. Business Vehicles			

Repeat the procedures to record the loan payment for office furniture/equipment
- When you enter the Payee as Sunshine Bank, the amount for the previous transaction (722.41) appears in Amount.

Enter the new amount, **82.56**
Click **Splits** button
Click the appropriate accounts and enter the correct amount for each item
- *Note*: The amounts for the previous loan payment automatically appear. You will need to enter the amounts for both accounts in this transaction.
- Refer to the bank statement for details regarding the amount of the payment for interest and the amount of the payment applied to principal.

ACCOUNT	AMOUNT	MEMO	CUSTOMER:JOB	BILLABLE?	
Interest Expense:Loan Interest	53.39	Office Furniture/Equipment Loan, Interest			Close
Loan Payable:Office Furniture/Equipment Loan	29.17	Office Furniture/Equipment Loan, Principal			Clear

Click **Close** to close the window for the information regarding the "split" between accounts
Enter the transaction Memo **Loan Pmt. Office Furniture/Equipment**
Click **Record** to record the loan payment

01/31/2013	Transfer	Sunshine Bank		82.56	✔	44,280.46
	CHK	-split-	Loan Pmt. Office Furniture/Equipment			

Close the **Checking** Register
- You should return to **Reconcile - Checking**.
Scroll through **Checks and Payments** until you find the two Transfers
Mark the two entries
- At this point, the **Ending Balance** and **Cleared Balance** should be equal—$49,318.46 with a difference of 0.00.

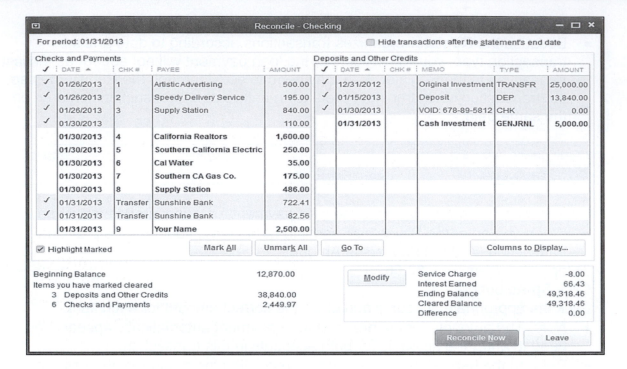

If your entries agree with the above, click **Reconcile Now** to finish the reconciliation

- If your reconciliation is not in agreement, do <u>not</u> click **Reconcile Now** until the errors are corrected.
- Once you click **Reconcile Now**, you may not return to this **Reconciliation - Checking** window.
- If you get an information screen regarding Online Banking, click **OK**.

PRINT A RECONCILIATION REPORT

As soon as the Ending Balance and the Cleared Balance are equal or when you finish marking transactions and click Reconcile Now, a screen appears allowing you to select the level of Reconciliation report you would like to print. You may select Summary and get a report that lists totals only or Detail and get all the transactions that were reconciled on the report. You may print the report at the time you have finished reconciling the account or you may print the report later by returning to the Reconciliation window. If you think you may want to print the report again in the future, print the report to a file to save it permanently.

 Print a **Detail Reconciliation Report**

On the **Select Reconciliation Report** screen, click **Detail**

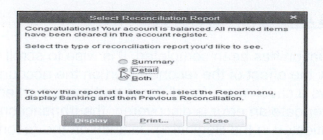

To view the report before you print, click Display;
If you get a Reconciliation Report message box, click **OK**.

Computer Consulting by Your Name
Reconciliation Detail
Checking, Period Ending 01/31/2013

Type	Date	Num	Name	Clr	Amount	Balance
Beginning Balance						12,870.00
Cleared Transactions						
Checks and Payments – 7 items						
Bill Pmt –Check	01/26/2013	3	Supply Station	✓	–840.00	–840.00
Bill Pmt –Check	01/26/2013	1	Artistic Advertising	✓	–500.00	–1,340.00
Bill Pmt –Check	01/26/2013	2	Speedy Delivery Service	✓	–195.00	–1,535.00
Transfer	01/30/2013			✓	–110.00	–1,645.00
Check	01/31/2013	Transfer	Sunshine Bank	✓	–722.41	–2,367.41
Check	01/31/2013	Transfer	Sunshine Bank	✓	–82.56	–2,449.97
Check	01/31/2013			✓	–8.00	–2,457.97
Total Checks and Payments					–2,457.97	–2,457.97
Deposits and Credits – 4 items						
Transfer	12/31/2012			✓	25,000.00	25,000.00
Deposit	01/15/2013			✓	13,840.00	38,840.00
Check	01/30/2013		Communication Telephone Co.	✓	0.00	38,840.00
Deposit	01/31/2013			✓	66.43	38,906.43
Total Deposits and Credits					38,906.43	38,906.43
Total Cleared Transactions					36,448.46	36,448.46
Cleared Balance					36,448.46	49,318.46
Uncleared Transactions						
Checks and Payments – 6 items						
Check	01/30/2013	4	California Realtors		–1,600.00	–1,600.00
Check	01/30/2013	8	Supply Station		–486.00	–2,086.00
Check	01/30/2013	5	Southern California Electric		–250.00	–2,336.00
Check	01/30/2013	7	Southern CA Gas Co.		–175.00	–2,511.00
Check	01/30/2013	6	Cal Water		–35.00	–2,546.00
Check	01/31/2013	9	Your Name		–2,500.00	–5,046.00
Total Checks and Payments					–5,046.00	–5,046.00
Deposits and Credits – 1 item						
General Journal	01/31/2013				5,000.00	5,000.00
Total Deposits and Credits					5,000.00	5,000.00
Total Uncleared Transactions					–46.00	–46.00
Register Balance as of 01/31/2013					36,402.46	49,272.46
Ending Balance					36,402.46	49,272.46

- The uncleared information may be different from the report above. This is due to the fact that your computer's date may be different than January 31, 2013. As long as the cleared balance is $49,318.46, your report should be considered correct.

Resize the columns in report as previously instructed; and then, print the report in Portrait orientation

If your report printed correctly, close the report

VIEW THE CHECKING ACCOUNT REGISTER

Once the bank reconciliation has been completed, it is wise to scroll through the Checking account register to view the effect of the reconciliation on the account. You will notice that the check column shows a check mark for all items that were marked as cleared during the reconciliation. If at a later date an error is discovered, the transaction may be changed, and the correction will be reflected in the Beginning Balance on the reconciliation.

 View the register for the Checking account

> Open the Chart of Accounts and access the Checking account register as previously instructed
> To display more of the register, click the check box for **1-Line**
> Scroll through the register
> - Notice that the transactions are listed in chronological order and that cleared transactions have a check mark.

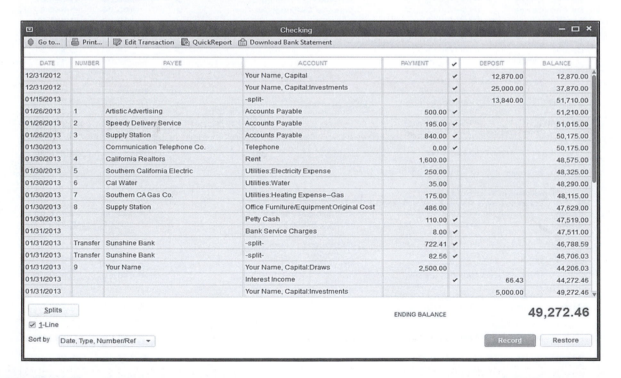

EDIT CLEARED TRANSACTIONS

 Edit a transaction that was marked and cleared during the bank reconciliation:

> Edit the **Petty Cash** transaction:
> Click in the entry for the transfer of funds to **Petty Cash** on January 30
> Change the **Payment** amount to **100**
> Click the **Record** button

Click **Yes** on the **Transaction Reconciled** dialog box
- The transaction amount has been changed.

Close the **Checking Register**

Do <u>not</u> close the **Chart of Accounts**

View the effects of the change to the Petty Cash transaction in the "Begin Reconciliation window":

Display the **Begin Reconciliation** window by:

Making sure **Checking** is highlighted, clicking the **Activities** button, and clicking **Reconcile**

- Notice that the Opening Balance has been increased by $10 and shows $49,328.46.

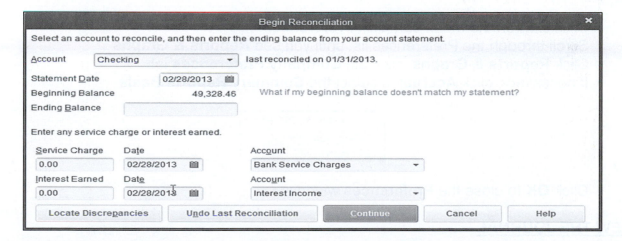

Click the **Cancel** button on the bottom of the **Begin Reconciliation** screen and, if open, return to the Chart of Accounts

Open the **Checking** account register

Change the amount for the **Petty Cash** transaction back to **110**

Click **Record** to record the change

Click **Yes** on the **Transaction Reconciled** dialog box

Reopen the **Begin Reconciliation** following the steps presented earlier

- Make sure the Beginning Balance shows **49,318.46**

Close the **Checking Register**, and, if open, the **Chart of Accounts**

SELECT ACCRUAL-BASIS REPORTING PREFERENCE

QuickBooks allows a business to customize the program and select certain preferences for reports, displays, graphs, accounts, and so on. There are two report preferences available in QuickBooks: Cash and Accrual. You need to choose the one you prefer. If you select Cash as the report preference, income on reports will be shown as of the date payment is received and expenses will be shown as of the date you pay the bill. If Accrual is selected, QuickBooks shows the income on the report as of the date of the invoice and expenses as of the bill date. Prior to printing end-of-period reports, it is advisable to verify which reporting basis is selected. If cash has been selected and you are using the accrual basis, it is imperative that you change your report basis.

MEMO
DATE: January 31, 2013

Prior to printing reports, check the report preference selected for the company. If necessary, choose Accrual.

 Select **Accrual** as the **Summary Reports Basis**

      Click **Edit** on the menu bar, click **Preferences**
      Scroll through the Preferences list until you see **Reports & Graphs**
      Click **Reports & Graphs**, click the **Company Preferences** tab
      If necessary, click **Accrual** to select the **Summary Reports Basis**

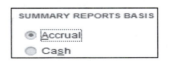

      Click **OK** to close the **Preferences** window

VIEW THE JOURNAL

After entering several transactions, it is helpful to view the Journal. In the Journal, all transactions, regardless of the method of entry are shown in traditional debit/credit format. (Remember, you may have learned this as the General Journal in your concepts course.)

 View the **Journal** for January

      Click the **Reports** icon, use the view you prefer, click **Accountant & Taxes** as the type of report, and double-click **Journal**
- If you will be preparing several reports, using the Report Center is much more efficient than using the Reports menu.

Tab to or click **From**
- If necessary, delete existing date.

Enter **01/01/13**

Tab to or click **To**

Enter **01/31/13**

Tab to generate the report

Scroll through the report

Verify the total of $57,919.69

- If your total does not match, you may have an error in a date used, an amount entered, a transaction not entered, etc.

Computer Consulting by Your Name

Journal

January 2013

Trans #	Type	Date	Num	Adj	Name	Memo	Account	Debit	Credit
73	Check	01/31/2013	Transfer		Sunshine Bank	Loan Pmt. Business Vehicles	Checking		722.41
					Sunshine Bank	Business Vehicles Loan, Interest	Loan Interest	255.22	
					Sunshine Bank	Business Vehicles Loan, Principal	Business Vehicles Loan	467.19	
								722.41	722.41
74	Check	01/31/2013	Transfer		Sunshine Bank	Loan Pmt. Office Furniture/Equipment	Checking		82.56
					Sunshine Bank	Office Furniture/Equipment Loan, Interest	Loan Interest	53.39	
					Sunshine Bank	Office Furniture/Equipment Loan, Principal	Office Furniture/Equipment Loan	29.17	
								82.56	82.56
75	Check	01/31/2013				Service Charge	Checking		8.00
						Service Charge	Bank Service Charges	8.00	
								8.00	8.00
76	Deposit	01/31/2013				Interest	Checking	66.43	
						Interest	Interest Income		66.43
								66.43	66.43
TOTAL								57,919.69	57,919.69

Partial Report

Close the **Journal** without printing

Do <u>not</u> close the Report Center

PREPARE TRIAL BALANCE

After all adjustments have been recorded and the bank reconciliation has been completed, it is wise to prepare the Trial Balance. As in traditional accounting, the QuickBooks Trial Balance proves that debits equal credits.

MEMO

DATE: January 31, 2013

Because adjustments have been entered, prepare a Trial Balance.

Prepare and print the Trial Balance

Double-click **Trial Balance** in the Accountant & Taxes section of the Report Center
Enter the dates from **01/01/13** to **01/31/13**, and Tab to generate the report
Scroll through the report and study the amounts shown
  • Notice that the final totals of debits and credits are equal: $138,119.07.

Computer Consulting by Your Name
Trial Balance
As of January 31, 2013

	Jan 31, 13	
	Debit	Credit
Your Name, Capital		53,135.00
Your Name, Capital:Draws	2,500.00	
Your Name, Capital:Investments		33,000.00
Income:Installation Income		175.00
Income:Technical Support Income		900.00
Income:Training Income		7,850.00
Advertising Expense	260.00	
Bank Service Charges	8.00	
Business Vehicles Expense	588.88	
Depreciation Expense	725.00	
Dues and Subscriptions	79.00	
Equipment Rental	25.00	
Insurance:Business Vehicles Insurance	237.50	
Interest Expense:Loan Interest	308.61	
Office Supplies Expense	368.57	
Postage and Delivery	195.34	
Rent	1,600.00	
Telephone	0.00	
Utilities:Electricity Expense	250.00	
Utilities:Heating Expense--Gas	175.00	
Utilities:Water	35.00	
Interest Income		66.43
TOTAL	138,119.07	138,119.07

Partial Report

Resize the columns and **Print** the **Trial Balance** in Portrait orientation as previously
  instructed
Do <u>not</u> close the **Report Center** or the **Trial Balance**

EXPORTING REPORTS TO EXCEL (OPTIONAL)

Many of the reports prepared in QuickBooks can be exported to Microsoft® Excel. This
allows you to take advantage of extensive filtering options available in Excel, hide detail for
some but not all groups of data, combine information from two different reports, change
titles of columns, add comments, change the order of columns, and to experiment with
"what if" scenarios. In order to use this feature of QuickBooks you must also have
Microsoft® Excel.

 <u>Optional Exercise</u>: Export a report from QuickBooks to Excel

With the **Trial Balance** on the screen, click the ⎡Excel ▼⎤ button on the Trial Balance
  icon bar
Click **Create New Worksheet**

On the Send Report to Excel message screen, make sure **Create new worksheet In a new workbook** are marked

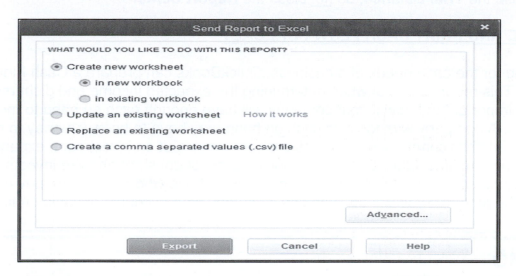

Click **Export**
- The **Trial** Balance will be displayed in Excel.
- The Book number may change depending on how many reports have been sent to Excel. The following example shows Book2.

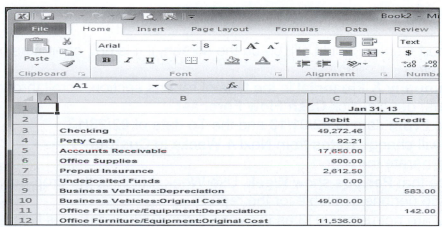

Partial Trial Balance in Excel

Click in Cell C1, change the heading by typing **JANUARY 31, 2013**
Click in Cell C2, type **DEBIT** to change Debit to all capitals
Click in Cell E2, type **CREDIT** to change Credit to all capitals

Click the **Close** button in the top right corner of the Excel title bar to close Excel
Click **Don't Save** to close Excel without saving the Trial Balance
Close the **Trial Balance**, do <u>not</u> close the **Report Center**

PREPARE AND PRINT CASH FLOW FORECAST

In planning for the cash needs of a business, QuickBooks can prepare a Cash Flow Forecast. This report is useful when determining the expected income and disbursement of cash. It is important to know if your company will have enough cash on hand to meet its obligations. A company with too little cash on hand may have to borrow money to pay its bills, while another company with excess cash may miss out on investment, expansion, or dividend opportunities. QuickBooks Cash Flow Forecast does not analyze investments. It simply projects the amount you will be receiving if all those who owe you money pay on time and the amounts you will be spending if you pay your accounts payable on time.

MEMO
DATE: January 31, 2013

Since this is the end of January, prepare Cash Flow Forecast for February 1-28, 2013.

 Prepare Cash Flow Forecast for February

The Report Center should still be on the screen; if it is not, open it as previously
    instructed
Click **Company & Financial** in the type of reports section, scroll through the list of
    reports, double-click **Cash Flow Forecast**
Enter the **From** date of **02/01/13** and the **To** date of **02/28/13**
- This will change **Dates** from Next 4 Weeks to **Custom**
Tab to generate the report
- Notice that **Periods** show **Week**. Use Week, but click the drop-down list arrow to
  see the periods available for the report.
- If you are not using 2013 as the year, the individual amounts listed per week may
  be different from the report shown. As long as the totals are the same, consider
  the report as being correct.
- Analyze the report for February: The Beginning Balance for Accounts Receivable
  shows the amounts due from customers as of 1/31/13.
- Depending on whether or not you applied the Credit Memo to Invoice 4 in
  Chapter 2, you may have a $400 difference in the Accounts Receivable detail

and the Projected Balance; however, the Ending Balance for Accounts Receivable and Projected Balance will still be the same.

- The amounts for Accnts Receivable and Accts Payable for the future weeks are for the customer payments you expect to receive and the bills you expect to pay. This information is based on the due dates for invoices and bills and on the credit memos recorded.
- The Bank Accnts amount for future weeks is based on deposits made or deposits that need to be made.
- Net Inflows summarizes the amounts that should be received and the amounts that should be paid to get a net inflow of cash.
- The Proj Balance is the total in all bank accounts if all customer and bill payments are made on time.

Computer Consulting by Your Name

Cash Flow Forecast

February 2013

	Accnts Receivable	Accnts Payable	Bank Accnts	Net Inflows	Proj Balance
Beginning Balance	9,570.00	0.00	49,364.67		58,934.67
Feb 1 - 2, 13	300.00	0.00	0.00	300.00	59,234.67
Week of Feb 3, 13	7,780.00	0.00	0.00	7,780.00	67,014.67
Week of Feb 10, 13	0.00	260.00	0.00	-260.00	66,754.67
Week of Feb 17, 13	0.00	3,504.00	0.00	-3,504.00	63,250.67
Feb 24 - 28, 13	0.00	0.00	0.00	0.00	63,250.67
Feb 13	8,080.00	3,764.00	0.00	4,316.00	
Ending Balance	17,650.00	3,764.00	49,364.67		63,250.67

If necessary, adjust the column widths; print the report for February in **Landscape** Close the report; do not close the Report Center

STATEMENT OF CASH FLOWS

Another report that details the amount of cash flow in a business is the Statement of Cash Flows. This report organizes information regarding cash in three areas of activities: Operating Activities, Investing Activities, and Financing Activities. The report also projects the amount of cash at the end of a period.

MEMO

DATE: January 31, 2013

Prepare Statement of Cash Flows for January 1-31, 2013.

 Prepare Statement of Cash Flows for January

Double-click **Statement of Cash Flows** in the **Company & Financial** list of reports

Enter the **From** date of **01/01/13** and the **To** date of **01/31/13**
Tab to generate the report

Computer Consulting by Your Name

Statement of Cash Flows
January 2013

	Jan 13
OPERATING ACTIVITIES	
Net Income	▶ 4,135.53 ◀
Adjustments to reconcile Net Income	
to net cash provided by operations:	
Accounts Receivable	4,915.00
Office Supplies	-100.00
Prepaid Insurance	-2,612.50
Accounts Payable	2,914.00
Net cash provided by Operating Activities	9,252.03
INVESTING ACTIVITIES	
Business Vehicles:Depreciation	583.00
Office Furniture/Equipment:Depreciation	142.00
Office Furniture/Equipment:Original Cost	-3,486.00
Net cash provided by Investing Activities	-2,761.00
FINANCING ACTIVITIES	
Loan Payable:Business Vehicles Loan	-467.19
Loan Payable:Office Furniture/Equipment Loan	-29.17
Your Name, Capital:Draws	-2,500.00
Your Name, Capital:Investments	8,000.00
Net cash provided by Financing Activities	5,003.64
Net cash increase for period	11,494.67
Cash at beginning of period	37,870.00
Cash at end of period	49,364.67

Print the report in **Portrait** mode following previous instructions
Close the report; do <u>not</u> close the Report Center

VIEW STANDARD PROFIT AND LOSS STATEMENT

Because all income, expenses, and adjustments have been made for the period, a Profit and Loss Statement can be prepared. This statement is also known as the Income Statement and shows the income and the expenses for the period and the net income or the net loss for the period (Income-Expenses=Net Profit or Net Loss).

QuickBooks has several different types of Profit and Loss statements available: <u>Standard</u>—summarizes income and expenses; <u>Detail</u>—shows the year-to-date transactions for each income and expense account. The other Profit and Loss reports are like the Standard Profit and Loss but have additional information displayed as indicated in the following: <u>YTD Comparison</u>—summarizes your income and expenses for this month and compares them to your income and expenses for the current fiscal year; <u>Prev Year Comparison</u>—summarizes your income and expenses for both this month and this month last year; <u>By Job</u>—has columns for each customer and job and amounts for this year to date; <u>By Class</u>—has columns for each class and sub-class with the amounts for this year to date, and <u>Unclassified</u>—shows how much you are making or losing within segments of your business that are not assigned to a QuickBooks class.

 Prepare a **Standard Profit and Loss Report**

Double-click **Profit & Loss Standard** as the type of Profit & Loss (Income
Statement) to prepare in the list of Company & Financial reports
Enter the dates From **01/01/13** to **01/31/13**
Tab to generate the report
Scroll through the report to view the income and expenses listed

Computer Consulting by Your Name
Profit & Loss
January 2013

	Jan 13
Total Expense	4,855.90
Net Ordinary Income	4,069.10
Other Income/Expense	
Other Income	
Interest Income	66.43
Total Other Income	66.43
Net Other Income	66.43
Net Income	4,135.53

Partial Report

- Make note of the Net Income of $4,135.53.
Close the report without printing, do <u>not</u> close Report Center

PREPARE A STANDARD BALANCE SHEET

The Balance Sheet proves the fundamental accounting equation: Assets = Liabilities +
Owner's Equity. When all transactions and adjustments for the period have been recorded,
a balance sheet should be prepared. QuickBooks has several different types of Balance
Sheet statements available: <u>Standard</u>—shows as of the report dates the balance in each
balance sheet account with subtotals provided for assets, liabilities, and equity; <u>Detail</u>—for
each account, the report shows the starting balance, transactions entered, and the ending
balance during the period specified in the From and To dates; <u>Summary</u>—shows amounts
for each account type but not for individual accounts; and <u>Prev. Year Comparison</u>—has
columns for the report date, the report date a year ago, $ change, and % change; <u>By
Class</u>—has information by the class assigned to accounts, if no class is assigned, there will
be columns for Unclassified and Total.

 Prepare a **Standard Balance Sheet Report**

Double-click **Balance Sheet Standard** as the type of Balance Sheet to prepare in
the list of Company & Financial reports
Tab to or click **As of**, enter **01/31/13**, tab to generate the report
Scroll through the report to view the assets, liabilities, and equities listed
- Notice the Net Income listed in the Equity section of the report. This is the same
amount of Net Income shown on the Profit and Loss report.

- Your Name, Capital – Other is the balance of the Your Name, Capital account. The word Other is used by QuickBooks so that it is not confused with the Equity Section heading Your Name, Capital.
- Also note the Total Assets of $130,038.17. Compare that to the Total Liabilities & Equity of $130,038.17. This proves the Fundamental Accounting Equation of Assets=Liabilities + Owner's Equity.

Computer Consulting by Your Name **Balance Sheet** As of January 31, 2013	Jan 31, 13
Total Liabilities	42,267.64
Equity	
Your Name, Capital	
Draws	-2,500.00
Investments	33,000.00
Your Name, Capital - Other	53,135.00
Total Your Name, Capital	83,635.00
Net Income	4,135.53
Total Equity	87,770.53
TOTAL LIABILITIES & EQUITY	130,038.17

Partial Report

Do <u>not</u> print or close the **Standard Balance Sheet**

CLOSING ENTRIES

In accounting, there are four closing entries that need to be made in order to close the books for a period. They include closing all income and expense accounts, closing the drawing account, and transferring the net income or net loss to the owner's capital account.

In QuickBooks, setting a closing date will replace closing the income and expense accounts. QuickBooks automatically transfers net income into retained earnings, which is appropriate for corporations but not for a sole proprietor. The following section will illustrate the transfer of Net Income into the Your Name, Capital account. QuickBooks does not close the owner's drawing account. This will also be completed in this chapter.

ADJUSTMENT TO TRANSFER NET INCOME/RETAINED EARNINGS INTO YOUR NAME, CAPITAL

Because Computer Consulting by Your Name is a sole proprietorship, the amount of net income should appear as part of your capital account rather than set aside in Retained Earnings as QuickBooks does automatically. In many instances, this is the type of adjustment the CPA makes on the Accountant's Copy of the QuickBooks company files. The adjustment may be made before the closing date for the fiscal year, or it may be made after the closing has been performed. Because QuickBooks automatically transfers Net Income into Retained Earnings, the closing entry will transfer the net income into Your Name, Capital account. This adjustment is made in a General Journal entry that debits

Retained Earnings and credits Your Name, Capital. When you view a report before the end of the year after you enter the adjustment, you will see an amount in Net Income and the same amount as a negative in Retained Earnings. If you view a report after the end of the year, you will not see any information regarding Retained Earnings or Net Income because the adjustment correctly transferred the amount to Your Name, Capital.

If you prefer to use the power of the program and not make the adjustment, QuickBooks simply carries the amount of Retained Earnings forward. Each year net income is added to Retained Earnings. On the Balance Sheet, Retained Earnings and/or Net Income appears as part of the equity section. The owner's drawing and investment accounts are kept separate from Retained Earnings at all times.

To make the transfer of net income, you will record the entry in the General Journal. (Once the transaction is recorded in the General Journal, the entry and all other transactions will be displayed in debit/credit format in the report called the Journal.)

 Transfer the net income into Your Name, Capital account

> Open the General Journal by clicking on **Company** on the menu bar, and clicking **Make General Journal Entries…**
> If you get a screen regarding Assigning Numbers to Journal Entries, click **Do not display this message in the future**, and then click **OK**
> Enter the date of **01/31/13**
> Since this a closing entry, click the checkbox for Adjusting Entry to remove the check mark
> The first account used is **Retained Earnings**
> Debit **Retained Earnings** for the amount of Net Income **4,135.53**,
> - Note: if the entire General Journal disappears during the transaction entry, simply open the Journal again and continue recording the transaction.
> The Memo is **Transfer Net Income into Capital**
> The other account used is **Your Name, Capital**
> **4,135.53** should appear as the credit amount for **Your Name, Capital**
> If the memo does not appear when pressing tab, enter the same Memo

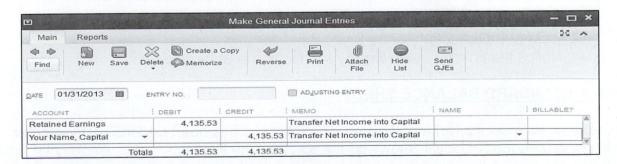

> Click **Save & New** to record and close the **General Journal**
> If a Retained Earnings screen appears, click **OK**

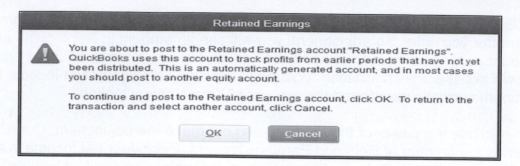

CLOSE DRAWING AND TRANSFER INTO YOUR NAME, CAPITAL ACCOUNT

The closing entry to transfer the net income into Your Name, Capital has already been made. While this is not the actual end of the fiscal year for Computer Consulting by Your Name, the closing entry for the Drawing account will be entered at this time so that you will have experience in recording this closing entry.

 Close Draws into Your Name, Capital

On the new **Make General Journal Entries** screen, make sure the **DATE** is
01/31/13
Since this a closing entry, make sure the check box for ADJUSTING ENTRY is not
marked
Debit **Your Name, Capital**, for the amount of the drawing account **2,500**
The Memo for the transaction is **Close Drawing**
Credit **Draws**, for **2,500**

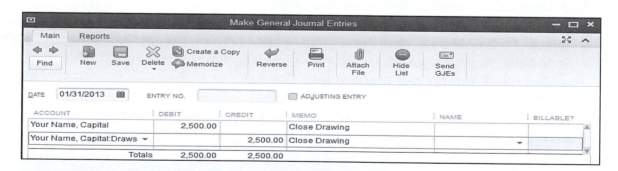

Click **Save & Close** and return to the Balance Sheet
- Notice the change in the **Equity** section of the Balance Sheet.

VIEW A STANDARD BALANCE SHEET

Once the adjustment for Net Income/Retained Earnings has been performed, viewing or printing the Balance Sheet will show you the status of the Equity.

View the **Standard Balance Sheet** as of January 31, 2013

> The Standard Balance Sheet should still be showing on the screen
> Scroll through the report
> - Notice the Equity section, especially Retained Earnings and Net Income.

Computer Consulting by Your Name
Balance Sheet
As of January 31, 2013

	Jan 31, 13
Equity	
Retained Earnings	-4,135.53
Your Name, Capital	
Investments	33,000.00
Your Name, Capital – Other	54,770.53
Total Your Name, Capital	87,770.53
Net Income	4,135.53
Total Equity	87,770.53
TOTAL LIABILITIES & EQUITY	130,038.17

Partial Report after Adjusting Entry

- Remember, Your Name, Capital – Other is the balance of the Your Name, Capital account and is used by QuickBooks to avoid confusion between the actual account and the section heading.
- The amount of Net Income has been added to Your Name, Capital - Other. The Retained Earnings and Net Income amounts shown cancel out each other (notice the positive Net Income and the negative Retained Earnings).
- Draws is no longer shown on the Balance Sheet.
- Verify these two transactions by adding the net income of 4,135.53 to 53,135.00, which was shown as the balance of the Your Name, Capital - Other account on the Balance Sheet prepared before the adjusting entry was made. Then subtract 2,500.00, which is the amount of the owner withdrawals that were subtracted from Capital. The Total Your Name, Capital - Other should be 54,770.53.

Change the **As of** date on the Balance Sheet to **01/31/14**, press **Tab**
- Notice the Equity section.
- Nothing is shown for Retained Earnings or Net Income.

Computer Consulting by Your Name
Balance Sheet
As of January 31, 2014

	Jan 31, 14
Equity	
Your Name, Capital	
Investments	33,000.00
Your Name, Capital – Other	54,770.53
Total Your Name, Capital	87,770.53
Total Equity	87,770.53
TOTAL LIABILITIES & EQUITY	130,038.17

Partial Report

Close the **Balance Sheet** without printing and close the Report Center

JOURNAL

Normally, you would prepare a Journal before completing the end-of-period procedures so you have a printed or "hard copy" of the data for January. At this point, we will postpone printing until all of the closing procedures have been completed.

END-OF-PERIOD BACKUP

Once all end-of-period procedures have been completed, a regular backup and a second/archival backup of the company data should be made. Preferably the archive copy will be located someplace other than on the business premises. The archive copy is set aside in case of emergency or in case damage occurs to the original company file and current backup copies of the company data. Normally, a backup and an archive copy would be made before closing the period. Since we will be making changes to transactions for the closed period, the archive will be made after that.

 Prepare an archive copy of your company file

> For training purposes, use your USB drive
> Follow the procedures given previously to make your backup files
> Name the file **Computer (Archive 01-31-13)**
> - In actual practice, the company (.qbw) file would be on your hard drive and the backup (.qbb) file would be stored on a separate disk, USB drive, online, or in the cloud.
> - If you get a QuickBooks screen regarding the files location, click **Use this Location**.
> Once the archive copy has been made, click **OK** on the QuickBooks Information dialog box to acknowledge the successful backup

PASSWORDS

Not every employee of a business should have access to all the financial records for the company. In some companies, only the owner will have complete access. In others, one or two key employees will have full access while other employees are provided limited access based on the jobs and tasks they perform. Passwords are secret words used to control access to data. QuickBooks has several options available when assigning passwords.

In order to assign any passwords at all, you must have an administrator. The administrator has unrestricted access to all QuickBooks functions, sets up users and user passwords for QuickBooks and for Windows, and assigns areas of transaction access for each user. Areas of access can be limited to transaction entry for certain types of transactions or a user may have unrestricted access into all areas of QuickBooks and company data. To obtain more information regarding QuickBooks' passwords, refer to Help.

A password should be kept secret at all times. It should be something that is easy for the individual to remember, yet difficult for someone else to guess. Birthdays, names, initials, and similar devices are not good passwords because the information is too readily available. Never write down your password where it can be easily found or seen by someone else. In QuickBooks passwords are case sensitive. It is wise to use a complex password. The requirements for a password to be accepted as complex are: a minimum of seven characters including at least one number and one uppercase letter. Use of special characters is also helpful. Complex passwords should be changed every 90 days. Make sure your password is something you won't forget. Otherwise, you will not be able to access your Company file.

Since the focus of the text is in training in all aspects of QuickBooks, no passwords will be assigned. Also, if you set a password and then forget it, you will not be able to access QuickBooks; and your instructor will not be able to override your password.

SET THE CLOSING DATE FOR THE PERIOD

Instead of closing entries for income and expense accounts, QuickBooks uses a closing date to indicate the end of a period. When a closing date is assigned, income and expenses are effectively closed. When a transaction involving income or expenses is recorded after the closing date, it is considered part of the new period and will not be used in calculating net income (or loss) for the previous period.

A closing date assigned to transactions for a period prevents changing data from the closed period without acknowledging that a transaction has been changed. This is helpful to discourage casual changes or transaction deletions to a period that has been closed. Setting the closing date is done by accessing Preferences in QuickBooks.

MEMO
DATE: January 31, 2013

Alhandra, protect the data by setting the closing date to 1/31/13.

 Assign the closing date of **01/31/13** to the transactions for the period

    Click **Edit** on the menu bar, click **Preferences**
    Click **Accounting** in the list of Preferences
    Click **Company Preferences**
      OR
    Click **Accountant** on the menu bar; and then click **Set Closing Date...**
    Click the **Set Date/Password** button

Enter **01/31/13** as the closing date.

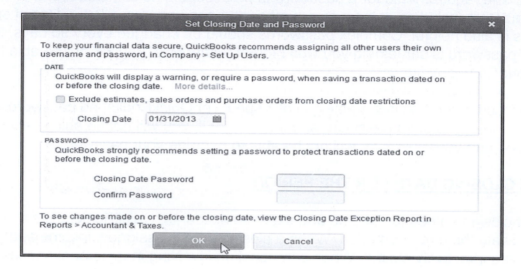

Do not enter anything in the text boxes for Password, click the **OK** button
On the No Password Entered screen, click **Do not display this message in the future**; and then click **No**.
Click **OK** to close the period and to close Preferences

EDIT TRANSACTIONS FROM PREVIOUS PERIOD

Even though the month of January has been "closed," transactions still appear in the account registers, the Journal, and so on. If it is determined that an error was made in a previous period, QuickBooks does allow the correction. The edited transactions may not be changed unless you click Yes on the screen warning you that you have changed a transaction to a closed period. Changes to transactions involving income and expense will also necessitate a change to the transfer of net income into the owner's capital account.

MEMO
DATE: January 31, 2013

After reviewing the journal for January, you determine that the amount of supplies used was $325, not $350. Make the correction to the adjusting entry of January 31. This will also require a change to the closing entry to transfer Net Income.

 Change Office Supplies adjusting entry to $325 from $350

Access the **Office Supplies** account register as previously instructed
Click the **DECREASE** column for the Adjusting Entry recorded to the account on
     01/31/13
Change 350 to **325**
Click **Record**
Click **Yes** on the Recording Transaction dialog box
The **QuickBooks** warning dialog box regarding the closed period appears

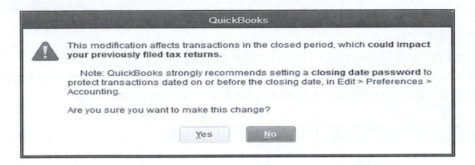

Click **Yes**
- Notice that the Balance for the Office Supplies account now shows 625 instead
  of 600.

01/31/2013			325.00		625.00
	GENJRN	Office Supplies Exp Supplies Used			

Close the Register for **Office Supplies** and close the **Chart of Accounts**
- The adjusting entry used to transfer retained earnings/net income into the
  owner's capital account also needs to be adjusted as a result of any changes to
  transactions.
- Since the correction to Office Supplies decreased the amount of the expense by
  $25, there is an increase in net income of $25 (Income – Expenses = Net
  Income).
Change the Adjusting Entry where Net Income was transferred from Retained
     Earnings into Your Name, Capital
Click **Make General Journal Entries...** on the Accountant or the Company menus

Click ◄ on the Make General Journal Entries icon bar until you find the entry
     adjusting Retained Earnings
Change the Debit to Retained Earnings by 25.00 from 4135.53 to **4160.53**
Change the Credit to Your Name, Capital by 25.00 from 4135.53 to **4160.53**

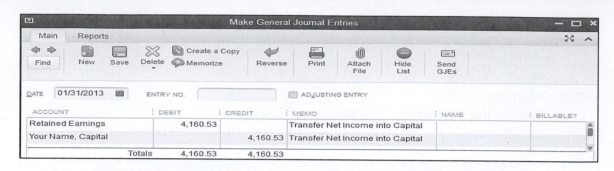

Click **Save & Close**
Click **Yes** on the Recording Transaction dialog box
Click **Yes** on the QuickBooks dialog box regarding transactions in a closed period
Click **OK** on the QuickBooks dialog box for Retained Earnings

REDO THE ARCHIVE COPY OF THE COMPANY FILE

Since we have made changes to transactions for the closed period, the archive copy of the company file should be redone.

 Create an archive copy of the company data

Replace the previous file **Computer (Backup Archive 1-31-13)**
Follow the procedures given previously to make your backup files

PRINT JOURNAL

Normally, you would have printed the Journal prior to closing the period. Since changes to the "previous" period have been made, the Journal would need to be reprinted to replace the one printed before closing.

 Print the Journal for January

Open the Report Center, click **Accountant & Taxes** as the type of report
Double-click **Journal**
On the Collapsing and Expanding Transactions dialog box click **Do not display this message in the future** and then click **OK**
Enter the dates From **01/01/13** To **01/31/13**
- Notice that the report contains all the transactions from Chapters 2, 3, and 4
Click the **Expand** button
Resize the columns to display the information in full
Verify that the final total for debits and credits is **$64,555.22**
- If it is not, make the necessary corrections to incorrect transactions. Frequent errors include incorrect dates, incorrect accounts used, incorrect amounts, and incorrect sales items.

Computer Consulting by Your Name

Journal

January 2013

Trans #	Type	Date	Num	Adj	Name	Memo	Account	Debit	Credit
75	Check	01/31/2013				Service Charge	Checking		8.00
						Service Charge	Bank Service Charges	8.00	
								8.00	8.00
76	Deposit	01/31/2013				Interest	Checking	66.43	
						Interest	Interest Income		66.43
								66.43	66.43
77	General Journal	01/31/2013				Transfer Net Income into Capital	Retained Earnings	4,160.53	
						Transfer Net Income into Capital	Your Name, Capital		4,160.53
								4,160.53	4,160.53
78	General Journal	01/31/2013				Close Drawing	Your Name, Capital	2,500.00	
						Close Drawing	Draws		2,500.00
								2,500.00	2,500.00
TOTAL								64,555.22	64,555.22

Partial Report

Adjust column widths to display information in full, print in **Landscape** orientation after selecting **Fit report to one page wide**
Close the **Journal** do <u>not</u> close the **Report Center**

PRINT TRIAL BALANCE

After the adjustments have been recorded and the "closing" has been completed, it is helpful to print reports. A Trial Balance is printed to prove that debits still equal credits. Post-closing reports are typically prepared as of the last day of the fiscal year after all closing entries for the year have been recorded. Since our closing was simply for a period, this means that income and expenses will be shown in the Trial Balance and in the Profit & Loss reports for January.

MEMO

DATE: January 31, 2013

Print a Trial Balance, a Profit and Loss Statement, and a Balance Sheet for Computer Consulting by Your Name. The dates should be as of or for 01/31/13.

 Print a Trial Balance to prove that debits equal credits

Click **Accountant & Taxes** in the **Report Center**, double-click **Trial Balance**
Enter the **From** and **To** dates as **01/31/13**, tab to generate the report
Click the **Customize Report** button
Scroll through the report and study the amounts shown
- Notice that the final totals of debits and credits are equal.

- Notice that Office Supplies has a balance of $625.00 and Office Supplies Expense is $343.57, which is the 25.00 change you made in the register after the period was closed.

Computer Consulting by Your Name
Trial Balance
As of January 31, 2013

	Jan 31, 13	
	Debit	Credit
Advertising Expense	260.00	
Bank Service Charges	8.00	
Business Vehicles Expense	588.88	
Depreciation Expense	725.00	
Dues and Subscriptions	79.00	
Equipment Rental	25.00	
Insurance:Business Vehicles Insurance	237.50	
Interest Expense:Loan Interest	308.61	
Office Supplies Expense	343.57	
Postage and Delivery	195.34	
Rent	1,600.00	
Telephone	0.00	
Utilities:Electricity Expense	250.00	
Utilities:Heating Expense--Gas	175.00	
Utilities:Water	35.00	
Interest Income		66.43
TOTAL	139,779.60	139,779.60

Partial Report

Print the report in **Portrait** orientation

USE QUICKZOOM IN TRIAL BALANCE

QuickZoom is a QuickBooks feature that allows you to make a closer observation of transactions, amounts, and other entries. With QuickZoom you may zoom in on an item when the mouse pointer turns into a magnifying glass with a Z inside. If you point to an item and you do not get a magnifying glass with a Z inside, you cannot zoom in on the item. For example, if you point to Interest Expense, you will see the magnifying glass with the Z inside. If your Trial Balance had Retained Earnings and you pointed to the account, the mouse pointer would not change from the arrow. This means that you can see transaction details for Interest Expense but not for Retained Earnings.

 Use QuickZoom to view the details of Office Supplies Expense

Scroll through the Trial Balance until you see Office Supplies Expense
Position the mouse pointer over the amount of Office Supplies Expense, **343.57**
- Notice that the mouse pointer changes to
Double-click the primary mouse button
- A Transactions by Account report appears on the screen showing the transactions for Office Supplies Expense as of 01/31/2013.
If necessary, enter the From date **010113** and the To date **013113**
- QuickBooks will enter the / in a date and convert the year to four digits.
Tab to generate the report
Scroll through the report

Computer Consulting by Your Name
Transactions by Account
As of January 31, 2013

Type	Date	Num	Adj	Name	Memo	Clr	Split	Debit	Credit	Balance
Office Supplies Expense										
Bill	01/18/2013	1035A		Supply Station	Fax Supplies for the Month		Accounts Payable	20.00		20.00
Credit	01/26/2013	789		Supply Station	Returned Damaged Fax Paper		Accounts Payable		5.00	15.00
Check	01/30/2013	1					Petty Cash	3.57		18.57
General Journal	01/31/2013		✓		Supplies Used		Office Supplies	325.00		343.57
Total Office Supplies Expense								348.57	5.00	343.57
TOTAL								348.57	5.00	343.57

Close the Transactions by Account report without printing; close the **Trial Balance**

PRINT PROFIT AND LOSS STATEMENT

Since the closing was done as of January 31, 2013, the Profit and Loss Statement for January 31, 2013 will give the same data as a Profit and Loss Statement prepared manually on January 31. To verify the closing of income and expense accounts for January, you would prepare a Profit and Loss statement for February 1. Since no income had been earned or expenses incurred in the new period, February, the Net Income will show $0.00.

Print a Profit & Loss Standard report for January and view the report for February

Click **Company & Financial** in the **Report Center**, double-click **Profit & Loss Standard**
The **Dates** are From **01/01/13** To **01/31/13**

Computer Consulting by Your Name
Profit & Loss
January 2013

	Jan 13
Total Expense	4,830.90
Net Ordinary Income	4,094.10
Other Income/Expense	
Other Income	
Interest Income	66.43
Total Other Income	66.43
Net Other Income	66.43
Net Income	**4,160.53**

Partial Report

- Note the Net Income of **4,160.53**

Print the report in **Portrait** orientation
To view the effect of closing the period, prepare a Profit & Loss for February
Change the dates From **02/01/13** to **02/01/13**
Tab to generate the report

```
        Computer Consulting by Your Name
                   Profit & Loss
                  February 1, 2013
                     ◇ Feb 1, 13 ◇
            Net Income   ▶      0.00  ◀
```

- Note the Net Income of **0.00**.
Close the **Profit & Loss Report**

PRINT BALANCE SHEET

Proof that assets are equal to liabilities and owner's equity needs to be displayed in a Balance Sheet. Because this report is for a month, the adjustment to Retained Earnings and Net Income will result in both accounts being included on the Balance Sheet. If, however, this report were prepared for the year, neither account would appear.

 Prepare and print a **Balance Sheet** report for January 31, 2013, and view the report as of February 1, 2014

Prepare a **Balance Sheet Standard** as previously instructed
Tab to or click **As of**, enter **01/31/13**
Tab to generate the report
Scroll through the report to view the assets, liabilities, and equities listed
- Because this report is for a one-month period, both Retained Earnings and Net Income are included on this report.
- Also notice that the amount of Retained Earnings shows -4,160.53 and Net Income shows 4,160.53. This is the amount of the adjusting entry after the change in supplies of $25.00.

```
          Computer Consulting by Your Name
                  Balance Sheet
                As of January 31, 2013
                              ◇      Jan 31, 13      ◇
    Total Liabilities                      42,267.64

  ▽ Equity
      Retained Earnings                    -4,160.53
    ▽ Your Name, Capital
        Investments                        33,000.00
          Your Name, Capital - Other       54,795.53
      Total Your Name, Capital             87,795.53

      Net Income                            4,160.53
    Total Equity                           87,795.53

    TOTAL LIABILITIES & EQUITY            130,063.17
```

Partial Report

Print the report in **Portrait** orientation
Change the date to **01/31/14**, tab to generate the report
Scroll through the report to view the assets, liabilities, and equities listed

- Because this report is prepared after the end of the fiscal year, neither Retained Earnings nor Net Income is included on this report.

Computer Consulting by Your Name	
Balance Sheet	
As of January 31, 2014	
	Jan 31, 14
Total Liabilities	42,267.64
Equity	
Your Name, Capital	
Investments	33,000.00
Your Name, Capital - Other	54,795.53
Total Your Name, Capital	87,795.53
Total Equity	87,795.53
TOTAL LIABILITIES & EQUITY	130,063.17

Partial Report

Close the **Balance Sheet** for **January 2014** without printing and Close the **Report Center**

END-OF-CHAPTER BACKUP AND CLOSE COMPANY

As in previous chapters, you should back up your company and then close the company. This backup file will contain all of your work for Chapters 1-4.

 Follow instructions previously provided to back up company files, close the company, and make a duplicate disk

Name the backup **Computer (Backup Ch. 4)**

SUMMARY

In this chapter, end-of-period adjustments were made, a bank reconciliation was performed, backup and archive copies were prepared, and a period was closed. The use of Net Income and Retained Earnings accounts was explored and interpreted for a sole proprietorship. Account name changes were made, and the effect on subaccounts was examined. Even though QuickBooks focuses on entering transactions on business forms, a Journal recording each transaction is kept by QuickBooks. This chapter presented transaction entry directly into the General Journal in Debit/Credit format, which were then displayed in the Journal. The differences between accrual-basis and cash-basis accounting were discussed. Company preferences were established for reporting preferences. Owner withdrawals and additional owner investments were made. Many of the different report options available in QuickBooks were examined, and the exporting of reports to Excel was explored. A variety of reports were printed. Correction of errors was explored, and changes to transactions in "closed" periods were made. The fact that QuickBooks does not require an actual closing entry at the end of the period was examined.

END-OF-CHAPTER QUESTIONS

TRUE/FALSE

ANSWER THE FOLLOWING QUESTIONS IN THE SPACE PROVIDED BEFORE THE QUESTION NUMBER.

_____ 1. Accrual-basis accounting matches the income from the period and the expenses for the period in order to determine the net income or net loss for the period.

_____ 2. In QuickBooks, the Journal is called the book of final entry.

_____ 3. Adjusting entries are recorded when cash basis accounting is used.

_____ 4. In a sole proprietorship, an owner's name is added to the Vendor List for recording withdrawals.

_____ 5. Additional investments made by an owner may be cash or noncash items.

_____ 6. QuickBooks records every transaction in the Journal.

_____ 7. A Reconciliation Detail Report prints the last two bank reconciliation reports.

_____ 8. Once an account has been used in a transaction, no changes may be made to the account name.

_____ 9. When completing a bank reconciliation, anything entered as a service charge or as interest earned will be entered in the Journal automatically when the reconciliation is complete.

_____ 10. A Balance Sheet is prepared to prove the equality of debits and credits.

MULTIPLE CHOICE

WRITE THE LETTER OF THE CORRECT ANSWER IN THE SPACE PROVIDED BEFORE THE QUESTION NUMBER.

_____ 1. To close a period, you must ___.
    A. have a closing password
    B. enter a closing date in the Company Preferences for Accounting
    C. enter a closing date in the Company Preferences for Reports
    D. enter the traditional closing entries in debit/credit format in the General Journal

_____ 2. When a master account name such as "cars" is changed to "automobiles," the subaccount "depreciation" ___.
A. needs to be changed to a subaccount of automobiles
B. is automatically becomes a subaccount of automobiles
C. cannot be changed
D. must be deleted and re-entered

_____ 3. The report that proves Assets = Liabilities + Owner's Equity is the ___.
A. Trial Balance
B. Income Statement
C. Profit and Loss Statement
D. Balance Sheet

_____ 4. If the adjusting entry to transfer net income/retained earnings into the owner's capital account is made prior to the end of the year, the Balance Sheet shows ___.
A. Retained Earnings
B. Net Income
C. both Net Income and Retained Earnings
D. none of the above because the income/earnings has been transferred into capital

_____ 5. The type of Profit and Loss report showing year-to-date transactions instead of totals for each income and expense account is a(n) ___ Profit and Loss Report.
A. Standard
B. YTD Comparison
C. Prev Year Comparison
D. Detailed

_____ 6. A bank statement may ___.
A. show service charges or interest not yet recorded
B. be missing deposits in transit or outstanding checks
C. show automatic payments
D. all of the above

_____ 7. The Journal shows ___.
A. all transactions no matter where they were recorded
B. only those transactions recorded in the General Journal
C. only transactions recorded in account registers
D. only those transactions that have been edited

_____ 8. A QuickBooks backup file ___.
          A. is a condensed file containing company data
          B. is prepared in case of emergencies or errors
          C. must be restored before information can be used
          D. all of the above

_____ 9. An error known as a transposition can be found by ___.
          A. dividing the amount out of balance by 9
          B. dividing the amount out of balance by 2
          C. multiplying the difference by 9, then dividing by 2
          D. dividing the amount out of balance by 5

_____ 10. The type of Balance Sheet Report showing information for today and a year ago is a(n) ___ Balance Sheet.
          A. Standard
          B. Summary
          C. Comparison
          D. Detailed

FILL-IN

IN THE SPACE PROVIDED, WRITE THE ANSWER THAT MOST APPROPRIATELY COMPLETES THE SENTENCE.

1. Bank reconciliations should be performed on a(n) _____ basis.

2. Exporting report data from QuickBooks to _____ can be made in order to perform "what if" scenarios.

3. An owner's paycheck is considered a(n)_____.

4. The Summary Report Basis for _____ or _____ is selected as a Report Preference.

5. The Cash Flow Forecast Projected Balance column shows the total in all bank accounts if all _____ and _____ payments are made on time.

SHORT ESSAY

Describe the five types of Balance Sheet Reports available in QuickBooks.

_____

_____

_____

_____

NAME_____

TRANSMITTAL

CHAPTER 4: COMPUTER CONSULTING BY YOUR NAME

Attach the following documents and reports:

Account Listing
Check No. 9: Your Name
Reconciliation Detail Report
Trial Balance, January 1-31, 2013
Cash Flow Forecast, February 1-28, 2013
Statement of Cash Flows, January 2013
Journal, January 1-31, 2013
Trial Balance, January 31, 2013
Profit and Loss, January 31, 2013
Balance Sheet, January 31, 2013

END-OF-CHAPTER PROBLEM

YOUR NAME LANDSCAPE AND POOL SERVICE

Chapter 4 continues with the end-of-period adjustments, bank reconciliation, archive copies, and closing the period for Your Name Landscape and Pool Service. The company does use a certified public accountant for guidance and assistance with appropriate accounting procedures. The CPA has provided information for use in recording adjusting entries and so on.

INSTRUCTIONS

Continue to use the company file **Landscape.qbw** that you used for Chapters 1, 2, and 3. Record the adjustments and other transactions as you were instructed in the chapter. Always read the transaction carefully and review the Chart of Accounts when selecting transaction accounts. Expand reports, adjust columns so they display in full, and print the reports and journals as indicated.

RECORD TRANSACTIONS

January 31
► Change the names of the following accounts:
- o **Student's Name, Capital** to **Your Name, Capital**
  - • Remember to use your actual name.
- o **Business Trucks** to **Business Vehicles** (Notice that the names of the subaccounts were not affected by this name change.)
- o **Business Trucks Depreciation** to **Business Vehicles Depreciation** and **Business Trucks Original Cost** to **Business Vehicles Original Cost** (These remain subaccounts of Business Vehicles.)
- o **Business Trucks Loan** to **Business Vehicles Loan**
- o **Automobile Expense** to **Business Vehicles Expense** (Delete the description)
- o **Auto Insurance Expense** to **Business Vehicles Insurance**
► Make the following accounts inactive:
- o **Recruiting**
- o **Travel & Ent** (Notice that the subaccounts are also made inactive.)
► Delete the following accounts:
- o **Sales**
- o **Services**
- o **Amortization Expense**
- o **Interest Expense: Mortgage**
- o **Taxes: Property**
► Print the Chart of Accounts by clicking **Reports** on the menu bar, pointing to **List**, clicking **Account Listing.** Adjust the column widths so that all information is displayed, hide the Tax Line and Description columns. Use Portrait orientation.

January 31

▶ Enter adjusting entries in the Journal for:
- ○ Office Supplies Used, $185. Memo: January Supplies Used
- ○ Business vehicles insurance expense for the month, $250.
  Memo: January Insurance Expense
- ○ Depreciation for the month (Use a compound entry), Memo: January Depreciation
  - • Business Vehicles, $950
  - • Equipment, $206.25

▶ Enter transactions for Owner's Equity (These are not adjusting entries):
- ○ Owner withdrawal $1,000. Memo: January Withdrawal (Add your name as "Other," include the memo on the check face and in the Memo column in the detail section of the check, print the check.)
- ○ Additional cash investment by you, $2,000. Memo: Investment: Cash
- ○ Additional noncash investment by owner, $1,500 of lawn equipment. Memo: Investment: Equipment (Note: The value of the lawn equipment is the original cost of the asset.)

▶ Prepare Bank Reconciliation and Enter Adjustments for the Reconciliation for January 31, 2013 (Be sure to enter automatic payments, service charges, and interest. Pay close attention to the dates.

<table>
<tr><td colspan="4">SANTA BARBARA BANK
1234 Coast Highway
Santa Barbara, CA 93100 (805) 555-9310</td></tr>
<tr><td colspan="4">BANK STATEMENT FOR</td></tr>
<tr><td colspan="3">Your Name Landscape and Pool Service
18527 State Street
Santa Barbara, CA 93103
Acct. #987-352-9152</td><td>January 31, 2013</td></tr>
<tr><td>Beginning Balance, January 2, 2013</td><td></td><td></td><td>$23,850.00</td></tr>
<tr><td>1/18/13, Check 1</td><td></td><td>485.00</td><td>23,365.00</td></tr>
<tr><td>1/18/13, Check 2</td><td></td><td>180.00</td><td>23,185.00</td></tr>
<tr><td>1/18/13, Check 3</td><td></td><td>669.00</td><td>22,516.00</td></tr>
<tr><td>1/18/13, Check 4</td><td></td><td>375.00</td><td>22,141.00</td></tr>
<tr><td>1/31/13, Service Charge</td><td></td><td>10.00</td><td>22,131.00</td></tr>
<tr><td>1/31/13, Business Vehicles Loan Pmt.:
Interest, 795.54; Principal, 160.64</td><td></td><td>956.18</td><td>21,174.82</td></tr>
<tr><td>1/31/13, Interest</td><td>59.63</td><td></td><td>21,234.45</td></tr>
<tr><td>Ending Balance, 1/31/13</td><td></td><td></td><td>$21,234.45</td></tr>
</table>

▶ Print a Detailed Reconciliation Report in Portrait orientation

► Change Reports & Graphs Preferences: Verify or change Summary Reports Basis to accrual

► Transfer Net Income/Retained Earnings into Capital Account (Did you prepare a Profit & Loss report to find out the amount of Net Income?) Use the Memo: Transfer Net Income into Capital

► Close the Draws account. Use the Memo: **Close Drawing**

► Prepare the archive backup file: **Landscape (Backup Archive 01-31-13)**

► Close the period. The closing date is **01/31/13** (Do <u>not</u> use a password.)

► Edit a Transaction from a closed period: Discovered an error in the amount of office supplies used. The amount used should be **$175**, not $185. (Don't forget to adjust Retained Earnings and Capital.)

► Replace the archive backup file: **Landscape (Backup Archive 01-31-13)**

January 31, 2013

Use the dates given for each report, expand, resize columns, and print the following in Portrait orientation unless specified as Landscape:

► Cash Flow Forecast for February 1-28, 2013 (Landscape orientation)

► Statement of Cash Flows, January 1-31, 2013

► Journal for January, 2013 (Expand the report. Use Landscape orientation, and Fit report to one page wide)

► Trial Balance, January 31, 2013

► Profit & Loss Statement, January 31, 2013

► Balance Sheet, January 31, 2013

► Backup your work to **Landscape (Backup Ch. 4)**

NAME_____

TRANSMITTAL

CHAPTER 4: YOUR NAME LANDSCAPE AND POOL SERVICE

Attach the following documents and reports:

Account Listing, January 31, 2013
Check No. 8: Your Name
Reconciliation Detail Report
Cash Flow Forecast, February 1-28, 2013
Statement of Cash Flows, January 2013
Journal, January 2013
Trial Balance, January 31, 2013
Profit and Loss, January 31, 2013
Balance Sheet, January 31, 2013

SECTION 1 PRACTICE SET, SERVICE BUSINESS: YOUR NAME AT YOUR SERVICE

The following is a comprehensive practice set combining all the elements of QuickBooks studied in Chapters 1-4. In this practice set, you will keep the books for a company for one month. Entries will be made to record invoices, receipt of payments on invoices, cash sales, bills and bill payments, credit memos for invoices and bills. Account names will be added, changed, deleted, and made inactive. Customer, vendor, owner names, and items will be added to the appropriate lists. Adjusting entries for depreciation, supplies used, and insurance expense will be recorded. A bank reconciliation will be prepared. Reports will be prepared to analyze sales, bills, and receipts. Formal reports including the Trial Balance, Profit and Loss Statement, and Balance Sheet will be prepared.

YOUR NAME AT YOUR SERVICE

Located in Beverly Hills, California, Your Name At Your Service is a service business providing assistance with errands, shopping, home repairs, and simple household chores The company is going to start providing transportation for children and others who do not drive. Rates are on a per-hour basis and differ according to the service performed.

Your Name At Your Service is a sole proprietorship owned and operated by you. You have one assistant, Barbara Rogers, helping you with errands, scheduling of duties, and doing the bookkeeping for Your Name At Your Service. In addition, a part-time employee, Angela Brown, works weekends for Your Name At Your Service.

INSTRUCTIONS

Use the company file **Service.qbw**. If you get a message to update the file, follow the steps listed in QuickBooks.

The following lists are used for all sales items, customers, and vendors. You will be adding additional customers and vendors as the company is in operation. When entering transactions, you are responsible for any memos or customer messages you wish to include in transactions. Unless otherwise specified, the terms for each sale or bill will be the terms specified on the Customer or Vendor List. (View the terms for the individual customers or vendors in the Customer Center and Vendor Center.)

Customers:

Vendors:

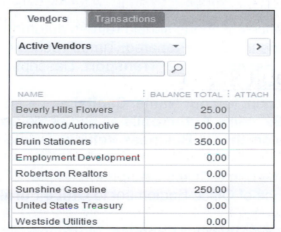

Sales Items:

Each Item is priced per hour. Unless otherwise specified within the transactions, a minimum of one hour is charged for any service provided. As you can see, there is no difference in amount between the first hour of a service and subsequent hours of service.

RECORD TRANSACTIONS

Enter the transactions for Your Name At Your Service and print as indicated. When preparing invoices, use an Intuit Service Invoice form, a message of your choosing, and do not e-mail invoices or accept online payments. Start numbering the Invoices with number 35 and Sales Receipts with the number 22. Use the standard terms provided by QuickBooks unless the transaction indicates something different and print invoices and sales receipts without lines. Provide transaction memos when needed for clarification. Print invoices, sales receipts, and checks as they are entered. Unless instructed to do so by your professor, do not print Payment Receipts and Bills (even if not printed, they are included on the transmittal sheet). Always resize the columns in reports to display information in full.

Week 1: January 1-6, 2013:
► Add your name to the company name and legal name. The name will be **Your Name At Your Service**. (Type your actual name. For example, Mark Randall would enter Mark Randall At Your Service)
► Change Report Preferences: Reports should refresh automatically, Report Header/Footer should *not* include the Date Prepared, Time Prepared, or the Report Basis
► Add a new Item: Type: **Service**, Name: **Transport**, Description: **Transportation**; Rate: **35.00**, Account: **Services**
► Change the Capital account to **Your Name, Capital**.
► Find all accounts with the name **Automobile** as part of the account name. Change every occurrence of Automobile to **Business Vehicle**. Delete any unwanted descriptions.
► Find all accounts with the name **Office Equipment** as part of the account name. Change every occurrence of Office Equipment to **Office Furniture/Equipment**. Delete any unwanted descriptions.
► Make the following inactive: **Interest Expense: Mortgage**; **Taxes: Property**; **Travel & Ent**
► Delete the following accounts: **Sales, Amortization Expense, Professional Development,** and **Recruiting**
► Add **Petty Cash** to the Chart of Accounts. Transfer **$100** from Checking to Petty Cash to fund the account. Use January 1, 2013 as the transaction date.
► Print an Account Listing in Portrait orientation. Hide the columns for Description and Tax Line and resize any columns that are not displayed in full.
► Prior to recording any transactions, print a Trial Balance as of January 1, 2013.

1/1/13
► We were out of paper, toner cartridges for the laser printer, and various other office supplies that we need to have on hand. Received a bill—Invoice No. 1806-1—from Bruin Stationers for $450 for the office supplies we received today. (Even though the Bills are listed on the transmittal sheet, check with your instructor to see if you should print them.)
► Dr. Ricardo Sanchez has arranged for you to take his dogs to the vet for shots and to feed and walk his dogs 1 hour per day every day. Bill Dr. Sanchez for 3 hours transport and pet sitting for one hour a day for 14 days, terms Net 30. (Refer to the Item Detail

List for the appropriate sales item and put this all on Invoice No. 35. Remember to use an Intuit Service Invoice as the business form.) Use an appropriate customer message and print the invoice without lines. Use an appropriate customer message and print the invoice without lines. On the Name Information Changed dialog box, click "No" so you do not change the terms for Dr. Sanchez from Net 15 to Net 30

▶ Samantha Waters is having a party in two weeks. Bill Samantha Waters for 12 hours of party planning. Invoice No. 36, terms Net 30.

1/2/13

▶ Mr. Pirosky's mother has several doctor appointments. He has asked Your Name At Your Service to take her to these appointments. Bill Mikhail Pirosky for 8 hours of transportation.

1/3/13

▶ Gloria Bailey needed to have her shelves relined. You did part of the house this week and will return next week to continue the work. Bill her for 12 hours of household chores for this week.

1/4/13

▶ Record the bill from Western Insurance, (7654 Western Avenue, Hollywood, CA 90721, Main Phone 310-555-1598, Fax 310-555-8951, terms Net 30) for Business Vehicle Insurance for the year, $2,400.00, Invoice 2280.

▶ Received checks for payments on account from the following customers: Dr. John Anderson, $275, Check No. 713; Jorge Perez, $250, Check No. 36381; Mikhail Pirosky, $450, Check No. 6179; Jeff Jackson, $1,000, Check No. 38142. (Even though the Payment Receipts are listed on the transmittal sheet, check with your instructor to see if you should print them.)

1/5/13

▶ Prepare Sales Receipt No. 22 to record a cash sale. Received Check No. 2894 for 2 hours of errands and 1 hour of household chores for a new customer: Fatema Nasseri, 18062A Beverly Drive, Beverly Hills, CA 90210, Main Phone 310-555-7206, Fax 310-555-6027, Main E-mail FNasseri@abc.com, Payment Terms Net 10. (*Note:* Remember to key the last name first for the customer name.) Print the sales receipt.

1/6/13

▶ Prepare Unpaid Bills Detail Report for January 6, 2013. Print the report.

▶ Pay bills for the amount owed to Beverly Hills Flowers and Sunshine Gasoline on December 31. (Refer to the Vendor List shown on the second page of the practice set or to the Unpaid Bills Detail Report to determine the amounts for the checks. Remember that the due dates will not be 12/31/12 they will be 01/10/13.) Print the checks using a Standard check style—they may be printed on one page or individually.

▶ Make the bank deposit for the week. Deposit date is 1/6/13. Print a Deposit Summary.

▶ Print Trial Balance from 01/01/13 to 01/06/13.

▶ Back up your work for the week. Use **Service (Backup Week 1)** as the file name.

Week 2: January 7-13, 2013

1/9/13

▶ Received checks for payment on accounts from the following customers: Dr. Sanchez, $500, No. 7891; Ms. Lim, $200, No. 97452; Ms. Brankowski, $600, No. 605; Mr. Evans, $50, No. 178; and Mr. Ashford, $750, No. 3916.

▶ Received a bill—Invoice No. 81085—from Sunshine Gasoline, $325 for the bi-weekly gasoline charge.

▶ Every week we put fresh flowers in the office in order to provide a welcoming environment for any customers who happen to come to the office. Received a bill— Invoice No. 9287—from Beverly Hills Flowers for $60 for office flowers for two weeks. (Miscellaneous Expense)

1/10/13

▶ Willow Brankowski really likes the floral arrangements in the office of Your Name At Your Service. She has asked that flowers be brought to her home and arranged throughout the house. When you complete the placement of the flowers in the house, Willow gives you Check No. 387 for $180 for 3 hours of errands and 3 hours of household chores. This is payment in full for three weeks of floral arrangements. Prepare the Sales Receipt

▶ Jeff Jackson has arranged for Your Name At Your Service to supervise and coordinate the installation of new tile in his master bathroom. Bill Mr. Jackson for 5 hours of repair service for hiring the subcontractor, scheduling the installation for 1/14, 1/15 and 1/16, and contract preparation.

1/11/13

▶ Returned faulty printer cartridge that we had purchased in December to have on hand. Received Credit Memo No. 5 from Bruin Stationers, $95.

1/13/13

▶ Pay all bills for the amounts due on or before January 13. (*Hint:* Are there any credits to apply?) There should be two checks. Print the checks–all on one page or individually.

▶ Correct the invoice issued to Gloria Bailey on 1/03/13. The number of hours billed should be 14 instead of 12. Print the corrected invoice.

▶ Make the bank deposit for the week. Deposit date is 1/13/13. Print a Deposit Summary.

▶ Print Trial Balance from 01/01/13 to 01/13/13.

▶ Back up your work for the week. Use **Service (Backup Week 2)** as the file name.

Week 3: January 14-20, 2013

1/15/13

▶ Pay postage due 64 cents. Use Petty Cash. Number is 1 for Petty Cash.

▶ Print Petty Cash Account QuickReport in by clicking the Report button at the bottom of the Chart of Accounts. Print in Landscape orientation.

1/17/13

▶ Mr. Jackson's bathroom tile was installed on 1/14, 1/15 and 1/16. The installation was completed to his satisfaction. Bill him for 24 hours of repair service.

1/18/13
► Willow Brankowski's neighbor, Avi Levin, really liked the flowers in Willow's house and asked you to bring flowers to his home and office. This week he gave you Check No. 90-163 for 1 hour of errands and 1 hour of household chores. Add him to the customer list: Avi Levin, 236 West Camden Drive, Beverly Hills, CA 90210, Main Phone 310-555-0918, Payment Terms Net 10.

1/19/13
► Tonight is Samantha's big party. She has arranged for both you and Angela to supervise the party from 3 p.m. until 1 a.m. Bill Samantha Waters for 20 hours of party planning and supervision.
► Print a Customer Balance Summary Report.

1/20/13
► Record the checks received from customers for the week: Mr. Pirosky, $280, No. 9165; Dr. Sanchez, $455, No. 89162, Ms. Bailey, $150, No. 7-303, and Mr. Jackson, $325, No. 38197.
► Make the bank deposit for the week. Deposit date is 1/20/13. Print a Deposit Summary.
► Print Trial Balance from 01/01/13 to 01/20/13.
► Back up your work for the week. Use **Service (Backup Week 3)** as the file name.

Week 4: January 21-27, 2013
1/23/13
► Samantha's party went so smoothly on the 19th that you went home at 11 p.m. rather than 1 a.m. Issue a Credit Memo to Samantha Waters for 2 hours of party planning and supervision. Apply the credit to Invoice 41 dated January 19, 2013.
► Drake Evans arranged to have his pets cared for by Your Name At Your Service during the past 7 days. Bill him for 1 hour of pet sitting each day. Drake wants to add a doggie door and a fenced area for his dog. Bill him 24 hours of repair service for the planning and overseeing of the project.
► Use Petty Cash to pay for a box of file folders to be used immediately in reorganizing some of the files in the office, $14.84. (This is an expense and is Check 2 for Petty Cash.)
► Print a Petty Cash Account QuickReport in Landscape. Fit the report to one page wide.

1/24/13
► You arranged for theater tickets, dinner reservations, and an after-theater surprise party for Dr. Anderson to celebrate his wife's birthday. Bill him for 4 hours of errands, 3 hours shopping for the gift, and 5 hours of party planning.
► Received a bill—Invoice No. 9802—from Beverly Hills Flowers for $60 for office flowers for two weeks.
► Received a bill—Invoice No. 81116—from Sunshine Gasoline, $355 for the bi-weekly gasoline charge.
► Write a check to Bruin Stationers for the purchase of a new printer for the office, $500. (*Note:* If you get a warning to use Pay Bills because we owe the company money, click Continue Writing Check.) Print the check using standard-style checks.

1/27/13

▶ Dr. Sanchez has arranged for Your Name At Your Service to feed and walk his dogs every day. Bill him for pet sitting, 1 hour per day for the past two weeks. In addition, Dr. Sanchez is going to have a party and wants Your Name At Your Service to plan it for him. Bill him for 20 hours party planning. When the dogs were puppies they did some damage to the interior of the house. In order to prepare for the party several areas in the house need to be reorganized and repaired. Bill him for 18 hours of household chores and 20 hours of repairs.

▶ Write checks to pay for telephone, rent, and utilities. The telephone company will need to be added to the Vendor List. Vendor information is provided in each transaction. Print the checks using standard-style checks. They may be printed as a batch or individually.
  - Monthly telephone bill: $150, Bel Air Telephone. Add the vendor: Bel Air Telephone, Main Phone 310-555-4972, 2015 Beverly Boulevard, Bel Air, CA 90047, Payment Terms Net 30.
  - Monthly rent for office space: $1,500, Robertson Realtors
  - Monthly utility bill $477 for: water $183 and gas and electric $294, Westside Utilities.

▶ Prepare and print in Portrait orientation an Unpaid Bills Detail Report for January 27.

▶ Pay bills for all amounts due on or before January 27. Print check(s).

▶ Prepare a Check Detail Report from 1/1/13 to 1/27/13. Use Landscape orientation and fit report to one page wide.

▶ Record payments received from customers: Ms. Waters, $600, No. 4692; Dr. Sanchez, $1,550, No. 7942; Mr. Evans, $735, No. 235; Dr. Anderson, $495, No. 601; Ms. Bailey, $140, No. 923-10. (If any of the payments are not payments in full, leave as an underpayment. Include the Memo: Partial Payment.)

▶ Make the bank deposit for the week. Deposit date is 1/27/13. Print a Deposit Summary.

▶ Print Customer Balance Detail Report in Portrait orientation for All Transactions.

▶ Print Trial Balance from 01/01/13 to 01/27/13.

▶ Back up your work for the week. Use **Service (Backup Week 4)** as the file name.

Week 5: January 28-30, 2013
1/30/13

▶ Write a check for your monthly withdrawal, $1,200.

▶ Because a fax machine is a business necessity, you decided to give your new fax machine to Your Name At Your Service. Record this additional $350 investment of equipment by you.

▶ Because they are remodeling the offices, Robertson Realtors decreased the amount of rent to $1,000 per month. Correct and reprint the check for rent.

▶ Record adjusting entries for:
  - Business Vehicle Insurance, $200
  - Office Supplies Used, $150
  - Depreciation: Business Vehicles, $500 and Office Furniture/Equipment, $92

▶ Print Trial Balance from 01/01/13 to 01/30/13.

▶ Back up your work for the week. Use **Service (Backup Week 5)** as the file name.

End of the Month: January 31, 2013

Beverly Hills Bank		
1234 Rodeo Drive		
Beverly Hills, CA 90210		

Your Name At Your Service
2789 Robertson Boulevard
Beverly Hills, CA 90210

Beginning Balance, 1/1/13			$25,350.00
1/1/13, Transfer		100.00	25,250.00
1/6/13, Deposit	2,070.00		27,320.00
1/7/13, Check 1		25.00	27,295.00
1/7/13, Check 2		250.00	27,045.00
1/13/13, Deposit	2,280.00		29,325.00
1/15/13, Check 3		500.00	28,825.00
1/16/13, Check 4		255.00	28,570.00
1/20/13, Deposit	1,270.00		29,840.00
1/28/13, Check 5		500.00	29,340.00
1/29/13, Check 7		1,000.00	28,340.00
1/31/13, Payment: Business Vehicle Loan: interest $551.87; principal $177.57		729.44	27,610.56
1/31/13, Payment: Office Furniture/ Equipment Loan: interest $59.45; principal $15.44		74.89	27,535.67
1/31/13, Service Charge		25.00	27,510.67
1/31/13, Interest	53.00		27,563.67
1/31/13, Ending Balance			$27,563.67

► Prepare the bank reconciliation using the following bank statement. Record any adjustments necessary as a result of the bank statement.
► Print a Reconciliation Detail Report.
► Print the following reports as of 1/31/13:
  o Trial Balance from 1/1/13 through 1/31/13 in Portrait.
  o Cash Flow Forecast from 2/1/13 through 2/28/13 in Landscape.
  o Statement of Cash Flows from 1/1/13 through 1/31/13 in Portrait.
  o Standard Profit and Loss Statement from 1/1/13 through 1/31/13 in Portrait.
► Transfer the net income/retained earnings to owner's capital account.
► Close the Drawing account
► Close the period as of 01/31/13. Do not use any passwords.
► Prepare a Standard Balance Sheet as of 1/31/13. Print in Portrait
► Prepare the Journal from 1/1/13 through 1/31/13, expand the report, print in Landscape orientation, and Fit to 1 page wide.
► Create an Archive Backup named **Service (Backup Archive 01-31-13).qbb**
► Back up your work for the week. Use **Service (Backup Complete)** as the file name.

NAME _____

TRANSMITTAL

SECTION 1 PRACTICE SET: YOUR NAME AT YOUR SERVICE

Attach the following documents and reports:

Week 1
Account Listing
Trial Balance, January 1, 2013
Bill: Bruin Stationers (Optional
Invoice No. 35: Ricardo Sanchez
Invoice No. 36: Samantha Waters
Invoice No. 37: Mikhail Pirosky
Invoice No. 38: Gloria Bailey
Bill: Western Insurance (Optional))
Payment Receipt: John Anderson
    (Optional)
Payment Receipt: Jorge Perez (Optional)
Payment Receipt: Mikhail Pirosky
    (Optional)
Payment Receipt: Jeff Jackson (Optional)
Sales Receipt No. 22: Fatema Nasseri
Unpaid Bills Detail, January 6, 2013
Check No. 1: Beverly Hills Flowers
Check No. 2: Sunshine Gasoline
Deposit Summary, January 6, 2013
Trial Balance, January 6, 2013

Week 2
Payment Receipt: Ricardo Sanchez
    (Optional)
Payment Receipt: Keiko Lim (Optional)
Payment Receipt: Willow Brankowski
    (Optional)
Payment Receipt: Drake Evans (Optional)
Payment Receipt: Will Ashford (Optional)
Bill: Sunshine Gasoline (Optional)
Bill: Beverly Hills Flowers (Optional)
Sales Receipt No. 23: Willow Brankowski
Invoice No. 39: Jeff Jackson
Credit Memo: Bruin Stationers
Check No. 3: Brentwood Automotive
Check No. 4: Bruin Stationers
Invoice No. 38 (Corrected): Gloria Bailey
Deposit Summary, January 13, 2013

Week 3
Petty Cash QuickReport, January 15, 2013
Invoice No. 40: Jeff Jackson
Sales Receipt No. 24: Avi Levin
Invoice No. 41: Samantha Waters
Customer Balance Summary
Payment Receipt: Mikhail Pirosky (Optional)
Payment Receipt: Ricardo Sanchez (Optional)
Payment Receipt: Gloria Bailey (Optional)
Payment Receipt: Jeff Jackson (Optional)
Deposit Summary, January 20, 2013

Week 4
Credit Memo No. 42: Samantha Waters
Invoice No. 43: Drake Evans
Petty Cash QuickReport, January 23, 2013
Invoice No. 44: John Anderson
Check No. 5: Bruin Stationers
Invoice No. 45: Ricardo Sanchez
Check No. 6: Bel Air Telephone
Check No. 7: Robertson Realtors
Check No. 8: Westside Utilities
Unpaid Bills Detail, January 27, 2013
Check No. 9: Beverly Hills Flowers
Check Detail, January 1-27, 2013
Payment Receipt: Samantha Waters (Optional)
Payment Receipt: Ricardo Sanchez (Optional)
Payment Receipt: Drake Evans (Optional)
Payment Receipt: John Anderson (Optional)
Payment Receipt: Gloria Bailey (Optional)
Deposit Summary, January 27, 2013
Customer Balance Detail
Trial Balance, January 27, 2013

Week 5
Check 10 Your Name
Check No. 7 (Corrected): Robertson Realtors
Trial Balance, January 30, 2013

End of the Month
Bank Reconciliation Detail Report
Trial Balance, January 31, 2013
Cash Flow Forecast, February 2013
Statement of Cash Flows, January 2013
Profit and Loss, January 2013
Balance Sheet January 31, 2013
Journal, January 2013

SALES AND RECEIVABLES: MERCHANDISING BUSINESS

LEARNING OBJECTIVES

At the completion of this chapter, you will be able to:

1. Enter sales transactions for a retail business.
2. Prepare invoices that use sales tax, have sales discounts, and exceed a customer's credit limit.
3. Prepare sales orders; and then, once fulfilled, use to prepare a Custom S. O. Invoice
4. Prepare transactions for cash sales with sales tax.
5. Prepare transactions for customers using credit cards.
6. Add new accounts to the Chart of Accounts and new sales items to the Item List.
7. Add new customers and modify existing customer records.
8. Delete and void invoices.
9. Prepare credit memos with and without refunds.
10. Record customer payments on account with and without discounts.
11. Deposit checks and credit card receipts for sales and customer payments.
12. Record a transaction for a NSF check.
13. Customize report preferences and prepare and print Customer Balance Detail Reports, Open Invoice Reports, Sales Reports, and Inventory Valuation Reports.
14. View a QuickReport and use the QuickZoom feature.
15. Use the Customer Center to obtain information regarding credit customers.

ACCOUNTING FOR SALES AND RECEIVABLES IN A MERCHANDISING BUSINESS

Rather than using a traditional Sales Journal to record transactions using debits and credits and special columns, QuickBooks uses an invoice to record sales transactions for accounts receivable in the Accounts Receivable Register. Because cash sales do not involve accounts receivable, a Sales Receipt is prepared, and QuickBooks puts the money from a cash sale into the Undeposited Funds account until a bank deposit is made. Instead of being recorded within special journals, cash receipts transactions are entered as activities. However, all transactions, regardless of the activity, are placed in the Journal behind the scenes. A new account, sales item, or customer can be added *on the fly* as transactions are entered. Customer information may be changed by editing the Customer List.

For a retail business, QuickBooks tracks inventory, maintains information on reorder limits, tracks the quantity of merchandise on hand, maintains information on the value of the inventory, computes the cost of goods sold using the average cost basis, and can inform you of the percentage of sales for each inventory item. Early-payment discounts as well as discounts to certain types of customers can be given. Different price levels may be created for sales items and/or customers.

Unlike many computerized accounting programs, QuickBooks makes error correction easy. A sales form may be edited, voided, or deleted in the same window where it was created or via an account register. If a sales form has been printed prior to correction, it may be reprinted after the correction has been made.

A multitude of reports are available when using QuickBooks. Accounts receivable reports include Customer Balance Summary and Customer Balance Detail reports. Sales reports provide information regarding the amount of sales by item. Transaction Reports by Customer are available as well as the traditional accounting reports such as Trial Balance, Profit and Loss, and Balance Sheet. QuickBooks also has graphing capabilities so that you can see and evaluate your accounts receivable and sales at the click of a button. Reports created in QuickBooks may be exported to Microsoft® Excel.

DOWNLOAD COMPANY FILES

Refer to Chapter 1 procedures for downloading company files. When you follow the steps for downloading company files, use

Company Master Files Chapters 5-8 (Student Data Files)

Once the files have been downloaded, make sure they are not marked as "Read Only" or "Archive" and then continue with Chapter 5.

TRAINING TUTORIAL

The following tutorial is a step-by-step guide to recording receivables (both cash and credit) for a fictitious company with fictitious employees. This company is called Student's Name Mountain Sports. In addition to recording transactions using QuickBooks, you will prepare several reports and graphs for the company. The tutorial for Student's Name Mountain Sports will continue in Chapters 6 and 7, when accounting for payables, bank reconciliations, financial statement preparation, and closing an accounting period for a merchandising business will be completed.

Since the company used in training is fictitious, there are transactions that will be entered for illustration but will not be able to be entered in a way that will take full advantage of QuickBooks. For example, in an actual business when a credit card is accepted for payment, the payment would be processed. QuickBooks can accept E-Checks, but cannot be done in the training. If there are supplemental or subscription enhancements to QuickBooks, they may be noted but will not be utilized.

COMPANY PROFILE: STUDENT'S NAME MOUNTAIN SPORTS

Student's Name Mountain Sports is a sporting goods store located in Mammoth Lakes, California. Previously, the company was open only during the winter. As a result Student's Name Mountain Sports specializes in equipment, clothing, and accessories for skiing and snowboarding. You have plans to expand into a year-round operation and will eventually provide merchandise for summer sports and activities. The company is a partnership between you and Larry Muir. Each partner has a 50 percent share of the business, and both of you devote all of your efforts to Student's Name Mountain Sports. You have several part-time employees who work in the evenings and on the weekends during ski season. There is a full-time bookkeeper and manager, Ruth Morgan, who oversees purchases, maintains the inventory, and keeps the books for the company.

DATES

As in Chapters 1-4, the year used for the screen shots is 2013, which is the same year as the version of the program. You may want to check with your instructor to see if you should use 2013 as the year for the transactions. The year you use in Chapter 5 should be the same year you use in Chapters 6 and 7.

PRINTING

As in Chapters 1-4, you will be instructed when to print business documents and reports. Everything that is to be printed within the chapter is listed on a transmittal sheet. The end-of- chapter problem also has everything to be printed listed on a transmittal sheet. In some instances, your instructor may direct you to change what you print. Always verify items to be printed with your instructor.

BASIC INSTRUCTIONS

In this chapter you will be entering both accounts receivable and cash sale transactions for a retail company that sells merchandise and charges its customers sales tax. As in previous chapters, all transactions are listed on memos. The transaction date will be the same date as the memo date unless otherwise specified within the transaction. Customer names, when necessary, will be given in the transaction. Unless otherwise specified, all terms for customers on account are Net 30 days.

Even when you are instructed to enter a transaction step-by-step, you should always refer to the memo for transaction details. Once a specific type of transaction has been entered in a step-by-step manner, additional transactions will be made without having instructions provided. Of course, you may always refer to instructions given for previous transactions for ideas or for steps used to enter those transactions.

OPEN A COMPANY—STUDENT'S NAME MOUNTAIN SPORTS

Use the Sports.qbw file to complete the training in Chapters 5, 6, and 7.

 Use the **Sports.qbw** file that you downloaded in the folder for **Company Master Files Chapters 5-8 (Student Data Files)** (instructions in Chapter 1), open **QuickBooks**, and open **Sports.qbw**

- If QuickBooks has received an update from Intuit, you may get a screen to Update Company. If so, click **Yes**

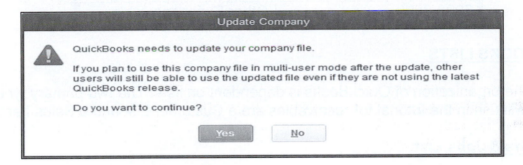

ADD YOUR NAME TO THE COMPANY NAME

As with previous companies, each student in the course will be working with the same company and printing the same documents. Personalizing the company name to include your name will help identify many of the documents you print during your training.

 Add your name to the company name

Click **Company** on the menu bar, click **Company Information**
In the Company Name textbox, drag through the words **Student's Name** to highlight
Type **your real name**
- Type your real name, *not* the words *Your Real Name*. For example, Pamela Powers would type—**Pamela Powers**.
Repeat for the Legal Name
Click **OK**
- The title bar now shows Your Name Mountain Sports and has a colored flag that is used as an additional identifier.

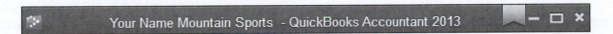

ACCOUNT NUMBERS

QuickBooks has a choice to use or not use account number for the accounts in the Chart of Accounts. In this section of the text, account numbers will be used.

The account numbering may be four or five digits. The structure is:

ACCOUNT NUMBER	TYPE OF ACCOUNT
1000-1999	Assets
2000-2999	Liabilities
3000-3099	Capital
4000-4999	Income or Revenue
5000-5999	Cost of Goods Sold
6000-6999	Expenses
7000-7999	Other Income
8000-8999	Other Expenses

QUICKBOOKS LISTS

Much of the organization of QuickBooks is dependent on lists. The two primary types of lists you will use in the tutorial for receivables are a Customer List and a Sales Item List.

Customers & Jobs List

The names, addresses, telephone numbers, credit terms, credit limits, balances, and tax terms for all established credit customers are contained in the Customers & Jobs List. The Customers & Jobs List is also the Accounts Receivable Ledger. You will be using the following Customers & Jobs List for established credit customers:

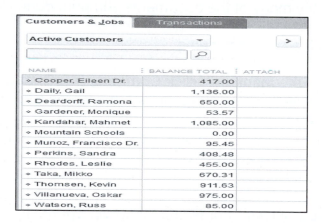

Item List

Sales are often made up of various types of income. In Your Name Mountain Sports there are several income accounts. In order to classify income regarding the type of sale, the sales account may have subaccounts. When recording a transaction for a sale, QuickBooks requires that a Sales Item be used. When the sales item is created, a sales account is required. When the sales item is used in a transaction, the income is credited to the appropriate sales/income account. For example, Ski Boots is a sales item and uses Equipment Income, a subaccount of Sales, when a transaction is recorded.

QuickBooks uses lists to organize sales items. Using lists for sales items allows for flexibility in billing and a more accurate representation of the way in which income is earned. If the company charges a standard price for an item, the price of the item will be included on the list. Your Name Mountain Sports sells all items at different prices, so the price given for each item is listed at 0.00. In a retail business with an inventory, the number of units on hand can be tracked; and, when the amount on hand gets to a predetermined limit, an order can be placed. The following Item List for the various types of merchandise and sales categories will be used for Your Name Mountain Sports:

NAME	DESCRIPTION	TYPE	ACCOUNT	TOTAL QUANTITY ON HAND	ON SALES ORDER	PRICE	ATTACH
Accessories	Sunglasses, Ski Wax, Sunscreen, Ski Holders, Boot Carriers, etc.	Inventory Part	4011 · Clothing & Accessory Sales	800	0	0.00	
Bindings-Skis	Ski Bindings	Inventory Part	4012 · Equipment Sales	50	0	0.00	
Bindings-Snow	Snowboard Bindings	Inventory Part	4012 · Equipment Sales	50	0	0.00	
Boots	After Ski Boots and Shoes	Inventory Part	4011 · Clothing & Accessory Sales	20	0	0.00	
Boots-Ski	Ski Boots	Inventory Part	4012 · Equipment Sales	15	0	0.00	
Boots-Snowbrd	Snowboard Boots	Inventory Part	4012 · Equipment Sales	12	0	0.00	
Gloves	Gloves	Inventory Part	4011 · Clothing & Accessory Sales	22	0	0.00	
Hats	Hats and Scarves	Inventory Part	4011 · Clothing & Accessory Sales	30	0	0.00	
Pants-Ski	Ski Pants	Inventory Part	4011 · Clothing & Accessory Sales	95	0	0.00	
Pants-Snowbrd	Snowboard Pants	Inventory Part	4011 · Clothing & Accessory Sales	50	0	0.00	
Parkas	Parkas and Jackets	Inventory Part	4011 · Clothing & Accessory Sales	75	0	0.00	
Poles-Ski	Ski Poles	Inventory Part	4012 · Equipment Sales	18	0	0.00	
Skis	Snow Skis	Inventory Part	4012 · Equipment Sales	50	0	0.00	
Snowboard	Snowboard	Inventory Part	4012 · Equipment Sales	30	0	0.00	
Socks	Ski and Snowboard Socks	Inventory Part	4011 · Clothing & Accessory Sales	75	0	0.00	
Sweaters	Sweaters & Shirts	Inventory Part	4011 · Clothing & Accessory Sales	75	0	0.00	
Underwear	Long Underwear	Inventory Part	4011 · Clothing & Accessory Sales	33	0	0.00	
CA Sales Tax	CA Sales Tax	Sales Tax Item	2200 · Sales Tax Payable			8.0%	
Out of State	Out-of-state sale, exempt from sales tax	Sales Tax Item	2200 · Sales Tax Payable			0.0%	

CUSTOMIZE REPORT PREFERENCES

The report format used in one company may not be appropriate for all companies that use QuickBooks. The preferences selected in QuickBooks are only for the current company. In Section 1 of the text, report preferences were changed for Computer Consulting by Your Name, but those changes have no effect on Your Name Mountain Sports. The header/footer for reports in Your Name Mountain Sports must be customized to eliminate the printing of the date prepared, time prepared, and report basis as part of a report heading.

MEMO
DATE: January 1, 2013

Before recording any transactions or preparing any reports, customize the report format by removing the date prepared, time prepared, and report basis from report headings.

Customize the preferences as indicated in the memo

> Click **Edit**, click **Preferences**
> Click **Reports and Graphs**
> Click the **Company Preferences** tab
> Click the **Format** button
> Click the **Header/Footer** tab
> Click **Date Prepared**, **Time Prepared**, and **Report Basis** to deselect

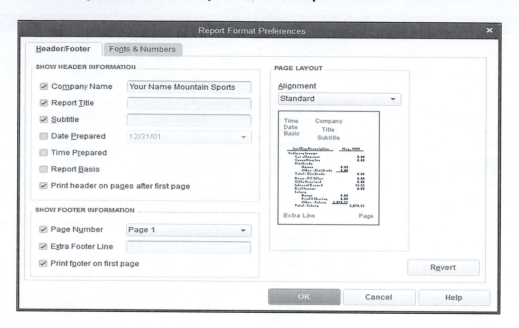

> Click **OK** to save the change
> Click **OK** to close **Preferences**

CUSTOMIZE BUSINESS FORMS

In QuickBooks it is possible to customize the business forms used in recording transactions. Forms that may be customized include Credit Memo, Estimate, Invoice, Purchase Order, Sales Order, Sales Receipt, Statement, and Donation. In addition to customizing the forms within QuickBooks, Intuit allows users to download templates of forms without charge by accessing the Forms/Intuit Community. To do this, click Lists menu, click Templates, click the Templates button, and click Download Templates.

In earlier chapters some student names included as part of the company name may not have printed on the same line as the company name. In order to provide more room for the company title, QuickBooks' Layout Designer must be used. Some business forms may be changed directly within the form, while others need to have the form duplicated. When you access an invoice, for example, QuickBooks uses a ready-made form. This is called a *template*. In order to make changes to an invoice, you must first duplicate the template and then make changes to it.

> # MEMO
> **DATE:** January 2, 2013
>
> Customize the Sales Receipt form, the Credit Memo form, the Custom Sales Order, and the template used for Product Invoices.

 Customize the Sales Receipt, the Credit Memo, and the Product Invoice

> Click the **Create Sales Receipts** icon to open a sales receipt
> Click the **Formatting** tab in the Sales Receipt Icon bar
> Click the **Customize Data Layout** icon

> - Look at the tabs for Header, Columns, Footer, and Print. Each tab has selections that you may select to indicate what is shown on the form when it is displayed on the screen or when it is printed.
> Click in the Default Title text box for Sales Receipt, highlight and delete the words Sales Receipt, key in **SALES RECEIPT**
> Click the **Layout Designer** button at the bottom of the Additional Customization screen
> - If you get a Layout Designer Message regarding overlapping fields, click **Do not display this message in the future**, and then click **OK**
> Once again, click the **Layout Designer** button at the bottom of the Additional Customization screen
> Point to one of the black squares (sizing handles) on the left border of the frame around the words SALES RECEIPT
> When the cursor turns into a double arrow, hold the primary (left) mouse button and drag until the size of the frame begins at **5 ½** on the ruler bar

> Click in the textbox for **Your Name Mountain Sports**
> Drag the right border of the frame until it is a **5 ¼** on the ruler bar

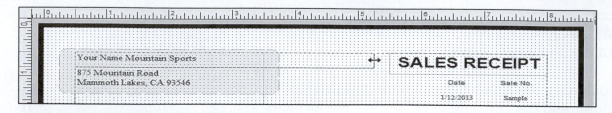

Click **OK** on Layout Designer

Click **OK** on the Additional Customization screen

Close the **Enter Sales Receipts** screen

Repeat the steps to customize the **Credit Memo** and the **Custom Sales Order**

- The Default Title should be in all capital letters, and the company name and form names should be resized.

When finished with the customization of the Credit Memo and Custom Sales Order, click **Lists** on the menu bar

Click **Templates**

- A template is a predesigned form. It defines what is shown on the form, determines the structure of the form, and contains the visual elements of the form.
- *Note:* The Custom Credit Memo, Custom Sales Receipt, and Custom Sales Order and have been added to the Template list.

From the Templates List, click **Intuit Product Invoice**

- The Intuit Product Invoice is designed to work on Intuit preprinted forms. In order to customize the invoice, a duplicate copy of the Intuit Product Invoice must be made.

Click the **Templates** button

Click **Duplicate**

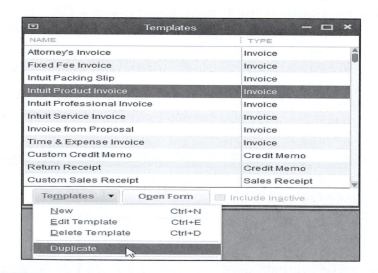

On the Select Template Type make sure Invoice is selected and click **OK**

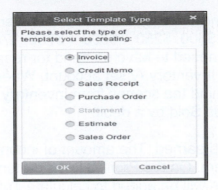

Make sure **Copy of: Intuit Product Invoice** is selected
Click the **Templates** button, click **Edit Template**

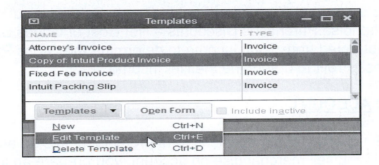

Click the **Additional Customization** button
Change the Default Title to **INVOICE**
Click the **Layout Designer** button
* If you get the Layout Designer message, click **OK**; and, then, click the Layout Designer button again.
Change the layout as instructed for SALES RECEIPTS

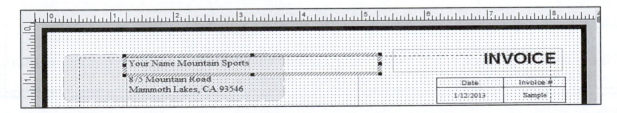

Click **OK** until you return to the Template List
Close the Template List

INVENTORY

When your company sells inventory items, QuickBooks keeps track of each inventory item, the number of items on hand, and the value of the items. Unless you use the Enterprise version of QuickBooks, the only inventory valuation method available for use is Average Cost. Average Cost adds the cost of all the inventory items together, divides by the total number of items on hand, and the result is the average cost. For example, if your company purchased 50 widgets for $5 and 50 widgets for $10, the average cost of the widgets would be: 50 * $5 = $<u>250</u>, 50 * $10 = $<u>500</u>, $250 + $500 = $750, $750 / 100 = $<u>7.50</u> When inventory items are purchased to have on hand for resale, QuickBooks shows the average cost of the item in the Inventory Asset account. When the item is sold, the average cost of the item is removed behind the scenes from Inventory Asset by a credit and transferred to the Cost of Goods Sold by a debit.

When an item is sold, income is earned. The amount of income earned will be different from the average cost of the item. On the Profit & Loss Statement all the income earned from different revenue accounts will be added to calculate Total Income. Since the income was earned by selling items, the cost of the items sold must be subtracted from income in order to calculate gross profit.

On the Profit & Loss Statement the total of Cost of Goods Sold is calculated as: Cost of Goods Sold – Merchandise Purchases Discounts = Net Cost of Goods Sold. The Net Cost of Goods Sold is subtracted from Total Income to determine the Gross Profit. Expenses are subtracted from Gross Profit to determine the Net Income.

ENTER SALES ON ACCOUNT

Because QuickBooks operates on a business form premise, a sale on account is entered via an invoice. When you sell merchandise on account, you prepare an invoice including sales tax and payment terms and QuickBooks records the transaction in the Journal and updates the customer's account automatically. QuickBooks allows you to set up different price levels for customers. Since our small company has not established sales prices for each item it sells, we will not be using Price Levels in this tutorial. For information on Price Levels, refer to Appendix B.

> **MEMO**
> **DATE:** January 2, 2013
>
> Bill the following: Invoice No. 1—An established customer, Russ Watson, purchased a pair of after-ski boots for $75.00 on account. Terms are Net 15.

 Record the sale on account shown in the transaction above.

Access a blank invoice as previously instructed in Chapter 2
If you do not want to display customer's history on the invoice, click the
   Hide history tab
- If you hide the history and the invoice becomes wider, resize by pointing to the right edge of the invoice until you get a double arrow, and then hold down the primary mouse button and drag to the left
Click the drop-down list arrow next to **CUSTOMER:JOB**, click **Watson, Russ**

Click the drop-down list arrow next to Intuit Product Invoice
Click **Copy of: Intuit Product Invoice** to use your customized invoice

- QuickBooks does not allow you to permanently change the default invoice. It should remember to use the same invoice if you enter several invoices at a time, but it may or may not revert back to the default invoice the next time you enter an invoice.
- Notice the change in the format when using a product invoice rather than a service invoice.

Tab to **Date** and enter the date of **01/02/2013**
Invoice No. **1** should be showing in the **Invoice #** box
There is no PO Number to record, Terms should be indicated as **Net 15**
Tab to or click **QUANTITY**, type **1**

- The quantity is 1 because you are billing for one pair of after-ski boots.

Click the drop-down list arrow next to **ITEM CODE**

- Refer to the memo above and the Item list for appropriate billing information.

Click **Boots** to bill for one pair of after-ski boots

- The Description **After Ski Boots and Shoes** is automatically inserted.

Once the ITEM CODE has been entered (Boots), an icon appears in the Quantity column

Click on the icon to see the current availability of Boots in stock

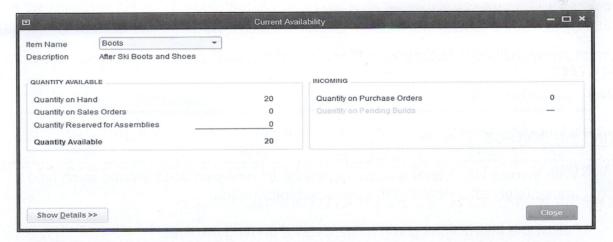

Click **Close** on the Current Availability screen
Tab to or click **PRICE EACH**
Type in the amount of the after-ski boots **75**

- Because the price on ski boots differs with each style, QuickBooks has not been given the price in advance. It must be inserted during the invoice preparation. If you chose to set up separate sales items for each type of ski boot, sales prices could be and should be assigned. In addition, different price levels could be designated for the item.

Click in the drop-down list arrow for **CUSTOMER MESSAGE**

- If you get a dialog box regarding Price Levels, click **Do not display this message in the future**, and click **OK**. (For information regarding Price Levels, refer to Appendix B.)
- QuickBooks will automatically calculate the total in the **AMOUNT** column.
- Because this is a taxable item, QuickBooks inserts the word **Tax** in the **TAX** column.

Click the message **Thank you for your business.**

- Message is inserted in the **CUSTOMER MESSAGE** box.
- Notice that QuickBooks automatically calculates the tax for the invoice and adds it to the invoice total.

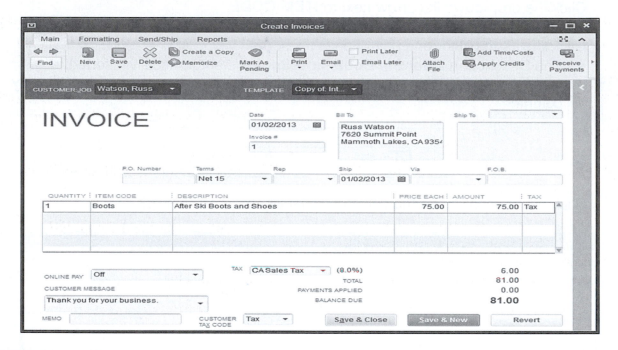

PRINT AN INVOICE

 With Invoice No. 1 on the screen, print the invoice with lines around each field immediately after entering the corrected information

Follow the instructions given previously for printing invoices

- If you get a message regarding printing Shipping Labels, click the **Do not display this message in the future** checkbox, click **OK**

Make sure that the check box for **Do not print lines around each field** does **not** have a check mark; if it does, click the box to remove the check mark.

When finished printing, click the **Save & Close** button on the bottom of the **Create Invoices** screen to record the invoice

ANALYZE AN INVOICE IN THE JOURNAL

As learned previously, QuickBooks records all transactions in the Journal. When recording sales in a merchandizing business, QuickBooks will not only debit Accounts Receivable and credit Sales, it will also debit Cost of Goods Sold, credit Inventory Asset, debit Sales Discounts (if a discount was used), and credit Sales Tax Payable. This is important because it allows QuickBooks to keep an accurate record of inventory on hand, to calculate the Cost of Goods Sold, keep track of sales discounts used, and record the liability for sales taxes.

 Prepare a Journal for January 1-2, 2013 as previously instructed and analyze the entry for Invoice 1

Click the **Do not display this message in the future** on the Collapsing and Expanding Transactions dialog box, then click **OK**
Click the **Expand** button
Enter the dates **From 01/01/13** and **To 01/02/13**, press **Tab**

Your Name Mountain Sports									
Journal									
January 1 - 2, 2013									
Trans # ◇	Type ◇	Date ◇	Num ◇	Adj ◇	Name ◇	Memo ◇	Account ◇	Debit ◇	Credit
48	Invoice	01/02/2013	1		Watson, Russ		1200 · Accounts Receivable	81.00	
					Watson, Russ	After Ski Boots and Shoes	4011 · Clothing & Accessory Sales		75.00
					Watson, Russ	After Ski Boots and Shoes	1120 · Inventory Asset		30.00
					Watson, Russ	After Ski Boots and Shoes	5000 · Cost of Goods Sold	30.00	
					State Board of Equalization	CA Sales Tax	2200 · Sales Tax Payable		6.00
								111.00	111.00
TOTAL								111.00	111.00

- Note the $81.00 debit to Accounts Receivable is for the total amount of the invoice. This amount is matched with corresponding credits to Clothing & Accessory Sales for $75.00 (the amount of the sale) and to Sales Tax Payable for $6.00 (the sales tax collected)
- There is also a debit to Cost of Goods Sold for $30 (the average cost of the item) and credits to Inventory Asset for $30 (the average cost of the item). Since you

no longer have the item available for sale, this removes it from the inventory on hand and places the value into the cost of goods sold.
- Because QuickBooks removes the average cost of the asset from Inventory Assets and puts it into Cost of Goods Sold, the Total of the transaction recorded for Invoice 1 includes this and becomes $111.00 not $81.00

Close the Journal without printing
- If you get a Memorize Report dialog box, click **Do not display this message in the future**; and then, click **No**

INVENTORY ASSETS, COST OF GOODS SOLD, SALES TAX LIABILITY

The following illustrates the type of accounts and calculations used in the Journal for an invoice entered for the sale of a pair of after ski boots:

Sales: The amount for which an inventory item is sold is entered into the revenue account. The pair of after ski boots was sold for $75 and is recorded as a credit to increase income.

Inventory Assets: When a merchandise item is on hand it is an asset. QuickBooks uses Inventory Asset as the account. To reduce an asset, you credit the account for the value of the item. QuickBooks uses the Average Cost method of inventory valuation. As previously illustrated, the average cost of an item is calculated by dividing the total value of the item by the number of items. If, for example, there are 20 pairs of after ski boots in stock, the Average Cost is calculated:

> 10 pair cost $40 to purchase = $400
> 10 pair cost $20 to purchase = $200
> Total value = $600
> $600 total value / 20 pairs of boots = $30 average cost per pair

Cost of Goods Sold: Is used when there is merchandise to keep track of the amount the merchandise cost the company. This amount is deducted from sales to determine the amount of gross profit earned when the merchandise sold. If the pair of after ski boots is sold for $75 and it cost the company $30, the amount of gross profit is $45. (Sales - Cost of Goods Sold = Gross Profit). Since the cost of goods sold will ultimately decrease the revenue, you debit the account.

Sales Tax: When sales tax is collected, it is a liability that is owed to the government. To record the liability, you credit the liability account—Sales Tax Payable

ENTER TRANSACTIONS USING MORE THAN ONE SALES ITEM AND SALES TAX

Frequently, sales to customers will be for more than one item. For example, new bindings are usually purchased along with a new pair of skis. Invoices can be prepared to bill a customer for several items at once.

MEMO
DATE: January 3, 2013

Bill the following: Invoice No. 2—Every year Dr. Francisco Munoz gets new ski equipment. Bill him for his equipment purchase for this year: skis, $425; ski bindings, $175; ski boots, $250; and ski poles, $75.

 Record a transaction on account for a sale involving several taxable sales items:

Click the **Create Invoices** icon, and then click the drop-down list arrow next to
  CUSTOMER:JOB
Click **Munoz, Francisco Dr.**
Verify the Template as **Copy of: Intuit Product Invoice**
• Since QuickBooks does not let you select a specific invoice as the default, you will need to verify that you are using the Copy of: Intuit Product Invoice.
Tab to or click **Date**, enter **01/03/13** as the date
Make sure the number **2** is showing in the **Invoice #** box
There is no PO No. to record, Terms should be indicated as **2% 10 Net 30**
• The terms mean that if Dr. Munoz's payment is received within ten days, he will get a two percent discount. Otherwise, the full amount is due in 30 days.
Tab to or click **QUANTITY**, type **1**
Click the drop-down list arrow next to **ITEM CODE**
Click **Skis**
• **Skis** is inserted as the item code.
• **Snow Skis** is inserted as the **DESCRIPTION**.
Tab to or click **PRICE EACH,** enter **425**
• Because Dr. Munoz is a taxable customer and Skis are a taxable item, sales tax is indicated by **Tax** in the **TAX** column.
Tab to or click the second line for **QUANTITY**, type **1**
Click the drop-down list arrow next to **ITEM CODE**
Click **Bindings-Skis**
• **Ski Bindings** is inserted as the **DESCRIPTION**.
Tab to or click **PRICE EACH**, enter **175**
• Notice that sales tax is indicated by **Tax** in the **TAX** column.
Repeat the above steps to enter the information for the ski boots and the ski poles and use a quantity of 1 for each item
Click the drop-down list arrow next to **CUSTOMER MESSAGE**
Click **Thank you for your business.**
• QuickBooks automatically calculated the tax for the invoice and added it to the invoice total.

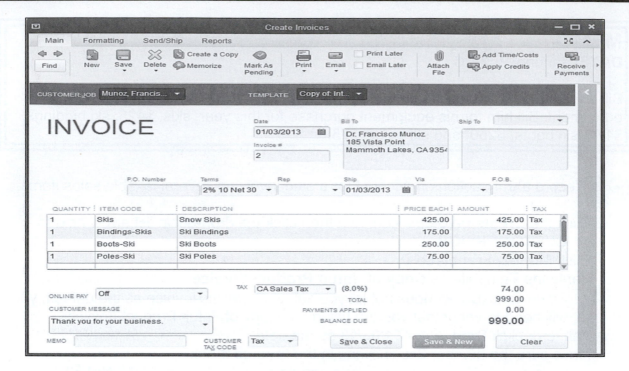

Print the invoice, and click **Save & New**

EMAIL INVOICES (READ FOR INFORMATION ONLY)

In addition to printing and mailing invoices, QuickBooks® Pro 2013 allows invoices to be sent to customers via email. While this text will not actually require sending invoices by email, it is important to be aware of this time-saving feature. In order to use the email feature of QuickBooks, you must subscribe to one of QuickBooks other services. However, QuickBooks now supports different Web Mail providers and can be used without charge or any QuickBooks subscriptions. Web mail providers include: Gmail, Hotmail, Yahoo Mail, Outlook, Outlook Express, Windows Mail, or your own SMTP email provider.

 Information only: To email an invoice:

In order to activate email, click **Edit** on the menu bar, click **Preferences**, and click **Send Forms**
- If you have an active subscription for QuickBooks Connect, Intuit Data Protect, QuickBooks Attached Documents, Intuit Commissions Manager, or QuickBooks Time and Billing Manager, you may use QuickBooks Email

Since Your Name Mountain Sports does not have any subscriptions, click **Web Mail**

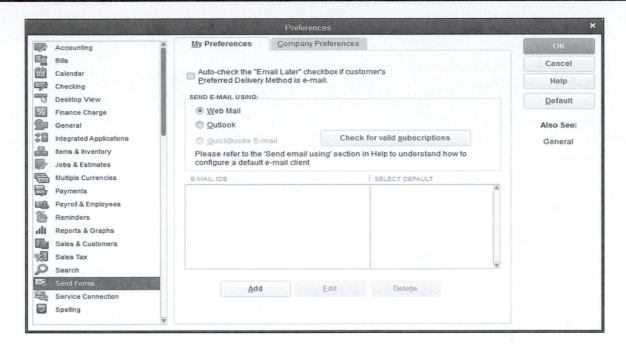

Click the **Add** button to create your Email Id

On the Add Email Info dialog box, enter your Email ID, click the drop-down list arrow for Email Provider, click the one you use, the information for Server Name and Port should automatically be entered on the form, click **OK**

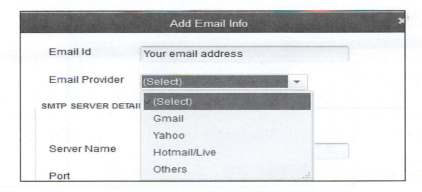

Click **OK** to close the Preferences screen

With the invoice for Dr. Munoz showing on the Create Invoices screen, click the drop-down list arrow next to **Send**

Click **Email Invoice**

- Web Mail and your Email address is being used
- To: should be the email address of your customer
  - From: is your email address
  - Subject should be: Invoice 2 from Your Name Mountain Sports
  - The Email Text is prewritten but may be changed
  - The Invoice will be attached to the message as a PDF file

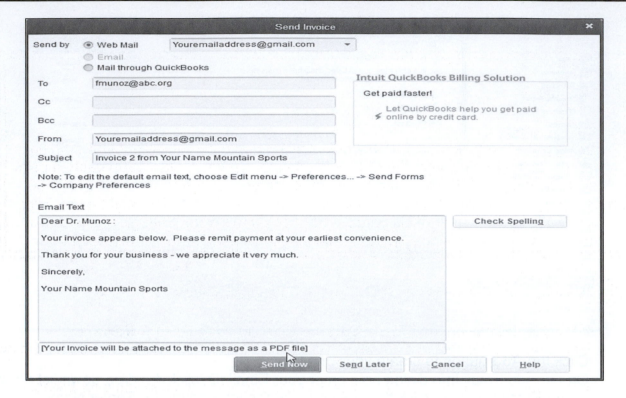

Click **Send Now**
On the Provide Email Information, enter the Password for your email account, click
  OK to send the email

When the email has been sent, you will get a QuickBooks Information box, click **OK**

PREPARE INVOICES WITHOUT STEP-BY-STEP INSTRUCTIONS

MEMO

DATE: January 3, 2013

Bill the following:

Invoice No. 3—We give Mountain Schools a special rate on equipment and clothing for the ski team. This year the school purchases 5 pairs of skis, $299 each; 5 pairs of ski bindings, $100 each; and 5 sets of ski poles, $29 each. Terms 2/10 Net 30.

Invoice No. 4—Sandra Perkins purchased a new ski outfit: 1 parka, $249; a hat, $25; a sweater, $125; 1 pair of ski pants, $129; long underwear, $68; gloves, $79; ski socks, $15.95; sunglasses, $89.95; and a boot carrier, $2.95. Terms Net 15.

 Prepare and print invoices without step-by-step instructions.

If Invoice 2 is still on the screen, click the **Next** arrow or **Save & New**
Enter the two transactions in the memo above. Refer to instructions given for the two previous transactions entered.

- Always use the Item List to determine the appropriate sales items for billing.
- Use *"Thank you for your business."* as the message for these invoices.
- If you make an error, correct it.
- Print each invoice immediately after you enter the information for it, and print lines around each field.
- To go from one invoice to the next, click **Save & New** at the bottom of the **Create Invoices** screen or click **New** at the top of the invoice.
- If you get a Check Spelling on Form message for Snowboard, click **Ignore All**
- Click **Save & Close** after Invoice No. 4 has been entered and printed.

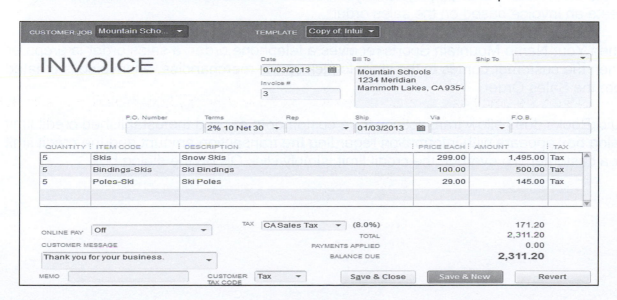

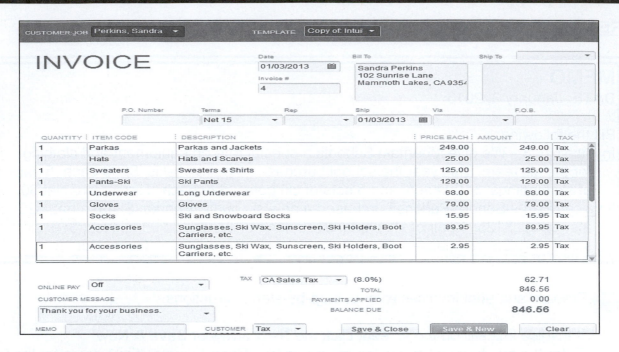

ENTER SALES ORDERS

Sales orders help you manage the sale of the products your customers order. Using sales orders is optional and must be selected as a Preference. Typically, when a customer places an order, a sales order is filled out with the customer information and the items ordered. The sales order is fulfilled when you get the products to your customer. Once the sales order is fulfilled, you create an invoice based on your sales order.

When you create and fill out a sales order, you haven't recorded the sale—you've only recorded the information you need to fulfill the order. The sale is recorded only after you create an invoice. For example, items you sell are not deducted from inventory until you create an invoice based on the sales order.

When Your Name Mountain Sports receives a telephone order, a sales order is prepared. When the customer comes to the store to pick up the merchandise, an invoice is created from the Sales Order.

QuickBooks does allow transactions for a customer to exceed the established credit limit. A dialog box appears with information regarding the transaction amount and the credit limit for a customer. To override the credit limit, simply click OK on the dialog box.

MEMO

DATE: January 3, 2013

Sales Order 1—Kevin Thomsen broke his snowboard when he was going down his favorite run, Dragon's Back. He called the store and ordered a new one without bindings for $499.95

Sales Order 1—Russ Watson called the store to order some new skis and bindings. Prepare Sales Order 2 for snow skis, $599, and ski bindings, $179. In case he doesn't come to the store to pick up his order, add his shipping address: 7620 Summit Point, Mammoth Lakes, CA 93546.

 Prepare Sales Orders

Click the **Sales Orders** icon on the Home Page

Click the drop-down list arrow for Customer:Job, click **Kevin Thomsen**

The form should be Custom Sales Order

- If it is not, click the drop-down list arrow and click Custom Sales Order
- Tab to or click **Date**, enter **01/03/13** as the date
- Make sure the number **1** is showing in the **S.O. No.** box
- Since Kevin is picking up the snowboard at the store, do not enter a Ship To address

Click in the drop-down list arrow in the **ITEM** column

Click **Snowboard**, press Tab until you get to the **ORDERED** column

Enter **1** for **ORDERED**, press Tab

Enter the **RATE** of **499.95**, press Tab

Click the drop-down list arrow for **CUSTOMER MESSAGE**, and click **Thank you for your business**

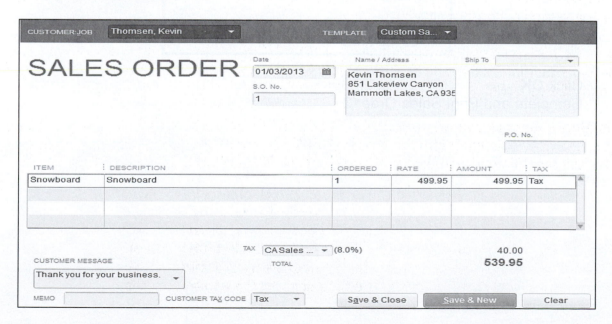

Click **Print** and print the Sales Order

- If you get a Check Spelling on Form message for Snowboard, click **Ignore All**
- If you get a message regarding Shipping Labels, click **Do not display this message in the future** and then, click **OK**
- After printing the Sales Order, notice the addition of the Invoiced and Clsd columns.

Click **Save & New**

Prepare Sales Order 2 for Russ Watson as previously instructed

Add the Ship To address

Click the drop-down list arrow for **Ship To**

Click **<Add New>**

The Address Name **Ship To 1** should appear automatically

Tab to **Address**

Key **Russ Watson**, press Enter

Key **7620 Summit Point**, press Tab

City is **Mammoth Lakes**, press Tab

State is **CA**, press Tab

Zip Code is **93546**

- Leave the check marks in **Show this window again when address is incomplete or unclear** and in **Default shipping address**

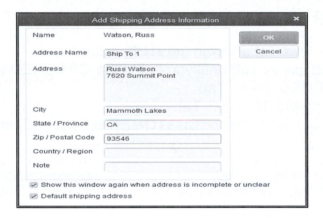

Click **OK**

Complete and Print Sales Order 2

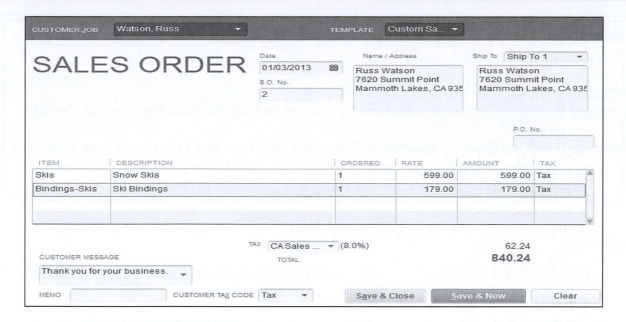

Print the Sales Order

Since this transaction puts Russ over his established credit limit, a Recording Transaction message appears

- If you click **No**, you are returned to the sales in order to make changes.
- If you click **Yes**, the sales order will be printed.

Click **Yes** to exceed the credit limit go to the Print One Invoice screen

After printing, click **Save & Close**

CREATE INVOICES FOR SALES ORDERS

When a sales order is filled, shipped, or picked up at the store, an invoice is created. Creating an invoice enters the sale in the Journal, decreases inventory on hand, and increases accounts receivable and sales.

MEMO
DATE: January 3, 2013

Create invoices from the following sales orders:
Invoice 5—Kevin Thomsen came to the store to pick up his new snowboard. Terms 1% 10 Net 30.
Invoice 6—Russ Watson decided to come into the store and pick up his new skis, and bindings. He decided to add a ski carrier for $10.99 to his purchase Payment Terms 1% 10 Net 30. (Include the additional purchase on Invoice 6.)

 Create Invoices from Sales Orders 1 and 2

Click the **Sales Orders** icon and click **Previous** until the Sales Order 1 is shown
Click **Create Invoice** on the Create Sales Orders Icon bar

Make sure **Create invoice for all of the sales order(s).** is selected, and then click **OK**

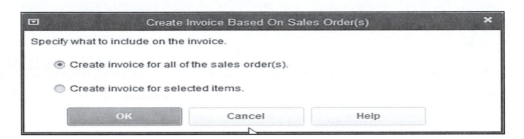

- Invoice 5 appears on the screen. The template used is Custom S. O. Invoice.
Customize the form to allow room for your name and to print the default title as
INVOICE
Click **Formatting** on the Create Invoices Icon bar
Click **Customize Data Layout**
Key in **INVOICE** for the Default Title
Click **Layout Designer** and adjust the size of the area for Your Name Mountain Sports and for INVOICE
  - If you get the message regarding Layout Designer, click **OK**; click Layout Designer again; and then resize.
Click **OK** to close Layout Designer, and then click **OK** on Additional Customization
- Notice the columns for Ordered, Prev. Invoiced, Backordered, and Invoiced.

- The Terms of 1% 10 Net 30 automatically appear because they are the standard terms for Kevin Thomsen.

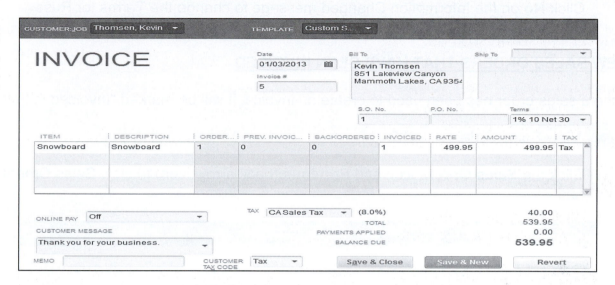

Click **Ignore All** on the Check Spelling on Form for Snowboard
Print the invoice and then close Create Invoices
Use Sales Orders to create the Invoice for Russ Watson
When Invoice 6 appears on the screen, add the additional item:

  Click the drop-down list arrow for ITEM, select **Accessories**, and enter **1** in the INVOICED COLUMN, and **10.99** in the RATE column

- If you get a message box for Custom Pricing, click **No**

Make sure you use **Terms** of **1% 10 Net 30**

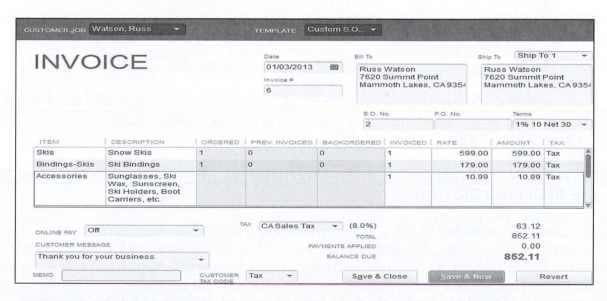

Print the invoice
Click **Yes** on the Recording Transaction message to exceed the credit limit

- If you get a Recording Transaction message about the sales order being linked to the invoice, click **Yes**

Click **No** on the Information Changed message to change the Terms for Russ

Close Create Invoices

VIEW SALES ORDERS THAT HAVE BEEN INVOICED

Once a sales order has been used to create an invoice, it will be marked "Invoiced in Full"

 View Sales Orders 1 and 2

Click the **Sales Orders** icon and **Previous** (back arrow icon) to view Sales Orders 1 and 2

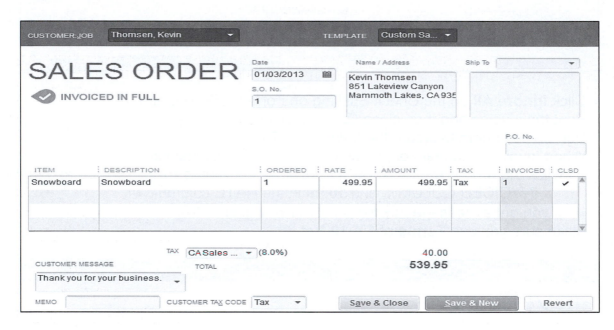

- Note the stamped "INVOICED IN FULL" on both Sales Orders and the 1 in the Invoice column and the check mark in the Clsd (Closed) column.

Close Sales Orders

ENTER A TRANSACTION EXCEDING A CUTOMER'S CREDIT LIMI AND ADD A WORD TO THE SPELLING DICTIONARY

When a customer is added to the Customer List and a complete setup is performed, the file tab for Address Info will appear and the address information is entered for the customer. To establish a credit limit for a customer, you click on the Payment Settings tab and enter the amount in the Credit Limit field. If a transaction is entered that exceeds the credit limit, you may choose to exceed the limit. This does not change the credit limit for the customer.

As was experienced in the last set of transactions, QuickBooks has a spelling check. When the previous invoices were printed, QuickBooks Spell Check identified snowboard as being misspelled. In fact, the word is spelled correctly. It just needs to be added to the QuickBooks dictionary. This is done by clicking the Add button when the word is highlighted in spell check.

MEMO

DATE: January 4, 2013

Bill the following: <u>Invoice No. 7</u>—Monique Gardener decided to get a new snowboard, $489.95; snowboard bindings, $159.99; snowboard boots, $249; and a special case to carry her boots, $49.95. Terms are Net 30.

 Prepare Invoice No. 7 as instructed previously
Make sure to use **Copy of: Intuit Product Invoice** for the Template

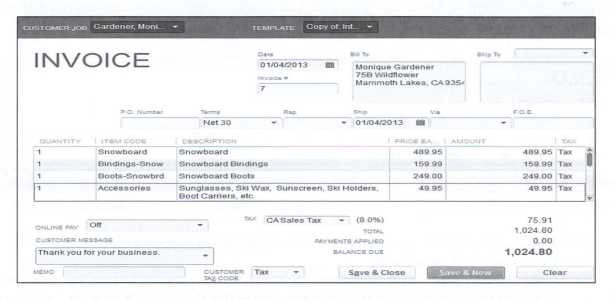

Print the invoice
When the **Check Spelling on Form** appears and the word **Snowboard** is
   highlighted, click the **Add** button

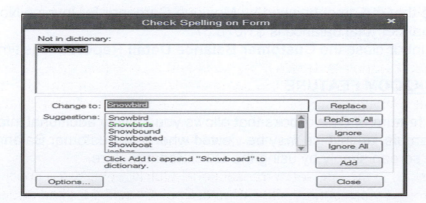

A Recording Transaction message box appears; click **Yes** to exceed the credit limit
After Invoice No. 7 has been entered and printed click **Save & Close**

ACCOUNTS RECEIVABLE REPORTS

A variety of reports are available regarding accounts receivable. Data regarding customers
may be displayed on the basis of account aging, open invoices, collections reports,
customer balances; or they may be itemized according to the sales by customer. Many
reports may be printed in a summarized form while other reports provide detailed
information.

PREPARE CUSTOMER BALANCE DETAIL REPORT

The Customer Balance Detail Report lists information regarding each customer. The
information provided includes the customer name, all invoices with a balance, the date of
the invoice, the invoice number, the account used to record the invoice, the amount of each
invoice, the balance after each invoice, and the total balance due from each customer.

MEMO
DATE: January 5, 2013

Prepare a Customer Balance Detail Report so that the owners can see exactly how
much each customer owes to Your Name Mountain Sports.

 Prepare a Customer Balance Detail Report for all customers for all transactions:

> Click **Reports** on the menu bar, point to **Customers & Receivables**, and click
> **Customer Balance Detail**
> - *Note:* When preparing a single report, it is more convenient to use the Reports
>   menu. When preparing several reports, using the Report Center is more efficient.
> Dates should be **All**
> - If not, click the drop-down list arrow next to the **Dates** text box, click **All**.
> - Scroll through the report. See how much each customer owes for each invoice.
> - Notice that the amount owed by Monique Gardener for Invoice No. 7 is $1,024.80
>   and that her total balance is $1,078.37.
> Do not print or close the **Customer Balance Detail Report** at this time

USE THE QUICKZOOM FEATURE

QuickZoom is a feature of QuickBooks that allows you to view additional information within
a report. For example, an invoice may be viewed when the Customer Balance Detail
Report is on the screen simply by using the QuickZoom feature.

MEMO

DATE: January 5, 2013

The bookkeeper, Ruth Morgan, could not remember if Invoice No. 7 was for ski equipment or snowboard equipment. With the Customer Balance Detail Report on the screen, use QuickZoom to view Invoice No. 7.

 Use QuickZoom in the Customer Balance Detail Report to view Invoice No. 7

Position the cursor over any part of the information about Invoice No. 7
- The cursor will turn into a magnifying glass with a letter **Z** inside.
Double-click
- Invoice No. 7 appears on the screen.
- Check to make sure the four items on the invoice are: Snowboard, Bindings-Snow, Boots-Snowbrd, and Accessories.
With Invoice No. 7 on the screen, proceed to the next section.

CORRECT AN INVOICE, PRINT THE CORRECTED FORM, AND PRINT THE CUSTOMER BALANCE DETAIL REPORT

QuickBooks allows corrections and revisions to an invoice even if the invoice has been printed. The invoice may be corrected by going directly to the original invoice or by accessing the original invoice via the Accounts Receivable Register. An invoice can be on view in QuickZoom and still be corrected.

MEMO

DATE: January 5, 2013

While viewing Invoice No. 7 for Monique Gardener in QuickZoom, the bookkeeper, Ruth Morgan, realizes that the snowboard should be $499.95, not the $489.95 that is on the original invoice. Make the correction and reprint the invoice.

 Correct Invoice No. 7 while showing on the screen in QuickZoom

Click in the **PRICE EACH** column
Change the amount for the snowboard to **499.95**
Press Tab to change the **AMOUNT** calculated for the Snowboard
Print the corrected Invoice No. 7
Click **Yes** on the Recording Transaction dialog box to record the change to the transaction

A **Recording Transaction** message box appears on the screen regarding the credit
limit of $500 for Monique Gardener

Click **Yes** to accept the current balance of $1,089.17

When the invoice has been printed, click **Save & Close** at the bottom of the **Create
Invoice** screen to record and close the invoice

• This closes the invoice and returns you to the Customer Balance Detail Report.

• Notice that the total amount for Invoice No. 7 is $1,035.60 and that Monique
Gardener's total balance is $1,089.17.

• As you can see, the Account column does not have the account names displayed
in full

Resize the columns as instructed in Chapter 2 so the Account names are displayed
in full as shown below

Your Name Mountain Sports
Customer Balance Detail
All Transactions

Type	Date	Num	Account	Amount	Balance
Gardener, Monique					
Invoice	12/31/2012		1200 · Accounts Receivable	53.57	53.57
Invoice	01/04/2013	7	1200 · Accounts Receivable	1,035.60	1,089.17 ◄
Total Gardener, Monique				1,089.17	1,089.17

After the columns have been resized, click **Print**

• Verify that **Fit report to one page wide** is not selected.

• If it is selected, click the check box to remove the check mark.

Click **Preview**

• The report will fit on one page wide and the account names will be shown in full.

Click **Close** to close the **Preview**

Click **Print**

Your Name Mountain Sports
Customer Balance Detail
All Transactions

Type	Date	Num	Account	Amount	Balance
Villanueva, Oskar					
Invoice	12/31/2012		1200 · Accounts Receivable	975.00	975.00
Total Villanueva, Oskar				975.00	975.00
Watson, Russ					
Invoice	12/31/2012		1200 · Accounts Receivable	85.00	85.00
Invoice	01/02/2013	1	1200 · Accounts Receivable	81.00	166.00
Invoice	01/03/2013	6	1200 · Accounts Receivable	852.11	1,018.11
Total Watson, Russ				1,018.11	1,018.11
TOTAL				13,607.86	13,607.86

Partial Report

After the report is printed, close the **Customer Balance Detail Report**
- If you get a Memorize Report dialog box, click **Do not display this message in the future**, and then click **No**

ADDING NEW ACCOUNTS TO THE CHART OF ACCOUNTS

Because account needs can change as a business is in operation, QuickBooks allows you to make changes to the Chart of Accounts at any time. Some changes to the Chart of Accounts require additional changes to other lists, such as the Item List. An account may be added by accessing the Chart of Accounts. It is also possible to add an account to the Chart of Accounts while adding an item to another list.

ADD NEW ITEMS TO LIST

In order to accommodate the changing needs of a business, all QuickBooks lists allow you to make changes at any time. New items may be added in the Item List or *on the fly* while entering invoice information. The Item List stores information about the items the company sells. Your Name Mountain Sports does not use price levels, so it would be appropriate to have an item allowing for sales discounts. Sales discounts decrease income and function as a contra account to income (similar to accumulated depreciation decreasing the value of an asset). Having a discount item allows discounts to be recorded on the sales form. A discount can be a fixed amount or a percentage. A discount is calculated only on the line above it on the sales form. To allow the entire amount of the invoice to receive the discount, an item for a subtotal will also need to be added. When you complete the sales form, the subtotal item will appear before the discount item.

MEMO
DATE: January 5, 2013

Add an item for Sales Discounts and a Subtotal Item. Add a new income account, 4050 Sales Discount, to the Chart of Accounts. The description for the account should be Discount on Sales.

 Add new items and accounts

Click the **Items & Services** icon on the QuickBooks Home Page
Use the keyboard shortcut **Ctrl + N** to add a new item
- If you get a New Feature screen regarding Add/Edit Multiple List Entries, click **OK**. Do not use this feature unless instructed to do so.
Item **TYPE** is **Discount**
Tab to or click **Item Name/Number**
Type **Nonprofit Discount**
Tab to or click **Description**
Type **10% Discount to Nonprofit Agencies**

Tab to or click **Amount or %**, key in **10%**

- The % sign must be included in order to differentiate between a $10 discount and a 10% discount.

Click the drop-down list arrow for **Account**

Scroll to the top of the list, and then, click **<Add New>**

Complete the information for a New Account:

Account Type should be **Income**

- If **not**, click the drop-down list arrow next to the text box for Type. Click **Income**.
- Giving a sales discount to a customer means that your profit for selling an inventory item is less. This will mean that revenue decreases, and this will ultimately decrease the amount of Net Income.

Tab to or click in the **Number** text box

Enter the Account Number **4050**

- Your Name Mountain Sports uses account numbers for all accounts.
- Numbers in the 4000 category are income.

Tab to or click **Account Name**

Enter **Sales Discounts**

Tab to or click **Description**

Enter **Discount on Sales**

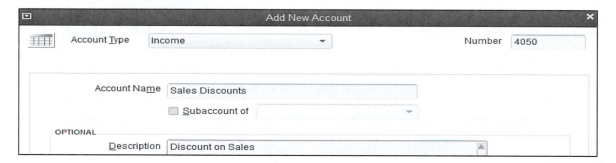

Click **Save & Close** to add the **Sales Discounts** account, close the **New Account** dialog box, and return to the New Item screen

- At the bottom of the screen you should see the Tax Code as **Tax** and the statement **Discount is applied before sales tax** should be displayed.

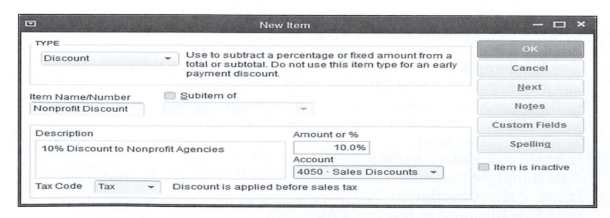

Click **Next** on the **New Item** dialog box
- A discount is calculated only on the line above it on the sales form. To allow the entire amount of the invoice to receive the discount, a subtotal needs to be calculated; so, an item for a subtotal will also need to be added.

Repeat the steps for adding a New Item to add **Subtotal**

TYPE should be **Subtotal**

Item Name/Number is **Subtotal**

The description is **Subtotal**

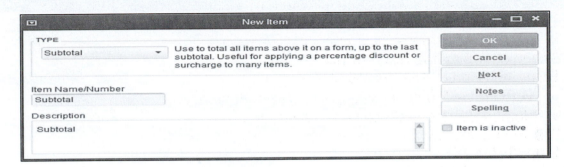

Click **OK** to add the new items and to close the **New Item** screen
- Verify the addition of Nonprofit Discount and Subtotal on the Item List. If everything is correct, close the **Item List**.
- If you find an error, click on the item with the error, use the keyboard shortcut **Ctrl + E**, and make corrections as needed.

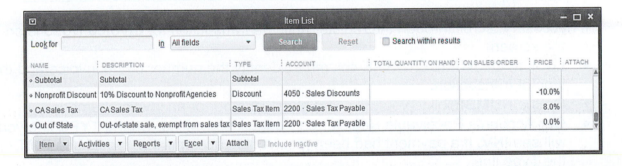

Close the **Item List**

CORRECT AN INVOICE TO INCLUDE SALES DISCOUNT

MEMO

DATE: January 6, 2013

Now that the appropriate accounts for sales discounts have been created, use the Accounts Receivable Register to correct Invoice 3 for Mountain Schools to give the schools a 10% discount as a nonprofit organization.

Correct the invoice to Mountain Schools in the Accounts Receivable Register

Use the keyboard shortcut, **Ctrl + A** to open the Chart of Accounts
In the Chart of Accounts, double-click **Accounts Receivable**
- Double-clicking opens the register
- The **Accounts Receivable Register** appears on the screen with information regarding each transaction entered into the account.

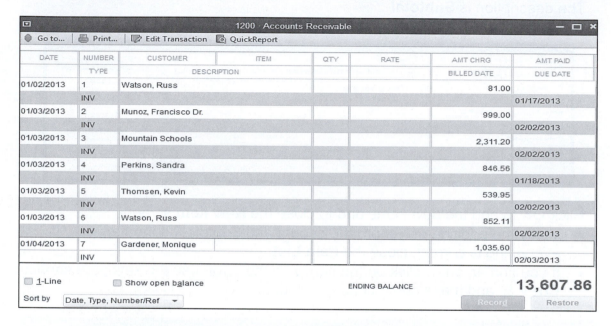

If necessary, scroll through the register until the transaction for **Invoice No. 3** is on the screen
- **Look** at the **NUMBER/TYPE** column to identify the number of the invoice and the type of transaction.
- On the **NUMBER** line you will see a <u>check number</u> or an <u>invoice number</u>.
- Our Accounts Receivable Register only contains invoices. On the **TYPE** line you will see **INV**. If a payment had been received on account, you would see **PMT** on the Type line
Click anywhere in the transaction for Invoice No. 3 to Mountain Schools
Click the **Edit Transaction** button at the top of the register or use the shortcut **Ctrl+E**
- Invoice No. 3 appears on the screen.
Click in **ITEM CODE** beneath the last item, Poles-Ski
Click the drop-down list arrow for **ITEM CODE**
Click **Subtotal**
- You may need to scroll through the Item List until you find Subtotal.
- Remember in order to calculate a discount for everything on the invoice, QuickBooks must calculate the subtotal for the items on the invoice.
Tab to or click the next blank line in **ITEM CODE**
Click **Nonprofit Discount**

- You may need to scroll through the Item List until you find Nonprofit Discount.

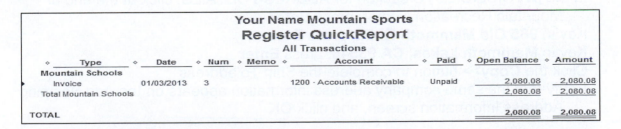

INVOICE

CUSTOMER:JOB Mountain Scho... ▼   TEMPLATE Copy of: Int... ▼

Date	01/03/2013	Bill To: Mountain Schools, 1234 Meridian, Mammoth Lakes, CA 9354
Invoice #	3	

P.O. Number	Terms	Rep	Ship	Via	F.O.B.
	2% 10 Net 30		01/03/2013		

QUANTITY	ITEM CODE	DESCRIPTION	PRICE EA...	AMOUNT	TAX
5	Skis	Snow Skis	299.00	1,495.00	Tax
5	Bindings-Skis	Ski Bindings	100.00	500.00	Tax
5	Poles-Ski	Ski Poles	29.00	145.00	Tax
	Subtotal	Subtotal		2,140.00	
	Nonprofit Discount	10% Discount to Nonprofit Agencies	-10.0%	-214.00	Tax

ONLINE PAY Off

TAX CA Sales Tax ▼ (8.0%)   154.08

TOTAL   2,080.08

CUSTOMER MESSAGE
Thank you for your business.

PAYMENTS APPLIED   0.00
BALANCE DUE   **2,080.08**

MEMO   CUSTOMER TAX CODE Tax ▼   Save & Close   Save & New   Revert

- Notice the subtotal of $2,140.00, the discount of $214, and the new invoice total of $2,080.08.

Print the corrected invoice with lines around each field
Click **Yes** on the **Recording Transaction** screen
After printing, click **Save & Close** on the **Create Invoices** screen to save the corrected invoice and return to the Accounts Receivable Register

- Notice the new Amt Chrg of $2,080.08 for Invoice No. 3 in the register.

Do not close the **Accounts Receivable Register**

VIEW AND ANALYZE A QUICKREPORT FOR MOUNTAIN SCHOOLS

After editing the invoice and returning to the register, you may get a detailed report regarding the customer's transactions by clicking the QuickReport button. 🔍 QuickReport

 With the cursor in Invoice No. 3, click the **QuickReport** button to view the **Mountain Schools** account

Your Name Mountain Sports
Register QuickReport
All Transactions

Type	Date	Num	Memo	Account	Paid	Open Balance	Amount
Mountain Schools							
Invoice	01/03/2013	3		1200 - Accounts Receivable	Unpaid	2,080.08	2,080.08
Total Mountain Schools						2,080.08	2,080.08
TOTAL						2,080.08	2,080.08

Notice that the total of Invoice No. 3 is $2,080.08
Close the **QuickReport** without printing
Close the **Accounts Receivable Register**
Close the **Chart of Accounts**

ADD A NEW CUSTOMER WITH A SHIPPING ADDRESS

QuickBooks allows customers to be added at any time. They may be added to the company records through the Customer List, through Add/Edit Multiple List entries, or they may be added *on the fly* as you create an invoice or sales receipt. When adding *on the fly*, you may choose between Quick Add (used to add only a customer's name) and Set Up (used to add complete information for a customer).

MEMO

DATE: January 8, 2013

Ruth was instructed to add a new customer. The information provided for the new customer is: Mountain Recreation Center, Main Phone: 909-555-2951, Main Email: mountainrec@abc.com Fax: 909-555-1592, Address Details: 985 Old Mammoth Road, Mammoth Lakes, CA 93546, Terms: 1%10 Net 30, Tax Code is Tax, Tax Item: CA Sales Tax, Credit Limit: 5,000, as of 1/8/2013 there is a 0.00 opening balance for the customer.

 Add a new customer in the Customer Center

> Click the **Customers** icon on the icon bar or the **Customers** button in the Customers section of the Home Page
> Use the keyboard shortcut **Ctrl + N** to create a new customer
> In the **Customer** text box, enter **Mountain Recreation Center**
> - Since there is no opening balance for a new customer, there is no need to worry about the AS OF date.
> Tab to or click **COMPANY NAME**
> Enter **Mountain Recreation Center** or copy the Customer Name as previously instructed
> Tab to or click in the text box for **Main Phone**, enter the telephone number
> Tab to or click in the text box for **Main Email**, enter the email address
> Tab to or click in the text box for **Fax**, enter the fax number
> In the INVOICE/BILL TO section for ADDRESS DETAILS, click at the end of Mountain Recreation Center, press **Enter**
> Key in **985 Old Mammoth Road**, press **Enter**
> Key in **Mammoth Lakes, CA 93546**, press **Enter**
> Click the **Copy>>** button to complete the Ship To address
> Verify that the same company address information appears on the Add Shipping Address Information screen, and click **OK**

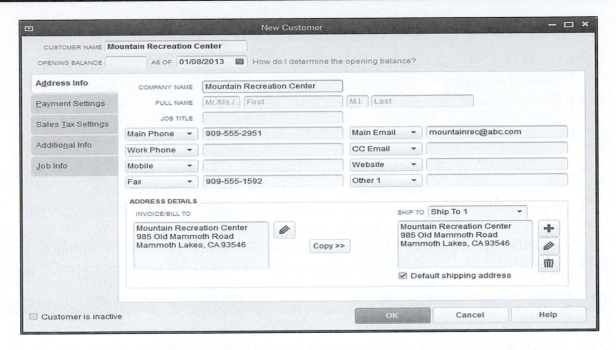

Click the **Payment Settings** tab
Tab to or click in the text box for **CREDIT LIMIT**, enter **5,000**
Click the drop-down list arrow for **PAYMENT TERMS**, click **1% 10 Net 30**

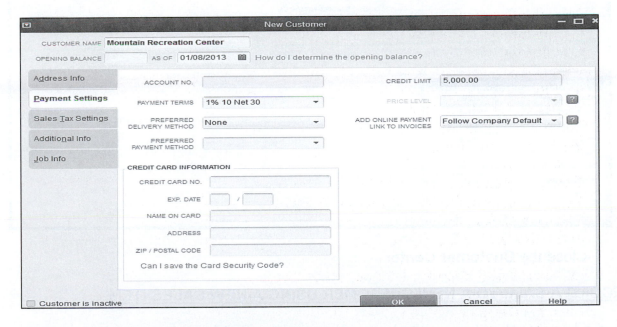

Click the **Sales Tax Settings**
Verify that the **TAX CODE** is **Tax** and that the **TAX ITEM** is **CA Sales Tax**
- If not, click the drop-down arrows for each and click on the proper selection.

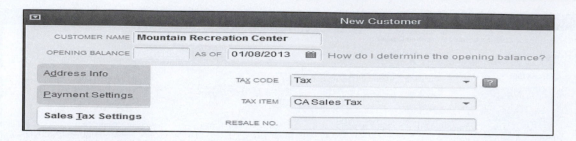

- The Additional Info tab allows you to include information regarding the customer type and sales rep info. In addition Custom Fields may be created.
- If you itemize customers based on contracted jobs, Job Info will allow you to include information about the jobs being performed.

Click **OK** to complete the addition of Mountain Recreation Center as a customer

- Verify the addition of Mountain Recreation Center to the Customer:Job List.

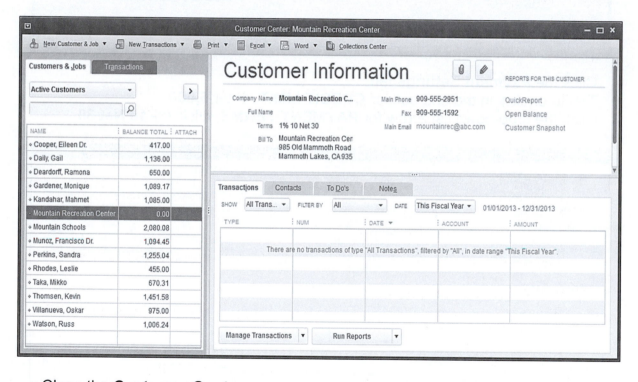

Close the **Customer Center**

RECORD A SALE TO A NEW CUSTOMER USING A NEW SALES ITEM

Once a customer has been added, sales may be recorded for a customer.

> **MEMO**
> **DATE:** January 8, 2013
>
> Record a sale of 5 sleds at $119.99 each, 5 toboggans at $229.95, and 5 helmets at $69.95 each to Mountain Recreation Center. Because the sale is to a nonprofit organization, include a nonprofit discount.

 Record the above sale on account and add three new sales items

Access a blank invoice by using the keyboard shortcut **Ctrl + I**
Enter invoice information for **Mountain Recreation Center** on the customized
  invoice copy as previously instructed
Date of the invoice is **01/08/2013**
Invoice #. is **8**
Tab to or click **QUANTITY**
Enter **5**
Tab to or click **ITEM CODE**
Key in the word **Sleds** for the **ITEM CODE**, press **Enter**
On the Item Not Found dialog box, click **Yes** to create the new item.

On the **New Item** screen, click **Inventory Part** for **TYPE**
- If necessary, click the drop-down list menu to get a list of choices for **TYPE**.
The Inventory Item is divided into three parts:
- <u>PURCHASE INFORMATION</u>: used when purchasing the inventory item
- <u>SALES INFORMATION</u>: used when selling the merchandise
- <u>INVENTORY INFORMATION</u>: used to: calculate the value of the item, calculate the average cost of the item, track the amount of inventory on hand, and prompt when inventory needs to be ordered
The **Item Name/Number** is **Sleds**
Do <u>not</u> enable Unit of Measure
- Unit of Measure is used to indicate what quantities, prices, rates, and costs are based on
Complete the **PURCHASE INFORMATION**:
  Description on Purchase Transactions enter **Sleds**
  Cost leave at **0.00**

- Your Name Mountain Sports has elected to keep the item list simple and not use different items for different styles and models of sleds. Thus, sleds are purchased at different prices so the Cost is left at 0.00.

COGS Account is **5000 - Cost of Goods Sold**

- If 5000 – Cost of Goods Sold is not shown, click the drop-down list arrow and click the account to select it.

Preferred Vendor: leave blank because we do not use the same vendor for this item every time we order it

Complete the **SALES INFORMATION**:

Description on Sales Transactions is **Sleds**

- If Sleds was not inserted at the same time as the Purchase Information Description, enter **Sleds** for the description.

Sales Price leave at **0.00**

- Your Name Mountain Sports has elected to keep the item list simple and not use different items for different styles and models of sleds. Thus, sleds are sold at different prices; and the Sales Price remains as 0.00.

Tax Code is **Tax** because sales tax is collected on this item

Click the drop-down list arrow for **Income Account**

Click **4012 Equipment Sales**

Complete the **INVENTORY INFORMATION**:

Asset Account should be **1120 Inventory Asset**

- If this account is not in the **Asset Account** text box, click the drop-down list arrow, click **1120 Inventory Asset**. This asset account keeps track of the value of the inventory we have on hand.

Tab to **Reorder Point**, enter **5**

Tab to **On hand**, enter **10**

Tab to or click **Total Value**

- IMPORTANT: QuickBooks uses this amount and date to calculate the average cost
- To calculate the average cost, multiply the number of sleds by their purchase price; and then, add the value of all sleds together. For example, five of the ten sleds were purchased by Your Name Mountain Sports for $75 each (Total $375). The other five sleds were purchased for $60 each (Total $300) Total value: $375 + $300 = $675.

Total Value of the sleds is **$675**

Tab to **As of**

- The date is very important! A common error in training is to use the computer date—not the date in the text. An incorrect date may cause a change in the value of your inventory, and it is very difficult to correct the date later.

Enter the As of date **01/08/13**

Check your entry with the following screen shot:

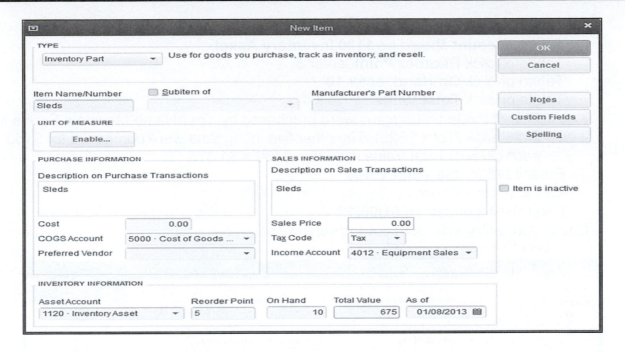

Click **OK** to add Sleds as a sales item
On the invoice, tab to or click **PRICE EACH**
Enter **119.99**
Tab to or click the second line in **QUANTITY**
Enter **5**
Tab to or click **ITEM CODE**
Click the drop-down list arrow for **ITEM CODE**
- There is no item listed for Toboggans.

Click **<Add New>** at the top of the **Item List**
Complete the information for **New Item**
On the **New Item** screen, click **Inventory Part** for **TYPE**
Tab to or click **Item Name/Number**
Enter **Toboggans**
Do <u>not</u> enable Unit of Measure
Complete **PURCHASE INFORMATION**:
    Tab to or click **Description on Purchase Transactions** enter **Toboggans**
    Cost is **0.00**
    COGS Account is **5000 Cost of Goods Sold**
- If 5000 – Cost of Goods Sold is not shown, click the drop-down list arrow and
  click **5000 Cost of Goods Sold** to select the account.

    Preferred Vendor leave blank
Complete **SALES INFORMATION**:
    Description on Sales Transactions should be **Toboggans**
    Sales Price leave at **0.00**
    Tax Code should be **Tax**
    Click the drop-down list arrow for **Income Account**
    Click **4012 Equipment Sales**

Complete the **INVENTORY INFORMATION**:
> **Asset Account** should be **1120 Inventory Asset**
> Tab to or click **Reorder Point**, enter **5**
> Tab to or click **On Hand**, enter **10**
> Tab to or click **Total Value**
> - Five of the ten toboggans were purchased by Your Name Mountain Sports for $125 each (Total $625). The other five toboggans were purchased for $150 each ($750). Total Value is $625 + $750 = $1,375
> Enter **1375** for the **Total Value**
> Tab to or click **As of**
> Enter the As of date of **01/08/13**

Check your entry with the following screen shot:

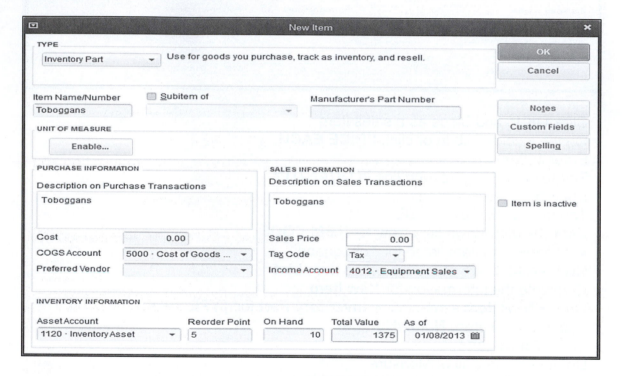

Click **OK** to add Toboggans as a sales item
Enter the Price for the Toboggans of **229.95**
Repeat the steps shown above to add **Helmets** as a sales item
Use **4011 Clothing & Accessory Sales** as the Income Account
Enter the **Reorder Point** of **5**, On Hand **25**
Calculate the Total Value: purchased 10 helmets @ $25 each, purchased 15 helmets @ $30 each, enter the amount of **Total Value** as of **01/08/2013**
Check your entry with the following screen shot:

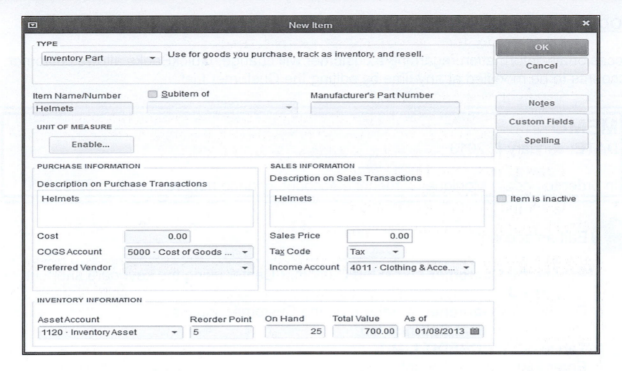

Use the information in the Memo to complete the invoice
- Remember that Mountain Recreation Center is a nonprofit organization and is entitled to a Nonprofit Discount.

The **CUSTOMER MESSAGE** is **Thank you for your business.**

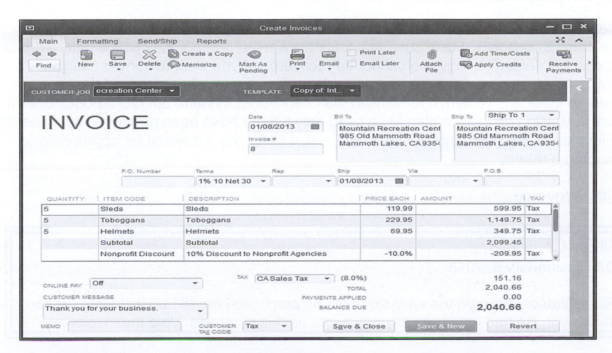

Print the invoice as previously instructed

Click **Save & Close** to record the invoice and close the transaction

MODIFY CUSTOMER RECORDS

Occasionally information regarding a customer will change. QuickBooks allows customer accounts to be modified at any time by editing the Customer List.

MEMO

DATE: January 8, 2013

In order to update Monique Gardener's account, change her credit limit to $2,500.00.

 Edit an account

> Access the **Customer List** in the Customer Center using the keyboard shortcut:
>   **Ctrl + J**.
> Double-click **Gardener, Monique** on the Customer:Job List.
> Click the **Payment Settings** tab
> Tab to or click **CREDIT LIMIT**
> Enter **2500** for the amount
> Click **OK** to record the change and exit the information for Monique Gardener
> Close the **Customer Center**

VOID AND DELETE SALES FORMS

Deleting an invoice or sales receipt completely removes it and any transaction information for it from QuickBooks. Make sure you definitely want to remove the invoice before deleting it. Once it is deleted, an invoice cannot be recovered. If you want to correct financial records for an invoice that is no longer viable, it is more appropriate to void the invoice. When an invoice is voided, it remains in the QuickBooks system, but QuickBooks does not count it. Voiding an invoice should be used only if there have been no payments made on the invoice. If any payment has been received, a Credit Memo would be appropriate for recording a return.

Void an Invoice

MEMO

DATE: January 8, 2013

Russ Watson returned the after-ski boots he purchased for $81.00 including tax on January 2. He had not made any payments on this purchase. Void the invoice.

 Void the transaction for Russ Watson using **Advanced Find** to locate the invoice:

Click **Find** on the **Edit** menu, click the **Advanced** tab

- **Advanced Find** is useful when you have a large number of invoices and want to locate an invoice for a particular customer.
- Using **Advanced Find** will locate the invoice without requiring you to scroll through all the invoices for the company. For example, if customer Sanderson's transaction was on Invoice No. 7 and the invoice on the screen was 784, you would not have to scroll through 777 invoices because Find would locate Invoice No. 7 instantly.

In the list displayed under **FILTER**, click **Name**

- A Filter allows you to specify the type of search to be performed.

In the **Name** text box, click the drop-down list arrow, click **Watson, Russ**

Click the **Find** button on the upper-right side of the **Find** dialog box

- QuickBooks will find all transactions recorded for Russ Watson.

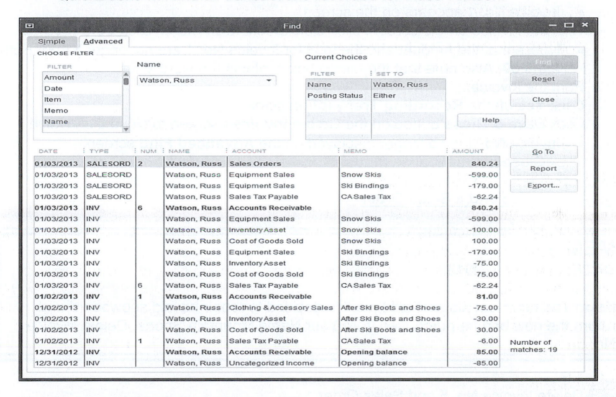

- Because there are several invoices, another filter would need to be defined in order to find the invoice with the exact amount of 81.00. This would be done by selecting a second filter.

Click **Amount** under **FILTER**

Click the circle in front of the **=** sign

Key in **81.00** in the text box

Press the **Tab** key

- The first two lines of the Current Choices Box shows *Filter: Amount* and *Set to: 81.00*: followed by *Filter: Name* and *Set to: Watson, Russ*.

Click the **Find** button

Click the line for **Invoice No. 1**

Click **Go To** button

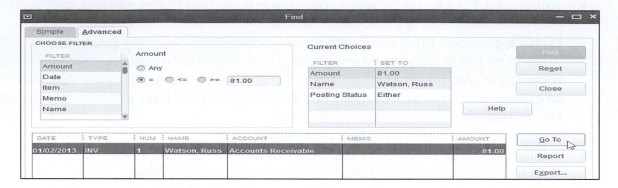

Click the **Go To** button
- Invoice No. 1 appears on the screen.

With the invoice on the screen, click QuickBooks **Edit** menu, click **Void Invoice**
- Notice that the amount and the total for Invoice No. 1 are no longer 81.00. Both are **0.00**. Also note that the Memo box contains the word Void.

Print the invoice

Click **Yes** on the **Recording Transaction** screen

Click **Save & Close** button on the **Create Invoices** screen to close the invoice
- Invoice No. 1 is no longer displayed on the **Advanced Find** screen.

Click **Close** button to close **Find**

Delete an Invoice and a Sales Order

MEMO

DATE: January 8, 2013

Kevin Thomsen lost his part-time job. He decided to repair his old snowboard and return the new one he purchased from Your Name Mountain Sports. Delete Invoice No. 5.

 Delete Invoice No. 5 and Sales Order 1

Access Invoice No. 5 as previously instructed

Click the **Edit** menu, click **Delete Invoice** or use the keyboard shortcut **Ctrl + D**

Click **OK** in the **Delete Transaction** dialog box
- The cursor is now positioned on Invoice No. 6.

Click **Previous** or **Back** arrow
- Now the cursor is positioned on Invoice No. 4.

Click **Save & Close** on the **Create Invoices** screen to close the invoice
- When you delete an invoice that was prepared from a sales order, the sales order must be deleted as well.

Access Sale Order 1 as previously instructed
- Notice that the Sales Order is no longer marked INVOICED IN FULL.

Delete the Sales Order following the same procedures used when deleting an invoice

Click **OK** when asked if you want to delete the transaction

Close **Create Sales Orders**

 View the **Customer Balance Detail Report**

Click the **Reports** icon to open the **Report Center**, click **Customers & Receivables,** and double-click **Customer Balance Detail**

Scroll through the report
- Look at Kevin Thomsen's account. Notice that Invoice No. 5 does not show up in the account listing. When an invoice is deleted, there is no record of it anywhere in the report.
- Look at Russ Watson's account. The amount for Invoice No. 1 shows as **0.00**. Nothing is shown for the Sales Order because a sales order is not recorded in accounts or journals.

Your Name Mountain Sports
Customer Balance Detail
All Transactions

Type	Date	Num	Account	Amount	Balance
Thomsen, Kevin					
Invoice	12/31/2012		1200 · Accounts Receivable	911.63	911.63
Total Thomsen, Kevin				911.63	911.63
Villanueva, Oskar					
Invoice	12/31/2012		1200 · Accounts Receivable	975.00	975.00
Total Villanueva, Oskar				975.00	975.00
Watson, Russ					
Invoice	12/31/2012		1200 · Accounts Receivable	85.00	85.00
Invoice	01/02/2013	1	1200 · Accounts Receivable	0.00	85.00
Invoice	01/03/2013	6	1200 · Accounts Receivable	852.11	937.11
Total Watson, Russ				937.11	937.11
TOTAL				**14,796.45**	**14,796.45**

Partial Report

Close the report without printing, do <u>not</u> close the Report Center

PREPARE THE VOIDED/DELETED TRANSACTIONS DETAIL REPORT

The report that lists the information regarding voided and deleted transactions is the Voided/Deleted Transaction Detail Report.

 View the Voided/Deleted Transactions Detail Report

Click **Accountant & Taxes** in the Report Center
Double-click **Voided/Deleted Transaction Detail**
The dates are **01/01/13 - 01/08/13**

- If the report does not match the text when preparing the report with the dates of 01/08/13, use **All** as the date selection.
- The Entered Last Modified column shows the actual date and time that the entry was made.
- In addition, your report may not match the one illustrated if you have voided or deleted anything else during your work session.

Scroll through the report to see the transactions

- Notice the entries for Invoice 1 include both the original entry and the voided entry.
- The entries for Invoice 5 show the original entry and the deleted entry.

Your Name Mountain Sports
Voided/Deleted Transactions Summary
Entered/Last Modified January 1 - 8, 2013

Num	Action	Entered/Last Modified	Date	Name	Memo	Account	Split	Amount
Transactions entered or modified by Admin								
Invoice 1								
1	Voided Transaction	01/08/2013 15:12:58	01/02/2013	Watson, Russ	VOID:	1200 · Accounts Receivable	-SPLIT-	0.00
1	Changed Transaction	01/03/2013 15:30:27	01/02/2013	Watson, Russ		1200 · Accounts Receivable	-SPLIT-	81.00
1	Added Transaction	01/02/2013 15:03:44	01/02/2013	Watson, Russ		1200 · Accounts Receivable	-SPLIT-	80.44
Invoice 5								
5	Deleted Transaction	01/08/2013 15:14:59						0.00
5	Added Transaction	01/03/2013 16:41:49	01/03/2013	Thomsen, Kevin		1200 · Accounts Receivable	-SPLIT-	539.95
Sales Order 1								
1	Deleted Transaction	01/08/2013 15:17:15						0.00
1	Added Transaction	01/03/2013 16:29:21	01/03/2013	Thomsen, Kevin		90200 · Sales Orders	-SPLIT-	539.95

Close the report without printing, and close the Report Center

PREPARE CREDIT MEMOS

A credit memo is prepared to show a reduction to a transaction and to notify a customer that a change has been made to a transaction. If the invoice has already been sent to the customer, it is more appropriate and less confusing to make a change to a transaction by issuing a credit memo rather than voiding an invoice and issuing a new one.

When applying a credit to an invoice, QuickBooks marks either the oldest invoice or the invoice that matches the amount of the credit.

MEMO

DATE: January 10, 2013

Credit Memo No. 9: Monique Gardener returned the boot carrying case purchased for $49.95 on Invoice No. 7.
Credit Memo No. 10: Russ Watson returned the ski carrier purchased for $10.99 on Invoice No. 6.

Prepare the Credit Memos shown above

Click the **Refunds and Credits** icon on the Home Page
Click the down arrow for the drop-down list box next to **CUSTOMER:JOB**
Click **Gardener, Monique**
Use the **Custom Credit Memo** Template
The **Date** of the Credit Memo is **01/10/13**
The **Credit No.** field should show the number **9**
- Because Credit Memos are included in the numbering sequence for invoices, this number matches the number of the next blank invoice.
There is no PO No.
Click the drop-down list arrow next to **ITEM**, click **Accessories**
Tab to or click in **QTY**, type in **1**
Tab to or click **RATE**, enter **49.95**
Press tab to enter 49.95 in the **AMOUNT** column
The **CUSTOMER MESSAGE** is **Thank you for your business.**

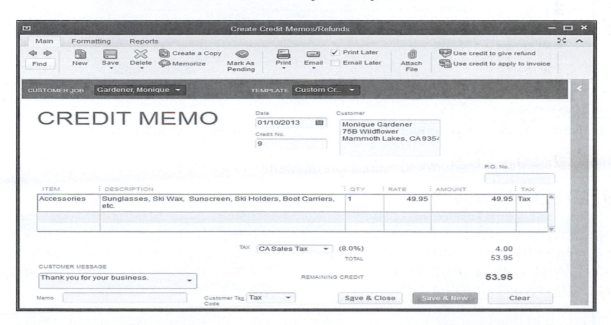

Since the return was for an item purchased on Invoice 7, it is appropriate to apply the credit to Invoice 7
Click the **Use Credit to apply to an invoice** on the Create Credit Memos/Refunds icon bar
Click **Yes** if you get a Recording Transaction message box
The Apply Credit to Invoices screen will appear.
- Unless an exact match in the Amt. Due occurs, QuickBooks applies the credit to the oldest item.
- You will see a checkmark in the column next to the date of 12/31/2012, which is the Opening Balance and the oldest transaction. You will also see a check mark for the Date 01/04/2013. This is because the oldest transaction is selected by

QuickBooks and because the amount of the credit is for more than the opening balance.

Since the credit is for a return to the boot carrier purchased on Invoice 7, click the **Clear Selections** button

Click in the check column to mark Invoice 7 on 01/04/2013

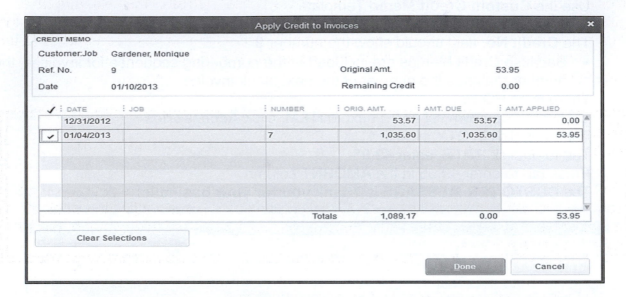

Click **Done**

Print the credit memo with lines around each field as previously instructed

Click **Save & New**

Repeat the procedures to record Credit Memo 10 for Russ Watson applying the credit to Invoice 6

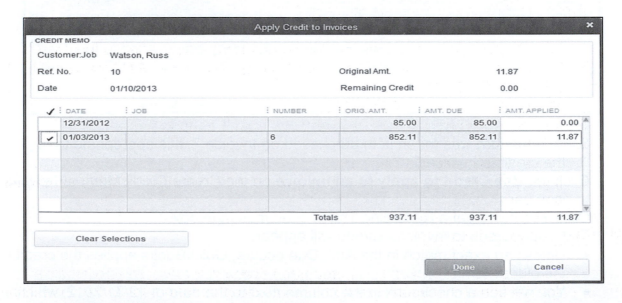

Print the credit memo

Click **Save & Close** on **Create Credit Memo/Refunds** to close the **Credit Memo**

PRINT OPEN INVOICES REPORT

To determine which invoices are still open—they have not been paid—QuickBooks allows you to print an Open Invoices report. This report lists unpaid invoices and statement charges grouped and subtotaled by customer. It also shows the transaction date, the Invoice number, a Purchase Order number (if there is one), terms of the sale, due date, aging, and the amount of the open balance. The total amount due from each customer for all open invoices less credit memos is also listed. If a credit memo has been applied to an invoice, the new total due is reflected in this report and the credit memo is not shown separately.

MEMO

DATE: January 10, 2013

Ruth needs to prepare and print an Open Invoices Report to give to Larry and you, so you can see which invoices are open. When preparing the report, adjust the width of the columns. The report should be one page wide without selecting the print option *Fit report to one page wide*.

 Prepare, resize, and print an Open Invoices Report

> Click **Reports** on the Menu bar, point to **Customers & Receivables**, and click **Open Invoices**
> Enter the date **011013**
> - QuickBooks will insert the / between the items in the date.
> Press the **Tab** key to generate the report
> - Notice the amount due for Invoice 7. It now shows $981.65 as the total rather than $1,035.60. This verifies that the credit memo was applied to Invoice 7.
> - The amount due for Invoice 6 to Russ Watson now shows $840.24 as the total rather than $852.11.
> - The total of the report is $14,730.63
> Resize the columns as previously instructed, print the report
> Click **Print**
> Close the **Open Invoices Report**
> - If you get a Memorize Report dialog box, click **Do not display this message in the future**; and then, click **No**

PREPARE A DAILY BACKUP

As previously discussed, a backup file is prepared in case you make an error. After a number of transactions have been recorded, it is wise to prepare a backup file. In addition, a backup should be made at the end of every work session. The Daily Backup file is an appropriate file to create for saving your work as you progress through a chapter.

By creating the backup file now, it will contain your work for Chapter 5 up through the preparation of the credit memo.

 Prepare the Sports (Daily Backup).qbb file

> Follow the steps presented in Chapter 1 for creating a backup file
> Name the file **Sports (Daily Backup)**
> The file type is **QBW Backup (* .QBB)**

RECORD CASH SALES WITH SALES TAX

Not all sales in a business are on account. In many instances, payment is made at the time the merchandise is purchased. This is entered as a cash sale. Sales with cash, credit cards, or checks as the payment method are entered as cash sales. When entering a cash sale, you prepare a Sales Receipt rather than an Invoice. QuickBooks records the transaction in the Journal and places the amount of cash received in an account called *Undeposited Funds*. The funds received remain in Undeposited Funds until you record a deposit to your bank account.

MEMO
DATE: January 11, 2013

Record the following cash sale: Sales Receipt No. 1—Received <u>cash</u> from a customer who purchased a pair of sunglasses, $29.95; a boot carrier, $2.99; and some lip balm, $1.19. Use the message *Thank you for your business.*

 Enter the above transaction as a cash sale to a cash customer

> Click the **Create Sales Receipts** icon on the Home Page
> - Depending on the size of your computer screen, the History can take up more room than you wish. You may want to hide the history panel.
> If the History panel is shown, click **Hide History**
> If your sales receipt, changes size, resize it by:
>> Point to the right edge of the form
>> The cursor will turn into a double-arrow
>> Hold down the primary mouse button and drag until the Sales Receipt is a smaller size
> If any of the columns in the Sales Receipt are not shown in full,
>> resize them by pointing between the column headings and dragging the double arrow until the column is shown in full
> Enter **Cash Customer** in the **CUSTOMER:JOB** text box, press Tab
> Because Your Name Mountain Sports does not have a customer named Cash Customer, a **Customer:Job Not Found** dialog box appears on the screen.

Click **Quick Add** to add the customer name Cash Customer to the Customer List

- Details regarding Cash Customer are not required, so Quick Add is the appropriate method to use to add the name to the list.
- Now that the customer name has been added to the Customer:Job List, the cursor moves to the **Template** field.

Template should be **Custom Sales Receipt**

- If not, click the drop-down list arrow and click Custom Sales Receipt.

Tab to or click **Date**, type **01/11/13**

- As shown in earlier chapters, the date may be entered 01/11/2013; 01/11/13; or 011113; or by clicking on the calendar, clicking the forward or back arrows until you get to the correct month, and then clicking on the date.

Sale No. should be **1**

Click the drop-down list arrow next to **Payment Method**, click **Cash**

- QuickBooks will allow you to accept cash, checks, credit cards, and e-checks.
- Your business must subscribe to the optional QuickBooks Merchant Accounts, to allow credit card and e-payment processing to be completed without additional software or hardware.

Use **Accessories** as the **ITEM** for each of the items sold and complete the Sales Receipt as instructed in Chapter 2

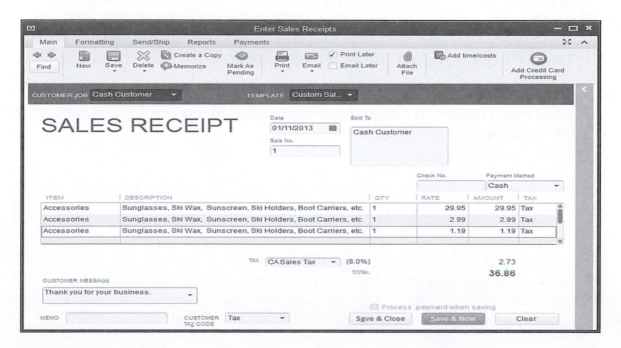

Print the Sales Receipt <u>with</u> lines around each field as previously instructed

Because QuickBooks saves automatically before printing, you may get a Recording Transaction dialog box after printing; if so, always click **Yes**

Click **Save & New** on the bottom of the **Enter Sales Receipts** screen to save the Sales Receipt and go to the next one

ENTERING A CREDIT CARD SALE

A credit card sale is treated exactly like a cash sale. When you prepare the Sales Receipt, the payment method selected is by clicking on the credit card. The credit cards available on the Payment Method List are American Express, Discover, MasterCard, and Visa. The amount of the sale using a credit card is placed into the Undeposited Funds account. When the actual bank deposit is made, the amount is deposited into the checking or bank account. The bank fees for the charge cards are deducted directly from the bank account.

MEMO

DATE: January 11, 2013

Enter a sale to a cash customer using a Visa card. Identify the customer as Cash Customer. The sale was for a sled, $199.95. Use the message *Thank you for your business.*

 Record the credit card sale

Click the drop-down list arrow next to **CUSTOMER:JOB**, click **Cash Customer**

The date of the transaction is **01/11/13**

Sale No. should be **2**

Click the drop-down list arrow next to **Payment Method**, click **VISA**

Complete the Sales Receipt as previously instructed

- At the bottom of the sales receipt is a check box to "Process VISA payment when saving," if your company had a subscription to QuickBooks Merchant Accounts, you would be able to click in the check box and to process a credit card payment when saving

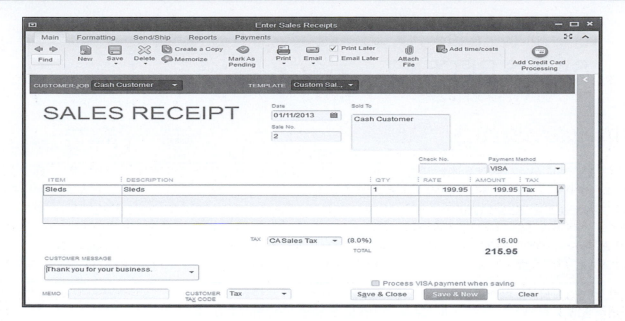

Print the sales receipt <u>with</u> lines around each field
Click **Save & New** to go to Sales Receipt No. 3

RECORD SALES PAID BY CHECK

A sale paid for with a check is considered a cash sale. A sales receipt is prepared to record the sale.

MEMO

DATE: January 11, 2013

We do take checks for sales even if a customer is from out of town. Record the sale of 2 pairs of socks at $15.99 each to a cash customer using Check No. 5589. The message for the Sales Receipt is *Thank you for your business.*

 With Sales Receipt No. 3 on the screen, enter the information for the transaction

The customer is **Cash Customer**
The Date is **01/11/13**
Sale No. should be **3**
Tab to or click **Check No.**, type **5589**
Click the drop-down list arrow next to **Payment Method**, click **Check**
Complete and print Sales Receipt No. 3 as previously instructed

Click **Next** or **Save & New** to go to Sales Receipt No. 4

ENTER CASH SALES TRANSACTIONS WITHOUT STEP-BY-STEP INSTRUCTIONS

MEMO

DATE: January 12, 2013

After a record snowfall, the store is really busy. Use Cash Customer as the customer name for the transactions. Record the following cash, check, and credit card sales:

Sales Receipt No. 4—A cash customer used Check No. 196 to purchase a ski parka, $249.95; ski pants, $129.95; and a sweater, $89.95.

Sales Receipt No. 5—A cash customer used a Master Card to purchase a snowboard, $389.95; snowboard bindings, $189.95; and snowboard boots, $229.95.

Sales Receipt No. 6—A cash customer purchased a pair of gloves for $89.95 and paid cash.

 Repeat the procedures used previously to record the additional transactions listed above

- Use the date 01/12/2013 (or the year you have used previously)
- Always use the Item List to determine the appropriate sales items for billing.
- Use **Thank you for your business.** as the CUSTOMER MESSAGE for these sales receipts.
- Print each Sales Receipt immediately after entering the information for it.
- If you get a Merchant Service message, click **Not Now**
- Click **Save & Close** after you have entered and printed Sales Receipt No. 6.

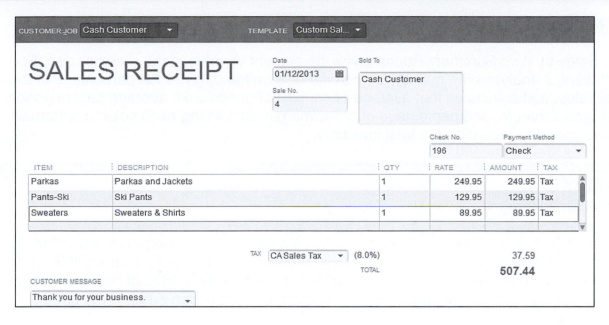

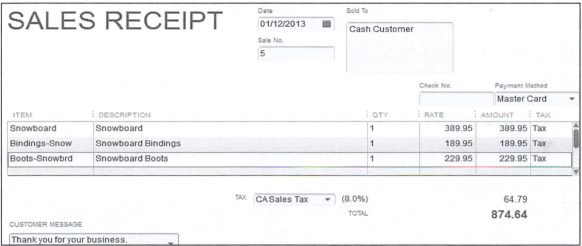

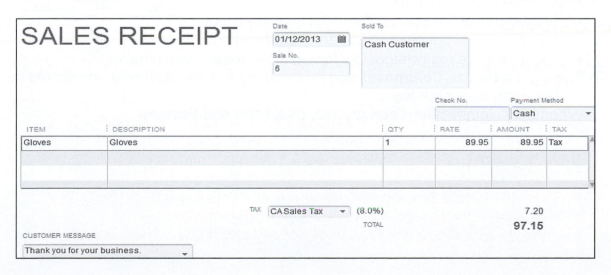

PRINT SALES BY ITEM SUMMARY REPORT

The Sales by Item Summary Report gives the amount or value of the merchandise. For each item, it analyzes the quantity of merchandise on hand, gives the percentage of the total sales, and calculates the: average price, cost of goods sold, average cost of goods sold, gross margin, and percentage of gross margin. By totaling each column, information is also provided regarding the total inventory.

MEMO

DATE: January 13, 2013

Near the middle of the month, Ruth prepares a Sales by Item Summary Report to obtain information about sales, inventory, and merchandise costs. Prepare this report in landscape orientation for 1/1/2013-1/13/2013. Adjust the widths of the columns so the report prints on one page without selecting the print option *Fit report to one page wide*

 Prepare the Sales by Item Summary report

Click **Reports** on the menu bar, point to **Sales**, and click **Sales by Item Summary**
The report dates are From **010113** To **011313**
Tab to generate the report
Scroll through the report
Click **Print**, select **Orientation: Landscape**
Click **Preview**, click **Next Page**
- Notice that the report does not fit on one page wide.
Click **Close** to close the Preview, and click **Cancel** to return to the report
Position the cursor on the diamond between columns
Drag to resize the columns
- The names of the column headings should appear   in full and should not have **...** as part of the heading.
- If columns are really large, Qty for example, make them smaller.
If you get a **Resize Columns** dialog box wanting to know if all columns should be the same size, click **No**
When the columns have been resized, click **Print** and **Preview**

Your Name Mountain Sports
Sales by Item Summary
January 1 - 13, 2013

	Qty	Amount	% of Sales	Avg Price	COGS	Avg COGS	Gross Margin	Gross Margin %
					Jan 1 - 13, 13			
Inventory								
Accessories	5	127.03	1.4%	25.41	18.30	3.66	108.73	85.6%
Bindings-Skis	7	854.00	9.7%	122.00	525.00	75.00	329.00	38.5%
Bindings-Snow	2	349.94	4%	174.97	150.00	75.00	199.94	57.1%
Boots	0	0.00	0.0%	0.00	0.00	0.00	0.00	0.0%
Boots-Ski	1	250.00	2.8%	250.00	75.00	75.00	175.00	70.0%
Boots-Snowbrd	2	478.95	5.4%	239.48	150.00	75.00	328.95	68.7%
Gloves	2	168.95	1.9%	84.48	30.00	15.00	138.95	82.2%
Hats	1	25.00	0.3%	25.00	8.00	8.00	17.00	68.0%
Helmets	5	349.75	4%	69.95	140.00	28.00	209.75	60%
Pants-Ski	2	258.95	2.9%	129.48	60.00	30.00	198.95	76.8%
Parkas	2	498.95	5.6%	249.48	116.66	58.33	382.29	76.6%
Poles-Ski	6	220.00	2.5%	36.67	180.00	30.00	40.00	18.2%
Skis	7	2,519.00	28.5%	359.86	700.00	100.00	1,819.00	72.2%
Sleds	6	799.90	9%	133.32	405.00	67.50	394.90	49.4%
Snowboard	2	889.90	10.1%	444.95	200.00	100.00	689.90	77.5%
Socks	3	47.93	0.5%	15.98	9.00	3.00	38.93	81.2%
Sweaters	2	214.95	2.4%	107.48	50.00	25.00	164.95	76.7%
Toboggans	5	1,149.75	13%	229.95	687.50	137.50	462.25	40.2%
Underwear	1	68.00	0.8%	68.00	8.00	8.00	60.00	88.2%
Total Inventory	61.00	9,270.95	104.8%	151.98	3,512.46	57.58	5,758.49	62.1%
Discounts								
Nonprofit Discount		-423.95	-4.8%					
Total Discounts		-423.95	-4.8%					
TOTAL	61	8,847.00	100.0%	145.03		57.58		

When the report fits on one page wide, print and close the report

CORRECT A SALES RECEIPT AND PRINT THE CORRECTED FORM

QuickBooks makes correcting errors user friendly. When an error is discovered in a transaction such as a cash sale, you can simply return to the form where the transaction was recorded and correct the error. Thus, to correct a sales receipt, you could click Customers on the menu bar, click Enter Sales Receipts, click the Previous or Back arrow until you found the appropriate sales receipt, and then correct the error. Since cash or checks received for cash sales are held in the Undeposited Funds account until the bank deposit is made, a sales receipt can be accessed through the Undeposited Funds account in the Chart of Accounts. Accessing the receipt in this manner allows you to see all the transactions entered in the account for Undeposited Funds.

When a correction for a sale is made, QuickBooks not only changes the form, it also changes all Journal and account entries for the transaction to reflect the correction. QuickBooks then allows a corrected sales receipt to be printed.

MEMO
DATE: January 13, 2013

After reviewing transaction information, you realize that the date for Sales Receipt No. 1 was entered incorrectly. Change the date to 1/8/2013.

 Use the Undeposited Funds account register to correct the error in the memo above, and print a corrected Sales Receipt

Open the **Chart of Accounts**, use the keyboard shortcut **Ctrl+A**
Double-click **Undeposited Funds**
- The register maintains a record of all the transactions recorded within the Undeposited Funds account.

Click anywhere in the transaction for **RCPT 1**
- Look at the **REF/TYPE** column to see the type of transaction.
- The number in the REF column indicates the number of the sales receipt or the customer's check number.
- Type shows **RCPT** for a sales receipt.

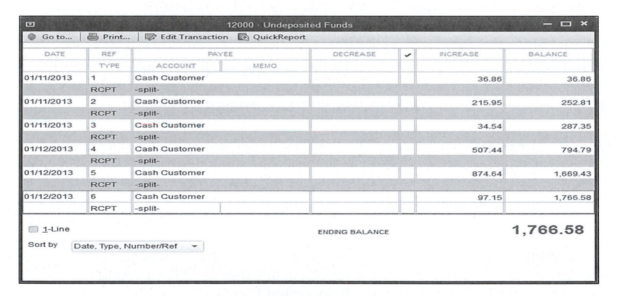

Click **Edit Transaction** or double-click the transaction
- The sales receipt appears on the screen.

Tab to or click **Date** field
Change the Date to **01/08/13**

SALES RECEIPT				Date 01/08/2013 🗓		Sold To Cash Customer			

Sale No.
1

Check No.   Payment Method
    Cash ▾

ITEM	DESCRIPTION	QTY	RATE	AMOUNT	TAX
Accessories	Sunglasses, Ski Wax, Sunscreen, Ski Holders, Boot Carriers, etc.	1	29.95	29.95	Tax
Accessories	Sunglasses, Ski Wax, Sunscreen, Ski Holders, Boot Carriers, etc.	1	2.99	2.99	Tax
Accessories	Sunglasses, Ski Wax, Sunscreen, Ski Holders, Boot Carriers, etc.	1	1.19	1.19	Tax

TAX   CA Sales Tax ▾   (8.0%)   2.73

TOTAL   **36.86**

CUSTOMER MESSAGE
Thank you for your business.   ▾

Print a corrected sales receipt as previously instructed
Click **Yes** on the **Recording Transactions** dialog box
- If you get a QuickBooks Merchant Services dialog box, click **OK**

Click **Save & Close**
Return to the **Register for Undeposited Funds** do <u>not</u> close the register

VIEW AND ANALYZE A QUICKREPORT FOR CASH CUSTOMER

After editing the sales receipt and returning to the register, you may get a detailed report regarding the customer's transactions by clicking the QuickReport button. If you use Cash Customer for all cash sales, a QuickReport will be for all the transactions of Cash Customer.

 Prepare a QuickReport for Cash Customer

After closing the sales receipt, you returned to the register for the Undeposited Funds account
Click the **QuickReport** button to display the Register QuickReport for **Cash Customer**
All transactions for Cash Customer appear in the report
Because there are no entries in the Memo and Clr columns, drag the diamond between columns to eliminate the columns for **Memo** and **Clr**
Widen the **Account** column until the account name **Undeposited Funds** appears in full

Your Name Mountain Sports
Register QuickReport
All Transactions

Type	Date	Num	Account	Split	Amount
Cash Customer					
Sales Receipt	01/08/2013	1	12000 · Undeposited Funds	-SPLIT-	36.86
Sales Receipt	01/11/2013	2	12000 · Undeposited Funds	-SPLIT-	215.95
Sales Receipt	01/11/2013	3	12000 · Undeposited Funds	-SPLIT-	34.54
Sales Receipt	01/12/2013	4	12000 · Undeposited Funds	-SPLIT-	507.44
Sales Receipt	01/12/2013	5	12000 · Undeposited Funds	-SPLIT-	874.64
Sales Receipt	01/12/2013	6	12000 · Undeposited Funds	-SPLIT-	97.15
Total Cash Customer					1,766.58
TOTAL					**1,766.58**

- Notice that the date for Sales Receipt No. 1 has been changed to **01/08/2013**.
  The account used is Undeposited Funds
  The Split column contains the other accounts used in the transactions
- For all the transactions you see the word **-SPLIT-** rather than an account name.
- Split means that more than one account was used for this portion of the transaction.
- In addition to a variety of sales items, sales tax was charged on all sales, so each transaction will show **-SPLIT-** even if only one item was sold as in Sales Receipt No. 2.

Verify that Sales Receipt No. 2 had one sales item by using QuickZoom to view the actual sales receipt
Use QuickZoom by double-clicking anywhere on the information for Sales Receipt No. 2

- The item sold is Sleds. Also note the CA Sales Tax.

Close **Sales Receipt No. 2**
Close the report without printing
Close the register for **Undeposited Funds**
Do <u>not</u> close the **Chart of Accounts**

VIEW SALES TAX PAYABLE REGISTER

The Sales Tax Payable Register shows a detailed listing of all transactions with sales tax. The option of 1-Line may be selected in order to view each transaction on one line rather than the standard two lines. The account register provides information regarding the vendor and the account used for the transaction.

 View the register for the Sales Tax Payable account

Double-click **2200-Sales Tax Payable** in the Chart of Accounts
Once the register is displayed, click **1-Line** to view the transactions

- The amount of sales tax for each sale, whether cash or credit, in which sales tax was collected is displayed

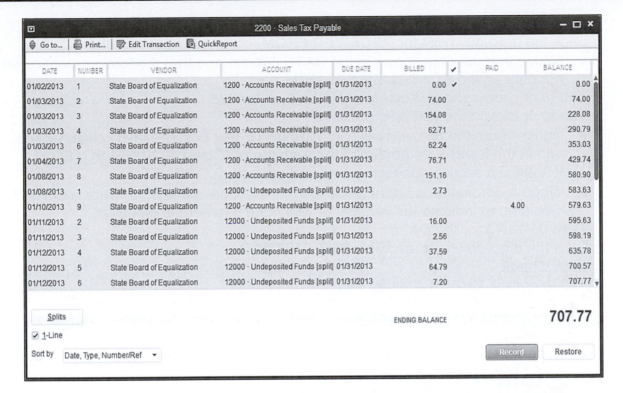

DATE	NUMBER	VENDOR	ACCOUNT	DUE DATE	BILLED	✓	PAID	BALANCE
01/02/2013	1	State Board of Equalization	1200 · Accounts Receivable [split]	01/31/2013	0.00	✓		0.00
01/03/2013	2	State Board of Equalization	1200 · Accounts Receivable [split]	01/31/2013	74.00			74.00
01/03/2013	3	State Board of Equalization	1200 · Accounts Receivable [split]	01/31/2013	154.08			228.08
01/03/2013	4	State Board of Equalization	1200 · Accounts Receivable [split]	01/31/2013	62.71			290.79
01/03/2013	6	State Board of Equalization	1200 · Accounts Receivable [split]	01/31/2013	62.24			353.03
01/04/2013	7	State Board of Equalization	1200 · Accounts Receivable [split]	01/31/2013	76.71			429.74
01/08/2013	8	State Board of Equalization	1200 · Accounts Receivable [split]	01/31/2013	151.16			580.90
01/08/2013	1	State Board of Equalization	12000 · Undeposited Funds [split]	01/31/2013	2.73			583.63
01/10/2013	9	State Board of Equalization	1200 · Accounts Receivable [split]	01/31/2013			4.00	579.63
01/11/2013	2	State Board of Equalization	12000 · Undeposited Funds [split]	01/31/2013	16.00			595.63
01/11/2013	3	State Board of Equalization	12000 · Undeposited Funds [split]	01/31/2013	2.56			598.19
01/12/2013	4	State Board of Equalization	12000 · Undeposited Funds [split]	01/31/2013	37.59			635.78
01/12/2013	5	State Board of Equalization	12000 · Undeposited Funds [split]	01/31/2013	64.79			700.57
01/12/2013	6	State Board of Equalization	12000 · Undeposited Funds [split]	01/31/2013	7.20			707.77

Splits

☑ 1-Line

Sort by   Date, Type, Number/Ref   ▼

ENDING BALANCE   **707.77**

Record   Restore

Close the register for **Sales Tax Payable**, and close the **Chart of Accounts**

RECORD CUSTOMER PAYMENTS ON ACCOUNT

As previously noted, whenever money is received, whether it is for a cash sale or when customers pay the amount they owe on account, QuickBooks uses the account called *Undeposited Funds* to record the receipt of funds. The money stays in the account until a bank deposit is made. The amount is then transferred into Checking. When you start to record a payment on account, you see the customer's balance, any credits or discounts, and a complete list of unpaid invoices. QuickBooks automatically applies the payment received to a matching amount or to the oldest invoice.

If a customer owes you money for a purchase made "on account" (an invoice) you record the payment in Receive Payments. If a customer paid you at the time the purchase was made, a sales receipt was prepared and the amount received was recorded at that time.

> **MEMO**
>
> **DATE:** January 13, 2013
>
> Record the following receipt of Check No. 765 for $975 from Oskar Villanueva as payment in full on his account.

 Record the above payment on account

Click the **Receive Payments** icon on the QuickBooks Home Page
Click the drop-down list for **RECEIVED FROM**, click **Villanueva, Oskar**

- Notice that the date shows in the DATE column and that the total amount owed appears as the CUSTOMER BALANCE.

Tab to or click in the text box for **AMOUNT**, enter **975**
Tab to or click in the text box for **DATE**

- Notice when the cursor moves into the **DATE** text box, the invoice is checked, and in the lower-right portion of the form the AMOUNT FOR SELECTED INVOICES section shows the payment amount as APPLIED.

- When recording a payment on account, QuickBooks places a check mark in the √ column to indicate the invoice for which the payment is received.

Type **01/13/13** for the DATE
Click the drop-down list arrow for **PMT. METHOD**
Click **Check**
Tab to or click **CHECK #**, enter **765**

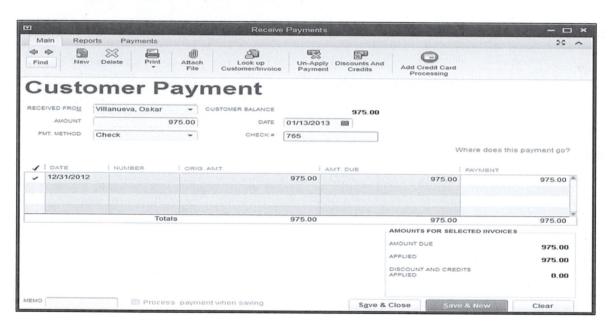

Click the **Print** icon at the top of the Receive Payments screen and print the Payment Receipt
Click the **Next** arrow or **Save & New** to record this payment and advance to the next **Receive Payments** screen

RECORD CUSTOMER PAYMENT ON ACCOUNT WITH AN APPLIED CREDIT

If there are any existing credits (such as a Credit Memo) on an account that have not been applied to the account, they may be applied to a customer's account when a payment is made. If a credit was recorded and applied to an invoice, the total amount due on the invoice will reflect the credit.

> **MEMO**
> **DATE:** January 13, 2013
>
> Monique Gardener sent Check No. 1026 for $1,035.22 to pay her account in full.
> Apply unused credits when recording her payment on account.

 Record the payment by Monique Gardener and apply her unused credits

Click the drop-down list for **RECEIVED FROM**, click **Gardener, Monique**
- Notice the Customer Balance shows the total amount owed by the customer.
- In the lower portion of the **Receive Payments** screen, notice the list of unpaid invoices for Monique Gardener.

Tab to or click **AMOUNT**, enter **1035.22**
Tab to or click **DATE**, type the date **01/13/13**
Check should still show as the payment method
Tab to or click **CHECK #**, enter **1026**
- Notice the ORIG. AMT. of the two transactions, the AMT. DUE, and the PAYMENT amounts. The AMT. DUE for Invoice 7 shows 981.65 this reflects the application of the Credit Memo 9 for $53.95 that was previously recorded.

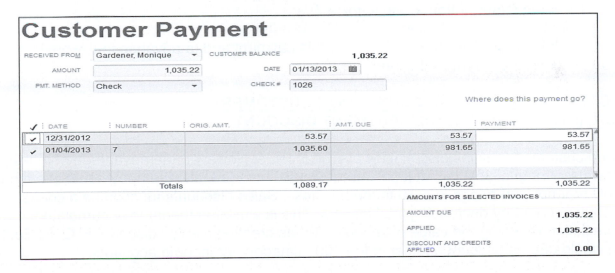

View the Credits
Double-click the transaction for Invoice 7
- You will see Invoice 7 shown on the screen.

Click the **Apply Credits** icon on the Create Invoices Icon bar
- The Apply Credits screen is shown on the screen.

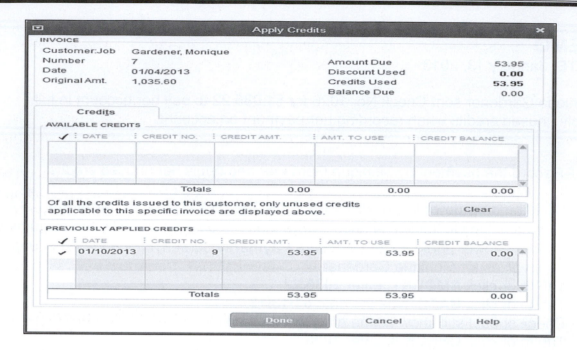

- If you did not apply a credit directly to an invoice, the Available Credits will show the information for Credit Memo 9. You may apply the credit now by clicking in the √ column in the AVAILABLE CREDITS section.

Click the **Done** button, close Invoice 7

Print the Payment Receipt

Click **Next** or **Save & New** to record this payment and to advance to the next **Receive Payments** screen.

RECORD PAYMENT ON ACCOUNT FROM CUSTOMER QUALIFYING FOR AN EARLY-PAYMENT DISCOUNT

Giving customers a sales discount lowers the income. However, the advantage of making a sales discount available is that it encourages customers to make their payments in a more timely manner and brings in cash to the business. Sales discounts function as a contra revenue account by decreasing total income. This is similar in theory to accumulated depreciation reducing the value of an asset. When creating a sales discount in QuickBooks you would use an account number in the 4000 category for income accounts.

Each customer may be assigned terms as part of the customer information. When terms such as 1% 10 Net 30 or 2% 10 Net 30 are given, customers whose payments are received within ten days of the invoice date are eligible to deduct 1% or 2% from the amount owed when making their payments.

QuickBooks will automatically calculate the amount of discount that is being applied to a payment. In certain circumstances, you should override QuickBooks calculations. For example, if a payment is postmarked before the due date, QuickBooks will not show a discount. You may change this by clicking the Discounts and Credits icon and entering the discount amount yourself. To do this, use QuickMath: key in the total amount owed in the Amount of Discount text box, press * to multiply, key in .02 (the discount percentage), and press Enter. The Balance Due is automatically calculated by QuickBooks.

Another instance in which an override is essential is if a customer has made a return. QuickBooks always calculates the amount of the discount on the original Amount Due. To override this, subtract the amount of the return from the original amount due to determine the actual amount owed; and then, calculate the discount amount by multiplying the corrected amount due by the discount percentage. For example: Using a transaction with an Amount Due of $500, a Credit Used of $50, and Discount Terms of 2%, calculating the 2% discount can have different results. If you allow QuickBooks to calculate the discount, (2% of $500 = $10) The Balance Due would be: $500 - $50 (return) - $10 (discount) = $440 Balance Due. More accurately, the amount due of $500 less a return of $50 equals a corrected amount due of $450. A 2% discount on $450 is $9, which leaves a Balance Due of $441.

MEMO

DATE: January 13, 2013

Received Check No. 981-13 for $2,020.25 from Mountain Recreation Center as full payment for Invoice No. 8. Record the payment and the 1% discount for early payment under the invoice terms of 1% 10 Net 30.

 Record the receipt of the check and apply the discount to the above transaction

Click the drop-down list for **RECEIVED FROM**
Click **Mountain Recreation Center**
- The total amount owed, $2,040.66, appears as the CUSTOMER BALANCE.
Tab to or click the **AMOUNT** text box and enter **2020.25**
- Notice that this amount is different from the balance of $2,040.66.
Tab to or click **DATE**
- Notice that the payment amount is entered in the **PAYMENT** column for Invoice 8.
You will get a message in the UNDERPAYMENT section, which is in the lower-left portion of Receive Payments

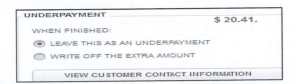

Type date **01/13/13**
The **PMT. METHOD** should show Check
Tab to or click **CHECK #**, enter **981-13**

Click in the text box for **MEMO** below the UNDERPAYMENT section
Key in **Includes Early Payment Discount**
- Since the column for DISC. DATE is displayed, you will see that the Invoice is being paid within the discount date and is eligible to receive a discount

Click the **Discounts and Credits** icon on the Receive Payments Icon bar
- QuickBooks displays the 1% discount amount, which was calculated on the total amount due

Click the drop-down list arrow for **Discount Account**, click **4050 Sales Discounts**

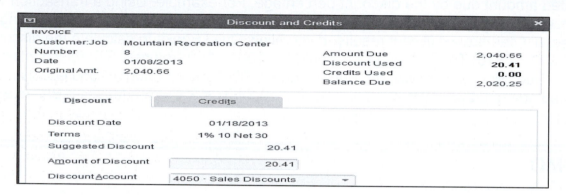

Click the **Done** button at the bottom of the Discounts and Credits screen to apply the discount of $20.41

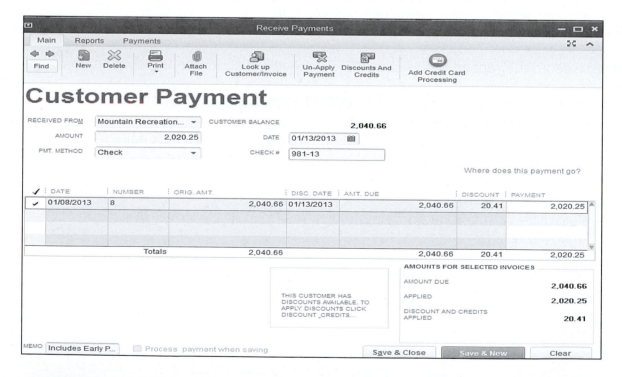

- Notice that ORIG. AMT. stays the same, $2,040.66; the AMT. DUE for Invoice Number 8 shows $2,040.66; the discount amount of $20.41 shows in the DISCOUNT column, and the PAYMENT shows $2,020.25.

- In the area for AMOUNTS FOR SELECTED INVOICES, you will see the AMOUNT DUE, 2,040.66; APPLIED, 2,020.25; and DISCOUNTS AND CREDITS APPLIED, 20.41.

Print the Payment Receipt

- Once the transaction has been saved, if find you made an error in applying the discount, click the **Revert** button and re-enter the transaction.

Click the **Next** arrow or **Save & New** to record this payment and to advance to the next **Receive Payments** screen

RECORD PAYMENT FOR A CUSTOMER WITH A CREDIT MEMO AND FOR A PAYMENT RECEIVED AFTER THE DUE DATE

As learned previously, QuickBooks will automatically calculate discounts. However, there are instances when the automatic calculation is not correct. For example when a payment is received and a return has been made. QuickBooks will apply the discount to the original amount owed, which gives a discount on returned merchandise. Another example is when a customer mails a payment before the due date yet it is received after the due date. When that occurs, QuickBooks will not calculate an automatic discount. The discount must be entered on the Discounts and Credit screen.

MEMO

DATE: January 14, 2013

Received Check No. 8252 dated January 10 and postmarked 1/11 for $2,038.48 from Mountain Schools. Date the payment receipt 01/14/13.
Received Check No. 152 dated January 11 and postmarked 1/12 from Russ Watson for $916.84. Date the payment receipt 01/13/13.

 Record the receipt of the payment and apply the appropriate discounts to the above transactions

Enter **Mountain Schools** in RECEIVED FROM as previously indicated
Enter **2038.48** in the AMOUNT text box
Use the DATE **01/14/2013**
PMT. METHOD is **Check** and the CHECK # is **8252**
- Note the UNDERPAYMENT of $41.60.
Click the **Discounts And Credits** icon on the Receive Payments icon bar
Make sure the **Discount** tab is selected
- Note that the Amount Due and the Balance Due are both 2,080.08. The Discount Date shows as 01/13/2013 with Terms of 2% 10 Net 30 and a Suggested Discount is shown as 0.00.
- Even though we are recording the payment after the discount date, the check was postmarked within the discount period. We will apply the discount for early payment to this transaction.

- Since the payment is being recorded after the discount date, you need to calculate and enter the amount of the 2% discount

Click in the **Amount of Discount** text box, and enter **2080.08,** then press the * (asterisk)

- This opens QuickMath

Enter **.02**, press **Enter**, press **Tab**

- QuickMath calculates the 2% discount of $41.60, enters it into the text box, and shows the amount as Discount Used.
- Once the Discount Used is applied, the Balance Due shows 2,038.48.

The Discount Account is **4050 Sales Discounts**

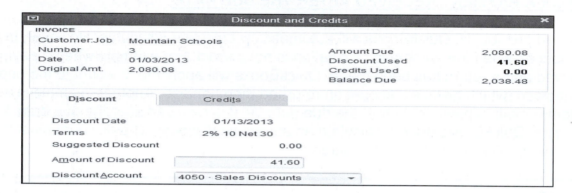

Click **Done** and return to the Customer Payment

Enter the MEMO: **Includes Early Payment Discount**

- Notice that the Customer Payment now shows a DISC. DATE of 01/14/2013 and that the AMOUNTS FOR SELECTED INVOICES includes the DISCOUNT AND CREDITS APPLIED of $41.60.

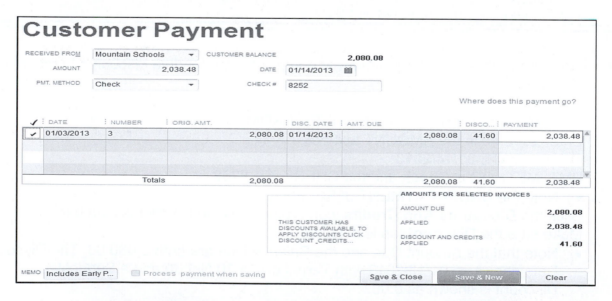

Print the Customer Payment and then click **Save & New** to continue

Enter the payment information for **Russ Watson** as previously instructed using the date the check was received **01/13/13** as the DATE

- Once all the transaction information is entered, notice the UNDERPAYMENT of $8.40.
- Since the payment was received within the discount period, the discount needs to be applied

Click the line for Number 6 on the Receive Payments window and then click the **Discounts And Credits** icon, make sure the **Discount** tab is selected and that Number is 6 is shown

- Analyze the information displayed:
    - o   852.11 is the original <u>Amount Due</u> for Invoice 6 is 852.11.
    - o   8.52 is the <u>Discount Used</u>, which is the amount QuickBooks calculates for the discount on the original <u>Amount Due</u> rather than the <u>Balance Due</u>
    - o   11.87 is the <u>Credits Used</u> (The credit of 11.87 was applied to the invoice when the return was recorded.)
    - o   831.72 is the <u>Balance Due</u> (This is incorrect because the discount should not be calculated before the Credit Used is subtracted. It should be calculated 852.11 – 11.87 = 840.24 Balance Due.)

The terms are **1% 10 Net 30**

Click in the **Amount of Discount** text box, delete the discount of 8.52

Use QuickMath to calculate the discount amount:

Amount Due **852.11** - Balance Due **840.24 * .01** (discount percentage) = a discount of **8.40**, press **Enter** to enter the discount, press **Tab** to update Discount Used

- Note that QuickBooks shows the Suggested Discount of 8.52, which is the discount for the Amount Due before subtracting the Credits Used. The Discount Used is 8.40, the amount calculated by QuickMath.

Use the Discount Account **4050 Sales Discounts**

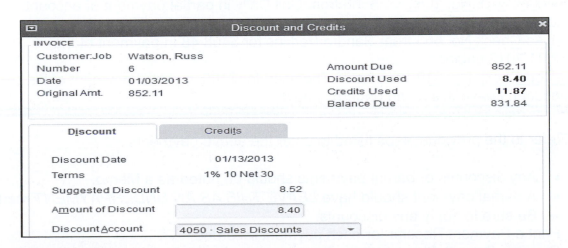

Click **Done**

Enter the MEMO: **Includes Early Payment Discount**

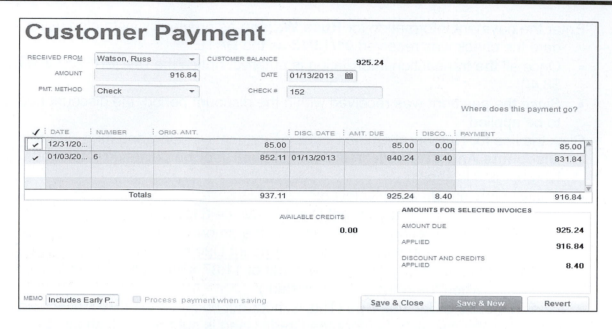

Print the Customer Payment, click **Save & New**

RECORD ADDITIONAL PAYMENTS ON ACCOUNT WITHOUT STEP-BY-STEP INSTRUCTIONS

MEMO

DATE: January 14, 2013

Received Check No. 3951 from Dr. Francisco Munoz for $1,094.45. Since he dropped off his check today, it does not qualify for an early payment discount.
Received Check No. 1051 for $500 from Gail Daily in partial payment of account. Record the memo: Partial Payment. Leave this as an underpayment.
Received Check No. 563 from Sandra Perkins for $408.48 in payment of the 12/31/2012 balance.
Received Check No. 819 from Kevin Thomsen for $100 in partial payment of his account. Leave this as an underpayment.

 Refer to the previous steps listed to enter the above payments:

- Any discounts or partial payments should be noted as a Memo.
- A partial payment should have *LEAVE THIS AS AN UNDERPAYMENT* marked.
- Be sure to apply any discounts.

Print a Payment Receipt for each payment recorded
Click the **Save & Close** button after all payments received have been recorded

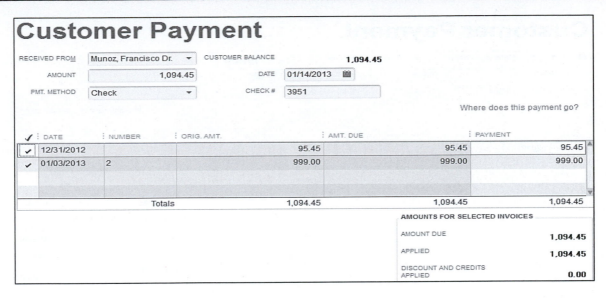

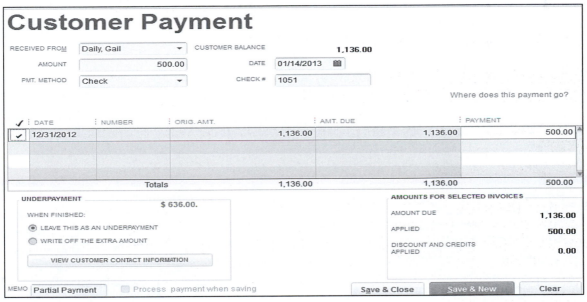

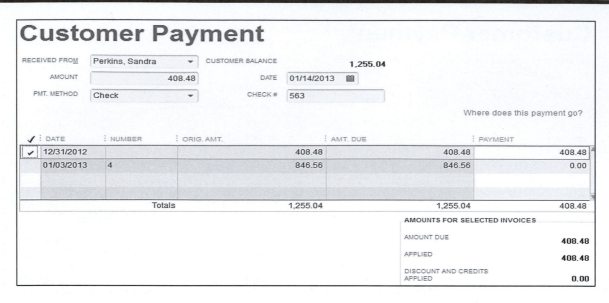

VIEW TRANSACTION LIST BY CUSTOMER

In order to see the transactions for customers, you need to prepare a report called Transaction List by Customer. This report shows all sales, credits, and payments for each customer on account and for the customer named Cash Customer. The report does not show the balance remaining on account for the individual customers.

 View the Transaction List by Customer

> Click the **Reports** icon to open the **Report Center**, click **Customers & Receivables**
> Double-click **Transaction List by Customer**
> Enter the dates from **01/01/13** to **01/14/13**
> Tab to generate the report and scroll through the report

Your Name Mountain Sports
Transaction List by Customer
January 1 - 14, 2013

Type	Date	Num	Memo	Account	Clr	Split	Debit	Credit
Cash Customer								
Sales Receipt	01/08/2013	1		12000 · Undeposited Funds		–SPLIT–	36.86	
Sales Receipt	01/11/2013	2		12000 · Undeposited Funds		–SPLIT–	215.95	
Sales Receipt	01/11/2013	3		12000 · Undeposited Funds		–SPLIT–	34.54	
Sales Receipt	01/12/2013	4		12000 · Undeposited Funds		–SPLIT–	507.44	
Sales Receipt	01/12/2013	5		12000 · Undeposited Funds		–SPLIT–	874.64	
Sales Receipt	01/12/2013	6		12000 · Undeposited Funds		–SPLIT–	97.15	
Daily, Gail								
Payment	01/14/2013	1051	Partial Payment	12000 · Undeposited Funds		1200 · Accounts Receivable	500.00	
Gardener, Monique								
Invoice	01/04/2013	7		1200 · Accounts Receivable		–SPLIT–	1,035.60	
Credit Memo	01/10/2013	9		1200 · Accounts Receivable		–SPLIT–		53.95
Payment	01/13/2013	1026		12000 · Undeposited Funds		1200 · Accounts Receivable	1,035.22	
Mountain Recreation Center								
Invoice	01/08/2013	8		1200 · Accounts Receivable		–SPLIT–	2,040.66	
Payment	01/13/2013	981–13	Includes Early Payment Discount	12000 · Undeposited Funds		1200 · Accounts Receivable	2,020.25	
Mountain Schools								
Invoice	01/03/2013	3		1200 · Accounts Receivable		–SPLIT–	2,080.08	
Payment	01/14/2013	8252	Includes Early Payment Discount	12000 · Undeposited Funds		1200 · Accounts Receivable	2,038.48	
Munoz, Francisco Dr.								
Invoice	01/03/2013	2		1200 · Accounts Receivable		–SPLIT–	999.00	
Payment	01/14/2013	3951		12000 · Undeposited Funds		1200 · Accounts Receivable	1,094.45	
Perkins, Sandra								
Invoice	01/03/2013	4		1200 · Accounts Receivable		–SPLIT–	846.56	
Payment	01/14/2013	563		12000 · Undeposited Funds		1200 · Accounts Receivable	408.48	
Thomsen, Kevin								
Payment	01/14/2013	819	Partial Payment	12000 · Undeposited Funds		1200 · Accounts Receivable	100.00	
Villanueva, Oskar								
Payment	01/13/2013	765		12000 · Undeposited Funds		1200 · Accounts Receivable	975.00	
Watson, Russ								
Invoice	01/02/2013	1	VOID:	1200 · Accounts Receivable	✔	–SPLIT–	0.00	
Sales Order	01/03/2013	2		90200 · Sales Orders		–SPLIT–	840.24	
Invoice	01/03/2013	6		1200 · Accounts Receivable		–SPLIT–	852.11	
Credit Memo	01/10/2013	10		1200 · Accounts Receivable		–SPLIT–		11.87
Payment	01/13/2013	152	Includes Early Payment Discount	12000 · Undeposited Funds		1200 · Accounts Receivable	916.84	

- Information is shown for the Invoices, Sales Receipts, Credit Memos, and Payments made on the accounts and the Num column shows the Invoice numbers, Sales Receipt numbers, Credit Memo numbers, and Check numbers. Nothing is shown for beginning balances.

Close the report <u>without</u> printing

PRINT CUSTOMER BALANCE SUMMARY

A report that will show you the balance owed by each customer is the Customer Balance Summary. The report presents the total balance owed by each customer as of a certain date.

MEMO
DATE: January 14, 2013

Larry and you want to see how much each customer owes to Your Name Mountain Sports. Print a Customer Balance Summary Report for All Transactions.

Prepare and print a **Customer Balance Summary** following the steps given previously for printing the report in Portrait orientation

Your Name Mountain Sports
Customer Balance Summary
All Transactions

	◇ Jan 14, 13 ◇
Cooper, Eileen Dr. ▶	417.00 ◀
Daily, Gail	636.00
Deardorff, Ramona	650.00
Kandahar, Mahmet	1,085.00
Perkins, Sandra	846.56
Rhodes, Leslie	455.00
Taka, Mikko	670.31
Thomsen, Kevin	811.63
TOTAL	5,571.50

Close the report and the Report Center

DEPOSIT CASH, CHECKS AND CREDIT CARD RECEIPTS

When cash sales are made and payments on accounts are received, QuickBooks places the money received in the *Undeposited Funds* account. Once the deposit is recorded, the funds are transferred from *Undeposited Funds* to the account selected when preparing the deposit, usually Cash or Checking.

MEMO

DATE: January 14, 2013

Deposit all cash, checks and credit card receipts for cash sales and payments on account into the Checking account.

 Deposit cash, checks and credit card receipts

Click the **Record Deposits** icon on the QuickBooks Home Page
The View payment method type should be **All types**
- The **Payments to Deposit** window shows all amounts received for cash sales (including bank credit cards) and payments on account that have not been deposited in the bank organized by category—Cash, Check, and finally Credit Cards.

Sort is by **Payment Method**
- Notice that the **check** column to the left of the Date column is empty.

Click the **Select All** button
- Notice the check marks in the check column.

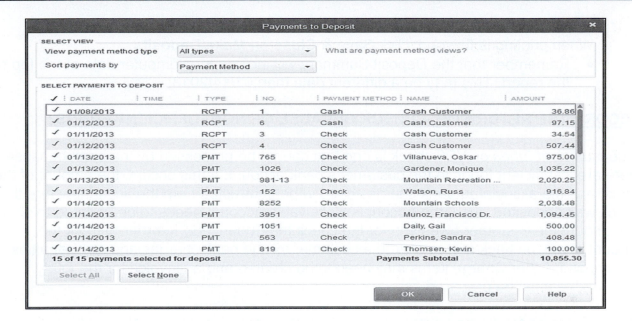

- Since not all transactions are displayed, scroll through the payments to view
Click **OK** to close the **Payments to Deposit** screen and go to the **Make Deposits** screen
On the **Make Deposits** screen, **Deposit To** should be **1100 Checking**
Date should be **01/14/2013**
- Tab to date and change if not correct.

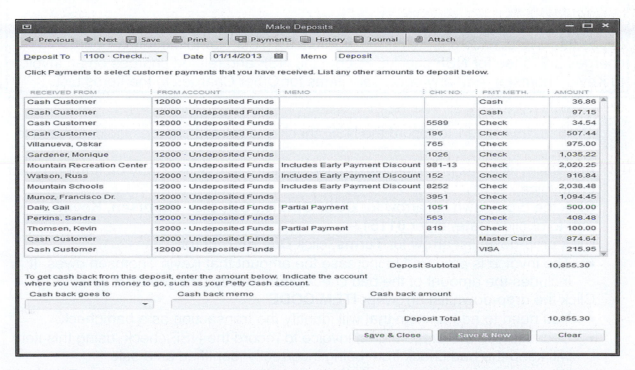

Click **Print** to print the **Deposit Summary**
Select **Deposit summary only** and click **OK** on the **Print Deposit** dialog box

Click **Print** on the **Print Lists** dialog box
When printing is finished, click **Save & Close** on **Make Deposits**
- Remember that the Deposit Summary will include the computer date at the top of the report. This may be a different date than 01/14/2013.

RECORD THE RETURN OF A CHECK BECAUSE OF NONSUFFICIENT FUNDS

A *nonsufficient funds* or *NSF* check is one that cannot be processed by the bank because there are insufficient funds in the customer's bank account. If this occurs, the amount of the check and the associated bank charges need to be subtracted from the account where the check was deposited. Also, the Accounts Receivable account needs to be updated to show the amount the customer owes you for the check that "bounced." In order to track the amount of a bad check and to charge a customer for the bank charges and any penalties you impose, Other Charge items may need to be created and an invoice for the total amount due must be prepared.

Money received for the bad check charges from the bank and for Your Name Mountain Sports is recorded as income. When the bank account is reconciled, the amount of bank charges will offset the income recorded on the invoice.

MEMO
DATE: January 15, 2013

The bank returned Kevin Thomsen's Check No. 819 for $100 marked NSF. The bank imposed a $10 service charge for the NSF check. Your Name Mountain Sports charges a $15 fee for NSF checks. Record the NSF and related charges on an invoice to Kevin Thomsen. Add any necessary items for Other Charges to the Items List.

 Prepare Invoice 11 to record the NSF check and related charges indicated above

Access invoices as previously instructed, be sure to use the Copy of: Intuit Product Invoice
Click the drop-down list arrow for **CUSTOMER:JOB**, click **Thomsen, Kevin**
Tab to or click **Date**, enter **011513**
Click drop-down list arrow for **Terms**, click **Due on receipt**
- The invoice is prepared to increase the amount that Kevin Thomsen owes. It includes the amount of the bad check and the fees charged for it.
Click the drop-down list arrow for **ITEM CODE**
- You need to add an item that will identify the transaction as a bad check.
- Because you are preparing an invoice to record the NSF check, using this item will keep the bad check from being incorrectly identified as a sale.
- When the invoice is prepared, the use of this item will debit Accounts Receivable (to increase the amount owed) and credit Checking (to decrease cash).

Click **<Add New>**
Click **Other Charge** for the **TYPE**
Enter **Bad Check** as the **Item Name/Number**
Tab to or click **Description**
Enter **Check Returned by Bank**
Amount or % should be **0.00**
Click the drop-down-list arrow for **Tax Code**
Click **Non-Taxable Sales**
Click the drop-down list arrow for **Account**
Click **1100 Checking**

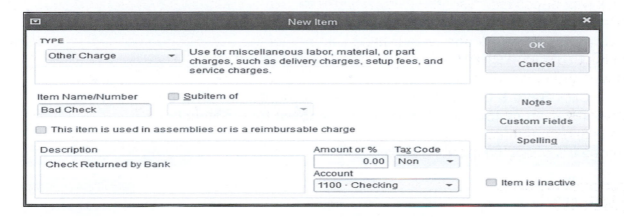

Click **OK**
Click or tab to **PRICE EACH** on the Invoice
Enter **100**
- This is the amount of Kevin's bad check.
Tab to or click the next line for **ITEM CODE**, click the drop-down list arrow for **ITEM CODE**
- Another item needs be added in order to identify the amount that Kevin owes for the NSF charges from both the bank and Your Name Mountain Sports.
Click **<Add New>**
Click **Other Charge** for **TYPE**
Enter **Bad Check Charges** as the **Item Name/Number**
Tab to or click **Description**
Enter **Bank and Other Charges for Returned Check**
Amount or % should be **0.00**
The **Tax Code** should be **Non-Taxable Sales**
Click the drop-down list arrow for **Account**
Scroll through the list of accounts
- There are no appropriate accounts for this item.
Add a new account to the Chart of Accounts by clicking **<Add New>** at the top of the Accounts list
TYPE of account is **Income**
- This account is an income account because we will be receiving money for the charges. When the bank statement is reconciled, the amount of bank service

charges will reduce the amount of income earned for the bad check charges leaving only the amount actually earned by Your Name Mountain Sports.

Enter **4040** for the **Number**

Tab to or click **Account Name**

Enter **Returned Check Service Charges**

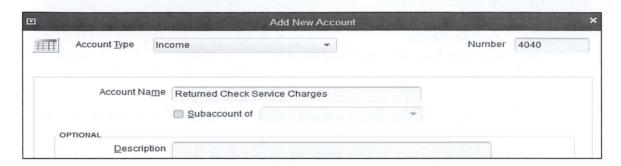

Click **Save & Close** to record the new account in the **Chart of Accounts**

- Account **4040** is inserted as the **Account** for the **New Item**

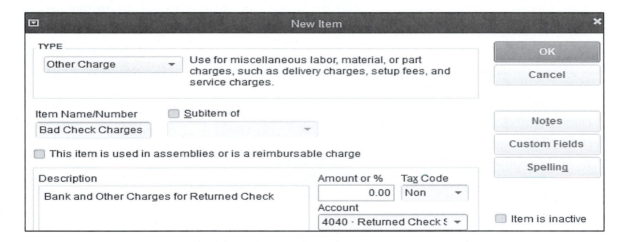

Click **OK** to add Bad Check Charges to the Item List

Tab to or click **PRICE EACH** on the Invoice

Enter **25**

- This is the total amount of the charges Kevin has incurred for the NSF check—$10 for the bank charges and $15 for Your Name Mountain Sports charges.

Click the drop-down list arrow for **CUSTOMER MESSAGE**, click **Please remit to above address.**

Customize the CUSTOMER MESSAGE by clicking between the **s** and the **.**

Type a **space** and then the word **immediately**

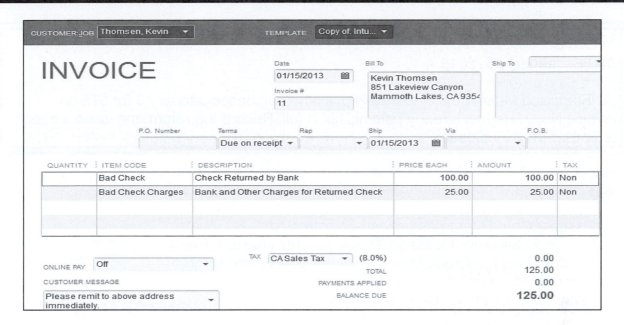

Print the Invoice
To add this to your Customer Messages List, click **Quick Add** on the Customer Message Not Found dialog box

- You may get a message box regarding the change in terms for Kevin Thomsen. Click **No**

After printing, click **Save & Close** to save and exit **Create Invoices**

ISSUE A CREDIT MEMO AND A REFUND CHECK

If merchandise is returned and the invoice has been paid in full or the sale was for cash, a refund check may be issued at the same time the credit memo is prepared. Simply clicking the "Use credit to give refund" icon instructs QuickBooks to prepare a refund check for you.

MEMO

DATE: January 15, 2013

Dr. Francisco Munoz returned the ski poles he purchased January 3 for $75 on Invoice No. 2. He has already paid his bill in full. Record the return and issue a check refunding the $75 plus tax.

 Prepare a Credit Memo to record the return and issue a refund check

Issue a Credit Memo as previously instructed
Use the Customer Message **Thank you for your business.**
At the top of the Credit Memo, click the **Use Credit to give refund** icon
The Issue a Refund dialog box appears.

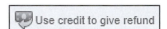

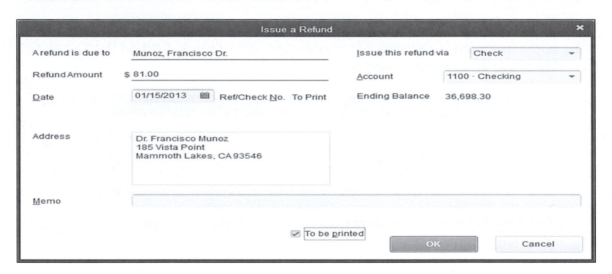

Verify the information and click **OK**.
The Credit Memo will be stamped "REFUNDED."

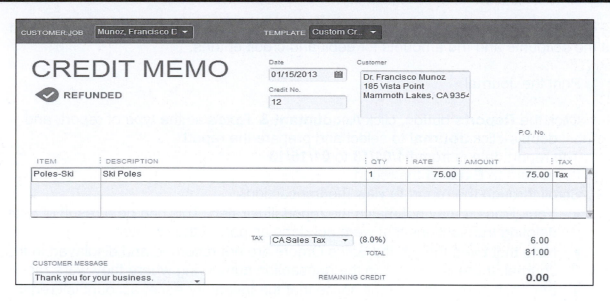

Print the Credit Memo with lines around each field
Click **Save & Close** to record the **Credit Memo** and exit
Click the **Write Checks** icon on the Home Page, click the **Previous** or back arrow until you get to the check for Dr. Munoz

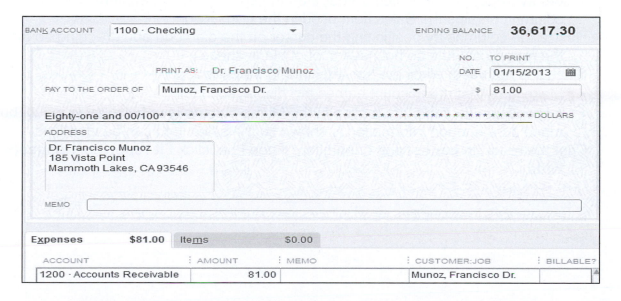

- Note that Munoz, Francisco Dr. appears in the CUSTOMER:JOB column on the Expenses tab.
Print Check No. 1 in <u>Standard</u> format as previously instructed
Click **Save & Close** on the **Write Checks** screen

PRINT THE JOURNAL

Even though QuickBooks displays registers and reports in a manner that focuses on the transaction—that is, entering a sale on account via an invoice rather than a Sales Journal or a General Journal—it still keeps a Journal. The Journal records each transaction and lists the accounts and the amounts for debit and credit entries.

 Print the Journal

> Click the **Reports** button, click **Accountant & Taxes** as the type of report, and
> double-click **Journal** to select and prepare the report
> The report date is from **01/01/13** to **01/15/13**
> Make sure to **Expand** the report
> Scroll through the report to view the transactions
> - Your Trans # may not match the report illustrated. This can be a result of your
>   deleting transactions that were not done as part of the chapter.
> - Note that even though the Sales Orders are not recorded and displayed in the
>   Journal, there is a space in the transaction numbering where they were recorded.
> - For each item sold, you will notice that the Inventory Asset account is credited
>   and the Cost of Goods Sold account is debited. This moves the value of the item
>   out of your assets and into the cost of goods sold. The amount is not the same
>   amount as the one in the transaction. This is because QuickBooks uses the
>   average cost method of inventory valuation and records the transaction based on
>   the average cost of an item rather than the specific cost of an item. The Memo
>   column contains the Sales Item used in the transaction.
> Resize the columns by positioning the cursor on the diamond and dragging so that
> the report columns do not have a lot of blank space
> Since it is not used, eliminate the **Adj** column from the report
> - Make sure that the account names are displayed in full
> - It is acceptable if the Information in the Memo column is not displayed in full, but
>   make sure enough information is shown so the sales item can be identified.
> Print the report in **Landscape** orientation; if need be, click **Fit report to 1 pages(s)
> wide**

Your Name Mountain Sports
Journal
January 1 - 15, 2013

Trans #	Type	Date	Num	Adj	Name	Memo	Account	Debit	Credit
78	Deposit	01/14/2013				Deposit	1100 · Checking	10,855.30	
					Cash Customer	Deposit	12000 · Undeposited Funds		36.86
					Cash Customer	Deposit	12000 · Undeposited Funds		97.15
					Cash Customer	Deposit	12000 · Undeposited Funds		34.54
					Cash Customer	Deposit	12000 · Undeposited Funds		507.44
					Villanueva, Oskar	Deposit	12000 · Undeposited Funds		975.00
					Gardener, Monique	Deposit	12000 · Undeposited Funds		1,035.22
					Mountain Recreation Center	Includes Early Payment Discount	12000 · Undeposited Funds		2,020.25
					Watson, Russ	Includes Early Payment Discount	12000 · Undeposited Funds		916.84
					Mountain Schools	Includes Early Payment Discount	12000 · Undeposited Funds		2,038.48
					Munoz, Francisco Dr.	Deposit	12000 · Undeposited Funds		1,094.45
					Daily, Gail	Partial Payment	12000 · Undeposited Funds		500.00
					Perkins, Sandra	Deposit	12000 · Undeposited Funds		408.48
					Thomsen, Kevin	Partial Payment	12000 · Undeposited Funds		100.00
					Cash Customer	Deposit	12000 · Undeposited Funds		874.64
					Cash Customer	Deposit	12000 · Undeposited Funds		215.95
								10,855.30	10,855.30
79	Invoice	01/15/2013	11		Thomsen, Kevin		1200 · Accounts Receivable	125.00	
					Thomsen, Kevin	Check Returned by Bank	1100 · Checking		100.00
					Thomsen, Kevin	Bank and Other Charges for Returned Check	4040 · Returned Check Service Charges		25.00
					State Board of Equalization	CA Sales Tax	2200 · Sales Tax Payable	0.00	
								125.00	125.00
80	Credit Memo	01/15/2013	12		Munoz, Francisco Dr.		1200 · Accounts Receivable		81.00
					Munoz, Francisco Dr.	Ski Poles	4012 · Equipment Sales	75.00	
					Munoz, Francisco Dr.	Ski Poles	1120 · Inventory Asset	30.00	
					Munoz, Francisco Dr.	Ski Poles	5000 · Cost of Goods Sold		30.00
					State Board of Equalization	CA Sales Tax	2200 · Sales Tax Payable	6.00	
								111.00	111.00
81	Check	01/15/2013	1		Munoz, Francisco Dr.		1100 · Checking		81.00
					Munoz, Francisco Dr.		1200 · Accounts Receivable	81.00	
								81.00	81.00
TOTAL								**36,718.89**	**36,718.89**

Partial Report

When the report is printed, close it.
Close the Journal
Do not close the Report Center

PRINT THE TRIAL BALANCE

When all sales transactions have been entered, it is important to print the trial balance and verify that the total debits equal the total credits.

 Double-click **Trial Balance** to select the type of report on the Accountant & Taxes section the Report Center

The report dates are from **01/01/2013** to **01/15/2013**

Your Name Mountain Sports
Trial Balance
As of January 15, 2013

	Jan 15, 13	
	Debit	Credit
1100 · Checking	36,617.30	
1200 · Accounts Receivable	5,696.50	
1120 · Inventory Asset	32,766.54	
12000 · Undeposited Funds	0.00	
1311 · Office Supplies	850.00	
1312 · Sales Supplies	575.00	
1340 · Prepaid Insurance	250.00	
1511 · Original Cost	5,000.00	
1521 · Original Cost	4,500.00	
2000 · Accounts Payable		8,500.00
2100 · Visa		150.00
2200 · Sales Tax Payable		701.77
2510 · Office Equipment Loan		3,000.00
2520 · Store Fixtures Loan		2,500.00
3000 · Retained Earnings	0.00	
3010 · Your Name & Muir Capital		26,159.44
3011 · Your Name, Investment		20,000.00
3012 · Larry Muir, Investment		20,000.00
4011 · Clothing & Accessory Sales		1,759.51
4012 · Equipment Sales		7,436.44
4040 · Returned Check Service Charges		25.00
4050 · Sales Discounts	494.36	
5000 · Cost of Goods Sold	3,482.46	
TOTAL	90,232.16	90,232.16

Print the Trial Balance in **Portrait** orientation
Close the report

PREPARE INVENTORY VALUATION DETAIL REPORT

To obtain information regarding the inventory, you may prepare an Inventory Valuation Summary or an Inventory Valuation Detail report. Both reports give you information regarding an item, the number on hand, the average cost, asset value. The summary report also gives information regarding an item's percentage of total assets, sales price, retail value, and percentage of total retail. The detail report includes information for transactions using inventory items. In addition to the information shown in both reports, the detail report includes the type of transaction, date of transaction, customer name, number, quantity, and cost.

Preparing the Inventory Valuation Detail will allow you to verify the inventory item used and average cost for each transaction. In addition, you will know the number of items on hand.

 Prepare and print an Inventory Valuation Detail report in Landscape orientation for January 1-15, 2013

    Click **Inventory** in the Report Center
Double-click **Inventory Valuation Detail**
Enter the dates From **01/01/13** To **01/15/13**
Resize the columns to display the information in full

Your Name Mountain Sports
Inventory Valuation Detail
January 1 - 15, 2013

Type	Date	Name	Num	Qty	Cost	On Hand	Avg Cost	Asset Value
Sweaters								
Invoice	01/03/2013	Perkins, Sandra	4	–1		74	25.00	1,850.00
Sales Receipt	01/12/2013	Cash Customer	4	–1		73	25.00	1,825.00
Total Sweaters						73		1,825.00
Toboggans								
Inventory Adjust	01/08/2013			10		10	137.50	1,375.00
Invoice	01/08/2013	Mountain Recreation Center	8	–5		5	137.50	687.50
Total Toboggans						5		687.50
Underwear								
Invoice	01/03/2013	Perkins, Sandra	4	–1		32	8.00	256.00
Total Underwear						32		256.00
Total Inventory						1,435		31,016.54
Assembly								
Total Assembly						0		0.00
TOTAL						1,435		31,016.54

Partial Report

Print the report and then close it
Close the Report Center

CUSTOMER CENTER

In the Customer Center, you will see the customer list. When pointing at a customer name, you may see a message regarding overdue or almost due invoices. As you click each customer, you will see the customer information and transaction details for the individual customer. You may also view transaction details for specific types of transactions by clicking the drop-down list arrow.

 View the Customer Center and the information for Cash Customer

Click the **Customers** icon, and then click **Cash Customer**
Click the drop-down list arrow next to **Show** to see the list of the types of transactions that may be displayed

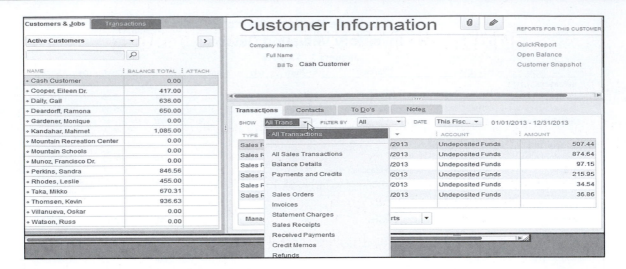

Close the Customer Center

BACK UP YOUR NAME MOUNTAIN SPORTS

Whenever an important work session is complete, you should always back up your data. If your data disk is damaged or an error is discovered at a later time, the backup disk may be restored and the information used for recording transactions. The backup being made will contain all of the transactions entered in Chapter 5. In addition, it is always wise to make a duplicate of your data disk just in case the disk is damaged in some way.

 Back up data for Your Name Mountain Sports to **Sports (Backup Ch. 5).qbb**. If you wish to make a duplicate disk, follow the instructions provided by your professor.

SUMMARY

In this chapter, cash, bank charge card, and credit sales were prepared for Your Name Mountain Sports, a retail business, using sales receipts, sales orders, and invoices. Credit memos and refund checks were issued, and customer accounts were added and revised. Invoices and sales receipts were edited, deleted, and voided. Sales orders were changed into invoices. Cash payments were received, and bank deposits were made. New accounts were added to the Chart of Accounts, and new items were added to the Item List while entering transactions. Inventory items were added and sold. All the transactions entered reinforced the QuickBooks concept of using the business form to record transactions rather than entering information in journals. However, QuickBooks does not disregard traditional accounting methods. Instead, it performs this function in the background. The Journal was accessed, analyzed, and printed. The importance of reports for information and decision-making was illustrated. Sales reports emphasized both cash and credit sales according to the customer or according to the sales item generating the revenue. Accounts receivable reports focused on amounts owed by credit customers. The traditional trial balance emphasizing the equality of debits and credits was prepared.

END-OF-CHAPTER QUESTIONS

TRUE/FALSE

ANSWER THE FOLLOWING QUESTIONS IN THE SPACE PROVIDED BEFORE THE QUESTION NUMBER.

_____ 1. If a return is made after an invoice has been paid in full, a refund check is issued along with a credit memo.

_____ 2. QuickBooks automatically applies a payment received to the most current invoice.

_____ 3. Sales tax will be calculated automatically on an invoice if a customer is marked taxable.

_____ 4. A new sales item may be added only at the beginning of a period.

_____ 5. Items on a Sales Order are immediately removed from inventory.

_____ 6. All business forms must be duplicated before they can be customized.

_____ 7. The Discounts and Credits icon on the Receive Payments window allows discounts to be applied to invoices being paid by clicking Cancel.

_____ 8. Cash sales are recorded in the Receive Payments window and marked paid.

_____ 9. If a customer issues a check that is returned marked NSF, you may charge the customer the amount of the bank charges and any penalty charges you impose.

_____ 10. Sales tax must be calculated manually and added to sales receipts.

MULTIPLE CHOICE

WRITE THE LETTER OF THE CORRECT ANSWER IN THE SPACE PROVIDED BEFORE THE QUESTION NUMBER.

_____ 1. Information regarding details of a customer's balance may be obtained by viewing ___.
A. the Trial Balance
B. the Customer Balance Summary Report
C. the Customer Balance Detail Report
D. the check detail report

_____ 2. Even though transactions are entered via business documents such as invoices and sales receipts, QuickBooks keeps track of all transactions ___.
A. in a chart
B. in the master account register
C. on a graph
D. in the Journal

_____ 3. If a transaction is ___, it will not show up in the Customer Balance Detail Report.
A. voided
B. deleted
C. corrected
D. canceled

_____ 4. A credit card sale is treated exactly like a ___.
A. cash sale
B. sale on account until reimbursement is received from a bank
C. sale on account
D. bank deposit

_____ 5. If the word -Split- appears in the Split column of a report rather than an account name, it means that the transaction is split between two or more ___.
A. accounts or items
B. customers
C. journals
D. reports

_____ 6. When adding a customer _on the fly_, you may choose to add just the customer's name by selecting ___.
A. Quick Add
B. Set Up
C. Condensed
D. none of the above—a customer cannot be added _on the fly_

_____ 7. The Item List stores information about ___.
    A. each item that is out of stock
    B. each item in stock
    C. each customer with an account
    D. each item a company sells

_____ 8. A report prepared to obtain information about sales, inventory, and merchandise costs is a ___.
    A. Stock Report
    B. Income Statement
    C. Sales by Vendor Summary Report
    D. Sales by Item Summary Report

_____ 9. If a customer has a balance for an amount owed and a return is made, a credit memo is prepared and ___.
    A. a refund check is issued
    B. the amount of the return is applied to an invoice
    C. the customer determines whether to apply the amount to an invoice or to get a refund check
    D. all of the above

_____ 10. Purchase information regarding an item sold by the company is entered ___.
    A. in the Invoice Register
    B. when adding a sales item
    C. only when creating the company
    D. when the last item in stock is sold

FILL-IN

IN THE SPACE PROVIDED, WRITE THE ANSWER THAT MOST APPROPRIATELY COMPLETES THE SENTENCE.

1. A report showing all sales, credits, and payments for each customer on account and the remaining balance on the account is the _____ report.

2. When a customer with a balance due on an account makes a payment, it is recorded in the _____ window.

3. If the Quantity and Price Each are entered on an invoice, pressing the _____ key will cause QuickBooks to calculate and enter the correct information in the Amount column of the invoice.

4. QuickBooks allows you to view additional information within a report by using the _____ feature.

5. When you receive payments from customers, QuickBooks places the amount received in an account called _____.

SHORT ESSAY

Describe the use of Find to locate an invoice. Based on chapter information, what is used to instruct Find to limit its search?

_____

_____

_____

_____

_____

NAME _____

TRANSMITTAL

CHAPTER 5: YOUR NAME MOUNTAIN SPORTS

Attach the following documents and reports:

Invoice No. 1: Russ Watson
Invoice No. 2: Francisco Munoz
Invoice No. 3: Mountain Schools
Invoice No. 4: Sandra Perkins
Sales Order 1: Kevin Thomsen
Sales Order 2: Russ Watson
Invoice No. 5: Kevin Thomsen
Invoice No. 6: Russ Watson
Invoice No. 7: Monique Gardener
Invoice No. 7 (Corrected): Monique Gardener
Customer Balance Detail
Invoice No. 3 (Corrected): Mountain Schools
Invoice No. 8: Mountain Recreation Center
Invoice 1 (Voided): Russ Watson
Credit Memo No. 9: Monique Gardener
Credit Memo No. 10: Russ Watson
Open Invoices by Customer, January 10, 2013
Sales Receipt No. 1: Cash Customer
Sales Receipt No. 2: Cash Customer
Sales Receipt No. 3: Cash Customer
Sales Receipt No. 4: Cash Customer
Sales Receipt No. 5: Cash Customer
Sales Receipt No. 6: Cash Customer
Sales by Item Summary, January 1-13, 2013
Sales Receipt No. 1 (Revised):
  Cash Customer
Payment Receipt: Oskar Villanueva
Payment Receipt: Monique Gardener
Payment Receipt: Mountain Recreation Center
Payment Receipt: Mountain Schools
Payment Receipt: Russ Watson
Payment Receipt: Francisco Munoz
Payment Receipt: Gail Daily
Payment Receipt: Sandra Perkins
Payment Receipt: Kevin Thomsen

Customer Balance Summary
Deposit Summary
Invoice No. 11: Kevin Thomsen
Credit Memo No. 12: Francisco Munoz
Check No. 1: Francisco Munoz
Journal, January 1-15, 2013
Trial Balance, January 1-15, 2013
Inventory Valuation Detail,
  January 1-15, 2013

END-OF-CHAPTER PROBLEM

YOUR NAME RESORT CLOTHING

Your Name Resort Clothing is a men's and women's clothing store located in San Luis Obispo, California, that specializes in resort wear. The store is owned and operated by you and your partner Karen Olsen. Karen keeps the books and runs the office for the store, and you are responsible for buying merchandise and managing the store. Both partners sell merchandise in the store, and they have some college students working part time during the evenings and on the weekends.

INSTRUCTIONS

As in previous chapters, use a copy of **Clothing.qbw** that you made following the directions presented in Chapter 1. If QuickBooks wants to update the program, click Yes. Open the company, and record the following transactions using invoices and sales receipts. Student's Name Resort Clothing accepts cash, checks, and credit cards for *cash* sales. Make bank deposits as instructed. Print the reports as indicated. Add new accounts, items, and customers where appropriate. Pay attention to the dates and note that the year is **2013**. Verify the year to use with your instructor and use the same year for Clothing in Chapters 5, 6, and 7.

When recording transactions, use the Item List to determine the item(s) sold. All transactions are taxable unless otherwise indicated. Terms for sales on account are the standard terms assigned to each customer individually. If a customer exceeds his or her credit limit, accept the transaction. When receiving payment for sales on account, always check to see if a discount should be given. A customer's beginning balance is not eligible for a discount. The date of the sale begins the discount period. A check should be received or postmarked within ten days of the invoice in order to qualify for a discount. If the customer has any credits to the account because of a return, apply the credits to the appropriate invoice. If the customer makes a return and does not have a balance on account, prepare a refund check for the customer.

Invoices begin with number 15, are numbered consecutively, and have lines printed around each field. Sales Receipts begin with number 25, are also numbered consecutively, and have lines printed around each field. Sales Orders are accepted for orders made by telephone, begin with the number 1, and have lines printed around each field. Each invoice, sales order and sales receipt should contain a message. Use the one you feel is most appropriate. If you write any checks, keep track of the check numbers used. QuickBooks does not always display the check number you are expecting to see. Remember that QuickBooks does not print check numbers on checks because most businesses use checks with the check numbers preprinted.

If a transaction can be printed, print the transaction when it is entered unless your instructor specifies the transactions to print.

LISTS

The Item List and Customers & Jobs List are displayed for your use in determining which sales item and customer to use in a transaction.

ITEM LIST

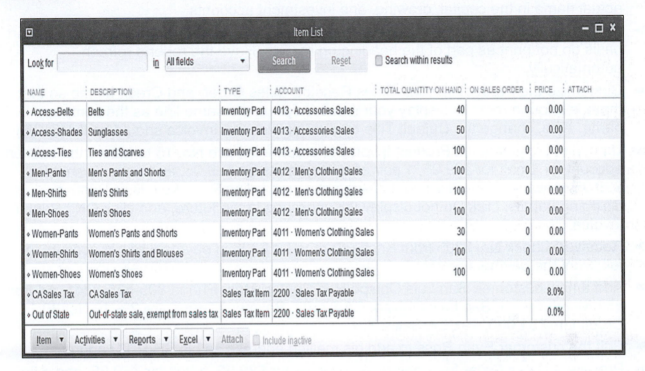

CUSTOMER & JOBS LIST

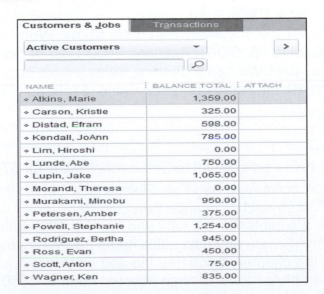

RECORD TRANSACTIONS

January 1, 2013:

► Add your name to the Company Name and the Legal Name. The name will be **Your Name Resort Clothing**— (Type your actual name, *not* the words *Your Name*.)

► Add your name to the owner's equity accounts. Replace "Student's Name" with your actual name in the capital, drawing, and investment accounts.

► Change the company preferences so that the date prepared, time prepared, and report basis do not print as part of the heading on reports. Have the reports refresh automatically.

► Customize the Product Invoice, Sales Receipt, Sales Order, and Credit Memo so that there is enough room to display your name in full on the same line as the company name. Also, change the Default Title to all capital letters (Invoice should be INVOICE)

► Use your Copy of: Intuit Product Invoice to prepare Invoice No. 15 to record the sale on account for 1 belt for $29.95, 1 pair of men's shorts for $39.95, and a man's shirt for $39.95 to Hiroshi Lim. (If you get dialog boxes regarding Price Levels or Printing Shipping Labels, click Do not display this message in the future, and click OK.) Print the invoice.

► Received Check No. 3305 from Kristie Carson for $325 in payment of her account in full. Print the payment receipt.

► Add a new customer: San Luis Obispo Rec Center, Main Phone 805-555-2241, Address 451 Marsh Street, San Luis Obispo, CA 93407, Payment Terms are 2% 10 Net 30, Credit Limit $1,000, Tax CA Sales Tax,.

► Edit the customer Evan Ross to add his mailing address as his SHIP TO address

► Prepare a Sales Order for 1 pair of sunglasses for $89.95, a belt for $69.95, and a tie for $39.95 to Evan Ross. Print the Sales Order. (Remember to approve any transaction that exceeds a customer's credit limit.)

► Add a new sales item—Type: Inventory Part, Item Name: Women-Dress, Description: Women's Dresses, Cost: 0.00, COGS Account: 5000-Cost of Goods Sold, Tax Code: Tax, Income Account: 4011 Women's Clothing Sales, Asset Account: 1120-Inventory Asset; Reorder Point: 20, On Hand: 25, Total Value: $750, as of 01/01/2013—be sure to use the correct date.

January 3, 2013:

► Record the sale of 1 dress on account to Stephanie Powell for $79.95.

► Sold 5 men's shirts on account to San Luis Obispo Rec Center for $29.95 each, 5 pair of men's shorts for $29.95 each. Because San Luis Rec Center is a nonprofit organization, include a subtotal for the sale and apply a 10% sales discount for a nonprofit organization. (Create any new sales items necessary by following the instructions given in the chapter. If you need to add an income account for Sales Discounts to the Chart of Accounts, assign account number 4050. The nonprofit discount is marked Taxable so the discount is applied before adding sales tax.)

▶ Sold 1 woman's blouse for $59.95 to a cash customer. Record the sale to Cash Customer. (If necessary, refer to steps provided within the chapter for instructions on creating a cash customer.) Received Check No. 378 for the full amount including tax. Prepare and print Sales Receipt No. 25 for this transaction.

▶ Received a belt returned by Ken Wagner. The original price of the belt was $49.95. Prepare a Credit Memo. Apply the credit to his Opening Balance.

▶ Sold a dress to a customer for $99.95. The customer paid with her Visa. Record the sale.

▶ Sold a scarf for $19.95 plus tax for cash. Record the sale.

▶ Received payments on account from the following customers:

  o   Efram Distad, $598.00, Check No. 145
  o   Amber Petersen, $375, Check No. 4015
  o   Abe Lunde, $750, Check No. 8915-02
  o   Ken Wagner, $781.05, Check No. 6726

January 5, 2013:

▶ Evan Ross came into the store to pick up his items on order. Create an invoice from the sales order. (Remember use the date 01/05/13, approve any transaction that exceeds a customer's credit limit, and customize the Sales Order Invoice as you did for other templates earlier.) Print the invoice.

▶ Deposit all cash, checks, and credit card receipts. Print a Deposit Summary.

January 7, 2013

▶ Evan Ross returned the tie he purchased on 01/05/13. (Did you apply this to an invoice?)

January 15, 2013:

▶ Received an NSF notice from the bank for the check for $325 from Kristie Carson. Enter the necessary transaction for this nonsufficient funds check to be paid on receipt. The bank's charges are $15, and Your Name Resort Clothing charges $15 for all NSF checks. (If necessary, refer to steps provided within the chapter for instructions on adding accounts or items necessary to record this transaction. If a new income account is needed, use 4040 as the account number.) Terms are "Due on receipt" and the message is "Please remit to above address immediately."

▶ Abe Lunde returned a shirt he had purchased for $54.99 plus tax. Record the return. Check the balance of his account. If there is no balance, issue a refund check.

▶ Sold 3 men's shirts to a cash customer, for $39.95 each plus tax. He used his Master Card for payment.

▶ Sold on account 1 dress for $99.99, 1 pair of women's sandals for $79.95, and a belt for $39.95 to JoAnn Kendall.

▶ Sold 1 pair of women's shorts for $34.95 to a cash customer. Accepted Check No. 8160 for payment.

▶ Received payments on account from the following customers:

- Partial payment from Jake Lupin, $250, Check No. 2395.
- Payment in full from Anton Scott, Check No. 9802.
- Received $1,338.62 from Stephanie Powell as payment in full on account, Check No. 2311. The payment was postmarked 1/11/2013. (Apply the discount to Invoice No. 16, click the line for Invoice No. 16; click the Discounts And Credits icon; calculate the 2 percent discount (be sure to round up to the nearest cent) and enter the amount on the Discounts and Credits screen, select the appropriate account for the sales discount, click Done to apply the discount.
- Received Check No. 2805 for $619.24 as payment in full from Evan Ross. (If eligible for a discount, apply it to the actual amount that is owed after the return rather than accept QuickBooks' discount on the original invoice amount.)

▶ Sold 3 pairs of men's pants for $75.00 each, 3 men's shirts for $50.00 each, 3 belts for $39.99 each, 2 pairs of men's shoes for $90.00 each, 2 ties for $55.00 each, and 1 pair of sunglasses for $75.00 to Bertha Rodriguez on account. (If the amount of the sale exceeds Bertha's credit limit, accept the sale anyway.)

▶ Change the Sales Item Access-Shades to Access-Sunglasses

▶ Sold on account 1 pair of sunglasses for $95.00, 2 dresses for $99.95 each, and 2 pairs of women's shoes for $65.00 each to Amber Petersen.

▶ Print Customer Balance Detail Report for All Transactions in Portrait orientation. Adjust column widths so the account names are shown in full and the report is one page wide without selecting Fit report to one page wide. The report length may be longer than one page.

▶ Print a Sales by Item Detail Report for 01/01/2013 to 01/15/2013 in Landscape orientation. Adjust column widths so the report fits on one page wide. Do not select Fit report to one page wide.

▶ Deposit all payments, checks, and charges received from customers. Print the Deposit Summary.

▶ Print a Journal for 01/01/2013 to 01/15/2013 in Landscape orientation. (Remember to Expand the report, adjust the column widths, and remove any unused columns from display. In order to print the report on one page wide, the information in the memo column may not show in full.)

▶ Print a Trial Balance for 01/01/2013 to 01/15/2013.

▶ Print an Inventory Valuation Detail for 01/01/2013 to 01/15/2013.

▶ Backup your work to Clothing (Backup Ch. 5).

NAME _____

TRANSMITTAL

CHAPTER 5: YOUR NAME RESORT CLOTHING

Attach the following documents and reports:

Invoice No. 15: Hiroshi Lim
Payment Receipt: Kristie Carson
Sales Order 1: Evan Ross
Invoice No. 16: Stephanie Powell
Invoice No. 17: San Luis Obispo Rec Center
Sales Receipt No. 25: Cash Customer
Credit Memo No. 18: Ken Wagner
Sales Receipt No. 26: Cash Customer
Sales Receipt No. 27: Cash Customer
Payment Receipt: Efram Distad
Payment Receipt: Amber Petersen
Payment Receipt: Abe Lunde
Payment Receipt: Ken Wagner
Invoice No. 19: Evan Ross
Deposit Summary, January 5, 2013
Credit Memo 20: Evan Ross
Invoice No. 21: Kristie Carson
Credit Memo No. 22: Abe Lunde
Check No. 1: Abe Lunde
Sales Receipt No. 28: Cash Customer
Invoice No. 23: JoAnn Kendall
Sales Receipt No. 29: Cash Customer
Payment Receipt: Jake Lupin
Payment Receipt: Anton Scott
Payment Receipt: Stephanie Powell
Payment Receipt: Evan Ross
Invoice No. 24: Bertha Rodriguez
Invoice No. 25: Amber Petersen
Customer Balance Detail
Sales by Item Detail Report, January 1-15, 2013
Deposit Summary, January 15, 2013
Journal, January 1-15-2013
Trial Balance, January 1-15, 2013
Inventory Valuation Detail, January 1-15, 2013

PAYABLES AND PURCHASES: MERCHANDISING BUSINESS

LEARNING OBJECTIVES

At the completion of this chapter you will be able to:

1. Understand the concepts for computerized accounting for payables in a merchandising business.
2. Customize a Purchase Order template.
3. Prepare, view, and print purchase orders and checks.
4. Enter items received against purchase orders.
5. Enter bills, enter vendor credits, and pay bills.
6. Edit and correct errors in bills and purchase orders.
7. Add new vendors, add new accounts.
8. Assign preferred vendors to sales items.
9. View accounts payable transaction history from the Enter Bills window.
10. View, use the QuickZoom feature, and/or print QuickReports for vendors, accounts payable register, and so on.
11. Record and edit transactions in the Accounts Payable Register.
12. Use various payment options including writing checks, using Pay Bills to write checks, and company credit cards.
13. Use early payment discounts.
14. Display and print a Sales Tax Liability Report, an Accounts Payable Aging Summary Report, an Unpaid Bills Detail Report, a Vendor Balance Summary Report, an Inventory Stock Status by Item Report, and an Inventory Valuation Detail Report.
15. Use the Vendor Center to obtain or modify vendor information, and to assign accounts to vendors.
16. Use the Inventory Center to view information about individual inventory items and to prepare an Inventory Stock Status report.

ACCOUNTING FOR PAYABLES AND PURCHASES

In a merchandising business, much of the accounting for purchases and payables consists of ordering merchandise for resale and paying bills for expenses incurred in the operation of the business. Purchases are for things used in the operation of the business. Some transactions will be in the form of cash purchases; others will be purchases on account.

Bills can be paid when they are received or when they are due. Merchandise received must be checked against purchase orders, and completed purchase orders must be closed. Rather than use cumbersome journals, QuickBooks continues to focus on recording transactions based on the business document; therefore, you use the Enter Bills and Pay Bills features of the program to record the receipt and payment of bills. While QuickBooks does not refer to it as such, the Vendor List is the same as the Accounts Payable Subsidiary Ledger.

QuickBooks can remind you when inventory needs to be ordered and when payments are due. Purchase orders are prepared when ordering merchandise and sent to a vendor who will process the order and send the merchandise to the company. When the merchandise is received, the quantity received is recorded. The program automatically tracks inventory and uses the average cost method to value the inventory.

If the bill accompanies the merchandise, both the bill and the merchandise receipt are recorded together on a bill. If the merchandise is received without a bill, the receipt of items is recorded; and, when it arrives, the bill is recorded. When the inventory receipt is recorded, the purchase order is closed automatically.

QuickBooks can calculate and apply discounts earned for paying bills early. Payments can be made by recording payments in the Pay Bills window or, if using the cash basis for accounting, by writing a check. Merchandise purchased may be paid for at the same time the items and the bill are received, or it may be paid for at a later date. A cash purchase can be recorded by writing a check, by using a credit card, or by using petty cash. Even though QuickBooks focuses on recording transactions on the business forms used, all transactions are recorded behind the scenes in the Journal.

As in previous chapters, corrections can be made directly on the bill or within the account register. New accounts and vendors may be added *on the fly* as transactions are entered. Purchase orders, bills, or checks may be voided or deleted. Reports illustrating vendor balances, unpaid bills, accounts payable aging, sales tax liability, transaction history, accounts payable registers, and inventory may be viewed and printed.

TRAINING TUTORIAL AND PROCEDURES

The following tutorial will once again work with the fictitious company, Your Name Mountain Sports. You will use the company file for Your Name Mountain Sports that contains the transactions you entered for Chapter 5. As with the earlier training in a service company, the merchandising section of the text has you enter the transactions for all three chapters—5, 6, and 7—within the same company file.

DATES

Throughout the text, the year used for the screen shots is 2013, which is the same year as the version of the program. You may want to check with your instructor to see if you should use 2013 as the year for the transactions. The year you used in Chapter 5 should be the same year you use in Chapters 6 and 7.

PRINTING

As in previous chapters, you will be instructed when to print business documents and reports. Everything that is to be printed within the chapter is listed on a transmittal sheet. The end-of- chapter problem also has everything to be printed listed on a transmittal sheet. Always check with your instructor for printing requirements.

OPEN QUICKBOOKS® AND YOUR NAME MOUNTAIN SPORTS

 Open QuickBooks and Your Name Mountain Sports as instructed in previous chapters

BEGINNING THE TUTORIAL

In this chapter you will be entering purchases of merchandise for resale in the business and entering bills incurred by the company in the operation of the business. You will also be recording the payment of bills and purchases using checks and credit cards.

The Vendor List keeps information regarding the vendors with which you do business. This information includes the vendor names, addresses, telephone number, fax number, e-mail address, payment terms, credit limits, and account numbers. You will be using the following list for vendors:

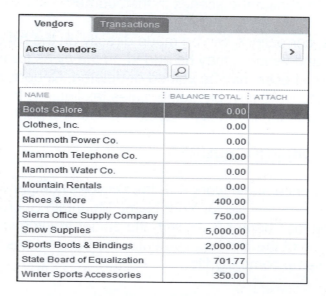

NAME	BALANCE TOTAL	ATTACH
Boots Galore	0.00	
Clothes, Inc.	0.00	
Mammoth Power Co.	0.00	
Mammoth Telephone Co.	0.00	
Mammoth Water Co.	0.00	
Mountain Rentals	0.00	
Shoes & More	400.00	
Sierra Office Supply Company	750.00	
Snow Supplies	5,000.00	
Sports Boots & Bindings	2,000.00	
State Board of Equalization	701.77	
Winter Sports Accessories	350.00	

As in previous chapters, all transactions are listed on memos. The transaction date will be the same date as the memo date unless otherwise specified within the transaction. Vendor names, when necessary, will be given in the transaction. Unless otherwise specified, terms are 2% 10 Net 30. Once a specific type of transaction has been entered in a step-by-step manner, additional transactions of the same or a similar type will be made without having instructions provided. Of course, you may always refer to instructions given for previous transactions for ideas or for steps used to enter those transactions. To determine the account used in the transaction, refer to the Chart of Accounts. When you enter account information on a bill, clicking the drop-down list arrow will show a copy of the Chart of Accounts.

VIEW REMINDERS TO DETERMINE MERCHANDISE TO ORDER

QuickBooks has a feature for Reminders that is used to remind you of things that need to be completed. The Company menu allows you to display Reminders. Information on Reminders may be displayed in summary (collapsed) form or in detailed (expanded) form. The information displayed is affected by the date of the computer; so, what you see on your screen may not match the text display.

MEMO
DATE: January 16, 2013

Display Reminders to determine which items need to be ordered.

 Display **Reminders**

Click **Company** on the Menu bar, click **Reminders**
- The Reminders List appears on the screen in Summary (Collapsed) form.

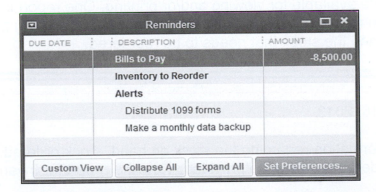

- Note: Your Reminders Summary (Collapsed) form and Reminders Detail (Expanded) form may <u>not</u> match the ones displayed in the text. This is due to the fact that your computer date may be different from the date used in the chapter. Disregard any differences.

Click the **Expand All** button to view detailed Reminders

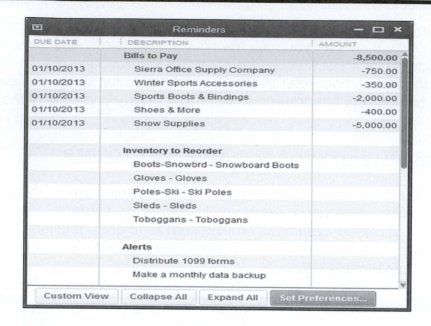

- The expanded view shows the bills that need to be paid as well as any overdue invoices, inventory to reorder, any items that need to be printed, and alerts.
- The Set Preferences button allows you to customize the data shown in Reminders.

Close Reminders

PREPARE AN INVENTORY STOCK STATUS BY ITEM REPORT

In addition to the Inventory Valuation Detail Report prepared in Chapter 5, several Inventory Reports are available for viewing and/or printing. One report is the Inventory Stock Status by Item report. This report provides information regarding the stock on hand, the stock on order, and the stock that needs to be reordered.

MEMO

DATE: January 16, 2013

More detailed information regarding the stock on hand, stock ordered, and stock needing to be ordered needs to be provided. View the report for Inventory Stock Status by Item.

 View the **Inventory Stock Status by Item Report**

Click **Reports** on the Menu bar, point to **Inventory,** click **Inventory Stock Status by Item**

The dates are From **01/01/13** and To **01/16/13**

Tab to generate the report

Your Name Mountain Sports
Inventory Stock Status by Item
January 1 - 16, 2013

	Pref Vendor	Reorder Pt	On Hand	On Sales Order	For Assemblies	Available	Order	On PO	Next Deliv	Sales/Week
Inventory										
Accessories	▶ Winter Sports Accessories	100	795	0	0	795		0		2.2
Bindings-Skis	Sports Boots & Bindings	10	43	0	0	43		0		3.1
Bindings-Snow	Sports Boots & Bindings	5	48	0	0	48		0		0.9
Boots	Shoes & More	10	20	0	0	20		0		0
Boots-Ski	Boots Galore	10	14	0	0	14		0		0.4
Boots-Snowbrd	Boots Galore	10	10	0	0	10	✔	0		0.9
Gloves	Clothes, Inc.	20	20	0	0	20	✔	0		0.9
Hats	Winter Sports Accessories	20	29	0	0	29		0		0.4
Helmets		5	20	0	0	20		0		2.2
Pants-Ski	Clothes, Inc.	10	93	0	0	93		0		0.9
Pants-Snowbrd	Clothes, Inc.	10	50	0	0	50		0		0
Parkas	Clothes, Inc.	25	73	0	0	73		0		0.9
Poles-Ski	Snow Supplies	15	13	0	0	13	✔	0		2.2
Skis	Snow Supplies	15	43	0	0	43		0		3.1
Sleds		5	4	0	0	4	✔	0		2.6
Snowboard	Snow Supplies	15	28	0	0	28		0		0.9
Socks	Boots Galore	25	72	0	0	72		0		1.3
Sweaters	Clothes, Inc.	25	73	0	0	73		0		0.9
Toboggans		5	5	0	0	5	✔	0		2.2
Underwear	Clothes, Inc.	30	32	0	0	32		0		0.4

- Notice the items marked in the Order column. This tells you that you need to prepare and send purchase orders
- QuickBooks performs the calculations to determine whether or not an item needs to be ordered.
- The items on hand are equal to or less than the number of items indicated in the reorder point so QuickBooks marks the Order column. These are the same items that were shown in Reminders.

Make note of the items that need to be ordered, and close the report

PURCHASE ORDERS

Using the QuickBooks Purchase Order feature helps you track your inventory. Information regarding the items on order or the items received may be obtained at any time. Once merchandise has been received, QuickBooks marks the purchase order *Received in full,* which closes the purchase order automatically. The Purchase Order feature must be selected as a Preference when setting up the company, or it may be selected prior to processing your first purchase order. QuickBooks will automatically set up an account called Purchase Orders in the Chart of Accounts. The account does not affect the balance sheet or the profit and loss statement of the company. As with other business forms, QuickBooks allows you to customize your purchase orders to fit the needs of your individual company or to use the purchase order format that comes with the program.

VERIFY PURCHASE ORDERS ACTIVE AS A COMPANY PREFERENCE

Verify that the Purchase Order feature of QuickBooks is active by checking the Company Preferences.

> # MEMO
> **DATE:** January 16, 2013
>
> Prior to completing the first purchase order, verify that Purchase Orders are active.

 Verify that Purchase Orders are active by accessing the Company Preferences

Click **Edit** menu, click **Preferences**

Click **Items & Inventory** on the Preferences List, click the **Company Preferences** tab

- Make sure there is a check mark in the check box for **Inventory and purchase orders are active**. If not, click the check box to select.

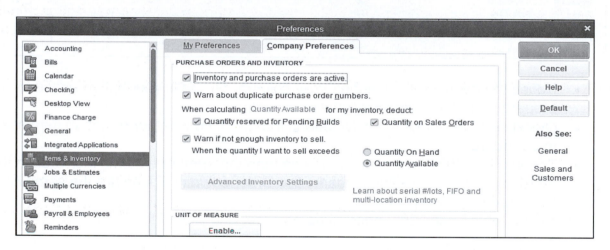

Click **OK** to accept and close the Preferences screen

CUSTOMIZE PURCHASE ORDERS

As instructed in Chapter 5, business forms may be customized. Prior to recording your first purchase order, it should be customized.

 Customize a Purchase Order

Click the **Purchase Orders** icon in the **Vendors** section of the Home Page

Click the **Formatting** tab on the Create Purchase Orders Icon bar, click **Customize Data Layout**

Change the Default Title in the Additional Customization screen to **PURCHASE ORDER**

On the Additional Customization screen, click the **Layout Designer...** button

- If you get a message regarding overlapping fields, click **Do not display this message in the future**, and then click **OK**, and then click **Layout Designer**

To change the size for **PURCHASE ORDER** to begin at **5:**

Point to the black squares (sizing handles) on the frame around the words
    PURCHASE ORDER
When the cursor turns into a double arrow, hold the primary (left) mouse button
    and drag until the size of the frame begins at **5** on the ruler bar
- For additional information and visual references, refer to Chapter 5.

Expand the area for **Your Name Mountain Sports** to **4 ¾**
Click **OK** to close the Layout Designer
Click **OK** to close the Additional Customization screen
Do not close the Purchase Order

PREPARE PURCHASE ORDER TO ORDER MERCHANDISE

Once the Purchase Order feature is selected, purchase orders may be prepared. Primarily, purchase orders are prepared to order merchandise; but they may also be used to order non-inventory items like supplies or services. The same purchase order may not be sent to several vendors. Each vendor should receive a separate purchase order. A purchase order, however, may have more than one item listed.

MEMO
DATE: January 16, 2013

With only 10 pairs of snowboard boots in stock in the middle of January an additional 25 pairs of boots in assorted sizes need to be ordered from Boots Galore for $75 per pair. Prepare Purchase Order No. 1.

 Prepare Purchase Order No. 1 for 25 pairs of snowboard boots

Purchase Order 1 should be on the screen
- If not, click the **Purchases Order** icon on the Home Page

If you wish to save space on the screen, click the Hide History button
To resize the purchase order so it is smaller, point to the edge of the
    form and drag the sizing handle

Click the drop-down list arrow for **Vendor**, click **Boots Galore**
The Template should be Custom Purchase Order, select if necessary
Tab to or click **Date**, enter **01/16/2013**
- P.O. No. should be 1. If not, enter 1 as the P.O. No.

Tab to or click **Item**, click **Boots-Snowbrd**
Tab to or click **Qty**, enter **25**
- The cost of the item was entered when Boots-Snowbrd was created. The Rate should appear automatically as **75.00**

Tab to generate Amount

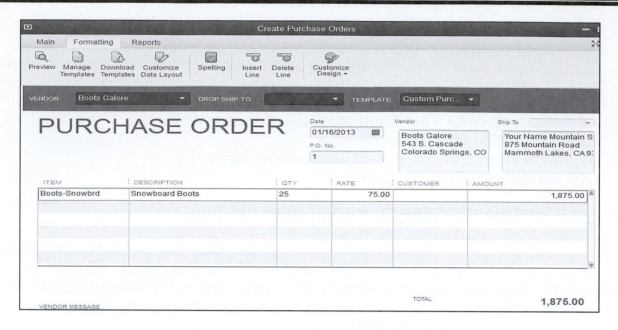

On the **Main** Icon bar, click **Print** to print the **Purchase Order**

Check printer settings

- Be sure to print lines around each field.

Click **Print**

- Sometimes, after printing, you will get a Recording Transaction message, if you have made no changes, always click **Yes**

Click **Save & Close**

ADD A NEW VENDOR

MEMO

DATE: January 16, 2013

Add a new vendor: Snow Stuff, 7105 Camino del Rio, Durango, CO 81302, Phone: 303-555-7765, Fax: 303-555-5677, E-mail: SnowStuff@ski.com, Terms: 2% 10 Net 30, Credit Limit: $2000.

 Add a new vendor

Open the **Vendor Center** as previously instructed

Click the **New Vendor…** button at the top of the Vendor Center

Click **New Vendor**

Enter **Snow Stuff** for the **Vendor** name and the **Company** name

There is no Opening Balance

Tab to or click in the text box for **Main Phone**, enter **303-555-7765**

Tab to or click in the text box for **Main E-mail**, enter **SnowStuff@ski.com**

Tab to or click in the text box for **FAX**, enter **303-555-5677**

Click at the end of the first line of the address in BILLED FROM, press **Enter**
Type the address **7105 Camino del Rio**, press **Enter**
Type **Durango, CO 81302**
Click the **Payment Settings** tab, click the drop-down list arrow for **PAYMENT TERMS**, and click **2% 10 Net 30**
Tab to or click **CREDIT LIMIT**, enter **2000**
Click **OK** to add Vendor

ASSIGN A PREFERRED VENDOR AND A COST TO A SALES ITEM

Most of the items in the Item List have a Preferred Vendor and a Cost entered as Purchase Information. This enables you to prepare a purchase order and have QuickBooks insert the Vendor Name and cost automatically when an Item Code is entered on a Purchase Order.

Assign Snow Stuff as the Preferred Vendor for Sleds and Toboggans. Also assign a Cost of $50 to Sleds and $110 to Toboggans

Open the **Item List** as previously instructed
Double-click **Sleds**
Click in the text box for **Cost**, enter **50**, press **Tab** twice
Click the drop-down list arrow for **Preferred Vendor**
Click **Snow Stuff**, click **OK**

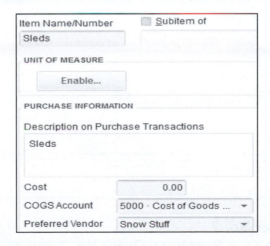

Repeat for Toboggans using **Snow Stuff** and a Cost of **$110**
Close the Item List

PREPARE A PURCHASE ORDER FOR MORE THAN ONE ITEM

If more than one item is purchased from a vendor, all items purchased can be included on the same purchase order.

MEMO

DATE: January 16, 2013

Prepare a purchase order for 3 sleds @ $50 each, and 2 toboggans @ $110 each from Snow Stuff

---

 Prepare a purchase order using an assigned vendor

- The **Date** should be **01/16/2013**. If it is not, delete the date shown and enter **01/16/13**.
- P.O. No. should be **2**. If it is not, enter **2**.

Tab to or click the first line in the column for **Item**
Click the drop-down list arrow for **Item**, click **Sleds**

- Vendor information for Snow Stuff is automatically completed.

Tab to or click **Qty**, enter **3**

- The purchase cost of $50 is automatically entered.

Tab to generate the total for **Amount**
Repeat steps necessary to enter the information to order 2 toboggans

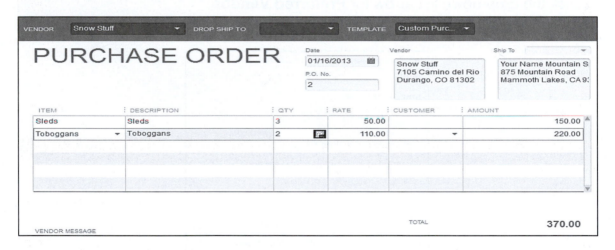

Print **Purchase Order No. 2**
Click **Save & New** to save **Purchase Order No. 2** and go to the next purchase order
- If you get a Recording Transaction message, click **Yes**.

ENTER PURCHASE ORDERS WITHOUT STEP-BY-STEP INSTRUCTIONS

MEMO

DATE: January 16, 2013

Prepare purchase orders for the following:
25 pairs of gloves @ 15.00 each from Clothes, Inc.
12 sets of ski poles @ 30.00 each from Snow Supplies.

 Prepare and print the purchase orders indicated above.

Compare your completed purchase orders with the ones following:

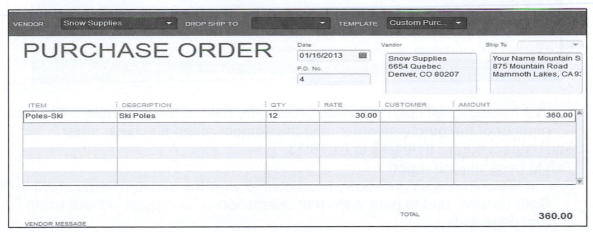

Save and **Close** after entering and printing Purchase Order No. 4

PREPARE AND PRINT A PURCHASE ORDERS QUICKREPORT

To see a list of purchase orders that have been prepared, open the Chart of Accounts, select Purchase Orders, click the Reports button, and choose QuickReport from the menu shown.

┌───┐
│ **MEMO**   │
│ **DATE:** January 16, 2013   │
│   │
│ Larry and you need to see which purchase orders are open. Prepare and print the │
│ Purchase Orders QuickReport.   │
└───┘

 View the open purchase orders for Your Name Mountain Sports

Click the **Chart of Accounts** icon on the Home Page
Scroll through the accounts until you get to the end of the accounts
Your will see **2 Purchase Orders** in the Name column and **Non-Posting** in the Type
    column
Click **2 Purchase Orders**
Click the **Reports** button
Click **QuickReport: 2 Purchase Orders**

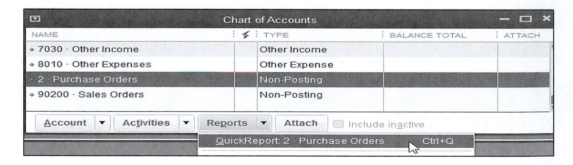

- The list shows all open purchase orders, the date of the purchase order, the number of the purchase order, and the amount of the purchase order.

The dates are from **01/01/13** to **01/16/13**
Tab to generate the report
Resize the columns as previously instructed to view the account name in full in the
    Split column, and to print in Portrait orientation on one page without using Fit to
    one page wide
Click **Print** to print the report

Your Name Mountain Sports
Account QuickReport
As of January 16, 2013

Type	Date	Num	Name	Memo	Split	Amount
2 · Purchase Orders						
Purchase Order	01/16/2013	1	Boots Galore		1120 · Inventory Asset	-1,875.00
Purchase Order	01/16/2013	2	Snow Stuff		-SPLIT-	-370.00
Purchase Order	01/16/2013	3	Clothes, Inc.		1120 · Inventory Asset	-375.00
Purchase Order	01/16/2013	4	Snow Supplies		1120 · Inventory Asset	-360.00
Total 2 · Purchase Orders						-2,980.00
TOTAL						-2,980.00

Close the **Purchase Order QuickReport** and the **Chart of Accounts**

CHANGE MINIMUM REORDER LIMITS FOR AN ITEM

Any time that you determine your reorder limits are too low or too high, you can change the Reorder Point by editing the Item in the Item List.

MEMO
DATE: January 16, 2013

View the Item List to see the amount on hand for each item. In viewing the list, Larry and you determine that there should be a minimum of 35 sets of long underwear on hand at all times. Currently, there are 32 sets of long underwear in stock. Change the reorder point for long underwear to 35.

 View the **Item List**

Click the **Items & Services** icon on the QuickBooks Home Page
Scroll through Item List, double-click **Underwear**
Click in **Reorder Point**
Change 30 to **35**
- Notice the Average Cost. For example, 32 on hand * $8 average cost = $256 total value. If 16 pair cost $10, the value would be $160. If the other 16 pair cost $6, the value would be $96. The total value for all 16 would be $160 + $96 = $256. Remember $256 / 32 = $8 average cost.

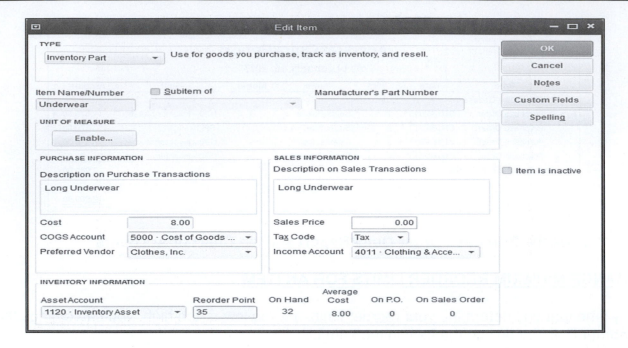

Click **OK** to save and exit
Close the **Item List**

VIEW EFFECT OF REORDER POINT ON REMINDERS

Once the reorder point has been changed and the quantity on hand is equal to or falls below the new minimum, the item will be added to Reminders so you will be reminded to order it.

MEMO

DATE: January 16, 2013

Look at Reminders to see what items need to be ordered.

 Look at **Reminders**

Open and Expand **Reminders** as previously instructed
- The items shown previously on the Reminders List as Inventory to Reorder (Snowboard Boots, Gloves, Ski Poles, Sleds, and Toboggans) are no longer present because they have been ordered. Underwear appears because the reorder point has been changed.
- If your computer date is not January 16, 2013 your Reminders screen will be different

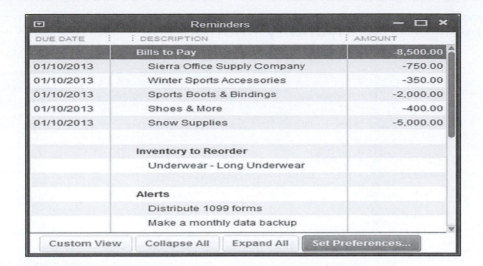

Close **Reminders**

USE THE INVENTORY CENTER TO VIEW INVENTORY STOCK STATUS BY ITEM REPORT

QuickBooks 2013 has an Inventory Center that gives information about each inventory item. Changes may be made to inventory items in the Center as well as on the Items & Services List. Several Inventory Reports are available for viewing and/or printing when you are in the Inventory Center. One report is the Inventory Stock Status by Item report. This report provides information regarding the stock on hand, the stock on order, and the stock that needs to be reordered.

> # MEMO
> **DATE:** January 16, 2013
>
> More detailed information regarding the stock on hand, stock ordered, and stock needing to be ordered needs to be provided. Open the Inventory Center and prepare the report for Inventory Stock Status by Item.

 Open the Inventory Center and view the **Inventory Stock Status by Item Report**

Click the **Vendors** menu, point to **Inventory Activities,** click **Inventory Center**
Click **Underwear**
- Note the Reorder Point of 35 that was changed earlier in the chapter and the Quantity on Hand
- At the bottom of Inventory Information, you will see that Underwear was sold on Invoice 4

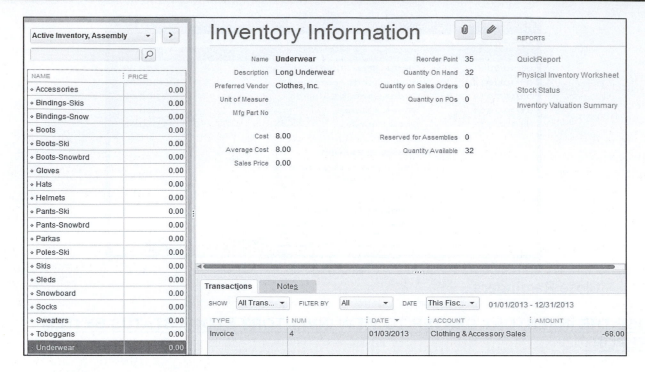

In the Reports area on the right side of Inventory Information, click **Stock Status**
The dates are From **01/01/13** to **01/16/13**
Tab to generate the report

Your Name Mountain Sports
Inventory Stock Status by Item
January 1 - 16, 2013

	Pref Vendor	Reorder Pt	On Hand	On Sales Order	For Assemblies	Available	Order	On PO	Next Deliv	Sales/Week
Inventory										
Accessories	▶ Winter Sports Accessories	100	795	0	0	795		0		2.2
Bindings-Skis	Sports Boots & Bindings	10	43	0	0	43		0		3.1
Bindings-Snow	Sports Boots & Bindings	5	48	0	0	48		0		0.9
Boots	Shoes & More	10	20	0	0	20		0		0
Boots-Ski	Boots Galore	10	14	0	0	14		0		0.4
Boots-Snowbrd	Boots Galore	10	10	0	0	10		25	01/16/2013	0.9
Gloves	Clothes, Inc.	20	20	0	0	20		25	01/16/2013	0.9
Hats	Winter Sports Accessories	20	29	0	0	29		0		0.4
Helmets		5	20	0	0	20		0		2.2
Pants-Ski	Clothes, Inc.	10	93	0	0	93		0		0.9
Pants-Snowbrd	Clothes, Inc.	10	50	0	0	50		0		0
Parkas	Clothes, Inc.	25	73	0	0	73		0		0.9
Poles-Ski	Snow Supplies	15	13	0	0	13		12	01/16/2013	2.2
Skis	Snow Supplies	15	43	0	0	43		0		3.1
Sleds	Snow Stuff	5	4	0	0	4		3	01/16/2013	2.6
Snowboard	Snow Supplies	15	28	0	0	28		0		0.9
Socks	Boots Galore	25	72	0	0	72		0		1.3
Sweaters	Clothes, Inc.	25	73	0	0	73		0		0.9
Toboggans	Snow Stuff	5	5	0	0	5		2	01/16/2013	2.2
Underwear	Clothes, Inc.	35	32	0	0	32	✔	0		0.4

Scroll through the report
- Notice the items in stock.
- Notice the reorder point for items.
- Find the items marked as needing to be ordered. They are marked with a √.

- Notice the Next Deliv dates of the items that have been ordered. Close the report without printing, and close the Inventory Center

RECEIVING ITEMS ORDERED

The form used to record the receipt of items in QuickBooks depends on the way in which the ordered items are received. Items received may be recorded in three ways. If the items are received without a bill and you pay later, record the receipt on an item receipt. If the items are received at the same time as the bill, record the item receipt on a bill. If the items are received and paid for at the same time, record the receipt of items on a check or a credit card.

When items are received in full, the purchase order will be closed automatically. If items are not received in full and you do not think you will receive them at a later date, a purchase order may be closed manually.

RECORD RECEIPT OF ITEMS NOT ACCOMPANIED BY A BILL

The ability to record inventory items prior to the arrival of the bill keeps quantities on hand, quantities on order, and the inventory up to date. Items ordered on a purchase order that arrive before the bill is received are recorded on an item receipt. When the bill arrives, it is recorded.

+---+
| **MEMO** |
| **DATE:** January 18, 2013 |
| |
| The sleds and toboggans ordered from Snow Stuff arrive without a bill. |
| Record the receipt of the 3 sleds and 2 toboggans. |
+---+

 Record the receipt of the items above

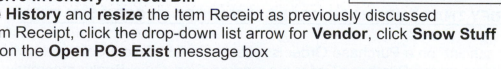

Click the **Receive Inventory** icon on the Home Page
Click **Receive Inventory without Bill**
Click **Hide History** and **resize** the Item Receipt as previously discussed
On the Item Receipt, click the drop-down list arrow for **Vendor**, click **Snow Stuff**
Click **Yes** on the **Open POs Exist** message box

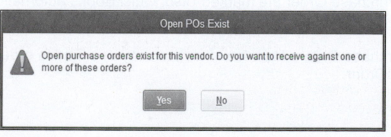

- An **Open Purchase Orders** dialog box appears showing all open purchase orders for the vendor, Snow Stuff

Point to any part of the line for P.O. No. 2
Click to select **Purchase Order No. 2**

- This will place a check mark in the check mark column.

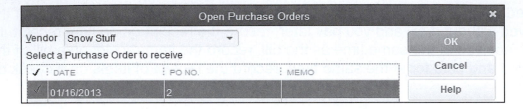

Click **OK**
Change the date to **01/18/2013**.

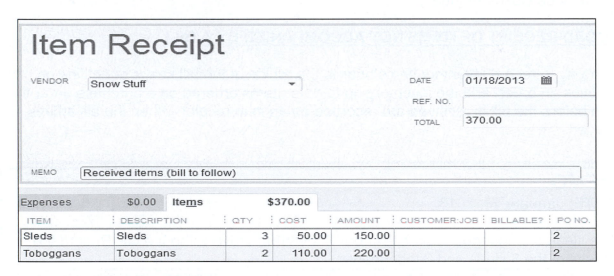

- Notice the completed information for the **Items** tab indicating how many sleds and toboggans were received.
- Notice the **Memo** of *Received items (bill to follow)*.

Click **Save & Close**

VERIFY THAT PURCHASE ORDER IS MARKED RECEIVED IN FULL

As each line on a Purchase Order is received in full, QuickBooks marks it as *Clsd*. When all the items on the Purchase Order are marked *Clsd*, QuickBooks automatically stamps the P.O. as *Received in Full* and closes the purchase order.

On the Create Purchase Orders Main Icon bar, you may use Find in order to locate a specific Purchase Order.

MEMO
DATE: January 18, 2013

View the original Purchase Order No. 2 to verify that it has been stamped "Received in Full" and each item received is marked "Clsd."

 Verify that Purchase Order No. 2 is marked Received in Full and all items received are Closed and access Purchase Orders by using **Find** within Purchase Orders

Open Create Purchase Orders as previously instructed
Click the **Find** button on the Main Icon bar
Click the drop-down list arrow for **Vendor**
Click **Snow Stuff**, click the **Find** button
Purchase Order 2 will be shown
- Next to the **Amount** column, you will see two new columns: **Rcv'd** and **Clsd**.
  - **Rcv'd** indicates the number of the items received.
  - **Clsd** indicates that the number of items ordered was received in full so the Purchase Order has been closed for that Item
- With all the items ordered marked as **Clsd**, the Purchase Order is stamped **RECEIVED IN FULL**.

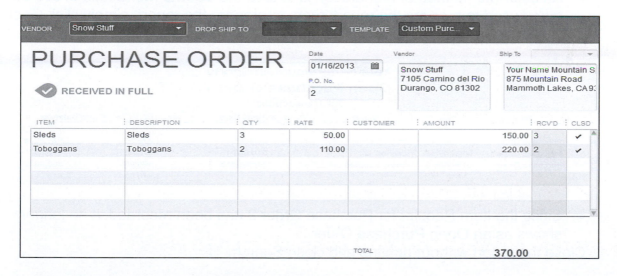

Close **Create Purchase Orders** window

PREPARE AN OPEN PURCHASE ORDERS REPORT FROM SEARCH

When using search to find purchase orders, reports pertaining to purchase orders were also found. These may be prepared directly from Search. Once the report is selected, you may locate the Menu for the report, launch the report, or add the report to favorites.

Prepare the Open Purchase Orders report using **Search**

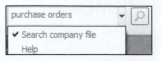

Type **Purchase Orders** in the Search textbox on the Icon bar
Click **Search company file**
- You may search through the company file or through Help.
Click the **Search** icon
In order to make sure all current information is shown, click **Update search information** (on the lower-left side of the Search screen)
Click **OK** on the Search Update message
- Search will find the purchase orders that have been prepared. It will also give you a list of Menu Items that may be used to prepare reports
Scroll through the Search results until you get to **Menu Item**
Point to the Menu Item **Open Purchase Orders** on the Search screen
- Action items of Locate Menu, Launch, and Add to Favorites should appear.

Click the **Launch** icon and the report will be shown on the screen
- An alternate method of preparation is to click the **Locate Menu** icon to see the menu used to prepare the report; then, to prepare the report, simply click Open Purchase Orders on the menu

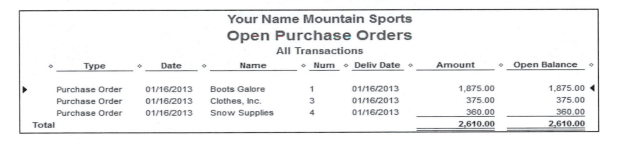

	Type	Date	Name	Num	Deliv Date	Amount	Open Balance
	Purchase Order	01/16/2013	Boots Galore	1	01/16/2013	1,875.00	1,875.00
	Purchase Order	01/16/2013	Clothes, Inc.	3	01/16/2013	375.00	375.00
	Purchase Order	01/16/2013	Snow Supplies	4	01/16/2013	360.00	360.00
Total						2,610.00	2,610.00

- Since the Item Receipt for Purchase Order 2 has been recorded, it no longer shows as an Open Purchase Order
Close the report without printing and close Search

ENTER RECEIPT OF A BILL FOR ITEMS ALREADY RECEIVED

For items that have been received prior to the bill, the receipt of items is recorded as soon as the items arrive. When the bill is received, it must be recorded. To do this, indicate that the bill is entered against Inventory. When completing a bill for items already received, QuickBooks fills in all essential information on the bill.

A bill is divided into two sections: a <u>vendor-related</u> section (the upper part of the bill that looks similar to a check and has a memo text box under it) and a <u>detail</u> section (the area that has two tabs marked Items and Expenses). The vendor-related section of the bill is where information for the actual bill is entered, including a memo with information about the transaction. The detail section is where the information regarding the items ordered, the quantity ordered and received, and the amounts due for the items received is indicated.

MEMO

DATE: January 19, 2013

Record the bill for the sleds and toboggans already received from Snow Stuff, Vendor's Invoice No. 97 dated 01/18/2013, Terms 2% 10 Net 30.

 Record the above bill for items already received

Enter Bills Against Inventory

Click the **Enter Bills Against Inventory** icon on the Home Page
On the **Select Item Receipt** screen, click the drop-down list arrow for **Vendor**, click **Snow Stuff**
- Snow Stuff is entered as the vendor.
Click anywhere on the line **01/18/2013 Received items (bill to follow)** to select the Item Receipt
- The line for the item receipt will be highlighted.
- Unlike many of the other screens, there is no check column so the line must be highlighted to be selected.

Click **OK**
- QuickBooks displays the **Enter Bills** screen and the completed bill for Snow Stuff
- The date shown is the date of the Vendor's bill **01/18/2013**.
Tab to or click **Ref No.**, type the vendor's invoice number **97**
- Notice that the **Amount Due** of **370** has been inserted.
- Terms of **2% 10 Net 30** and the Discount Date and the Due Date are shown.

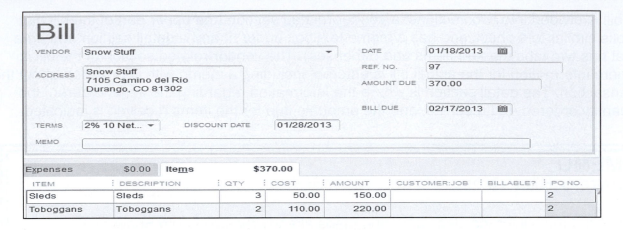

- If instructed to do so by your instructor, print the Bill

Click **Save & Close**

- If you get a Recording Transaction message box regarding the fact that the transaction has been changed, always click **Yes**.

RECORD RECEIPT OF ITEMS AND A BILL

When ordered items are received and accompanied by a bill, the receipt of the items is recorded while entering the bill.

MEMO

DATE: January 19, 2013

Received 25 pairs of snowboard boots and a bill from Boots Galore. Record the bill dated 01/18/2013 and the receipt of the items.

 Record the receipt of the items and the bill

Click **Receive Inventory** icon on the QuickBooks Home Page
Click **Receive Inventory with Bill**
Click the drop-down list for **Vendor**, click **Boots Galore**
Click **Yes** on the **Open POs Exist** message box
On the Open Purchase Orders screen, click anywhere in P.O. No. 1 line to select and insert a check mark in the √ column

Click **OK**

- The bill appears on the screen and is complete.
- Because no invoice number was given, leave the **Ref. No.** blank.

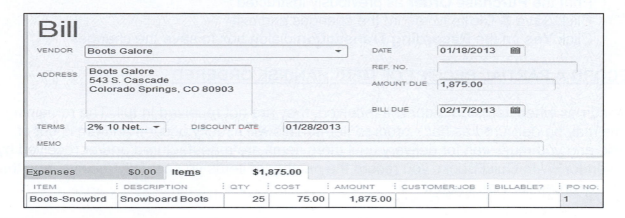

- If instructed, print the bill
Click **Save & Close**

EDIT A PURCHASE ORDER

As with any other form, purchase orders may be edited once they have been prepared. Purchase orders may be accessed by clicking on the Purchase Order icon on the QuickBooks Home Page.

MEMO

DATE: January 19, 2013

Ruth realized that Purchase Order No. 4 should be for 15 pairs of ski poles. Change the purchase order and reprint.

 Change Purchase Order No. 4

Access Purchase Order No. 4 as previously instructed
Click in **Qty**; change the number from 12 to **15**
Tab to recalculate the amount due for the purchase order

- Notice the columns for Rcv'd and Clsd. Those are included on the Purchase Order once it has been saved.

Print the **Purchase Order** as previously instructed

Click **Save & Close** to record the changes and exit

Click **Yes** on the **Recording Transaction** dialog box to save the changes

RECORD A PARTIAL RECEIPT OF MERCHANDISE ORDERED

Sometimes when items on order are received, they are not received in full. The remaining items may be delivered as back-ordered items. This will usually occur if an item is out of stock, and you must wait for delivery until more items are manufactured and/or received by the vendor. With QuickBooks you record the number of items you actually receive, and the bill is recorded for that amount.

MEMO

DATE: January 19, 2013

Record the bill and the receipt of 20 pairs of gloves ordered on Purchase Order No. 3. On the purchase order, 25 pairs of gloves were ordered. Clothes, Inc. will no longer be carrying these gloves, so the remaining 5 pairs of gloves on order will not be shipped. Manually close the purchase order. The date of the bill is 01/18/2013.

 Record the receipt of and the bill for 20 pairs of gloves from Clothes, Inc.

Access **Receive Inventory with Bill** as previously instructed

If necessary, change the **Date** of the bill to **01/18/2013**

Click the drop-down list arrow for **Vendor**, click **Clothes, Inc.**

Click **Yes** on **Open POs Exist** dialog box

Click anywhere in the line for **P.O. 3** on **Open Purchase Orders** dialog box

Click **OK**

Click the **Qty** column on the Items tab in the middle of the bottom half of the Enter Bills window

Change the quantity to **20**

Tab to change **Amount** to **300**

- Notice the **Amount Due** on the bill also changes.

Print if instructed to do so

Click **Save & Close** to record the items received and the bill

CLOSE PURCHASE ORDER MANUALLY

If you have issued a purchase order and it is determined that you will not be receiving the remaining items on order, a purchase order can be closed manually.

 Close Purchase Order No. 3 using **Advanced Find** to locate Purchase Order No. 3

Use the keyboard shortcut **Ctrl+F**; and then, click the **Advanced Find** tab
Scroll through **Choose Filter**
- Filter helps to narrow the search for locating something.

Click **Transaction Type**
Click the drop-down list arrow for **Transaction Type**, click **Purchase Order**
Click **Find**
- A list of all purchase orders shows on the screen.
- The information shown includes the purchase order number, vendor name, account used, the item(s) ordered, and the amount of the purchase order.
- Unlike Search, no reports are shown.

Click **Purchase Order No. 3** for **Clothes, Inc**.
Click **Go To**

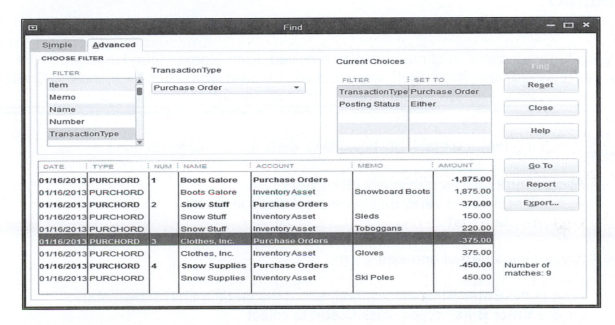

- P.O. 3 will show on the screen
- Notice that the ordered **Qty** is 25, **Backordered** is 5, and **Rcv'd** is 20.

Click the **Clsd** column for Gloves to mark and close the purchase order
- Notice the check mark in the Clsd column. Backordered is now 0.
- Below PURCHASE ORDER you will see a check mark and the word CLOSED.

Click **Save & Close**, click **Yes** on the Recording Transactions dialog box
Close **Find**

ENTER A CREDIT FROM A VENDOR

Credit memos are prepared to record a reduction to a transaction. With QuickBooks you use the Enter Bills window to record credit memos received from vendors acknowledging a return of items purchased or an allowance for a previously recorded bill and/or payment. The amount of a credit memo can be applied to the amount owed to a vendor when paying bills.

MEMO
DATE: January 21, 2013

Upon further inspection of merchandise received, Ruth Morgan found that one of the sleds received from Snow Stuff, was cracked. The sled was returned. Received Credit Memo No. 9912 from Snow Stuff for $50 (the full amount on the return of 1 sled).

 Check the **Item List** to verify how many sleds are currently on hand

Access **Item List** as previously instructed
•   Look at Sleds to verify that there are 7 sleds in stock.
Close the **Item List**

 Record the return of one sled

Access the **Enter Bills** window and record the credit memo shown above
On the **Enter Bills** screen, click **Credit** to select
•   The word *Bill* changes to *Credit*.
Click the **Items** tab
Tab to or click the first line in the **Item** column, click the drop-down list arrow
Click **Sleds**
•   The Vendor **Snow Stuff**, the Amount Due **50**, and the Cost **50** are entered automatically
Tab to or click **Qty**, enter **1**
Tab to enter the **50** for **Amount**
Click in the text box for **Date**, enter **01/21/13**
Tab to or click **Ref. No.**, type **9912**
Memo, enter **Returned 1 Sled**

Credit

VENDOR	Snow Stuff		DATE	01/21/2013
			REF. NO.	9912
			CREDIT AMOUNT	50.00

MEMO	Returned 1 Sled

Expenses	$0.00	Items	$50.00				
ITEM	DESCRIPTION	QTY	COST	AMOUNT	CUSTOMER:JOB	BILLABLE?
Sleds	Sleds	1	50.00	50.00		

Print the Credit Memo if instructed to do so

Click **Save & Close** to record the credit and exit the **Enter Bills** window

- QuickBooks decreases the quantity of sleds on hand and creates a credit with the vendor that can be applied when paying the bill. The Credit Memo also appears in the Accounts Payable account in the **Paid** column, which decreases the amount owed and shows the transaction type as BILLCRED in the Accounts Payable register.

Verify that there are 6 sleds in stock after the return.

Access the **Item List**

Verify the number of sleds and then close the list

View the return in the Accounts Payable register

Access the **Chart of Accounts** as previously instructed

Double-click **Accounts Payable** to open the Register

Scroll through the register until you see the BILLCRED for Snow Stuff

01/21/2013	9912	Snow Stuff				50.00	10,995.00
		BILLCRE 1120 - Inventory Asset Returned 1 Sled					

Close the **Accounts Payable Register** and the **Chart of Accounts**

MAKE A PURCHASE USING A CREDIT CARD

Some businesses use credit cards as an integral part of their finances. Many companies have a credit card that is used primarily for gasoline purchases for company vehicles. Other companies use credit cards as a means of paying for expenses or purchasing merchandise or other necessary items for use in the business.

MEMO

DATE: January 21, 2013

Ruth discovered that she was out of paper. She purchased a box of paper to have on hand to be used for copies, for the laser printer, and for the fax machine from Sierra Office Supply Company for $21.98. Rather than add to the existing balance owed to the company, Ruth pays for the office supplies using the company's Visa card.

 Purchase the above office supplies using the company's Visa card

Click the **Enter Credit Card Charges** icon in the **Banking** section of the Home Page

Credit Card should indicate **2100 Visa**

- The radio button for Purchase/Charge should be selected; if not, click to mark.

Click the drop-down list arrow for **Purchased From**, click **Sierra Office Supply Company**

Click **OK** on the **Warning** screen

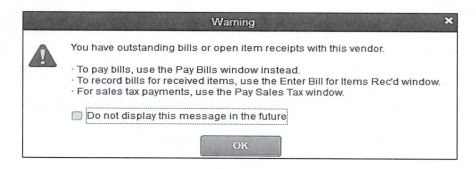

Date should be **01/21/2013**

Ref No. is blank

Tab to or click **AMOUNT**, enter **21.98**

Tab to or click **Memo**, enter **Purchase Paper**

Tab to or click the **Account** column on the **Expenses** tab, click the drop-down list arrow for **Account**, click **1311 Office Supplies**

- This transaction is for supplies to have on hand, so the Asset Account Office Supplies is used.

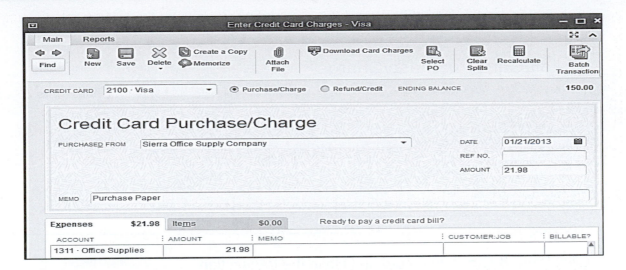

Click **Save & New** to record the charge and go to the next credit card entry

PAY FOR INVENTORY ITEMS ON ORDER USING A CREDIT CARD

It is possible to pay for inventory items using a credit card. The payment may be made using the Pay Bills window, or it may be made by recording an entry for Credit Card Charges. If you are purchasing something that is on order, you may record the receipt of merchandise on order first, or you may record the receipt of merchandise and the credit card payment at the same time.

MEMO

DATE: January 21, 2013

Note from You: Ruth, record the receipt of 10 ski poles from Snow Supplies. Pay for the ski poles using the company's Visa credit card.

 Pay for the ski poles received using the company's Visa credit card

Click the drop-down list for **Purchased From** click **Snow Supplies**
Click the **Yes** button on the **Open POs Exist** message box
To select P.O. No. 4, click the line containing information regarding P.O. No. 4 on the **Open Purchase Orders** dialog box
Click **OK**
- If you get a warning screen regarding outstanding bills, click **OK**.
Click the **Clear Qtys** button on the bottom of the screen to clear 15 from the Qty column
Tab to or click **Qty**, enter **10**
Tab to change the Amount to 300

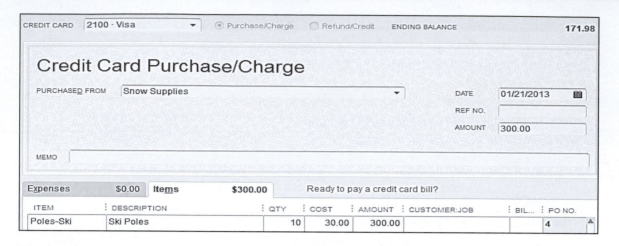

Click **Save & Close** to record and close the transaction

CONFIRM THE RECORDING OF THE SKI POLES RECEIVED ON PURCHASE ORDER NO. 4

MEMO

DATE: January 21, 2013

View Purchase Order No. 4 to determine whether or not the amount of ski poles received was recorded.

 Access Purchase Order No. 4 as previously instructed

- The **Rcv'd** column should show **10** and **Backordered** shows **5**.
- Notice that the **Qty** column shows **15** and **Clsd** is not marked. This indicates that 5 sets of ski poles are still on order.

  Close Purchase Order No. 4 without changing

CUSTOMIZE ADD/EDIT MULTIPLE LIST ENTRIES AND ADD A VENDOR

Vendors, customers, and list items may be added through the add/edit multiple list entries on the list menu. This feature is especially useful when importing data from Excel spreadsheets into QuickBooks. In addition, it may be used to quickly add one or more records to a list.

MEMO
DATE: January 23, 2013

Add a new vendor, *Mammoth News*, 1450 Main Street, Mammoth Lakes, CA 93546, Main Phone: 909-555-2525, Fax: 909-555-5252, E-mail: mammothnews@ski.com.

 Add the new vendor using Add/Edit Multiple List Entries

> Click the **Lists** menu
> Click **Add/Edit Multiple List Entries**
> Click the drop-down list arrow next to **List**
> Click **Vendors**
> Click the **Customize Columns** button and remove unwanted columns
> Click **Alt. Phone** in the Chosen Columns
> Click **Remove**

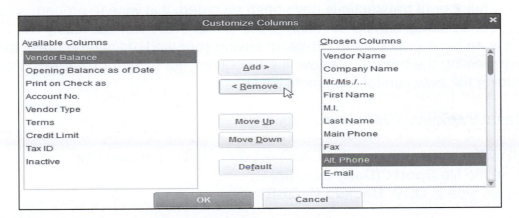

> Repeat to remove **Mr./Ms./**, **First Name**, **M.I.**, **Last Name**, **Address 5**
> When finished removing columns, click **OK**
> Click on the Vendor Name, **Mammoth Power Co.**
> Right-click on Mammoth Power Co., click **Insert Line**
> • If you get a Time Saving tip, click **OK**.
> In the Vendor Name column, enter **Mammoth News**
> Press, **Tab**
> Enter the Company Name **Mammoth News**
> Tab to or click in the column for **Main Phone**, enter **909-555-2525**
> Tab to or click **FAX**, enter **909-555-5252**
> Tab to or click **E-mail**, enter **mammothnews@ski.com**
> Tab to or click **Address 1**, enter **Mammoth News**
> Tab to or click **Address 2**, enter **1450 Main Street**
> Tab to or click **Address 3**, enter **Mammoth Lakes, CA 93546**

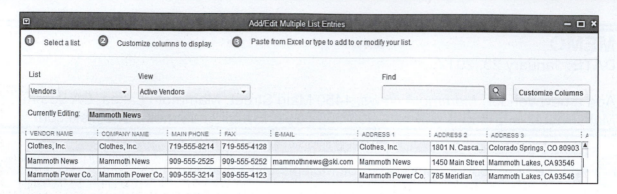

Click **Save Changes**
Click **OK** on the Record(s) Saved dialog box
Click **Close**

PREPARE A DAILY BACKUP

As previously discussed, a backup file is prepared as a precaution in case you make an error. After a number of transactions have been recorded, it is wise to prepare a backup file. In addition, a backup should be made at the end of every work session. The Daily Backup file is an appropriate file to create for saving your work as you progress through a chapter. By creating the backup file now, it will contain your work for Chapters 5 and 6 up through adding the new vendor Mammoth News.

 Prepare the Sports (Daily Backup).qbb file

Follow the steps presented in Chapter 1 for creating a backup file
Name the file **Sports (Daily Backup)**
The file type is **QBW Backup (* .QBB)**

ENTER BILLS

Whether the bill is to pay for expenses incurred in the operation of a business or to pay for merchandise to sell in the business, QuickBooks provides accounts payable tracking for all vendors to which the company owes money. Entering bills as soon as they are received is an efficient way to record your liabilities. Once bills have been entered, QuickBooks will be able to provide up-to-date cash flow reports, and QuickBooks will remind you when it's time to pay your bills.

As previously stated, a bill is divided into two sections: a <u>vendor-related</u> section and a <u>detail</u> section. The vendor- related section of the bill is where information for the actual bill is entered. If the bill is for paying an expense, the Expenses tab is used for the detail section. Using this tab allows you to indicate the expense accounts for the transaction, to enter the amounts for the various expense accounts, and to provide transaction explanations. If the bill is for merchandise, the Items tab will be used to record the receipt of the items ordered.

If you use the Document Center, you may scan the bill you receive, store it in the Doc Center, and attach it to the bill electronically. (Refer to Appendix B for more detailed information and examples of using the Document Center and Attaching electronically.)

MEMO
DATE: January 23, 2013

Placed an ad in the *Mammoth News* announcing our February sale. Record the receipt of the bill from *Mammoth News* for $95.00, Terms Net 30, Invoice No. 381-22.

 Enter the bill

Click the **Enter Bills** icon on the Home Page
Complete the **Vendor Section** of the bill:
Click the drop-down list arrow for Vendor, and click **Mammoth News**
Tab to Date, enter **01/23/13** as the date
Tab to **Ref No.**, type the vendor's invoice number **381-22**
Tab to **Amount Due**, type **95**
Tab to **Terms**, click the drop-down list arrow next to **Terms**, click **Net 30**
- QuickBooks automatically changes the Bill Due date to show 30 days from the transaction date.
- Since the terms are Net 30, there is no Discount Date.
- At this time no change will be made to the Bill Due date, and nothing will be inserted as a memo.
Complete the **Detail Section** of the bill:
- If necessary, click the **Expenses** tab so it is the area of the detail section in use.
Tab to or click in the column for **Account**, click the drop-down list arrow next to **Account**, scroll through the list to find **Advertising Expense**
Because the account does not appear, click **<Add New>**
- **Type** of account should show **Expense**. If not, click **Expense**.
Click **Continue**
Enter **6140** as the account number in Number
Tab to or click **Account Name**, enter **Advertising Expense**

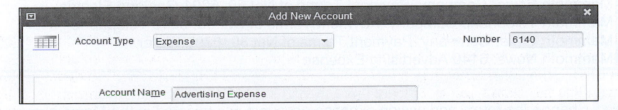

Click **Save & Close**
6140 Advertising Expense shows as the Account

- Based on the accrual method of accounting, Advertising Expense is selected as the account for this transaction because this expense should be matched against the revenue of the period.
- The Amount column already shows 95.00—no entry required
- Tab to or click the first line in the column for **Memo**

Enter the transaction explanation of **Ad for February Sale**

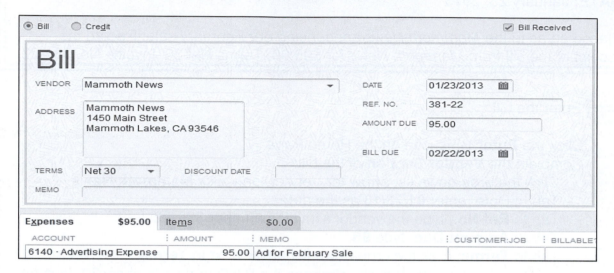

Print if instructed to do so, and then click **Save & Close**

Since no terms were assigned when the company was added to the Vendor List, click **Yes** on the **Name Information Changed** dialog box

CHANGE EXISTING TERMS AND ASSIGN AN EXPENSE ACCOUNT TO A VENDOR

Once a vendor has been established, changes can be made to the vendor's account information. The changes will take effect immediately and will be reflected in any transactions recorded for the vendor.

MEMO
DATE: January 23, 2013

Ruth Morgan wants to add information for the following vendors:
Mammoth Power Company: Payment Terms of Net 30, 6391 Gas and Electric
Mammoth Telephone Company: Payment Terms of Net 30, 6340 Telephone
Mammoth Water Company: Payment Terms of Net 30, 6392 Water
Mammoth News: 6140 Advertising Expense

 Change the terms and assign expense accounts as indicated in the Memo above

Access the **Vendor List** in the Vendor Center as previously instructed

Double-click on **Mammoth Power Co.**
Click **Payment Settings** tab
Click the drop-down list arrow for PAYMENT TERMS, click **Net 30**
Click the **Account Settings** tab, click the drop-down list arrow, click the expense
    account **6391 Gas and Electric**
Click **OK**
Repeat for the other vendors indicated in the memo above
When you enter the information for Mammoth News, check to verify that the terms
    are Net 30; and then add the expense account
Close the **Vendor Center** when all changes have been made

PAY BILLS USING ASSIGNED EXPENSE ACCOUNTS

Once expense accounts have been assigned to a vendor, the account will automatically be
used when a bill is entered.

MEMO
DATE: January 25, 2013

Record the bill to Mammoth Power Company electrical power for January:
Invoice No. 3510-1023, $359.00

 Record the bill to Mammoth Power Company

Access **Enter Bills** as previously instructed
Click the drop-down list arrow for Vendor, click **Mammoth Power Company**
- Notice that the terms and account are entered automatically
Complete the bill by entering the **DATE**, **REF NO.** and **AMOUNT DUE** shown in the
    Memo

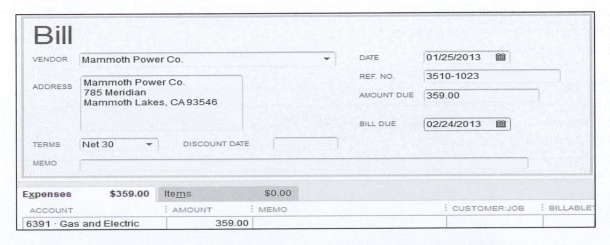

Print if instructed to do so; and then, click **Save & New** to continue

PREPARE BILLS WITHOUT STEP-BY-STEP INSTRUCTIONS

It is more efficient to record bills in a group or batch than it is to record them one at a time. If an error is made while preparing the bill, correct it. Your Name Mountain Sports uses the accrual basis of accounting. In the accrual method of accounting the expenses of a period are matched against the revenue of the period. Unless otherwise instructed, use the accrual basis of accounting when recording entries.

MEMO

DATE: January 25, 2013

Record the following bills:
Mammoth Telephone Company telephone service for January: Invoice No. 7815-21, $156.40
Mammoth Water Company water for January: Invoice No. 3105, $35.00

 Enter the two transactions in the memo above.

- Refer to the instructions given for previous transactions.
- Enter information for Memos if transaction explanation is needed for clarification.
- Print if instructed to do so.
- To go from one bill to the next, click the **Next** arrow on the Main Icon bar or click the **Save & New** button at the bottom of the bill.
- After entering the last bill, click **Save & Close** to record and exit the **Enter Bills** screen.

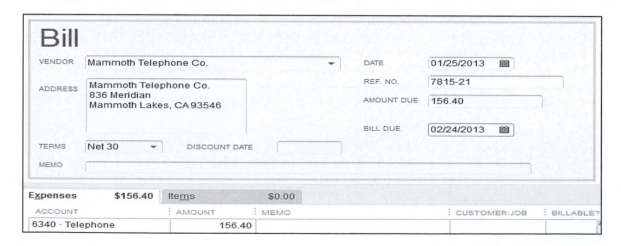

Bill

VENDOR	Mammoth Water Co.	▼	DATE	01/25/2013 📅
			REF. NO.	3105
ADDRESS	Mammoth Water Co. 903 Meridian Mammoth Lakes, CA 93546		AMOUNT DUE	35.00
			BILL DUE	02/24/2013 📅
TERMS	Net 30 ▼ DISCOUNT DATE			
MEMO				

Expenses	$35.00	Items	$0.00			
ACCOUNT		AMOUNT	MEMO		CUSTOMER:JOB	BILLABLE?
6392 - Water		35.00				

ENTER A BILL USING THE ACCOUNTS PAYABLE REGISTER

The Accounts Payable Register maintains a record of all the transactions recorded within the Accounts Payable account. Not only is it possible to view all of the account activities through the account's register, it is also possible to enter a bill directly into the Accounts Payable register. This can be faster than filling out all of the information through Enter Bills.

MEMO

DATE: January 25, 2013

Received a bill for the rent from Mountain Rentals. Use the Accounts Payable Register and record the bill for rent of $950, Invoice No. 7164, due February 4, 2013.

 Use the Accounts Payable Register to record the above transaction:

Use the keyboard shortcut, **Ctrl+A** to access the Chart of Accounts
Double-click **Accounts Payable** to open the Accounts Payable register
The date is highlighted in the blank entry, key in **01/25/13** for the transaction date
The word *Number* is in the next column
Tab to or click **Number**
- The word *Number* disappears.

Enter the Vendor's Invoice Number **7164**
Click the drop-down list arrow for the VENDOR, click **Mountain Rentals**
- When there is a drop-down list arrow, you do not need to tab or click in the field.

Tab to or click **DUE DATE**; and, if necessary, enter the due date **02/04/13**
Tab to or click **BILLED**, enter the amount **950**
Click the drop-down list arrow for **Account**
Determine the appropriate account to use for rent
- If all of the accounts do not appear in the drop-down list, scroll through the accounts until you find the one appropriate for this entry.

Click **6300 Rent**
Click **Record** to record the transaction

| 01/25/2013 | 7164 | Mountain Rentals | 02/04/2013 | 950.00 | | | 12,590.40 |
| | BILL | 6300 · Rent | | | | | |

Do not close the register

EDIT A TRANSACTION IN THE ACCOUNTS PAYABLE REGISTER

Because QuickBooks makes corrections extremely user friendly, a transaction can be edited or changed directly in the Accounts Payable Register as well as on the original bill. By eliminating the columns for Type and Memo, it is possible to change the register to show each transaction on one line. This can make the register easier to read.

MEMO
DATE: January 25, 2013

Upon examination of the invoices and the bills entered, Ruth discovers an error: The actual amount of the bill from the water company was **$85**, not $35. Change the transaction amount for this bill.

 Correct the above transaction in the Accounts Payable Register

Click the check box for **1-line** to select
- Each Accounts Payable transaction will appear on one line.

Click the transaction for Mammoth Water Co.

Change the amount of the transaction from $35.00 to **$85.00**

To record the change in the transaction, click the **Record** button at the bottom of the register and click **Yes** on the Record Transaction dialog box

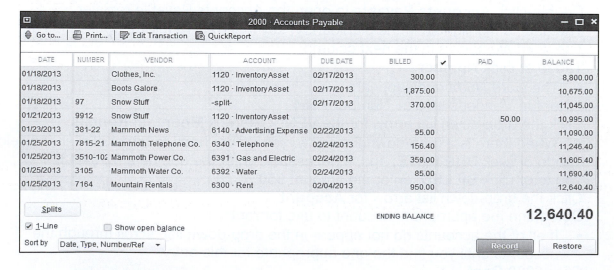

DATE	NUMBER	VENDOR	ACCOUNT	DUE DATE	BILLED	✔	PAID	BALANCE
01/18/2013		Clothes, Inc.	1120 · Inventory Asset	02/17/2013	300.00			8,800.00
01/18/2013		Boots Galore	1120 · Inventory Asset	02/17/2013	1,875.00			10,675.00
01/18/2013	97	Snow Stuff	-split-	02/17/2013	370.00			11,045.00
01/21/2013	9912	Snow Stuff	1120 · Inventory Asset				50.00	10,995.00
01/23/2013	381-22	Mammoth News	6140 · Advertising Expense	02/22/2013	95.00			11,090.00
01/25/2013	7815-21	Mammoth Telephone Co.	6340 · Telephone	02/24/2013	156.40			11,246.40
01/25/2013	3510-10:	Mammoth Power Co.	6391 · Gas and Electric	02/24/2013	359.00			11,605.40
01/25/2013	3105	Mammoth Water Co.	6392 · Water	02/24/2013	85.00			11,690.40
01/25/2013	7164	Mountain Rentals	6300 · Rent	02/04/2013	950.00			12,640.40

ENDING BALANCE   **12,640.40**

Do not close the register

PREVIEW AND PRINT A QUICKREPORT
FROM THE ACCOUNTS PAYABLE REGISTER

After editing the transaction, you may want to view information about a specific vendor. Clicking the vendor's name within a transaction and clicking the QuickReport button at the top of the register can do this quickly and efficiently.

MEMO

DATE: January 25, 2013

More than one transaction has been entered for Snow Stuff. you and Larry like to view transaction information for all vendors that have several transactions within a short period of time.

 Prepare a QuickReport for Snow Stuff

Click any field in any transaction for Snow Stuff
Click the **QuickReport** button at the top of the Register
- The Register QuickReport for All Transactions for Snow Stuff appears on the screen.

Resize the columns and print in Portrait orientation

Your Name Mountain Sports
Register QuickReport
All Transactions

Type	Date	Num	Memo	Account	Paid	Open Balance	Amount
Snow Stuff							
Bill	01/18/2013	97		2000 · Accounts Payable	Unpaid	370.00	370.00
Credit	01/21/2013	9912	Returned 1 Sled	2000 · Accounts Payable	Unpaid	-50.00	-50.00
Total Snow Stuff						320.00	320.00
TOTAL						320.00	320.00

Click the **Close** button to close the report
Close the Accounts Payable register and the Chart of Accounts

PREPARE AND PRINT UNPAID BILLS DETAIL REPORT

It is possible to get information regarding unpaid bills by simply preparing a report. No more digging through tickler files, recorded invoices, ledgers, or journals. QuickBooks prepares an Unpaid Bills Detail Report listing each unpaid bill grouped and subtotaled by vendor.

> # MEMO
> **DATE:** January 25, 2013
>
> Ruth Morgan prepares an Unpaid Bills Report for you and Larry each week. Because Your Name Mountain Sports is a small business, you like to have a firm control over cash flow so you can determine which bills will be paid during the week.

 Prepare and print an **Unpaid Bills Detail Report**

     Click **Reports** on the menu bar, point to **Vendors & Payables**, click **Unpaid Bills Detail**
     Enter the date of **01/25/13** as the report date
     Tab to generate report
     Adjust column size as necessary to display all data in the columns in full
- Notice the Due Dates for the bills. Bills from the end of the previous year are due on January 10.
- The days shown for Aging will be different from the report shown because the aging is based on the date of your computer.

Your Name Mountain Sports
Unpaid Bills Detail
As of January 25, 2013

Type	Date	Num	Due Date	Aging	Open Balance
Snow Stuff					
Credit	01/21/2013	9912			-50.00
Bill	01/18/2013	97	02/17/2013		370.00
Total Snow Stuff					320.00
Snow Supplies					
Bill	12/31/2012		01/10/2013	15	5,000.00
Total Snow Supplies					5,000.00
Sports Boots & Bindings					
Bill	12/31/2012		01/10/2013	15	2,000.00
Total Sports Boots & Bindings					2,000.00
Winter Sports Accessories					
Bill	12/31/2012		01/10/2013	15	350.00
Total Winter Sports Accessories					350.00
TOTAL					12,640.40

Partial Report

     Print in Portrait orientation
     Click **Close** to close the report

PAYING BILLS

When using QuickBooks, you may choose to pay your bills directly from the Pay Bills command and let QuickBooks write your checks for you, or you may choose to write the checks yourself. If you recorded a bill, you should use the Pay Bills feature of QuickBooks to pay the bill. If no bill was recorded, you should pay the bill by writing a check in QuickBooks. Using the Pay Bills window enables you to determine which bills to pay, the method of payment—check, or credit card—and the appropriate account. When you are determining which bills to pay, QuickBooks allows you to display the bills by due date, discount date, vendor, or amount. All bills may be displayed, or only those bills that are due by a certain date may be displayed. In addition, when a bill has been recorded and is paid using the Pay Bills feature of QuickBooks, the bill will be marked *Paid in Full* and the amount paid will no longer be shown as a liability. If you record a bill and pay it by writing a check and *not* using the Pay Bills feature of QuickBooks, the bill won't be marked as paid and it will show up as a liability.

MEMO

DATE: January 25, 2013

Whenever possible, Ruth Morgan pays the bills on a weekly basis. Show all the bills in the Pay Bills window. Select the bills for Boots Galore and Clothes, Inc. with discounts dates of 1/28/2013 for payment.

 Pay the bills that are eligible for a discount

> Click **Pay Bills** on the QuickBooks Home Page
> Click **Show All Bills** to select
> Filter By **All vendors**
> Sort By **Due Date**
> In the PAYMENT section at the bottom of the **Pay Bills** window, verify and/or select
> > the following items:
> > **Date** is **01/25/13**
> > **Method** is **Check**
> > **To be printed** should be selected
> > **Account** is **1100 Checking**
> Scroll through the list of bills
> - The bills will be shown according to the date due.

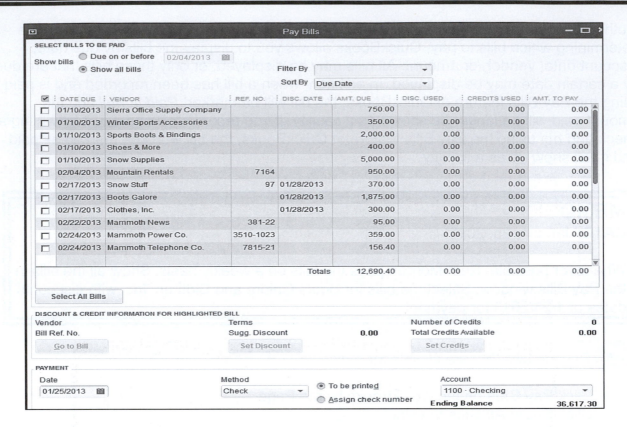

Select the bills to be paid and apply the discounts:

Click in the check mark column for the transaction for **Boots Galore** with a DUE DATE of 2/17/2013 and a DISC Date of 01/28/2013

Click the **Set Discount** button

- Verify the Suggested Discount of **37.50**.

Click the drop-down list arrow for the Discount Account

- Scroll through the list of accounts.
- There is account 4030 Purchases Discounts but it is not appropriate for this transaction. This income account is used for purchases of things used by the business <u>not</u> for merchandise.
- There is 4050 Sales Discounts. This income account is used when we give discounts to customers.
- The bill payment is for merchandise purchased to sell in the business. A cost of goods sold discount account needs to be created for merchandise discounts

Click **<Add New>**

Click the drop-down list arrow for **Account Type**, click **Cost of Goods Sold**

- Remember the Cost of Goods sold is the average cost you pay for an item you sell and is calculated on the Profit & Loss Statement using the formula: Total Income – Cost of Goods Sold = Gross Profit; Gross Profit – Expenses = Net Profit

- Using Merchandise Discounts for early payment will decrease the overall Cost of Goods Sold and increase Profit or Net Income. Example: Cost of Goods Sold – Merchandise Discounts = Net Cost of Goods Sold.
- If Cost of Goods Sold is $1,000 and you subtract Merchandise Discounts of $100 the Net Cost of Goods Sold is $900. Without the discount, Cost of Goods Sold is $1,000.

Enter **5200** as the account number
Enter the account name **Merchandise Discounts**
Click **Subaccount** and select **5000 Cost of Goods Sold** as the account

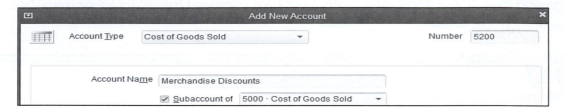

Click **Save & Close**

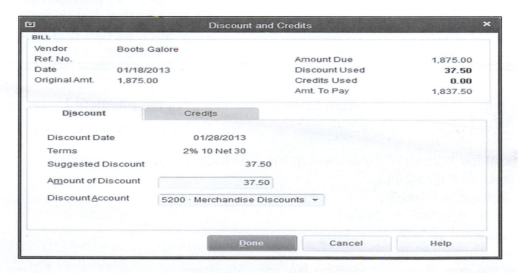

Click **Done** to record the discount
Repeat the steps for the bill from Clothes, Inc. that is eligible for a discount

☑	02/17/2013	Boots Galore		01/28/2013	1,875.00	37.50	0.00	1,837.50
☑	02/17/2013	Clothes, Inc.		01/28/2013	300.00	6.00	0.00	294.00
☐	02/22/2013	Mammoth News	381-22		95.00	0.00	0.00	0.00
☐	02/24/2013	Mammoth Power Co.	3510-1023		359.00	0.00	0.00	0.00
☐	02/24/2013	Mammoth Telephone Co.	7815-21		156.40	0.00	0.00	0.00
				Totals	12,690.40	43.50	0.00	2,131.50

- Once you click **Done** to accept the discount, the amount due and amount paid amounts change to reflect the amount of the discount taken.

- Notice the totals provided indicating the DISC. USED and the AMT. TO PAY for the two selected bills

Click the **Pay Selected Bills** button,

- Notice the two payments shown.

Click the **Pay More Bills** button on the **Payment Summary** screen

PAY A BILL QUALIFYING FOR A MERCHANDISE DISCOUNT AND APPLY CREDIT AS PART OF PAYMENT

When paying bills, it is a good idea to apply credits received for returned or damaged merchandise to the accounts as payment is made.

MEMO

DATE: January 25, 2013

As she is getting ready to pay bills, Ruth looks for any credits that may be applied to the bill as part of the payment. In addition, Ruth looks for bills that qualify for an early-payment discount. Apply the credit received from Snow Stuff, as part of the payment for the bill, then apply the discount, and pay the bill within the discount period.

 Apply the credit received from Snow Stuff, as part of the payment for the bill and pay bill within the discount period

Look at the bottom of the screen in the PAYMENT section and verify:
    Date of **01/25/2013**
    Method is **Check**
    To be printed is marked
    Account is **1100 Checking**
Select **Show all bills**
Click the drop-down list for **Sort By**, click **Vendor**
Scroll through transactions until you see the transaction for Snow Stuff
Click the check mark column next to the transaction to select it

- *Note:* This must be completed before applying the discount or credit to the bill.
- Notice that both the Set Credits and Set Discount buttons are now active and that information regarding credits and discounts is displayed.

☑ 02/17/2013	Snow Stuff	97	01/28/2013	370.00	0.00	0.00	370.00
			Totals	10,515.40	0.00	0.00	370.00

Clear Selections

DISCOUNT & CREDIT INFORMATION FOR HIGHLIGHTED BILL

Vendor	**Snow Stuff**	Terms	2% 10 Net 30	Number of Credits	1
Bill Ref. No. 97		Sugg. Discount	7.40	Total Credits Available	50.00
Go to Bill		**Set Discount**		**Set Credits**	

Click the **Set Discount** button
- Verify the amount of the discount **7.40** and the discount account **5200 Merchandise Discounts**

Click the **Credits** tab

Click the Check Mark column for the credit amount of **50.00**
- On the Discounts and Credits screen, verify the amount due of **370**, the discount used of **7.40**, and the credits used of **50.00**, leaving an amount to pay of **312.60**

- QuickBooks calculates the discount on the original amount of the invoice rather than the amount due after subtracting the credit. You need to recalculate the discount on the amount due after the credit.

Use QuickMath to calculate the correct amount of discount:

Amount Due **370** – Credits Used **50** * Discount Percentage **.02** = Discount **6.40**

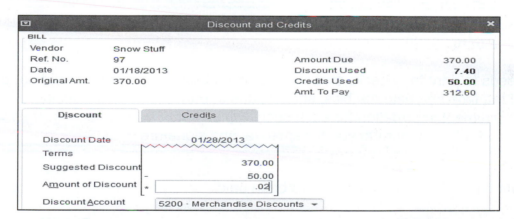

Press **Enter** to enter the discount amount, press **Tab** to update Discount Used
Click the **Done** button

☑	02/17/2013	Snow Stuff	97	01/28/2013	370.00	6.40	50.00	313.60
				Totals	10,515.40	6.40	50.00	313.60

Click **Pay Selected Bills**, click **Done** on the payment summary screen, click **Pay Selected Bills**, click **Done** on the Payment Summary

VERIFY THAT BILLS ARE MARKED PAID

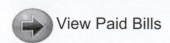 View Paid Bills

Access **Enter Bills** as previously instructed

Click **Previous** (Back arrow icon) and view all the bills that were paid in Pay Bills to verify that they are marked as paid

- Notice that the Credit for Snow Stuff is *not* marked in any way to indicate that it has been used.

Close the Enter Bills screen

PRINT CHECKS TO PAY BILLS

Once bills have been selected for payment and any discounts taken or credits applied, the checks should be printed, signed, and mailed. QuickBooks has three methods that may be used to print checks. Checks may be printed immediately after a bill has been paid, which is the most efficient method. Secondly, checks may be accessed and printed one at a time using the Write Checks window. This allows you to view the Bill Payment Information for each check. The third way is to print a batch of checks. This is done by clicking the File menu and selecting checks from the Print Forms menu. This method will print all checks that are marked *To be printed* but will not allow you to view the bill payment information for any of the checks as you would if you printed each check separately. QuickBooks does not separate checks it writes in Pay Bills from the checks that are written when using the Write Checks feature of the program.

MEMO

DATE: January 25, 2013

Ruth needs to print the checks for bills that have been paid. Since she did not print them at the time she paid the bills, she decides to print checks individually so she can view bill payment information for each check while printing. When she finishes with the checks, she will give them to you for approval and signature.

 Print the checks for bills that have been paid

Access the Write Checks window using the keyboard shortcut **Ctrl+W**
- A blank check will show on the screen.

Click **Previous** (Back arrow icon) until you get to the check for **Boots Galore**

Click **Print** at the top of the window to print the check

Click **OK** on the Print Check screen to select Check No. 2
- Check No. 1 was issued in Chapter 5 to Dr. Francisco Munoz for a return. If Check No. 2 is not on the Print Check screen, change the screen so that the check number is 2.

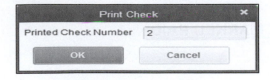

- On the **Print Checks** screen, verify the printer name, printer type, and the selection of Standard check style.

Print Company Name and Address should be selected

- If is not marked with a check, click the check box to insert a check mark and select.

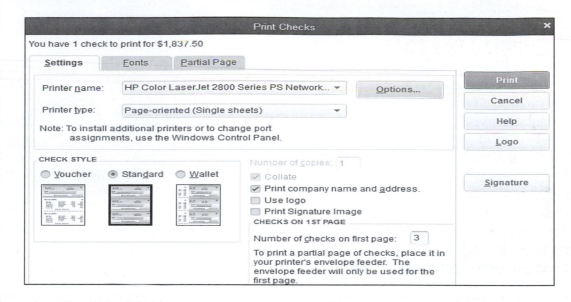

Click **Print** to print the check

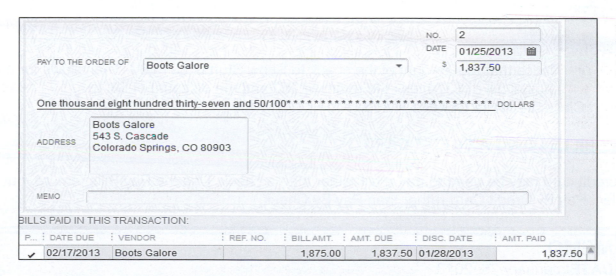

Click **OK** on the **Print Checks – Confirmation** screen

Click **Previous** or **Next** arrow icons and repeat the steps to print Check No. 3 for Clothes, Inc., and Check No. 4 for Snow Stuff

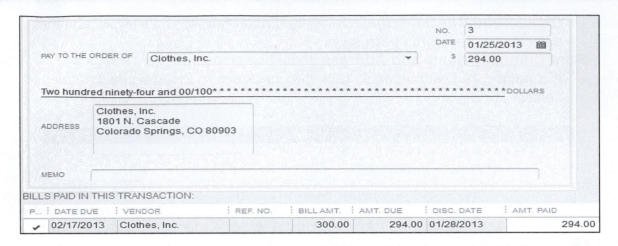

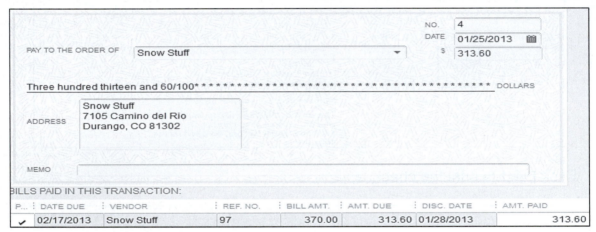

- Notice that the amount of the check to Snow Stuff is $313.60. This allows for the original bill of $370 less the return of $50 and the discount of $6.40.

Close the **Write Checks** window.

PAY BILLS USING A CREDIT CARD

A credit card may be used to pay a bill rather than a check. Use the Pay Bills feature, but select Pay By Credit Card rather than Pay By Check.

MEMO

DATE: January 25, 2013

In viewing the bills due, you direct Ruth to pay the bills to Winter Sports Accessories and Shoes & More using the Visa credit card.

 Pay the above bills with a credit card

Access **Pay Bills** as previously instructed

Select **Show all bills**

Filter By **All vendors** and Sort By **Vendor**

Scroll through the list of bills and select **Shoes & More** and **Winter Sports Accessories** by clicking in the check mark column

Make the following selections in the **PAYMENT** section:

Date should be **01/25/2013**

For **Method** click the drop-down list arrow, click **Credit Card** to select

- Account should show 2100 Visa. If it does not, click the drop-down list arrow and click **2100 Visa**.

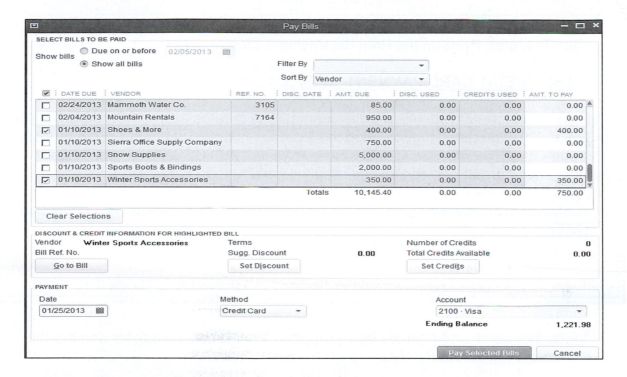

Click **Pay Selected Bills** to record the payment

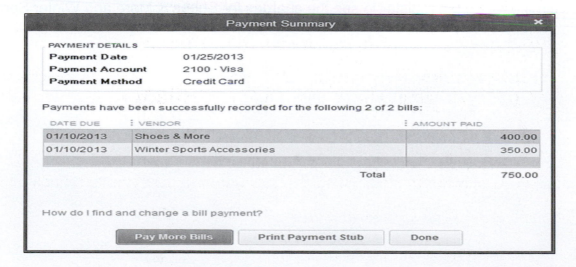

In order to have a printed record of your payment, click Print Payment Stub

Click **OK**, click **Print** on the Print Bill Payment Stubs

VERIFY THE CREDIT CARD PAYMENT OF BILLS

Paying bills with a credit card in Pay Bills automatically creates a Credit Card transaction in QuickBooks. This can be verified through the Visa account register in the Chart of Accounts and through Enter Credit Card Charges. The entry into QuickBooks does not actually charge the credit card. It only records the transaction.

MEMO

DATE: January 25, 2013

Verify the credit card charges for Winter Sports Accessories and Shoes & More.

Verify the credit card charges by viewing the Visa Account Register and the Bill Payments (Credit Card)- Visa

Access the **Visa Account Register** in the **Chart of Accounts**
Scroll through the register to see the charges for Shoes & More and Winter Sports Accessories

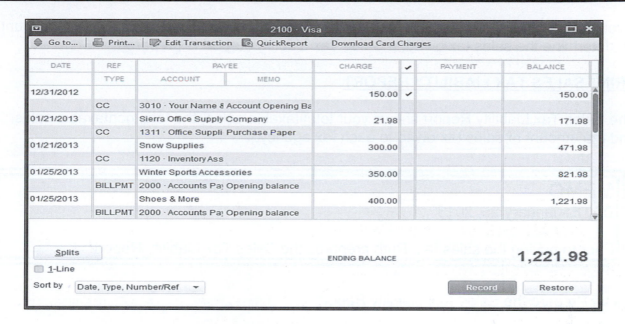

Close the **Visa Account Register** and the **Chart of Accounts**
Click the **Enter Credit Card Charges** icon
Click **Previous** arrow on the Enter Credit Card Charges – Visa screen until you see
   the payments to Shoes & More and Winter Sports Accessories
- Notice that the form title changes to Bill Payments (Credit Card) – Visa.

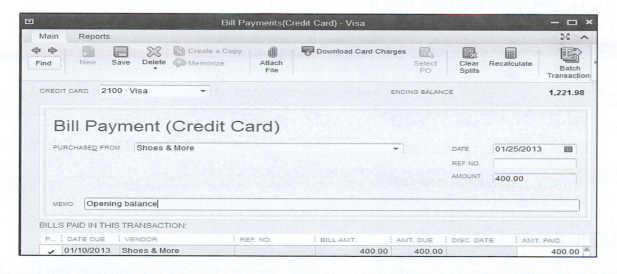

Close Bill Payments

SALES TAX

When a company is set up in QuickBooks, a Sales Tax Payable liability account is automatically created if the company indicates that it charges sales tax on sales. The Sales Tax Payable account keeps track of as many tax agencies as the company needs. As invoices are written, QuickBooks records the tax liability in the Sales Tax Payable account. To determine the sales tax owed, a Sales Tax Liability Report is prepared.

PRINT SALES TAX LIABILITY REPORT

The Sales Tax Liability Report shows your total taxable sales, the total nontaxable sales, and the amount of sales tax owed to each tax agency.

MEMO

DATE: January 25, 2013

Prior to paying the sales tax, Ruth prepares the Sales Tax Liability Report.

 Prepare the Sales Tax Liability Report

Click **Reports** on the Menu bar, point to **Vendors & Payables** as the type of report, click **Sales Tax Liability**
The Report Dates are **From 01/01/2013 To 01/25/2013**
- If necessary, adjust the column widths so the report will fit on one page.
- If you get a message box asking if all columns should be the same size as the one being adjusted, click **No**.

Your Name Mountain Sports
Sales Tax Liability
January 1 - 25, 2013

	Total Sales	Non-Taxable Sales	Taxable Sales	Tax Rate	Tax Collected	Sales Tax Payable As of Jan 25, 13
State Board of Equalization						
CA Sales Tax	▶ 8,897.00 ◄	125.00	8,772.00	8.0%	701.77	701.77
Total State Board of Equalization	8,897.00	125.00	8,772.00		701.77	701.77
TOTAL	8,897.00	125.00	8,772.00		701.77	701.77

Print in Landscape orientation
Close the report after printing

PAYING SALES TAX

Use the Manage Sales Tax window to determine how much sales tax you owe and to write a check to the tax agency. QuickBooks will update the sales tax account with payment information.

MEMO

DATE: January 25, 2013

Note from Larry: Ruth, pay the sales taxes owed.

Pay the sales taxes owed

Click the **Manage Sales Tax** icon in the Vendors section of the Home Page
Click the **Pay Sales Tax** button on the Manage Sales Tax screen.

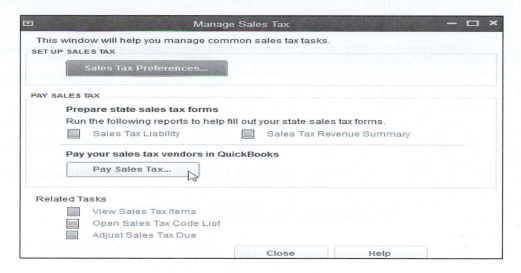

Pay From Account is **1100 Checking**
Check Date is **01/25/2013**
Show sales tax due through is **01/25/2013**
Starting Check No. should be **To Print**
Click the **Pay All Tax** button or click in the Pay column to mark the transaction

- Once the transaction has been marked, the Pay All Tax button changes to Clear Selections

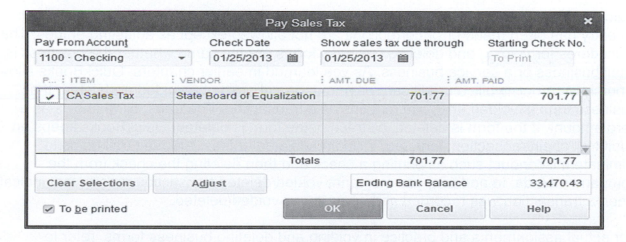

- Once **Pay All Tax** has been clicked and the Sales Tax item is selected, the **Ending Bank Balance** changes to reflect the amount in checking after the tax has been paid.

Click **OK**, and then click **Close** on the Manage Sales Tax screen

Use Print Forms to print Check No. 5 for the payment of the Sales Tax

Click **File** on the Menu bar, point to **Print Forms**, click **Checks**
- Verify the Bank Account 1100 Checking, the First Check No. 5, and the check mark in front of State Board of Equalization. If your screen does not match the following, make the appropriate changes.

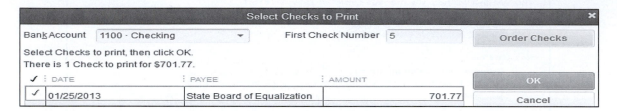

Select Checks to Print			✖
Bank Account 1100 · Checking ▼	First Check Number 5		Order Checks
Select Checks to print, then click OK. There is 1 Check to print for $701.77.			
✓ : DATE	: PAYEE	: AMOUNT	OK
✓ 01/25/2013	State Board of Equalization	701.77	Cancel

Click **OK**, click **Print**, click **OK** on the **Print Checks – Confirmation** screen

VIEW CHECK FOR TAX PAYMENT IN THE CHECK REGISTER

Whenever a check is prepared, it will show in the Register for the Checking account.

 View the payment made for sales tax

Click the **Check Register** icon on the Banking section of the Home Page
- The register for 1100-Checking is shown
Scroll through the register to view the information for Check 5, and then close it

VOIDING AND DELETING

QuickBooks allows any business form to be deleted. In some accounting programs, once an entry has been made error corrections are not allowed except as adjusting entries. The procedures for voiding and deleting business forms are the same whether the business is a retail business or a service business. As you learned in earlier chapters, QuickBooks allows a purchase order, a bill, a credit card payment, or a check to be voided or deleted. If a business form is voided, the form remains as a transaction. The transaction shows as a zero amount. If the form is deleted, all trace of the form is deleted. QuickBooks keeps an audit trail of all transactions entered, including deleted entries. An audit trail helps to eliminate misconduct such as printing a check and then deleting the check from the company records. In addition, you may print voided/deleted transaction reports that indicate when a transaction was recorded and when it was voided/deleted.

For actual assignments and practice in voiding and deleting business forms, refer to Chapters 2, 3, and 5.

PRINT THE TRIAL BALANCE

When all sales transactions have been entered, it is important to print the trial balance and verify that the total debits equal the total credits.

 Prepare and print the Trial Balance
Open the **Report Center** as previously instructed
Select **Accountant & Taxes** section, double-click **Trial Balance**
The report dates are from **01/01/2013** to **01/25/2013**

Your Name Mountain Sports
Trial Balance
As of January 25, 2013

	Jan 25, 13	
	Debit	Credit
1100 · Checking	33,470.43	
1200 · Accounts Receivable	5,696.50	
1120 · Inventory Asset	35,551.54	
12000 · Undeposited Funds	0.00	
1311 · Office Supplies	871.98	
1312 · Sales Supplies	575.00	
1340 · Prepaid Insurance	250.00	
1511 · Original Cost	5,000.00	
1521 · Original Cost	4,500.00	
2000 · Accounts Payable		9,395.40
2100 · Visa		1,221.98
2200 · Sales Tax Payable	0.00	
2510 · Office Equipment Loan		3,000.00
2520 · Store Fixtures Loan		2,500.00
3000 · Retained Earnings	0.00	
3010 · Your Name & Muir Capital		26,159.44
3011 · Your Name, Investment		20,000.00
3012 · Larry Muir, Investment		20,000.00
4011 · Clothing & Accessory Sales		1,759.51
4012 · Equipment Sales		7,436.44
4040 · Returned Check Service Charges		25.00
4050 · Sales Discounts	494.36	
5000 · Cost of Goods Sold	3,492.46	
5200 · Merchandise Discounts		49.90
6140 · Advertising Expense	95.00	
6300 · Rent	950.00	
6340 · Telephone	156.40	
6391 · Gas and Electric	359.00	
6392 · Water	85.00	
TOTAL	91,547.67	91,547.67

Print the Trial Balance in **Portrait** orientation
Close the report, do **not** close the Report Center

PRINT THE JOURNAL

The Journal records each transaction and lists the accounts and the amounts for debit and credit entries. The Journal is very useful; especially if you are trying to find errors. Always check the transaction dates, the account names, and the items listed in the Memo column. If a transaction does not appear in the Journal, it may be due to using an incorrect date. Remember, only the transactions entered within the report dates will be displayed.

 Print the Journal for Chapter 6 transactions

In the **Accountant & Taxes** section double-click **Journal**
Click the **Expand** button to show all information
Enter the dates for Chapter 6 transactions: From **01/18/13** and To **01/25/13**
- Using the chapter transaction dates means that the Journal will not show the transactions for Chapter 5. If you wish to see the transactions for Chapters 5 and 6, the From date should be 01/01/13.

Resize the columns so information shows in full

Your Name Mountain Sports
Journal
January 18 - 25, 2013

Trans #	Type	Date	Num	Adj	Name	Memo	Account	Debit	Credit
99	Bill Pmt -Check	01/25/2013	4		Snow Stuff		1100 · Checking		313.60
					Snow Stuff		2000 · Accounts Payable	313.60	
					Snow Stuff		2000 · Accounts Payable	6.40	
					Snow Stuff		5200 · Merchandise Discounts		6.40
								320.00	320.00
100	Bill Pmt -CCard	01/25/2013			Shoes & More	Opening balance	2100 · Visa		400.00
					Shoes & More	Opening balance	2000 · Accounts Payable	400.00	
								400.00	400.00
101	Bill Pmt -CCard	01/25/2013			Winter Sports Accessories	Opening balance	2100 · Visa		350.00
					Winter Sports Accessories	Opening balance	2000 · Accounts Payable	350.00	
								350.00	350.00
102	Sales Tax Payment	01/25/2013	5		State Board of Equalization		1100 · Checking		701.77
					State Board of Equalization		2200 · Sales Tax Payable	701.77	
								701.77	701.77
TOTAL								8,519.15	8,519.15

Partial Report

Print the Journal in Landscape orientation
Close the **Journal**, do <u>not</u> close the **Report Center**

PREPARE INVENTORY VALUATION SUMMARY REPORT

To obtain information regarding the inventory, you may prepare an Inventory Valuation Summary or an Inventory Valuation Detail report. Both reports give you information regarding an item, the number on hand, the average cost, and asset value. The summary report also gives information regarding an item's percentage of total assets, sales price, retail value, and percentage of total retail. The detail report includes information for transactions using inventory items. In addition to the information shown in both reports, the detail report includes type of transaction, date of transaction, customer name, number, quantity, and cost.

Preparing the Inventory Valuation Summary will allow you to verify the number on hand, average cost, asset value, percentage of Total Assets, sales price, retail value, and percentage of Total Retail value for each inventory item.

 Prepare and print an Inventory Valuation Summary report in Landscape orientation as of January 25, 2013

In the Inventory section of the Report Center, click **Inventory Valuation Summary**
Enter the date **01/25/13**, press **Tab**

- Since we use different sales prices within an item, the Sales Price, Retail Value, and % of Total Retail are not calculated

Remove the columns for Sales Price, Retail Value, and % of Tot Retail
Resize the columns to display them in full

	On Hand	Avg Cost	Asset Value	% of Tot Asset
Your Name Mountain Sports				
Inventory Valuation Summary				
As of January 25, 2013				
Inventory				
Accessories	795	3.66	2,906.70	8.2%
Bindings-Skis	43	75.00	3,225.00	9.1%
Bindings-Snow	48	75.00	3,600.00	10.1%
Boots	20	30.00	600.00	1.7%
Boots-Ski	14	75.00	1,050.00	3.0%
Boots-Snowbrd	35	75.00	2,625.00	7.4%
Gloves	40	15.00	600.00	1.7%
Hats	29	8.00	232.00	0.7%
Helmets	20	28.00	560.00	1.6%
Pants-Ski	93	30.00	2,790.00	7.8%
Pants-Snowbrd	50	35.00	1,750.00	4.9%
Parkas	73	58.33	4,258.34	12.0%
Poles-Ski	23	30.00	690.00	1.9%
Skis	43	100.00	4,300.00	12.1%
Sleds	6	60.00	360.00	1.0%
Snowboard	28	100.00	2,800.00	7.9%
Socks	72	3.00	216.00	0.6%
Sweaters	73	25.00	1,825.00	5.1%
Toboggans	7	129.64	907.50	2.6%
Underwear	32	8.00	256.00	0.7%
Total Inventory	**1,544**		**35,551.54**	**100.0%**
TOTAL	**1,544**		**35,551.54**	**100.0%**

Print in Landscape orientation, and then close the report and the Report Center

BACK UP YOUR NAME MOUNTAIN SPORTS

 Follow the instructions given in previous chapters to back up data for Your Name Mountain Sports, use the file name **Sports (Backup Ch. 6)**.

SUMMARY

In this chapter, purchase orders were completed, inventory items were received, and bills were recorded. Payments for purchases and bills were made by cash and by credit card and early payment discounts were applied. Sales taxes were paid. Vendors, inventory items, and accounts were added while transactions were being recorded. Accounts were assigned to vendors and preferred vendors were added to sales items. Various reports were prepared to determine unpaid bills, account and vendor QuickReports, and sales tax liability.

END-OF-CHAPTER QUESTIONS

TRUE/FALSE

ANSWER THE FOLLOWING QUESTIONS IN THE SPACE PROVIDED BEFORE THE QUESTION NUMBER.

_____ 1. Receipt of purchase order items is never recorded before the bill arrives.

_____ 2. A bill can be paid by check or credit card.

_____ 3. The Cost of Goods Sold account Merchandise Discounts is used to record discounts to customers.

_____ 4. Voiding a purchase order removes every trace of the purchase order from the company records.

_____ 5. The Vendor Center displays the vendor list and information about individual vendors.

_____ 6. A single purchase order can be prepared and sent to several vendors.

_____ 7. A Sales Tax account is automatically created if a company indicates that it charges sales tax on sales.

_____ 8. When a credit is received from a vendor for the return of merchandise, it may be applied to a payment to the same vendor.

_____ 9. A new vendor cannot be added while recording a transaction.

_____ 10. A purchase order is closed automatically when a partial receipt of merchandise is recorded.

MULTIPLE CHOICE

WRITE THE LETTER OF THE CORRECT ANSWER IN THE SPACE PROVIDED BEFORE THE QUESTION NUMBER.

_____ 1. If you change the reorder point for an item, it becomes effective ___.
   A. immediately
   B. the beginning of next month
   C. as soon as outstanding purchase orders are received
   D. the beginning of the next fiscal year

_____ 2. If an order is received with a bill but is incomplete, QuickBooks will ___.
  A. record the bill for the full amount ordered
  B. record the bill only for the amount received
  C. not allow the bill to be prepared until all the merchandise is received
  D. close the purchase order

_____ 3. The Purchase Order feature must be selected as a preference ___.
  A. when setting up the company
  B. prior to recording the first purchase order
  C. is automatically set when the first purchase order is prepared
  D. either A or B

_____ 4. A faster method of entering bills can be entering the bills ___.
  A. while writing the checks for payment
  B. in the Pay Bills window
  C. in the Accounts Payable Register
  D. none of the above

_____ 5. A Preferred Vendor is selected for an existing Item ___.
  A. in the Vendor Center
  B. on the Edit Item screen
  C. on the Purchase Order
  D. when entering the Bill

_____ 6. Sales tax is paid by using the ___ window.
  A. Pay Bills
  B. Manage Sales Tax
  C. Write Check
  D. Credit Card

_____ 7. A Purchase Order may be customized using the ___.
  A. Layout Designer
  B. Drawing menu
  C. Customize Form button on the Home Page
  D. a form may not be changed

_____ 8. Checks to pay bills may be printed ___.
  A. individually
  B. all at once
  C. as the checks are written
  D. all of the above

_____ 9. When items ordered are received with a bill, you record the receipt ___.
   A. on an item receipt form
   B. on the bill
   C. on the original purchase order
   D. in the Journal

_____ 10. Expense accounts for individual vendors may be assigned in the _____.
   A. Check Register
   B. General Journal
   C. Expense Account Register
   D. Vendor Center

FILL-IN

IN THE SPACE PROVIDED, WRITE THE ANSWER THAT MOST APPROPRIATELY COMPLETES THE SENTENCE.

1. Orders for merchandise are prepared using the QuickBooks _____ form.

2. Information on the Reminders List may be displayed in _____ or _____ form.

3. The _____ Report shows the total taxable sales and the amount of sales tax owed.

4. A purchase order can be closed _____ or _____.

5. To see the bill payment information, checks must be printed _____.

SHORT ESSAY

Describe the cycle of obtaining merchandise. Include the process from ordering the merchandise through paying for it. Include information regarding the QuickBooks forms prepared for each phase of the cycle, the possible ways in which an item may be received, and the ways in which payment may be made.

_____

_____

_____

_____

_____

NAME_____

TRANSMITTAL

CHAPTER 6: YOUR NAME MOUNTAIN SPORTS

Attach the following documents and reports:

Purchase Order No. 1: Boots Galore
Purchase Order No. 2: Snow Stuff
Purchase Order No. 3: Clothes, Inc.
Purchase Order No. 4: Snow Supplies
Account QuickReport, Purchase Orders, January 16, 2013
Bill: Snow Stuff (Optional)
Bill: Boots Galore (Optional)
Purchase Order No. 4 (Corrected): Snow Supplies
Bill: Clothes, Inc. (Optional)
Purchase Order No. 3 (Closed): Clothes, Inc.
Bill Credit: Snow Stuff (Optional)
Bill: Mammoth News (Optional)
Bill: Mammoth Power (Optional)
Bill: Mammoth Telephone (Optional)
Bill: Mammoth Water (Optional)
Register QuickReport, Snow Stuff
Unpaid Bills Detail, January 25, 2013
Check No. 2: Boots Galore
Check No. 3: Clothes, Inc.
Check No. 4: Snow Stuff
Bill Payment Stub: Shoes & More
Bill Payment Stub: Winter Sports Accessories
Sales Tax Liability Report, January 1-25, 2013
Check No. 5: State Board of Equalization
Trial Balance, January 25, 2013
Journal, January 18-25, 2013
Inventory Valuation Summary, January 25, 2013

END-OF-CHAPTER PROBLEM

YOUR NAME RESORT CLOTHING

Chapter 6 continues with the transactions for purchase orders, merchandise receipts, bills, bill payments, and sales tax payments. Your partner, Karen Olsen, prints the checks, purchase orders, and any related reports; and you sign the checks. This procedure establishes cash control procedures and lets both owners know about the checks being processed.

INSTRUCTIONS

Continue to use the copy of Your Name Resort Clothing you used in Chapter 5. Open the company—the file used is **Clothing.qbw**. Record the purchase orders, bills, payments, and other transactions as instructed within the chapter. Always read the transactions carefully and review the Chart of Accounts when selecting transaction accounts. Add new vendors and minimum quantities where indicated. Verify with your instructor the required printing and whether or not to print Bills. Otherwise, print all purchase orders, bills, and checks. Print reports as indicated making sure to resize columns so all information is displayed in full. The first purchase order used is Purchase Order No. 1. When paying bills, always check for credits that may be applied to the bill, and always check for discounts.

In addition to the Item List and the Chart of Accounts, you will need to use the Vendor List when ordering merchandise and paying bills.

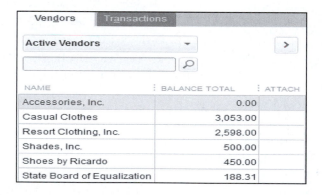

RECORD TRANSACTIONS

January 5, 2013:
- ► Customize a Purchase Order template so the Default Title is **PURCHASE ORDER**, Company Name is expanded to **4 ¾**, and PURCHASE ORDER begins at **5**.
- ► Hide the History and resize the Purchase Order to make it smaller on the screen
- ► Change the reorder point for dresses from 20 to 25.
- ► Change the reorder point for women's pants from 25 to 30.

▶ Prepare and print an Inventory Stock Status by Item Report for January 1-5, 2013 in Landscape orientation. Manually adjust column widths so vendors' names are shown in full. (Note: In Chapter 5, transactions were entered through January 15. If you prepare the report based on January 15, it will be different from this one.)

▶ Prepare Purchase Orders for all items marked Order on the Stock Status by Item Inventory Report. Use the vendor Casual Clothes. for the dresses. Since a vendor has been assigned for Women-Pants, VENDOR information will be completed when the Item is entered. The quantity for each item ordered is 10. The rate is $35 for dresses and $20 for pants. Print purchase orders with lines around each field.

  ○ If you get an Item's Cost Changed dialog box asking if you want to update the item with the new cost, click **Do not display this message in the future**, and click **No**.

▶ Change the Vendor Name Resort Clothing, Inc. to Trendy Clothing, Inc. Make sure to change the vendor name, company name, billed from name, and print name on checks as (on the Payment Settings tab). Also, change the Main Email to TrendyClothing@abc.com.

▶ Reprint Purchase Order 2.

▶ Add a new vendor: Clothes Time, Main Phone 805-555-5512, Main Email clothestime@slo.com, Fax 805-555-2155, 9382 Grand Avenue, San Luis Obispo, CA 93407, Credit terms 2% 10 Net 30, Credit limit $2000.

▶ Assign Clothes Time as the Preferred Vendor for dresses.

▶ Order an additional 10 dresses from Clothes Time. The rate for the dresses is $25.

▶ Print a Purchase Order QuickReport for January 1-5.

January 8, 2013:
▶ Received pants that were ordered on Purchase Order 2 from Trendy Clothing, Inc. without the bill. Enter the receipt of merchandise. The transaction date is 01/08/2013.

▶ Received dresses that were ordered on Purchase Order 1 from Casual Clothes with Bill Use date of 01/08/2013. Enter the receipt of the merchandise and the bill. Print the Bill.

▶ Received 8 dresses from Clothes Time ordered on Purchase Order 3. Enter the receipt of the merchandise and Bill 406. Print the bill. Manually close the Purchase Order, and print it.

▶ After recording the receipt of merchandise, view the three purchase orders. Notice which ones are marked *Received in Full* and *Closed*.

January 9, 2013:
▶ Received Bill 239 from Trendy Clothing, Inc. for the pants received on 01/08/13. The bill was dated 01/08/2013 (use this date for the bill).

January 10, 2013:
▶ Discovered unstitched seams in two pairs of women's pants ordered on PO 2. Return the pants for credit. Use 2340 as the Reference number.

January 12, 2013
▶ Pay for the dresses from Clothes Time with a credit card. (Take a purchase discount if the transaction qualifies for one. Use a Cost of Goods Sold account 5200 Merchandise

Discounts for the discount. Create any necessary accounts.) Print the Bill Payment Stub.

January 15, 2013:
▶ Add new vendors:
  ○ SLO Rental Company, Main Phone 805-555-4100, Fax 805-555-0014, 301 Marsh Street, San Luis Obispo, CA 93407, Payment Terms Net 30. Assign 6280 Rent as the account.
  ○ SLO Telephone Co., Main Phone 805-555-1029, 8851 Hwy. 58, San Luis Obispo, CA 93407. Payment Terms Net 30. Assign the account 6340 Telephone Expense
▶ Record and print the bills for rent of $1,150.00 and telephone service of $79.85.

January 18, 2013:
▶ Pay all bills that are eligible for a discount. Take any discounts for which you are eligible. If there are any credits, apply the credit and calculate the appropriate discount (if eligible) prior to paying the bill. Pay the bill(s) by check.
▶ Print Check Nos. 2 and 3 for the bills that were paid. (They may be printed individually or as a batch.)

January 25, 2013:
▶ Purchase office supplies to have on hand for $250 with a credit card from a new vendor (Office Masters, Main Phone 805-555-9915, Main Email OfficeMasters@slo.com, Fax 805-555-5199, 8330 Grand Avenue, Arroyo Grande, CA 93420, Terms Net 30, Credit limit $500).
▶ Print Unpaid Bills Detail Report in Portrait orientation.
▶ Pay bills for rent and telephone. Print the checks prepared for these bills. (They may be printed individually or as a batch.)

January 30, 2013:
▶ Prepare Sales Tax Liability Report from 01/01/2013 to 01/30/2013. Print the report in Landscape orientation. Change columns widths, if necessary, so the report will fit on one page.
▶ Pay Sales Tax for the amount due through 01/30/13, and print the check.
▶ Prepare a Vendor Balance Detail Report for All Transactions. Do __not__ print but leave on the screen.
▶ When reviewing the Vendor Balance Detail Report, realized that the Ref. No. C309 for the 01/08/13 bill from Casual Clothes was missing. Correct and reprint the bill.
▶ Print the Vendor Balance Detail Report in Portrait orientation.
▶ Print a Trial Balance for 01/01/2013 to 01/30/2013.
▶ Print a Journal for 01/01/2013 to 01/30/2013 (Size columns to display all information.)
▶ Print an Inventory Valuation Summary Report for 01/30/2013 in Portrait (Remove the columns for Sales Price, Retail Value, and % of Tot Retail).
▶ Back up data.

NAME_____

TRANSMITTAL

CHAPTER 6: YOUR NAME RESORT CLOTHING

Attach the following documents and reports:

Inventory Stock Status by Item, January 1-5, 2013
Purchase Order No. 1: Casual Clothes
Purchase Order No. 2: Trendy Clothing, Inc.
Purchase Order No. 2: Reprint: Trendy Clothing, Inc.
Purchase Order No. 3: Clothes Time
Account QuickReport, Purchase Orders
Bill: Casual Clothes
Bill: Clothes Time
Purchase Order No. 3 Closed: Clothes Time
Bill: Trendy Clothing, Inc.
Bill Credit: Trendy Clothing, Inc.
Bill Payment Stub: Clothes Time
Bill: SLO Rental, Inc.
Bill: SLO Telephone Co.
Check No. 2: Casual Clothes
Check No. 3: Trendy Clothing, Inc.
Unpaid Bills Detail, January 25, 2013
Check No. 4: SLO Rental Company
Check No. 5: SLO Telephone Company
Sales Tax Liability Report
Check No. 6: State Board of Equalization
Bill Corrected: Casual Clothes
Vendor Balance Detail, January 30, 2013
Trial Balance, January 1-30, 2013
Journal, January 1-30, 2013
Inventory Valuation Summary, January 30, 2013

GENERAL ACCOUNTING AND END-OF-PERIOD PROCEDURES: MERCHANDISING BUSINESS

LEARNING OBJECTIVES

At the completion of this chapter, you will be able to:

1. Complete the end-of-period procedures.
2. Change the name of existing accounts in the Chart of Accounts, view the account name change, and view the effect of an account name change on subaccounts.
3. Delete an existing account from the Chart of Accounts.
4. Enter the adjusting entries required for accrual-basis accounting.
5. Make an adjustment to inventory.
6. Understand how to record owners' equity transactions for a partnership.
7. Transfer Capital – Other to the individual partners.
8. Enter transactions for owner withdrawals, close the owners' drawing accounts, and transfer net income to the owners' capital accounts.
9. Reconcile the bank statement, record bank service charges, and mark cleared transactions.
10. Reconcile a credit card statement and Undo a reconciliation
11. Enter a correcting entry after a period has been closed.
12. Print the Journal and other reports; such as, Trial Balance, Profit and Loss Statement, and Balance Sheet.
13. Export a report to Microsoft® Excel and import data from Excel
14. Perform end-of-period backup, close a period, record transactions in a closed period, and adjust inventory quantities.

GENERAL ACCOUNTING AND END-OF-PERIOD PROCEDURES

As stated in previous chapters, QuickBooks operates from the standpoint of the business document rather than an accounting form, journal, or ledger. While QuickBooks does incorporate all of these items into the program, in many instances they operate behind the scenes. While many accounting programs require special closing procedures at the end of a period, QuickBooks does not. At the end of the fiscal year, QuickBooks transfers the net income into the Retained Earnings account and allows you to protect the data for the year by assigning a closing date to the period. All of the transaction detail is maintained and viewable, but it will not be changed unless OK is clicked on a warning screen.

Even though a formal closing does not have to be performed within QuickBooks, when using accrual-basis accounting, several transactions must be recorded in order to reflect all expenses and income for the period accurately. For example, bank statements and credit cards must be reconciled; and any charges or bank collections need to be recorded. Adjusting entries such as depreciation, office supplies used, and so on will also need to be made. These adjustments may be recorded by the CPA or by the company's accounting personnel. At the end of the year, net income for the year and the owner withdrawals for the year should be transferred to the owners' capital accounts.

As in a service business, the CPA for the company will review things such as account names, adjusting entries, depreciation schedules, owner's equity adjustments, and so on.

If the CPA makes the changes and adjustments, they may be made on the Accountant's Copy of the business files. An Accountant's Copy is a version of your company file that your accountant can use to make changes. You record the day-to-day business transactions; and, at the same time, your accountant works using the Accountant's Copy. The changes made by the CPA are imported into your company file. There are certain restrictions to the types of transactions that may be made on an Accountant's Copy of the company file. There are also restrictions regarding the types of entries that may be made in the company file that you are using.

Once necessary adjustments have been made, reports reflecting the end-of-period results of operations should be prepared. For archive purposes, at the end of the fiscal year, an additional backup is prepared and stored.

TRAINING TUTORIAL AND PROCEDURES

The following tutorial will once again work with Your Name Mountain Sports. As in Chapters 5 and 6, transactions will be recorded for this fictitious company. Refer to procedures given in Chapter 2 to maximize training benefits.

As in the other chapters in the text, the year used for the screen shots is 2013, which is the same year as the version of the program. You may want to check with your instructor to see if you should use 2013 as the year for the transactions. Be sure to use the same year for all the transactions in Chapters 5, 6, and 7.

While everything that may be printed is listed on the transmittal sheet, check with your instructor for exact printing assignments and instructions.

OPEN QUICKBOOKS® AND YOUR NAME MOUNTAIN SPORTS

 Open **QuickBooks** and **Your Name Mountain Sports** as previously instructed

BEGINNING THE TUTORIAL

In this chapter you will be recording end-of-period adjustments, reconciling bank and credit card statements, changing account names, and preparing traditional end-of-period reports. Because QuickBooks does not perform a traditional closing of the books, you will close the period to protect transactions and data recorded during previous accounting periods.

As in previous chapters, all transactions are listed on memos. The transaction date will be the same as the memo date unless otherwise specified within the transaction. To determine the account used in the transaction, refer to the Chart of Accounts.

CHANGE THE NAME OF EXISTING ACCOUNTS IN THE CHART OF ACCOUNTS

Even though transactions have been recorded during the month of January, QuickBooks makes it a simple matter to change the name of an existing account. Once the name of an account has been changed, all transactions using the old name are updated and show the new account name.

MEMO

DATE: January 31, 2013

On the recommendation of the company's CPA, you decided to change the account named Freight Income to Delivery Income.

 Change the account name of Freight Income

Access the Chart of Accounts using the keyboard shortcut **Ctrl+A**
Scroll through accounts until you see 4020 Freight Income, click **4020 Freight Income**
Use the keyboard shortcut **Ctrl+E**
On the **Edit Account** screen, highlight **Freight Income**
Enter the new name **Delivery Income**
Since the account name is self-explanatory, delete the description
Click **Save & Close** to record the name change and to close the **Edit Account** screen
- Notice that the name of the account appears as Delivery Income in the Chart of Accounts.

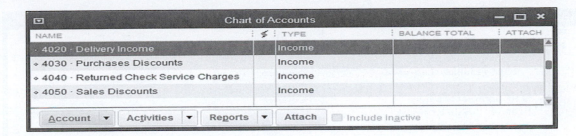

Do <u>not</u> close the **Chart of Accounts**

MAKE AN ACCOUNT INACTIVE

If you are not using an account and do not have plans to do so in the near future, the account may be made inactive. The account remains available for use, yet it does not appear on your Chart of Accounts unless you check the Show All check box.

MEMO
DATE: January 31, 2013

At this time, Your Name Mountain Sports does not plan to rent any equipment. The account 6170 - Equipment Rental should be made inactive. In addition, the company does not plan to use 6290 - Franchise Fees. Make these accounts inactive.

 Make the accounts listed above inactive

> Click **6170 - Equipment Rental**
> Click the **Account** button at the bottom of the Chart of Accounts, click **Make Account Inactive**
> • The account no longer appears in the Chart of Accounts.
> Make **6290 - Franchise Fees** inactive
> Click **6290 - Franchise Fees**
> Use the keyboard shortcut **Ctrl+E**
> On the Edit Account screen, click the **Account is inactive** check box in the lower-left portion of the screen
> Click **Save & Close**
> To view all accounts, including the inactive ones, click the **Include Inactive** check box at the bottom of the Chart of Accounts
> • Notice the icons that mark Equipment Rental and Franchise Fees as inactive accounts.

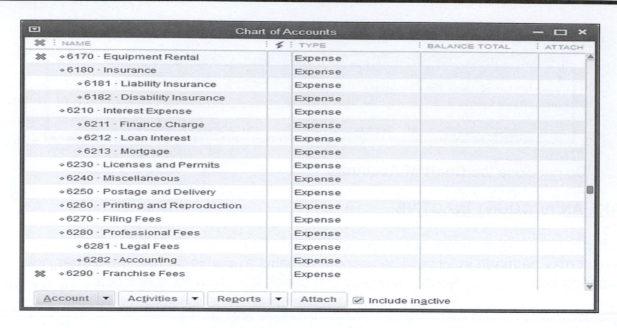

Do <u>not</u> close the **Chart of Accounts**

DELETE AN EXISTING ACCOUNT FROM THE CHART OF ACCOUNTS

If you do not want to make an account inactive because you have not used it and do not plan to use it at all, QuickBooks allows the account to be deleted at any time. However, as a safeguard, QuickBooks does prevent the deletion of an account once it has been used even if it simply contains an opening or an existing balance.

MEMO

DATE: January 31, 2013

In addition to previous changes to account names, you find that you do not use and will not use the expense accounts: Account 6213 Interest Expense: Mortgage, Account 6523 Taxes: Property, and Account 6350 Travel & Ent. and its subaccounts. Delete these accounts from the Chart of Accounts.

 Delete the accounts listed in the memo

     Scroll through Chart of Accounts until you see Account 6213: Mortgage, a
         subaccount of 6210 Interest Expense
     Click **6213 - Mortgage** to select the account
     Click the **Account** button at the bottom of the Chart of Accounts, click **Delete**
         Account
     Click **OK** on the **Delete Account** dialog box
     •   The account has now been deleted.
     Click **6523 – Property**, a subaccount of 6520 Taxes, to select the account

Use the keyboard shortcut **Ctrl+D** to delete and then click **OK** on the **Delete Account** dialog box

Follow the same procedures to delete the subaccounts of 6350 Travel & Ent.:
6351 - Entertainment, **6352 - Meals**, and **6353 - Travel**

- *Note:* Whenever an account has subaccounts, the subaccounts must be deleted before QuickBooks will let you delete the main account. This is what you must do before you can delete Travel & Ent. A subaccount is deleted the same as any other account.

When the subaccounts have been deleted; delete **6350 - Travel & Ent.**

Do <u>not</u> close the Chart of Accounts

CREATE AN INDIVIDUAL CAPITAL ACCOUNT FOR EACH OWNER

Currently, all of the owners' accounts are grouped together. A better display of owners' equity would be to show all equity accounts for each owner grouped by owner. In addition, each owner should have an individual capital account.

Your equity accounts should have both your first and last name as part of the title, just like Larry Muir's accounts. For the joint capital account, you should have your last name & Muir.

MEMO
DATE: January 31, 2013

Edit Your Name & Muir, Capital to change the account number to 3100 and add your Last Name to the account name. Create separate Capital accounts for (Your) First and Last Name and Larry Muir. Name the accounts 3110 First and Last Name, Capital, and 3120 Larry Muir, Capital. In addition, change your Investment account to 3111 First and Last Name, Investment and your Drawing account to 3112 First and Last Name, Drawing. Make these subaccounts of 3110 First and Last Name, Capital. Do the same for Larry's accounts: 3121 Investment and 3122 Drawing.

 Create separate Capital accounts and change subaccounts for existing owners' equity accounts

Click **3010 - Your Name & Muir, Capital**
- In the controlling account 3010 you will just use your <u>last</u> name. However, in the individual capital accounts, such as, Your Name, Investment, you will use both your <u>first</u> and <u>last</u> names.

Click **Account** at the bottom of the **Chart of Accounts**, click **Edit Account**

Change the account number to **3100**

Tab to or click **Account Name**

Highlight the words Your Name and replace them with your <u>last</u> name to name the account and add a comma between Muir and Capital

- In the textbook **3100 - Your Last Name & Muir, Capital** is shown as the account name, but your work will show your own last name. For example, the author's account name would be 3100 Horne & Muir, Capital.

Click **Save & Close**

Click **Account** at the bottom of the **Chart of Accounts**, click **New**

Click **Equity** as the account type, click **Continue**

Tab to or click **Number**, enter **3120**

Tab to or click **Account Name**, enter **Larry Muir, Capital**

Click **Subaccount**; click the drop-down list arrow next to **Subaccount**, click **3100 - Your Last Name & Muir, Capital**

Click **Save & Close**

Edit the account **3012 - Larry Muir, Investment** following steps previously listed to change the Account number to **3121**. It is a **Subaccount of: 3120**

Edit **3014 - Larry Muir, Drawing**, Account number is **3122**, **Subaccount of: 3120**

NAME	TYPE	BALANCE TOTAL	ATTACH
◇ 3120 - Larry Muir, Capital	Equity	20,000.00	
◇ 3121 - Larry Muir, Investment	Equity	20,000.00	
◇ 3122 - Larry Muir, Drawing	Equity	0.00	

Use the keyboard shortcut **Ctrl+N** to create a new account

Click **Equity** as the account type, click **Continue**

Tab to or click **Number**, enter **3110**

Tab to or click **Account Name**, enter **First and Last Name, Capital**

- Remember to use your real <u>first</u> and <u>last</u> name.
- In the textbook **3110 - First and Last Name, Capital** is shown as the account name, but your work will show your own name. For example, the author's account name would be 3110 - Janet Horne, Capital.
- In QuickBooks, there is not enough room for the words "Your First and Last Name, Capital" so the account name is First and Last Name, Capital, which is used to indicate that the account name contains your actual first and last names.

Click **Subaccount**; click the drop-down list arrow next to **Subaccount**, click **3100 - Your Last Name & Muir, Capital**

Click **Save & Close**

Edit the account **3011 - Your Name, Investment** following steps presented previously

Change the **Number** to **3111**

Change the **Account Name** to **First and Last Name, Investment**

- In QuickBooks there is not enough room for the words "Your First and Last Name, Investment" so the account name is First and Last Name, Investment, which is used to indicate that the account name contains your actual first and last names.

Make this a **Subaccount of: 3110 - First and Last Name, Capital**

- In the textbook **3111 - First and Last Name, Investment** is shown as the account name, but your work will show your own name. For example, the

author's account name would be Janet Horne, Investment, a subaccount of
3110 - Janet Horne, Capital.

Click **Save & Close** when the changes have been made

Make the following changes to **3013 Your Name, Drawing:**

Account number is **3112**; Account name is **First and Last Name, Drawing**; the
account is a **Subaccount of: 3110**

- In the text **3112 - First and Last Name, Drawing** is shown as the account name,
but your work will show your own name. For example, the author's account name
would be Janet Horne, Drawing, a subaccount of 3110 - Janet Horne, Capital.

- The capital accounts appear as follows:

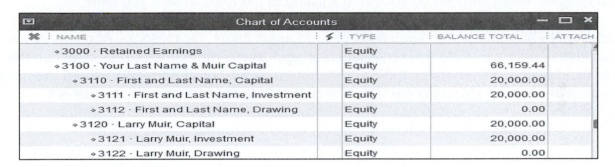

Close the **Chart of Accounts**

Use the **Reports** menu **List** category to print the **Account Listing** in Portrait
orientation

Use the date **01/31/13** for the report

- Since the report is prepared using the date of your computer, it will need to be
changed to 01/31/13

Click the **Customize Report** button at the top of the report, and then click the
Header/Footer tab

Change **Subtitle** from the current date to **January 31, 2013**, and then, click **OK**

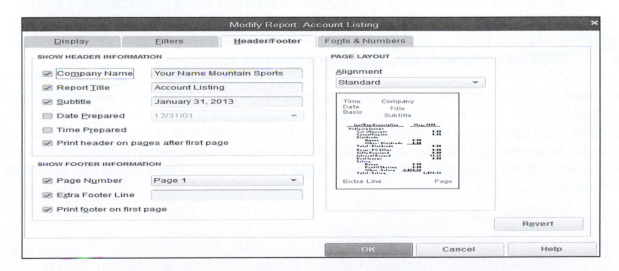

Resize the columns to display the Account Names in full—including subaccounts

Hide the columns for Description, Accnt. #, and Tax Line by dragging the sizing
   diamond from the right side of the column to the left
Print and close the Report

FIXED ASSETS AND FIXED ASSET MANAGER

Fixed assets are the long-term assets that are used in in the business for longer than one
year. The asset does wear out or needs to be replaced over time. During the time the asset
is in use by the company, the amount of the asset that is "used up" needs to be recorded to
reflect the current value of the asset item. If the company owns fixed assets, it is helpful to
create a fixed asset item list so you have a listing of the fixed assets you own.

In addition to allowing you to keep a list of fixed asset items, QuickBooks Accountant and
Enterprise versions include a Fixed Asset Manager that is more comprehensive than the
list of fixed assets. When used, the Fixed Asset Manager pulls information about the fixed
assets from an open company file. The Fixed Asset Manager allows you to use six
depreciation bases—Federal, AMT, ACE, Book, State, and Other. The accountant can use
the Fixed Asset Manager to determine the depreciation for the assets and then post a
journal entry back to the company file. The Fixed Asset Manager also integrates with
Intuit's ProSeries Tax products and must have tax forms identified prior to use. It provides a
wide variety of built-in depreciation reports, forms, and multiple ways to import and export
data. The Fixed Asset Manager is synchronized with QuickBooks and has its own data files
that allow for more detailed asset information than a company file. The Fixed Asset
Manager will not be used at this time since it is designed to be used by the company's
accountant to calculate depreciation schedules based on the taxation information entered.

FIXED ASSET ITEM LIST

As with other QuickBooks lists, you may keep a record of your company's fixed assets in
the Fixed Asset Item List. In the list, you record information about your company's fixed
assets including the purchase date and cost, whether the item was new or used when
purchased, and the sales price if the item is sold. Note that Depreciation and Book Value
are not calculated or stored in the Fixed Asset Item List.

The Fixed Asset List provides a way to keep important information about your assets in one
convenient place. This is useful to do whether or not your accountant uses the Fixed Asset
Manager. You can create an item to track a fixed asset at several points during the asset's
life cycle; however, it is recommended that you create the item when you buy the asset or
setup the company. You can create a fixed asset item from the Fixed Asset List or from a
Transaction.

MEMO

DATE: January 31, 2013

When Your Name Mountain Sports was setup in QuickBooks, the Fixed Item Asset List was not created. Create the Fixed Asset Item List:
<u>Store Fixtures</u>: Asset Name/Number, Purchase Description, and Asset Description: Store Fixtures; Item is New; Date: 12/31/12; Cost: $4,500; Asset Account: 1520.
<u>Office Equipment</u>: Asset Name/Number, Purchase Description, and Asset Description: Office Equipment; Item is New; Date: 12/31/12; Cost: $5,000; Asset Account: 1510.

 Create a Fixed Asset Item List

Click **Lists** on the menu bar
Click **Fixed Asset Item List**
Use the keyboard shortcut **Ctrl+N** to create a new item
Complete the information for the new item:
The **Asset Name/Number** is **Store Fixtures**
The **Asset Account** is **1520**
Complete the PURCHASE INFORMATION:
> The Item is **new**
> The **Purchase Description** should be **Store Fixtures**
> The **Date** is **12/31/12**
> The **Cost** is **4500**
- There is no SALES INFORMATION to record.

To complete the ASSET INFORMATION, enter **Store Fixtures** as the **Asset Description**

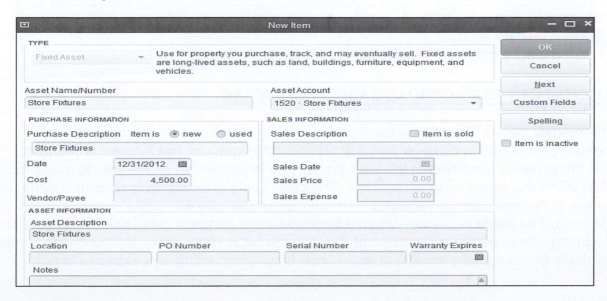

- Look at the bottom of the screen. Fields are provided to add information for the location, PO Number, Serial Number, and Warranty. There is also room to add Notes about the item.

When the information is entered for Store Fixtures, click **Next**

Repeat to add the new item **Office Equipment**, Asset Account **1510 – Office Equipment**, Date **12/31/12**, and Cost **$5,000.00** to the list

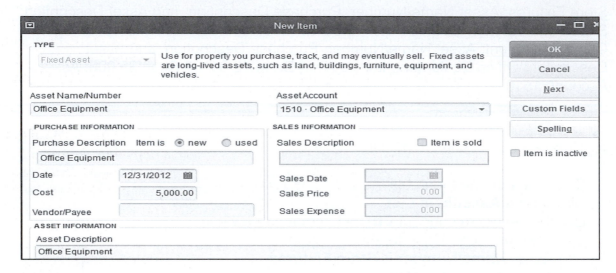

Click **OK**

Close the Fixed Asset Item List

ADJUSTMENTS FOR ACCRUAL-BASIS ACCOUNTING

As previously stated, the accrual basis of accounting matches the income and the expenses of a period in order to arrive at an accurate figure for net income or net loss. Thus, the revenue is earned at the time the service is performed or the sale is made no matter when the actual cash is received. The cash basis of accounting records income or revenue at the time cash is received no matter when the sale was made or the service performed. The same holds true when a business buys things or pays bills. In accrual-basis accounting, the expense is recorded at the time the bill is received or the purchase is made regardless of the actual payment date. In cash-basis accounting, the expense is not recorded until it is paid. In QuickBooks, the Summary Report Basis for either Accrual or Cash is selected as a Report Preference. The default setting is Accrual.

For example, if $1,000 sales on account and one year of insurance for $600 were recorded in November: Accrual basis would record $1,000 as income or revenue and $600 as a prepaid expense in an asset account—Prepaid Insurance. Month by month, an adjusting entry for $50 would be made to record the amount of insurance used for the month. Using the same figures, Cash basis would have no income and $600 worth of insurance recorded as an expense for November and nothing the rest of the year or during the early portion of the next year for insurance. A Profit and Loss report prepared in November would show: Accrual method—income of $1,000 and insurance expense of $50. Profit of $950. Cash method—no income and insurance expense of $600. Loss of $600.

There are several internal transactions that must be recorded when using the accrual basis of accounting. These entries are called adjusting entries. Typically, adjusting entries are entered in the General Journal by accountants to make after-the-fact changes to specific accounts. For example, equipment does wear out and will eventually need to be replaced. Rather than waiting until replacement to record the use of the equipment, an adjusting entry is made to allocate the use of equipment as an expense for a period. This is called *depreciation*. Certain items that will eventually become expenses for the business may be purchased or paid for in advance. When these things are purchased or paid for, they are recorded as an asset, and are referred to as prepaid expenses. As these are used, they become expenses of the business. For example, insurance is billed and usually paid for six-months or an entire year in advance. Until the insurance is used, it is an asset (something we own). Each month the portion of the insurance used becomes an expense for the month. Another similar adjustment is made to record the amount of supplies that have been used during the month. Supplies on hand are assets and the amount of the supplies used during the period is the expense.

ADJUSTING ENTRIES—PREPAID EXPENSES

A prepaid expense is an item that is paid for in advance. Examples of prepaid expenses include: Insurance—policy is usually for six months or one year; Office Supplies—buy to have on hand and use as needed. (This is different from supplies that are purchased for immediate use.) A prepaid expense is an asset until it is used. As the insurance or supplies are used, the amount used becomes an expense for the period. In accrual basis accounting, an adjusting entry is made in the General Journal at the end of the period to allocate the amount of prepaid expenses (assets) used to expenses.

The transactions for these adjustments may be recorded in the asset account register or they may be entered in the General Journal.

MEMO
DATE: January 31, 2013

The monthly adjustment for Prepaid Insurance needs to be recorded. The $250 currently in Prepaid Insurance is the amount we paid for two months of liability insurance coverage. Also, we have a balance of $521.98 in office supplies and a balance of $400 in sales supplies. Please adjust accordingly.

 Record the adjusting entries for insurance expense, office supplies expense, and sales supplies expense in the General Journal.

Access the **General Journal**:
Click **Company,** click **Make General Journal Entries**
Record the adjusting entry for Prepaid Insurance
If you get a screen regarding Assigning Numbers to Journal Entries, click **Do not display this message in the future**; and then, click **OK**
The General Journal Entries screen appears
- Note the checkbox for Adjusting Entry and the List of Entries
- A list of entries made Last Month is shown
  - If the date of your computer does not match the text, you may not have anything showing in the List of Selected General Journal Entries.
To remove the list of entries, click the **Hide List** icon on the Make General Journal Entries Icon bar
Enter **01/31/13** as the **Date**
- **Entry No.** is left blank unless you wish to record a specific number.
- Because all transactions entered for the month have been entered in the Journal as well as on an invoice or a bill, all transactions automatically have a Journal entry number. When the Journal is printed, your transaction number may be different from the answer key. Disregard the transaction number because it can change based on how many times you delete transactions, etc.
Notice the checkbox for **Adjusting Entry** is marked
- Adjusted journal entries are entered by accountants to make after-the-fact changes to specific accounts.
- Accountants make adjustments for a variety of reasons, including depreciation, prepaid income or expenses; adjusting sales tax payable; and entering bank or credit card fees or interest.
- The Adjusting Entry checkbox allows QuickBooks to indicate whether or not an entry is an adjustment.
- You can view a list of all adjusting journal entries in the Adjusting Journal Entries report.
- By default, this checkbox is selected for new transactions in the Accountant version.

Tab to or click the **Account** column, click the drop-down list arrow for **Account**, click
6181 Liability Insurance

Tab to or click **Debit**

- The $250 given in the memo is the amount for two months.

Use the QuickBooks Calculator to determine the amount of the adjustment for the
month:

Enter **250** in the Debit column

Press **/** for division

Key **2**

Press **Enter**

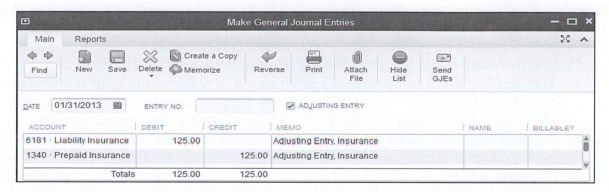

- The calculation is performed and the amount is entered in the Debit column.

Tab to or click the **Memo** column, type **Adjusting Entry, Insurance**

Tab to or click **Account**, click the drop-down list arrow for Account, click **1340
Prepaid Insurance**

The amount for the **Credit** column should have been entered automatically. If not,
enter **125**.

The Memo should have been entered automatically

- If not, enter the Memo information by using the copy command:

    Click the **Memo** column for the Debit entry

    Drag through the memo **Adjusting Entry, Insurance**

    When the memo is highlighted, use the keyboard command **Ctrl+C** to copy the
    memo

    Click in the **Memo** column for the Credit entry

    Use the keyboard command **Ctrl+V** to paste the memo into the column

Click **Save & New** or **NEXT** (forward arrow icon) to record the adjustment and to
advance to the next General Journal Entry screen

Record the adjustment for the office supplies used

The DATE is **01/31/2013**

Click in the **ACCOUNT** column

Click the drop-down list arrow, and then click the expense account **6472 – Office**, a
subaccount of 6470 Supplies Expense

- The amount given in the memo is the balance of the account after the supplies
have been used.

- The actual amount of the supplies used in January must be calculated.

Tab to the **DEBIT** column

Determine the current balance of asset account 1311 Office Supplies by using the keyboard shortcut **Ctrl+A** to access the Chart of Accounts

Make note of the balance and then close the Chart of Accounts

Use the QuickBooks Calculator to determine the amount of the adjustment

In the Debit column, enter the amount of the asset 1311 Office Supplies, press **-**, enter the amount of supplies on hand listed the in memo

Press **Enter** for QuickBooks to enter the amount of the adjustment

Enter an appropriate description and complete the adjustment for office supplies

Click in the **ACCOUNT** column, click the drop-down list arrow, and click **1311 Office Supplies** as the account to be credited

When the entry is complete, click **Next** or **Save & New**

Repeat the procedures to record the adjustment for the sales supplies used

- The amount given in the memo is the balance of the account after the supplies have been used. The actual amount of the supplies used in January must be calculated. Remember to subtract the $400 balance in the memo from the account total in order to get the amount of sales supplies used.

Close the Chart of Accounts after referring to the balance for Account 1312 Sales Supplies

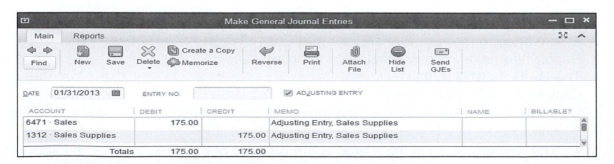

When the entry is complete, click **Save & New** or **Next**

ADJUSTING ENTRIES—DEPRECIATION

Using the accrual basis of accounting requires companies to record an expense for the decrease in value of equipment used in the operation of the business. Unlike supplies, where you can actually see the paper supply diminishing, it is very difficult to see how much of a cash register has been "used up" during the month. To account for the fact that machines do wear out and need to be replaced, an adjustment is made for depreciation. This adjustment correctly matches the expenses of the period against the revenue of the period.

MEMO

DATE: January 31, 2013

Having received the necessary depreciation schedules from the accountant, Ruth records the adjusting entry for depreciation: Office Equipment, $85 per month and Store Fixtures, $75 per month

---

 Record a compound adjusting entry for depreciation of the office equipment and the store fixtures in the General Journal:

The Date is **01/31/13**
Entry No. is left blank
- In order to use the automatic calculation feature of QuickBooks, the credit entries will be entered first.

Tab to or click the **Account** column, click the drop-down list arrow for **Account**, click **1512 Depreciation** under **Office Equipment**

Tab to or click **Credit**, enter **85**

Tab to or click **Memo**, enter **Adjusting Entry, Depreciation**

Tab to or click the **Account** column, click the drop-down list arrow for **Account**, click **1522 Depreciation** under **Store Fixtures**

- Disregard the 85 that shows as a debit. Entering an amount in the credit column and pressing the tab key will eliminate the debit.

Tab to or click **Credit**, enter **75**

- **Memo** column should show **Adjusting Entry, Depreciation**, if not enter it

Tab to or click the **Account** column, click the drop-down list arrow for **Account**, click **6150 Depreciation Expense**

Debit column should automatically show **160**

- **Memo** column should show **Adjusting Entry, Depreciation**, if not enter it

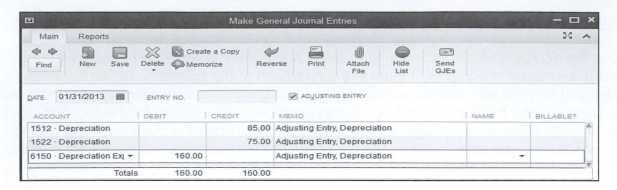

Verify that you entered Credits to accounts 1512 and 1522 and a Debit to account 6150

Click **Save & Close** to record the adjustment and close the General Journal

- If you get a message regarding Tracking Fixed Assets on Journal Entries, click **Do not display this message in the future** and click **OK**.

VIEW JOURNAL

Once transactions have been entered in the General Journal, it is important to view them. QuickBooks refers to the General Journal as the location of a transaction entry. To differentiate between the location of an entry and a report, QuickBooks refers to the report as the Journal. Even with the special ways in which transactions are entered in QuickBooks through invoices, bills, checks, and account registers, the Journal is still considered the book of original entry. All transactions recorded for the company may be viewed in the Journal even if they were entered elsewhere. The Journal may be viewed or printed at any time.

 View the Journal for January

Click **Reports** on the menu bar, point to **Accountant & Taxes**, and click **Journal**
Click the **Expand** button.
The Dates are from **01/01/13** to **01/31/13**
Tab to generate the report
Scroll through the report to view all transactions recorded in the Journal

- Only the transactions made from January 1 through January 31, 2013 are displayed. Since opening balances were entered during the creation of the company, note that the first transaction shown is 48—Invoice No. 1.
- If corrections or changes are made to entries, the transaction numbers may differ from the key. Since QuickBooks assigns transaction numbers automatically, disregard any discrepancies in transaction numbers.
- Viewing the Journal and checking the accounts used in transactions, the dates entered for transactions, the sales items used, and the amounts recorded for the transactions is an excellent way to discover errors and determine corrections that need to be made.

Verify the total Debit and Credit Columns of **$46,048.04**

- If your totals do not match, check for errors and make appropriate corrections.
- Since the adjusting entries were marked as adjustments when entered in the General Journal, the Adj column shows checks for these entries.

Your Name Mountain Sports
Journal
January 2013

Trans #	Type	Date	Num	Adj	Name	Memo	Account	Debit	Credit
103	General Journal	01/31/2013		✔		Adjusting Entry, Insurance	6181 · Liability Insurance	125.00	
				✔		Adjusting Entry, Insurance	1340 · Prepaid Insurance		125.00
								125.00	125.00
104	General Journal	01/31/2013		✔		Adjusting Entry, Office Supplies	6472 · Office	350.00	
				✔		Adjusting Entry, Office Supplies	1311 · Office Supplies		350.00
								350.00	350.00
105	General Journal	01/31/2013		✔		Adjusting Entry, Sales Supplies	6471 · Sales	175.00	
				✔		Adjusting Entry, Sales Supplies	1312 · Sales Supplies		175.00
								175.00	175.00
106	General Journal	01/31/2013		✔		Adjusting Entry, Depreciation	1512 · Depreciation		85.00
				✔		Adjusting Entry, Depreciation	1522 · Depreciation		75.00
				✔		Adjusting Entry, Depreciation	6150 · Depreciation Expense	160.00	
								160.00	160.00
TOTAL								46,048.04	46,048.04

Partial Report

Close the report without printing

DEFINITION OF A PARTNERSHIP

A partnership is a business owned by two or more individuals. Because it is unincorporated, each partner owns a share of all the assets and liabilities based on the percentage of his or her investment in the business or according to any partnership agreement drawn up at the time the business was created. In addition, each partner receives a portion of the profits or losses of the business. Because the business is owned by the partners, they do not receive a salary. Any funds obtained by the partners are in the form of withdrawals against their share of the profits. QuickBooks makes it easy to set up a partnership and create separate accounts, if desired, for each partner's equity, investment, and withdrawals.

OWNER WITHDRAWALS

In a partnership, owners cannot receive a paycheck because they own the business. An owner withdrawing money from a business—even to pay personal expenses—is similar to an individual withdrawing money from a savings account. A withdrawal simply decreases the owners' capital. QuickBooks allows you to establish a separate account for owner withdrawals for each owner. If a separate account is not established, owner withdrawals may be subtracted directly from each owner's capital or investment account.

> **MEMO**
> **DATE:** January 31, 2013
>
> Because both partners work in the business full time, they do not earn a paycheck. Prepare separate checks for monthly withdrawals of $1,000 for both Larry and you.

 Write the checks for the owner withdrawals

> Use the keyboard shortcut **Ctrl+W** to open the **Write Checks - Checking** window:
> • Make sure there is a check in the check box **Print Later**, and the NO. shows **TO PRINT**. If it is not checked, click **Print Later**.
> **BANK ACCOUNT** should be **1100 – Checking**, if not click the drop-down arrow and select
> **DATE** should be **01/31/13**
> Enter **Your First and Last Name** on the **PAY TO THE ORDER OF** line, press **Tab**
> • Since QuickBooks allows enough room, "Your First and Last Name" is shown to indicate you should use both your real <u>first</u> and <u>last</u> names. For example, the author's withdrawal would show Pay to the Order of Janet Horne.
> Because your name was not added to any list when the company was created, the **Name Not Found** dialog box appears on the screen.
> Click **Quick Add** to add your name to a list
> The **Select Name Type** dialog box appears
> Click **Other** and click **OK**
> • Your name is added to a list of *Other* names, which is used for owners, partners, and other miscellaneous names.
> Tab to or click in the area for the amount of the check
> • If necessary, delete any numbers showing for the amount (0.00).
> Enter **1000**
> Tab to or click **Memo**, enter **Owner Withdrawal, January**
> Use the **Expenses** tab at the bottom of the check
> Tab to or click in the Account column, click the drop-down list arrow, click the Equity account **3112 - First and Last Name, Drawing**
> • The amount 1,000.00 should appear in the Amount column.
> • If it does not, tab to or click in the Amount column and enter 1000.

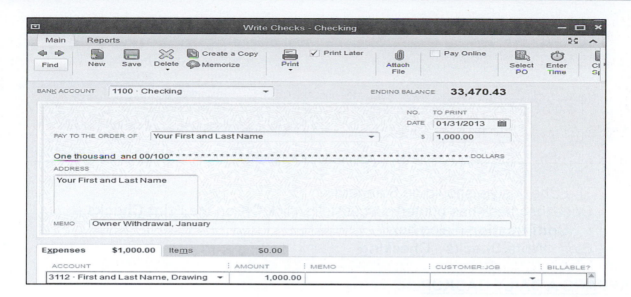

Click the **Next** arrow icon or **Save & New** and repeat the above procedures to prepare the check to Larry Muir for his $1,000 withdrawal
- Use his drawing account **3122 – Larry Muir, Drawing**

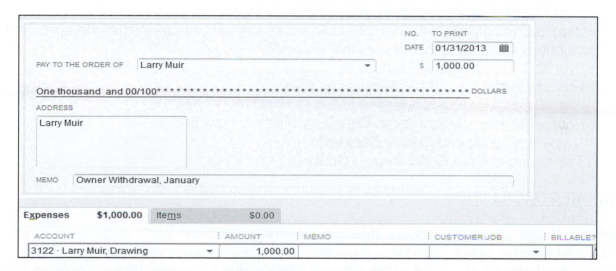

Click the **Next** arrow icon or **Save & New**
On the blank check, click the drop-down list arrow for **Print**
Click **Batch**
The **Select Checks to Print** dialog box appears
Bank Account is **1100- Checking**
The **First Check Number** should be **6**
- If necessary, change the number to **6**.
If both checks have a check mark, click **OK**, if not, click **Select All** and then click **OK**

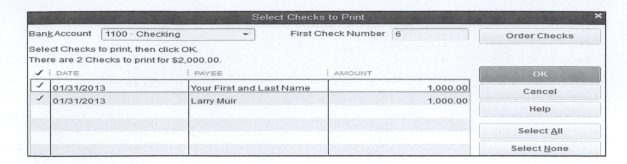

The Check style should be Standard

Once the check has printed successfully, click **OK** on the **Print Checks –
Confirmation** dialog box

Close **Write Checks - Checking**

PREPARE A DAILY BACKUP

A backup file is prepared as a safeguard in case you make an error. After a number of
transactions have been recorded, it is wise to prepare a backup file. In addition, a backup
should be made at the end of every work session. The Daily Backup file is an appropriate
file to create for saving your work as you progress through a chapter.

By creating the backup file now, it will contain your work for Chapters 5, 6, and up through
the distribution of capital to the owners in Chapter 7.

 Prepare the Sports (Daily Backup).qbb file

Follow the steps presented in Chapter 1 for creating a backup file

Name the file **Sports (Daily Backup)**

The file type is **QBW Backup (* .QBB)**

BANK RECONCILIATION

Each month the Checking account should be reconciled with the bank statement to make
sure both balances agree. The bank statement will rarely have an ending balance that
matches the balance of the Checking account. This is due to several factors: outstanding
checks, deposits in transit, bank service charges, interest earned on checking accounts,
collections made by the bank, errors made in recording checks and/or deposits by the
company or by the bank, etc.

In order to have an accurate amount listed as the balance in the Checking account, it is
important that the differences between the bank statement and the Checking account be
reconciled. If something such as a service charge or a collection made by the bank appears
on the bank statement, it needs to be recorded in the Checking account.

Reconciling a bank statement is an appropriate time to find any errors that may have been
recorded in the Checking account. The reconciliation may be out of balance because a

transposition was made, a transaction was recorded backwards, a transaction was recorded twice, or a transaction was not recorded at all.

ENTER BANK STATEMENT INFORMATION AND COMPLETE BEGIN RECONCILIATION

The Begin Reconciliation screen initiates the account reconciliation. On this screen, information regarding the ending balance, service charges, and interest earned is entered.

MEMO
DATE: January 31, 2013

Received the bank statement from Old Mammoth Bank dated January 31, 2013. Reconcile the bank statement and print a Reconciliation Report.

 Reconcile the bank statement for January

Use the bank statement on the following page to complete the reconciliation
Click the **Reconcile** icon on the QuickBooks Home Page
Enter preliminary information on the **Begin Reconciliation** screen
- *Note:* If you need to exit the Begin Reconciliation screen before it is complete, click **Cancel**.

The **Account To Reconcile** should be **1100 Checking**
- If not, click the drop-down list arrow, click **Checking**.
- The **Statement Date** should be **01/31/13**
- **Beginning Balance** should be **25,943.00**. This is the same amount as the Checking account starting balance and is shown on the bank statement.

Bank Statement

OLD MAMMOTH BANK
12345 Old Mammoth Road
Mammoth Lakes, CA 93546
(909) 555-3880

Your Name Mountain Sports
875 Mountain Road
Mammoth Lakes, CA 93546

Acct. # 123-456-7890   **January 2013**

Beginning Balance 1/1/13	25,943.00		$25,943.00
1/18/13 Deposit	10,855.30		36,798.30
1/20/13 NSF Returned Check		100.00	36,698.30
1/20/13 Check 1		81.00	36,617.30
1/25/13 Check 3		294.00	36,323.30
1/25/13 Check 2		1,837.50	34,485.80
1/25/13 Check 4		313.60	34,172.20
1/25/13 Check 5		701.77	33,470.43
1/31/13 Office Equip. Loan Pmt.: $10.33 Principal, $53.42 Interest		63.75	33,406.68
1/31/13 Store Fixtures Loan Pmt.: $8.61 Principal, $44.51 Interest		53.12	33,353.56
1/31/13 Service Chg.		8.00	33,345.56
1/31/13 NSF Charge		10.00	33,335.56
1/31/13 Interest	54.05		33,389.61
Ending Balance 1/31/13			33,389.61

Enter the **Ending Balance** from the bank statement, **33,389.61**
Tab to or click **Service Charge**, enter the **Service Charge**, **18.00**
- Note that this includes both the service charge of $8.00 and the $10.00 charge for Kevin Thomsen's NSF check in Chapter 5.

Tab to or click Service Charge **Date**, the date should be **01/31/13**
- Since the date of your computer may appear, double-check the date to avoid errors.

Tab to or click **Account**, click the drop-down list arrow for **Account**, click **6120 Bank Service Charges**
Tab to or click **Interest Earned**, enter **54.05**
Tab to or click Interest Earned **Date**, the date should be **01/31/13**

Tab to or click **Account**, enter the account number **7010** for **Interest Income** and press Tab or Enter

---

Begin Reconciliation

Select an account to reconcile, and then enter the ending balance from your account statement.

Account	1100 · Checking ▼ last reconciled on 12/31/2012.
Statement Date	01/31/2013 📅
Beginning Balance	25,943.00 What if my beginning balance doesn't match my statement?
Ending Balance	33,389.61

Enter any service charge or interest earned.

Service Charge	Date	Account
18.00	01/31/2013 📅	6120 · Bank Service Charges ▼

Interest Earned	Date	Account
54.05	01/31/2013 📅	7010 · Interest Income ▼

| Locate Discrepancies | Undo Last Reconciliation | Continue | Cancel | Help |

Click **Continue**

MARK CLEARED TRANSACTIONS FOR BANK RECONCILIATION

Once bank statement information for the ending balance, service charges, and interest earned has been entered, compare the checks and deposits listed on the statement with the transactions for the Checking account. If a deposit or a check is listed correctly on the bank statement and in the Reconcile - Checking window, it has cleared and should be marked. An item may be marked individually by positioning the cursor on the deposit or the check and clicking the primary mouse button. If all deposits and checks match, click the Mark All button to mark all the deposits and checks at once. To remove all the checks, click the Unmark All button. To unmark an individual item, click the item to remove the check mark.

 Mark cleared checks and deposits

- *Note:* If you need to exit the Reconcile - Checking screen before it is complete, click **Leave**. If you click **Reconcile Now**, you must Undo the reconciliation and start over.
- If you need to return to the Begin Reconciliation window, click the **Modify** button.
- Notice that the **Highlight Marked** is selected. When an item has been selected or marked, the background color changes.

Compare the bank statement with the **Reconcile - Checking** window
- On the bank statement, dates may not be the same as the actual check or deposit dates.

Click the items that appear on both statements
When finished, look at the bottom of the **Reconcile - Checking** window
You have marked cleared:
    1 Deposits and Other Credits for 10,855.30
    6 Checks and Payments for 3,327.87
The Service Charge of -18.00 and Interest Earned of 54.05 are shown

The Ending Balance is 33,389.61
The Cleared Balance is 33,506.48
There is a Difference of -116.87

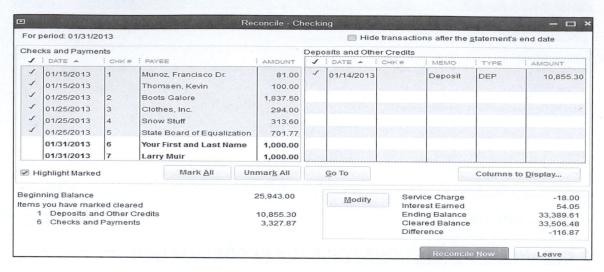

The bank statement should remain on the screen while you complete the next
section

ADJUSTING AND CORRECTING ENTRIES—BANK RECONCILIATION

As you complete the reconciliation, you may find errors that need to be corrected or
transactions that need to be recorded. Anything entered as a service charge or interest
earned will be entered automatically when the reconciliation is complete and the Reconcile
Now button is clicked. To correct an error such as a transposition, click on the entry then
click the Go To button. The original entry will appear on the screen. The correction can be
made and will show in the Reconcile - Checking window. If there is a transaction, such as
an automatic loan payment to the bank, access the register for the balance sheet account
used in the transaction and enter the payment.

 Enter the automatic loan payments shown on the bank statement

Use the keyboard shortcut **Ctrl+R** to open the register for the **1100 Checking**
account:
- Notice that the checks and the deposit marked in the reconciliation now have an
  * in the √ column.
In the blank transaction at the bottom of the register, enter the **Date, 01/31/13**
Tab to or click **Number**, enter **Transfer**
Tab to or click **Payee**, enter **Old Mammoth Bank**
Tab to or click the **Payment** column
- Because Old Mammoth Bank does not appear on any list, you will get a **Name
  Not Found** dialog box when you move to another field.
Click the **Quick Add** button to add the name of the bank to the Name List

Click **Other**, and click **OK**

- Once the name of the bank has been added to the Other List, the cursor will be positioned in the **Payment** column.

Enter **63.75** in the **Payment** column

Click **Splits** at the bottom of the register

Click the drop-down list arrow for **Account**, click **6212 Loan Interest**

Tab to or click **Amount**, delete the amount 63.75 shown

Enter **53.42** as the amount of interest

Tab to or click **Memo**, enter **Office Equipment Loan, Interest**

Tab to or click **Account**, click the drop-down list arrow for **Account**, click **2510 Office Equipment Loan**

- The correct amount of principal, 10.33, should be shown as the amount.
- Tab to or click **Memo**, enter **Office Equipment Loan, Principal**

ACCOUNT	AMOUNT	MEMO	CUSTOMER:JOB	BILLABLE?	
6212 · Loan Interest	53.42	Office Equipment Loan, Interest			Close
2510 · Office Equipment Loan	10.33	Office Equipment Loan, Principal			Clear

Click **Close** on the Splits window

- This closes the window for the information regarding the way the transaction is to be "split" between accounts. Notice the work –split- in the ACCOUNT column.

For the **Memo** in the Checking Register, record **Office Equipment Loan, Payment**

Click the **Record** button to record the transaction

- Transfers are shown before checks prepared on the same date; thus, the loan payment does not appear as the last transaction in the register.

01/31/2013	Transfer	Old Mammoth Bank		63.75		33,406.68
	CHK	-split-	Office Equipment Loan, Payment			

Repeat the procedures to record the loan payment for store fixtures

- When you enter the Payee as Old Mammoth Bank, the amount for the previous transaction (63.75) appears in amount.

Enter the new amount **53.12**

Click **Splits**

Click the appropriate accounts and enter the correct amount for each item

- The accounts and amounts for the office equipment loan payment may appear. Click the drop-down list arrow and select the appropriate accounts for the store fixture loan payment. Be sure to use the information for Store Fixtures <u>not</u> the information for Office Equipment.
- Refer to the bank statement for details regarding the amount of the payment for interest and the amount of the payment applied to principal.

ACCOUNT	AMOUNT	MEMO	CUSTOMER:JOB	BILLABLE?	
6212 · Loan Interest	44.51	Store Fixtures Loan, Interest			Close
2520 · Store Fixtures Loan	8.61	Store Fixtures Loan, Principal			Clear

Click **Close** to close the window for the information regarding the "split" between accounts

Enter the transaction **Memo**: **Store Fixtures Loan, Payment**

Click **Record** to record the loan payment

01/31/2013	Transfer	Old Mammoth Bank		53.12		33,353.56
	CHK	-split-	Store Fixtures Loan, Payment			

Close the **Checking Register**

- You should return to the **Reconcile – Checking** screen

Scroll to the bottom of **Checks and Payments**

- Notice the two entries for the loan payments in Checks and Payments.

Mark the two entries

- At this point the Ending Balance and Cleared Balance should be equal— $33,389.61 with a difference of 0.00.

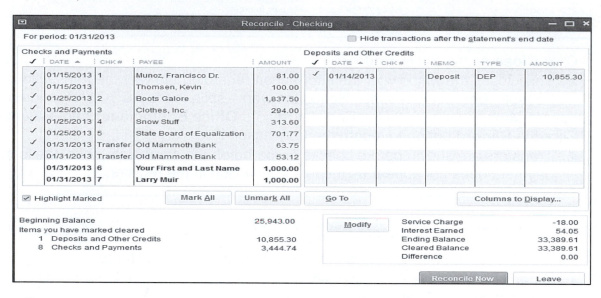

If your entries agree with the above, click **Reconcile Now** to finish the reconciliation

- If your reconciliation is not in agreement, do not click **Reconcile Now** until the errors are corrected.
- Once you click **Reconcile Now**, you may not return to this **Reconcile - Checking** window. You would have to Undo the reconciliation and start over.
- If you get an **Information** screen regarding Online Banking, click **OK**.

PRINT A RECONCILIATION REPORT

As soon as the Ending Balance and the Cleared Balance are equal or when you finish marking transactions and click Reconcile Now, a screen appears allowing you to select the level of Reconciliation Report you would like to print. You may select Summary and get a report that lists totals only or Detail and get all the transactions that were reconciled on the report. You may print the report at the time you have finished reconciling the account or you may print the report later by clicking the Reports menu, clicking Banking, and then clicking Previous Reconciliation. If you think you may want to print the report again in the future, print the report to a file to save it permanently.

 Print a Detail Reconciliation report

On the **Reconciliation Complete** screen, click **Detail**, click **Display**
- If you get a Reconciliation Report message, click **Do not display this message in the future**, and click **OK**

Adjust the column widths so the report will print on one page and all information is displayed in full

Your Name Mountain Sports
Reconciliation Detail
1100 · Checking, Period Ending 01/31/2013

Type	Date	Num	Name	Clr	Amount	Balance
Beginning Balance						25,943.00
Cleared Transactions						
Checks and Payments – 9 items						
▶ Invoice	01/15/2013	11	Thomsen, Kevin	✓	–100.00	–100.00 ◀
Check	01/15/2013	1	Munoz, Francisco Dr.	✓	–81.00	–181.00
Bill Pmt –Check	01/25/2013	2	Boots Galore	✓	–1,837.50	–2,018.50
Sales Tax Payment	01/25/2013	5	State Board of Equalization	✓	–701.77	–2,720.27
Bill Pmt –Check	01/25/2013	4	Snow Stuff	✓	–313.60	–3,033.87
Bill Pmt –Check	01/25/2013	3	Clothes, Inc.	✓	–294.00	–3,327.87
Check	01/31/2013	Transfer	Old Mammoth Bank	✓	–63.75	–3,391.62
Check	01/31/2013	Transfer	Old Mammoth Bank	✓	–53.12	–3,444.74
Check	01/31/2013			✓	–18.00	–3,462.74
Total Checks and Payments					–3,462.74	–3,462.74
Deposits and Credits – 2 items						
Deposit	01/14/2013			✓	10,855.30	10,855.30
Deposit	01/31/2013			✓	54.05	10,909.35
Total Deposits and Credits					10,909.35	10,909.35
Total Cleared Transactions					7,446.61	7,446.61
Cleared Balance					7,446.61	33,389.61
Uncleared Transactions						
Checks and Payments – 2 items						
Check	01/31/2013	7	Larry Muir		–1,000.00	–1,000.00
Check	01/31/2013	6	Your First and Last Name		–1,000.00	–2,000.00
Total Checks and Payments					–2,000.00	–2,000.00
Total Uncleared Transactions					–2,000.00	–2,000.00
Register Balance as of 01/31/2013					5,446.61	31,389.61
Ending Balance					5,446.61	31,389.61

Print as previously instructed in Portrait orientation then close the report

VIEW THE CHECKING ACCOUNT REGISTER

Once the bank reconciliation has been completed, it is wise to scroll through the Check Register to view the effect of the reconciliation on the account. You will notice that the check column shows a check mark for all items that were marked as cleared during the reconciliation. If at a later date an error is discovered, the transaction may be changed, and the correction will be reflected in the Beginning Balance on the reconciliation.

 View the register for the Checking account

Access the register as previously instructed

To display more of the register, click the check box for **1-Line**

Scroll through the register

- Notice that the transactions are listed in chronological order and that each item marked in the Bank Reconciliation now has a check mark in the check column.
- The interest earned and bank service charges appear in the register.
- Even though the bank reconciliation transactions for loan payments were recorded after the checks written on January 31, the bank reconciliation transactions appear before the checks because they were recorded as a Transfer.

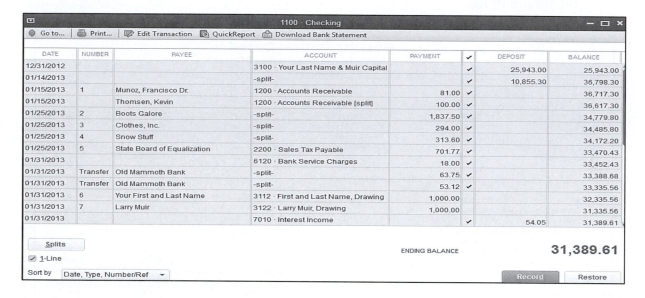

DATE	NUMBER	PAYEE	ACCOUNT	PAYMENT	✓	DEPOSIT	BALANCE
12/31/2012			3100 · Your Last Name & Muir Capital		✓	25,943.00	25,943.00
01/14/2013			-split-		✓	10,855.30	36,798.30
01/15/2013	1	Munoz, Francisco Dr.	1200 · Accounts Receivable	81.00	✓		36,717.30
01/15/2013		Thomsen, Kevin	1200 · Accounts Receivable [split]	100.00	✓		36,617.30
01/25/2013	2	Boots Galore	-split-	1,837.50	✓		34,779.80
01/25/2013	3	Clothes, Inc.	-split-	294.00	✓		34,485.80
01/25/2013	4	Snow Stuff	-split-	313.60	✓		34,172.20
01/25/2013	5	State Board of Equalization	2200 · Sales Tax Payable	701.77	✓		33,470.43
01/31/2013			6120 · Bank Service Charges	18.00	✓		33,452.43
01/31/2013	Transfer	Old Mammoth Bank	-split-	63.75	✓		33,388.68
01/31/2013	Transfer	Old Mammoth Bank	-split-	53.12	✓		33,335.56
01/31/2013	6	Your First and Last Name	3112 · First and Last Name, Drawing	1,000.00			32,335.56
01/31/2013	7	Larry Muir	3122 · Larry Muir, Drawing	1,000.00			31,335.56
01/31/2013			7010 · Interest Income		✓	54.05	31,389.61

ENDING BALANCE   **31,389.61**

- Notice that the final balance of the account is $31,389.61.

Close the register and; if necessary, the Chart of Accounts

CREDIT CARD RECONCILIATION

Any balance sheet account used in QuickBooks may be reconciled. These include assets, liabilities, and owner's equity accounts. Income, expense, and cost of goods sold accounts are not balance sheet accounts and may not be reconciled.

As with a checking account, it is a good practice to reconcile the Credit Card account each month. When the credit card statement is received, the transactions entered in QuickBooks should agree with the transactions shown on the credit card statement. A reconciliation of the credit card should be completed on a monthly basis.

> **MEMO**
>
> **DATE:** January 31, 2013
>
> The monthly bill for the Visa has arrived and is to be paid. Prior to paying the monthly credit card bill, reconcile the Credit Card account.

 Reconcile and pay the credit card bill

Click the **Reconcile** icon on the Home Page
Click the drop-down list arrow for Account
Click **2100 Visa** to select the account
Use the following credit card statement to complete the reconciliation of the Visa credit card

OLD MAMMOTH BANK
VISA
12345 Old Mammoth Road
Mammoth Lakes, CA 93546
(619) 555-3880

Your Name Mountain Sports
875 Mountain Road
Mammoth Lakes, CA 93546

Acct. # 098-776-4321

Beginning Balance 1/1/13		150.00	$150.00
1/23/13 Sierra Office Supply Company		21.98	171.98
1/23/13 Snow Supplies		300.00	471.98
1/25/13 Winter Sports Accessories		350.00	821.98
1/25/13 Shoes & More		400.00	1,221.98
Ending Balance 1/31/13			1,221.98

Minimum Payment Due: $50.00   Payment Due Date: February 15, 2013

Enter the **Statement Date** of **01/31/13**
Enter the **Ending Balance** of **1,221.98** in the **Begin Reconciliation** window

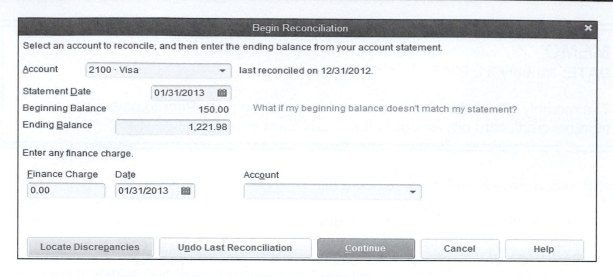

Click the **Continue** button

Mark each item that appears on both the statement and in the reconciliation **EXCEPT** for the $**400** transaction for Shoes & More

RECORD AN ADJUSTMENT TO A RECONCILIATION

In QuickBooks 2013, adjustments to reconciliations may be made during the reconciliation process..

 Verify that all items are marked **EXCEPT** the charge for $**400** for Shoes & More

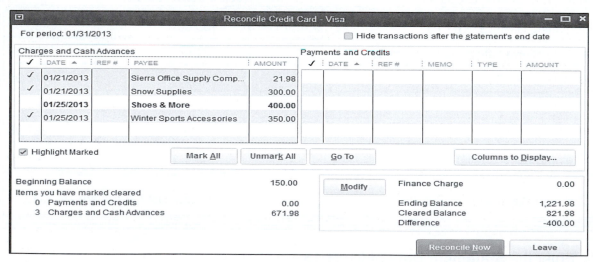

Click **Reconcile Now**

- The Reconcile Adjustment screen appears because there was a $400 Difference shown at the bottom of the reconciliation.
- Even though the error on the demonstration reconciliation is known, an adjustment will be entered and then deleted at a later time.

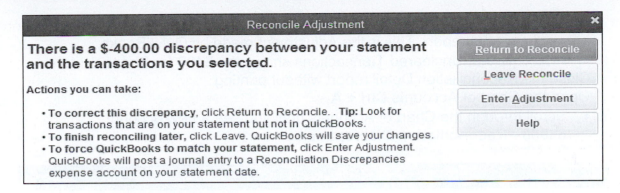

Click **Enter Adjustment**
Click **Cancel** on the Make Payment screen

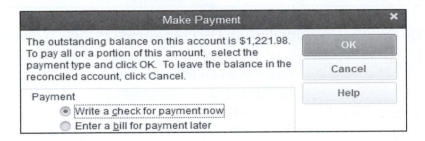

- The Reconciliation report is generated

Click **Detail** and then click **Display**

Your Name Mountain Sports
Reconciliation Detail
2100 · Visa, Period Ending 01/31/2013

Type	Date	Num	Name	Clr	Amount	Balance
Beginning Balance						150.00
Cleared Transactions						
Charges and Cash Advances – 4 items						
▶ Credit Card Charge	01/21/2013		Snow Supplies	✓	–300.00	–300.00 ◀
Credit Card Charge	01/21/2013		Sierra Office Supply Company	✓	–21.98	–321.98
Bill Pmt –CCard	01/25/2013		Winter Sports Accessories	✓	–350.00	–671.98
General Journal	01/31/2013			✓	–400.00	–1,071.98
Total Charges and Cash Advances					–1,071.98	–1,071.98
Total Cleared Transactions					–1,071.98	–1,071.98
Cleared Balance					1,071.98	1,221.98
Uncleared Transactions						
Charges and Cash Advances – 1 item						
Bill Pmt –CCard	01/25/2013		Shoes & More		–400.00	–400.00
Total Charges and Cash Advances					–400.00	–400.00
Total Uncleared Transactions					–400.00	–400.00
Register Balance as of 01/31/2013					1,471.98	1,621.98
Ending Balance					1,471.98	1,621.98

- Because the date of your computer may be different from the date used in the text, there may be some differences in the appearance of the Reconciliation Detail report. As long as the appropriate transactions have been marked, disregard any discrepancies.

- Notice that there is a General Journal entry for $400 in the Cleared Transactions section of the report. This is the Adjustment made by QuickBooks.
- Also note that Uncleared Transactions shows the $400 for Shoes & More.

Close the Reconciliation Detail report without printing

Open the Chart of Accounts **Ctrl + A**

- Scroll through the Chart of Accounts until you see a new account, **66900 - Reconciliation Discrepancies**

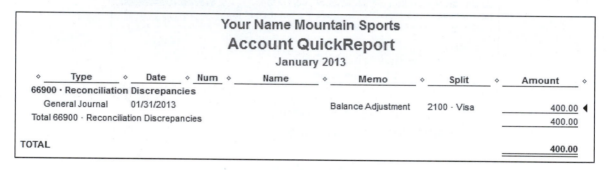

Double-click **66900 – Reconciliation Discrepancies** to view a QuickReport

Your Name Mountain Sports
Account QuickReport
January 2013

Type	Date	Num	Name	Memo	Split	Amount
66900 · Reconciliation Discrepancies						
General Journal	01/31/2013			Balance Adjustment	2100 · Visa	400.00 ◄
Total 66900 · Reconciliation Discrepancies						400.00
TOTAL						400.00

- Note the General Journal entry for Balance Adjustment

Close the QuickReport without printing and close the Chart of Accounts

UNDO A PREVIOUS RECONCILIATION, DELETE AN ADJUSTMENT, AND REDO A RECONCILIATION

If an error is discovered after an account reconciliation has been completed, the reconciliation may be removed by using the Undo Last Reconciliation feature located on the Begin Reconciliation screen. If an adjusting entry for a reconciliation has been made, it may be deleted. This is useful if you had a discrepancy when making the reconciliation and found the error at a later date.

 Undo the credit card reconciliation and delete the adjusting entry made by QuickBooks

       Click the **Reconcile** icon on the Home Page
       Click the drop-down list arrow for Account, select **2100 - Visa**
       Click **Undo Last Reconciliation** on the Begin Reconciliation screen

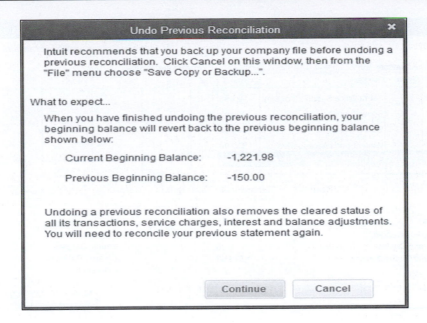

Click the **Continue** button
Click **OK** on the **Undo Previous Reconcile** dialog box

- Remember that service charges, interest, and balance adjustments are <u>not</u> removed. If you have entered any of these items on the previous reconciliation, they will need to be deleted from the Journal manually. None of the items were entered on the previous reconciliation so there is nothing to be deleted.
- You will return to the Begin Reconciliation screen.

Make sure the **Account** is **2100 – Visa** and the **Statement Date** is **01/31/13**
The **Beginning Balance** is once again **$150.00**
Enter the **Ending Balance** of **1221.98**
Click **Continue**
Click **Mark All**

- All of the items listed on the Credit Card Statement <u>**INCLUDING**</u> the **$400** for Shoes & More will be marked.

Click the **Adjusting Entry** for **01/31/13**

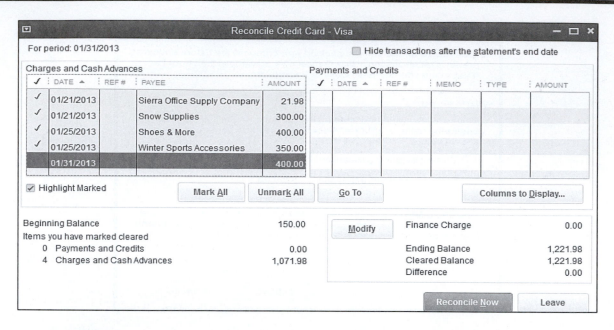

Click **Go To**

- You will go to the Make General Journal Entries screen

Use the keyboard shortcut **Ctrl+D** to delete the entry

Click **OK** on the **Delete Transaction** screen

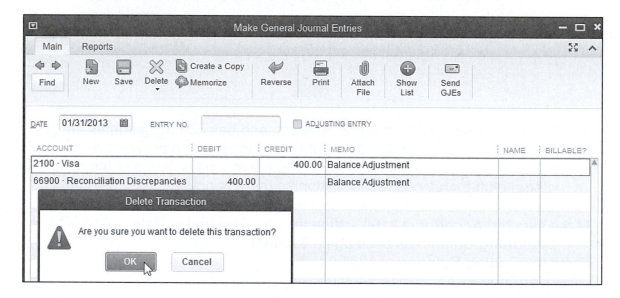

Close the **Make General Journal Entries** screen

Verify that the adjusting entry has been deleted and that the **Ending** and **Cleared Balances** are **1,221.98** and the **Difference** is **0.00**

| Reconcile Credit Card - Visa | | | | | | | | |

For period: 01/31/2013   ☐ Hide transactions after the statement's end date

Charges and Cash Advances

✓	DATE ▲	REF #	PAYEE	AMOUNT
✓	01/21/2013		Sierra Office Supply Company	21.98
✓	01/21/2013		Snow Supplies	300.00
✓	01/25/2013		Shoes & More	400.00
✓	01/25/2013		Winter Sports Accessories	350.00

Payments and Credits

✓	DATE ▲	REF #	MEMO	TYPE	AMOUNT

☑ Highlight Marked   [Mark All]   [Unmark All]   [Go To]   [Columns to Display...]

Beginning Balance	150.00	[Modify]	Finance Charge 0.00
Items you have marked cleared			Ending Balance 1,221.98
0 Payments and Credits	0.00		Cleared Balance 1,221.98
4 Charges and Cash Advances	1,071.98		Difference 0.00

[Reconcile Now]   [Leave]

Click **Reconcile Now**
When the **Make Payment** dialog box appears on the screen
Make sure **Write a check for payment now** is selected, click **OK**

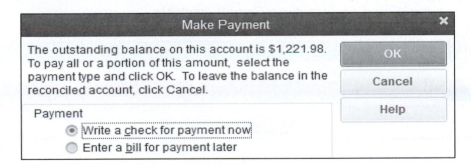

The outstanding balance on this account is $1,221.98. To pay all or a portion of this amount, select the payment type and click OK. To leave the balance in the reconciled account, click Cancel.

Payment
◉ Write a check for payment now
◯ Enter a bill for payment later

[OK] [Cancel] [Help]

Display and print a **Reconciliation Detail Report** following the procedures given for the Bank Reconciliation Report

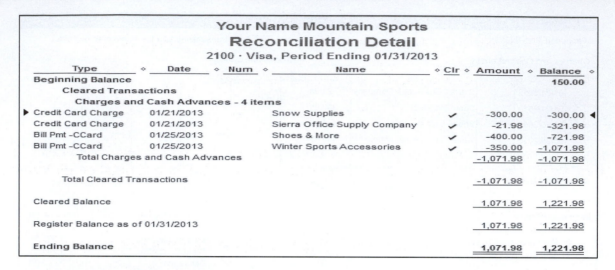

Close the Reconciliation Detail report

The payment check should appear on the screen

Enter **8** as the check number

The **DATE** of the check should be **01/31/13**

Click the drop-down list next to **PAY TO THE ORDER OF**, click **Old Mammoth Bank**

- If you get a dialog box for **Auto Recall**, click **No**.

Tab to or click **Memo** on the bottom of the check

Enter **January Visa Payment** as the memo

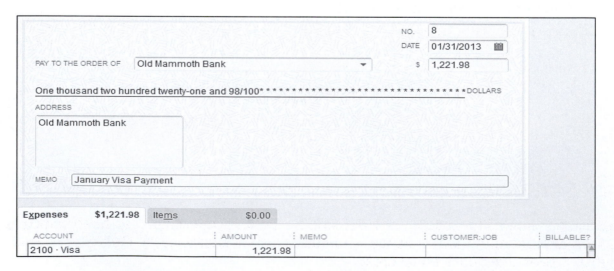

Print the standard-style check as previously instructed
When the check has printed successfully, click **OK** on the Print Checks –
Confirmation
Click **Save & Close** to record, and exit **Write Checks**

VIEW THE JOURNAL

After entering several transactions, it is helpful to view the Journal. In the Journal all transactions regardless of the method of entry are shown in traditional debit/credit format.

 View the **Journal** for January

Since you will be preparing several reports, click the **Reports** icon to open the
Report Center
Click **Accountant & Taxes** as the type of report, double-click **Journal**
- If necessary, Expand the report
The dates are from **01/01/13** to **01/31/13**, press **Tab**
Expand the Journal
Scroll through the report and view all the transactions that have been made

Your Name Mountain Sports
Journal
January 2013

Trans #	Type	Date	Num	Adj	Name	Memo	Account	Debit	Credit
109	Check	01/31/2013	Transfer		Old Mammoth Bank	Office Equipment Loan, Payment	1100 · Checking		63.75
					Old Mammoth Bank	Office Equipment Loan, Interest	6212 · Loan Interest	53.42	
					Old Mammoth Bank	Office Equipment Loan, Principal	2510 · Office Equipment Loan	10.33	
								63.75	63.75
110	Check	01/31/2013	Transfer		Old Mammoth Bank	Store Fixtures Loan, Payment	1100 · Checking		53.12
					Old Mammoth Bank	Store Fixtures Loan, Interest	6212 · Loan Interest	44.51	
					Old Mammoth Bank	Store Fixtures Loan, Principal	2520 · Store Fixtures Loan	8.61	
								53.12	53.12
111	Check	01/31/2013				Service Charge	1100 · Checking		18.00
						Service Charge	6120 · Bank Service Charges	18.00	
								18.00	18.00
112	Deposit	01/31/2013				Interest	1100 · Checking	54.05	
						Interest	7010 · Interest Income		54.05
								54.05	54.05
114	Check	01/31/2013	8		Old Mammoth Bank	January Visa Payment	1100 · Checking		1,221.98
					Old Mammoth Bank	January Visa Payment	2100 · Visa	1,221.98	
								1,221.98	1,221.98
TOTAL								**49,458.94**	**49,458.94**

Partial Report

Close the **Journal** <u>without</u> printing
The **Report Center** should remain on the screen

PREPARE TRIAL BALANCE

After all adjustments have been recorded and the bank reconciliation has been completed, it is wise to prepare the Trial Balance. As in traditional accounting, the QuickBooks Trial Balance proves that debits equal credits.

MEMO

DATE: January 31, 2013

Because adjustments have been entered, prepare a Trial Balance.

 Prepare a trial balance using the Report Center

Verify that the type of report is **Accountant & Taxes**
Double-click **Trial Balance**
- If necessary, enter the dates **From 01/01/13** and **To 01/31/13**
Scroll through the report and study the amounts shown

Your Name Mountain Sports
Trial Balance
As of January 31, 2013

	Jan 31, 13	
	Debit	Credit
1100 · Checking	30,167.63	
1200 · Accounts Receivable	5,696.50	
1120 · Inventory Asset	35,551.54	
12000 · Undeposited Funds	0.00	
1311 · Office Supplies	521.98	
1312 · Sales Supplies	400.00	
1340 · Prepaid Insurance	125.00	
1511 · Original Cost	5,000.00	
1512 · Depreciation		85.00
1521 · Original Cost	4,500.00	
1522 · Depreciation		75.00
2000 · Accounts Payable		9,395.40
2100 · Visa	0.00	
2200 · Sales Tax Payable	0.00	
2510 · Office Equipment Loan		2,989.67
2520 · Store Fixtures Loan		2,491.39
3000 · Retained Earnings	0.00	
3100 · Your Last Name & Muir, Capital		26,159.44
3110 · First and Last Name, Capital	0.00	
3111 · First and Last Name, Investment		20,000.00
3112 · First and Last Name, Drawing	1,000.00	
3120 · Larry Muir, Capital	0.00	
3121 · Larry Muir, Investment		20,000.00
3122 · Larry Muir, Drawing	1,000.00	
4011 · Clothing & Accessory Sales		1,759.51
4012 · Equipment Sales		7,436.44
4040 · Returned Check Service Charges		25.00
4050 · Sales Discounts	494.36	
5000 · Cost of Goods Sold	3,492.46	
5200 · Merchandise Discounts		49.90
6120 · Bank Service Charges	18.00	
6140 · Advertising Expense	95.00	
6150 · Depreciation Expense	160.00	
6181 · Liability Insurance	125.00	
6212 · Loan Interest	97.93	
6300 · Rent	950.00	
6340 · Telephone	156.40	
6391 · Gas and Electric	359.00	
6392 · Water	85.00	
6471 · Sales	175.00	
6472 · Office	350.00	
7010 · Interest Income		54.05
TOTAL	**90,520.80**	**90,520.80**

- Notice that the final totals of debits and credits are equal: $90,520.80.
Do <u>not</u> close the report

USE QUICKZOOM IN TRIAL BALANCE

 Use QuickZoom to view the details of Office Supplies:

Scroll through the Trial Balance until you see **1311 Office Supplies**
Position the mouse pointer over the amount of Office Supplies, **521.98**
- Notice that the mouse pointer changes to a magnifying glass with a Z.
Double-click the primary mouse button
- A **Transactions by Account Report** appears on the screen showing the two transactions entered for office supplies.
Scroll through the report

Your Name Mountain Sports										
Transactions by Account										
As of January 31, 2013										
Type	Date	Num	Adj	Name	Memo	Clr	Split	Debit	Credit	Balance
1310 · Supplies										850.00
1311 · Office Supplies										850.00
Credit Card Charge	01/21/2013			Sierra Office Supply Company	Purchase Paper		2100 · Visa	21.98		871.98
General Journal	01/31/2013		✓		Adjusting Entry, Office Supplies		6472 · Office		350.00	521.98
Total 1311 · Office Supplies								21.98	350.00	521.98
Total 1310 · Supplies								21.98	350.00	521.98
TOTAL								21.98	350.00	521.98

Close the Transactions by Account and Trial Balance reports <u>without</u> printing
Do <u>not</u> close the Report Center

VIEW STANDARD PROFIT AND LOSS STATEMENT

Because all income, expenses, and adjustments have been made for the period, a Profit and Loss Statement can be prepared. This statement is also known as the Income Statement and shows the income and the expenses for the period and the net income or the net loss for the period (Income – Expenses = Net Profit or Net Loss). QuickBooks has several different types of Profit and Loss statements available: <u>Standard</u>—summarizes income and expenses; <u>Detail</u>—shows the year-to-date transactions for each income and expense account. The other Profit and Loss reports are like the Standard Profit and Loss but have additional information displayed as indicated in the following: <u>YTD Comparison</u>—summarizes your income and expenses for this month and compares them to your income and expenses for the current fiscal year; <u>Prev Year Comparison</u>—summarizes your income and expenses for both this month and this month last year; <u>By Job</u>—has columns for each customer and job and amounts for this year to date; <u>By Class</u>—has columns for each class and sub-class with the amounts for this year to date, and <u>Unclassified</u>—shows how much you are making or losing within segments of your business that are not assigned to a QuickBooks class

 View a **Standard Profit and Loss Report**

In the Report Center, click **Company & Financial** as the type of report, double-click
   Profit & Loss Standard
The dates are from **01/01/13** to **01/31/13**, press **Tab** to generate the report

Your Name Mountain Sports	
Profit & Loss	
January 2013	
	Jan 13
Total Expense	2,571.33
Net Ordinary Income	2,712.70
Other Income/Expense	
Other Income	
7010 · Interest Income	54.05
Total Other Income	54.05
Net Other Income	54.05
Net Income	2,766.75

Partial Report

Scroll through the report to view the income and expenses listed
- Remember, accrual basis accounting calculates the net income based on income earned at the time the service was performed or the sale was made and the expenses incurred at the time the bill was received or incurred whether or not they have been paid.
- The calculations shown below may not have all the subtotals shown in the report; but the example is given to help with understanding the calculations made
- Total Income is calculated
  - Sales:
    - Clothing & Accessory Sales $1,759.51
    - Equipment Sales   7,436.44
    - Equals Total Sales   9,195.95
    - Plus: Returned Check Service Charges   25.00
    - Less: Sales Discounts   494.36
  - Equals Total Income $8,726.59
- Cost of Goods Sold is calculated:
  - Less: Merchandise Discounts   -49.90
  - Plus: Cost of Goods Sold-Other   3,492.46
    (The amount for the merchandise purchased)
  - Equals Total COGS   3,442.56
- Note the calculation to obtain the Net Income:
  - Total Income $8,726.59
  - Less: Total COGS   3,442.56
  - Equals Gross Profit   5,284.03
  - Less: Total Expenses   2,571.33
  - Plus: Interest Income   54.05
  - Equals Net Income $2,766.75

Close the **Profit and Loss Report**, do **not** close the Report Center

VIEW A STANDARD BALANCE SHEET

The Balance Sheet proves the fundamental accounting equation: Assets = Liabilities + Owner's Equity. When all transactions and adjustments for the period have been recorded, a balance sheet should be prepared. QuickBooks has several different types of Balance Sheet statements available: Standard—shows as of the report dates the balance in each balance sheet account with subtotals provided for assets, liabilities, and equity; Detail—for each account the report shows the starting balance, transactions entered, and the ending balance during the period specified in the From and To dates; Summary—shows amounts for each account type but not for individual accounts; Prev. Year Comparison—has columns for the report date, the report date a year ago, $ change, and % change; and By Class—shows the value of your company or organization by class.

Since Your Name Mountain Sports is a partnership, separate equity accounts for each partner were established earlier in the chapter. You may explore the owner information in the Balance Sheet.

 View a **Standard Balance Sheet Report**

Double-click **Balance Sheet Standard**
Tab to or click **As of,** enter **01/31/13**, tab to generate the report
Scroll through the report to view the assets, liabilities, and equities listed
- Notice the Equity section, especially the Investment and Drawing accounts for each owner.
- You will see that your investment and drawing accounts are separate from Larry's.
- Total 3100 Your Last Name & Muir, Capital shows a total of the capital for both owners.
- Notice that there is an amount shown for 3100 - Your Last Name & Muir, Capital – Other of $26,159.44. This balance shows how much "other" capital the owners share. Other capital can include things such as opening balances that represent value belonging to the owners. Originally, the capital for both owners was combined into one account. The report does not indicate how much of the "other" capital is for each owner.
- Notice the Net Income account listed in the **Equity** section of the report. This is the same amount of Net Income shown on the Profit and Loss Statement.

Your Name Mountain Sports
Balance Sheet
As of January 31, 2013

	Jan 31, 13
Equity	
3100 · Your Last Name & Muir, Capital	
3110 · First and Last Name, Capital	
3111 · First and Last Name, Investment	20,000.00
3112 · First and Last Name, Drawing	-1,000.00
Total 3110 · First and Last Name, Capital	19,000.00
3120 · Larry Muir, Capital	
3121 · Larry Muir, Investment	20,000.00
3122 · Larry Muir, Drawing	-1,000.00
Total 3120 · Larry Muir, Capital	19,000.00
3100 · Your Last Name & Muir, Capital - Other ▶	26,159.44 ◀
Total 3100 · Your Last Name & Muir, Capital	64,159.44
Net Income	2,766.75
Total Equity	66,926.19
TOTAL LIABILITIES & EQUITY	81,802.65

Partial Report

Do not close the report

USE QUICKZOOM TO VIEW THE CAPITAL – OTHER ACCOUNT

As you learned earlier, QuickZoom is a QuickBooks feature that allows you to make a closer observation of transactions, amounts, etc. With QuickZoom, you may zoom in on an item when the mouse pointer turns into a magnifying glass with a Z inside. If you point to an item and you do not get a magnifying glass with a Z inside, you cannot zoom in on the item.

As you view the Balance Sheet, you will notice that the balance for 3100 - Your Last Name & Muir, Capital - Other is $26,159.44. To determine why there is an amount in the Other Capital, use QuickZoom to see the Transactions by Account report. You will see that the amounts for the beginning balances of the assets, liabilities, and the owners' equity have been entered in this account. Thus, the value of the Other Capital account proves the fundamental accounting equation of Assets = Liabilities + Owner's Equity.

 Use QuickZoom to view the Your Last Name & Muir, Capital – Other account

Point to the amount 26,159.44, and double-click the primary mouse button
Change the report dates **From** is **12/01/12** and **To** is **01/31/13**, press Tab to generate the report

Your Name Mountain Sports
Transactions by Account
As of January 31, 2013

Type	Date	Num	Adj	Name	Memo	Clr	Split	Debit	Credit	Balance
3100 · Your Last Name & Muir, Capital										0.00
Inventory Adjust	12/31/2012				Pants Opening balance	✔	1120 · Inventory Asset		1,750.00	1,750.00
Inventory Adjust	12/31/2012				Accessories Opening balance	✔	1120 · Inventory Asset		2,925.00	4,675.00
Inventory Adjust	12/31/2012				Bindings-Skis Opening balance	✔	1120 · Inventory Asset		3,750.00	8,425.00
Inventory Adjust	12/31/2012				Bindings-Snow Opening balance	✔	1120 · Inventory Asset		3,750.00	12,175.00
Inventory Adjust	12/31/2012				Boots Opening balance	✔	1120 · Inventory Asset		600.00	12,775.00
Inventory Adjust	12/31/2012				Boots-Ski Opening balance	✔	1120 · Inventory Asset		1,125.00	13,900.00
Inventory Adjust	12/31/2012				Boots-Snowbrd Opening balance	✔	1120 · Inventory Asset		900.00	14,800.00
Inventory Adjust	12/31/2012				Gloves Opening balance	✔	1120 · Inventory Asset		330.00	15,130.00
Inventory Adjust	12/31/2012				Hats Opening balance	✔	1120 · Inventory Asset		240.00	15,370.00
Inventory Adjust	12/31/2012				Pants-Ski Opening balance	✔	1120 · Inventory Asset		2,850.00	18,220.00
Inventory Adjust	12/31/2012				Parkas Opening balance	✔	1120 · Inventory Asset		4,375.00	22,595.00
Inventory Adjust	12/31/2012				Poles-Ski Opening balance	✔	1120 · Inventory Asset		540.00	23,135.00
Inventory Adjust	12/31/2012				Skis Opening balance	✔	1120 · Inventory Asset		5,000.00	28,135.00
Inventory Adjust	12/31/2012				Snowboard Opening balance	✔	1120 · Inventory Asset		3,000.00	31,135.00
Inventory Adjust	12/31/2012				Socks Opening balance	✔	1120 · Inventory Asset		225.00	31,360.00
Inventory Adjust	12/31/2012				Sweaters Opening balance	✔	1120 · Inventory Asset		1,875.00	33,235.00
Inventory Adjust	12/31/2012				Underwear Opening balance	✔	1120 · Inventory Asset		264.00	33,499.00
Credit Card Charge	12/31/2012				Account Opening Balance		2100 · Visa	150.00		33,349.00
General Journal	12/31/2012				Account Opening Balance		2510 · Office Equipment Loan	3,000.00		30,349.00
General Journal	12/31/2012				Account Opening Balance		2520 · Store Fixtures Loan	2,500.00		27,849.00
Deposit	12/31/2012				Account Opening Balance		1100 · Checking		25,943.00	53,792.00
Deposit	12/31/2012				Account Opening Balance		1311 · Office Supplies		850.00	54,642.00
General Journal	12/31/2012				Account Opening Balance		1511 · Original Cost		5,000.00	59,642.00
General Journal	12/31/2012				Account Opening Balance		1521 · Original Cost		4,500.00	64,142.00
Deposit	12/31/2012				Account Opening Balance		1340 · Prepaid Insurance		250.00	64,392.00
General Journal	12/31/2012				Account Opening Balance		3111 · First and Last Name, Investment	20,000.00		44,392.00
General Journal	12/31/2012				Account Opening Balance		3121 · Larry Muir, Investment	20,000.00		24,392.00
Deposit	12/31/2012				Account Opening Balance		1312 · Sales Supplies		575.00	24,967.00
General Journal	12/31/2012						4999 · Uncategorized Income		6,942.44	31,909.44
General Journal	12/31/2012						6999 · Uncategorized Expenses	8,500.00		23,409.44
Inventory Adjust	01/08/2013				Sleds Opening balance	✔	1120 · Inventory Asset		675.00	24,084.44
Inventory Adjust	01/08/2013				Toboggans Opening balance	✔	1120 · Inventory Asset		1,375.00	25,459.44
Inventory Adjust	01/08/2013				Helmets Opening balance	✔	1120 · Inventory Asset		700.00	26,159.44
Total 3100 · Your Last Name & Muir, Capital								54,150.00	80,309.44	26,159.44
TOTAL								**54,150.00**	**80,309.44**	**26,159.44**

- Notice that the amounts shown include the amounts for the opening balances of all the assets including each inventory item, all the liabilities, the original investment amounts (equity), and uncategorized income and expenses.
- Uncategorized Income and Expenses reflect the income earned and expenses incurred prior to the current period. This prevents previous income/expenses being included in the calculation for the net income or loss for the current period.
  Close the Transactions by Account report without printing
  Do not close the Balance Sheet

DISTRIBUTE CAPITAL TO EACH OWNER

The Balance Sheet does not indicate how much of the Other Capital should be distributed to each partner because 3100 - Your Last Name & Muir, Capital, is a combined Capital account. In order to clarify this section of the report, the capital should be distributed between the two owners. Each owner has contributed an equal amount as an investment in the business, so the Other Capital should be divided equally between Larry and you. The $26,159.44 represents equity for the owners that has not been previously recorded as an investment or a withdrawal. This could include net income from previous business periods and other equity items.

 Make an adjusting entry to distribute capital between the two owners

Access the **Make General Journal Entries** screen as previously instructed
The **Date** is **01/31/13**
This is not an adjusting entry, so remove the check mark
Transfer the amount in the account **3100 - Your Last Name & Muir, Capital –Other** to the owners' individual capital accounts by debiting Account **3100** for **26159.44**
Memo for all entries in the transaction is **Transfer Capital to Partners**
Transfer one-half of the amount entered in the DEBIT column to **3110 – First and Last Name, Capital**, by crediting this account
- To determine one-half of the amount use QuickMath as follows: Click after the credit amount, press **/**, enter **2,** and press **Enter**.
Credit **3120 - Larry Muir, Capital**, for the other half of the amount

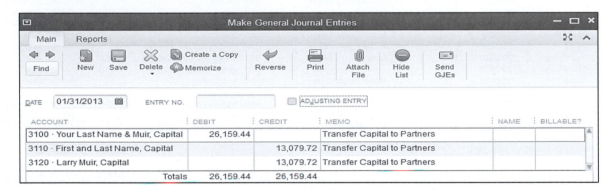

Click **Save & Close** to record and return to the Balance Sheet
- If the report does not automatically refresh, click **Yes**
- Notice the change in the Equity section of the Balance Sheet.
- The total of 3100 - Your Last Name & Muir, Capital, is still $64,159.44. There is no longer a 3100 - Your Last Name & Muir, Capital – Other account. Now, each owner has a Capital-Other account that shows 13,079.72.
- Look closely at the following balance sheet's equity section. Verify that your account setup matches the one shown in the text. Keep in mind that 3100 – Your Last Name & Muir, Capital, will show your actual last name. For example, the author's account would be Horne & Muir, Capital.
- Accounts 3110, 3111, 3112, and 3110 – Other should all have your actual <u>first</u> and <u>last</u> name rather than the words First & Last Name. For the author, Accounts 3110, 3111, 3112, and 3110 – Other would all have Janet Horne rather than First and Last Name.

Your Name Mountain Sports
Balance Sheet
As of January 31, 2013

	Jan 31, 13
Equity	
▼ 3100 · Your Last Name & Muir, Capital	
▼ 3110 · First and Last Name, Capital	
3111 · First and Last Name, Investment	20,000.00
3112 · First and Last Name, Drawing	–1,000.00
3110 · First and Last Name, Capital – Other	13,079.72
Total 3110 · First and Last Name, Capital	32,079.72
▼ 3120 · Larry Muir, Capital	
3121 · Larry Muir, Investment	20,000.00
3122 · Larry Muir, Drawing	–1,000.00
3120 · Larry Muir, Capital – Other	13,079.72
Total 3120 · Larry Muir, Capital	32,079.72
Total 3100 · Your Last Name & Muir, Capital	64,159.44
Net Income	2,766.75
Total Equity	66,926.19
TOTAL LIABILITIES & EQUITY	81,802.65

Partial Report

Do <u>not</u> close the report

CLOSING ENTRIES

In traditional accrual-basis accounting, there are four entries that need to be made at the end of a fiscal year. These entries close income, expenses, and the drawing accounts and transfer the net income into owners' equity.

Income and Expense accounts are closed when QuickBooks is given a closing date. This will occur later in this chapter. When preparing reports during the next fiscal year, QuickBooks will not show any amounts in the income and expense accounts for the previous year once the closing date has been entered.

However, QuickBooks does not close the owners' drawing accounts, nor does it transfer the net income into the owners' Capital accounts. If you prefer to use the power of the program and omit the last two closing entries, QuickBooks will keep a running account of the owner withdrawals, and it will put net income into a Retained Earnings account. However, transferring the net income and drawing into the owners' Capital accounts provides a clearer picture of the value of the owners' equity.

ADJUSTMENT TO TRANSFER NET INCOME/RETAINED EARNINGS
INTO FIRST AND LAST NAME, CAPITAL AND LARRY MUIR, CAPITAL

Because Your Name Mountain Sports is a partnership, the amount of net income should appear as part of each owner's capital account rather than appear as Retained Earnings. In many instances, this is the type of adjustment the CPA makes on the Accountant's Copy of the QuickBooks company files. The adjustment may be made before the closing date for the fiscal year, or it may be made after the closing has been performed. Because

QuickBooks automatically transfers the amount in the Net Income account into Retained Earnings, the closing entry for a partnership will transfer the net income into each owner's capital account. This adjustment is made by debiting Retained Earnings and crediting the owners' individual capital accounts. When you view a report before the end of the year, you will see an amount in Net Income and the same amount as a negative in Retained Earnings. If you view a report after the end of the year, you will not see any information regarding Retained Earnings or Net Income because the adjustment correctly transferred the amount to the owners' capital accounts.

On the Balance Sheet, Retained Earnings and/or Net Income appear as part of the equity section. The owners' Drawing and Investment accounts are kept separate from Retained Earnings at all times.

 Evenly divide and transfer the net income into the 3110 - First and Last Name, Capital and 3120 - Larry Muir, Capital accounts

Open the **General Journal** as previously instructed
- Since the transfer of net income into capital could be considered an adjustment, leave Adjusting Entry marked

The **Date** is **01/31/13**
The first account used is **3000 Retained Earnings**
Debit **3000 Retained Earnings**, **2,766.75**
For the Memo record **Transfer Net Income into Capital**
Click the drop-down list arrow on the second line and select **3110 - First and Last Name, Capital** as the account
Use QuickMath to divide the 2,766.75 in half
Click after the 2,766.75 in the credit column, type **/**, type **2**, press **Enter**
- A credit amount of **1,383.38** should be entered for **3110 - First and Last Name, Capital**.
- QuickBooks enters **1,383.37** as the credit amount for the next line

Click the drop-down list arrow and select **3120 Larry Muir, Capital** as the account, press Tab
- Because QuickBooks accepts only two numbers after a decimal point, the cents must be rounded. Thus, there is a 1¢ difference in the distribution between the two owners. If there is an uneven amount in the future, Larry will receive the extra amount.

The Memo should be the same for all three lines

DATE 01/31/2013 📅	ENTRY NO.		☑ ADJUSTING ENTRY		
ACCOUNT	DEBIT	CREDIT	MEMO	NAME	BILLABLE?
3000 - Retained Earnings	2,766.75		Transfer Net Income into Capital		
3110 - First and Last Name, Capital		1,383.38	Transfer Net Income into Capital		
3120 - Larry Muir, Capital ▾		1,383.37	Transfer Net Income into Capital	▾	
Totals	2,766.75	2,766.75			

- Not all companies have a profit each month. If your business has a negative amount for net income, in other words, a loss, the appropriate adjustment would be to debit each owner's individual capital account and to credit Retained Earnings. For example, if Net Income (Loss) was -500.00, you would record the following: 3110 - First and Last Name, Capital—debit 250; 3120 - Larry Muir, Capital—debit 250; and 3000 Retained Earnings—credit 500.

Click **Save & Close** to record and close the **General Journal**

- If you get a Retained Earnings dialog box regarding posting a transaction to the Retained Earnings account, click **OK**

VIEW STANDARD BALANCE SHEET

Once the adjustment for Net Income/Retained Earnings has been performed, viewing or printing the Balance Sheet will show you the status of the Owners' Equity. If you keep the year as 2013, both Retained Earnings and Net Income are shown in the report. However, a Balance Sheet prepared for 2014 will show nothing for Retained Earnings or Net Income because the net income was transferred into the owners' Capital accounts

 Observe the effect of the adjustment to the owners' equity

Since you did not close the report, the Balance Sheet should still be on the screen.

Your Name Mountain Sports
Balance Sheet
As of January 31, 2013

	Jan 31, 13
▼ Equity	
3000 · Retained Earnings	-2,766.75
▼ 3100 · Your Last Name & Muir, Capital	
▼ 3110 · First and Last Name, Capital	
3111 · First and Last Name, Investment	20,000.00
3112 · First and Last Name, Drawing	-1,000.00
3110 · First and Last Name, Capital - Other	14,463.10
Total 3110 · First and Last Name, Capital	33,463.10
▼ 3120 · Larry Muir, Capital	
3121 · Larry Muir, Investment	20,000.00
3122 · Larry Muir, Drawing	-1,000.00
3120 · Larry Muir, Capital - Other	14,463.09 ◄
Total 3120 · Larry Muir, Capital	33,463.09
Total 3100 · Your Last Name & Muir, Capital	66,926.19
Net Income	2,766.75
Total Equity	66,926.19
TOTAL LIABILITIES & EQUITY	81,802.65

Partial Report

- Notice the change in the **Equity** section of the Balance Sheet. Both Net Income and Retained Earnings are shown.

View a **Standard Balance Sheet** for **January 2014**

Change the **As of** date to **01/31/2014**, press **Tab**

- Notice the Equity section. Nothing is shown for Retained Earnings or Net Income.
- The net income has been added to the owners' capital accounts.

Your Name Mountain Sports
Balance Sheet
As of January 31, 2014

	Jan 31, 14
Equity	
3100 · Your Last Name & Muir, Capital	
3110 · First and Last Name, Capital	
3111 · First and Last Name, Investment	20,000.00
3112 · First and Last Name, Drawing	-1,000.00
3110 · First and Last Name, Capital - Other	14,463.10
Total 3110 · First and Last Name, Capital	33,463.10
3120 · Larry Muir, Capital	
3121 · Larry Muir, Investment	20,000.00
3122 · Larry Muir, Drawing	-1,000.00
3120 · Larry Muir, Capital - Other	14,463.09
Total 3120 · Larry Muir, Capital	33,463.09
Total 3100 · Your Last Name & Muir, Capital	66,926.19
Total Equity	66,926.19
TOTAL LIABILITIES & EQUITY	81,802.65

Partial Report

Change the **As of** date for the Balance Sheet to **01/31/13**
- The Equity section once again shows both Retained Earnings and Net Income.
Do <u>not</u> close the report

CLOSE DRAWING AND TRANSFER INTO OWNERS' CAPITAL ACCOUNTS

The entry transferring the net income into the owners' Capital accounts has already been made. While this is not the actual end of the fiscal year for Your Name Mountain Sports, the closing entry for the Drawing accounts will be entered at this time so that you will have experience in recording this closing entry.

MEMO
DATE: January 31, 2013

Record the closing entry to close 3112 – First and Last Name, Drawing, and 3122 - Larry Muir, Drawing, into each owner's Capital account.

 Record the closing entry for each owner's Drawing account

  Access **Make General Journal Entries** as previously instructed
- Since a closing entry could be considered an adjustment, leave Adjusting Entry marked

Debit **3110 – First and Last Name, Capital**, for the amount of the drawing account
1,000
The Memo for the transaction is **Close Drawing**
Credit **3112 – First and Last Name, Drawing**, for **1,000**
Use the same Memo for this portion of the transaction

DATE 01/31/2013	ENTRY NO.			✓ ADJUSTING ENTRY		
ACCOUNT	DEBIT	CREDIT	MEMO		NAME	BILLABLE?
3110 · First and Last Name, Capital	1,000.00		Close Drawing			
3112 · First and Last Name, Drawing		1,000.00	Close Drawing			
Totals	1,000.00	1,000.00				

Click the **New** icon on the Main Icon bar
Repeat the above steps to close **3122 - Larry Muir, Drawing** to his Capital account

DATE 01/31/2013	ENTRY NO.			✓ ADJUSTING ENTRY		
ACCOUNT	DEBIT	CREDIT	MEMO		NAME	BILLABLE?
3120 · Larry Muir, Capital	1,000.00		Close Drawing			
3122 · Larry Muir, Drawing		1,000.00	Close Drawing			
Totals	1,000.00	1,000.00				

Click **Save & Close** and return to the Balance Sheet
- Notice the change in the **Equity** section of the Balance Sheet.

Your Name Mountain Sports
Balance Sheet
As of January 31, 2013

	Jan 31, 13
Equity	
3000 · Retained Earnings	-2,766.75
3100 · Your Last Name & Muir, Capital	
3110 · First and Last Name, Capital	
3111 · First and Last Name, Investment	20,000.00
3110 · First and Last Name, Capital – Other	13,463.10
Total 3110 · First and Last Name, Capital	33,463.10
3120 · Larry Muir, Capital	
3121 · Larry Muir, Investment	20,000.00
3120 · Larry Muir, Capital – Other	13,463.09
Total 3120 · Larry Muir, Capital	33,463.09
Total 3100 · Your Last Name & Muir, Capital	66,926.19
Net Income	2,766.75
Total Equity	66,926.19
TOTAL LIABILITIES & EQUITY	81,802.65

Partial Report

If you are going to do the following optional exercise, do <u>not</u> close the report

EXPORTING REPORTS TO EXCEL (OPTIONAL)

Many of the reports prepared in QuickBooks can be exported to Microsoft® Excel. This allows you to take advantage of extensive filtering options available in Excel, hide detail for some but not all groups of data, combine information from two different reports, change titles of columns, add comments, change the order of columns, and experiment with "what if" scenarios. In order to use this feature of QuickBooks you must also have Microsoft Excel available for use on your computer.

 Optional Exercise: Export a report from QuickBooks to Excel

> With the **Balance Sheet** showing on the screen, click the **Excel** button, click **Create New Worksheet**
> On the Send Report to Excel message, make sure **Create New Worksheet** and **in a new workbook** are selected or click to select

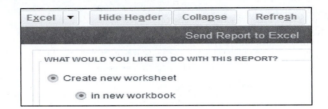

> Click **Export**
> • The Balance Sheet will be displayed in Excel.

	A	B	C	D	E	F
1						Jan 31, 13
2	ASSETS					
3		Current Assets				
4			Checking/Savings			
5				1100 · Checking		30,167.63
6			Total Checking/Savings			30,167.63
7			Accounts Receivable			
8				1200 · Accounts Receivable		5,696.50
9			Total Accounts Receivable			5,696.50
10			Other Current Assets			
11				1120 · Inventory Asset		35,551.54
12				1310 · Supplies		
13					1311 · Office Supplies	521.98
14					1312 · Sales Supplies	400.00
15				Total 1310 · Supplies		921.98
16				1340 · Prepaid Insurance		125.00
17			Total Other Current Assets			36,598.52
18			Total Current Assets			72,462.65

> Scroll through the report and click in Cell A60
> Type **BALANCE SHEET EXPORTED TO EXCEL**

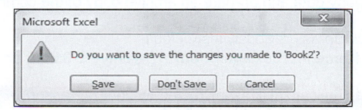

	A	B	C	D	E	F
1						Jan 31, 13
42		Equity				
43			3000 · Retained Earnings			-2,766.75
44			3100 · Your Last Name & Muir, Capital			
45				3110 · First and Last Name, Capital		
46					3111 · First and Last Name, Investment	20,000.00
47					3110 · First and Last Name, Capital – Other	13,463.10
48				Total 3110 · First and Last Name, Capital		33,463.10
49				3120 · Larry Muir, Capital		
50					3121 · Larry Muir, Investment	20,000.00
51					3120 · Larry Muir, Capital – Other	13,463.09
52				Total 3120 · Larry Muir, Capital		33,463.09
53				Total 3100 · Your Last Name & Muir, Capital		66,926.19
54				Net Income		2,766.75
55		Total Equity				66,926.19
56	TOTAL LIABILITIES & EQUITY					81,802.65
57						
58						
59						
60	BALANCE SHEET EXPORTED TO EXCEL					

Click the **Close** button in the upper right corner of the Excel title bar to close **Excel**

Microsoft Excel

⚠ Do you want to save the changes you made to 'Book2'?

Save   Don't Save   Cancel

Click **Don't Save** to close **Book2** without saving
- The Book number changes depending on how many times you export reports to Excel.

Return to QuickBooks, close the Balance Sheet, and the Report Center

IMPORTING DATA FROM EXCEL

There are several ways to import data into QuickBooks: You may use Intuit Interchange Format (IIF) files to import lists, transactions, vendors, employees, customers, bank transactions, and others. IIF files are ASCII text or CSV files that QuickBooks uses to import/export lists and to import transactions. You may also import an existing Excel or CSV file; you can enter data into a specially formatted spreadsheet and then add it to QuickBooks; or you can copy and paste data from Excel into QuickBooks by using the Add/Edit Multiple List Entries. An import file must conform to a specific structure for QuickBooks to interpret the data in the file correctly. QuickBooks has a built in Reference Guide for Importing Files that may be accessed and printed through Help. (Refer to Appendix B for more detailed information.)

JOURNAL FOR JANUARY

It is always wise to have a printed or hard copy of the data on disk. After all entries and adjustments for the month have been made, the Journal for January should be printed. This copy should be kept on file as an additional backup to the data stored on your disk. If something happens to your disk to damage it, you will still have the paper copy of your transactions available for re-entry into the system. Normally, the Journal would be printed before closing the period; however, we will print the Journal at the end of the chapter so that all entries are included.

END-OF-PERIOD BACKUP

Once all end-of-period procedures have been completed, in addition to a regular backup copy of company data and a duplicate disk, a second duplicate disk of the company data should be made and filed as an archive disk. Preferably, this copy will be located someplace other than on the business premises. The archive disk or file copy is set aside in case of emergency or in case damage occurs to the original and current backup copies of the company data.

 Back up company data and prepare an archive copy of the company data

Prepare a Back Up as previously instructed
- In the **File Name** text box enter **Sports (Archive 1-31-13)** as the name for the backup

Also prepare a duplicate disk as instructed by your professor
- Label this disk **Sports Archive, 1-31-13**

PASSWORDS

Not every employee of a business should have access to all the financial records. In some companies, only the owner(s) will have complete access. In others, one or two key employees will have full access while other employees are provided limited access based on the jobs they perform. Passwords are secret words used to control access to data. QuickBooks has several options available to assign passwords.

In order to assign any passwords at all, you must have an administrator. The administrator has unrestricted access to all QuickBooks functions and sets up users, user passwords, and assigns areas of transaction access for each user. Areas of access can be limited to transaction entry for certain types of transactions or a user may have unrestricted access into all areas of QuickBooks and company data. To obtain more information regarding QuickBooks' passwords, refer to Help.

A password should be kept secret at all times. It should be something that is easy for the individual to remember, yet difficult for someone else to guess. Birthdays, names, initials, and other similar devices are not good passwords because the information is too readily available. Never write down your password where it can be easily found or seen by someone else. In QuickBooks passwords are case sensitive. It is wise to use a complex password. The requirements for a password to be accepted as complex are: a minimum of seven characters including at least one number and one uppercase letter. Use of special characters is also helpful. Complex passwords should be changed every 90 days. Make sure your password is something you won't forget. Otherwise, you will not be able to access your Company file.

Since the focus of the text is in training in all aspects of QuickBooks, no passwords will be assigned.

SET THE CLOSING DATE FOR THE PERIOD

A closing date assigned to transactions for a period prevents changing data from the closed period without acknowledging that a transaction from a previous period has been changed. This is helpful to discourage casual changes or transaction deletions to a period that has been closed. Setting the closing date is done by accessing Accounting Preferences in QuickBooks. Setting a closing date also closes the income and expenses for the period.

MEMO
DATE: January 31, 2013

Now that the closing entries have been made, you want to protect the data and close income and expenses for the period by setting the closing date to 1/31/13.

 Assign the closing date of **01/31/13** to the transactions for the period ending 1/31/13

>   Click **Edit** on the menu bar, click **Preferences**
>   Click **Accounting**
>   Click **Company Preferences** tab
>   Click the **Set Date/Password** button.
>   Enter **01/31/13** as the closing date in the Closing Date section of the Company
>   Preferences for Accounting
>   Do not set any passwords at this time

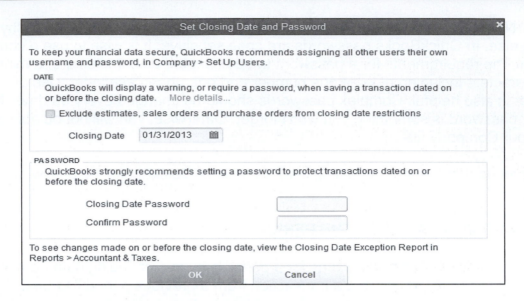

Click **OK**
Click **No** on the No Password Entered dialog box

Click **OK** to close Preferences

ENTER A CORRECTION TO A CLOSED PERIOD

If it is determined that an error was made in a previous period, QuickBooks does allow the correction. Before it will record any changes for previous periods, QuickBooks requires that Yes is clicked on the dialog box warning of the change to a transaction date that is prior to the closing date for the company.

MEMO
DATE: January 31, 2013

After entering the closing date, Ruth reviews the Journal and reports printed at the end of January. She finds that $25 of the amount of Office Supplies should have been recorded as Sales Supplies. Record an entry in the Journal to transfer $25 from Office Supplies to Sales Supplies.

Transfer $25 from Office Supplies to Sales Supplies

> Access the **General Journal** as previously instructed
> ADJUSTING ENTRY should be marked
> Enter the DATE of **01/31/13**
> Tab to or click in the **ACCOUNT** column, click the drop-down list arrow for
>   **ACCOUNT**, click **1312 - Sales Supplies**
> Enter the DEBIT of **25.00**
> Enter the MEMO **Correcting Entry**
> Tab to or click in the **ACCOUNT** column, enter the account number **1311** press Tab
> - The account 1311-Office Supplies will be shown
> - A credit amount of 25.00 should already be in the CREDIT column. If not, enter the amount.
> - The MEMO **Correcting Entry** should appear

DATE	01/31/2013	ENTRY NO.		✓ ADJUSTING ENTRY			
ACCOUNT		DEBIT	CREDIT	MEMO		NAME	BILLABLE?
1312 · Sales Supplies		25.00		Correcting Entry			
1311 · Office Supplies			25.00	Correcting Entry			
	Totals	25.00	25.00				

> Click **Save & Close**
> Click **Yes** on the **QuickBooks** dialog box

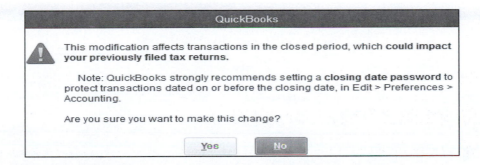

QuickBooks

> ⚠ This modification affects transactions in the closed period, which **could impact your previously filed tax returns.**
>
> Note: QuickBooks strongly recommends setting a **closing date password** to protect transactions dated on or before the closing date, in Edit > Preferences > Accounting.
>
> Are you sure you want to make this change?
>
> Yes   No

VERIFY THE CORRECTION TO OFFICE AND SALES SUPPLIES

Once the correction has been made, it is important to view the change in the accounts. The transfer of an amount of one asset into another will have no direct effect on the total assets in your reports. The account balances for Office Supplies and Sales Supplies will be changed. To view the change in the account, open the Chart of Accounts and look at the balance of each account. You may also use the account register to view the correcting entry as it was recorded in each account.

MEMO

DATE: January 31, 2013

Access the Chart of Accounts and view the change in the account balances and the correcting entry in each account's register.

 View the correcting entry in each account

Open the **Chart of Accounts** as previously instructed
- Notice that the balance for Office Supplies has been changed from 521.98 to 496.98.
- Notice that the balance for Sales Supplies has been changed from 400.00 to 425.00.

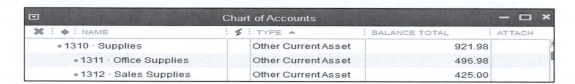

NAME	TYPE ▲	BALANCE TOTAL	ATTACH
◇ 1310 · Supplies	Other Current Asset	921.98	
◇ 1311 · Office Supplies	Other Current Asset	496.98	
◇ 1312 · Sales Supplies	Other Current Asset	425.00	

Double-click **Office Supplies** to open the account register
- Verify that the correcting entry was recorded for Office Supplies.

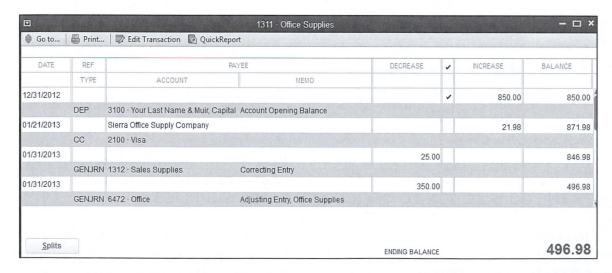

1311 · Office Supplies

DATE	REF	PAYEE		DECREASE	✔	INCREASE	BALANCE
	TYPE	ACCOUNT	MEMO				
12/31/2012					✔	850.00	850.00
	DEP	3100 · Your Last Name & Muir, Capital	Account Opening Balance				
01/21/2013		Sierra Office Supply Company				21.98	871.98
	CC	2100 · Visa					
01/31/2013				25.00			846.98
	GENJRN	1312 · Sales Supplies	Correcting Entry				
01/31/2013				350.00			496.98
	GENJRN	6472 · Office	Adjusting Entry, Office Supplies				

Splits

ENDING BALANCE   **496.98**

Close the **Office Supplies Register**
Repeat the steps to view the correcting entry in Sales Supplies

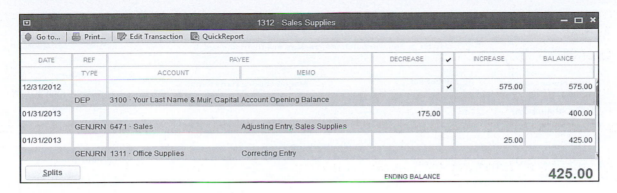

			1312 · Sales Supplies					— □ ×

DATE	REF	PAYEE		DECREASE	✔	INCREASE	BALANCE
	TYPE	ACCOUNT	MEMO				
12/31/2012					✔	575.00	575.00
	DEP	3100 · Your Last Name & Muir, Capital	Account Opening Balance				
01/31/2013				175.00			400.00
	GENJRN	6471 · Sales	Adjusting Entry, Sales Supplies				
01/31/2013						25.00	425.00
	GENJRN	1311 · Office Supplies	Correcting Entry				

Splits   ENDING BALANCE   **425.00**

Close the **Sales Supplies Register**
Close the **Chart of Accounts**

INVENTORY ADJUSTMENTS

In a business that has inventory, it is possible that the number of items on hand is different from the quantity shown in QuickBooks when a physical inventory is taken. This can be caused by a variety of items: loss due to theft, fire, or flood; damage to an item in the stockroom; an error in a previous physical inventory. Even though QuickBooks uses the average cost method of inventory valuation, the value of an item can be changed as well. For example, assume that several pairs of after-ski boots are discounted and sold for a lesser value during the summer months. QuickBooks allows the quantity and value of inventory to be adjusted.

MEMO

DATE: January 31, 2013

After taking a physical inventory, you discover two hats were placed next to the cleaning supplies and are discolored because bleach was spilled on them. These hats must be discarded. Record this as an adjustment to the quantity of inventory. Use the Expense account 6190 Merchandise Adjustments to record this adjustment.

 Adjust the quantity of hats

QuickBooks values inventory using the Average Cost Method
Open the Item List as previously instructed, double-click **Hats**

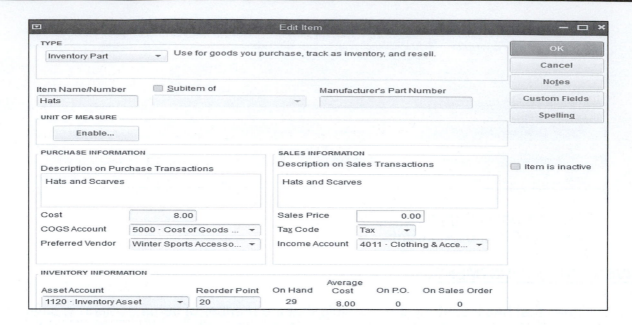

- Note the Avg. Cost of 8.00 for Hats

Close the Edit Item screen and the Item List

Click the **Inventory Activities** icon in the Company section of the QuickBooks Home Page

Click **Adjust Quantity/Value On Hand...** in the list shown

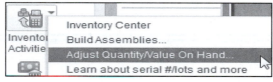

Enter the adjustment date of **013113**

Click the drop-down list arrow next to **Adjustment Account**

Click **<Add New>**

Enter the new account information:

Type **Expense**

Number **6190**

Name **Merchandise Adjustments**

Click **Save & Close** to add the account

Click in the **ITEM** column, click the drop-down list arrow, and click **Hats**

Click in the **NEW QUANTITY** column for Hats

Enter **27**

Press **Tab** to enter the change

- Notice that the Total Value of the Adjustment is -16.00, which is -8.00 for each hat. The number of Item Adjustments is one. The Quantity on Hand is 27, Avg. Cost per Item is 8.00, and the Value is 216.00.

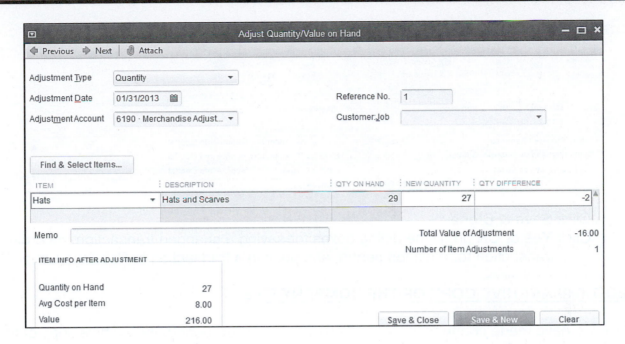

Click **Save & Close**
Click **Yes** on the **QuickBooks** dialog box regarding changing a transaction for a
closed period

ADJUST THE JOURNAL ENTRY FOR NET INCOME/RETAINED EARNINGS

The adjustment to inventory reduced the value of the inventory asset by $16.00 and
increased the expenses of the business by $16.00. The change decreased the net income
by $16.00; thus, the adjusting entry for net income/retained earnings made previously
needs to be changed.

 Adjust the net income

Access **General Journal** transactions as previously instructed
Click **Previous** (back arrow icon) until you get to the entry debiting Retained
Earnings for 2,766.75
To reduce the amount by $16.00, click after the **5**, press **–**, key in **16**, press **Enter** to
change the debit to Retained Earnings to **2,750.75**
Change the credit to 3110 – First and Last Name, Capital by half of the amount of
the adjustment (16 / 2 = 8) thus, 1383.38 – 8 = **1,375.38**
Change the credit to 3120 - Larry Muir, Capital by half the amount to **1,375.37**

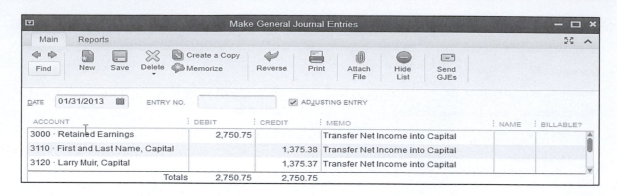

Click **Save & Close**

Click **Yes** or **OK** on all the dialog boxes for saving a changed transaction, recording a transaction for a closed period, and posting a transaction to Retained Earnings

REDO THE ARCHIVE COPY OF THE COMPANY FILE

Since we have made changes to transactions for the closed period, the archive copy of the company file should be redone.

 Create an archive copy of the company data

Replace the previous file **Sports (Backup Archive 1-31-13)**
Follow the procedures given previously to make your backup files

PRINT REPORTS

After closing entries have been entered, it is important to print post-closing reports. Normally, those reports are dated as of the last day of or for the period. The only exception to the reports is the Profit & Loss Statement. In order to see that the income and expenses have been closed, the report has to be prepared as of the first day of the next period.

> **MEMO**
> **DATE:** January 31, 2013
>
> Print the following reports for Your Name Mountain Sports as of or for 01/31/13: Journal, Trial Balance, Profit and Loss Statement, and Balance Sheet.

PRINT THE JOURNAL

Since the Journal was not printed before closing the period, it should be printed at this time. This will give a printed copy of all the transactions made in Chapters 5, 6, and 7.

 Print the **Journal** for January

Access the Journal as previously instructed
Expand the report
The dates are from **01/01/13** to **01/31/13**
Tab to generate the report
Resize the columns so all names and accounts are shown in full and the report prints on one-page wide

- Names, Memos, and Accounts may not necessarily be shown in full; however, make sure enough of the information shows so you can identify the names, sales items, and accounts used in transactions.

Your Name Mountain Sports
Journal
January 2013

Trans #	Type	Date	Num	Adj	Name	Memo	Account	Debit	Credit
115	General Journal	01/31/2013				Transfer Capital to Partners	3100 · Your Last Name & Muir, Capital	26,159.44	
						Transfer Capital to Partners	3110 · First and Last Name, Capital		13,079.72
						Transfer Capital to Partners	3120 · Larry Muir, Capital		13,079.72
								26,159.44	26,159.44
116	General Journal	01/31/2013		✓		Transfer Net Income into Capital	3000 · Retained Earnings	2,750.75	
				✓		Transfer Net Income into Capital	3110 · First and Last Name, Capital		1,375.38
				✓		Transfer Net Income into Capital	3120 · Larry Muir, Capital		1,375.37
								2,750.75	2,750.75
117	General Journal	01/31/2013		✓		Close Drawing	3110 · First and Last Name, Capital	1,000.00	
				✓		Close Drawing	3112 · First and Last Name, Drawing		1,000.00
								1,000.00	1,000.00
118	General Journal	01/31/2013		✓		Close Drawing	3120 · Larry Muir, Capital	1,000.00	
				✓		Close Drawing	3122 · Larry Muir, Drawing		1,000.00
								1,000.00	1,000.00
119	General Journal	01/31/2013		✓		Correcting Entry	1312 · Sales Supplies	25.00	
				✓		Correcting Entry	1311 · Office Supplies		25.00
								25.00	25.00
120	Inventory Adjust	01/31/2013	1				6190 · Merchandise Adjustments	16.00	
						Hats Inventory Adjustment	1120 · Inventory Asset		16.00
								16.00	16.00
TOTAL								80,410.13	80,410.13

Partial Report

Print the report in **Landscape** orientation
Close the **Journal** and the **Report Center**

PRINT THE TRIAL BALANCE

After closing the period has been completed, it is helpful to print a Trial Balance. This proves that debits still equal credits.

 Print a **Trial Balance** to prove debits still equal credits

Prepare a **Trial Balance** as previously instructed
The dates are from **01/01/13** to **01/31/13**
Scroll through the report and study the amounts shown

- Notice that the final totals of debits and credits are equal.

Your Name Mountain Sports
Trial Balance
As of January 31, 2013

	Jan 31, 13	
	Debit	Credit
6120 · Bank Service Charges	18.00	
6140 · Advertising Expense	95.00	
6150 · Depreciation Expense	160.00	
6181 · Liability Insurance	125.00	
6190 · Merchandise Adjustments	16.00	
6212 · Loan Interest	97.93	
6300 · Rent	950.00	
6340 · Telephone	156.40	
6391 · Gas and Electric	359.00	
6392 · Water	85.00	
6471 · Sales	175.00	
6472 · Office	350.00	
7010 · Interest Income		54.05
TOTAL	91,271.55	91,271.55

Partial Report

Print in **Portrait** orientation
Close the report

PRINT PROFIT AND LOSS STATEMENT

Since the closing was done as of January 31, 2013, the Profit and Loss Statement for January 31, 2013 will give the same data as a Profit and Loss Statement prepared manually on January 31. To verify the closing of income and expense accounts for January, you would prepare a Profit and Loss statement for February 1. Since no income had been earned or expenses incurred in the new period, February, the Net Income will show $0.00.

 Print a Profit & Loss Standard report for January and view the report for February

Click **Company & Financial** in the **Report Center**, double-click **Profit & Loss Standard**
The **Dates** are From **01/01/13** To **01/31/13**

Your Name Mountain Sports
Profit & Loss
January 2013

	Jan 13
Total Expense	2,587.33
Net Ordinary Income	2,696.70
▼ Other Income/Expense	
▼ Other Income	
7010 · Interest Income	54.05
Total Other Income	54.05
Net Other Income	54.05
Net Income	2,750.75

Partial Report

- Note the Net Income of $2,750.75.

Print the report in **Portrait** orientation
To view the effect of closing the period, prepare a Profit & Loss for February
Change the dates From **02/01/13** to **02/01/13**
Tab to generate the report

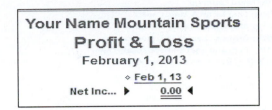

- Note the Net Income of **0.00**.

Close the **Profit & Loss Report**

PRINT THE BALANCE SHEET

The proof that assets equal liabilities and owners' equity after the closing entries have been made needs to be displayed in a Balance Sheet. Because this report is for a month, the adjustment to Retained Earnings and Net Income will result in both of the accounts being included on the Balance Sheet. If, however, this report were prepared for the year, neither account would appear.

 Print a Standard Balance Sheet report for January 31, 2013

Prepare a **Standard Balance Sheet** as previously instructed
If necessary, enter the as of date as **01/31/13**
Scroll through the report to view the assets, liabilities, and equities listed
- Because this report is for a one-month period, both Retained Earnings and Net Income are included on this report.

Your Name Mountain Sports
Balance Sheet
As of January 31, 2013

	Jan 31, 13
Total Liabilities	14,876.46
Equity	
3000 · Retained Earnings	-2,750.75
3100 · Your Last Name & Muir, Capital	
3110 · First and Last Name, Capital	
3111 · First and Last Name, Investment	20,000.00
3110 · First and Last Name, Capital - Other	13,455.10
Total 3110 · First and Last Name, Capital	33,455.10
3120 · Larry Muir, Capital	
3121 · Larry Muir, Investment	20,000.00
3120 · Larry Muir, Capital - Other	13,455.09
Total 3120 · Larry Muir, Capital	33,455.09
Total 3100 · Your Last Name & Muir, Capital	66,910.19
Net Income	2,750.75
Total Equity	66,910.19
TOTAL LIABILITIES & EQUITY	81,786.65

Partial Report

Print the report, orientation is **Portrait**
Close the **Balance Sheet**

BACKUP YOUR NAME MOUNTAIN SPORTS

As in previous chapters, you should back up your company and then close the company.

 Follow instructions previously provided to back up company files, name the backup **Sports (Backup Ch. 7)**, close the company, and make a duplicate disk

SUMMARY

In this chapter, end-of-period adjustments were made, a bank reconciliation and a credit card reconciliation were performed, backup (duplicate) and archive disks were prepared, and adjusting entries were made. A credit card reconciliation was "undone" and then completed correctly. The use of Drawing, Net Income, and Retained Earnings accounts were explored and interpreted for a partnership. The closing date for a period was assigned. Account names were changed, and new accounts were created. Even though QuickBooks focuses on entering transactions on business forms, a Journal recording each transaction is kept by QuickBooks. This chapter presented transaction entry directly into the General Journal. The difference between accrual-basis and cash-basis accounting was discussed. Owner withdrawals and distribution of capital to partners were examined. Many of the different report options available in QuickBooks were explored, and a report was exported to Microsoft® Excel. A variety of reports were printed after closing the period. Correction of errors was analyzed, and corrections were made after the period was closed and adjustments were made to inventory. The fact that QuickBooks does not require an actual closing entry at the end of the period was addressed.

END-OF-CHAPTER QUESTIONS

TRUE/FALSE

ANSWER THE FOLLOWING QUESTIONS IN THE SPACE PROVIDED BEFORE THE QUESTION NUMBER.

_____ 1. The owner's drawing account should be transferred to capital each week.

_____ 2. Even if entered elsewhere, all transactions are recorded in the Journal.

_____ 3. You must access the General Journal in order to close a period.

_____ 4. If Show All is selected, inactive accounts will not appear in the Chart of Accounts.

_____ 5. When you reconcile a bank statement, anything entered as a service charge will automatically be entered as a transaction when the reconciliation is complete.

_____ 6. Once an account has been used, the name cannot be changed.

_____ 7. Once an account reconciliation is completed, it may not be undone.

_____ 8. At the end of the year, QuickBooks transfers the net income into retained earnings.

_____ 9. A withdrawal by an owner in a partnership reduces the owner's capital.

_____ 10. As with other accounting programs, QuickBooks requires that a formal closing be performed at the end of each year.

MULTIPLE CHOICE

WRITE THE LETTER OF THE CORRECT ANSWER IN THE SPACE PROVIDED BEFORE THE QUESTION NUMBER.

_____ 1. To print a Reconciliation Report that lists only totals, select ___.
   A. none
   B. summary
   C. detail
   D. complete

_____ 2. The report that proves debits equal credits is the ___.
A. Sales Graph
B. Balance Sheet
C. Profit & Loss Statement
D. Trial Balance

_____ 3. If reports are prepared for the month of January, net income will appear in the ___ .
A. Profit & Loss Statement
B. Balance Sheet
C. both A and B
D. neither A nor B

_____ 4. In QuickBooks, you export reports to Microsoft® Excel in order to ___.
A. print the report
B. explore "what if" scenarios with data from QuickBooks
C. prepare checks
D. all of the above

_____ 5. QuickBooks uses the ___ method of inventory valuation
A. LIFO
B. average cost
C. FIFO
D. Actual Cost

_____ 6. If a transaction is recorded in the Journal, it may be viewed ___.
A. in the Journal
B. in the register for each balance sheet account used in the transaction
C. by preparing an analysis graph
D. in both A and B

_____ 7. Entries for bank collections of automatic payments ___.
A. are automatically recorded at the completion of the bank reconciliation
B. must be recorded after the bank reconciliation is complete
C. should be recorded when reconciling the bank statement
D. should be recorded on the first of the month

_____ 8. The account(s) that may be reconciled is (are) ___.
A. Checking
B. Credit Card
C. the Customer list account
D. both A and B

_____ 9. The closing entry for a drawing account transfers the balance of an owner's drawing account into the ___ account.
- A. Retained Earnings
- B. Net Income
- C. Owner's Capital
- D. Investment

_____ 10. A Balance Sheet that shows amounts for each account type but not for individual accounts is the ___ Balance Sheet.
- A. Standard
- B. Summary
- C. Detail
- D. Comparison

FILL-IN

IN THE SPACE PROVIDED, WRITE THE ANSWER THAT MOST APPROPRIATELY COMPLETES THE SENTENCE.

1. _____-basis accounting matches income and expenses against a period, and _____-basis accounting records income when the money is received and expenses when the purchase is made or the bill is paid.

2. The _____ proves that Assets = Liabilities + Owners' Equity.

3. In a partnership, each owner has a share of all the _____ and _____ based on the percentage of his or her investment in the business or according to any partnership agreements.

4. In order to close a period, a closing _____ must be provided.

5. No matter where transactions are recorded, they all appear in the _____.

SHORT ESSAY

Describe the entry that is made to transfer net income into the owner's capital account. Include the reason this entry should be made and how income will be listed if it is not made.

_____

_____

_____

_____

_____

NAME_____

TRANSMITTAL

CHAPTER 7: YOUR NAME MOUNTAIN SPORTS

Attach the following documents and reports:

Account Listing
Check No. 6: Your First and Last Name
Check No. 7: Larry Muir
Bank Reconciliation Detail Report, January 31, 2013
Visa Reconciliation Detail Report, January 31, 2013
Check No. 8: Old Mammoth Bank
Journal, January, 2013
Trial Balance, January 31, 2013
Profit and Loss, January 2013
Balance Sheet, January 31, 2013

END-OF-CHAPTER PROBLEM

YOUR NAME RESORT CLOTHING

Chapter 7 continues with the end-of-period adjustments, bank and credit card reconciliations, archive disks, and closing the period for Your Name Resort Clothing. The company does use a certified public accountant for guidance and assistance with appropriate accounting procedures. The CPA has provided information for Karen to use for adjusting entries, etc.

INSTRUCTIONS

Continue to use the copy of Your Name Resort Clothing you used in the previous chapters. Open the company—the file used is **Clothing.qbw**. Record the adjustments and other transactions as you were instructed in the chapter. Always read the transaction carefully and review the Chart of Accounts when selecting transaction accounts. Print the reports and journals as indicated and resize columns for a full display of information.

RECORD TRANSACTIONS

January 31, 2013—Enter the following:
► Change the names and/or the account numbers of the following accounts.
- o **6260 - Printing and Reproduction** to **6260 Printing and Duplication**
- o **6350 - Travel & Ent** to **6350 - Travel Expenses**
- o **3010 - Your Name & Olsen, Capital** to **3100 - Your Last Name & Olsen, Capital**
  - ▪ Remember to use your actual <u>last</u> name.
► Add the following accounts:
- o Equity account **3110 - First and Last Name, Capital** (subaccount of **3100**)
  - ▪ Remember to use both your real first and last name.
- o Equity account **3120 - Karen Olsen, Capital** (subaccount of **3100**)
► Change the following accounts:
- o **3011 - Your Name, Investment** to **3111 - First and Last Name, Investment** (subaccount of **3110**)
  - ▪ Remember to use both your real first and last name.
- o **3013 - Your Name, Drawing** to **3112 - First and Last Name, Drawing** (subaccount of **3110**)
  - ▪ Remember to use both your real first and last name.
- o **3012 - Karen Olsen, Investment** to **3121 - Karen Olsen, Investment** (subaccount of **3120**)
- o **3014 - Karen Olsen, Drawing** to **3122 Karen Olsen, - Drawing** (subaccount of **3120**)
- o **6422 – Office** to **6422 – Office Supplies** (subaccount of 6420 - Supplies Expense)

► Make the following accounts inactive:
  o **6291 - Building Repairs**
  o **6351 - Entertainment**
► Delete the following accounts:
  o **6182 - Disability Insurance**
  o **6213 - Mortgage**
  o **6823 - Property**
► Print an Account Listing in Landscape orientation
  o Do _not_ show inactive accounts (If necessary, click Include inactive to remove the check mark)
  o Click the Reports button at the bottom of the Chart of Accounts, and click Account Listing to display the report
  o Resize the columns to display the Account Names in full and to hide the columns for Description, Accnt. #, and Tax Line
  o Change the Header/Footer so the report date is January 31, 2013
  o Print the report
► Create a Fixed Asset Item List for:
  o Asset Name/Number: **Office Equipment**, Item is: **New**, Purchase and Asset Description: **Office Equipment**, Date: **12/31/12**, Cost: **$8,000**, Asset Account: **1510**
  o Asset Name/Number: **Store Fixtures**, Item is: **New**, Purchase and Asset Description: **Store Fixtures**, Date: **12/31/12**, Cost: **$9,500**, Asset Account: **1520**
► Enter adjusting entries in the Journal and use the memo Adjusting Entry for the following:
  o Office Supplies Used, the amount used is $35
  o Sales Supplies Used, account balance (on hand) at the end of the month is $1,400
  o Record a compound entry for depreciation for the month: Office Equipment, $66.67 and Store Fixtures, $79.17
  o The amount of insurance remaining in the Prepaid Insurance account is for six months of liability insurance. Record the liability insurance expense for the month
► Each owner withdrew $500. (Memo: January Withdrawal) Print Check Nos. 7 and 8 for the owners' withdrawals.
► Prepare Bank Reconciliation and Enter Adjustments for the Reconciliation: (Refer to the chapter for appropriate Memo notations)

CENTRAL COAST BANK
1234 Coast Highway
San Luis Obispo, CA 93407
(805) 555-9300

Your Name Resort Clothing
784 Marsh Street
San Luis Obispo, CA 93407

Acct. # 987-352-9152   January 31, 2013

Beginning Balance, January 1, 2013			$32,589.00
1/15/13, Deposit	3,023.30		35,612.30
1/15/13, Deposit	2,450.05		38,062.35
1/15/13, NSF Returned Check		325.00	37,737.35
1/15/13, Check 1		59.39	37,677.96
1/18/13, Check 3		156.80	37,521.16
1/18/13, Check 2		343.00	37,178.16
1/25/13, Check 4		1,150.00	36,028.16
1/25/13, Check 5		79.85	35,948.31
1/31/13, Service Charge 10.00, NSF Charge 15.00		25.00	35,923.31
1/31/13, Office Equipment Loan Pmt.: $44.51 Interest, $8.61 Principal		53.12	35,870.19
1/31/13, Store Fixtures Loan Pmt.: $53.42 Interest, $10.33 Principal		63.75	35,806.44
1/31/13, Interest	73.30		35,879.74
Ending Balance, 1/31/13			35,879.74

▶ Print a Detailed Reconciliation Report in Portrait. Adjust column widths so the report fits on one page
▶ Reconcile the Visa account using the statement on the following page

---

CENTRAL COAST BANK
1234 Coast Highway
San Luis Obispo, CA 93407

Your Name Resort Clothing
784 Marsh Street
San Luis Obispo, CA 93407
VISA Acct. # 9187-52-9152   **January 31, 2013**

		Balance
Beginning Balance, January 2, 2013		0.00
1/9/13, Clothes Time	196.00	196.00
1/18/13, Office Masters	250.00	446.00
Ending Balance, 1/31/13		446.00

Minimum Payment Due: $50.00	**Payment Due Date: February 5, 2013**

► Print a Detailed Reconciliation Report in Portrait. Pay Central Coast Bank for the Visa bill using Check No. 9. Print Check No. 9

► After completing the Visa reconciliation, distribute capital to each owner: divide the balance of 3100 - Your Last Name & Olsen, Capital - Other equally between the two partners. (View a Standard Balance Sheet to see the balance of the Capital – Other account.) Record an entry to transfer each owner's portion of the Capital Other to the individual capital accounts. (Memo: Transfer Capital to Partners) Remember, this is not an adjusting entry

► Divide in half and transfer Net Income/Retained Earnings into owners' individual Capital accounts. Remember, this is an adjusting entry

► Close Drawing accounts into owner's individual Capital accounts

► Prepare an archive copy of the company file

► Close the period as of January 31, 2013 (Do not assign passwords)

► After closing the period on 01/31/13, discovered an error in the amount of Office Supplies and Sales Supplies: Transfer $40 from Office Supplies to Sales Supplies

► After closing the period on 01/31/13, found one damaged tie. Adjust the quantity of ties on 01/31/13 using the Expense account 6190 Merchandise Adjustments

► Change the net income/retained earnings adjustment to reflect the merchandise adjustment for the ties

► Backup the company and redo the archive copy of the company file as well

► Print the Journal for January, 2013 (Landscape orientation, Fit to one page wide)

► Print the following reports:
   o Trial Balance, January 1-31, 2013
   o Profit and Loss Statement, January 31, 2013
   o Balance Sheet, January 31, 2013

NAME_____

TRANSMITTAL

CHAPTER 7: YOUR NAME RESORT CLOTHING

Attach the following documents and reports:

Account Listing
Check No. 7: Your First and Last Name
Check No. 8: Karen Olsen
Bank Reconciliation Detail Report, January 31, 2013
Visa Reconciliation Detail Report, January 31, 2013
Check No. 9: Central Coast Bank
Journal, January 1-31, 2013
Trial Balance, January 31, 2013
Profit and Loss, January, 2013
Balance Sheet, January 31, 2013

SECTION 2 PRACTICE SET, MERCHANDISING BUSINESS: YOUR NAME'S ULTIMATE GOLF

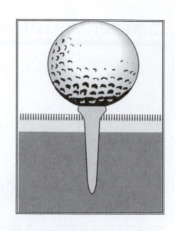

The following is a comprehensive practice set combining all the elements of QuickBooks studied in the merchandising section of the text. Since the version of QuickBooks is 2013, the text shows the year as 2013. In this practice set, you are instructed to keep the books for a company for the month of January 2013. Check with your instructor to find out what year you should use when recording transactions. Entries will be made to record invoices, sales orders, receipt of payments on invoices, cash sales, credit card sales, receipt and payment of bills, orders and receipts of merchandise, credit memos for invoices and bills, sales tax payments, and credit card payments. Account names will be added, changed, deleted, and made inactive. Customers, vendors, owners, and fixed assets will be added to the appropriate lists. Reports will be prepared to analyze sales, bills, receipts, and items ordered. Formal reports including the Trial Balance, Profit and Loss Statement, and Balance Sheet will be prepared. Adjusting entries for depreciation, supplies used, insurance expense, and automatic payments will be recorded. Both bank and credit card reconciliations will be prepared. Entries to display partnership equity for each partner will be made. The owners' drawing accounts will be closed and the period will be closed.

STUDENT'S NAME'S ULTIMATE GOLF

Located in La Quinta, California, Student's Name's Ultimate Golf is a full-service golf shop that sells golf equipment and golf clothing. Even though Valerie's name is not part of the company name, Student's Name's Ultimate Golf is a partnership owned and operated by Valerie Childers and you. Each partner contributed an equal amount to the partnership. You buy the equipment and manage the store. Valerie buys the clothing and accessory items and keeps the books for the company. There are several part-time employees working for the company selling merchandise.

INSTRUCTIONS

Use the file **Golf.qbw**.

When entering transactions, you are responsible for entering any memos you wish to include in transactions. Unless otherwise specified, the terms for each sale or bill will be the terms specified on the Customer or Vendor List. (Look at the Terms shown for each individual customer or vendor in the Information area or double-click the customer or vendor and select the Payment Settings tab to see the terms.) Customer Message is usually *Thank you for your business*. However, any other message that is appropriate may be used. If a customer's order exceeds the established credit limit, accept the order and process it.

If the terms allow a discount for a customer, make sure to apply the discount if payment is made within the discount period. Use the Income account 4050 Sales Discounts as the discount account. On occasion, a payment may be made within the discount period but not received or recorded within the discount period. Information within the transaction will indicate whether or not the payment is equivalent to a full payment. For example, if you received $98 for an invoice for $100 shortly after the discount period and the transaction indicated payment in full, apply the discount. If a customer has a credit and has a balance on the account, apply the credit to the appropriate invoice for the customer. If a customer pays a bill within the discount period and has a credit, make sure to calculate the discount on the payment amount after subtracting the credit. If there is no balance for a customer and a return is made, issue a credit memo and a refund check.

Always pay bills in time to take advantage of purchase discounts. Use the Cost of Goods Sold Account 5200 Merchandise Discounts for the discount account. Remember that the discount due date will be ten days from the date of the bill.

Invoices, sales orders, purchase orders, and other business forms should be printed as they are entered. To save time, you do not need to print Payment Receipts or Bills unless your professor requests that you do so. (Everything that may be printed is included on the transmittal sheet just in case you are required to print the documents.)

Print business forms with lines around each field. Most reports will be printed in Portrait orientation; however, if the report (such as the Journal) will fit across the page using Landscape, use Landscape orientation. Whenever possible, adjust the column widths so that account names, amounts, and item names are displayed in full and so that reports fit on one page wide *without* selecting Fit report to one page wide.

Back up your work at the end of each week.

The following lists are used for all vendors, customers, and sales items. You will be adding additional customers and vendors as the company is in operation.

Vendors:

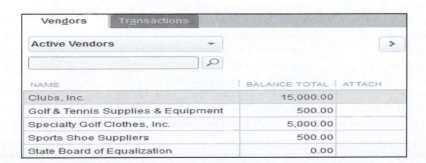

Customers:

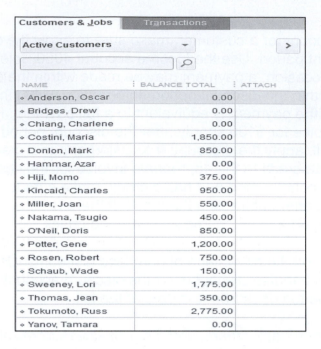

Sales Items:

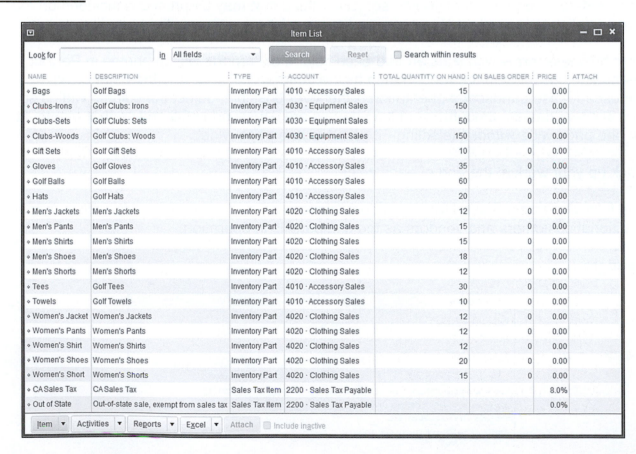

Note: Individual golf clubs are categorized as irons or woods. A complete set of clubs would be categorized as a set. The type of material used in a golf club makes no difference in a sales item. For example, graphite is a material used in the shaft of a golf club. A set of graphite clubs would refer to a set of golf clubs. Titanium is a type of metal used in the head of a golf club. A titanium wood would be sold as a wood. Golf balls are sold in packages called sleeves; thus, a quantity of one would represent one package of golf balls.

RECORD TRANSACTIONS:

Enter the transactions for Student's Name Ultimate Golf and print as indicated. If you get message boxes that you do not want, click the selection that will <u>not</u> display this in the future.

Week 1—January 2-8, 2013:
- ▶ Add your First and Last name to both the company name and legal name for Student's Name Ultimate Golf. Even though this is a partnership, the company name will be **Your Name's Ultimate Golf**. (Type your actual name *not* the words Your Name. Don't forget the apostrophe s after your last name. For example, Sue Smith would be Sue Smith's Ultimate Golf.)
- ▶ Change Report Preferences: The Report Header/Footer should *not* include the Date Prepared, Time Prepared, or Report Basis.
- ▶ Change the names and delete the descriptions of the following accounts:
  - o **3000** change the words Your Name to your actual last name to make the account name **Last Name & Childers, Capital**
  - o **4200 Sales Discounts** to **4200 Purchases Discounts**
  - o **4050 Reimbursed Expenses** to **Sales Discounts**
  - o **6350 Travel & Ent** to **6350 Travel Expenses**
  - o **6381 Marketing** to **6381 Sales Supplies Expense** (this is a subaccount of 6380 Supplies Expense)
  - o **6382 Office** to **6382 Office Supplies Expense** (this is a subaccount of 6380 Supplies Expense)
- ▶ Delete the following accounts:
  - o **4070 Resale Discounts**
  - o **4090 Resale Income**
  - o **4100 Freight Income**
  - o **6130 Cash Discounts**
  - o **6213 Mortgage**
  - o **6265 Filing Fees**
  - o **6285 Franchise Fees**
  - o **6351 Entertainment**
- ▶ Make the following accounts inactive:
  - o **6182 Disability Insurance**
  - o **6311 Building Repairs**
  - o **6413 Property**

▶ Add the following accounts:
- o Equity account: **3010 First and Last Name, Capital** (subaccount of **3000**) Use your real first and last name.
- o Equity account: **3020 Valerie Childers, Capital** (subaccount of **3000**)
- o Cost of Goods Sold account: **5200 Merchandise Discounts** (subaccount of **5000**)

▶ Change the following accounts:
- o **3400 Student's Name, Investment** to **3011 First and Last Name, Investment** (subaccount of **3010**). Use your real first and last name.
- o **3300 Student's Name, Drawing** to **3012 First and Last Name, Drawing** (subaccount of **3010**). Use your real first and last name.
- o **3200 Valerie Childers, Investment** to **3021 Valerie Childers, Investment** (subaccount of **3020**)
- o **3100 Valerie Childers, Drawing** to **3022 Valerie Childers, Drawing** (subaccount of **3020**)

▶ Use the Reports Menu to access the List reports. Print the Account Listing in portrait orientation. Resize the columns so the Account Names, Type, and Balance Total show in full. Do *not* show the Description, Accnt. #, or Tax Line columns. Click the Customize Report button and on the Header/Footer tab, change the report date to January 2, 2013.

▶ Create Fixed Asset Item List
- o Asset Name: Office Equipment, Item is: New, Purchase and Asset Description: Office Equipment, Date: 12/31/(use the end of previous year), Cost: 5,000.00, Asset Account: 1510 Office Equipment
- o Asset Name: Store Fixtures, Item is: New, Purchase and Asset Description: Store Fixtures, Date: 12/31/(use the end of previous year), Cost: 6,000.00, Asset Account: 1520 Store Fixtures

▶ Customize Sales Receipts, Purchase Orders, Sales Orders, Credit Memos, and Intuit Product Invoices so that the Default Title is in all capital letters and so that your name will print in full on the same line as the company name.

▶ Print invoices, checks, sales orders, and other items as they are entered in the transactions. Check with your instructor to see if you should print Payment Receipts. They are listed on the Transmittal just in case you print them.

1/2/2013

▶ Sold 2 pairs of women's shorts @ $64.99 each, 2 women's shirts @ $59.99 each, 1 women's jacket @ $129.99, and 1 pair of women's shoes @ $179.99 to Tamara Yanov on account. (Remember: Use your Copy of: Intuit Product Invoice. Print Invoice No. 1 when the transaction is entered.)

▶ Having achieved her goal of a handicap under 30, Maria Costini treated herself to the new clubs she had been wanting. Sold on account 1 set of graphite clubs for $750, 1 golf bag for $129.95, and 5 sleeves (packages) of golf balls @ $6.95 each. (Remember to accept sales that are over the credit limit.)

▶ Change Maria Costini's credit limit to $3,000.00.

▶ Change Azar Hammar's credit limit to $2,500.

▶ Azar heard that titanium would give him extra yardage with each shot. Sold 4 titanium woods (Clubs-Woods) on account to Azar Hammar @ $459.00 each.

▶ Sold 5 golf bags @ $59.99 each and 5 sets of starter clubs @ $159.99 each to Palm Springs Schools on account for the high school golf team. Palm Springs Schools, Main Phone: 760-555-4455, Main Email: PSSchools@ps.edu, Address: 99-4058 South Palm Canyon Drive, Palm Springs, CA 92262 is a nonprofit organization, Payment Terms: Net 30. Credit Limit: $1,500. Even though this is a nonprofit organization, it does pay California Sales Tax on all purchases. Include a subtotal for the sale and apply a 10% sales discount for a nonprofit organization. (Create any new sales items necessary.)

▶ Received a telephone sales order from Wade Schaub for 2 pairs of men's shorts @ $49.95 each, 2 men's shirts @ $59.99 each, 1 pair of men's golf shoes @ $119.99, a starter set of golf clubs for his son @ $250.00, and a new titanium driver for himself @ $549.95 (a driver is a Golf Club: Woods). Prepare a Sales Order.

▶ Correct the invoice to Maria Costini. The price of the golf bag should be $179.95. Reprint the invoice.

▶ Received Check No. 102-33 from Russ Tokumoto, $2,175, in partial payment of his account. (Did you leave this as an underpayment?)

1/3/2013

▶ Sold 3 gift sets @ $14.99 each and 3 sleeves (packages) of golf balls @ $8.95 each, and 5 Golf Hats @ $25.99 to Dr. Dr. Lori Sweeney on account to be given away as door prizes at an upcoming ladies' club tournament.

▶ Wade Schaub came into the store to pick up the merchandise on his Sales Order. Create the invoice from the sales order. (Use the pick-up date of January 3, 2013 for this invoice.) Since the Sales Order Invoice is different from a regular Product Invoice, customize the Sales Order Invoice so the Default Title is INVOICE and resize the title INVOICE and Your Name's Ultimate Golf so there is room for your name on the same line.

▶ Received Check No. 515 from Mark Donlon for $850 in full payment of his account.

▶ Sold a golf bag @ $99.95 and 2 golf towels @ $9.95 each to a cash customer using a Visa card. (Remember to print Sales Receipt No. 1.) Did you use QuickAdd to add the Cash Customer?

▶ Took a telephone sales order from a new customer Laura Hansen for 1 pair of women's golf shoes @ $149.95 and a set of golf clubs @ $895.00. New Customer info: Laura Hansen (Remember, last name first in the Customer List), Main Phone: 760-555-3322, Address: 45-2215 PGA Drive, Rancho Mirage, CA 92270, Payment Terms: 1% 10 Net 30, Credit Limit $1,500, taxable customer for California Sales Tax.

▶ Received Check No. 2233 for $950 from Gene Potter in partial payment of his account.

1/5/2013

▶ Laura Hansen came into the store to pick up the merchandise recorded on Sales Order 2. Create the invoice from the sales order and use the date of the sales order (January 3, 2013) for the invoice date.

► In the Item List, change the Item Name/Number from Hats to Men's Hats. The purchase and sales descriptions should be Men's Golf Hats. Change the reorder point from 15 to 12.

► Prepare and print an Inventory Stock Status by Item Report for January 1-5, 2013. Resize the columns, use Landscape orientation, and select Fit Report to 1 page wide.

► Prepare Purchase Orders for all items marked Order on the Inventory Stock Status by Item Report. Place all orders with the preferred vendors. Prepare only one purchase order per vendor. For all items ordered, the Qty on Hand should exceed the Reorder Point by 10 when the new merchandise is received. (For example, if the reorder point is 5 and you have 4 items on hand, you will need to order 11 items. This would make the quantity 15 when the order is received. This would exceed the reorder point by 10.) The cost of golf bags are $40 each, gift sets are $3 each, men's shorts are $20 each, towels are $2 each, and women's shirts are $20 each. (Remember to print the purchase orders. If you get a message to change the cost for the item, click No.)

► Order 5 women's hats @ $10.00 each from a new vendor: Head Gear, Inc., Main Phone: 310-555-8787, Main Email: HeadGear@la.com, Fax: 310-555-7878, Address: 45980 West Los Angeles Street, Los Angeles, CA 90025, Credit Limit $500, Payment Terms: 2% 10 Net 30. Add a new inventory sales item: Women's Hats. The purchase and sales description is Women's Golf Hats. Leave the purchase and sales price at 0.00. The COGS account is 5000. Head Gear, Inc. is the preferred vendor (Click the drop-down list arrow for Vendor, click Head Gear, Inc.). The hats are taxable. The Income account is 4010-Accessory Sales. The Asset account is 1120-Inventory Asset. The reorder point is 10. Quantity on Hand is 0 as of 01/05/2013.

► Print a Purchase Order QuickReport in Landscape orientation for January 1-5, 2013.

1/8/2013

► Received Check No. 1822 for a cash sale of 2 men's golf hats @ $49.95 each.

► Deposit all receipts (checks, credit cards, and/or cash) for the week. Print the Deposit Summary.

► Backup your work for Week 1. Name your backup file **Golf (Backup Week 1)**

Week 2—January 9-15:
1/10/2013

► Received the order from Head Gear, Inc. without the bill.

► Use 01/10/2013 for the bill date for both of the following transactions. Received the merchandise ordered and the bill from Golf & Tennis Supplies & Equipment. All items were received in full except the golf bags. Of the 12 bags ordered, only 8 were received. The remaining golf bags are on backorder. Also received all of the merchandise ordered and the bill from Specialty Golf Clothes, Inc.

► Dr. Dr. Lori Sweeney returned 1 of the gift sets purchased on January 3. Issue a credit memo and apply to Invoice 5.

► Mark Donlon returned 1 pair of men's golf shorts that had been purchased for $59.95. (The shorts had been purchased previously and were part of his $850 opening balance.) Issue the appropriate items.

► Received a telephone order for 1 complete set of golf clubs from Russ Tokumoto for $1,600.00.
► Sold a graphite sand wedge and a graphite gap wedge @ $119.95 each to a customer using a Visa card. (Both clubs are classified as irons.)

1/12/2013
► Russ Tokumoto came to the store and picked up the merchandise from his sales order. Create the invoice from the sales order and use the sales order date for the invoice.
► Received the telephone bill for the month, $85.15 from Desert Telephone Co., Main Phone: 760-555-9285, Address: 11-092 Highway 111, Palm Springs, CA 92262, Payment Terms: Net 30, Account Settings: 6340 Telephone.
► Used the company Visa card to purchase $175 of <u>office supplies</u> to have on hand from Indio Office Supply, Main Phone: 760-555-1535, Fax 760-555-5351, Address: 3950 46th Avenue, Indio, CA 92201.

1/14/2013
► Received the bill for the order from Head Gear, Inc. Use 01/14/2013 for the bill date.
► Received Check No. 3801 for $1,963.05 from Azar Hammar in full payment of his bill. (The transaction date is 01/14/13. The payment appropriately includes the discount since the check was dated 01/10/13.)
► Received Check No. 783 for $598.69 from Tamara Yanov in full payment of her bill. (The payment includes the discount since the check was dated 01/11/13.)
► Deposit all receipts (checks, credit cards, and/or cash) for the week. Print the Deposit Summary.
► Back up your work for Week 2. Name the file **Golf (Backup Week 2)**.

Week 3—January 16-22:
1/17/2013
► Dr. Charles Kincaid purchased 1 set of golf clubs, $1,200.00, 1 golf bag, $250.00, 1 pair of men's shoes, $195.00, and 1 putter (iron), $195.00 on account.
► Received Check No. 1822 back from the bank. This check was for $107.14 from a cash customer: William Jones, Main Phone: 760-555-0100, Address: 8013 Desert Drive, Desert Hot Springs, CA 92270. Payment Terms: Due on receipt. Charge William the bank charge of $15 plus Your Name's Ultimate Golf's own NSF charge of $15. Add any necessary customers, items and/or accounts. (Returned Check Service Charges should be Income account 4040.)
► Received Check No. 67-08 for $1,976.72 from Dr. Dr. Lori Sweeney in full payment of her account.
► Received the remaining 4 golf bags and the bill from Golf & Tennis Supplies & Equipment on earlier purchase order. The date of the bill is 01/16/2013.

1/18/2013
► Pay all bills that are eligible to receive a discount if paid between January 18 and 22. Use account 5200 Merchandise Discounts as the Discount Account. (Print the checks. To print the checks, you may use Print Forms or you may print them individually.)

▶ Sold 1 golf bag @ $199.95, 1 set of graphite golf clubs @ $1,200.00, 1 putter @ $129.95 (record the putter as Golf Clubs: Irons), and 3 sleeves of golf balls @ $9.95 each on account to Dr. Dr. Lori Sweeney.

▶ Returned 2 men's shirts that had poorly stitched seams at a cost of $20 each to Specialty Golf Clothes, Inc. Received Credit Memo 1045 from the company.

1/20/2013

▶ Dr. Charles Kincaid returned the putter he purchased on January 17. Issue a Credit Memo and apply to Invoice 11.

▶ Sold 1 men's golf hat @ $49.95, 1 men's jacket @ $89.95, 1 towel @ $9.95, 2 packages of golf tees @ $1.95 each, and 16 sleeves of golf balls at $5.95 to a customer using a Master Card.

▶ A businessman in town with his wife bought them each a set of golf clubs @ $1,495.00 per set and a new golf bag for each of them @ $249.95 per bag. He purchased 1 men's jacket for $179.95. His wife purchased 1 pair of golf shoes for $189.99 and 1 women's jacket for $149.99. He used his Visa to pay for the purchases.

▶ Prepare and print an Inventory Stock Status by Item Report for January 1-20.

▶ Edit the Item Golf Balls insert a space in the Purchase Description between Golf and Balls.

▶ Prepare Purchase Orders to order any inventory items indicated on the report. As with earlier orders, use the preferred vendor, issue only one purchase order per vendor, and order enough to exceed the Reorder Point by 10. (Golf balls cost $3.50 per sleeve, men's and women's jackets cost $20 each, and men's and women's hats cost $10 each.)

▶ Deposit all receipts (checks, credit cards, and/or cash) for the week. Print the Deposit Summary.

▶ Back up your work for Week 3. Name the file **Golf (Backup Week 3)**.

Week 4 and End of Period—January 23-31:
1/23/2013

▶ Pay all bills eligible to receive a discount if paid between January 23 and 30.

▶ Dr. Lori Sweeney was declared Club Champion and won a prize of $500. She brought in the $500 cash as a partial payment to be applied to the amount she owes on her account.

1/24/2013

▶ Received the bill and all the items ordered from Specialty Golf Clothes, Inc., and Golf & Tennis Supplies & Equipment. The bills are dated 01/23/2013.

▶ Received Check No. 1205 from Maria Costini as payment in full on her account. (No discounts applicable.)

▶ Received a letter of apology for the NSF check and a new check for $137.14 from William Jones to pay his account in full. The new check is Check No. 9015.

1/25/2013

▶ Received Check 305 for $1,741.07 as payment in full for Invoice 11 from Dr. Dr. Charles Kincaid. Since a Credit Memo was issued for Invoice 11, recalculate the discount to determine the appropriate amount. Since his account is not being paid in full include a memo of Partial Payment.

▶ Received the bill and all the hats ordered from Head Gear, Inc. The date of the bill is 01/23/2013.

▶ Received the bill dated 01/25/13 for $2,800 rent from Palm Springs Rentals, Main Phone: 760-555-8368, Fax 760-555-8638, Address: 11-2951 Palm Canyon Drive, Palm Springs, CA 92262, Payment Terms: Net 10. Account Settings: 6280 Rent.

▶ Purchased sales supplies to have on hand for $150 from Indio Office Supply. Used the company Visa for the purchase.

▶ Prepare an Unpaid Bills Detail Report for January 25, 2013. Print the report.

▶ Pay the following bills (Note: Bills for 12/31/2012 will have a due date of 01/10/13.) and print the checks:

   o $1,000 to Specialty Golf Clothes, Inc., for the amount owed on 12/31/2012. (NOTE: Select the bill you want to pay. Apply the credit you have from Specialty Golf Clothes, Inc., because of returned merchandise. You want to pay $1,000 plus use the $40 credit and reduce the amount owed by $1,040, *not* $960. Once the credit is applied, you will see the Amount To Pay as $4,960. Since you are not paying the full amount owed, click in Amt. To Pay column and enter the amount you are paying. In this case, enter 1,000 as the amount you are paying. When the payment is processed, $1,000 will be deducted from cash to pay for this bill and the $40 credit will be applied.)

   o Pay $5,000 to Clubs, Inc. toward the amount owed on 12/31/2012. (Again, change the payment amount in the Amt. To Pay column.)

   o Pay $500 to Golf & Tennis Supplies & Equipment to pay the amount owed on 12/31/2012

   o Pay $500 to Sports Shoe Suppliers to pay the amount owed on 12/31/2012

   o Pay the rent

1/26/2013

▶ Prepare and print an Unpaid Bills Detail Report for January 26, 2013. (*Note:* check Specialty Golf Clothes, Inc., the amount owed should be $4,360. If your report does not show this, check to see how you applied the credit when you paid bills. If necessary, QuickBooks does allow you to delete the previous bill payment and redo it. If this is the case, be sure to apply the credit, and record $1,000 as the payment amount.)

▶ Received $1,600 from Russ Tokumoto, Check No. 102-157 as a partial payment.

1/29/2013

▶ Deposit all checks and credit card receipts for the week.

1/30/2013

▶ Prepare Sales Tax Liability Report from January 1-30, 2013. Adjust the column widths and print the report in Landscape orientation. The report should fit on one page.

► Pay sales tax due as of January 30, 2013 and print the check.
► Print a Sales by Item Summary Report for January 1-30. Use Landscape orientation and, if necessary, adjust column widths so the report fits on one page wide.
► Print a Trial Balance for January 1-30, 2013 in Portrait orientation.
► Enter the following adjusting entries:
  o Office Supplies Used for the month is $125.
  o The balance of the Sales Supplies is $600 on January 30.
  o The amount of Prepaid Insurance represents the liability insurance for 12 months. Record the adjusting entry for the month of January.
  o Depreciation for the month is: Office Equipment, $83.33, Store Fixtures, $100.
► Record the transactions for owner's equity:
  o Each owner's withdrawal for the month of January is $2,000.
  o Divide the amount in account 3000-Your Last Name & Childers, Capital - Other, and transfer one-half the amount into each owner's individual Capital account. (View a Standard Balance Sheet for January 30 to determine the amount to divide.)
► Back up your work for Week 4. Name the file **Golf (Backup Week 4)**.

01/31/2013

► Use the following bank statement to prepare a bank reconciliation. Enter adjustments.

DESERT BANK
1234-110 Highway 111
Palm Springs, CA 92270

(760) 555-3300

Your Name's Ultimate Golf
55-100 PGA Boulevard
Palm Springs, CA 92270   Acct. # 9857-32-922   January 2013

Beginning Balance, January 1, 2013			$35, 275.14
1/8/2013, Deposit	4,212.33		39,487.47
1/10/2013, Check 1		64.75	39,422.72
1/14/2013, Deposit	2,820.83		42,243.55
1/16/2013, NSF Check		107.14	42,136.41
1/18/2013, Check 2		365.54	41,770.87
1/25/2013, Check 3		392.00	41,378.87
1/23/2013, Check 4		156.80	41,222.07
1/23/2013, Check 5		49.00	41,173.07
1/25/2013, Deposit	6,576.21		47,749.28
1/25/2013, Check 9		1,000.00	46.749.28
1/25/2013, Check 10		500.00	46,249.28
1/25/2013, Check 8		2,800.00	43,449.28
1/25/2013, Check 7		500.00	42,949.28
1/25/2013, Check 6		5,000.00	37,949.28
1/31/2013, Service Charge, $15, and NSF Charge, $15		30.00	37,919.28
1/31/2013, Store Fixtures Loan Pmt.: Interest, $89.03; Principal, $17.21		106.24	37,813.04
1/31/2013, Office Equipment Loan Pmt: Interest, $53.42; Principal, $10.33		63.75	37,749.29
1/31/2013, Interest	76.73		37,826.02
Ending Balance, 1/31/2013			**37,826.02**

► Print a Detailed Reconciliation Report.
► Received the Visa bill. Prepare a Credit Card Reconciliation

DESERT BANK **VISA DEPARTMENT** 1234-110 Highway 111 Palm Springs, CA 92270			(760) 555-3300
Your Name's Ultimate Golf 55-100 PGA Boulevard Palm Springs, CA 92270 VISA Acct. # 9287-52-952			January 2013
Beginning Balance, January 1, 2013			0.00
1/12/2013, Indio Office Supply		175.00	175.00
1/25/2013, Indio Office Supply		150.00	325.00
Ending Balance, 1/25/2013			325.00
Minimum Payment Due, $50.00		**Payment Due Date: February 7, 2013**	

▶ Print the check for payment to Desert Bank and a Reconciliation Summary Report
▶ View a Statement of Profit & Loss to get the information needed to divide the net income in half. Close the report without printing.
▶ Divide the Net Income/Retained Earnings in half and transfer one-half into each owner's individual capital account.
▶ Close the drawing account for each owner into the owner's individual capital account.
▶ Close the period using the closing date of 01/31/2013. Do not use a password.
▶ Edit a transaction from the closed period: Discovered an error in the Supplies accounts. Transfer $50 from 1320-Sales Supplies to 1310-Office Supplies.
▶ Adjust the number of tees on hand to 24. Use the expense account 6190 for Merchandise Adjustments. Be sure to correct the adjustment for net income/ retained earnings.
▶ Prepare an Archive Backup named **Golf (Archive 01-31-13)**

Print Reports and Back Up
▶ Print the following:
  o Journal (Landscape orientation, Fit on one page wide) for January , 2013
  o Trial Balance, January 31, 2013 (Portrait orientation)
  o Standard Profit and Loss Statement, January 1-31, 2013
  o Standard Balance Sheet, January 31, 2013
▶ Back up your work to **Golf (Backup Complete)**.

NAME_____

TRANSMITTAL

YOUR NAME'S ULTIMATE GOLF: PRACTICE SET MERCHANDISING BUSINESS

Attach the following documents and reports:

Week 1
Account Listing
Invoice No. 1: Tamara Yanov
Invoice No. 2: Maria Costini
Invoice No. 3: Azar Hammar
Invoice No. 4: Palm Springs Schools
Sales Order No. 1: Wade Schaub
Invoice No. 2 (Corrected): Maria Costini
Payment Receipt: Russ Tokumoto
Invoice No. 5: Dr. Lori Sweeney
Invoice No. 6: Wade Schaub
Payment Receipt: Mark Donlon
Sales Receipt No. 1: Cash Customer
Sales Order No. 2: Laura Hansen
Payment Receipt: Gene Potter
Invoice No. 7: Laura Hansen
Inventory Stock Status by Item Report,
    January 1-5, 2013
Purchase Order No. 1: Golf & Tennis
    Supplies & Equipment
Purchase Order No. 2: Specialty Golf
    Clothes, Inc.
Purchase Order No. 3: Head Gear, Inc.
Purchase Order QuickReport,
    January 5, 2013
Sales Receipt No. 2: Cash Customer
Deposit Summary, January 8, 2013

Week 2
Bill: Golf & Tennis Supplies & Equipment
    (Optional)
Bill: Specialty Golf Clothes, Inc. (Optional)
Credit Memo No. 8: Dr. Lori Sweeney
Credit Memo No. 9: Mark Donlon
Check No. 1: Mark Donlon
Sales Order No. 3: Russ Tokumoto
Sales Receipt No. 3: Cash Customer
Invoice No. 10: Russ Tokumoto
Bill: Desert Telephone Co. (Optional)
Bill: Head Gear, Inc. (Optional
Payment Receipt: Azar Hammar
Payment Receipt: Tamara Yanov
Deposit Summary, January 14, 2013

Week 3

Invoice No. 11: Dr. Dr. Charles Kincaid
Invoice No. 12: William Jones
Payment Receipt: Dr. Lori Sweeney
Bill: Golf & Tennis Supplies & Equipment (Optional)
Check No. 2: Golf & Tennis Supplies & Equipment
Check No. 3: Specialty Golf Clothes, Inc.
Invoice No. 13: Dr. Lori Sweeney
Bill Credit: Specialty Golf Clothes, Inc. (Optional)
Credit Memo No. 14: Dr. Dr. Charles Kincaid
Sales Receipt No. 4: Cash Customer
Sales Receipt No. 5: Cash Customer
Inventory Stock Status by Item, January 1-20, 2013
Purchase Order No. 4: Golf & Tennis Supplies & Equipment
Purchase Order No. 5: Specialty Golf Clothes, Inc.
Purchase Order No. 6: Head Gear, Inc.
Deposit Summary, January 20, 2013

Week 4 and End of Period

Check No. 4: Golf & Tennis Supplies & Equipment
Check No. 5: Head Gear, Inc.
Payment Receipt: Dr. Lori Sweeney
Bill: Specialty Golf Clothes, Inc. (Optional)
Bill: Golf & Tennis Supplies & Equipment (Optional)
Payment Receipt: Maria Crostini
Payment Receipt: William Jones
Payment Receipt: Dr. Charles Kincaid
Bill: Head Gear, Inc. (Optional)
Bill: Palm Springs Rentals (Optional)
Unpaid Bills Detail, January 25, 2013
Check No. 6: Clubs, Inc.
Check No. 7: Golf & Tennis Supplies & Equipment
Check No. 8: Palm Springs Rentals
Check No. 9: Specialty Golf Clothes, Inc.
Check No. 10: Sports Shoe Suppliers
Unpaid Bills Detail, January 26, 2013
Payment Receipt: Russ Tokumoto
Deposit Summary, January 29, 2013
Sales Tax Liability Report, January 1-30, 2013
Check No. 11: State Board of Equalization
Sales by Item Summary, January 1-30, 2013
Trial Balance, January 30, 2013
Check No. 12: Your First and Last Name
Check No. 13: Valerie Childers
Bank Reconciliation, January 31, 2013
Credit Card Reconciliation, January 31, 2013
Check No. 14: Desert Bank
Journal, January 2013
Trial Balance, January 31, 2013
Standard Profit and Loss Statement, January 1-31, 2013
Standard Balance Sheet, January 31, 2013

PAYROLL

LEARNING OBJECTIVES

At the completion of this chapter, you will be able to:

1. Create, preview, and print payroll checks.
2. Adjust pay stub information.
3. Correct, void, and delete paychecks.
4. Change employee information and add a new employee.
5. Print a Payroll Summary by Employee Report.
6. View an Employee Earnings Summary Report.
7. Print a Payroll Liabilities Report.
8. Pay Taxes and Other Liabilities.
9. Print a Journal

PAYROLL

Many times, a company begins the process of computerizing its accounting system simply to be able to do the payroll using the computer. It is much faster and easier to let QuickBooks look at the tax tables and determine how much withholding should be deducted for each employee than to have an individual perform this task. Because tax tables change frequently, QuickBooks requires its users to enroll in a payroll service plan in order to obtain updates. In order to enroll in a payroll service plan, you must have a company tax identification number and a registered copy of QuickBooks. QuickBooks has a variety of payroll service plans that are available for an additional charge. If you do not subscribe to a payroll plan, you must calculate and enter the payroll taxes manually.

Intuit's payroll plans are changed and updated frequently; however, at the time of writing, Intuit has the following Payroll Plans available on a subscription basis:

Online Payroll: Different levels available: Basic, and Enhanced. (Basic is available for $19.00 per month, Enhanced is $29 per month. Both versions charge an additional $1.50 per month for each employee). Subscribing to either of these plans enables you to pay your employees directly from Intuit and you may even use your iPhone or Android. Federal taxes are calculated for you, you may have an unlimited number of payrolls each month, free direct deposit. With the Enhanced version, state and federal tax payments are paid electronically. Quarterly and year-end tax filings are made, state and federal payroll tax forms are prepared and filed, and W-2s are processed. QuickBooks is not required, but the Online Plans do integrate with QuickBooks.

Payroll Basic: Essentially, paychecks only. ($19 per month plus $1.50 per month per employee) Subscribing to this plan enables you to download up-to-date tax tables into

QuickBooks. If you use this, you enter your employee information once. Each pay period you will enter the hours and QuickBooks will use this information to automatically calculate deductions and prepare paychecks for your employees. Direct deposit is available for no additional fee. Since no tax forms are included, you will work with your accountant; or use QuickBooks reports to generate the data you need in order to fill in state and federal tax forms by hand.

Payroll Enhanced: Primarily paychecks and taxes. ($29 per month plus $1.50 per employee) a more comprehensive do-it-yourself payroll solution used to calculate deductions, earnings, and payroll taxes using QuickBooks. Enter hours and get instant paychecks. Enhanced payroll includes federal and most state tax forms, tools for tracking payroll expenses and workers compensation. Direct deposit is available for no additional fee. Enhanced payroll automatically fills in your data on quarterly federal and state tax forms. Just print, sign & mail your tax filings or use E-File to file and pay payroll taxes electronically with QuickBooks. Year-end W-2s are included.

Payroll Assisted: Plan is a combo plan— Help with setup for do it yourself paychecks; and then, State and Federal taxes and filings are done for you. (Starting at $79 per month) Assistance from an Intuit payroll specialist is available for help during the setup procedures and when running your first payroll. You calculate earnings, deductions, and net pay and print paychecks using your QuickBooks software. Direct deposit is included. Your federal and state payroll taxes will be filed, tax deposits will be made, and W-2s will be processed for you. You are guaranteed that, if you provide accurate information, everything submitted for you will be accurate and on-time. And, if any issues come up with the IRS or state tax agencies, you will receive help to resolve them.

Full Service Payroll: Setup, paychecks, taxes, filings, and reports are done for you. ($75 per month plus $2 per employee) Complete setup done for you. Receive guidance when submitting employee hours online. Unlimited payrolls each month may be prepared, free direct deposit, free new hire reporting, free W-2 and 1099 printing and processing. Alerts for discrepancies are generated and each payroll you submit is reviewed for accuracy by Intuit's experts. Payroll taxes are filed and tax payments are made for you. The service is completely integrated with QuickBooks.

Payroll for Accounting Professionals: Intuit offers two payroll plans for accountants:

Online—run live payroll for clients from web, iPhone/iPad, or Android. Guaranteed to be accurate on tax calculations. (Priced per client at $10.99 – 19.99 per month plus $0.50 per employee) There is a one-click data sync with QuickBooks. Direct deposit, electronic payments and filings, and an employee website are included. For an additional fee of $2 per month, time tracking is available. Job Costing is included.

Enhanced—for accountants with live or after-the-fact payroll. (Priced from $230.30 to $300.30 annually depending on the number of employees) Works within QuickBooks, supports up to 50 clients, has client-ready payroll reports, and all of the benefits of the regular Enhanced Payroll.

MANUAL PAYROLL

The ability to process the payroll manually is part of the QuickBooks program and does not require a subscription or cost additional fees. However, if you use manual payroll for your business, it is your responsibility to obtain up-to-date payroll tax tables and tax forms.

Since all of our businesses in this text are fictitious and we do not have a FEIN, (Federal Employer's Identification Number), we will not be subscribing to any of the QuickBooks Payroll Services. As a result, we will be entering all tax information for paychecks manually based on data provided in the text. Calculations will be made for vacation pay, sick pay, medical and dental insurance deductions, and so on. Paychecks will be created, printed, corrected, and voided. Tax reports, tax payments, and tax forms will be explored.

Payroll is an area of accounting that has frequent changes; for example, tax tables are frequently updated, changes in withholding or tax limits are made, etc. As a result, QuickBooks is modified via updates to implement changes to payroll. As a word of caution, the materials presented in this chapter are current at the time of writing. It may be that as Intuit updates QuickBooks some of the things displayed in the chapter may change. If this happens, please read the information and ask your professor how to proceed.

TRAINING TUTORIAL AND PROCEDURES

The tutorial will work with the sole proprietorship, Student's Name Fitness Solutions, which has a gym with memberships, personal training, exercise classes, and a small boutique with fitness clothing, accessories, and equipment. You should use the company file **Fitness**. Once you open your copy of the company file, transactions will be recorded for the fictitious company. To maximize training benefits, you should follow the procedures listed in earlier chapters.

You have four employees Mark Argento, who provides the management and supervision of the gym; Stan Mendelson, who is a personal trainer; Leslie Shephard, who manages the boutique shop and is the bookkeeper; and Laura Waters, who is the Pilates instructor.

Mark Argento and Leslie Shephard are salaried employees. Stan Mendelson and Laura Waters are paid on an hourly basis, and any hours in excess of 160 for the pay period will be paid as overtime. Paychecks for all employees are issued on a monthly basis.

DATES, REPORT PREFERENCES, AND PRINTING

Throughout the text, the year used for the screen shots is 2013, which is the same year as the version of the program. You may want to check with your instructor to see if you should use 2013 as the year for the transactions. As in earlier chapters, verify the printing assignment with your instructor. The text will continue to include all printable items on the transmittal. Turn off the Date Prepared, Time Prepared, and Report Basis in the Header/Footer.

ADD YOUR NAME TO THE COMPANY NAME

As with previous companies, each student in the course will be working with the same company and printing the same documents. Personalizing the company name to include your name will help identify many of the documents you print during your training.

 Add your first and last name to the Company Name and Legal Name as previously instructed

CHANGE THE NAME OF THE CAPITAL ACCOUNTS

Since the owner's equity accounts have the words Student's Name as part of the account name, replace *Student's Name* with your actual name.

 Change the owner equity account names as previously instructed. Change the following:

- Remember to use your real name.
  Student's Name, Capital to **First and Last Name, Capital**
  Student's Name, Investment to **First and Last Name, Investment**
  Student's Name, Withdrawals to **First and Last Name, Withdrawal**

SELECT A PAYROLL OPTION

Before entering any payroll transactions, QuickBooks must be informed of the type of payroll service you are selecting. Once QuickBooks knows what type of payroll process has been selected for the company, you will be able to create paychecks. In order to create paychecks manually, you must go through the Help menu to designate this choice.

 Select a **Manual** payroll option

Press **F1** to access Help
Type **Manual Payroll**; click the Search button
Search preferences should be Help
- If Help is not marked with a check, click to mark

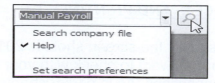

On the Have a Question? screen, which shows the Results in Help, click **Process payroll manually (without a subscription to QuickBooks Payroll)**

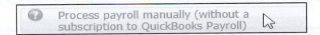

In the Help Article for **"Process payroll manually,"** click the words **manual payroll calculations**

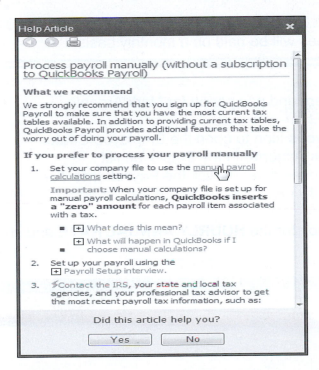

In the article **"Are you sure you want to set your company file to use manual calculations"**, read the article and then click **Set my company file to use manual calculations**

The manual calculations setting is applied immediately
Once QuickBooks processes the selection, you will get a message

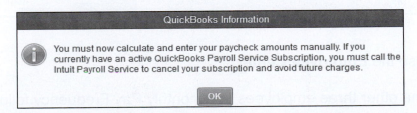

Click **OK**, and close **Help**

CHANGE EMPLOYEE INFORMATION

Whenever a change occurs for an employee, it may be entered at any time.

MEMO

DATE: January 30, 2013

Effective today, Mark Argento will receive a pay raise to $30,000 annually. In addition, all employees will be paid on a monthly basis.

 Change the salary and pay period for Mark Argento

Click the **Employees** icon to open the Employee Center
Double-click **Mark Argento** in the Employee list
On the Edit Employee screen, click the **Payroll Info Tab**
On the **Payroll Info** tab, click the drop-down list arrow for PAY FREQUENCY, click **Monthly**
Click in the text box for the **HOURLY/ANNUAL RATE** and change the amount to **30,000**

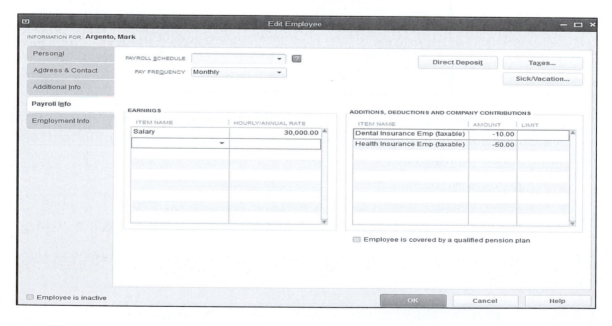

Click **OK**
Do <u>not</u> close the **Employee Center**

 Change the other three employees to a monthly Pay Frequency following the steps listed above

ADD A NEW EMPLOYEE

As new employees are hired, they should be added.

MEMO

DATE: January 30, 2013

Effective 01/30/13 hired a part-time employee to teach yoga classes. Ms. Lindsey King, SS. No. 100-55-6936, Female, Birth date 02/14/80, 2379 Bayshore Drive, Venice, CA 90405, 310-555-6611. Paid an hourly rate of $15.00 and an overtime rate of $22.50. Pay frequency is monthly. Federal and state withholding: Single, 0 Allowances. No local taxes, dental insurance, medical insurance, sick time, or vacation time.

 Add the new employee, Lindsey King

Click the **New Employee** button at the top of the Employee Center
On the **Personal** tab, click in the text box for **LEGAL NAME**, enter **Ms.**
Using the information provided in the memo, tab to or click in each field and enter
    the information for the **Personal** tab

Click the **Address & Contact** tab; enter the information provided in the memo

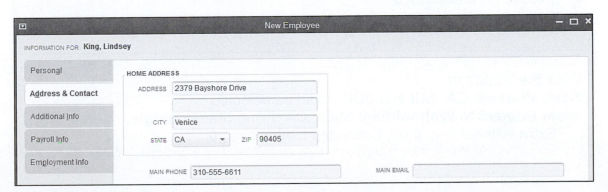

Click the **Payroll Info** tab

Select a **Monthly** pay frequency

Click in the **ITEM NAME** column under **EARNINGS**, click the drop-down list arrow that appears, and click **Hourly Rate**

Tab to or click in the text box for **HOURLY/ANNUAL RATE**, enter the **15.00** hourly rate she will be paid

Click in the **ITEM NAME** column under **Hourly Rate**, click the drop-down list arrow that appears, click **Overtime Rate**

- QuickBooks enters the rate of 22.50.

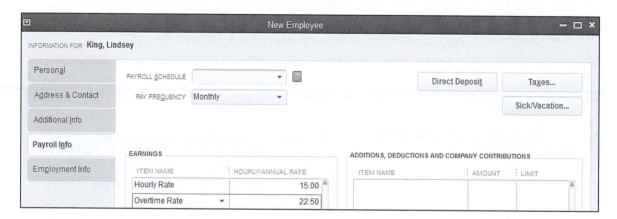

Click the **Taxes** button and complete the tax information:

Federal should show Filing Status: **Single,** Allowances: **0,** Extra Withholding: **0.00**

Subject to **Medicare, Social Security,** and **Federal Unemployment Tax (Company Paid)** should have a check mark

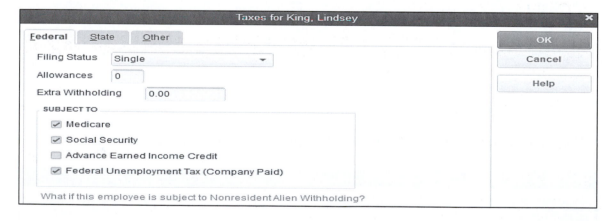

Click the **State** tab:

State Worked: **CA**, **SUI** and **SDI** should be selected

State Subject to Withholding: State: **CA**, Filing Status: **Single**, Allowances: **0**, Extra Withholding: **0.00**; Estimated Deductions: **0**

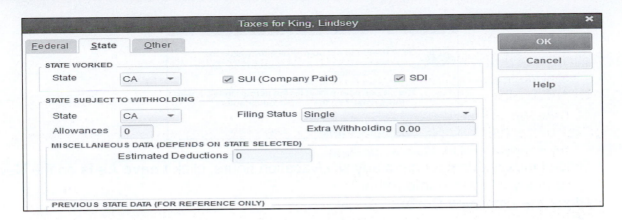

Click the **Other** tab

CA – Employment Training Tax should be showing

- If not, click the drop-down list arrow for **ITEM NAME**, and click **CA-Employment Training Tax**

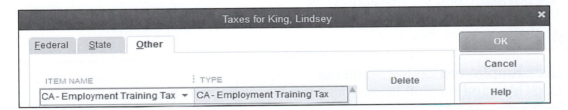

Click **OK** to complete the tax information

Click **Employment Info**

The **HIRE DATE** is **01/30/13** and in the **EMPLOYMENT DETAILS** section the **EMPLOYMENT TYPE** is **Regular**

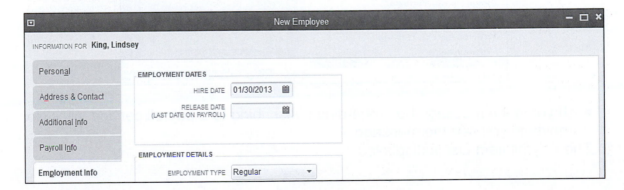

Click **OK** to complete the addition of the new employee

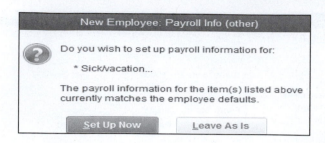

Since Lindsey does not have any sick/vacation hours, click **Leave As Is** on the New
Employee: Payroll Info (other)
Close the Employee Center

VIEW THE PAYROLL ITEM LIST

The Payroll Item list contains a listing of all payroll items, and information regarding the
item type, amount of deduction, annual limit for deductions (if applicable), tax tracking,
vendor for payment, and the account ID.

 View the Payroll Item List

Click **Employees** on the Menu bar
Click **Manage Payroll Items**, click **View/Edit Payroll Item List**

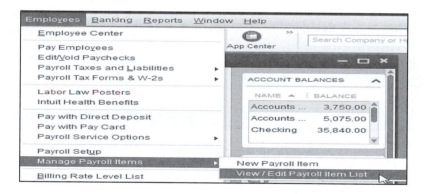

- If you get a message box regarding subscribing to a payroll service, click No
  anytime you see the message.
The Payroll Item List is displayed.

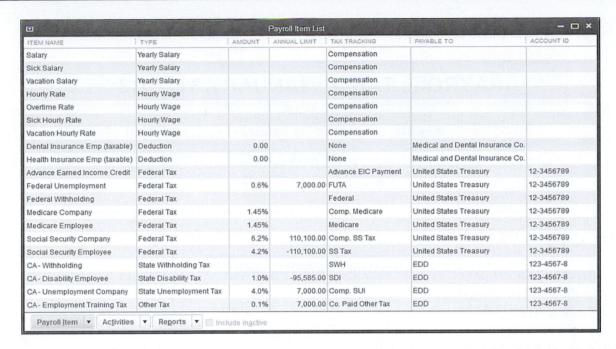

View the Payroll Item List to see the ITEM NAME, TYPE, AMOUNT, ANNUAL
    LIMIT, TAX TRACKING, PAYABLE TO, and ACCOUNT ID

- Remember, Annual Limits and Amounts are subject to change so this chart may
  not match the one you see at a later date
- As you learned when printing reports, you may resize the columns by pointing to
  the line between columns, holding down the primary mouse button, and dragging
  to resize the column.

Close the list without printing

CREATE PAYCHECKS

Once the manual payroll option has been selected, paychecks may be created. You may
enter hours and preview the checks before creating them, or, if using a payroll service, you
may create the checks without previewing. Once the payroll has been processed, checks
may be printed.

Since you chose to process the payroll manually, the payroll data for withholdings and
deductions must be entered manually. QuickBooks will enter other payroll items such as
medical and dental insurance deductions, and it will calculate the total amount of the
checks.

MEMO

DATE: January 31, 2013

Create and print paychecks for January 31, 2013. Use the above date as the pay
period ending date and the check date.

Pay all employees using the hours and deductions listed in the following table.

PAYROLL TABLE: JANUARY 31, 2013					
	Mark Argento	**Lindsey King**	**Stan Mendelson**	**Leslie Shephard**	**Laura Waters**
HOURS					
REGULAR	160	8	72	140	160
OVERTIME					8
SICK			8		
VACATION				20	
DEDUCTIONS OTHER PAYROLL ITEMS: EMPLOYEE					
DENTAL INS.	10.00			10.00	
MEDICAL INS.	50.00			50.00	
DEDUCTIONS: COMPANY					
CA-EMPLOYMENT TRAINING TAX	2.50	0.00	2.00	1.67	2.58
SOCIAL SECURITY	155.00	7.44	124.00	103.33	159.96
MEDICARE	36.25	1.74	29.00	24.17	37.41
FEDERAL UNEMPLOYMENT	15.00	0.00	12.00	10.00	15.48
CA-UNEMPLOYMENT	100.00	4.80	80.00	66.67	103.20
DEDUCTIONS: EMPLOYEE					
FEDERAL WITHHOLDING	312.00	0.00	132.50	124.60	276.34
SOCIAL SECURITY	155.00	7.44	124.00	103.33	159.96
MEDICARE	36.25	1.74	29.00	24.17	37.41
CA-WITHHOLDING	75.00	0.00	30.31	34.06	42.48
CA-DISABILITY	25.00	1.20	20.00	16.67	25.80

 Create checks for the above employees

Click **Pay Employees** icon in the **Employees** section of the **Home Page**
The **Enter Payroll Information** screen appears
Enter the **PAY PERIOD ENDS** date of **01/31/13**
Enter the **CHECK DATE** of **01/31/13**
The **BANK ACCOUNT** is **Checking** with a **BANK ACCOUNT BALANCE** of
    35,840.00
Click the **Check All** button to select all of the employees

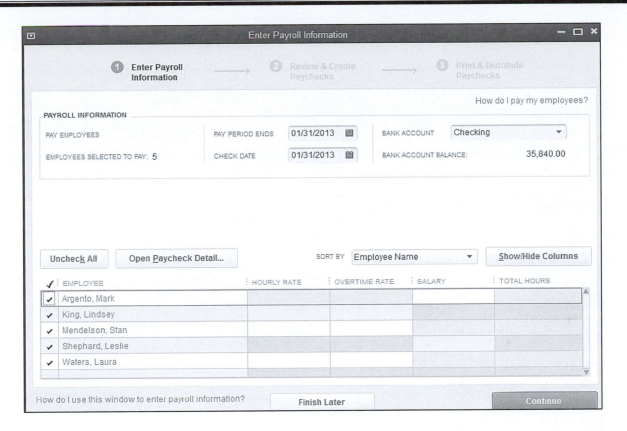

- Notice the check mark in front of each employee name.

Click the **Continue** button

On the **Review and Create Paychecks** screen, make sure that **Print Paychecks from QuickBooks** is selected

- Notice the amounts given for each employee. There is nothing listed for taxes, employer taxes, contributions, or total hours. This information needs to be entered because we are doing payroll manually.
- Remember, if you do subscribe to a QuickBooks payroll service, you will not enter the taxes manually. QuickBooks will calculate them and enter them for you. Since tax tables change frequently, the taxes calculated by QuickBooks may not be the same as the amounts listed on the Payroll Table in the text.
- As you record the information for each employee, refer to the payroll chart listed earlier in the chapter.

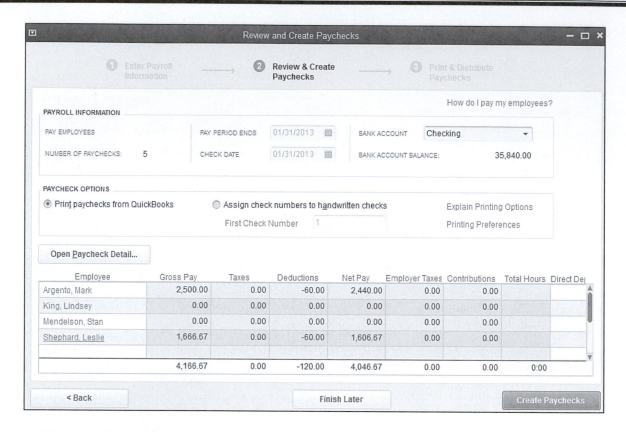

Click the **Open Paycheck Detail...** button on the Review and Create Paychecks screen

The **Preview Paycheck** screen for Mark Argento appears.

- Notice that QuickBooks calculated the monthly salary based on the annual salary.

Tab to or click in the **HOURS** column, enter **160**

The section for Other Payroll Items is automatically completed by QuickBooks

- Because these deductions were set up previously for Mark, the amounts deducted for Dental and Health Insurance paid by the employee shows.

Complete the **Company Summary (adjusted)** information:

Click in the **AMOUNT** column for **CA-Employment Training Tax,** enter **2.50**

Tab to or click in the **AMOUNT** column for **Social Security Company**, enter **155.00**

Tab to or click in the **Medicare Company** line, enter **36.25**

Tab to or click in the **Federal Unemployment** line, enter **15.00**

Tab to or click in the **CA-Unemployment Company** line, enter **100.00**

Complete the **Employee Summary (adjusted)** information:

- QuickBooks will automatically insert the – in front of the amount.

Click in the **AMOUNT** column for **Federal Withholding**, enter **312.00**

Tab to or click in the **Social Security Employee** line, enter **155.00**

Tab to or click in the **Medicare Employee** line, enter **36.25**

Tab to or click in the **CA-Withholding** line, enter **75.00**

Tab to or click in the **CA-Disability Employee** line, enter **25.00**, press **Tab**

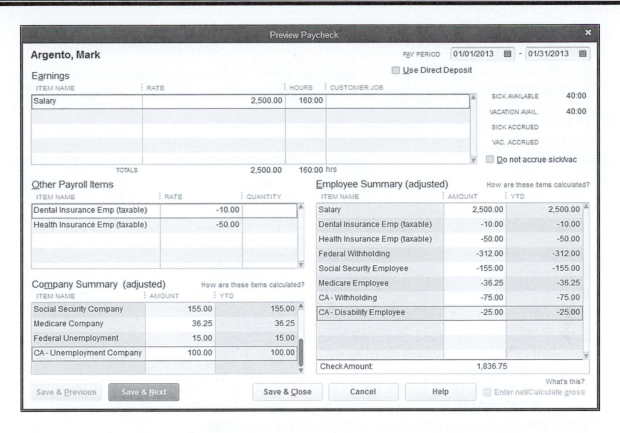

- In the Company Summary for all of the paychecks, the line for CD – Employment Training Tax is not shown in the screen shot.

After verifying that everything was entered correctly, click **Save & Next**

The next Preview Paycheck screen should be for **Lindsey King**

Tab to or click the **Hours** column next to **Hourly Rate** for **Lindsey King**, enter **8**

Refer to the Payroll Table for January 31, 2013, and enter the information

- You may need to use the scroll bar in the Company Summary section in order to complete the information for CA – Employment Training Tax.

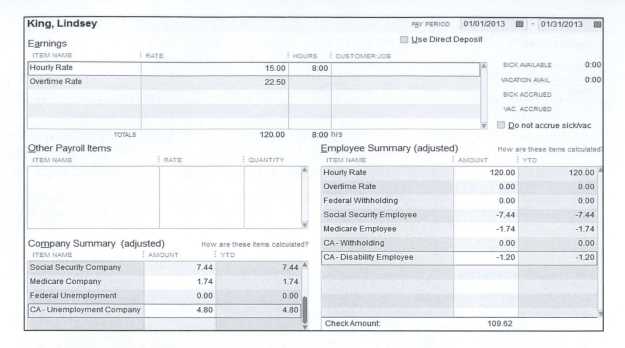

Click **Save & Next**

Pay **Stan Mendelson** for **72** hours of **Hourly Regular Rate**

In the **ITEM NAME** column for **Earnings**, click the line below Overtime Rate

Click the drop-down list arrow, click **Sick Hourly Rate**

Enter **8** for the number of hours Stan was out sick

Enter the company and employee deductions from the Payroll Table for January 31, 2013

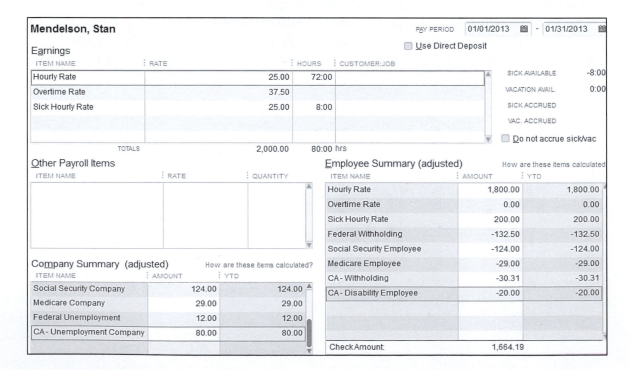

Click **Save & Next**

Pay **Leslie Shephard** for **140** hours of **Salary**

- Notice that the number of Vacation Hours listed in **Vacation Avail.** is **20.00**.

In the **ITEM NAME** column under **Earnings**, click on the blank line beneath Salary

Click the drop-down list arrow that appears, click **Vacation Salary**, tab to or click the **Hours** column, enter **20**, press **Tab**

- The Vacation Avail. will show 0.00 and the Rates for Salary and Vacation Salary will change to reflect the amount paid for vacation.

Complete the paycheck information using the Payroll Table for January 31, 2013

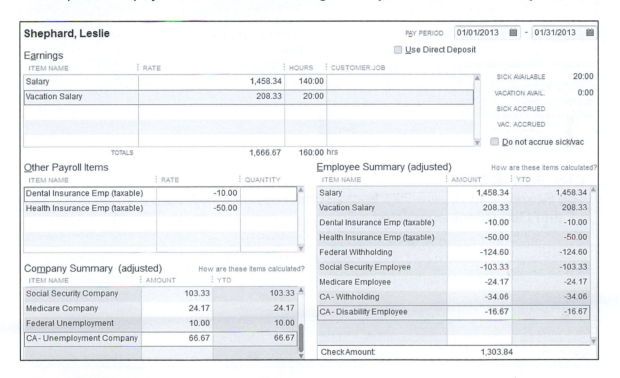

Click **Save & Next**

Process the paycheck for **Laura Waters**

Record **160** for her Hourly Rate Hours

Record **8** as her Overtime Rate Hours

Enter the remaining payroll information as previously instructed

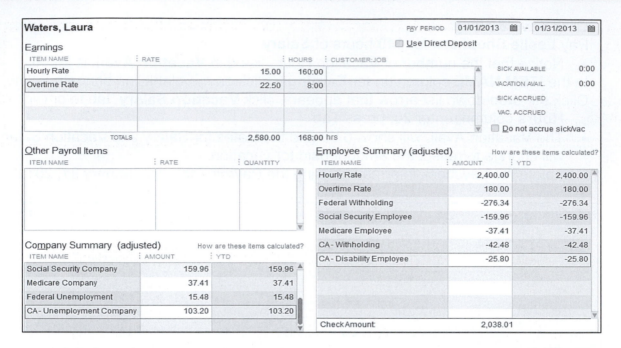

Click **Save & Close**

The Review and Create Paychecks screen appears with the information for Taxes and Deductions completed

Employee	Gross Pay	Taxes	Deductions	Net Pay	Employer Taxes	Contributions	Total Hours	Direct De
Argento, Mark	2,500.00	-603.25	-60.00	1,836.75	308.75	0.00	160:00	
King, Lindsey	120.00	-10.38	0.00	109.62	13.98	0.00	8:00	
Mendelson, Stan	2,000.00	-335.81	0.00	1,664.19	247.00	0.00	80:00	
Shephard, Leslie	1,666.67	-302.83	-60.00	1,303.84	205.84	0.00	160:00	
	8,866.67	-1,794.26	-120.00	6,952.41	1,094.20	0.00	576:00	

< Back		Finish Later		Create Paychecks

Click **Create Paychecks**

PRINT PAYCHECKS

Paychecks may be printed one at a time or all at once. You may use the same printer setup as your other checks in QuickBooks or you may print using a different printer setup. If you use a voucher check, the pay stub is printed as part of the check. If you do not use a voucher check, you may print the pay stub separately. The pay stub information includes the employee's name, address, Social Security number, the pay period start and end dates, pay rate, the hours, the amount of pay, all deductions, sick and vacation time used and available, net pay, and year-to-date amounts.

MEMO
DATE: January 31, 2013

Print the paychecks for all employees using a voucher-style check with 2 parts. Print the company name on the checks.

 Print the January 31 paychecks

The **Confirmation and Next Steps** screen shows on the screen

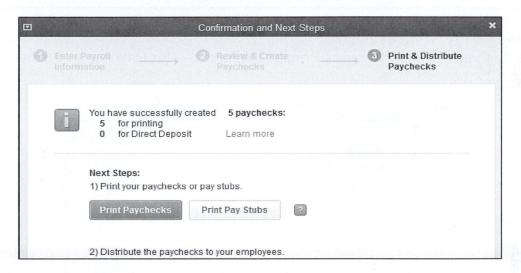

Click the **Print Paychecks** button
On the Select Paychecks to Print screen:
> **Bank Account** should be **Checking**; if it is not, click the drop-down list for Bank Account, and click **Checking**
> **First Check Number** is **1**; if it is not, change it to 1
> All the employees should have a check mark in the √ column, if not click the **Select All** button,

- Notice that there are 5 Paychecks to be printed for a total of $6,952.41.
- QuickBooks can process payroll for direct deposit or printed paychecks. Even though we are not processing direct deposit paychecks, leave **Show** as **Both**.

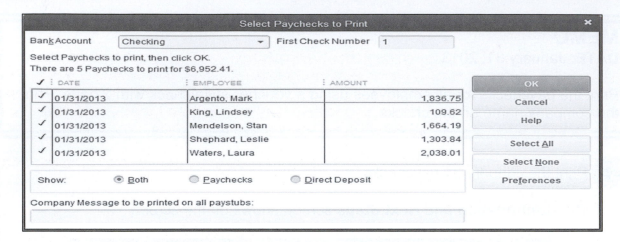

Click the **Preferences** button

Verify that all items for Payroll Printing Preferences for Paycheck Vouchers and Pay stubs have been selected

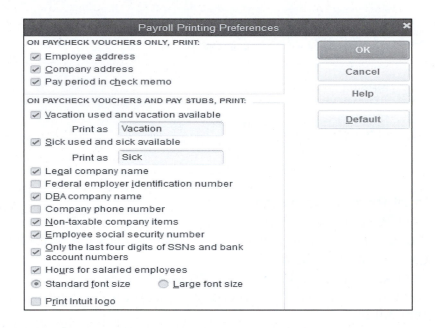

Click **OK**

Click **OK** on the Select Paychecks to Print screen

- Printer Name and Printer Type will be the same as in the earlier chapters.

Click **Voucher Checks** to select as the check style

- If necessary, click **Print company name and address** to select. There should not be a check mark in Use logo. **Number of copies** should be **1**.

Click **Print**

- *Note*: The pay stub information may be printed on the check two times. This is acceptable.

If the checks print correctly, click **OK** on the **Print Checks Confirmation** screen, and then click **Close** on the **Confirmation and Next Steps** screen

PREVIEW PAYCHECK DETAIL, EDIT AN EMPLOYEE, AND REPRINT PAYCHECK

As in earlier chapters, checks may be viewed individually and printed one at a time. A paycheck differs from a regular check. Rather than list accounts and amounts, it provides a Payroll Summary and an option to view Paycheck Detail at the bottom of the screen. When you are viewing the paycheck detail, corrections may be made and will be calculated for the check by unlocking net pay and entering the appropriate corrections.

MEMO

DATE: January 31, 2013

After reviewing the printed checks, you notice that Stan Mendelson shows -8.00 for Available Sick time. He should have had 20 hours available. Go to his paycheck and view his Paycheck Detail. Open the Employee Center and change his employee information to show 12.00 hours of Available Sick Time. He should also have 20 hours of vacation time available as of January 31, 2013. Change this to 20 hours. Return to his Paycheck Detail, Unlock the Net Pay, and re-enter the correct amounts of Sick and Vacation Hours Available. Reprint his check.

 View the paycheck detail for Stan Mendelson

> Click the **Write Checks** icon to open the **Paycheck – Checking** window
> Click **Previous** (Back Arrow icon) until you get to the check for Stan Mendelson
> Click the **Paycheck Detail** button
> Notice the **Sick Available** is **-8:00** and the **Vacation Avail.** is **0:00**
> Close the **Paycheck Detail** but leave Stan's check showing on the screen
> Click the **Employees** icon to open the **Employee Center**
> Double-click **Stan Mendelson** to **Edit Employee**
> Click the **Payroll Info** tab
> Click the **Sick/Vacation** button
> Enter **12:00** for the Sick Hours available as of **01/31/13**
> - Since Stan should have had 20 hours available, you would subtract the 8 hours of sick time he used. This leaves 12 hours available.
> If necessary, enter the date of **12/31/12** for **Begin accruing sick time on**
> Enter **20:00** for the Vacation Hours available as of **01/31/13**
> If necessary, enter the date of **12/31/12** for **Begin accruing vacation time on**

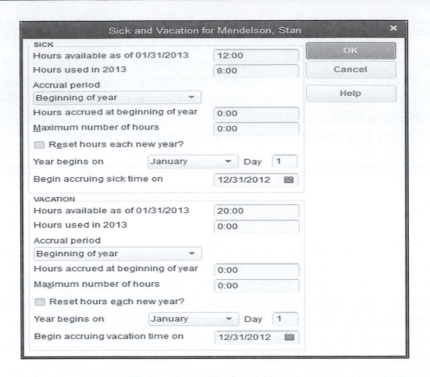

Click **OK** for Sick/Vacation, and click **OK** on the Edit Employee Screen
- If you get a Save message box, click **Yes**

Close the **Employee Center** and return to Stan Mendelson's check
- The change in sick and vacation hours entered in the Employee Center will be effective for automatic calculation on the next paycheck but will not be updated on the paycheck prepared January 31, 2013.

On the check for **Stan Mendelson** for **01/31/13**, click the **Paycheck Detail**
- Notice that the Sick Available shows 12:00 and Vacation Avail. shows 20:00.
- Even though the correct hours appear, the check will need to be unlocked and the information changed before the corrected hours will appear on the paycheck voucher stub.

Click **Unlock Net Pay** at the bottom of the Review Paycheck screen

You will get a **Special Paycheck Situation** screen to allow the paycheck to be changed

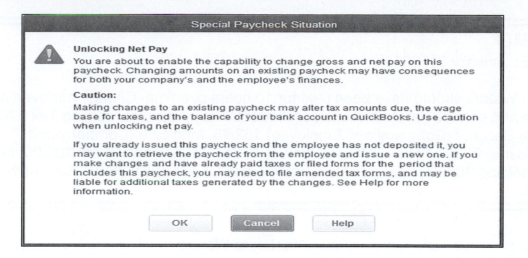

Click **OK**

Even though the correct hours show, delete the hours and re-enter them: Sick
Available is **12:00** and Vacation Avail. is **20:00**

Click **OK**

- Even though the amount of the check is not changed by this adjustment, the
  check should be reprinted so the correct sick leave information is shown.

To reprint Check **3**, click **Print**

- Click **Yes** on the Recording Transaction dialog box to record the changes.

If 3 is not shown as the check number, enter **3** as the Printed Check Number, and
click **OK**

Verify the information on the Print Checks screen including the selection of Voucher
checks, click **Print**

When the check has printed successfully, click **OK** on the **Print Checks
Confirmation** screen

Do <u>not</u> close the Paycheck – Checking window

MAKE CORRECTIONS TO PAYCHECK DETAIL AND REPRINT A PAYCHECK

When you need to make changes to Paycheck Detail that effect the amount of pay, you
may do so by unlocking the Net Pay, entering the required changes, and reprinting the
check.

MEMO

DATE: January 31, 2013

Laura Waters should have been paid for 10 hours overtime. Change her overtime hours and change her deductions as follows: CA-Employment Training Tax 2.63, Social Security (Company and Employee) 162.75, Medicare (Company and Employee) 38.06, Federal Unemployment 15.75, CA-Unemployment 105.00, Federal Withholding 330.65, CA Withholding 45.45, and CA Disability 26.25. Reprint the check

---

 Correct and reprint the paycheck for Laura Waters

Click **Next** (Forward Arrow icon) until you get to **Laura Waters'** paycheck
Click **Paycheck Detail**
- Since paychecks are not distributed to the employees until after they have been reviewed, it is acceptable to change this paycheck rather than voiding and reissuing a new one.

Change the Overtime Rate Hours to **10**
Press the **Tab** key
You may get a message regarding Net Pay Locked

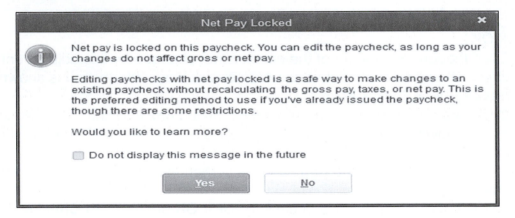

Click **No**
At the bottom of the paycheck, click **Unlock Net Pay**
Click **OK** on the **Special Paycheck Situation** screen
Enter the changes to the tax amounts as indicated in the Memo

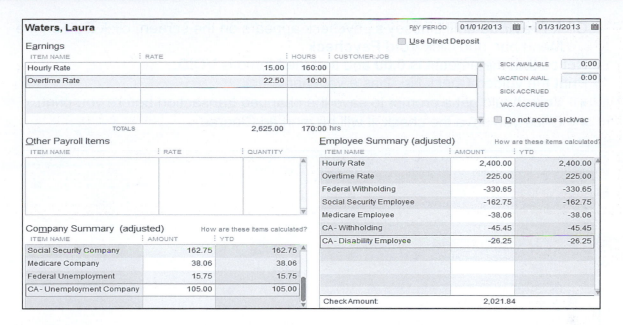

Waters, Laura				PAY PERIOD 01/01/2013 🗓 - 01/31/2013 🗓		
Earnings				☐ Use Direct Deposit		
ITEM NAME	RATE	HOURS	CUSTOMER:JOB			
Hourly Rate	15.00	160:00		SICK AVAILABLE		0:00
Overtime Rate	22.50	10:00		VACATION AVAIL.		0:00
				SICK ACCRUED		
				VAC. ACCRUED		
TOTALS	2,625.00	170:00 hrs		☐ Do not accrue sick/vac		

Other Payroll Items				**Employee Summary (adjusted)**		How are these items calculated?
ITEM NAME	RATE	QUANTITY		ITEM NAME	AMOUNT	YTD
				Hourly Rate	2,400.00	2,400.00
				Overtime Rate	225.00	225.00
				Federal Withholding	-330.65	-330.65
				Social Security Employee	-162.75	-162.75
				Medicare Employee	-38.06	-38.06
Company Summary (adjusted)		How are these items calculated?		CA- Withholding	-45.45	-45.45
ITEM NAME	AMOUNT	YTD		CA- Disability Employee	-26.25	-26.25
Social Security Company	162.75	162.75				
Medicare Company	38.06	38.06				
Federal Unemployment	15.75	15.75				
CA- Unemployment Company	105.00	105.00		Check Amount:	2,021.84	

Click **OK**

- If you return to the Paycheck Detail, you will find that Lock Net Pay is once again selected.

Reprint Check 5

Save the changes to the paycheck

Do <u>not</u> close the Paycheck-Checking window

VOIDING AND DELETING CHECKS

As with regular checks, paychecks may be voided or deleted. A voided check still remains as a check, but it has an amount of 0.00 and a Memo that says VOID. If a check is deleted, it is completely removed from the company records. The only way to have a record of the deleted check is in the Voided/Deleted Transactions reports and the audit trail, which keeps a behind the scenes record of every entry in QuickBooks. If you have prenumbered checks and the original check is misprinted, lost, or stolen, you should void the check. If an employee's check is lost or stolen and needs to be replaced and you are not using prenumbered checks, it may be deleted and reissued. For security reasons, it is better to void a check than to delete it.

MEMO

DATE: January 31, 2013

The checks have been distributed and Lindsey King spilled coffee on her paycheck for the January 31 pay period. Void the check, issue and print a new one.

 Void Lindsey's January 31 paycheck and issue a new one

Click **Previous** until Lindsey's paycheck appears on the screen, click **Edit** on the Menu bar, and click **Void Paycheck**

Notice that the amount is **0.00** and that the Memo is **VOID:**.

Print the voided Check No. **2** as a voucher check

* You should get a prompt to save the changed transaction before you print.
* Once you save the check, it will be marked Cleared.

Click **Save & Close** on **Paycheck-Checking** screen

To issue Lindsey's replacement check, click **Pay Employees** in the Employees section of the Home Page

The **Pay Period Ends 01/31/13** and the **Check Date** is **01/31/13**

The Bank Account is **Checking**

Click in the check column for **Lindsey King** to select her

Click **Continue**

Click the **Open Paycheck Detail** button

Pay Period is **01/01/13 - 01/31/13**

Lindsey worked **8** hours at the **Hourly Regular Rate**

Enter the deductions listed on the Payroll Table for January 31, 2013

Click **Save & Close**

Click the **Create Paychecks** button

Click **Print Paychecks**

Print the replacement check as Check No. **6**

Click **OK** on the **Confirmation and Next Steps** screen

Print the Voucher-style check

After the check has been printed successfully, click **OK**

Close the Paycheck – Checking window

MISSING CHECK REPORT

Since the same account is used for paychecks and regular checks, the Missing Check report will provide data regarding all the checks issued by Your Name Fitness Solutions After entering a number of checks, it is wise to review this report.

 View the Missing Check report

> Click the **Reports** icon to open the Report Center, click **Banking** for the type of report, double-click **Missing Checks**
> Specify the account as **Checking**

			Your Name Fitness Solutions				
			Missing Checks				
			All Transactions				
◇ Type ◇	Date ◇	Num ◇	Name ◇	Memo ◇	Account ◇	Split ◇	Amount ◇
Paycheck	01/31/2013	1	Argento, Mark		Checking	–SPLIT–	–1,836.75 ◄
Paycheck	01/31/2013	2	King, Lindsey	VOID:	Checking	–SPLIT–	0.00
Paycheck	01/31/2013	3	Mendelson, Stan		Checking	–SPLIT–	–1,664.19
Paycheck	01/31/2013	4	Shephard, Leslie		Checking	–SPLIT–	–1,303.84
Paycheck	01/31/2013	5	Waters, Laura		Checking	–SPLIT–	–2,021.84
Paycheck	01/31/2013	6	King, Lindsey		Checking	–SPLIT–	–109.62

> Review the report and close without printing, do not close the Report Center

PAYROLL SUMMARY REPORT

The Payroll Summary Report shows gross pay; the amounts and hours for salary, hourly, overtime, sick, and vacation; adjusted gross pay; taxes withheld; deductions from net pay; net pay; and employer-paid taxes and contributions for each employee individually and for the company.

 Print the Payroll Summary Report for January

> Since the Report Center is on the screen, click **Employees & Payroll**
> Double-click **Payroll Summary**
> Enter the report dates from **01/01/13** to **01/31/13**
> • View the information listed for each employee and for the company.
> Remove the Date Prepared and Time Prepared from the Header
> Print the report in Landscape orientation, and close the report

PREPARE THE EMPLOYEE EARNINGS SUMMARY REPORT

The Employee Earnings Summary Report lists the same information as the Payroll Summary Report above. The information for each employee is categorized by payroll items.

 Prepare the Employee Earnings Summary report

Double-click **Employee Earnings Summary** as the report
Use the dates from **01/01/13** to **01/31/13**
Scroll through the report
- Notice the way in which payroll amounts are grouped by item rather than employee.
Close the report without printing

PAYROLL LIABILITY BALANCES REPORT

Another payroll report is the Payroll Liability Balances Report. This report lists the company's payroll liabilities that are unpaid as of the report date. This report should be prepared prior to paying any payroll taxes.

 Prepare and print the Payroll Liability Balances report

Double-click **Payroll Liability Balances** as the report
The report dates should be **01/01/13** to **01/31/13**

Your Name Fitness Solutions **Payroll Liability Balances** January 2013	
	⬦ BALANCE ⬦
▼ Payroll Liabilities	
Federal Withholding	899.75
Medicare Employee	129.22
Social Security Employee	552.52
Federal Unemployment	52.75
Medicare Company	129.22
Social Security Company	552.52
CA - Withholding	184.82
CA - Disability Employee	89.12
CA - Unemployment Company	356.47
CA - Employment Training Tax	8.80
Dental Insurance Emp (taxable)	20.00
Health Insurance Emp (taxable)	100.00
Total Payroll Liabilities	3,075.19

Remove the Date Prepared and Time Prepared from the Header
Print the report in Portrait orientation; close the report and the Report Center

PAY TAXES AND OTHER LIABILITIES

QuickBooks keeps track of the payroll taxes and other payroll liabilities that you owe. When it is time to make your payments, QuickBooks allows you to choose to pay all liabilities or to select individual liabilities for payment. When the liabilities to be paid have been selected, QuickBooks will consolidate all the amounts for one vendor and prepare one check for that vendor.

MEMO

DATE: January 31, 2013

Based on the information in the Payroll Liabilities Report, pay all the payroll liabilities.

 Pay all the payroll liabilities

Click the **Pay Liabilities** icon in Employees section of the Home Page
Enter the dates of **01/01/13** to **01/31/13** on the **Select Date Range For Liabilities**
    screen

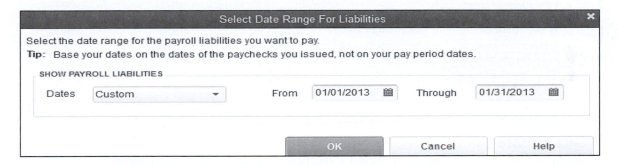

Click **OK**
On the Pay Liabilities screen, select **To be printed** if necessary
Bank Account should be **Checking**; if it is not, select it from the drop-down list.
Check Date is **01/31/13**
Sort by is **Payable To**
Select **Create liability check without reviewing**
Show payroll liabilities from **01/01/13** to **01/31/13**
Click in the check column to place a check mark next to each liability listed; be sure
    to scroll through the list to view and mark each liability

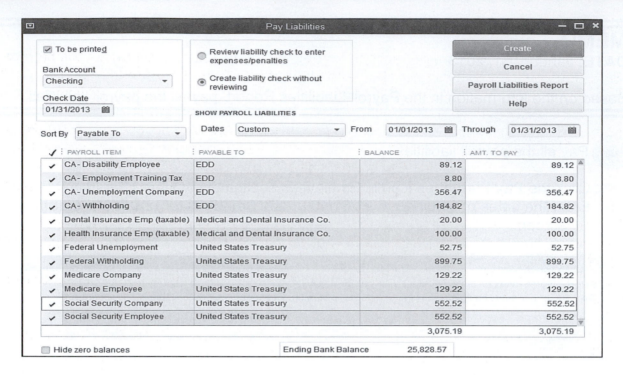

Click **Create**
To print the checks, access **Write Checks** as previously instructed
Click the drop-down list arrow next to **Print** at the top of the window
Click **Batch**, on the **Select Checks to Print** screen
The first check number should be **7**

- The names of the agencies receiving the checks and the check amounts should be listed and marked with a check. If not, click the **Select All** button.

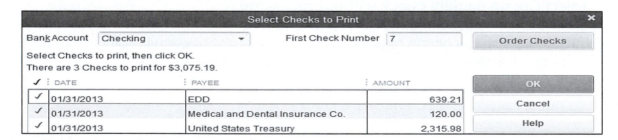

Click **OK**
Change the style of checks to **Standard**, click **Print**
When the checks have printed successfully, click **OK** on the confirmation screen

- Standard style checks print three to a page so all three checks will print on one page.
- If you wish to have each check printed separately, you would go to each check and print individually as previously instructed.

Close the Checks window

PAYROLL TAX FORMS

Depending on the type of payroll service to which you subscribe, QuickBooks will prepare, print, and sometimes submit your tax forms for Quarterly Form 941, Annual Form 944, Annual Form 940, Annual Form 943, Annual W-2/W-3, and State SUI Wage Listing.

Since we do not subscribe to a payroll service, QuickBooks will not allow us to prepare any of these forms. However, at the time of writing, QuickBooks includes several reports that enable you to link payroll data from QuickBooks to Excel workbooks. The workbooks provided contain worksheets designed to summarize payroll data collected and to organize data needed to prepare the state and federal tax forms listed above. Many of the worksheets are preset with an Excel Pivot Table. The worksheets may be used as designed or they may be modified to suit your reporting needs. You may only prepare these Excel reports if you have entered payroll data; i.e., paychecks and withholding, in QuickBooks and have Microsoft Excel 2000 or later installed on your computer with Macros enabled.

To access the various tax forms, click Employees on the menu bar, point to Payroll Tax Forms & W-2s; and then, click Tax Form Worksheets in Excel.

At this point you are taken to Excel where you need to turn on Macros. Once Macros have been enabled, you may select the form being prepared. Data from QuickBooks will be inserted into the Excel spreadsheet and may be used to manually complete the tax forms. We will not use this feature at this time.

PRINT THE JOURNAL

As in the previous chapters, it is always a good idea to print the Journal to see all of the transactions that have been made. If, however, you only want to see the transactions for a particular date or period of time, you can control the amount of data in the report by restricting the dates.

 Print the Journal for January 31 in landscape orientation

Prepare the report as previously instructed
Use the dates from **01/01/13** to **01/31/13**
Expand the report
Remove the Date Prepared and Time Prepared from the Header
Adjust column widths so the information in each column is displayed in full and print

BACK UP

Follow the instructions provided in previous chapters to make a backup file.

SUMMARY

In this chapter, paychecks were generated for employees who worked their standard number of hours, took vacation time, took sick time, and were just hired. Rather than have QuickBooks calculate the amount of payroll deductions, a table was provided and deductions to paychecks were inserted manually. Changes to employee information were made, and a new employee was added. Payroll reports were printed and/or viewed, and payroll liabilities were paid. Exporting payroll data to Excel workbooks was explored.

END-OF-CHAPTER QUESTIONS

TRUE/FALSE

ANSWER THE FOLLOWING QUESTIONS IN THE SPACE PROVIDED BEFORE THE QUESTION NUMBER.

_____ 1. When you process payroll manually, QuickBooks automatically prepares your paychecks and files all of your payroll tax reports.

_____ 2. Once a paycheck has been prepared, you must unlock the paycheck detail before editing it.

_____ 3. Paychecks may be printed only as a batch.

_____ 4. While a payroll check may voided, it may never be deleted.

_____ 5. Once an employee is hired, you may not change the pay period from semi-monthly to monthly.

_____ 6. An employee may be added at any time.

_____ 7. If several taxes are owed to a single agency, QuickBooks generates a separate check to the agency for each tax liability item.

_____ 8. If a salaried employee uses vacation pay, QuickBooks will automatically distribute the correct amount of earnings to Vacation Salary once the number of vacation hours has been entered.

_____ 9. Processing the Payroll Liabilities Balances Report also generates the checks for payment of the liabilities.

_____ 10. All payroll reports must be printed before payroll liabilities may be paid.

MULTIPLE CHOICE

WRITE THE LETTER OF THE CORRECT ANSWER IN THE SPACE PROVIDED BEFORE THE QUESTION NUMBER.

_____ 1. When completing paychecks manually, you ___.
    A. provide the information about hours worked
    B. provide the amounts for deductions
    C. provide the number of sick and/or vacation hours used
    D. all of the above

_____ 2. To change the amount of a deduction entered on an employee's check that has been created, you ___.
A. must void the check and issue a new one
B. adjust the next check to include the change
C. unlock and change the Paycheck Detail for the check and reprint it
D. must delete the check

_____ 3. When paying tax liabilities, you may ___.
A. pay all liabilities at one time
B. select individual tax liabilities and pay them one at a time
C. pay all the tax liabilities owed to a vendor
D. all of the above

_____ 4. A new employee may be added ___.
A. at any time
B. only at the end of the week
C. only at the end of the pay period
D. only when current paychecks have been printed

_____ 5. Pay stub information may be printed ___.
A. as part of a voucher check
B. separate from the paycheck
C. only as an individual employee report
D. both A and B

_____ 6. The Employee Earnings Summary Report lists payroll information for each employee categorized by ___.
A. employee
B. department
C. payroll item
D. date paid

_____ 7. A voided check ___.
A. shows an amount of 0.00
B. has a Memo of VOID
C. remains as part of the company records
D. all of the above

_____ 8. When the payroll liabilities to be paid have been selected, QuickBooks will ___.
A. create a separate check for each liability
B. consolidate the liabilities paid and create one check for each vendor
C. automatically process a Payroll Liability Balances Report
D. prepare any tax return forms necessary

_____ 9. The Journal may be prepared ___.
  A. for any range of dates
  B. for a specific month
  C. for a specific day
  D. all of the above

_____ 10. Changes made to an employee's pay rate will become effective ___.
  A. immediately
  B. at the end of the next payroll period
  C. at the end of the quarter
  D. after a W-2 has been prepared for the employee

FILL-IN

IN THE SPACE PROVIDED, WRITE THE ANSWER THAT MOST APPROPRIATELY COMPLETES THE SENTENCE.

1. In the _____, the individual employee's name, address, and telephone number is displayed in the Employee Information area.

2. The _____ is the report that lists transactions in debit/credit format.

3. The reports that show an employee's gross pay, sick and vacation hours and pay, deductions, taxes, and other details are the _____ and the _____.

4. When the Employee Center is on the screen, the _____ button is used to add a new employee.

5. The report listing the company's unpaid payroll liabilities as of the report date is the _____ Report.

SHORT ESSAY

What is the difference between voiding a paycheck and deleting a paycheck? Why should a business prefer to void paychecks rather than delete them?

_____

_____

_____

_____

_____

_____

NAME _____

TRANSMITTAL

CHAPTER 8: YOUR NAME FITNESS SOLUTIONS

Attach the following documents and reports:

Check No. 1: Mark Argento
Check No. 2: Lindsey King
Check No. 3: Stan Mendelson
Check No. 4: Leslie Shephard
Check No. 5: Laura Waters
Check No. 3: Stan Mendelson After Editing Sick Time
Check No. 5: Laura Waters After Editing Overtime
Check No. 2: Lindsey King Voided Check
Check No. 6: Lindsey King Replacement Check
Payroll Summary, January, 2013
Payroll Liability Balances, January, 2013
Check No. 7: EDD
Check No. 8: Medical and Dental Insurance Co.
Check No. 9: United States Treasury
Journal, January 31, 2013

END-OF-CHAPTER PROBLEM

YOUR NAME POOL & SPA

You will be working with a company called Your Name Pool & Spa. Transactions for employees, payroll, and payroll liabilities will be completed.

INSTRUCTIONS

For Chapter 8 use the company file, **Pool.qbw**. Open the company as previously instructed. If you get a message to update your company file, click Yes. You will select a manual payroll option; record the addition of and changes to employees; create, edit, and void paychecks; pay payroll liabilities; and prepare payroll reports.

RECORD TRANSACTIONS:

January 30, 2013
► Add your first and last name to the company name and the legal name
► Change the owner equity account names to: First and Last Name, Capital; First and Last Name, Drawing; and First and Last Name, Investment
► Turn off the Date Prepared, Time Prepared, and Report Basis in the Header/Footer.
► Select Manual processing for payroll
► Add a new employee, Reece Graham to help with pool supply sales. Social Security No.: 100-55-2145; Gender: Female, Date of Birth: 04/23/1977. Address: 2325 Summerland Road, Summerland, CA 93014, Main Phone: 805-555-9845. Reece is an hourly employee with a Regular Rate of $7.00 per hour and an Overtime Hourly Rate 1 of $10.50. Pay Frequency: Monthly. She is not eligible for medical or dental insurance. She is single, claims no exemptions or allowances, and is subject to Federal Taxes: Medicare, Social Security, and Federal Unemployment Tax (Company Paid), State Taxes for CA: SUI (Company Paid), and SDI; Other Taxes: CA-Employment Training Tax. Reece does not accrue vacation or sick leave. Hire Date: January 30, 2013, Employment Type: Regular.
► Dori Stevens changed her Main Phone number to 805-555-5111. Edit the employee on the employee list and record the change.

January 31, 2013
► Use the following Payroll Table to prepare and print checks for the monthly payroll. The pay period ends **January 31, 2013** and the check date is also **January 31, 2013**: Checking is the appropriate account to use. (Remember, if you get a screen regarding signing up for QuickBooks Payroll service, click **No**.)

PAYROLL TABLE: JANUARY 31, 2013

	Reece Graham	Joe Masterson	Morrie Miller	Dori Stevens
HOURS				
Regular	8	152	160	120
Overtime			20	
Sick		8		
Vacation				40
DEDUCTIONS OTHER PAYROLL ITEMS: EMPLOYEE				
Dental Ins.		25.00	25.00	25.00
Medical Ins.		25.00	25.00	25.00
DEDUCTIONS: COMPANY				
CA-Employment Training Tax	0.00	2.42	1.71	2.60
Social Security	3.47	149.83	106.00	161.20
Medicare	.81	35.04	24.80	37.70
Federal Unemployment	0.00	14.50	10.26	15.60
CA-Unemployment	2.24	96.67	68.40	104.00
DEDUCTIONS: EMPLOYEE				
Federal Withholding	0.00	188.75	145.90	168.75
Social Security	3.47	149.83	106.00	161.20
Medicare	.81	35.04	24.80	37.70
CA-Withholding	0.00	39.48	35.96	43.51
CA-Disability	0.00	24.17	17.10	26.00

► Verify the Payroll Printing Preferences: make sure the Intuit logo is not printed
► Print the company name and address on the voucher checks.
► Checks begin with number 1.
► Change Morrie Miller's check to correct the overtime hours. (Remember to Unlock Net Pay before recording the changes.) He worked 12 hours overtime. Because of the reduction in overtime pay, his deductions change as follows: CA-Employment Training Tax: 1.60; Social Security Company and Employee: 99.32; Medicare Company and Employee: 23.23; Federal Unemployment: 9.61; CA-Unemployment: 64.08; Federal Withholding: 129.70; CA-Withholding: 31.21; and CA-Disability: 16.02. Reprint Check No. 3.

► Reece spilled coffee on her check. Void her Check No. 1 for January 31, print the voided check.
► Reissue Reece's paycheck, and print it using Check No. 5. Remember to use 01/31/13 as the check and pay period ending date. The pay period is 01/01/13 to 01/31/13. Refer to the payroll table for information on hours and deductions.
► Prepare and print the Payroll Summary Report for January 1-31, 2013 in Landscape orientation.
► Prepare and print the Payroll Liability Balances Report for January 1-31, 2013 in Portrait orientation.
► Pay all the taxes and other liabilities for January 1-31, 2013. The Check Date is 01/31/13. Print the checks using a Standard check style with the company name and address.
► Prepare, expand, and print the Journal for January 31, 2013 in Landscape orientation.

NAME _____

TRANSMITTAL

<u>CHAPTER 8: YOUR NAME POOL & SPA</u>

Attach the following documents and reports:

Check No. 1: Reece Graham
Check No. 2: Joe Masterson
Check No. 3: Morrie Miller
Check No. 4: Dori Stevens
Check No. 3: Morrie Miller (Corrected)
Check No. 1: Reece Graham (Voided)
Check No. 5: Reece Graham
Payroll Summary, January, 2013
Payroll Liability Balances, January, 2013
Check No. 6: Dental and Medical Ins.
Check No. 7: Employment Development Department
Check No. 8: United States Treasury
Journal, January, 2013

CREATING A COMPANY IN QUICKBOOKS®

LEARNING OBJECTIVES

At the completion of this chapter, you will be able to:

1. Set up a company using the EasyStep Interview and QuickBooks Setup.
2. Establish a Chart of Accounts for a company.
3. Set up Company Info and start dates.
4. Create lists for receivables, payables, items, customers, vendors, employees, and others.
5. Complete the Payroll setup and create payroll items and employee defaults.
6. Customize reports and company preferences.

COMPUTERIZING A MANUAL SYSTEM

In previous chapters, QuickBooks was used to record transactions for businesses that were already set up for use in the program. In this chapter, you will actually set up a business, create a chart of accounts, create various lists, add names to lists, and delete unnecessary accounts. QuickBooks makes setting up the records for a business user-friendly by going through the process using the EasyStep Interview and QuickBooks Setup. Once the basic accounts, items, lists, and other items are established via the EasyStep Interview, QuickBooks Setup, and Payroll Setup, you will make some refinements to accounts, add detail information regarding customers, vendors, and employees, transfer Uncategorized Income and Expenses to the owner's equity account, and customize report and company preferences.

TRAINING TUTORIAL AND PROCEDURES

The following tutorial is a step-by-step guide to setting up the fictitious company Your Name's Dog Dayz. Company information, accounts, items, lists, and other items must be provided before transactions may be recorded in QuickBooks. The EasyStep Interview and the QuickBooks Setup will be used to set up company information; create Customer, Vendor, Employee, and Items lists; and add bank accounts. Once the basic company information has been entered via the EasyStep Interview and QuickBooks Setup, changes and modifications to the company data will be made. As in earlier chapters, information for the company setup will be provided in memos. Information may also be shown in lists or within the step-by-step instructions provided.

Please note that QuickBooks is updated on a regular basis. If your screens are not always an exact match to the text, check with your instructor to see if you should select something that is similar to the text. For example, QuickBooks has been known to change the type of businesses or industries that it uses in the EasyStep Interview. If that happens, your instructor may suggest that you select the company type closest to Your Name's Dog Dayz. A different company type may result in a different chart of accounts. This would mean adjusting the chart of accounts to match the one given in the text.

QUICKBOOKS UPDATES (READ ONLY)

QuickBooks has an update capability that is on by default when the program is installed. In addition to an automatic update by QuickBooks, you may also update the program manually. Always check with your professor to see if you should work with automatic update on or off. The following screens show you how to turn off/on automatic updates and to update manually. If you update QuickBooks 2013 and use a company file in the updated version, the company will not be able to be used on a computer that has not been updated.

Since updating is set by your professor, simply read the following:

Click **Help** on the Menu bar, click **Update QuickBooks**
Click the **Options** tab
Notice that Automatic Update is marked **Yes.** If you did not want Automatic Update, you
    would click the **No** radial dial.

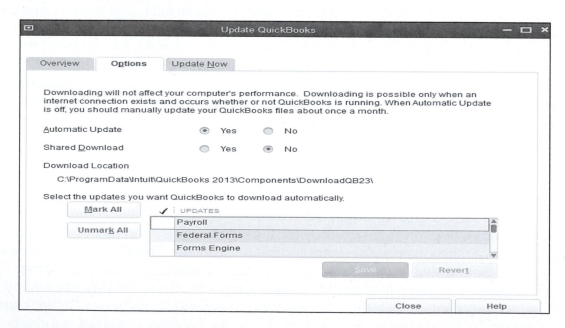

To update manually, click the **Update Now** tab and click **Get Updates**.
Even if your program is set for automatic updates, you may update manually.

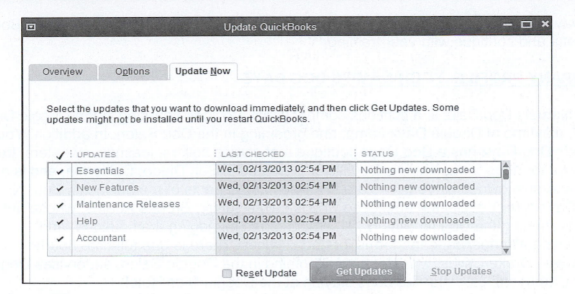

Once QuickBooks has been updated, the date of the computer is shown for LAST CHECKED.

You may also click the **Overview** tab and click the **Update Now** button.

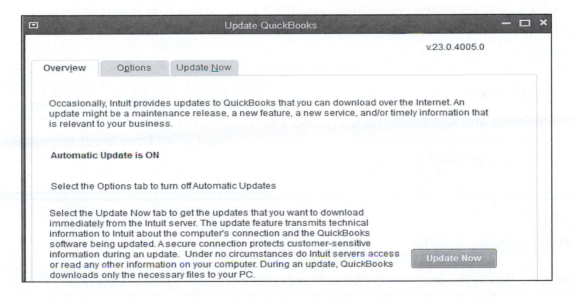

DATES

Throughout the text, the year used for the screen shots is 2013, which is the same year as the version of the program. You may want to check with your instructor to see if you should use 2013 as the year for the transactions. Sometimes, QuickBooks' screens will display in a slightly different manner than the text. This is due to the fact that the date of your computer is not the same as the date of the text. Instructions are given where this occurs. The main criterion is to be consistent with the year you use throughout the chapter. On certain screens, the difference in the computer and text dates will cause a slight variation in the way things are displayed. If you cannot change a date that is provided by QuickBooks, accept it and continue with your training.

COMPANY PROFILE: YOUR NAME'S DOG DAYZ

Your Name's Dog Dayz is a fictitious company that provides boarding in the Doggie Digs Hotel, playtime at Doggie Dayz camp, and grooming in the Dog Salon. In addition, Your Name's Dog Dayz has a Dog Dayz boutique that carries collars, leashes, sweaters, treats, and toys for dogs. Your Name's Dog Dayz is located in San Diego, California, and is a sole proprietorship owned by you. You are involved in all aspects of the business. Your Name's Dog Dayz has one full-time employee who is paid a salary: Brooke Adams, whose duties include running the Doggie Digs Hotel, ordering and managing the boutique, and completing all paperwork and forms for dog services. There is one full-time hourly employee: Drake Childs, who does the grooming in the Doggie Salon, supervises Doggie Dayz Camp, and cares for the dogs staying at the Doggie Digs Hotel.

CREATE A NEW COMPANY

Since Your Name's Dog Dayz is a new company, it does not appear as a company file. You may create a new company by clicking New Company on the File menu or the "Create a new company" button on the No Company Open screen.

There are three ways in which to setup a company. You may create a company using Express Start where you give QuickBooks a company name, the type of industry, type of ownership, tax ID#, legal name, address, telephone, email, and Web site. You may use the Advanced Setup and complete the EasyStep Interview, which provides more detailed company information than Express Start. You may convert a file from another program or an earlier version of QuickBooks.

MEMO
DATE: January 1, 2013

Because this is the beginning of the fiscal year for Your Name's Dog Dayz, it is an appropriate time to set up the company information in QuickBooks. Use the EasyStep Interview in QuickBooks.

 Open QuickBooks as previously instructed

> Insert a USB drive as previously instructed or use the storage location you have been using throughout the text
>
> Click **File** menu, click **New Company** or click the **Create a new Company** icon on the **No Company Open** dialog box
>
> - The "Let's get your business set up quickly!" screen will appear

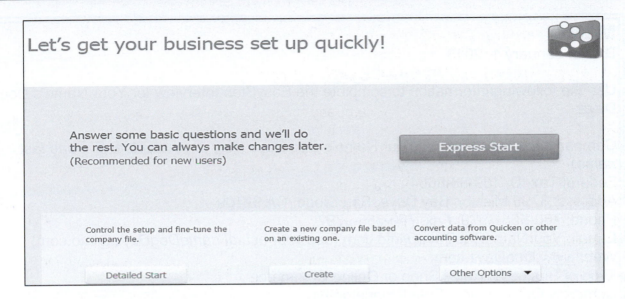

Let's get your business set up quickly!

Answer some basic questions and we'll do
the rest. You can always make changes later.
(Recommended for new users)

Express Start

Control the setup and fine-tune the   Create a new company file based   Convert data from Quicken or other
company file.   on an existing one.   accounting software.

Detailed Start   Create   Other Options ▼

THE EASYSTEP INTERVIEW

The EasyStep Interview is a step-by-step guide to entering your company information as of
a single date called a start date. It also provides tips regarding a chart of accounts,
standard industry practices, and other items for the type of company indicated. During the
Interview, general company information is entered; you may select a preset Chart of
Accounts; indicate preferences such as payroll, inventory, time tracking, and employees;
and select a start date.

Once a screen has been read and any required items have been filled in or questions
answered, the Next button is clicked to tell QuickBooks to advance to the next screen. If
you need to return to a previous screen, click the Back button. If you need to stop the
Interview before completing everything, you may exit by clicking the Leave button in the
bottom-left corner of the screen or by clicking the close button at the top-right corner of the
EasyStep Interview screen

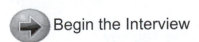 Begin the Interview

   Click **Detailed Start** to begin the EasyStep Interview

COMPLETE THE EASYSTEP INTERVIEW

The EasyStep Interview provides a series of screens with questions that, when answered,
enables QuickBooks to set up the company file, create a Chart of Accounts designed for
your specific type of business or industry, and establish the beginning of a company's fiscal
year and income tax year.

MEMO

DATE: January 1, 2013

Use the following information to complete the EasyStep Interview for Your Name's Dog Dayz:

Company and Legal Name: Your Name's Dog Dayz (*Key in your actual first and last name*)
Federal Tax ID: 159-88-8654
Address: 8795 Mission Bay Drive, San Diego, CA 92109
Phone: 760-555-7979; Fax: 760-555-9797
E-mail: YourNameDogDayz@info.com (use *your actual nameDogDayz*@info.com)
Web: www.DogDayz.com
Type of Business: Retail Shop or Online Commerce
Company Organization: Sole Proprietorship
Fiscal year starts in January
Do not use Passwords
File Name: Your Name's Dog Dayz
File Type: .qbw
Sell Both services and products
Record each sale individually, do charge sales tax
Do not use estimates, statements, progress invoicing, or track time
Do use invoices and track customer orders (sales orders)
Do track bills and inventory
Employees: Yes, W-2 Employees
Date to start tracking finances: 01/01/2013
Use QuickBooks to set up the Income and Expense Accounts. Add Service Sales and remove Merchant Account Fees

 Complete the Company Info screen

Enter the Company Name **Your Name's Dog Dayz**, press the Tab key
- Your Name's Dog Dayz is entered as the Legal name when the Tab key is pressed. To identify your work, type your own name, not the words "Your Name's" as part of the company name. For example, Selma Anderson would have **Selma Anderson's Dog Dayz**.

Tab to or click **Tax ID number**, enter **159-88-8654**
Enter the Company Address information in the spaces provided, tab to or click in the blanks to move from item to item
For the state, California, type **C** and QuickBooks will fill in the rest or click the drop-down list arrow for State and click CA
- The country is automatically filled in as US.

Enter the telephone number, fax number, e-mail address, and Web address as given in the Memo

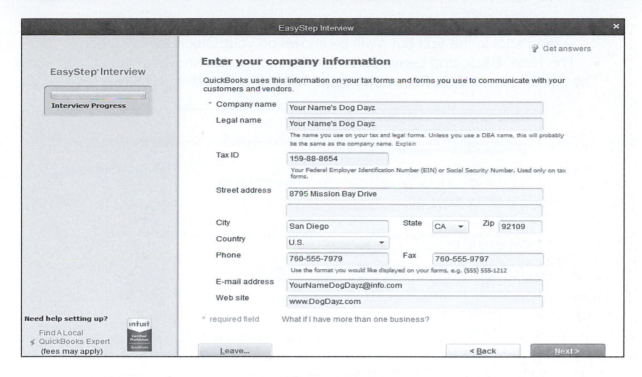

Click **Next**
Scroll through the list of industries
Click **Retail Shop or Online Commerce**, click **Next**

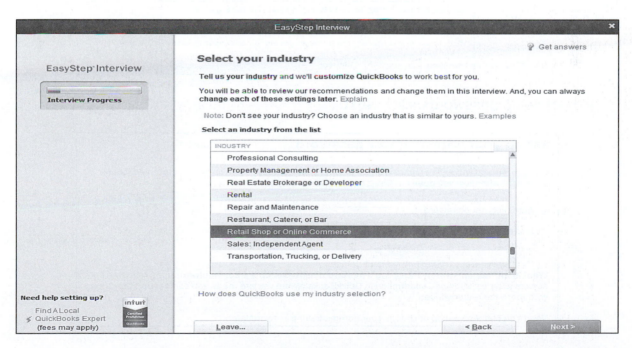

- Notice the Interview Progress in the upper-left side of the EasyStep Interview. This shows how much of the EasyStep Interview has been completed.

- This Interview Progress portion of the screen will no longer be shown in every screen shot in the text but it will be shown on your QuickBooks screen.
- The Next, Back, and Leave buttons will no longer be shown in the screen shots.

The company is a **Sole Proprietorship**, select this, and then click **Next**

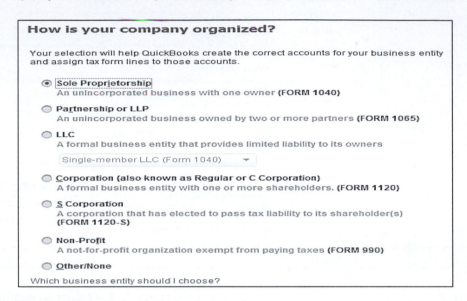

The fiscal year starts in **January**, click **Next**.

Do not setup passwords, click **Next**.

Read the screen to Create your company file, click **Next**

Click the drop-down list for **Save in:** and click the storage location you have been instructed to use (The example provided shows a USB drive in K: as the storage location.)

The File name is **Your Name's Dog Dayz**
Save as type: should show **QuickBooks Files (*.QBW, *.QBA)**

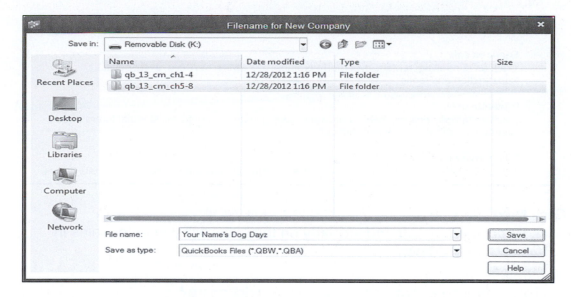

Click **Save**

- Once the company file has been saved, you may click **Leave** to exit the setup. When you reopen the company, QuickBooks will give you a Welcome Back screen. Simply click **OK** and resume the company setup.

Read the screen regarding Customizing QuickBooks for your business

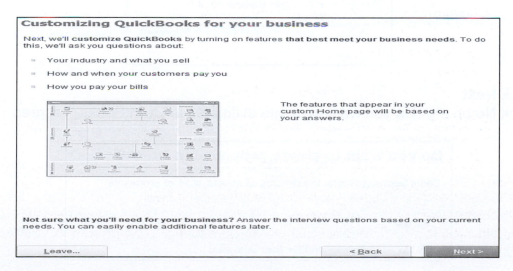

Click **Next**
Click **Both services and products** on the "What do you sell?" screen

What do you sell?

○ **Services only**
   Such as consulting, rentals, gym memberships, hair styling services, event services, construction and labor.

○ **Products only**
   Such as lamps, fertilizer, books, hardware, tickets, insurance policies. Manufacturers and distributors should also select this option.

◉ **Both services and products**
   Such as a bicycle repair shop that sells bikes, a carpet installation company that sells carpet.

Click **Next**
Click **Record each sale individually** on the "How will you enter sales in QuickBooks" screen

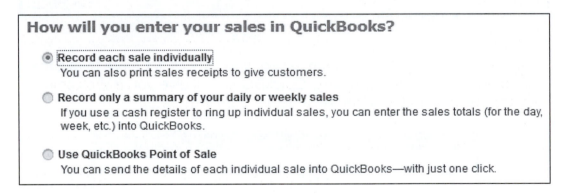

How will you enter your sales in QuickBooks?

◉ **Record each sale individually**
   You can also print sales receipts to give customers.

○ **Record only a summary of your daily or weekly sales**
   If you use a cash register to ring up individual sales, you can enter the sales totals (for the day, week, etc.) into QuickBooks.

○ **Use QuickBooks Point of Sale**
   You can send the details of each individual sale into QuickBooks—with just one click.

Click **Next**
You do plan to charge sales tax, click **Yes** on the "Do you charge sales tax?" screen

Do you charge sales tax?

◉ Yes   (recommended for your business)
○ No

Click **Next**
Click **No** on the "Do you want to create estimates in QuickBooks?" screen

Do you want to create estimates in QuickBooks?

Some businesses refer to estimates as **quotes, bids, or proposals**.

○ Yes
◉ No   (recommended for your business)

Click **Next**

Click **Yes** on the "Tracking customer orders in QuickBooks" screen

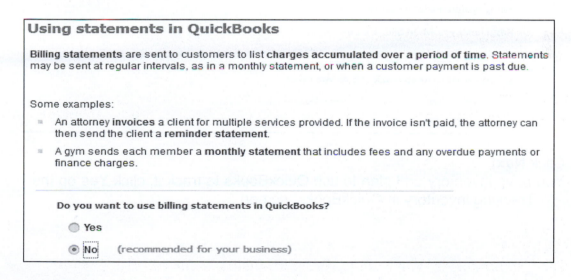

Click **Next**

You do not plan to send statements, click **No** on the "Using statements in QuickBooks" screen

Click **Next**

You do <u>not</u> plan to use progress invoicing, click **No**

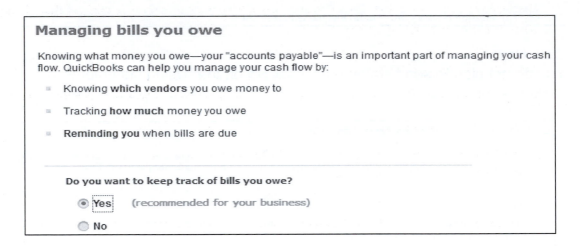

Click Next

You do want to keep track of the bills you owe, click **Yes** on the "Managing bills you owe" screen

Click Next

You have inventory and plan to use QuickBooks to track it, click **Yes** on the "Tracking inventory in QuickBooks" screen

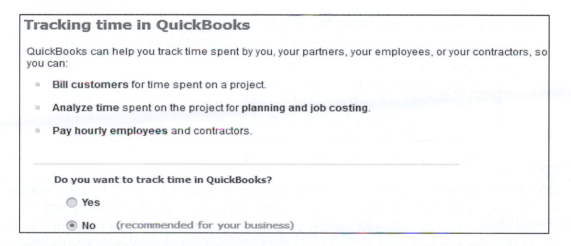

Click **Next**

Tracking time is used to keep track of the time spent on a particular job or with a particular client, which is not done in your company; so click **No** on the "Tracking time in QuickBooks" screen

Tracking time in QuickBooks

QuickBooks can help you track time spent by you, your partners, your employees, or your contractors, so you can:

- **Bill customers** for time spent on a project.
- **Analyze time** spent on the project for **planning and job costing**.
- **Pay hourly employees** and contractors.

Do you want to track time in QuickBooks?

○ Yes

◉ No   (recommended for your business)

Click **Next**

There are two employees who work for Dog Dayz, click **Yes** and click **We have W-2 employees.** On the "Do you have employees?" screen

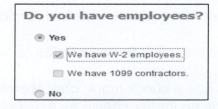

Click **Next**

You want to use QuickBooks to set up the Chart of Accounts

Using accounts in QuickBooks

Next, we'll help you set up your **Chart of Accounts**, which are categories of income, expenses and more that you'll use to track your business.

Why is the chart of accounts important?

To set up your chart of accounts, you'll need to:

- Decide on a date to use as the starting point to track your business finances in QuickBooks (e.g., beginning of fiscal year, first of this month, etc.)

- Understand how you want to categorize your business' income and expenses. (You may want to discuss this with your accountant, if you have one.)

Click **Next**
Click **Use today's date or the first day of the quarter or month.**
Enter the date **01/01/2013**

Select a date to start tracking your finances

The date you select will be your **start date** in QuickBooks.

○ **Beginning of this fiscal year: 01/01/2013**
- In order to complete this year's tax returns, you'll need to enter transactions from the beginning of this fiscal year to today.

◉ **Use today's date or the first day of the quarter or month.**
- You'll need to enter transactions from this date forward.

01/01/2013   🖩

Click **Next**
Scroll through the list of Income and Expense accounts created by QuickBooks
- The accounts recommended by QuickBooks are marked with a check. These accounts may or may not match your chart of accounts. You may make changes at this time to add and delete from this account list or you may customize your chart of accounts later.
- To customize the income and expense section of the chart of accounts now, you add an account by clicking the unmarked account name from the list of accounts shown.
- To remove an account that has been marked, click the account name to deselect it

Service Sales is not checked; click **Service Sales** to add the Income account to the Chart of Accounts
Merchant Account Fees has a check mark, click **Merchant Account Fees** to remove the check mark so it is no longer shown as a selected account

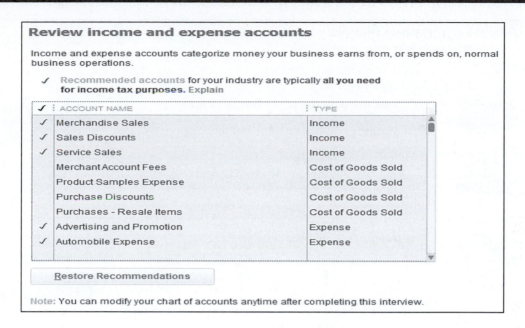

Other changes to the Chart of Accounts will be made later, click **Next**
On the **Congratulations** screen, click **Go to Setup**

USE QUICKBOOKS SETUP

Customers, vendors, employees, and items can be added individually via the appropriate centers as was done throughout the text. However, using QuickBooks Setup allows you to add multiple customers, vendors, employees, sales items, and bank accounts all at the same time. When using QuickBooks Setup, similar information such as names, addresses, and telephone are indicated for everything that is entered. Other more detailed information is added to the individual customer, vendor, or employee by going to the appropriate center and entering it later.

The QuickBooks Setup is divided into three sections. The first section is used to add customers, vendors, and employees. The second section is used to add the products and services you sell. The final section is used to add your bank accounts.

IMPORTANT: Once you begin QuickBooks Setup, you must complete all three sections. If you leave before it is complete, you will need to enter your customers, vendors, employees, items bank accounts and opening balances individually, as you did in the chapters.

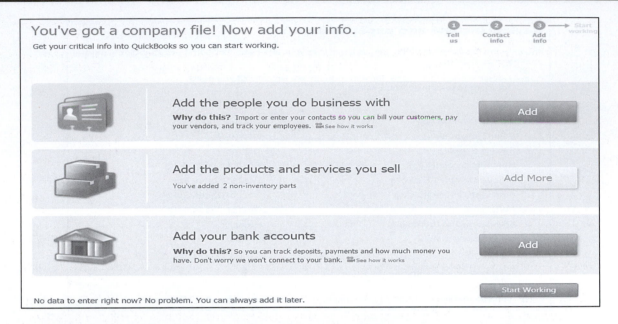

COMPLETE THE FIRST SECTION OF QUICKBOOKS SETUP

Customers, vendors, and employees are the three types of information that may be added in this section. QuickBooks Setup can import your customer, vendor, and employee lists from your address book in Outlook, Yahoo!, and Gmail. Customers, vendors, and employees may be added by pasting from Excel or they may be added manually.

Be extremely careful as you enter the information in this section of the Setup. Clicking an incorrect button may take you out of this step. If you exit or forget to enter something, you may not go back to it. Instead, you will need to enter the information manually after the setup is fully completed.

ADD CUSTOMERS

The Customer List is known as the Accounts Receivable Subsidiary Ledger. Whenever a transaction is entered for a customer, it is automatically posted to the General Ledger account and the Accounts Receivable Subsidiary Ledger.

Use QuickBooks Setup and the following chart to add multiple customers manually

Click the **Add** button on the "Add the people you do business with" section to begin adding customers, vendors, and employees

CUSTOMERS			
Customer Name	Gray, George	Moraga, Ellen	Phillips, Henry	Summer, Carol
Company Name				
First	George	Ellen	Henry	Carol
Last	Gray	Moraga	Phillips	Summer
Phone	760-555-8763	760-555-8015	760-555-1275	760-555-2594
Address	1980 A Street	719 4th Avenue	2190 State Street	2210 Columbia Street
City, State Zip	San Diego, CA 92101	San Diego, CA 92101	San Diego, CA 92101	San Diego, CA 92101

Since we are entering our information manually and are not importing customer information, click **Paste from Excel or enter manually**; and then, click the **Continue** button on the "Add the people you do business with" screen (button not shown)

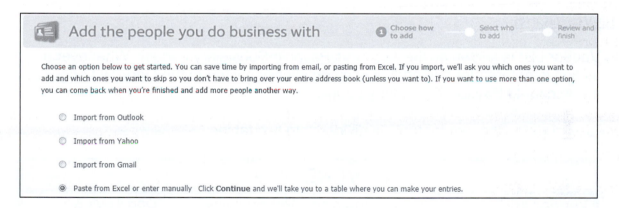

Click the **Customer** radial dial in the first empty row on the **Add people you do business with screen**, Tab to **Name**
Enter **Gray, George**
- Since you want your Customer List to be sorted according to the customer's last name, type the last name first
Tab to **First Name**, enter **George**
Tab to **Last Name**, enter **Gray**
Tab to **Phone**, enter **760-555-8763**

Skip	Customer	Vendor	Employee	Name	Company Name	First Name	Last Name	Email	Phone	Alt Phone	Fax
Select all	Select all	Select all	Select all								
○	◉	○	○	Gray, George		George	Gray		760-555-8763		

Tab to **Address**, enter **1980 A Street**
Tab to **City, State, Zip**, enter **San Diego, CA 92101**

Skip	Customer	Vendor	Employee	Name	Phone	Alt Phone	Fax	Address	City, State, Zip	Contact Name
Select all	Select all	Select all	Select all							
○	◉	○	○	Gray, George	760-555-8763			1980 A Street	San Diego, CA 92101	

In the next row, click **Customer** to identify the next entry
Tab to or click in the **Name** field
Add the remaining customers using the chart provided

Skip	Customer	Vendor	Employee	Name	Company Name	First Name	Last Name	Email	Phone	Alt Phone	Fax	Address	City, State, Zip
Select all	Select all	Select all	Select all										
○	◉	○	○	Gray, George		George	Gray		760-555-8763			1980 A Street	San Diego, CA 92101
○	◉	○	○	Moraga, Ellen		Ellen	Moraga		760-555-8015			719 4th Avenue	San Diego, CA 92101
○	◉	○	○	Phillips, Henry		Henry	Phillips		760-555-1275			2190 State Street	San Diego, CA 92101
○	◉	○	○	Summer, Carol		Carol	Summer		760-555-2594			2210 Columbia Street	San Diego, CA 92101

Before adding vendors, verify that you have selected customers for the four entries
above
Do **NOT** click Continue, you will use the same screen to add vendors

ADD VENDORS

The Vendor List is known as the Accounts Payable Subsidiary Ledger. Whenever a
transaction is entered for a vendor, it is automatically posted to the General Ledger account
and the Accounts Payable Subsidiary Ledger.

For ease of entry, the vendor table is divided into two tables.

VENDORS			
Vendor and Company Name	Canine Grooming Supplies	Pet Supplies, Inc.	Dog Toys & Treats
Phone	310-555-6971	760-555-2951	310-555-6464
Fax	310-555-1796	760-555-1592	310-555-4646
Address	10855 Western Avenue	7758 Broadway Avenue	1970 College Boulevard
City, State, Zip	Los Angeles, CA 90012	San Diego, CA 92101	Hollywood, CA 90028
Contact Person	Virginia Gonzalez	Delores Cooper	Carol Lewis

VENDORS				
Vendor and Company Name	Employment Development Department	San Diego Bank	Health Insurance, Inc.	State Board of Equalization
Phone	310-555-8877	760-555-9889	310-555-7412	916-555-0000
Fax	310-555-7788	760-555-9988	310-555-2147	916-555-1111
Address	11033 Wilshire Boulevard	350 Second Street	2085 Wilshire Boulevard	7800 State Street
City, State, Zip	Los Angeles, CA 90007	San Diego, CA 92114	Los Angeles, CA 90007	Sacramento, CA 94265

 Continue to use QuickBooks Setup and the charts above to add multiple vendors manually to the "People you do business with" screen

On the first blank line beneath the customer Summer, Carol, click **Vendor**, Tab to **Name**, enter **Canine Grooming Supplies**
Tab to **Company Name**, enter **Canine Grooming Supplies**
Tab to **Phone**, enter **310-555-6971**
Tab to **Fax**, enter **310-555-1796**

| ○ | ○ | ◉ | ○ | Canine Grooming Supplies | Canine Grooming Supplies | | | 310-555-6971 | 310-555-1796 |

Tab to **Address**, enter **10855 Western Avenue**
Tab to **City, State Zip**, enter **Los Angeles, CA 90012**
Tab to **Contact**, enter **Virginia Gonzalez**

| ○ | ○ | ◉ | ○ | Canine Grooming Supplies | 310-555-6971 | 310-555-1796 | 10855 Western Avenue | Los Angeles, CA 90012 | Virginia Gonzalez |

Repeat the steps above to enter all of the vendors in both charts
• After entering all of the vendors, you will see the completed list of both customers and vendors.
• Make sure all of the customers are marked as customers and vendors are marked as vendors

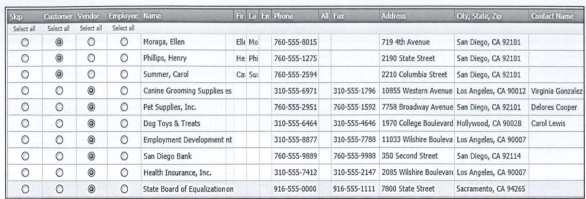

Skip	Customer	Vendor	Employee	Name	Fir	La	En	Phone	Al	Fax	Address	City, State, Zip	Contact Name
Select all	Select all	Select all	Select all										
○	◉	○	○	Moraga, Ellen	Elle	Mo		760-555-8015			719 4th Avenue	San Diego, CA 92101	
○	◉	○	○	Phillips, Henry	He	Phi		760-555-1275			2190 State Street	San Diego, CA 92101	
○	◉	○	○	Summer, Carol	Ca	Su		760-555-2594			2210 Columbia Street	San Diego, CA 92101	
○	○	◉	○	Canine Grooming Supplies es				310-555-6971		310-555-1796	10855 Western Avenue	Los Angeles, CA 90012	Virginia Gonzalez
○	○	◉	○	Pet Supplies, Inc.				760-555-2951		760-555-1592	7758 Broadway Avenue	San Diego, CA 92101	Delores Cooper
○	○	◉	○	Dog Toys & Treats				310-555-6464		310-555-4646	1970 College Boulevard	Hollywood, CA 90028	Carol Lewis
○	○	◉	○	Employment Development nt				310-555-8877		310-555-7788	11033 Wilshire Bouleva	Los Angeles, CA 90007	
○	○	◉	○	San Diego Bank				760-555-9889		760-555-9988	350 Second Street	San Diego, CA 92114	
○	○	◉	○	Health Insurance, Inc.				310-555-7412		310-555-2147	2085 Wilshire Boulevar	Los Angeles, CA 90007	
○	○	◉	○	State Board of Equalization on				916-555-0000		916-555-1111	7800 State Street	Sacramento, CA 94265	

Partial List

Do **NOT** click Continue, you will use the same screen to add employees

ADD EMPLOYEES

Multiple employees' names and address information may be added at the same time that customers and vendors are added. Other information will be added to the individual employees separately.

EMPLOYEES		
Employee Name	Adams, Brooke	Childs, Drake
First Name	Brooke	Drake
Last Name	Adams	Childs
Phone	760-555-8348	760-555-1386
Address	1077 Columbia Street	2985 A Street
City, State, Zip	San Diego, CA 92101	San Diego, CA 92101

 Continue to use QuickBooks Setup and the chart above to add the two employees manually to the "People you do business with" screen

If you do not see a blank line, tab to or scroll down to the next blank row
On the first blank line beneath the vendor State Board of Equalization, click
   Employee, Tab to **Name**
- Since you want your Employee List to be sorted according to the employee's last name, type the last name first
- Always double check the radial dial selection. If the selection doesn't hold, tab and then click the appropriate radial dial. (Employee in this case.)
Enter **Adams, Brooke**
Tab to **First Name**, enter **Brooke**
Tab to **Last Name**, enter **Adams**
Tab to **Phone**, enter **760-555-8348**
Tab to **Address**, enter **1077 Columbia Street**
Tab to **City, State, Zip**, enter **San Diego, CA 92101**

				Adams, Brooke	Brooke	Adams	760-555-8348			1077 Columbia Street	San Diego, CA 92101

Repeat the steps to add Drake Childs

Skip	Customer	Vendor	Employee	Name	First Name	Last Nam	En	Phone	Al	Fax	Address	City, State, Zip
Select all	Select all	Select all	Select all									
○	◉	○	○	Summer, Carol	Carol	Summer		760-555-2594			2210 Columbia Street	San Diego, CA 92101
○	○	◉	○	Canine Grooming Supplies				310-555-6971		310-555-1796	10855 Western Avenue	Los Angeles, CA 90012
○	○	◉	○	Pet Supplies, Inc.				760-555-2951		760-555-1592	7758 Broadway Avenue	San Diego, CA 92101
○	○	◉	○	Dog Toys & Treats				310-555-6464		310-555-4646	1970 College Boulevard	Hollywood, CA 90028
○	○	◉	○	Employment Development				310-555-8877		310-555-7788	11033 Wilshire Bouleva	Los Angeles, CA 90007
○	○	◉	○	San Diego Bank				760-555-9889		760-555-9988	350 Second Street	San Diego, CA 92114
○	○	◉	○	Health Insurance, Inc.				310-555-7412		310-555-2147	2085 Wilshire Boulevard	Los Angeles, CA 90007
○	○	◉	○	State Board of Equalization				916-555-0000		916-555-1111	7800 State Street	Sacramento, CA 94265
○	○	○	◉	Adams, Brooke	Brooke	Adams		760-555-8348			1077 Columbia Street	San Diego, CA 92101
○	○	○	◉	Childs, Drake	Drake	Childs		760-555-1386			2985 A Street	San Diego, CA 92101

13 contacts selected

- At the bottom of the list, you should see **13 contacts selected**. If you do not have this number, make sure that each of the names entered have the radial dial selected. If Skip is selected, that entry will not be included.
- You should have 4 customers, 7 vendors, and 2 employees.

Now that all customers, vendors, and employees have been added, click **Continue**

ENTER OPENING BALANCES

Opening balances for customers and vendors may be added at this time or they may be added later.

OPENING BALANCES			
Type	**Name**	**Balance**	**Opening Balance Date**
Customer	Gray, George	500.00	01/01/2013
Customer	Moraga, Ellen	800.00	01/01/2013
Customer	Phillips, Henry	1,500.00	01/01/2013
Customer	Summer, Carol	150.00	01/01/2013
Vendor	Canine Grooming Supplies	3,000.00	01/01/2013
Vendor	Pet Supplies, Inc.	2,000.00	01/01/2013

 Add the opening balances for customers and vendors with the opening Balance Date of 01/01/2013 using the information above

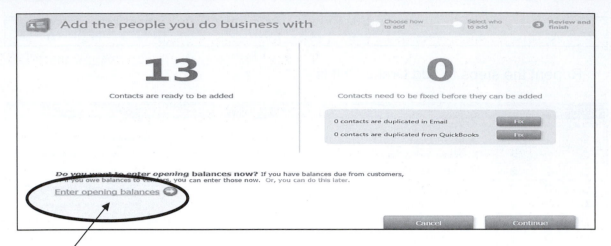

Click **Enter opening balances** in the lower-left corner of the **QuickBooks Setup screen**

- **CAUTION**: Be very, very, careful on this screen. If you click anything other than Enter opening balances, you will have to enter opening balances by creating an invoice or bill for each balance when you begin working in QuickBooks.
- If you do not see 13 contacts ready to be added, do **not** go back to check or add any missing customers, vendors, or employees. If you try to go back, everything you entered will disappear from the screen and you will have to add the opening balances later by preparing invoices and bills with opening balances.
- If you click "Or, you can do this later", you will have to create invoices and bills with opening balances for each customer and vendor when you begin working in QuickBooks.

Click the **Opening balance** column for **Gray, George**

Enter **500**, press Tab to the Opening Balance Date

Click the Calendar icon

Click the back button on the calendar until you get to **January, 2013**

Click **1** to select the date

Continue adding the opening balances and dates for the customers and vendors listed in the table including those with 0.00 balances

- If a vendor is not shown in the Opening Balances chart, select an Opening balance of **0.00** and the Opening balance date of **01/01/2013**.

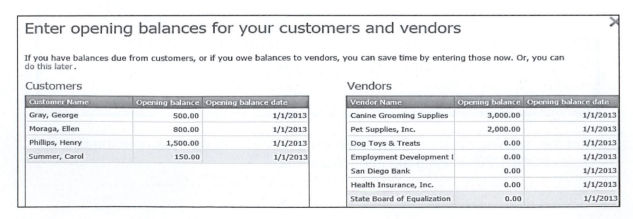

Enter opening balances for your customers and vendors

If you have balances due from customers, or if you owe balances to vendors, you can save time by entering those now. Or, you can do this later.

Customers

Customer Name	Opening balance	Opening balance date
Gray, George	500.00	1/1/2013
Moraga, Ellen	800.00	1/1/2013
Phillips, Henry	1,500.00	1/1/2013
Summer, Carol	150.00	1/1/2013

Vendors

Vendor Name	Opening balance	Opening balance date
Canine Grooming Supplies	3,000.00	1/1/2013
Pet Supplies, Inc.	2,000.00	1/1/2013
Dog Toys & Treats	0.00	1/1/2013
Employment Development [	0.00	1/1/2013
San Diego Bank	0.00	1/1/2013
Health Insurance, Inc.	0.00	1/1/2013
State Board of Equalization	0.00	1/1/2013

Click the **Continue** button on the Enter Opening Balances screen
Click the **Continue** button on the QuickBooks Setup screen
- The customers, vendors, employees, and any opening balances are added to the company.

COMPLETE THE SECOND SECTION OF THE QUICKBOOKS SETUP

Both service and inventory items are added in this section.

Add the products and services you sell

You've added 2 non-inventory parts

Add More

ITEMS LIST

The Items list contains information about all of the items sold or services performed by the business. The Items used to track services performed and products sold for income are created. The Items List is used in conjunction with the income accounts previously created.

ADD SERVICE ITEMS

Service items are used when you perform work for a customer that does not involve a product.

SERVICE ITEMS			
Item Name	Doggie Digs Hotel	Doggie Dayz Camp	Doggie Salon
Description	Boarding Services	Day Camp	Grooming
Price	55.00	30.00	0.00

 Add the three service items above to the Items List

Click the **Add More** button in the section: "Add the products and services you sell"
Click **Service** on the QuickBooks Setup screen, click the **Continue** button

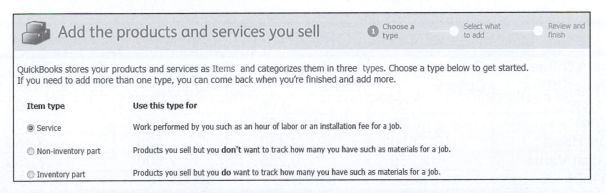

Click in the **Name** column, enter **Doggie Digs Hotel**
Tab to **Description**, enter **Boarding Services**
Tab to **Price**, enter **55.00**

Name	Description	Price
Doggie Digs Hotel	Boarding Services	55.00

Repeat for the other two service items

Name	Description	Price
Doggie Digs Hotel	Boarding Services	55.00
Doggie Dayz Camp	Day Camp	30.00
Doggie Salon	Grooming	0.00

Click the **Continue** button

- Review the screen to make sure 3 items are ready to be added and that none need to be fixed.

Click the **Continue** button

- Notice that the "Add the products and services you sell" screen shows 3 services and 2 non-inventory items.

ADD INVENTORY ITEMS

Now that the service items have been added, the Inventory part items should be entered. Inventory part items are the things you purchase, hold in inventory, and then sell.

INVENTORY PART ITEMS				
Item Name	Collars	Leashes	Sweaters	Toys & Treats
Description	Collars	Leashes	Sweaters	Toys & Treats
Price	0.00	0.00	0.00	0.00
Cost	0.00	0.00	0.00	0.00
On-Hand	650	450	325	3,450
Total Value	12,750	6,250	7,500	7,250
As Of	01/01/13	01/01/13	01/01/13	01/01/13

Use the information above to add the Inventory Part Items

Click the **Add More** button in the section: "Add the products and services you sell"
Click **Inventory Part**

Item type	Use this type for
○ Service	Work performed by you such as an hour of labor or an installation fee for a job.
○ Non-inventory part	Products you sell but you **don't** want to track how many you have such as materials for a job.
◉ Inventory part	Products you sell but you **do** want to track how many you have such as materials for a job.

Click the **Continue** button
Enter **Collars** as the Item Name
Tab to or click **Description**, enter **Collars**
Since the price of the collars vary, enter **0.00** for Price
- There is no manufacturing part number, leave the Mfg. Part # blank.

Since the cost of the collars vary, enter **0.00** for Cost
Tab to **On Hand**, enter **650**
Enter the Total Value of **12,750**
Tab to the As of date, click the Calendar icon
Click the back button on the calendar to get to **January, 2013**
Click **1** to select the date
- **CAUTION**: The only time a Total Value may be entered is at the time the Inventory Part item is created.

◀	January, 2013					
Su	**Mo**	**Tu**	**We**	**Th**	**Fr**	**Sa**
30	31	1	2	3	4	5
6	7	8	9	10	11	12
13	14	15	16	17	18	19
20	21	22	23	24	25	26
27	28	29	30	31	1	2

Name	Description	Price	Mfg Part #	Cost	On Hand	Total Value	As of date
Collars	Collars	0.00		0.00	650.00	12,750.00	1/1/2013

Add the remaining inventory part items

Name	Description	Price	Mfg Part #	Cost	On Hand	Total Value	As of date
Collars	Collars	0.00		0.00	650.00	12,750.00	1/1/2013
Leashes	Leashes	0.00		0.00	450.00	6,250.00	1/1/2013
Sweaters	Sweaters	0.00		0.00	325.00	7,500.00	1/1/2013
Toys & Treats	Toys & Treats	0.00		0.00	3,450.00	7,250.00	1/1/2013

Click the **Continue** button
- Make sure you see 4 Items are ready to be added

Click the **Continue** button

COMPLETE THE THIRD SECTION OF THE QUICKBOOKS SETUP

Bank accounts and balances are added in this section.

 Add the Checking Account using the information provided in the following steps

Click the **Add** button on the "Add your bank accounts" section
Click in the column for **Account name**, enter the name **Checking**
Tab to **Account number**, enter **123-456-78910**
Tab to **Opening balance**, enter the amount **29,385.00**
Tab to **Opening balance date**, enter the date **01/01/2013** as previously instructed

Account name	Account number	Opening balance	Opening balance date
Checking	123-456-78910	29,385.00	1/1/2013

Click the **Continue** button
On the screen to order checks, click **No Thanks**, click **Continue**
Click **Start Working** to end QuickBooks Setup
- **CAUTION**: Once you click Start Working you may not return to the QuickBooks Setup. If you need to add any missing or incomplete information go to the individual center, list, or account to add. You may edit information in these areas as well. (All of this will be done later in the chapter.)

The Quick Start Center is displayed
- If you did not enter a customer, vendor, service or inventory item, or a bank account, click **Return to Add Info** and add the missing information. You may not edit or correct something that had already been added.

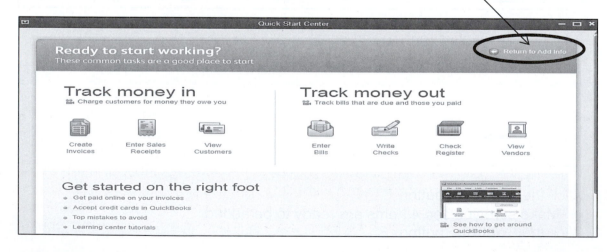

Close the **Quick Start Center**

COMPLETE COMPANY INFORMATION

Once the EasyStep Interview and the QuickBooks Setup have been completed, other information for the company must be entered. Information such as tax forms, Federal Employer Identification numbers, and payroll processing information may need to be provided. Preferences need to be entered. In addition, the chart of accounts, customers, vendors, employees, and sales items will need to be refined.

MEMO

DATE: January 1, 2013

The information necessary to complete the Company information is the Federal Employer Identification number. The number is 15-9888654.

 Enter the Federal Employer Identification number

Click **Company Information** on the Company menu
Click in the **Federal Employer Identification No.** text box, enter **15-9888654**

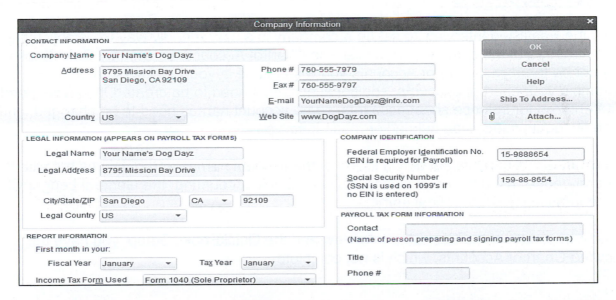

- View the other information on the page. Notice that the Report Information shows the Fiscal Year and Tax Year as January. The Income Tax Form Used is Form 1040 (Sole Proprietor). The Contact Information and Legal Information appear as it was entered during the EasyStep Interview. Do not make any other changes to the Company Information.

Click **OK**

SELECT A TOP ICON BAR

Throughout the textbook, the Top Icon Bar has been used. Currently the Left Icon Bar is shown as the default icon. QuickBooks allows you to use either of the icon bars. Since the Left Icon Bar takes up a lot of room on the screen, we will continue to use the Top Icon Bar.

 Select a Top Icon Bar

> Click **View** on the Menu Bar
> Click **Top Icon Bar**

- The Top Icon Bar is now shown in grayscale. We will change to color in Preferences later in the chapter.

CHART OF ACCOUNTS

Using the EasyStep Interview to set up a company is a user-friendly way to establish the basic structure of the company. However, the Chart of Accounts created by QuickBooks may not be the exact Chart of Accounts you wish to use in your business. In order to customize your chart of accounts, additional accounts need to be created, balances need to be entered for balance sheet accounts, some account names need to be changed, and some accounts need to be deleted or made inactive

The Chart of Accounts is not only a listing of the account names and balances but also the General Ledger used by the business. As in textbook accounting, the General Ledger/Chart of Accounts is the book of final entry.

At the completion of the EasyStep Interview and the QuickBooks Setup, you have the following Chart of Accounts, which is not complete:

NAME	⚡	TYPE	BALANCE TOTAL	ATTACH
◇ Checking		Bank	29,385.00	
◇ Accounts Receivable		Accounts Receivable	2,950.00	
◇ Inventory Asset		Other Current Asset	33,750.00	
◇ Accumulated Depreciation		Fixed Asset	0.00	
◇ Furniture and Equipment		Fixed Asset	0.00	
◇ Security Deposits Asset		Other Asset	0.00	
◇ Accounts Payable		Accounts Payable	5,000.00	
◇ Payroll Liabilities		Other Current Liability	0.00	
◇ Sales Tax Payable		Other Current Liability	0.00	
◇ Opening Balance Equity		Equity	63,135.00	
◇ Owners Draw		Equity	0.00	
◇ Owners Equity		Equity		
◇ Merchandise Sales		Income		
◇ Sales Discounts		Income		
◇ Sales Income		Income		
◇ Service Sales		Income		
◇ Uncategorized Income		Income		
◇ *Cost of Goods Sold		Cost of Goods Sold		
◇ Cost of Goods Sold		Cost of Goods Sold		
◇ Advertising and Promotion		Expense		
◇ Automobile Expense		Expense		
◇ Bank Service Charges		Expense		
◇ Computer and Internet Expenses		Expense		
◇ Depreciation Expense		Expense		
◇ Insurance Expense		Expense		
◇ Interest Expense		Expense		
◇ Janitorial Expense		Expense		
◇ Meals and Entertainment		Expense		
◇ Office Supplies		Expense		
◇ Payroll Expenses		Expense		
◇ Professional Fees		Expense		
◇ Rent Expense		Expense		
◇ Repairs and Maintenance		Expense		
◇ Telephone Expense		Expense		
◇ Uncategorized Expenses		Expense		
◇ Uniforms		Expense		
◇ Utilities		Expense		

- The account Ask My Accountant is not shown in the list above.
- Please be aware that the Chart of Accounts created in the EasyStep Interview may be different from the one shown above.

Use the Chart of Accounts and balances on the next page as a reference while you customize Your Name's Dog Dayz Chart of Accounts. Information regarding changes, additions, etc. is provided in the Memo that follows the Chart of Accounts. As usual, the steps used in making changes to the Chart of Accounts are detailed after the memo.

As you review the Chart of Accounts, look at the descriptions provided by QuickBooks. In many instances, the descriptions provided are explanatory and quite lengthy; and, frequently, they are unnecessary for clarification. In these instances, the descriptions should be deleted.

In addition to the changes you will be making in the Chart of Accounts, the Customer List, Vendor List, and Sales Items will also have information entered before your Chart of Accounts will match the following:

YOUR NAME'S DOG DAYZ
CHART OF ACCOUNTS

ACCOUNT	TYPE	BALANCE	ACCOUNT	TYPE
Checking	Bank	29,385.00	Sales	Inc.
Accounts Receivable (QB)	Accts. Rec.	2,950.00	Boarding	Inc.
Inventory Asset	Other C.A.	33,750.00	Merchandise	Inc.
Office Supplies	Other C.A.	350.00	Grooming	Inc.
Sales Supplies	Other C.A.	500.00	Sales Discounts	Inc.
Prepaid Insurance	Other C.A.	1,200.00	Cost of Goods Sold (QB)	COGS
Equipment	Fixed Asset	***	Advertising and Promotion	Exp.
Original Cost	Fixed Asset	8,000.00	Automobile Expense	Exp.
Depreciation	Fixed Asset	-800.00	Bank Service Charges	Exp.
Fixtures	Fixed Asset	***	Computer and Internet Expenses	Exp.
Original Cost	Fixed Asset	15,000.00	Depreciation Expense	Exp
Depreciation	Fixed Asset	-1,500.00	Insurance Expense	Exp.
Accounts Payable (QB)	Other C.L.	5,000.00	Interest Expense	Exp.
Payroll Liabilities	Other C.L.	0.00	Office Supplies Expense	Exp.
Sales Tax Payable	Other C.L.	0.00	Payroll Expenses	Exp.
Equipment Loan	Long Term L.	2,000.00	Professional Fees	Exp.
Fixtures Loan	Long Term L.	2,500.00	Rent Expense	Exp.
Retained Earnings (QB*)	Equity	***	Repairs and Maintenance	Exp.
First & Last Name, Capital	Equity	***	Sales Supplies Expense	Exp.
First & Last Name, Withdrawals	Equity	0.00	Telephone Expense	Exp.
First & Last Name, Investment	Equity	25,000.00	Utilities	Exp.
			Other Income	Other Inc
			Other Expenses	Other Exp

Chart Abbreviations:
(QB)=Account Created by QuickBooks
(QB*)=Account Created by QuickBooks. Name change required.
Indented Account Names indicate that the account is a subaccount
*** means that QuickBooks will enter the account balance
C.A.=Current Asset, F.A.=Fixed Asset; C.L.=Current Liability; Long Term L.=Long Term Liability; COGS=Cost of Goods Sold, Inc.=Income, Exp.=Expense.

MEMO

DATE: January 1, 2013

Since Your Name's Dog Dayz' Chart of Accounts/General Ledger needs to be customized, make the following changes to the accounts:

<u>Delete</u>: Accumulated Depreciation, Furniture and Equipment, Security Deposits Asset, Uniforms, and Ask My Accountant

<u>Make inactive</u>: Meals and Entertainment

<u>Edit Equity Accounts</u>: Change the name of Opening Balance Equity to **First & Last Name, Capital**; change Owners Equity to **Retained Earnings**, change Owners Draw to **First & Last Name, Withdrawals**; Subaccount of First & Last Name, Capital

<u>Add Equity Accounts</u>: **First & Last Name, Investment**; Subaccount of First & Last Name, Capital; Opening Balance $25,000 as of 01/01/13

<u>Edit Income Accounts</u>: Rename Sales Income to **Sales**; rename Merchandise Sales to **Merchandise** make it a subaccount of Sales, rename Service Sales to **Day Camp**, make it a subaccount of Sales

<u>Add Income Accounts</u>: add **Boarding**, a subaccount of Sales; add **Grooming**, a Subaccount of Sales; add **Other Income**

<u>Add Expense Accounts</u>: **Sales Supplies Expense**, and **Other Expenses**

<u>Edit Expense Accounts</u>: Rename Office Supplies to **Office Supplies Expense**

<u>Delete Account Descriptions</u>: Check each account and delete the descriptions entered by QuickBooks.

 Make the changes indicated above and delete the descriptions in the accounts

Click **Chart of Accounts** in the Company section of the Home Page

Click the account **Accumulated Depreciation** to highlight, use the keyboard **Ctrl+D** to delete the account, click **OK** to delete

Repeat to delete the other accounts listed in the memo

Position the cursor on the expense account, **Meals and Entertainment**, click the **Account** button, and click **Make Account Inactive**

Position the cursor on **Opening Balance Equity**, click the **Account** button, click **Edit Account**, enter **First & Last Name, Capital** as the account name (use your actual first and last name), delete the account description, click **Save & Close**

Edit **Owners Equity** and change the name to **Retained Earnings**, delete the description

Edit **Owners Draw** and rename it **First & Last Name, Withdrawals** (use your actual first and last name), click **Subaccount of**, click **First & Last Name, Capital**, delete the description, and click **Save & Close**

Click the **Account** button, click **New**, account type is **Equity**, click **Continue**

Enter the account name **First & Last Name, Investment** (use your first and last name), click **Subaccount**, click **First & Last Name, Capital**

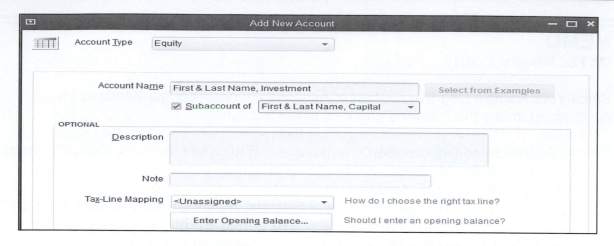

Click the **Enter Opening Balance** button, enter **25,000** as of **01/01/13**, click **OK**

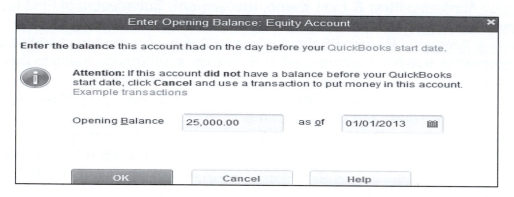

Click **Save & Close**

- If you get a screen warning about a transaction being 30 days in the future or 90 days in the past, click **Yes**

Click **Sales Income** in the Chart of Accounts, use the shortcut **Ctrl + E**, change the name to **Sales**, click **Save & Close**

Change **Merchandise Sales** to **Merchandise**, make it a subaccount of **Sales**, delete the description, click **Save & Close**

Rename **Service Sales** to **Day Camp**, make it a subaccount of **Sales**, and delete the description, click **Save & Close**

Click the **Account** button, click **New**, account type is **Income**, click **Continue**

Add the Income account **Boarding**, make this a subaccount of **Sales**

Click **Save & New**

Add the income account **Grooming,** make it a subaccount of **Sales**, click **Save & New**

Click the drop-down list arrow for type, click **Other Income**, the account name is **Other Income**, click **Save & New**

Change the type of account to **Expense**, the account name is **Sales Supplies Expense**, click **Save & New**

Change the type of account to **Other Expense**, the account name is **Other Expenses**, click **Save & Close**

Rename the Expense Account **Office Supplies** to **Office Supplies Expense**

In order to remove unwanted and lengthy account descriptions and a variety of tax-line mappings, use **Ctrl + E** to edit each account individually, <u>delete descriptions</u> added by QuickBooks, and change <u>tax-line mapping</u> to Unassigned, when finished, click **Save & Close**

Begin with Checking and repeat for all of the accounts

- Lengthy account descriptions are provided by QuickBooks when it establishes the Chart of Accounts. These descriptions are designed to help those with limited accounting. They will print on reports so removing them helps to streamline QuickBooks reports.

- QuickBooks will include appropriate tax-line mapping for some accounts but not others. Since our focus is not on tax-line mapping, making all of the tax lines <Unassigned> is appropriate.

At this point, the Chart of Accounts appears as follows:

NAME		TYPE	BALANCE TOTAL	ATTACH
Checking		Bank	29,385.00	
Accounts Receivable		Accounts Receivable	2,950.00	
Inventory Asset		Other Current Asset	33,750.00	
Accounts Payable		Accounts Payable	5,000.00	
Payroll Liabilities		Other Current Liability	0.00	
Sales Tax Payable		Other Current Liability	0.00	
First & Last Name, Capital		Equity	63,135.00	
First & Last Name, Investment		Equity	25,000.00	
First & Last Name, Withdrawals		Equity	0.00	
Retained Earnings		Equity		
Sales		Income		
Boarding		Income		
Day Camp		Income		
Grooming		Income		
Merchandise		Income		
Sales Discounts		Income		
Uncategorized Income		Income		
*Cost of Goods Sold		Cost of Goods Sold		
Cost of Goods Sold		Cost of Goods Sold		
Advertising and Promotion		Expense		
Automobile Expense		Expense		
Bank Service Charges		Expense		
Computer and Internet Expenses		Expense		
Depreciation Expense		Expense		
Insurance Expense		Expense		
Interest Expense		Expense		
Janitorial Expense		Expense		
Meals and Entertainment		Expense		
Office Supplies Expense		Expense		
Payroll Expenses		Expense		
Professional Fees		Expense		
Rent Expense		Expense		
Repairs and Maintenance		Expense		
Sales Supplies Expense		Expense		
Telephone Expense		Expense		
Uncategorized Expenses		Expense		
Utilities		Expense		
Other Income		Other Income		
Other Expenses		Other Expense		

- As you can see, income and expense accounts do not have opening balances. Only balance sheet accounts—assets, liabilities, and owner's equity accounts—have opening balances.
- Note that two Cost of Goods Sold accounts appear in the account listing.
- When creating a new company or adding your first sales item; sometimes, but not always, QuickBooks will duplicate the Cost of Goods sold. To differentiate between the two accounts, QuickBooks adds an * to the name.

If this occurs, it is important to determine which account is being used (by an item in this case) and delete to other account

- If you did not get a duplicate Cost of Goods Sold account, the following is information only.

With the Chart of Accounts still showing, click the **Lists** menu, click **Item List**
Double-click the inventory item **Collars**
Note that the COGS Account is ***Cost of Goods Sold**

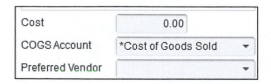

Close the Edit Item screen and the Item List and return to the Chart of Accounts
Click on the **Cost of Goods Sold** account without the *
Use the keyboard shortcut **Ctrl+D**; and then, click **OK** on the Delete Account
message

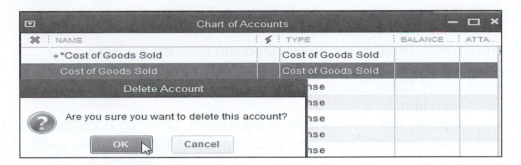

Click *****Cost of Goods Sold** to select the account
Use the keyboard shortcut **Ctrl+E** to edit the account
Delete the * from the account name, click **Save & Close**
- Now only one Cost of Goods Sold account appears in the Chart of Accounts

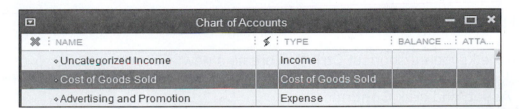

- As you review the Chart of Accounts above and compare it with the completed
  Chart of Accounts shown at the beginning of this section, note that a number of
  balance sheet accounts and their balances need to be added.

MEMO

DATE: January 1, 2013

Set up the following Balance Sheet accounts and balances. The as of dates for opening balances is 01/01/13.

Other Current Asset: Prepaid Insurance, Opening Balance $1,200
Other Current Asset: Office Supplies, Opening Balance $350
Other Current Asset: Sales Supplies, Opening Balance $500
Fixed Asset: Equipment
Fixed Asset: Original Cost, Subaccount of Equipment, Opening Balance $8,000
Fixed Asset: Depreciation, Subaccount of Equipment, Opening Balance -$800
Fixed Asset: Fixtures
Fixed Asset: Original Cost, Subaccount of Fixtures, Opening Balance $15,000
Fixed Asset: Depreciation, Subaccount of Fixtures, Opening Balance -$1,500
Long-term liability: Equipment Loan, Opening Balance $2,000
Long-term liability: Fixtures Loan, Opening Balance $2,500

 Add the accounts and balances listed above

Use the keyboard shortcut **Ctrl+N** to create a new account
Click the drop-down list arrow for **Other Account Types**, click **Other Current Asset**, and click **Continue**.
Enter **Prepaid Insurance** as the Account Name
Click the **Enter Opening Balance** button
Enter **1,200** as of **01/01/13**, and then click **OK**

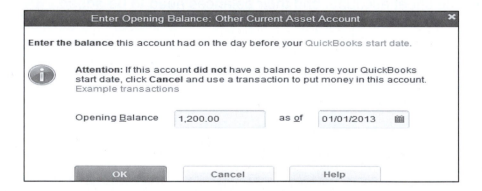

Verify the accuracy of your entry, and then, click **Save & New**

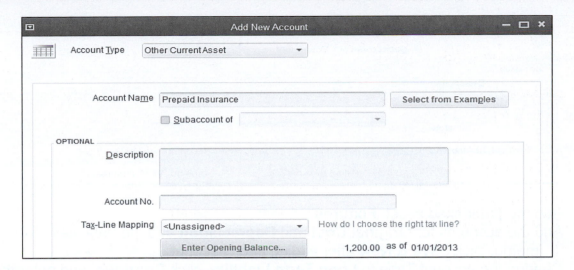

Add the Other Current Asset accounts: Office Supplies and Sales Supplies and the opening balances listed in the Memo, click **Save & New** after adding each account

After the current assets have been added, click the drop-down list arrow for Type, click **Fixed Asset**

Tab to or click in the textbox for **Account Name**, enter **Equipment**

Click **Save & New**

The type of account is still Fixed Asset, enter **Original Cost** as the Name

Click **Subaccount of** to enter a check mark

Click the drop-down list arrow for Subaccount, click **Equipment**

Click the **Enter Opening Balance** button, enter **8,000** as of **01/01/13**, click **OK**

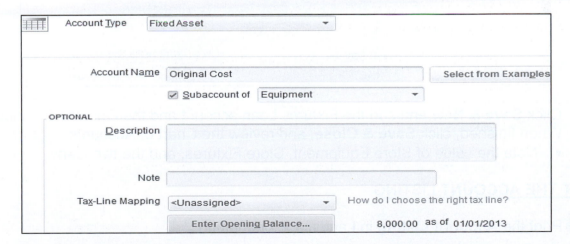

Click **Save & New** and repeat the procedure to add **Depreciation** as a Subaccount of Equipment with an Opening Balance of **-800** as of **01/01/13**

- Be sure to use a minus (-) sign in front of the 800. Remember, depreciation reduces the value of the asset.

Click **OK** on the Opening Balance screen, and then click **Save & New**

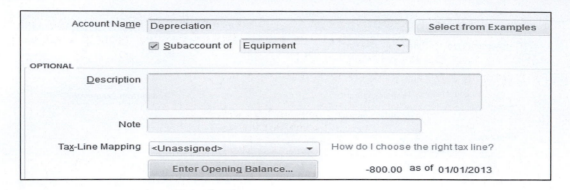

Add the other fixed asset, **Fixtures**

Add the accounts for **Original Cost** and **Depreciation** and the balances given in the memo, click **Save & New** after adding each account

Change the account Type to **Long Term Liability**, click **Continue**, and enter the name **Equipment Loan**

Click the **Enter Opening Balance** button; enter **2,000** as of **01/01/2013**, and then click **OK**

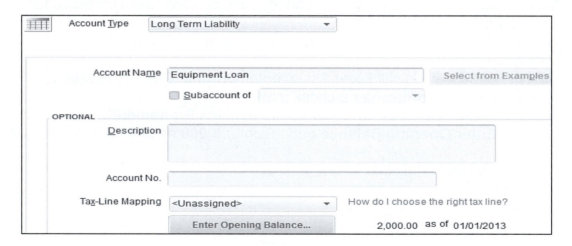

Click **Save & New** and add the Fixtures Loan account and the Opening Balance
When finished, click **Save & Close**, and review the Chart of Accounts
- Note the value of Store Equipment, Store Fixtures, and the two loans.

PRINT THE ACCOUNT LISTING

 Print the **Account Listing** in Landscape orientation

Click the **Reports** button at the bottom of the Chart of Accounts, click **Account Listing**
Resize columns to eliminate extra space, display columns in full, and remove Description and Tax Line from the report
- The Account column shows both the master and the subaccount in the report.

Click the **Customize Report** button, click the **Header/Footer** button, change the report date to **January 1, 2013**, click **Date Prepared** and **Time Prepared** to remove from the heading, click **OK**

Click the **Print** button, select **Portrait** orientation

Your Name's Dog Dayz
Account Listing
January 1, 2013

Account	Type	Balance Total
Checking	Bank	29,385.00
Accounts Receivable	Accounts Receivable	2,950.00
Inventory Asset	Other Current Asset	33,750.00
Office Supplies	Other Current Asset	350.00
Prepaid Insurance	Other Current Asset	1,200.00
Sales Supplies	Other Current Asset	500.00
Equipment	Fixed Asset	7,200.00
Equipment:Depreciation	Fixed Asset	–800.00
Equipment:Original Cost	Fixed Asset	8,000.00
Fixtures	Fixed Asset	13,500.00
Fixtures:Depreciation	Fixed Asset	–1,500.00
Fixtures:Original Cost	Fixed Asset	15,000.00
Accounts Payable	Accounts Payable	5,000.00
Payroll Liabilities	Other Current Liability	0.00
Sales Tax Payable	Other Current Liability	0.00
Equipment Loan	Long Term Liability	2,000.00
Fixtures Loan	Long Term Liability	2,500.00
First & Last Name, Capital	Equity	81,385.00
First & Last Name, Capital:First & Last Name, Investment	Equity	25,000.00
First & Last Name, Capital:First & Last Name, Withdrawals	Equity	0.00
Retained Earnings	Equity	
Sales	Income	
Sales:Boarding	Income	
Sales:Day Camp	Income	
Sales:Grooming	Income	
Sales:Merchandise	Income	
Sales Discounts	Income	
Uncategorized Income	Income	
Cost of Goods Sold	Cost of Goods Sold	
Advertising and Promotion	Expense	
Automobile Expense	Expense	
Bank Service Charges	Expense	
Computer and Internet Expenses	Expense	
Depreciation Expense	Expense	
Insurance Expense	Expense	
Interest Expense	Expense	
Janitorial Expense	Expense	
Office Supplies Expense	Expense	
Payroll Expenses	Expense	
Professional Fees	Expense	
Rent Expense	Expense	
Repairs and Maintenance	Expense	
Sales Supplies Expense	Expense	
Telephone Expense	Expense	
Uncategorized Expenses	Expense	
Utilities	Expense	
Other Income	Other Income	
Other Expenses	Other Expense	

When finished printing, close the Account Listing report and the Chart of Accounts

PREFERENCES

Many preferences used by QuickBooks are selected during the EasyStep Interview. However, there may be some preferences you would like to select, change, or delete. The Preferences section has two tabs where you may indicate My Preferences or Company Preferences. The Preferences that may be customized are: Accounting, Bills, Calendar, Checking, Desktop View, Finance Charge, General, Integrated Applications, Items & Inventory, Jobs & Estimates, Multiple Currencies, Payments, Payroll & Employees,

Reminders, Reports & Graphs, Sales & Customers, Sales Tax, Search, Send Forms, Service Connection, Spelling, Tax: 1099, and Time & Expenses. Not all the possible changes will be discussed in this chapter; however, some changes will be made. In previous chapters, some of the Preferences have been changed. In this chapter, all the Preferences available will be explored.

MEMO

DATE: January 1, 2013

Open the Preferences screen and explore the choices available for each of the areas. When you get to the following preferences, make the changes indicated below:

<u>Accounting</u>: Delete the Date Warnings for past and future transactions

<u>Checking</u>: My Preferences—Select Default Accounts to Checking for Open the Write Checks, Open the Pay Bills, Open the Pay Sales Tax, and Open the Make Deposits; Company Preferences— Select Default Accounts to use should be Checking for Open the Create Paychecks and Open the Pay Payroll Liabilities

<u>Desktop View</u>: My Preferences—Select Switch to colored icons/light background on the Top Icon Bar, use Green – Forest for the Company Flag Color

<u>Payroll & Employees</u>: Company Preferences—Display Employee List by Last Name

<u>Reports & Graphs</u>: My Preferences—Refresh reports automatically, Company Preferences—Display Report Items by Name only and modify the report Format for the Header/Footer to remove the Date Prepared, Time Prepared, and Report Basis from reports

<u>Sales & Customers</u>: Company Preferences—Deselect Use Price Levels

<u>Sales Tax</u>: Company Preferences—Most common sales tax is State Tax

---

 Access Preferences from the Edit menu

- In the following sections the Preferences are shown in the exact order listed on the Preferences screen.

  Click the icons for each category and explore the choices available on both the My Preferences tabs and the Company tabs

  When you get to a Preference that needs to be changed, make the changes indicated in the Memo above

ACCOUNTING PREFERENCES

On the Accounting Preferences screen the Company Preferences tab is accessed to select the use of account numbers. Selecting Use Account Numbers provides an area for each account to be given a number during editing. This screen instructs QuickBooks to automatically assign general journal entry numbers and to warn when posting a transaction to Retained Earnings. There are two check boxes for warning when transactions are 90 days within the past or 30 days within the future. The closing date for a period is entered after clicking the Set Date/Password button on this screen.

Remove the Date Warnings

Click **Accounting**, and then, if necessary, click the **Company Preferences** tab
Click the check boxes for **Date Warnings** to deselect the two warnings

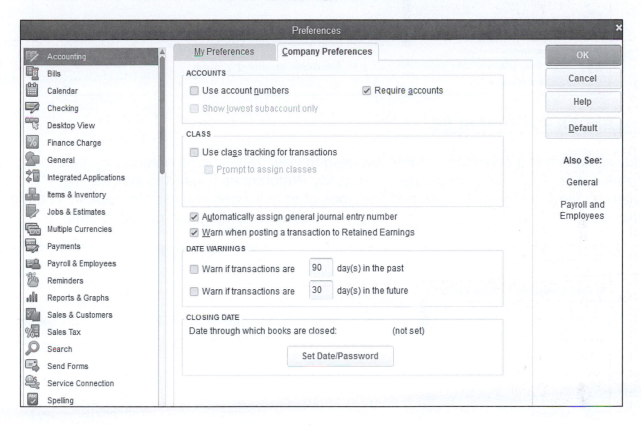

Click **Bills** in the list of **Preferences**
Each time you change a Preference and click on another Preference you get a
     dialog box to Save Changes to the Preference, always click **Yes**

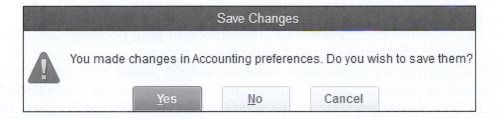

BILLS PREFERENCES

Bills Preferences has the selections on the Company Preferences tab for Entering Bills and
Paying Bills. You may tell QuickBooks the number of days after the receipt of bills that they
are due. You may also select to be warned about duplicate bill numbers from the same
vendor. When paying bills, you may tell QuickBooks to use discounts and credits
automatically.

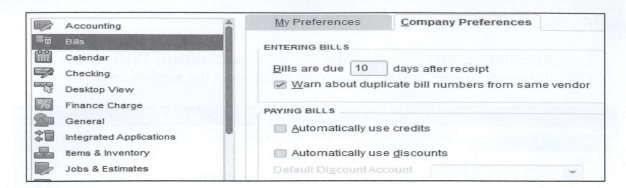

CALENDAR PREFERENCES

QuickBooks has a calendar that may be used to view transactions entered, transactions that are due, and to do's for a selected day. My Preferences is used to indicate the calendar view, the weekly view, and the types of transactions you wish to appear. You may also select settings for the number of days to display upcoming and past due data.

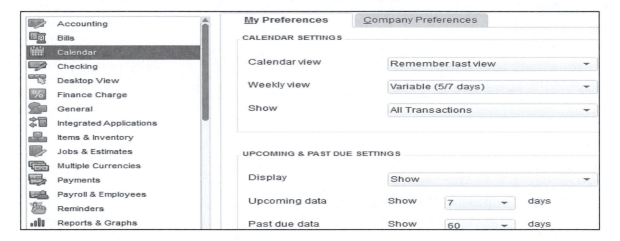

CHECKING PREFERENCES

The preferences listed for checking allows QuickBooks to print account names on check vouchers, change the check date when a non-cleared check is printed, start with the payee field on a check, warn of duplicate check numbers, autofill payee account number in check memo, set default accounts to use for checks, and to view and enter downloaded transactions in Online Banking in either the Side-by-Side Mode or the Register Mode.

 Select Default Accounts to use Checking

> Click **Checking** in the **Preferences** list
> Use the **Company Preferences** tab
> Click the check box for **Open the Create Paychecks**,
> Click **Checking** on the drop-down list for account
> Repeat for **Open the Pay Payroll Liabilities**

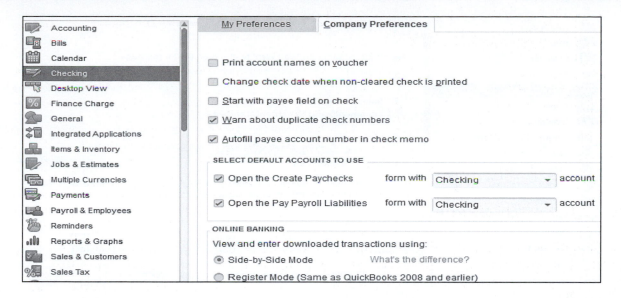

Click **My Preferences Tab**
Click the Check box for **Open the Write Checks** to select
Click the drop-down list arrow for Account
Click **Checking**
Repeat for **Open the Pay Bills**, **Open the Pay Sales Tax**, and **Open the Make Deposits**

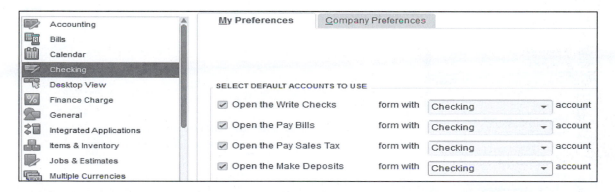

Click the **Desktop View Preference**, and then click **Yes** on **Save Changes**

DESKTOP VIEW PREFERENCES

The Desktop View Preference allows you to set My Preferences to customize your QuickBooks screens to view one or multiple windows, to display the Home Page, to save the desktop, to switch to colored icons on the Top Icon Bar, to select color schemes and sounds, and to add a Company Flag Color.

The Company Preferences tab allows you to select features that you want to show on the Home Page and to explore Related Preferences.

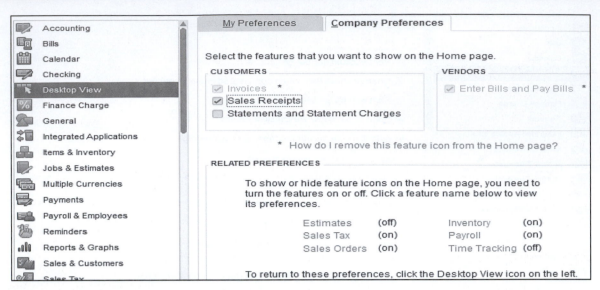

 Select colored icons with light backgrounds for the Top Icon Bar and add a Company Flag Color

On the **Desktop View Preference**, click **My Preferences Tab**
Click **Switch to colored icons/light background on the Top Icon Bar** to select
Click the drop-down list arrow for **Company Flag Color**, click **Green-Forest**

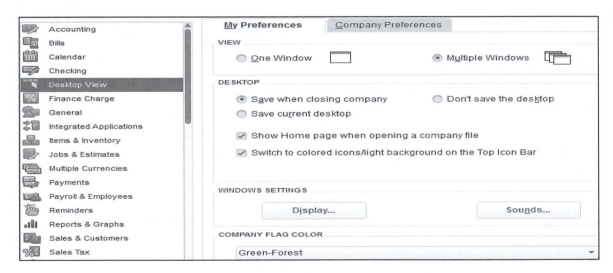

Click **Finance Charge** in the Preferences list, and then click **Yes** on **Save Changes**

FINANCE CHARGE PREFERENCES

This preference allows you to tell QuickBooks if you want to collect finance charges and to provide information about finance charges. The information you may provide includes the annual interest rate, the minimum finance charge, the grace period, the finance charge account, and whether to calculate finance charges from the due date or from the invoice/billed date.

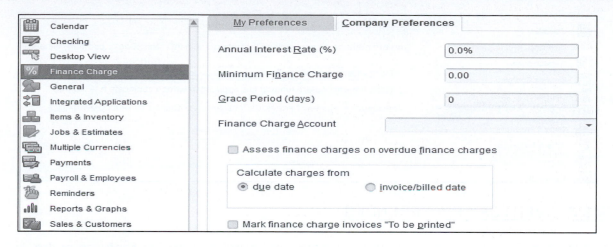

GENERAL PREFERENCES

General preferences use the Company Preferences tab to set the time format, to display the year as four digits, and save transactions before printing. My Preferences tab is used to indicate decimal point placement, to set warning screens and beeps, to turn on messages, to keep QuickBooks running for quick startups, to automatically recall the last transaction for a name, and to indicate which default date to use in new transactions.

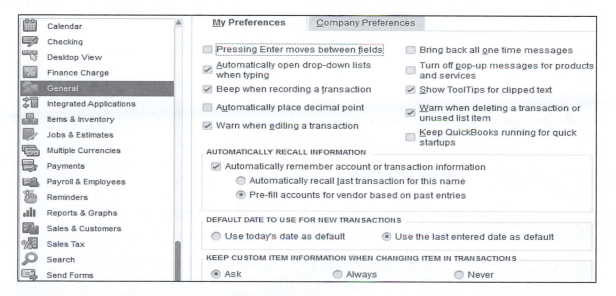

INTEGRATED APPLICATIONS PREFERENCES

Integrated preferences are used to manage all applications that interact with the current QuickBooks company file.

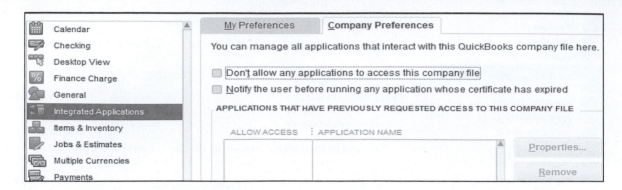

ITEMS & INVENTORY PREFERENCES

This section allows you to activate the inventory and purchase orders features of the program, have QuickBooks provide warnings if there is not enough inventory to sell, to warn if there are duplicate purchase order numbers, and to enable units of measure.

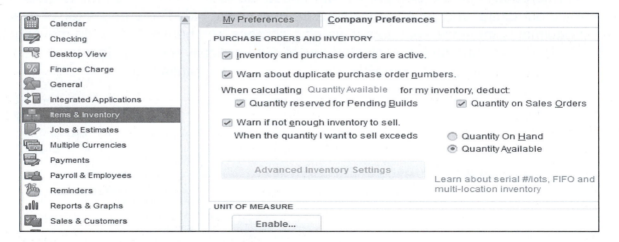

JOBS & ESTIMATES PREFERENCES

This preference allows you to indicate the status of jobs and to choose whether or not to use estimates.

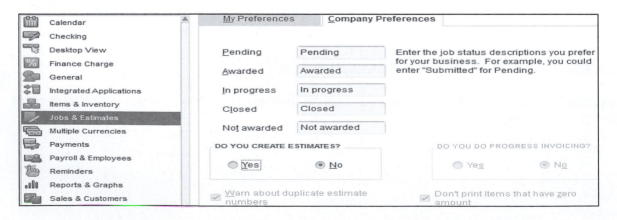

MULTIPLE CURRENCIES PREFERENCES

Using the Company Preferences tab, you may select to use more than one currency. You can assign a currency to customers, vendors, price levels, bank and credit card accounts as well as accounts receivable and accounts payable accounts. You must designate a home currency that will be used for income and expense accounts. Once you choose to use multiple currencies, you may not change the preference to discontinue the use of multiple currencies

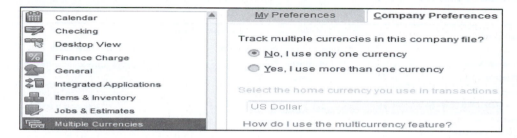

PAYMENTS PREFERENCES

On the Company Preferences tab of the Payments preference, you may specify Receive Payments to automatically apply payments, automatically calculate payments, and to use Undeposited Funds as a default deposit to account. You may sign up for the IntuitPaymentNetwork. In addition Invoice Payments may be marked to include the payment link on invoices.

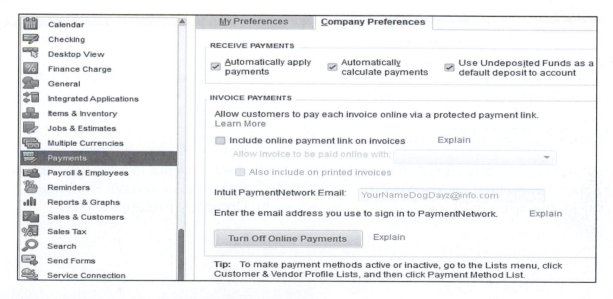

PAYROLL & EMPLOYEES PREFERENCES

Payroll preferences include selecting the payroll features, if any, you wish to use. Set Preferences for pay stub and voucher printing, workers compensation, and sick and vacation may be selected. Copying earnings details, recalling quantities and/or hours, and job costing for paycheck expenses may be marked or unmarked. You may choose the method by which employees are sorted. Employee Defaults may be accessed from this screen. Once accessed, the Employee Defaults may be changed and/or modified.

 Change the Display Employee List to Last Name

> Click **Payroll & Employees** to select
> Click the **Company Preferences** tab
> Click **Last Name** in the section for Display Employee List by

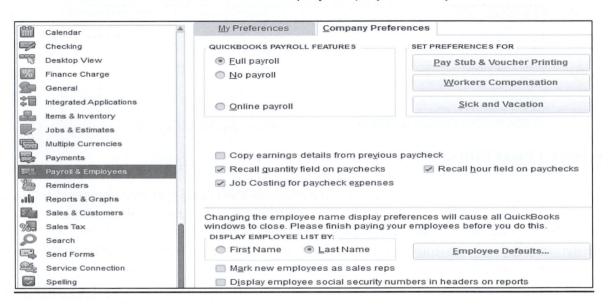

> Click the **Reminders Preference** click **Yes** on the Save Changes dialog box
> Click **OK** on the Warning screen
> • Preferences should reopen automatically. If it does not, click the Edit menu, click Preferences, click Reminders

REMINDERS PREFERENCES

In this section you may use My Preferences to select whether or not to have the Reminders List appear when the QuickBooks program is started. If you chose to have Reminders displayed, the specific Reminders are selected on the Company Preferences tab.

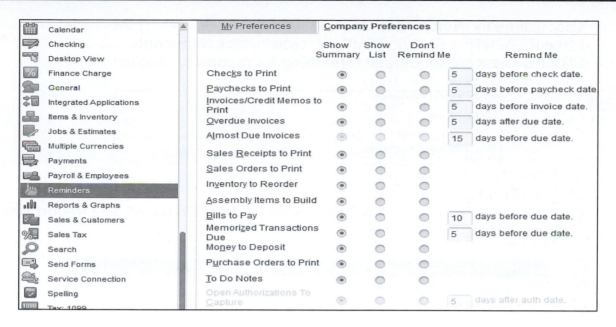

REPORTS & GRAPHS PREFERENCES

The My Preferences tab allows you to select whether to show a prompt to refresh reports and graphs or to refresh them automatically and whether to draw graphs in 2D or use patterns. The Company Preferences tab allows the selection of accrual or cash basis reporting. Preferences for report aging, how to display items in reports, and how to display accounts within reports are selected in this section. We can tell QuickBooks to assign accounts to the sections of the Statement of Cash Flows. In addition, report formats may be customized using this screen.

 Change My Preferences to have the reports refresh automatically

> Click **My Preferences** tab
> Click **Refresh Automatically**

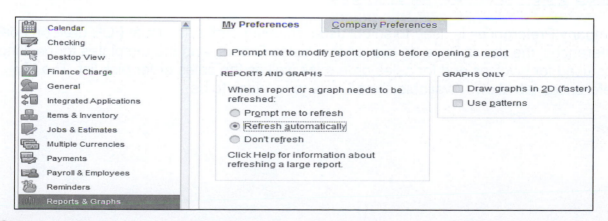

 Modify the report format to remove the Date Prepared, Time Prepared, and Report Basis and select Reports-Show Items By: Name only

Click **Company Preferences** tab
In the REPORTS – SHOW ITEMS BY: section, click **Name only**
Click the check box for **Default formatting for reports** to deselect

Click the **Format** button
On the Header/Footer tab, click **Date Prepared**, **Time Prepared**, and **Report Basis** to remove the check marks

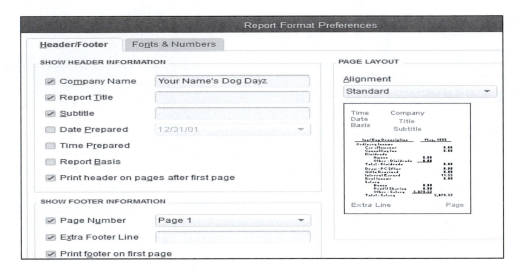

Click **OK**
Click **Sales & Customers** preferences, click **Yes** to save the changes

SALES & CUSTOMERS PREFERENCES

Company Preferences is used to select usual shipping methods, usual FOB (free on board) preferences, the use of Price Levels, enable Sales Orders, and the templates for packing slips used for invoices and for sales orders, as well as the sales order pick list. The My Preferences tab allows Available Time/Costs to Invoices to be.

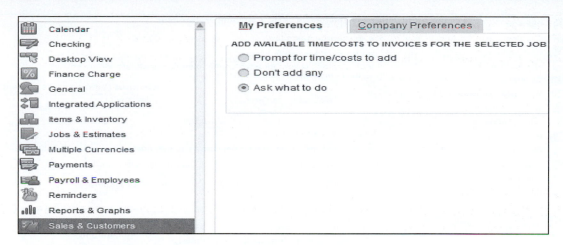

 Change Company Preferences to deselect Use Price Levels

Click the **Company Preferences** tab
Click **Use price levels** to remove the check mark

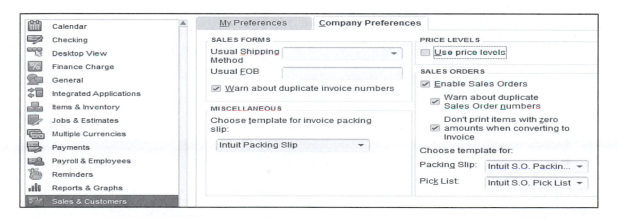

Click **Sales Tax Preferences**, and click **Yes to** Save the changes

SALES TAX PREFERENCES

The Sales Tax preferences indicate whether or not you charge sales tax. If you do collect sales tax, the default sales tax codes, when you need to pay the sales tax, when sales tax is owed, the most common sales tax, and whether or not to mark taxable amounts are selected on this screen.

 Change the default for the Most common sales tax to State Tax

Click the **Company Preferences** tab for **Sales Tax**
Click the drop-down list arrow for **Your most common sales tax item**
Click **State Tax**

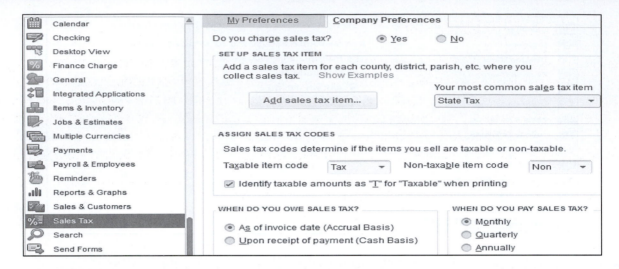

Click **Search** preferences and click **Yes** to save the change

SEARCH PREFERENCES

Company preferences for Search include how often to update search information and to update Search information. My Preferences allows the selection of "Show Search field in the Icon Bar" and of "Choose where to search by default."

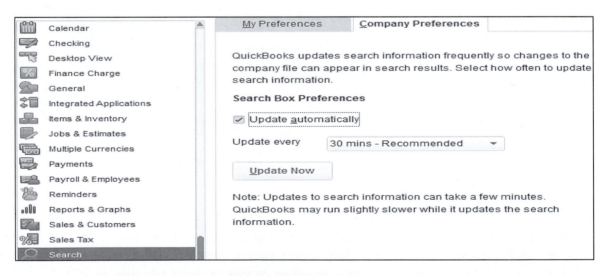

SEND FORMS PREFERENCES

Default text is provided for business documents that are sent by email. The text may be changed for invoices, estimates, statements, sales orders, sales receipts, credit memos, purchase orders, reports, pay stubs, overdue invoices, and almost due invoices. The My Preferences tab allows auto-check to determine if the customer's preferred send method is e-mail. You may also select whether to send e-mail using Web Mail, Outlook, or QuickBooks E-mail. To use QuickBooks E-mail, you must subscribe to Billing Solutions.

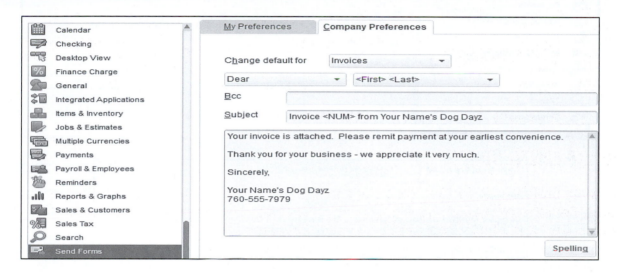

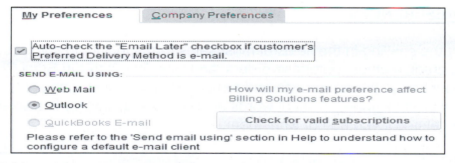

SERVICE CONNECTION PREFERENCES

On the Company Preferences tab, you can specify how you and other company file users log in to QuickBooks Business Services. You may select to automatically connect to QuickBooks Business Services network without passwords or require passwords before connecting. This preference is used to select whether or not Service updates are automatically downloaded from the Intuit server to your computer. The My Preferences tab allows settings for saving a file whenever Web Connect data is downloaded and leaving your browser open after Web Connect is done. Web Connect is used as a Web browser to connect to financial institutions and is used in online banking.

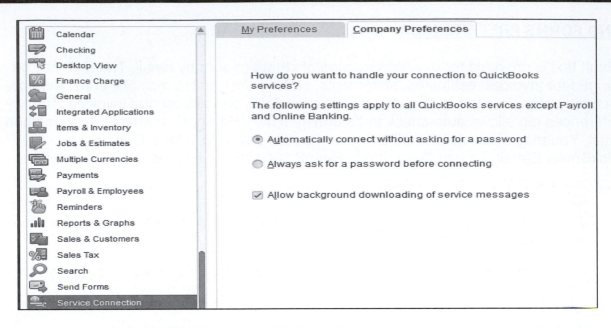

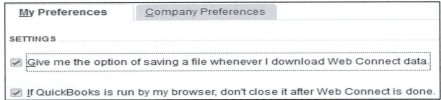

SPELLING PREFERENCES

You can check the spelling in the fields of most sales forms including invoices, estimates, sales receipts, credit memos, purchase orders, and lists. You can run Spell Checker automatically or change the preference and run the Spell Checker manually. There is also a selection for words to ignore. A list of words added to the dictionary is also shown. These words may be deleted if you do not want them.

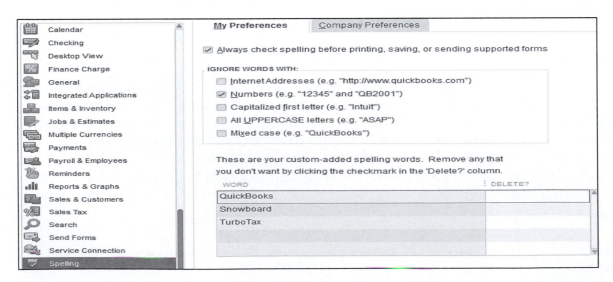

TAX: 1099 PREFERENCES

The only selection is on the Company Preferences screen. This is where you indicate whether or not you file 1099-MISC forms.

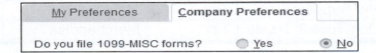

TIME & EXPENSES PREFERENCES

The Time Tracking preference is used to tell QuickBooks to track time. Tracking time is useful if you bill by the hour.

To close the Preferences screen, click **OK**

FINALIZE THE ITEMS LIST

The Items list contains information about all of the items sold or services performed by the business. The Items used to track services performed and products sold for income are created. These were added during the QuickBooks Setup. However, information needs to be added to each sales item. Finally, the Item List shows some items that we will not be using and they need to be deleted.

SERVICE ITEMS		
Item	**Tax Code**	**Income Account**
Doggie Dayz Camp	Non-Tax	Day Camp
Doggie Digs Hotel	Non-Tax	Boarding
Doggie Salon	Non-Tax	Grooming

INVENTORY ITEMS

Item	Preferred Vendor	Tax Code	Income Account	Reorder Point
Collars	Pet Supplies, Inc.	Tax	Merchandise	100
Leashes	Pet Supplies, Inc.	Tax	Merchandise	100
Sweaters	Pet Supplies, Inc.	Tax	Merchandise	100
Toys & Treats	Dog Toys & Treats	Tax	Merchandise	100

 Use the information in the preceding charts to edit each service item. Add the Tax Code, Income Account. Then, edit each inventory item and add the Preferred Vendor, if any; Tax Code; Income Account and Reorder Point. Finally, delete the following sales items: Consignment Item and Non-Inventory Item

If the Home Page is not shown, click **Home** on the icon bar
Open the **Items List**, and double-click **Doggie Dayz Camp** to open Edit Item
Click the drop-down list arrow for **Tax Code**, and click **Non - Taxable Sales**

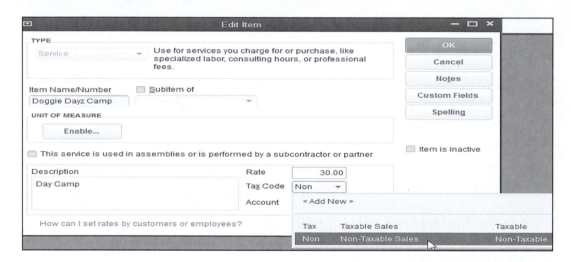

Click the drop-down list arrow for **Account**, and click **Day Camp**, which is a
    subaccount of Sales
Click **OK**
If you get an Account Change screen, click **Yes**. Do this for any other items that
    show the Account Change screen.

Edit the other service items

When the service items have been changed, edit the Inventory Item **Collars**
Click the drop-down list arrow for **Preferred Vendor**, click **Pet Supplies, Inc.**
Select the Tax Code **Tax** and the Income Account **Merchandise**
Enter **100** for the Reorder Point

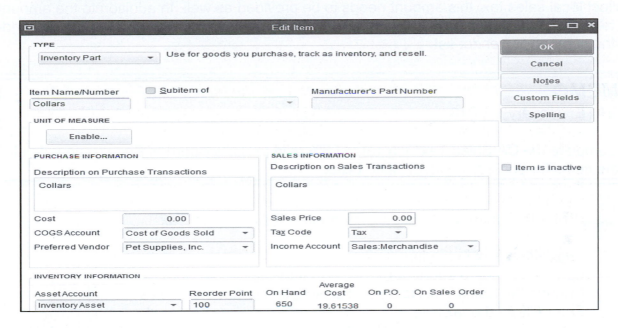

Click **OK**
Repeat for each inventory item
- Don't forget to enter the reorder point for inventory items.
After the service and inventory items have been edited, click **Consignment Item** in the Item list
Use the keyboard shortcut **Ctrl+D** to delete the item
Click **OK** on the Delete Item dialog box
Repeat the procedures to delete the Non-inventory Item
Your Item List should match the following:

ENTER SALES TAX INFORMATION

As you view the Item List, you will notice that the State Sales Tax shows 0.0%. This should be changed to show the appropriate amount of sales tax deducted for the state. If you also collect local sales tax, this amount needs to be provided as well. In addition to the amount of tax collected, the Tax Agency needs to be identified. The Tax Agency was already added to the company's vendor list.

MEMO

DATE: January 1, 2013

Complete the CA Sales Tax: Tax rate of 8% paid to State Board of Equalization, delete the items for Local and Out of State taxes.

 Enter the amount of sales tax information for CA Sales Tax

Click **State Tax** in the Item List
Use the keyboard shortcut **Ctrl+E** to edit the State Tax Item
Change the Sales Tax Name and Description to **CA Sales Tax**
Enter **8%** as the tax rate
- Since sales tax rates vary and may change at any given time, the rate of 8% is used as an example.

Click the drop-down list arrow for **Tax Agency**, click **State Board of Equalization**

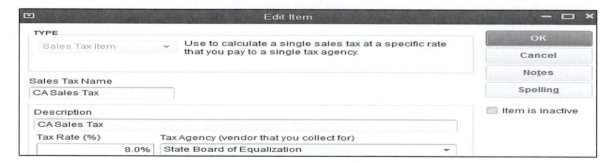

Click **OK** to close the Sales Tax Item
- Note the change to the State Tax on the Item List

Click **Local Tax** use **Ctrl + D** to delete the item as previously instructed
Repeat to delete **Out of State**
- The Item List appears as follows:

NAME	DESCRIPTION	TYPE	ACCOUNT	TOTAL QUANTITY ON HAND	ON SALES ORDER	PRICE	ATTACH
◇ Doggie Dayz Camp	Day Camp	Service	Sales:Day Camp			30.00	
◇ Doggie Digs Hotel	Boarding Services	Service	Sales:Boarding			55.00	
◇ Doggie Salon	Grooming	Service	Sales:Grooming			0.00	
◇ Collars	Collars	Inventory Part	Sales:Merchandise	650	0	0.00	
◇ Leashes	Leashes	Inventory Part	Sales:Merchandise	450	0	0.00	
◇ Sweaters	Sweaters	Inventory Part	Sales:Merchandise	325	0	0.00	
◇ Toys & Treats	Toys & Treats	Inventory Part	Sales:Merchandise	3,450	0	0.00	
◇ CA Sales Tax	CA Sales Tax	Sales Tax Item	Sales Tax Payable			8.0%	

To print the List, click the **Reports** button at the bottom of the screen
Click **Item Listing**
Click the **Customize Report** button, click the **Header/Footer** tab, change the
   Subtitle to show the report date of **January 1, 2013**, click **OK**
Adjust the column widths to remove extra space and to allow the information to
   display in full. Since all amounts are zero in the columns for Quantity on Sales
   Order and Quantity on Purchase Order hide the columns
Click **Print**, click **Landscape**, and click the **Print** button
Close the report and close the Item List

COMPLETE INDIVIDUAL INFORMATION FOR CUSTOMERS

The Customer List was created in the QuickBooks Setup; however, customers have
different terms, tax codes, tax items, and credit limits. This information needs to be added
to the individual customers. This is done in the Customer Center.

CUSTOMERS				
Customer Name	Gray, George	Moraga, Ellen	Phillips, Henry	Summer, Carol
Terms	Net 30	Net 30	Net 30	Net 30
Credit Limit	500	1,000	1,500	500
Tax Item	CA Sales Tax	CA Sales Tax	CA Sales Tax	CA Sales Tax

 Enter the additional information for each customer

Click the **Customers** icon to open the **Customer Center**
Double-click **Gray, George**
Click the **Payment Settings** tab
Click the drop-down list arrow for **PAYMENT TERMS**, click **Net 30**
Click in the text box for **CREDIT LIMIT**, enter **500**

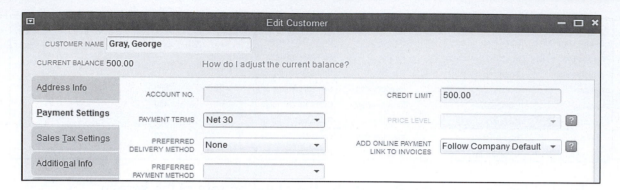

Click the **Sales Tax Settings** tab
Click the drop-down list arrow for **Tax Item**, click **CA Sales Tax**

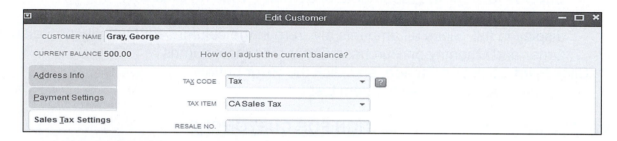

Click **OK**
Use the Customer Chart above and enter the information for the remaining customers
Click the **Print** icon in the Customer Center, click **Customer & Job List**, print in Portrait orientation

- The date of your computer will show as the report date.

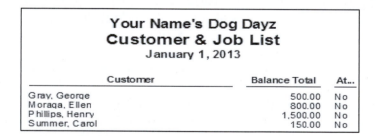

Close the Customer Center

COMPLETE INDIVIDUAL INFORMATION FOR VENDORS

The Vendor List was created in the QuickBooks Setup; however, individual vendors have different terms and credit limits. This information needs to be added to the individual vendors. This is done in the Vendor Center. Vendors used for tax payments, insurance, and banking will not need terms or credit limits entered.

VENDORS			
Vendor Name	Canine Grooming Supplies	Dog Toys & Treats	Pet Supplies, Inc.
Terms	2% 10, Net 30	Net 30	2% 10, Net 30
Credit Limit	10,000	5,000	8,500

 Enter the additional information for each vendor

Click the **Vendors** icon to open the **Vendor Center**
Double-click **Canine Grooming Supplies**
Click the **Payment Settings** tab
Click the drop-down list arrow for **PAYMENT TERMS**, click **2% 10, Net 30**
Click in the text box for **CREDIT LIMIT**, enter **10,000**, and click **OK**
Use the Vendors Chart and enter the information for the remaining vendors
Print the **Vendor List** in Portrait as previously instructed
- Remember, the date of your computer will show as the report date.

Your Name's Dog Dayz
Vendor List
January 1, 2013

Vendor	Balance Total	At...
Canine Grooming Supplies	3,000.00	No
Dog Toys & Treats	0.00	No
Employment Development Department	0.00	No
Health Insurance, Inc.	0.00	No
Pet Supplies, Inc.	2,000.00	No
San Diego Bank	0.00	No
State Board of Equalization	0.00	No

Close the Vendor Center

CORRECT DATES

When you created the company, inventory items that were added used the current date of your computer to record the quantity and value on hand. In addition, the opening balances for customers and vendors were included on invoices and bills. These should be dated January 1, 2013. These dates should be checked and, if necessary, changed to January 1, 2013.

 Correct the dates for opening balances

Click the **Inventory Activities** icon
Click **Adjust Quantity/Value on Hand**
Click **Previous,** if necessary, change the date for <u>each</u> inventory item to **01/01/13**, save the change

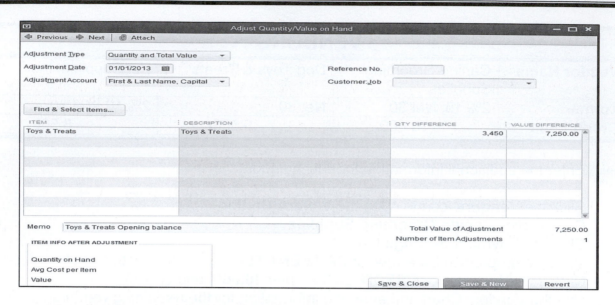

When finished, close **Adjust Quantity/Value on Hand**

To check the Opening balance dates for customers, click the **Create Invoices** icon on the Home Page

Click **Previous** (the back arrow icon), if the date is not 01/01/13 change it to **01/01/13**

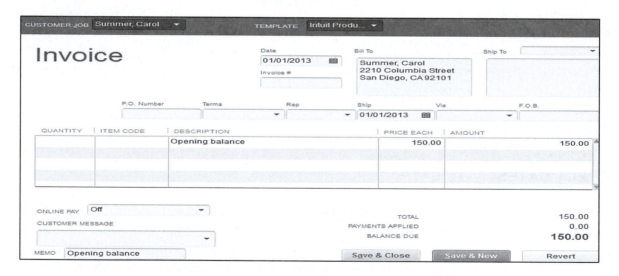

Click **Previous**, and check and, if necessary, change each customer's Opening balance date

- If you get a Recording Transaction dialog box, click **Yes**

When complete, close **Create Invoices**

Click the **Enter Bills** icon, click **Previous**, if the date on each bill is not **01/01/13**, change the date, save the change, and when finished close **Enter Bills**

PREPARE A DAILY BACKUP

A backup file is prepared as a safeguard in case you make an error. After a number of transactions have been recorded, it is wise to prepare a backup file. In addition, a backup should be made at the end of every work session. The Daily Backup file is an appropriate file to create for saving your work as you progress through a chapter.

 Prepare the Your Name's Dog Dayz (Daily Backup).qbb file

    Follow the steps presented in Chapter 1 for creating a backup file
    Name the file **Your Name's Dog Dayz (Daily Backup)**
    The file type is **QBW Backup (* .QBB)**

PAYROLL

When you completed the tutorial in Chapter 8, you paid the employees who worked for the company. In order to use QuickBooks to process payroll, you need to complete the Payroll Set up Interview and provide individual information regarding your employees.

SELECT A PAYROLL OPTION

Before entering any payroll transactions, QuickBooks must be informed of the type of payroll service you are selecting. Once QuickBooks knows what type of payroll process has been selected for the company, you will be able to create paychecks. As in you did in Chapter 8, you must go through the Help menu to designate the selection of the Manual payroll option.

 Select a **Manual** payroll option

    Press **F1** to access Help
    Type **Manual Payroll** and click the **Start Search** icon

    Click **Process payroll manually (without a subscription to QuickBooks Payroll)**
    In the **"Set your company file to use the manual payroll calculations setting"**
        section, click the words **manual payroll calculations**
    In the section **"If you are sure you want to manually calculate your payroll taxes**
        in QuickBooks," click **Set my company file to use manual calculations**
    Once QuickBooks processes the selection, you will get a message, which may be
        hidden behind the Help Article and the Help screen
    Close the Help Article, and close Help
    Click **OK** on the QuickBooks Information screen

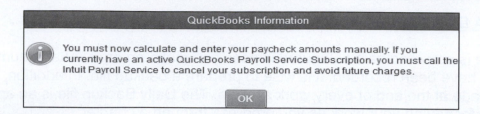

GENERAL NOTES ON QUICKBOOKS PAYROLL SETUP

Once the payroll processing method is selected, you must complete the QuickBooks Payroll Setup. QuickBooks is setup with Automatic Update turned on. Periodically, Intuit will send out program updates via the Internet that will be downloaded to your computer. It is important to note that sometimes information in the program changes. If your screens differ from the ones shown, do not be alarmed, you will enter the same information; but, perhaps, in a slightly different format or order.

You may find that some of your screens are different from the ones shown in the text. This is due to the fact that the computer date used when writing the text is January 1, 2013 and your computer will use the current date. If you see a different year on your screen, and you are not able to change it, just continue with the training and leave the date as it appears.

THE QUICKBOOKS PAYROLL SETUP

There are six sections in the QuickBooks Payroll Setup to guide you through the process of setting up the payroll in QuickBooks.

The first section is an introductory screen. The second section is the Company Setup for payroll. This section helps you identify and setup your methods of compensation, benefits your company offers, and additions and deductions your employees might have.

The third section leads you through adding employee information or setting up individual employees. When establishing the Employee Defaults, you will specify which payroll items apply to all or most of the employees of the company. Payroll items are used to identify and/or track the various amounts that affect a paycheck. There are items for salaries and wages, each kind of tax, each type of other deduction, commissions, and company-paid benefits.

The fourth section, Taxes, automatically sets up the payroll items for federal taxes, state taxes, and local taxes. Payroll tax liabilities and payroll withholding items need to be associated with a vendor in order to have payments processed appropriately.

The fifth section, Year-to-Date Payrolls, earnings and withholdings for the employees for the current year are entered and payroll liability payments are recorded. This is important if you are installing QuickBooks and have already made payroll payments during the calendar year.

The final section, Finishing Up, takes companies that subscribe to QuickBooks Payroll Services to the Payroll Center. If you are using manual payroll, you are taken to the Employee Center.

<u>**CAUTION**</u>: If you exit the payroll setup before everything is complete, be sure to click the **Finish Later** button. If you exit the payroll setup by any other method, you may lose all of the information you have entered. Sometimes, QuickBooks will retain the information and will re-enter it for you as you click through each of the sections in the QuickBooks Payroll Setup. Otherwise, you will need to re-enter all of your information.

BEGIN THE QUICKBOOKS PAYROLL SETUP

 Click the **Employees** menu, click **Payroll Setup**

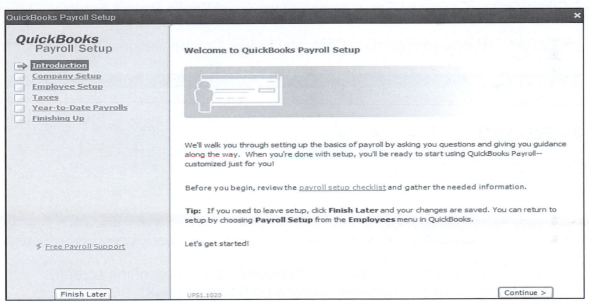

Read the Introduction screen
- If you click <u>payroll setup checklist</u> you will go to an Adobe pdf file that contains information about all of the information you need to gather in order to setup your payroll.

Click **Continue**

COMPANY SECTION OF THE QUICKBOOKS PAYROLL SETUP

In this section of the QuickBooks Payroll Setup, information about the methods of paying employees, deductions, and benefits is entered.

MEMO
DATE: January 1, 2013

Complete the Company portion of the QuickBooks Payroll Setup:

Methods used to compensate employees: Salary, Hourly Wage and Overtime
Insurance Benefits: Health Insurance, Dental Insurance both are fully paid by the
    employee after taxes have been deducted
Retirement Benefits: None
Paid Time Off: Sick Time and Vacation Time
Other Payments and Deductions: None

 Complete the Company Setup portion of the QuickBooks Payroll Setup

Read the first screen regarding Company Setup: Compensation and Benefits

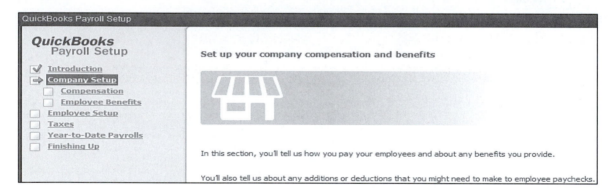

Click the **Continue** button (located in the lower-right corner of the screen)
Click **Bonus, award, or one-time compensation** to unmark

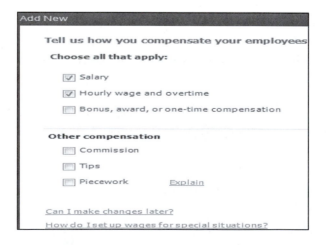

Click **Finish** (located in the lower-right corner of the screen)
Review the Compensation List

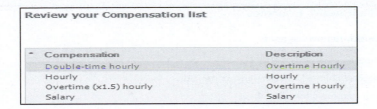

Click **Continue**

Read the screen regarding **Set up employee benefits**

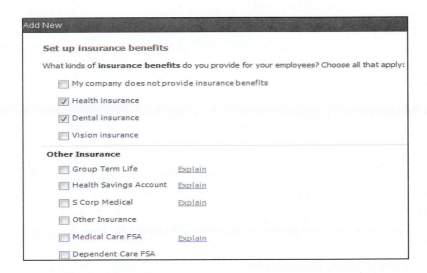

Click **Continue**

Click **Health insurance** and **Dental insurance** to select

Click **Next**

On the Health Insurance screen, click **Employee pays for all of it**
Payment is deducted after taxes should appear and be selected

Tell us about health insurance

How is Health Insurance paid?

- ○ Company pays for all of it
- ○ Both the employee and company pay portions
- ◉ Employee pays for all of it

Is the employee portion deducted before or after taxes are calculated?

- ◉ Payment is deducted after taxes
- ○ Payment is deducted BEFORE taxes (section 125)

Help me decide which one to choose.

Click **Next**

Click the drop-down list arrow for **Payee (Vendor)**, click **Health Insurance, Inc.** to select the Vendor that receives payment for health insurance premiums,

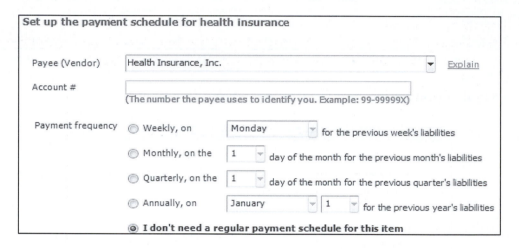

Set up the payment schedule for health insurance

Payee (Vendor)	Health Insurance, Inc. ▼ Explain
Account #	(The number the payee uses to identify you. Example: 99-99999X)

Payment frequency
- ○ Weekly, on   Monday ▼   for the previous week's liabilities
- ○ Monthly, on the   1 ▼   day of the month for the previous month's liabilities
- ○ Quarterly, on the   1 ▼   day of the month for the previous quarter's liabilities
- ○ Annually, on   January ▼   1 ▼   for the previous year's liabilities
- ◉ I don't need a regular payment schedule for this item

Click **Next**

On The Dental Insurance screen, click **Employee pays for all of it** and verify that **Payment is deducted after taxes** is checked

Click **Next**

The Payee for Dental Insurance is **Health Insurance, Inc.**

Click **Finish**

Review your Insurance Benefits list

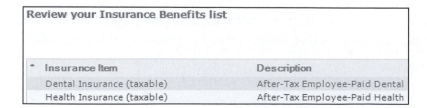

Review your Insurance Benefits list

Insurance Item	Description
Dental Insurance (taxable)	After-Tax Employee-Paid Dental
Health Insurance (taxable)	After-Tax Employee-Paid Health

Click **Continue**

The next screen allows you to select retirement benefits.

We do not provide any retirement benefits for our employees

Tell us about your company retirement benefits

What **retirement benefits** do you provide your employees? Select all that apply.

- ☑ My company does not provide retirement benefits
- ☐ 401(k) (most common)
  - ☐ My 401(k) plan includes a designated Roth contribution. (Roth 401(k))
- ☐ Simple IRA
- ☐ 403(b)
  - ☐ My 403(b) plan includes a designated Roth contribution. (Roth 403(b))
- ☐ 408(k)(6) SEP
- ☐ 457(b) Plan
  - ☐ My 457(b) plan includes a designated Roth contribution. (Roth 457(b))

What are these retirement benefits?

Click **Finish**, and then click **Continue**

For Paid Time Off, we do provide paid time off for Sick Leave and Vacation Leave, click **Paid sick time off** and **Paid vacation time off** to select

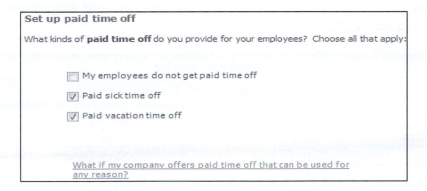

Set up paid time off

What kinds of **paid time off** do you provide for your employees? Choose all that apply:

- ☐ My employees do not get paid time off
- ☑ Paid sick time off
- ☑ Paid vacation time off

What if my company offers paid time off that can be used for any reason?

Click **Finish**

Review your Paid Time Off list

Paid Time Off	Description
Hourly Sick	Sick Taken
Hourly Vacation	Vacation Taken
Salary Sick	Sick Taken
Salary Vacation	Vacation Taken

Review the Paid Time Off list, click **Continue**

We do not have any other Additions or Deductions

Set up additions and deductions

Tell us about **anything else** that affects your employees' paychecks. Choose all that apply:

Additions

☐ Cash advance

☐ Taxable fringe benefits   Explain

☐ Mileage reimbursement   Explain

☐ Miscellaneous addition   Explain

Deductions

☐ Wage garnishment   Explain

☐ Union dues

☐ Donation to charity

☐ Miscellaneous deduction   Explain

Click **Finish**

Click **Continue** to complete the Employee Benefits section and the Company Setup

EMPLOYEE SECTION OF THE QUICKBOOKS PAYROLL SETUP

During the Employee section of the QuickBooks Payroll Setup, individual employees added during QuickBooks Setup may have information customized and employees not added at that time may be added here.

EMPLOYEES Brooke Adams and Drake Childs		
Name	Brooke Adams	Drake Childs
Employee Status	Active	Active
City	San Diego	San Diego
State	CA	CA
Zip	92101	92101
Employee Type	Regular	Regular
Social Security No.	100-55-2525	100-55-9661
Hire Date	04/23/1996	06/30/2004
Birth Date	12/28/1949	04/23/1977
Gender	Female	Male
Pay Period	Monthly	Monthly
Compensation	Salary: $26,000 per year	Hourly: Hourly wage: $15.50 Double-time hourly: $31.00 Overtime (x1.5) hourly: $23.25
Dental Insurance	$10 per month, annual limit $120	$10 per month, annual limit $120
Health Insurance	$50 per month, annual limit $600	$25 per month, annual limit $300
Sick Time Earns	40:00 at beginning of year	40:00 at beginning of year

EMPLOYEES Brooke Adams and Drake Childs		
Unused Hours (Sick)	Have an accrual limit	Have an accrual limit
Maximum Hours (Sick)	120:00	120:00
Earns (Sick)	Time off currently	Time off currently
Hours Available as of 01/01/13 (Your computer date will show) (Sick)	20:00	50:00
Vacation Time Earns	40:00 at beginning of year	40:00 at beginning of year
Unused Hours (Vacation)	Have an accrual limit	Have an accrual limit
Maximum Hours (Vacation)	120:00	120:00
Earns (Vacation)	Time off currently	Time off currently
Hours Available as of 01/01/13 (Your computer date will show) (Vacation)	20:00	40:00
Payment Method	Check	Check
State Subject to Withholding	CA	CA
State Subject to Unemployment Tax	CA	CA
Live or Work in Another State in 2013	No	No
Federal Filing Status	Single	Married
Allowances (Federal)	0	2
Extra Withholding	0.00	0.00
Nonresident Alien Withholding	Does not apply	Does not apply
HIRE Act Exemption	Not a qualified employee	Not a qualified employee
Subject to (Federal)	Medicare Social Security Federal Unemployment	Medicare Social Security Federal Unemployment
State Filing Status	Single	Married (two incomes)
Regular Withholding Allowances (State)	0	2
Subject to (State)	CA-Unemployment CA-Employment Training Tax CA-Disability	CA-Unemployment CA-Employment Training Tax CA-Disability
Wage Plan Code	S	S

Complete the Employee portion of the QuickBooks Payroll Setup using the chart above to add employee information not entered in the QuickBooks Setup

Read the screen about the Employee Setup

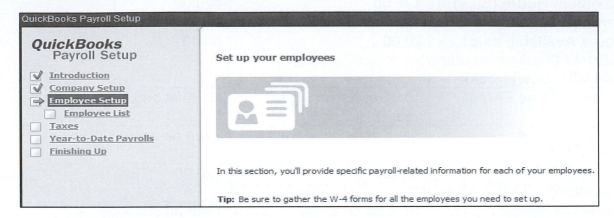

Click **Continue**

Click **Adams**, **Brooke**, and then click **Edit**
- Even though the complete address was entered during the QuickBooks Setup, QuickBooks marks the City, State, and Zip as being needed for W-2.

Before correcting the City, State and Zip, make sure Brooke's status is Active
- If her status is not Active, click the drop-down list arrow and select Active.
Click in the text box with San Diego, CA 92101 and delete all the information
Click in the text box for **City**, enter **San Diego**
Click drop-down list arrow for **State**, click **CA**
Click in the text box for **Zip**, enter **92101**

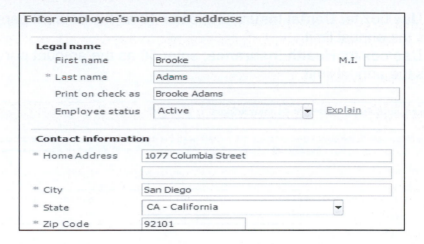

Click **Next**

Enter Brooke's missing information as given in the memo

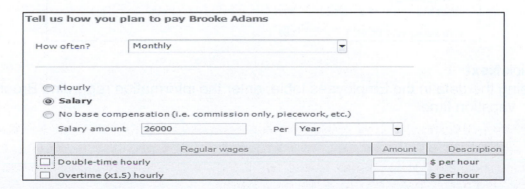

Click **Next**

Click the drop-down list arrow for **How often?** And click **Monthly**

Click the radial dial for **Salary**

For the **Salary amount** enter **26,000**

For **Per** click the drop-down arrow and click **Year**

Click **Next**

Click the **Use** box for **Dental Insurance**; enter **10** as the amount per paycheck and **120** as the annual limit

Click the **Use** box for **Health Insurance**; enter **50** as the amount per paycheck and **600** as the annual limit

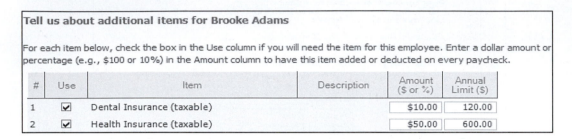

Click **Next**

Using the data provided in the Employees table, enter the information about Brooke's sick time

- Be sure to select hours "at beginning of year."
- In the **Current balances** section of the screen you may not see the dates of 1/1/2013. Use whatever date is automatically inserted by QuickBooks. The date shown may be the date of the computer.

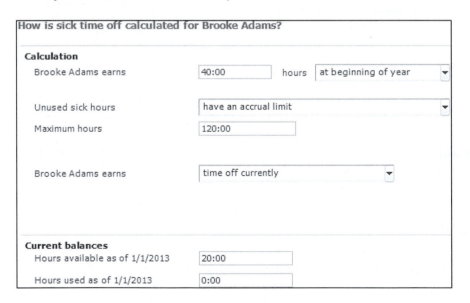

Click **Next**

Using the data in the Employees table, enter the information regarding Brooke's vacation time

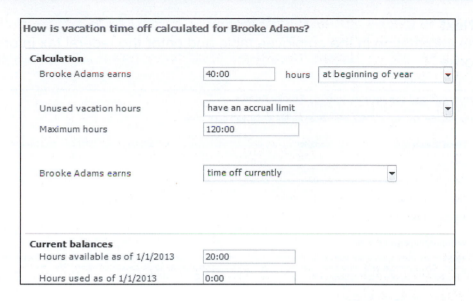

Click **Next**

Brooke is paid by Check, click **Check** if necessary

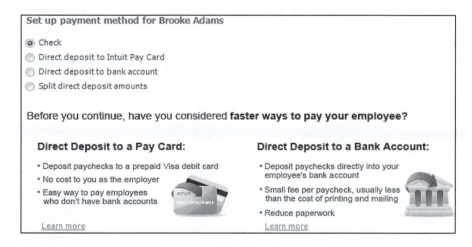

Click **Next**

Enter **CA** as the state where Brooke is subject to withholding and unemployment
tax. She has not lived or worked in another state in 2013

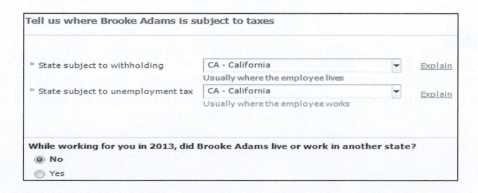

Click **Next**

Use the information in the employee table and enter the federal tax information for Brooke

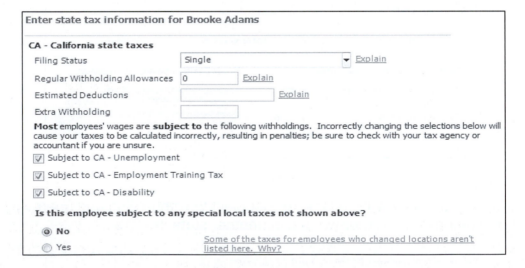

Click **Next**

Enter the state tax information for Brooke

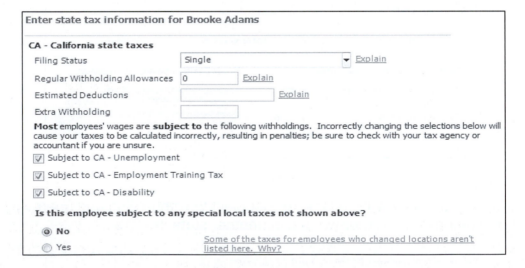

Click **Next**

The California Employment Development Department agency requires employers who file electronically to select a Wage Plan Code. Since you do participate in the state unemployment and disability insurance programs, select **S** as the code.

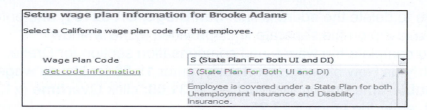

Click **Finish**
Click the **Summary** button to view the information entered for Brooke Adams

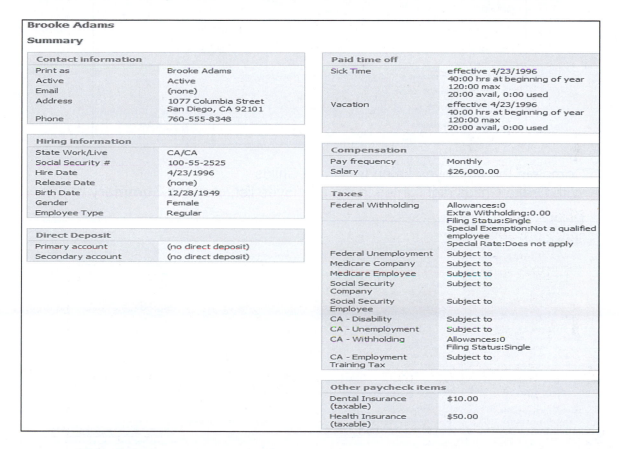

- Note that the Sick Time and Vacation Time are effective as of Brooke's hire date 04/23/1996. If a different effective date appears, disregard it at this time. The effective date can be corrected by going to the Employee Center, editing the employee, selecting the Payroll and Compensation Info tab, click Sick/Vacation, and changing the date to match the employee's hire date.
- If you selected 40:00 hours per year rather than 40:00 at the beginning of the year, your summary will show 3:20 per paycheck.

Click **Print** on the Summary screen and print Brooke's information
Close the **Employee Summary** window for Brooke
Click **Drake Childs** in the Employee List, click the **Edit** button
Add the information provided in the Employees Chart by following the steps provided for Brooke Adams

Make sure to delete the address line: **San Diego, CA 92101**, and enter the City, State and Zip on the separate lines provided in the window

When you complete the wages and compensation section for Drake, after selecting **Monthly** as How often?, click **Hourly**, enter **15.50** for Hourly wage

Click, **Double-time hourly** to select, enter **31.00**; click **Overtime (x1.5) hourly** to select, enter the amount **23.25**

Tell us how you plan to pay Drake Childs

| How often? | Monthly ▼ |

○ **Hourly**
○ Salary
○ No base compensation (i.e. commission only, piecework, etc.)

Hourly wage `15.50`

Regular wages	Amount	Description
☑ Double-time hourly	$31.00	$ per hour
☑ Overtime (x1.5) hourly	$23.25	$ per hour

Complete the employee setup for Drake Childs

With Drake Childs highlighted in the employee list, click the **Summary** button

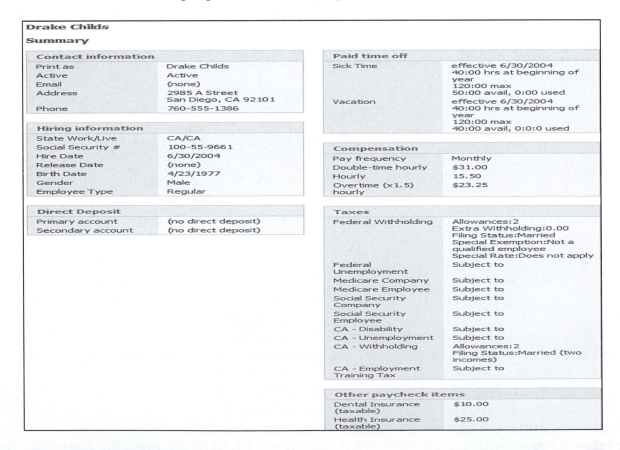

Drake Childs

Summary

Contact information

Print as	Drake Childs
Active	Active
Email	(none)
Address	2985 A Street
	San Diego, CA 92101
Phone	760-555-1386

Hiring information

State Work/Live	CA/CA
Social Security #	100-55-9661
Hire Date	6/30/2004
Release Date	(none)
Birth Date	4/23/1977
Gender	Male
Employee Type	Regular

Direct Deposit

| Primary account | (no direct deposit) |
| Secondary account | (no direct deposit) |

Paid time off

Sick Time	effective 6/30/2004
	40:00 hrs at beginning of year
	120:00 max
	50:00 avail, 0:00 used
Vacation	effective 6/30/2004
	40:00 hrs at beginning of year
	120:00 max
	40:00 avail, 0:0:0 used

Compensation

Pay frequency	Monthly
Double-time hourly	$31.00
Hourly	15.50
Overtime (x1.5) hourly	$23.25

Taxes

Federal Withholding	Allowances:2
	Extra Withholding:0.00
	Filing Status:Married
	Special Exemption:Not a qualified employee
	Special Rate:Does not apply
Federal Unemployment	Subject to
Medicare Company	Subject to
Medicare Employee	Subject to
Social Security Company	Subject to
Social Security Employee	Subject to
CA - Disability	Subject to
CA - Unemployment	Subject to
CA - Withholding	Allowances:2
	Filing Status:Married (two incomes)
CA - Employment Training Tax	Subject to

Other paycheck items

| Dental Insurance (taxable) | $10.00 |
| Health Insurance (taxable) | $25.00 |

- Before you print the Summary for Drake Childs, check the beginning date for accruing sick and vacation time. It should show his Hire date. If a different effective date appears, disregard it at this time. The effective date can be corrected by going to the Employee Center, editing the employee, selecting the Payroll and Compensation Info tab, click Sick/Vacation, and changing the date to match the employee's hire date.

Print **Drake Childs'** Summary, close the Summary

Review the Employee List

Employee	Social Security	Summary
Adams, Brooke	100-55-2525	
Childs, Drake	100-55-9661	

Click **Continue**

TAXES SECTION OF THE QUICKBOOKS PAYROLL SETUP

The Taxes section of the QuickBooks Payroll Setup allows you to identify federal, state, and local tax payments and agencies. You may also schedule tax payments in this section.

 Complete the Taxes section of the QuickBooks Payroll Setup

Read the screen for "Set up your payroll taxes"

QuickBooks Payroll Setup

QuickBooks
Payroll Setup
- ✔ Introduction
- ✔ Company Setup
- ✔ Employee Setup
- ⇨ **Taxes**
  - ☐ Federal taxes
  - ☐ State taxes
  - ☐ Schedule payments
- ☐ Year-to-Date Payrolls
- ☐ Finishing Up

Set up your payroll taxes

In this section, you'll confirm or provide rates for the federal and state taxes that apply to your payroll.

Tip: Before you start, be sure that you have state tax ID numbers, rates, and payment schedules. You can get this information from your state agencies. You can also find more information on the Intuit Payroll Tax Support web site.

Click **Continue**
Review the list of Federal taxes

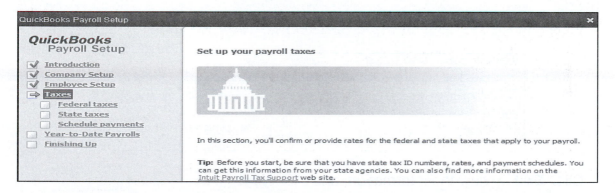

Here are the federal taxes we set up for you

Click **Edit** if you need to review or make changes to any of these taxes.

Federal Tax	Description
Federal Withholding	Also known as Federal Withholding Tax
Advance Earned Income Credit	Also known as AEIC
Federal Unemployment	Also known as FUTA
Medicare Company	Medicare Tax
Medicare Employee	Medicare Tax
Social Security Company	Also known as FICA
Social Security Employee	Also known as FICA

Click **Continue**

If you go directly to the screen for CA-EDD payments, Enter the California-Unemployment Company Rate of **3.4%**

- The rate for CA-Disability Employee Rate should be shown as 1% and the rate for CA-Employment Training Tax Company Rate should be shown as 0.1%, if not change as necessary.
- California has a variable rate schedule for Unemployment Insurance for companies. A new company will pay 3.4% for the first three years. After that, the rate is determined by a variety of factors and can range from 1.5 to 6.2%.

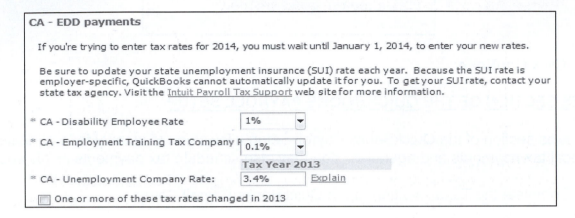

OR

If the Review your state taxes screen appears, click **CA –Unemployment**

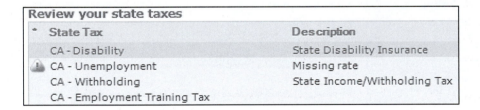

Click **Edit**, review the information, and click **Next**

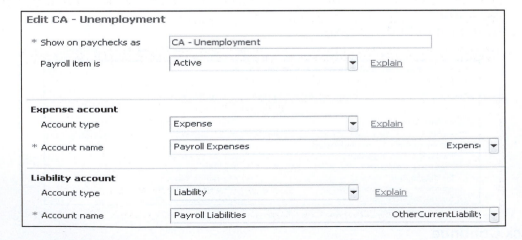

Enter the Company Rate of **3.4%**

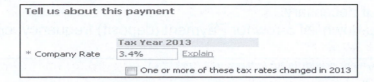

Click **Finish**
Review the state taxes and note the tax amounts

Click **Continue**
Read the screen regarding **Review your Scheduled Tax Payments** list
- QuickBooks might go into the area for Schedule Payments for Federal 940 before you have time to view the screen.

	Scheduled Payments	Description
⚠	Federal 940	Select a payment frequency
⚠	Federal 941/944/943	Select a payment frequency
⚠	CA Withholding and Disability Insurance	Missing account number; Select
⚠	CA UI and Employment Training Tax	Missing account number; Select

Review your Scheduled Tax Payments list

- Notice that each item is marked with Information is missing.

The Schedule Payments window for Federal 940 should appear
- If not, click it and then click Edit.
- For Federal Form 940, the Payee should be United States Treasury, the deposit frequency is Quarterly. Enter these if necessary.

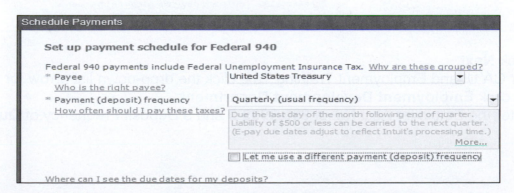

Click **Next** on the Schedule Payments window for Federal 940

- For Federal Form 941/944/943, the Payee should be United States Treasury, enter this if necessary.

Click the drop-down list arrow for Payment (deposit) frequency, click **Quarterly**

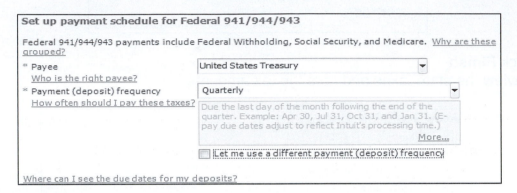

Click **Next**

- Sometimes the screens display in a different order than illustrated below. If that occurs, enter the information pertinent to the screen and continue until all payment schedule information is completed.

Complete the information for CA Withholding and Disability Insurance

Click the drop-down list arrow for Payee, and then click **Employment Development Department**

 Employer Acct No. is **999-9999-9**

Deposit Frequency is **Quarterly**

Set up payment schedule for CA Withholding and Disability Insurance

CA Withholding payments include Income Tax Withholdings and State Disability Insurance. Why are these grouped?

* Payee
Who is the right payee?
Employment Development Department

* CA Employment Development Dept
Employer Acct No.
What number do I enter?
999-9999-9

* Payment (deposit) frequency
How often should I pay these taxes?
Quarterly

Due the last day of the month following the end of the quarter. Example: Apr 30, Jul 31, Oct 31, and Jan 31. (E-pay due dates adjust to reflect Intuit's processing time.)
More...

☐ Let me use a different payment (deposit) frequency

Where can I see the due dates for my deposits?

Click **Next**

For CA UI and Employment Training Tax, click the drop-down list arrow for Payee, click **Employment Development Department**

Enter the Employer Acct No. of **999-9999-9** and a Deposit Frequency of **Quarterly**

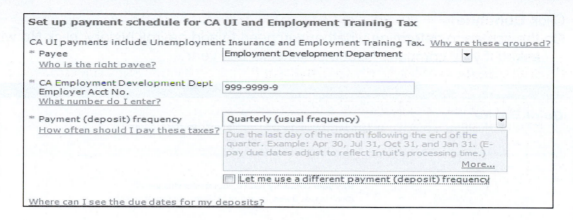

Click **Finish**, view the finalized **Scheduled Tax Payment List**

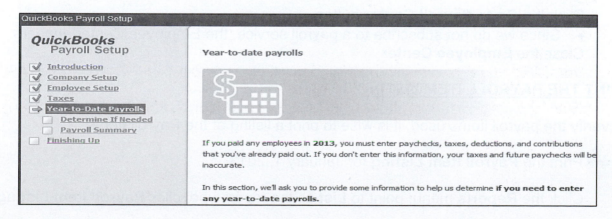

Click **Continue**

YEAR-TO-DATE PAYROLLS SECTION OF THE QUICKBOOKS PAYROLL SETUP

The Year-to-Date Payrolls is completed to enter year-to-date amounts for employees and to identify liability payments you made. Since there have been no payroll payments processed or paid for 2013, there is no payroll history to enter.

 Read the screen, click **Continue**

- Depending on the date of your computer, your screens for Payroll History may not be an exact match for the following screen shots. Your screen may show all four quarters listed under payroll history. This will not affect your setup. (Some examples of screens that you might see appear below.)

Click **Continue**

On the screen to determine whether you need to add payroll history, click **No** when asked if your company issued paychecks this year

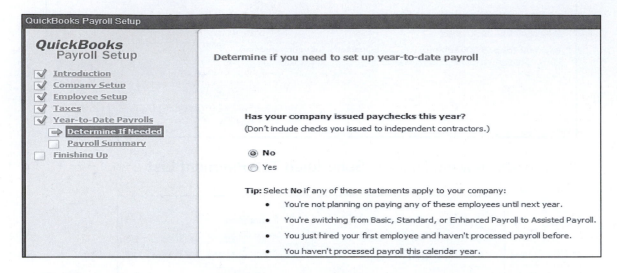

Click **Continue**

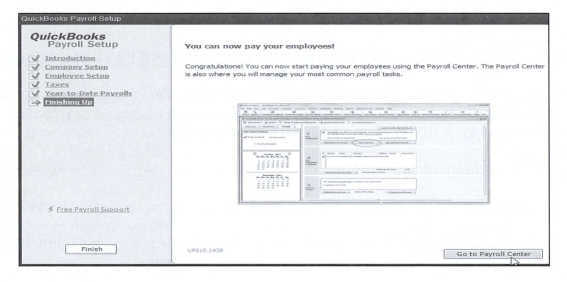

Click the **Go to Payroll Center** button
- Since we do not subscribe to a payroll service, the Employee Center appears.

Close the **Employee Center**

PRINT THE PAYROLL ITEM LISTING

To verify the payroll items used, it is wise to print a listing of the Payroll Items.

 Print the **Payroll Item Listing** for January 1, 2013

Click the **Reports** menu; point to **List** as the report type, click **Payroll Item Listing**

Adjust the column widths and print the report in **Landscape** orientation

Your Name's Dog Dayz
Payroll Item Listing

Payroll Item	Type	Amount	Limit	Expense Account	Liability Account	Tax Tracking
Salary	Yearly Salary			Payroll Expenses		Compensation
Salary Sick	Yearly Salary			Payroll Expenses		Compensation
Salary Vacation	Yearly Salary			Payroll Expenses		Compensation
Double-time hourly	Hourly Wage			Payroll Expenses		Compensation
Hourly	Hourly Wage			Payroll Expenses		Compensation
Hourly Sick	Hourly Wage			Payroll Expenses		Compensation
Hourly Vacation	Hourly Wage			Payroll Expenses		Compensation
Overtime (x1.5) hourly	Hourly Wage			Payroll Expenses		Compensation
Dental Insurance (taxable)	Deduction	0.00			Payroll Liabilities	None
Health Insurance (taxable)	Deduction	0.00			Payroll Liabilities	None
Advance Earned Income Credit	Federal Tax				Payroll Liabilities	Advance EIC Payment
Federal Unemployment	Federal Tax	0.6%	7,000.00	Payroll Expenses	Payroll Liabilities	FUTA
Federal Withholding	Federal Tax				Payroll Liabilities	Federal
Medicare Company	Federal Tax	1.45%		Payroll Expenses	Payroll Liabilities	Comp. Medicare
Medicare Employee	Federal Tax	1.45%			Payroll Liabilities	Medicare
Social Security Company	Federal Tax	6.2%	110,100.00	Payroll Expenses	Payroll Liabilities	Comp. SS Tax
Social Security Employee	Federal Tax	4.2%	110,100.00		Payroll Liabilities	SS Tax
CA – Withholding	State Withholding Tax				Payroll Liabilities	SWH
CA – Disability	State Disability Tax	1.0%	95,585.00		Payroll Liabilities	SDI
CA – Unemployment	State Unemployment Tax	3.4%	7,000.00	Payroll Expenses	Payroll Liabilities	Comp. SUI
CA – Employment Training Tax	Other Tax	0.1%	7,000.00	Payroll Expenses	Payroll Liabilities	Co. Paid Other Tax

Close the report and the Report Center

ADJUSTING ENTRIES

When the company setup is completed, all existing balances are placed into the Uncategorized Income and Uncategorized Expenses accounts so that the amounts listed will not be interpreted as income or expenses for the current period. This adjustment transfers the amount of income and expenses recorded prior to the current period into the owner's capital account. In actual practice this adjustment would be made at the completion of the company setup. In traditional accounting, Income is credited to the owner's capital account and expenses are debited. The same process is used in recording a Journal entry in QuickBooks.

MEMO
DATE: January 1, 2013

Make the adjusting entry to transfer Uncategorized Income and Uncategorized Expenses to First & Last Name, Capital.

 Transfer the Uncategorized Income and Expenses to the owner's capital account

Prepare a Profit & Loss Statement (not shown)
OR
Click **Chart of Accounts** in the Company Section of the Home Page

Double-click on the account **Uncategorized Income**, enter the to and from dates as **01/01/13**, tab to generate the report, note the amount of Uncategorized Income **$2,950.00**

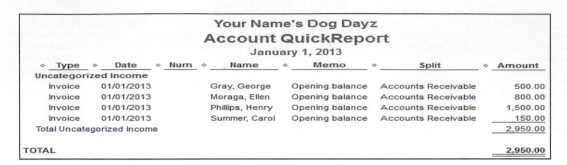

Close the QuickReport

Repeat the steps given to view the balance of the Uncategorized Expenses account of **5,000.00**

Your Name's Dog Dayz
Account QuickReport
January 1, 2013

Type	Date	Num	Name	Memo	Split	Amount
Uncategorized Expenses						
Bill	01/01/2013		Canine Grooming Supplies	Opening balance	Accounts Payable	3,000.00
Bill	01/01/2013		Pet Supplies, Inc.	Opening balance	Accounts Payable	2,000.00
Total Uncategorized Expenses						5,000.00
TOTAL						**5,000.00**

Close the QuickReport

Click the **Activities** button at the bottom of the Chart of Accounts, click **Make General Journal Entries**

Enter the date **01/01/13** (Your Entry No. may or may not match the illustration.)

Leave **Adjusting Entry** marked

Tab to or click **Account**, click the drop-down list arrow, click **Uncategorized Income**, tab to or click **Debit** enter **2950**, tab to or click **Account**, click the drop-down list arrow, click **First & Last Name, Capital**

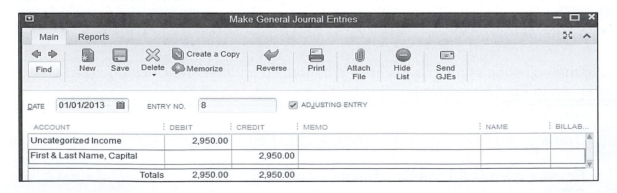

Click **Save & New**

Enter the adjustment to transfer the amount of **Uncategorized Expenses** to **First & Last Name, Capital**

- Remember, you will debit the Capital account and credit the Uncategorized Expenses account.

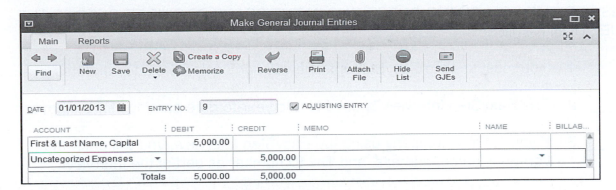

Click **Save & Close**, and close the Chart of Accounts

Print a **Standard Balance Sheet** for **January 1, 2013** in Portrait orientation

Total Assets of **$88,835.00** should equal the Total Liabilities + Owners Equities of **$88,835.00**

BACKUP

As in previous chapters, a backup of the data file for Your Name's Dog Dayz should be made.

 Back up the company file to **Dog Dayz (Backup Ch. 9)** as instructed in earlier chapters and make a duplicate disk as instructed by your professor.

SUMMARY

In this chapter a company was created using the EasyStep Interview and QuickBooks Setup. Once the interview and setup was complete, the Chart of Accounts/General Ledger was customized. Detailed information was given for items, customers and vendors. Preferences were customized. The Payroll Setup was completed, and employees were added. Adjusting entries were made.

END-OF-CHAPTER QUESTIONS

TRUE/FALSE

ANSWER THE FOLLOWING QUESTIONS IN THE SPACE PROVIDED BEFORE THE QUESTION NUMBER.

_____ 1. You must use the EasyStep Interview to add customers and vendors.

_____ 2. The EasyStep Interview is used to add year-to-date earnings for employees.

_____ 3. If you setup a company using the EasyStep Interview, you will enter the company name, address, and Tax ID number as part of the Interview.

_____ 4. Permanently removing the date prepared and time prepared from a balance sheet heading is done the first time you complete a balance sheet.

_____ 5. The start date is the date you select to begin tracking financial information for your company in QuickBooks.

_____ 6. The EasyStep Interview allows you to have QuickBooks generate a chart of accounts.

_____ 7. When the EasyStep Interview is complete, the Uncategorized Expenses account contains a balance that reflects the total amount of all receivables accounts.

_____ 8. When using the EasyStep Interview to set up income and expenses, you must type in the name of every income and expense account you use.

_____ 9. The Item List is automatically generated in the EasyStep Interview.

_____ 10. Customer names, addresses, credit terms, and credit limits are entered after the EasyStep Interview.

MULTIPLE CHOICE

WRITE THE LETTER OF THE CORRECT ANSWER IN THE SPACE PROVIDED BEFORE THE QUESTION NUMBER.

_____ 1. Send Forms preferences contain default text for business documents sent by ___.
A. Fax
B. E-mail
C. Fed-Ex
D. All of the above

_____ 2. Adjusting entries that must be made after the company setup are ___.
A. Close Uncategorized Income to Capital
B. Close Uncategorized Expenses to Capital
C. Both of the above
D. None of the above

_____ 3. When creating customer, vendor, and employee lists all at once, you use the ___.
A. QuickBooks Setup
B. EasyStep Interview
C. Chart of Accounts
D. None of the above

_____ 4. The EasyStep Interview is accessed on the ___.
A. File menu
B. QuickBooks Company Preferences screen
C. Activities menu
D. All of the above

_____ 5. In order to process payroll manually, you must go through the __ to designate this choice.
A. Payroll menu
B. Help menu
C. EasyStep Interview
D. Company Configuration

_____ 6. The Company File has a _____ extension.
A. .qbb
B. .qbi
C. .qbp
D. .qbw

_____ 7. When a(n) ___ account is created, you must provide an opening balance.
   A. Income
   B. Expense
   C. Asset
   D. Posting

_____ 8. Select to display employee names by last name on the ___.
   A. Payroll & Employees Preferences
   B. Employee List
   C. Employee Center
   D. None of the above

_____ 9. Employee deductions for medical and dental insurance may be created ___.
   A. during the EasyStep Interview
   B. during the QuickBooks Payroll Setup
   C. by clicking the Reports button at the bottom of the employee list
   D. on the Employee Menu

_____ 10. Sales tax is listed on the ___.
   A. Vendor List
   B. Company List
   C. Banking List
   D. Item List

FILL-IN

IN THE SPACE PROVIDED, WRITE THE ANSWER THAT MOST APPROPRIATELY COMPLETES THE SENTENCE.

1. The asset account used for Inventory sales items is _____.

2. In the Chart of Accounts, only _____ accounts have opening balances.

3. Accounts that are listed individually but are grouped together under a main account are called _____.

4. _____ Preferences warns you of duplicate check numbers.

5. The _____ section of the QuickBooks Payroll Setup allows information for earnings, withholding, and payroll liabilities to be entered for the year-to-date.

SHORT ESSAY

List the six sections in the Payroll Setup and describe the purpose of each section.

_____
_____
_____
_____
_____
_____
_____

NAME_____

TRANSMITTAL

CHAPTER 9: YOUR NAME'S DOG DAYZ

Attach the following documents and reports:

Account Listing
Item Listing
Customer & Job List
Vendor List
Brooke Adams Employee Summary
Drake Childs Employee Summary
Payroll Item Listing
Balance Sheet, January 1, 2013

END-OF-CHAPTER PROBLEM

YOUR NAME'S COFFEE CORNER

Your Name's Coffee Corner is a fictitious company that sells coffee and pastries. You also provide catering service for meetings and lunches. The company is located in San Francisco, California, and is a sole proprietorship owned by you. You are involved in all aspects of the business. There is one full-time employee, Barbara Olsen, who is paid a salary. She manages the store, is responsible for the all the employees, and keeps the books. There is one full-time hourly employee, Colleen Anders, who works in the shop and provides the catering service.

CREATE A NEW COMPANY

▶ Use the following information to complete the EasyStep Interview for Your Name's Coffee Corner.
   o **Your Name's Coffee Corner** *(Use your actual name)* is the Company Name and the Legal Name
   o Federal Tax ID 45-6221346
   o Address: 550 Powell Street, San Francisco, CA 94102
   o Phone: 415-555-4646; Fax: 415-555-6464
   o E-mail: YourNameCoffeeCorner@info.com *(Use your actual name)*
   o Web: www.CoffeeCorner.com
   o Type of business: Retail shop or online commerce
   o The company is a Sole Proprietorship
   o Fiscal year starts in January
   o Do not use passwords
   o File Name: Your Name's Coffee Corner
   o File Type: qbw
   o Sell both services and products.
   o Record each sale individually, do charge sales tax
   o Do not use estimates, statements, progress invoicing, or track time
   o Do use invoices and track customer orders (sales orders)
   o Do track bills and inventory
   o Employees: Yes, W-2 Employees
   o Date to start tracking finances is: 01/01/2013 (If your date is not 01/01/13, select "Use today's date or the first day of the quarter" and enter 01/01/13.)
   o Scroll through the list of the income and expense accounts created by QuickBooks, remove the check marks for Merchant Account Fees, Uniforms, and Ask My Accountant

USE QUICKBOOKS SETUP

▶ In the first section of the QuickBooks Setup, use the following charts to add customers, vendors, employees, opening balances.

CUSTOMERS

Customer Name	Jenkins, Sally, Inc.	Training, Inc.
Company Name	Sally Jenkins, Inc.	Training, Inc.
Phone	415-555-1248	415-555-8762
Address	785 Mason Street	490 Harvard Street
City, State Zip	San Francisco, CA 94102	San Francisco, CA 94102

VENDORS

Vendor and Company Name	Coffee Royale	Deluxe Pastries
Phone	415-555-3614	415-555-8712
Fax	415-555-4163	415-555-2178
Address	195 N. Market Street	701 7th Street
City, State, Zip	San Francisco, CA 94103	San Francisco, CA 94103
Contact Person	Ron Richards	Katie Carlson

VENDORS

Vendor and Company Name	Employment Development Department	Hill Street Bank	Insurance Organization of California	State Board of Equalization
Phone	415-555-5248	415-555-9781	415-555-2347	916-555-0000
Fax	415-555-8425	415-555-1879	415-555-7432	916-555-1111
Address	10327 Washington Street	205 Hill Street	20951 Oakmont Avenue	7800 State Street
City, State, Zip	San Francisco, CA 94107	San Francisco, CA 94104	San Francisco, CA 94103	Sacramento, CA 94265

EMPLOYEES

Employee Name	Olsen, Barbara	Anders, Colleen
First Name	Barbara	Colleen
Last Name	Olsen	Anders
Phone	415-555-7801	415-555-7364
Address	9077 Harvard Avenue	1808 17th Street
City, State, Zip	San Francisco, CA 94101	San Francisco, CA 94103

OPENING BALANCES

Type	Name	Balance	Opening Balance Date
Customer	Jenkins, Sally, Inc.	1,500.00	01/01/2013
Customer	Training, Inc.	5,245.00	01/01/2013
Vendor	Coffee Royale	1,000.00	01/01/2013
Vendor	Deluxe Pastries	500.00	01/01/2013

▶ Complete the second section of the QuickBooks Setup to add service and inventory items.

SERVICE ITEM

Item Name	Catering
Description	Catering
Price	50.00

INVENTORY ITEMS

Item Name	Coffee	Pastry
Description	Coffee	Pastry
Price	0.00	0.00
Cost	0.00	0.00
On-Hand	1,500	1,750
Total Value	12,000	1,750
As Of	01/01/13	01/01/13

▶ Complete the final section of the QuickBooks Setup to add your bank account: Account name: **Checking**; Account number **123-654-98755**; Opening balance: **35,871** Opening balance date **01/01/2013**.

▶ You do not want to order checks.

▶ Start Working.

▶ Close the Quick Start Center.

COMPANY INFORMATION

▶ Verify the company information and enter if necessary. Federal Employer Identification No.: 45-6221346; Social Security Number: 456-22-1346; First Month in Tax and Fiscal Year: January.

SELECT A TOP ICON BAR

▶ Rather than use the Left Icon Bar, use the View menu to select a Top Icon Bar.

CHART OF ACCOUNTS

After the EasyStep Interview and QuickBooks Setup have been completed, you have created a partial Chart of Accounts. The Chart of Accounts must be customized to reflect the actual accounts used by Your Name's Coffee Corner.

▶ Customize the Chart of Accounts provided by QuickBooks:
   o Delete: Accumulated Depreciation, Furniture and Equipment, and Security Deposits Asset
   o Make Inactive: Janitorial Expense and Meals and Entertainment
   o Edit Equity Accounts:
      ▪ Change the name of Opening Balance Equity to **First & Last Name, Capital** (use your real name) and delete the description
      ▪ Change Owners Equity to **Retained Earnings**, delete the description
      ▪ Change Owners Draw to **First & Last Name, Withdrawals;** Subaccount of First & Last Name, Capital; Opening Balance, $0.00 as of 01/01/13
   o Add Equity Accounts: **First & Last Name, Investment**; Subaccount of First & Last Name, Capital; Opening Balance **$35,000** as of **01/01/13**.
   o Edit Income Accounts:
      ▪ Rename Sales Income to **Sales**
      ▪ Rename Merchandise Sales to **Pastry Sales**, subaccount of Sales
   o Add Income Accounts:
      ▪ Add **Coffee Sales**, subaccount of Sales
      ▪ Add **Catering Sales**, subaccount of Sales
   o Add Other Income Account: **Other Income**
   o Add Expense Account: **Store Supplies Expense**
   o Add Other Expense Account: **Other Expenses**
   o Edit Expense Accounts: Rename Office Supplies to **Office Supplies Expense**
   o Delete Duplicate Cost of Goods Sold Account: If you get a duplicate Cost of Goods Sold account with an *, delete it
   o Delete: Descriptions for each account
   o Change: Tax-Line Mapping to **Unassigned** for each account
▶ Set up the following Balance Sheet accounts and balances. The Opening Balance date is **01/01/2013**.

CHART OF ACCOUNTS

Account Type	Account Name	Sub-Account of	Opening Balance 01/01/13
Other Current Asset	Prepaid Insurance		$1,200.00
Other Current Asset	Office Supplies		$950.00
Other Current Asset	Store Supplies		$1,800.00
Fixed Asset	Store Fixtures		
Fixed Asset	Original Cost	Store Fixtures	$18,000.00
Fixed Asset	Depreciation	Store Fixtures	$-1,800.00
Long-Term Liability	Store Fixtures Loan		$2,000.00

▶ Print an Account Listing in Landscape orientation. Remove the date and time prepared, change the Subtitle to show the date **January 1, 2013**. Resize columns and do not include the Description or Tax Line columns in your report.

Your Name's Coffee Corner
Account Listing
January 1, 2013

Account	Type	Balance Total
Checking	Bank	35,871.00
Accounts Receivable	Accounts Receivable	6,745.00
Inventory Asset	Other Current Asset	13,750.00
Office Supplies	Other Current Asset	950.00
Prepaid Insurance	Other Current Asset	1,200.00
Store Supplies	Other Current Asset	1,800.00
Store Fixtures	Fixed Asset	16,200.00
Store Fixtures:Depreciation	Fixed Asset	-1,800.00
Store Fixtures:Original Cost	Fixed Asset	18,000.00
Accounts Payable	Accounts Payable	1,500.00
Payroll Liabilities	Other Current Liability	0.00
Sales Tax Payable	Other Current Liability	0.00
Store Fixtures Loan	Long Term Liability	2,000.00
First & Last Name, Capital	Equity	67,771.00
First & Last Name, Capital:First & Last Name, Investment	Equity	35,000.00
First & Last Name, Capital:First & Last Name, Withdrawals	Equity	0.00
Retained Earnings	Equity	
Sales	Income	
Sales:Catering Sales	Income	
Sales:Coffee Sales	Income	
Sales:Pastry Sales	Income	
Sales Discounts	Income	
Uncategorized Income	Income	
Cost of Goods Sold	Cost of Goods Sold	
Advertising and Promotion	Expense	
Automobile Expense	Expense	
Bank Service Charges	Expense	
Computer and Internet Expenses	Expense	
Depreciation Expense	Expense	
Insurance Expense	Expense	
Interest Expense	Expense	
Office Supplies Expense	Expense	
Payroll Expenses	Expense	
Professional Fees	Expense	
Rent Expense	Expense	
Repairs and Maintenance	Expense	
Store Supplies Expense	Expense	
Telephone Expense	Expense	
Uncategorized Expenses	Expense	
Utilities	Expense	
Other Income	Other Income	
Other Expenses	Other Expense	

▶ Close the Chart of Accounts.

CUSTOMIZE PREFERENCES

► Make the following changes to Preferences:
- o Accounting: Company Preferences—Deselect the Date Warnings for past and future transactions
- o Checking Preferences: Company Preferences—Select Default Accounts for Open the Create Paychecks and Open the Pay Payroll Liabilities to Checking
- o Checking Preferences: My Preferences—Select Default Accounts to Checking for Open the Write Checks, Open the Pay Bills, Open the Pay Sales Tax, and Open the Make Deposits
- o Desktop View: My Preferences—Switch to colored icons/light background on the Top Icon Bar and select a Company Flag Color of Blue-Light
- o Payroll & Employees: Company Preferences—Display Employee List by Last Name
- o Reports & Graphs: My Preferences—Refresh reports automatically
- o Reports & Graphs: Company Preferences— For Reports-Show Items By: Select Name only, modify the report Format for the Header/Footer to remove the Date Prepared, Time Prepared, and Report Basis from reports
- o Sales & Customers: Company Preferences—Deselect "Use Price Levels"
- o Sales Tax: Company Preferences—Most common sales tax is State Tax

FINALIZE THE ITEMS LIST

► Add information to individual items and click Yes on the Account Change text box for each item:
- o Catering: Tax Code: Non; Income Account: Catering Sales
- o Coffee: Preferred Vendor: Coffee Royals; Tax Code: Tax; Income Account: Coffee Sales; Reorder Point: 500
- o Pastry: Preferred Vendor: Deluxe Pastries; Tax Code: Tax; Income Account: Pastry Sales; Reorder Point: 600

► Delete the following sales items: Consignment Item, Non-Inventory Item, Local Tax, and Out of State.

COMPLETE SALES TAX INFORMATION

► Edit the State Tax item. The name and description should be CA Sales Tax The rate is 8.75% and is paid to the State Board of Equalization.

► Print the Item List in Landscape orientation. Resize the columns and do not display the columns for Quantity on Sales Order and Quantity on Purchase Order. The report date is January 1, 2013.

COMPLETE INDIVIDUAL INFORMATION FOR CUSTOMERS

► Use the following information to add terms, tax codes, tax items, and credit limits to individual customers.

CUSTOMER LIST		
Customer Name	Jenkins, Sally, Inc.	Training, Inc.
Payment Terms	Net 30	Net 30
Credit Limit	2,000.00	8,000.00
Tax Item	CA Sales Tax	CA Sales Tax

▶ Print the Customer & Job List in Portrait orientation.

COMPLETE INDIVIDUAL INFORMATION FOR VENDORS

▶ Use the following Vendor List to add terms and credit limits to individual vendors:

VENDOR LIST		
Vendor Name	Coffee Royale	Deluxe Pastries
Payment Terms	2% 10, Net 30	2% 10, Net 30
Credit Limit	3,000.00	2,500.00

▶ Print the Vendor List in Portrait orientation.

CORRECT OPENING BALANCES DATES

▶ Check and, if necessary, change the opening balances dates to 01/01/13 for customers, vendors, and items by accessing invoices, bills, and adjust quantity/value on hand.

QUICKBOOKS PAYROLL SETUP

▶ Prior to completing the QuickBooks Payroll Setup, select **Manual Payroll**.
▶ Begin the QuickBooks Payroll Setup.

QUICKBOOKS PAYROLL SETUP

▶ Complete the **Company** portion of the QuickBooks Payroll Setup:
   o Payroll List Items for Wages, Tips, and Taxable Fringe Benefits: Salary, Hourly Wage and Overtime, deselect Bonus, award, and one-time compensation
   o Insurance Benefits: Health Insurance, Dental Insurance (both are fully paid by the employee after taxes have been deducted) (The vendor for Health and Dental insurance is Insurance Organization of California.) You do not need a payment schedule
   o Retirement Benefits: None
   o Paid Time Off: Sick Time and Vacation Time
   o Additions and Deductions: None
▶ Use the following information to add additional information for employees and to complete the **Employee** portion of the QuickBooks Payroll Setup. Print a Summary Report for each employee.

EMPLOYEES Colleen Anders and Barbara Olsen		
Name	Colleen Anders	Barbara Olsen
Employee Status	Active	Active
City	San Francisco	San Francisco
State	CA	CA
City, State Zip	94103	94101
Employee Type	Regular	Regular
Social Security No.	100-55-9107	100-55-5201
Hire Date	06/30/2007	02/19/2001
Birth Date	07/17/1980	09/29/1975
Gender	Female	Female
Pay Period	Monthly	Monthly
Compensation	Hourly wage: $9.50 Double-time hourly: $19.00 Overtime (x1.5) hourly: $14.25	Salary: $21,000 per year
Dental Insurance	$10 per month, annual limit $120	$10 per month, annual limit $120
Health Insurance	$25 per month, annual limit $300	$35 per month, annual limit $420
Sick Time Earns	40:00 at beginning of year	40:00 at beginning of year
Unused Hours (Sick)	Have an accrual limit	Have an accrual limit
Maximum Hours (Sick)	120:00	120:00
Earns (Sick)	Time off currently	Time off currently
Sick Hours Available as of 01/01/2013 (your computer date will show)	20:00	30:00
Vacation Time Earns	40:00 at beginning of year	40:00 at beginning of year
Unused Hours (Vacation)	Have an accrual limit	Have an accrual limit
Maximum Hours (Vacation)	120:00	120:00
Earns (Vacation)	Time off currently	Time off currently
Vacation Hours Available as of 01/01/13 (Your computer date will show)	20:00	40:00
Payment Method	Check	Check
State Subject to Withholding	CA	CA
State Subject to Unemployment Tax	CA	CA

EMPLOYEES Colleen Anders and Barbara Olsen		
Live or Work in Another State in 2013	No	No
Federal Filing Status	Married	Single
Allowances (Federal)	2	0
Extra Withholding	0.00	0.00
Nonresident Alien Withholding	Does not apply	Does not apply
HIRE Act Exemption	Not a qualified employee	Not a qualified employee
Subject to	Medicare Social Security Federal Unemployment	Medicare Social Security Federal Unemployment
State Filing Status	Married (two incomes)	Single
Regular Withholding Allowances	2	0
Subject to	CA-Unemployment CA-Employment Training Tax CA-Disability	CA-Unemployment CA-Employment Training Tax CA-Disability
Wage Plan Code	S	S

▶ Print the Summary for each employee.
▶ Complete the **Taxes** section of the QuickBooks Payroll Setup.
   o State Payroll Tax Rates— CA-Disability Employee Rate: 1%; CA-Employment Training Tax Company: 0.1%; California-Unemployment Company Rate: 3.4%
   o Federal Payroll Taxes— Schedules 940 and 941/944/943: Payee: United States Treasury, Frequency: Quarterly
   o State Payroll Taxes—Payee: Employee Development Department; Employer Account No.: 999-9999-9, Payment frequency: Quarterly
▶ Complete the **Year-to-Date Payrolls** section of the QuickBooks Payroll Setup. No paychecks have been issued this year.
▶ After completing the Payroll Setup, print the Payroll Item Listing in Landscape orientation using the Report menu or Report Center.

MAKE ADJUSTMENTS, PRINT THE BALANCE SHEET, AND PREPARE BACKUP

▶ Record the adjusting entry to transfer Uncategorized Income and Uncategorized Expenses to Your Name's, Capital.
▶ Print the Balance Sheet for January 1, 2013 in Portrait orientation.
▶ Backup your company file to **Your Name's Coffee Corner (Backup Ch. 9)**.

NAME_____

TRANSMITTAL

CHAPTER 9: YOUR NAME'S COFFEE CORNER

Attach the following documents and reports:

Account Listing
Item Listing
Customer & Job List
Vendor List
Colleen Anders Employee Summary
Barbara Olsen Employee Summary
Payroll Item Listing
Balance Sheet, January 1, 2013

COMPREHENSIVE PRACTICE SET: YOUR NAME'S CAPITOL BOOKS

The following is a comprehensive practice set that combines all the elements of QuickBooks studied throughout the text. In this practice set you will set up a company and keep the books for January 2013 (or the year that your instructor specifies). You will use the EasyStep Interview to create Your Name's Capitol Books. Once the company has been created, use QuickBooks Setup to add customers, vendors, employees, items, and bank accounts. Additional information will be provided for entry to individual items, customers, vendors, and employees. The QuickBooks Payroll Setup will be completed. Adjustments will be made to accounts and various items, transactions will be recorded, and reports will be prepared.

- During the month, new customers, vendors, and employees will be added.
- You are responsible for any memos you wish to include in transactions.
- Unless otherwise specified, the terms for each sale or bill will be the one specified in the Customer or Vendor List.
- If a customer's order exceeds the established credit limit, accept the order.
- If the terms allow a discount for a customer, make sure to apply the discount if payment is received in time for the customer to take it. Remember, the discount period starts with the date of the invoice. If an invoice or bill date is not provided, use the transaction date to begin the discount period.
- Use Sales Discounts as the discount account.
- If a customer has a credit and has a balance on the account, apply the credit to the invoice used for the sale. If there is no balance for a customer and a return is made, issue a credit memo and a refund check.
- If a transaction is eligible for a discount and there is a credit, always subtract the amount of the credit and recalculate the discount amount.
- Always pay bills in time to take advantage of purchase discounts.
- Invoices, purchase orders, and other similar items should be printed.
- Unless instructed to do so, you do not need to print Payment Receipts.
- It is your choice whether or not to print lines around each field.
- Most reports will be printed in Portrait orientation; however, if the report (such as the Journal) will fit across the page using Landscape orientation, use Landscape.
- Whenever possible, adjust the column widths so that reports fit on one-page wide without selecting Fit report to one page wide.

YOUR NAME'S CAPITOL BOOKS

Your Name's Capitol Books is a fictitious company that provides a typing service and sells books and educational supplies. Your Name's Capitol Books is located in Sacramento, California, and is a sole proprietorship owned by you. You do all the purchasing and are involved in all aspects of the business. Your Name's Capitol Books has one full-time employee who is paid a salary, Ms. Andrea Nahid, who manages the store, is responsible for the all the employees, and keeps the books. Cassie Egkan is a full-time hourly employee who works in the shop. The store is currently advertising for a part-time employee who will provide word processing/typing services.

CREATE A NEW COMPANY

▶ Use the following information to complete the EasyStep Interview:
o Company and Legal Name: **Your Name's Capitol Books** (*Key in your actual name*)
o Federal Tax ID: **466-52-1446**
o Address: **1055 Front Street, Sacramento, CA 95814**
o Phone: **916-555-9876**; Fax: **916-555-6789**
o E-mail: **YourNameCapitolBooks@reader.com** (don't forget to use your real name)
o Web: **www.CapitolBooks.com**
o Type of Business: **Retail Shop or Online Commerce**
o Company Organization: **Sole Proprietorship**
o Fiscal Year Starts: **January**
o Passwords: **No**
o File Name: **Your Name's Capitol Books.qbw (**don't forget to use your real name)
o Sell **Both Services and Products**, record each sale **individually**
o Charge Sales tax: **Yes**
o Estimates, statements, progress invoicing, or track time: **No**
o Use invoices, track customer orders, track bills, track inventory: **Yes**
o Employees**: Yes, W-2 Employees**
o Date to start tracking finances: **01/01/13** (If your date is not 01/01/13 select, "Use today's date or the first day of the quarter" and enter 01/01/13.)
o Use QuickBooks to set up the **Income and Expense Accounts**
o Start Date: **01/01/2013** (or the year you have been instructed to use)
o Review Income and Expense Accounts: Refer to the Chart of Accounts on Page 684.
  ▪ Remove Merchant Account Fees, Merchandise Sales, Sales Discounts, Automobile Expense, , Meals and Entertainment, Uniforms, and Ask My Accountant by clicking the √ column to remove the checkmark
  ▪ Add Purchase Discounts, Equipment Rental, Miscellaneous Expense, Postage and Delivery, Printing and Reproduction, and Interest Income

COMPLETE QUICKBOOKS SETUP

▶ Complete the first section to **Add Customers, Vendors, Employees, Opening and Balances**:

CUSTOMERS

Customer Name	Complete Training, Inc.	Newman, Helen	Sacramento Schools	Yu, Charlie
Company Name	Complete Training, Inc.		Sacramento Schools	
First Name		Helen		Charlie
Last Name		Newman		Yu
Phone	916-555-8762	916-555-8961	916-555-1235	916-555-2264
Address	785 Harvard Street	8025 Richmond Street	1085 2nd Street	253 Mason Street
City, State, Zip	Sacramento, CA 95814	Sacramento, CA 95814	Sacramento, CA 95814	Sacramento, CA 95814

VENDORS

Vendor and Company Name	Textbook Co.	Exotic Pens	Supplies Co.
Phone	916-555-2788	415-555-3224	916-555-5759
Fax	916-555-8872	415-555-4223	916-555-9575
Address	559 4th Street	2785 Market Street	95 8th Street
City, State, Zip	Sacramento, CA 95814	San Francisco, CA 94103	Sacramento, CA 95814
Contact Person	Al Daruty	Dennis Johnson	Raymond Ahrens

VENDORS

Vendor Name	State Board of Equalization	Employment Development Department	Sacramento State Bank	Medical Ins., Inc.
Phone	916-555-0000	916-555-8877	916-555-9889	415-555-4646
Fax	916-555-1111	916-555-7788	916-555-9988	415-555-6464
Address	7800 State Street	1037 California Street	102 8th Street	20865 Oak Street
City, State, Zip	Sacramento, CA 95814	Sacramento, CA 95814	Sacramento, CA 95814	San Francisco, CA 94101

EMPLOYEES

Name	Egkan, Cassie	Nahid, Andrea
First Name	Cassie	Andrea
Last Name	Egkan	Nahid
Phone	916-555-7862	916-555-1222
Address	833 Oak Avenue	1777 Watt Avenue
City, State, Zip	Sacramento, CA 95814	Sacramento, CA 95814

OPENING BALANCES

Type	Name	Balance	Opening Balance Date
Customer	Complete Training, Inc.	1,400.00	01/01/2013
Customer	Newman, Helen	100.00	01/01/2013
Customer	Sacramento Schools	1,000.00	01/01/2013
Customer	Yu, Charlie	350.00	01/01/2013
Vendor	Textbook Co.	1,000.00	01/01/2013
Vendor	Exotic Pens	500.00	01/01/2013
Vendor	Supplies Co.	800.00	01/01/2013

► Complete the second section to **Add Service and Inventory Items**:

SERVICE ITEM

Name	WP/Typing
Description	Word Processing/Typing Service
Price	0.00

INVENTORY ITEMS

Item Name	Textbooks	Paperback Books	Paper	Stationery	Pens, etc.
Description	Textbooks	Paperback Books	Paper Supplies	Stationery	Pens, etc.
Price	0.00	0.00	0.00	0.00	0.00
Cost	0.00	0.00	0.00	0.00	0.00
On-Hand	2,000	45	200	30	50
Total Value	100,000.00	180.00	1,000.00	225.00	250.00
As of Date	01/01/2013	01/01/2013	01/01/2013	01/01/2013	01/01/2013

► Complete the third section to **Add Bank Accounts**:

BANK ACCOUNTS

Account Name	Account Number	Opening Balance	Opening Balance Date
Checking	123-456-78910	130,870.25	01/01/2013

► Do not order checks.
► Close the Quick Start Center

COMPLETE THE COMPANY INFORMATION

► Add the Federal Employer Identification number **46-6521146** to the Company Information and verify the Social Security Number **466-52-1446**

SELECT A TOP ICON BAR (OPTIONAL)

▶ If you wish to use a Top Icon Bar, use the View Menu to change from the Left Icon Bar

CHANGE PREFERENCES

▶ Change the following preferences:
- **Accounting**: Deselect the **Date Warnings** for past and future transactions
- **Checking**: My Preferences—Default Accounts to use is **Checking** for Open the Write Checks, Open the Pay Bills, Open the Pay Sales Tax, and Open the Make Deposits; Company Preferences— Select Default Accounts to use is **Checking** for Open the Create Paychecks and Open the Pay Payroll Liabilities
- **Desktop** View: Switch to **colored icons/light background** on the Top Icon Bar (if using)
- **Payroll & Employees**: Company Preferences—Display Employee List by **Last Name**
- **Reports & Graphs**: My Preferences—**Refresh** reports automatically, Company Preferences—Reports – Show Items By: **Name only**; Reports – Show Accounts By: **Name only**; modify the report Format for the Header/Footer to remove the **Date Prepared, Time Prepared, and Report Basis** from reports
- **Sales & Customers**: Company Preferences—do **not** use **Price Levels**
- **Sales Tax**: Company Preferences—Most common sales tax is **State Tax**

FINALIZE THE ITEMS LIST

▶ Use the following charts for Service Item and Inventory Items to finalize the Items List
- Add: Preferred Vendor, Tax Codes and Income Accounts to individual items. (If information is not provided, use the default information)
- Add: Income accounts for **Word Processing/Typing Service**, **Supplies Sales**, and **Book Sales** (All are subaccounts of Sales Income)

SERVICE ITEM			
Item	**Tax Code**	**Income Account**	**Subaccount of**
WP/Typing	Non-taxable	Word Processing/Typing Service	Sales Income

INVENTORY ITEMS

Item Name	Paper	Paperback Books	Pens, etc.	Stationery	Textbooks
Preferred Vendor	Supplies Co.	Textbook Co.	Exotic Pens	Supplies Co.	Textbook Co.
Tax Code	Tax	Tax	Tax	Tax	Tax
Income Account	Supplies Sales	Book Sales	Supplies Sales	Supplies Sales	Book Sales
Subaccount of	Sales Income	Sales Income	Sales Income	Sales Income	Sales Income
Reorder Point	150	30	50	25	2,000

o **Delete**: the following sales items: Local Tax, and Out of State (If Consignment or Non-inventory Part Item appear, delete them as well).

o **Edit**: the State Sales Tax Item, change the name and description to CA Sales Tax, tax rate of 8.0%, paid to State Board of Equalization.

FINALIZE THE CUSTOMER LIST

▶ Since individual customers have different terms, tax codes, tax items, and credit limits, use the Customer Center to add the information shown in the Customers chart.

CUSTOMERS

Customer Name	Complete Training, Inc.	Newman, Helen	Sacramento Schools	Yu, Charlie
Terms	Net 30	2% 10 Net 30	2% 10 Net 30	Net 30
Credit Limit	$1,500	$500	$5,000	$350
Tax Code	Tax	Tax	Tax	Tax
Tax Item	CA State Tax	CA State Tax	CA State Tax	CA State Tax

FINALIZE THE VENDOR LIST

▶ Since individual vendors have different terms and credit limits, use the Vendor Center to add the information shown in the Vendors chart.

VENDOR LIST

Vendor Name	Exotic Pens	Supplies Co.	Textbook Co.
Terms	2% 10, Net 30	2% 10, Net 30	2% 10, Net 30
Credit Limit	$5,000	$15,000	$25,000

CHART OF ACCOUNTS

► Use the following chart of accounts and balances to customize the chart of accounts for Your Name's Capitol Books:

o To save space when printing, delete account descriptions for all accounts.

o Use <Unassigned> for tax line mapping

o <u>Delete</u>: Security Deposits Asset, Advertising and Promotion, and Professional Fees

o <u>Edit Equity Accounts</u>:
  - Change Opening Balance Equity to **First & Last Name, Capital** (use your real name)
  - Change Owners Equity to **Retained Earnings**
  - Change Owners Draw to **First & Last Name, Withdrawals**, subaccount of First & Last Name, Capital; Opening Balance **0.00** as of **01/01/13**

o <u>Add Equity Accounts</u>: **First & Last Name, Investment**; Subaccount of First & Last Name, Capital; Opening Balance **75,000** as of **01/01/13**

o <u>Edit Income Accounts</u>: Change Sales Income to **Sales and Services Income**

o <u>Add Master Card</u>: Type: Credit Card, Account Name: **Master Card**, Opening Balance/Statement Ending Balance: **$500.00**, Statement Ending Date: **12/31/12**

o <u>Add Other Current Assets</u>:
  - **Prepaid Insurance**, Opening Balance **1,200** as of **01/01/13**
  - **Supplies**, Opening Balance **1,950** as of **01/01/13**

o <u>Edit Fixed Assets</u>:
  - Change Furniture and Equipment to **Store Equipment & Fixtures**
  - Change Accumulated Depreciation to **Depreciation**, Subaccount of Store Equipment & Fixtures, Opening Balance **0.00** as of **01/01/13**

o <u>Add Fixed Assets</u>: Type: Fixed Asset, Account Name: **Original Cost**, Subaccount of: Store Equipment & Fixtures, Opening Balance: **18,000** as of **01/01/13**

o <u>Add Long-Term Liability</u>: **Store Equipment & Fixtures Loan**, Opening Balance **8,000** as of **01/01/13**

o <u>Edit Cost of Goods Sold</u>: Change Purchase Discounts to **Merchandise Discounts**, Subaccount of Cost of Goods Sold

o <u>Add Income Account</u>: **Sales Discounts**

o <u>Add Expense Accounts</u>:
  - **Fire Insurance**, Subaccount of Insurance Expense
  - **Liability Insurance**, Subaccount of Insurance Expense

o <u>Edit Expense Accounts</u>: Change Office Supplies to **Supplies Expense**

o Make any other changes necessary to match your Chart of Accounts with the one on the next page

o Chart Abbreviations:
  - (QB)=Account Created by QuickBooks—Do not do anything for these
  - *** means that QuickBooks will enter the account balance
  - Indented Account Names indicate that the account is a subaccount
  - C.A.=Current Asset, F.A.=Fixed Asset, C.L.=Current Liability, Long Term L.=Long Term Liability, COGS=Cost of Goods Sold

YOUR NAME'S CAPITOL BOOKS
CHART OF ACCOUNTS
January 1, 2013

ACCOUNT	TYPE	BALANCE	ACCOUNT	TYPE
Checking	Bank	130,870.25	Cost of Goods Sold (QB)	COGS
Accounts Receivable(QB)	Accts. Rec.	2,850.00	Merchandise Discounts	COGS
Inventory Asset	Other C.A	101,655.00	Bank Service Charges	Expense
Prepaid Insurance	Other C.A.	1,200.00	Computer and Internet Expenses	Expense
Supplies	Other C.A.	1,950.00	Depreciation Expense	Expense
Undeposited Funds (QB)	Other C.A.	***	Equipment Rental	Expense
Store Equipment & Fixtures	F.A.	***	Insurance Expense	Expense
Depreciation	F.A.	0.00	Fire Insurance	Expense
Original Cost	F.A.	18,000.00	Liability Insurance	Expense
Accounts Payable	Acct. Pay.	2,300.00	Interest Expense	Expense
Master Card (Statement Date: 12/31/12)	Credit Card	500.00	Janitorial Expense	Expense
Payroll Liabilities	Other C.L.	0.00	Miscellaneous Expense	Expense
Sales Tax Payable	Other C.L.	0.00	Payroll Expenses	Expense
Store Equipment & Fixtures Loan	Long Term L.	8,000.00	Postage and Delivery	Expense
First & Last Name, Capital	Equity	***	Printing and Reproduction	Expense
First & Last Name, Investment	Equity	75,000.00	Rent Expense	Expense
First & Last Name, Withdrawals	Equity	0.00	Repairs and Maintenance	Expense
Retained Earnings (QB)	Equity	***	Supplies Expense	Expense
Sales and Services Income	Income		Telephone Expense	Expense
Book Sales	Income		Uncategorized Expenses (QB)	Expense
Supplies Sales	Income		Utilities	Expense
Word Processing/Typing Service	Income		Interest Income	Other Income
Sales Discounts	Income			
Uncategorized Income (QB)	Income			

CORRECT DATES

► Unless you changed your computer's date when completing QuickBooks Setup to add customers, vendors, and items, the value and quantity of Inventory items will be dated the current date not January 1, 2013. The invoices and bills that contain the opening balances may also have the current date. As a safeguard, double-check the dates and change if needed.

o Open Inventory Activities and Adjust Quantity/Value on Hand, click Previous, and, if necessary, change the date to 01/01/13.

o Open Invoices, click Previous, and change the date, if necessary, for each invoice to 01/01/13.

o Open Bills, click Previous, and change the date, if necessary, for each bill to 01/01/13.

MAKE ADJUSTMENTS

▶ Transfer the Uncategorized Income and Uncategorized Expenses to the owner's capital account

PAYROLL

▶ Select Manual as the payroll option
▶ Complete the Payroll Setup (Remember that on some screens QuickBooks will show you the current computer date or current year. This should not make a difference as long as, whenever you enter a date, you use the same year as the one you used in the EasyStep Interview.)
  o Complete the Company portion of the setup
   • Payroll List Items for Wages, Tips, and Taxable Fringe Benefits: **Salary, Hourly Wage and Overtime**
   • Insurance Benefits: **Health Insurance**, **Dental Insurance**. Both are fully **paid by the employee after taxes** have been deducted. The Payee/Vendor is **Medical Ins., Inc.**, you do not need a payment schedule.
   • Retirement Benefits: **None**
   • Paid Time Off: **Sick Time** and **Vacation Time**
   • Other Payments and Deductions: **None**
  o Use the Employee List below to edit the employees and add additional information
   • Remember to delete the City, State, Zip and enter them individually
   • Print the Summary for <u>each</u> employee

EMPLOYEE LIST Cassie Egkan and Andrea Nahid		
Name	Cassie Egkan	Andrea Nahid
City	Sacramento	Sacramento
State	CA	CA
Zip	95814	95814
Social Security No.	100-55-6886	100-55-5244
Hire Date	04/03/96	02/17/10
Birth Date	12/07/70	11/28/85
Gender	Female	Female
Pay Period	Monthly	Monthly
Compensation	$10.00 per hour $20.00 Double-time hourly $15.00 Overtime (x1.5) hourly	$26,000 per year
Dental Insurance	$20 per month, annual limit $240	$30 per month, annual limit $360
Health Insurance	$20 per month, annual limit $240	$30 per month, annual limit $360

EMPLOYEE LIST Cassie Egkan and Andrea Nahid		
Sick Time Earns	40:00 at beginning of year	40:00 at beginning of year
Unused Hours (Sick)	Have an accrual limit	Have an accrual limit
Maximum Hours (Sick)	120:00	120:00
Earns (Sick)	Time off currently	Time off currently
Hours Available as of 01/01/13 (Sick)	40:00	40:00
Hours Used	0:00	0:00
Vacation Time Earns	40:00 at beginning of year	40:00 at beginning of year
Unused Hours (Vacation)	Have an accrual limit	Have an accrual limit
Maximum Hours (Vacation)	120:00	120:00
Earns (Vacation)	Time off currently	Time off currently
Hours Available as of 01/01/13 (Vacation)	40:00	40:00
Hours Used	0:00	0:00
Payment Method	Check	Check
State Subject to Withholding	CA	CA
State Subject to Unemployment Tax	CA	CA
Live or Work in Another State in 2013	No	No
Federal Filing Status	Married	Single
Allowances	1	0
Nonresident Alien Withholding	Does not apply	Does not apply
HIRE Act Exemption	Not a qualified employee	Not a qualified employee
Subject to	Medicare Social Security Federal Unemployment	Medicare Social Security Federal Unemployment
State Filing Status	Married (one income)	Single
Regular Withholding Allowances	1	0
Subject to	CA-Unemployment CA-Employment Training Tax CA-Disability	CA-Unemployment CA-Employment Training Tax CA-Disability
Local Taxes	No	No
Wage Plan Code	S	S

- (Did you print each employee's summary?)

o   Enter Payroll Tax information
- California-Unemployment Company Rate is **3.4%**, the rate for CA-Disability Employee Rate 1% and the rate for CA-Employment Training Tax Company Rate is 0.1%
- For all Federal Payroll Taxes use: Payee **United States Treasury**, **Quarterly** deposits
- For all California State Taxes use: Payee: is **Employment Development Department**, the Employer Account is **999-9999-9**, use **Quarterly** deposits

o   Determine if you need to enter the Year-to-Date Payrolls
- No paychecks have been issued

PRINT

► Print an Account Listing for the Chart of Accounts for January 1, 2013 in Portrait orientation after resizing the columns to display the names in full and removing the Description and Tax Line columns

► Print an Item Listing in Landscape orientation after resizing the columns to display all information in full (This will print on two pages)

► Use the Report menu or Reports Center to print a Transaction List by Customer for January 1, 2013 in Landscape orientation after resizing the columns to display all information in full

► Use the Report menu or Reports Center to print a Transaction List by Vendor for January 1, 2013 in Landscape orientation after resizing the columns to display all information in full

► Print a Balance Sheet as of January 1, 2013.

CUSTOMIZE

► Customize business forms: Make the default title all capital letters, and use Layout Designer to make the area for the company name wide enough for your name. Use a duplicate of a Product Invoice. Then, customize Sales Receipts, Credit Memos, Sales Orders, and Purchase Orders so they have the same format as the invoice.

ENTER TRANSACTIONS

► Print invoices, sales receipts, purchase orders, checks, and other items as they are entered in the transactions.

► Use the customized product invoice for all invoices (except those prepared from sales orders), and the customized credit memo for customer returns, voucher checks for payroll, and standard checks for all other checks. Create new items, accounts, customers, vendors, etc., as necessary. Refer to information given at the beginning of the problem for additional transaction details and information.

► Prepare an Inventory Stock Status by Item Report every five days as the last transaction of the day to see if anything needs to be ordered. Print the report and hide the For Assemblies column. If anything is indicated, order enough so you will have 10 more than the number of items shown for the Reorder Point. (For example, if you needed to order textbooks and the Reorder Point is 100, you would order enough books to have 110 available. If sales orders have been recorded, the number of items available may be less than shown for the number of items on hand so base your order on the number of items available. If you have 100 items on hand and 75 items available, you would order 35 items—25 to reach the 100 Reorder Point plus 10 more.) For this problem, the price per book ordered is **$50** per **textbook** and **$5** per **paperback**; **pens** are **$3.00** each, **paper** is **$4.00** per ream, **stationery** is **$7.50** per box, and **gift ware** is **$5.00** each.

▶ Full-time employees usually work 160 hours during a payroll period. Hourly employees working in excess of 160 hours in a pay period are paid overtime. In this problem, use the regular checking account to pay employees.

▶ Check every five days to see if any bills are due and eligible for a discount. If any bills can be paid and a discount received, pay the bills; otherwise, wait for instructions to pay bills. Remember that an opening balance is not eligible for a discount.

▶ If a bill or customer payment is eligible for a discount and a return has been made, subtract the amount of the credit from the amount due and recalculate the discount based on the actual amount owed.

▶ Backup the company file every five days. Create your first backup file before recording transactions. Name the file **Your Name's Capitol Books (Backup Company)**, name subsequent files with the date. For example, your first backup that includes transactions would be named **Your Name's Capitol Books (Backup 01-05-13)**. The final backup should be made at the end of the practice set. Name it **Your Name's Capitol Books (Backup Complete)**.

January 1

▶ Create a backup file and name it **Your Name's Capitol Books (Backup Company)**
▶ Add a new part-time hourly employee:
o Personal Info:
- Katie Gonzalez
- Social Security No.: 100-55-3699
- Gender: Female
- Birthday: 1/3/90
- Address: 1177 Florin Road
- City: Sacramento
- State: CA
- Zip: 95814
- Main Phone: 916-555-7766
o Payroll Info:
- Pay Frequency: Monthly
- Hourly: $8.00, Overtime (x1.5) hourly: $12.00, Double-time hourly: $16.00
- Dental and Health Insurance: None
- Federal Taxes:
  • Filing Status and Allowance: Single, 0
  • Subject to: Medicare, Social Security, Federal Unemployment

- State Taxes:
  - State Worked and State Subject to Withholding: California
  - Subject to, CA Unemployment (SUI), CA Disability taxes (SDI)
  - Filing Status and Allowance: Single, 0
- Other Taxes:
  - CA Employment Training Tax
- Sick and Vacation Hours: Does not qualify so leave as is
- Employment Info:
  - Hire Date: 01/01/13
  - Type: Regular

January 2:

▶ Katie typed a five-page paper at the rate of $5 per page, sold one $80 textbook, and three paperback books at $6.99 each to a Cash Customer. Received Check 2951 for the full payment.

▶ Complete Training, Inc. purchased 30 copies of a textbook on account for $95 each.

▶ Received Check 1096 from Helen Newman for $100 as payment in full on her account. (An opening balance is not eligible for a discount.)

▶ Received a telephone call for a Sales Order from Sacramento Schools for 25 pens on account at $8.99 each and five reams of paper at $6.99 per ream.

▶ Sold one textbook at $79.99, one textbook for $95.99, one textbook for $125.00, one textbook for $139.95, and one textbook for $145.00 for the new quarter to a student using a Visa.

▶ Prepare an Inventory Stock Status by Item report to see if anything needs to be ordered. After resizing the columns and removing the column "For Assemblies," print in Landscape (do this for all future Inventory Stock Status by Item reports). (Are pens and textbooks marked?)

▶ Prepare and print Purchase Orders for any merchandise that needs to be ordered.

▶ Check bills for discount eligibility between January 1-4. Pay any bills that qualify for a discount. (Opening balances do not qualify for an early payment discount.)

January 3:

▶ Sacramento Schools picked up the merchandise from Sales Order 1. Create the invoice dated January 2, 2013 from the Sales Order. (Even though the "Product Invoice" was customized earlier in the practice set, the Sales Order Invoice was not. Once you create the invoice from the sales order, you should customize the Sales Order Invoice so that the default title, INVOICE, is all capital letters; and then, use Layout Designer to make room for your full name to print.

▶ Received Check 915 for $350 from Charlie Yu for the full amount due on his account.

▶ Sold two pens on account at $12.99 each and five boxes of stationery at $10.99 per box to Helen Newman.

▶ Received payment of $1,400 from Complete Training, Inc., Check 7824.

January 5:

▶ Sold two textbooks on account at $125 each to a new customer: Hector Gomez, Main Phone: 916-555-6841, Main E-mail: HGomez@email.com, 478 Front Street, Sacramento, CA 95814, Payment Terms: Net 10 (Do you need to add a new Standard Term for Net 10?), Credit Limit $500, Taxable, CA Sales Tax.

▶ Received the pens ordered from Exotic Pens with the bill.

▶ Received the textbooks ordered from Textbook Co. without the bill

▶ Prepare and print Inventory Stock Status by Item Report for January 1-5, 2013. Order any items indicated. (Stationery) (Remember to hide the For Assemblies column.)

▶ Check bills for discount eligibility. Pay any bills that qualify for a discount between January 5-9.

▶ Deposit all cash, checks, and credit card payments received.

▶ Backup the company file.

January 7:

▶ Helen Newman returned two pens purchased on January 3. She did not like the color. Apply the credit to the invoice and print after you apply the credit to the invoice.

▶ Received the bill for the textbooks ordered from Textbook Co. Use the transaction date January 5, 2013.

▶ The nonprofit organization, State Schools, bought a classroom set of 30 computer training textbooks on account for $110.00 each and 15 reams of paper at $4.99 each. Add the new customer: State Schools, Main Phone: 916-555-8787, Fax: 916-555-7878, 451 State Street, Sacramento, CA 95814, Payment Terms Net 30, Credit Limit $5,000, Taxable, CA Sales Tax. Include a subtotal for the sale and apply a 10% sales discount for a nonprofit organization. (Create any new sales items necessary. Use Sales Discounts as the account for the nonprofit discount.)

▶ Add a new inventory part sales item for Gift Ware, Purchase Description: Gift Ware, Cost: 0.00, COGS Account: Cost of Goods Sold (Cost of Goods Sold is an account setup by QuickBooks when you add your first inventory item. If you get a duplicate Cost of Goods Sold account marked with an asterisk *, click the drop-down list arrow for COGS Account and select the Cost of Goods Sold account that does not have the asterisk.), Preferred Vendor: Gifts Galore (Main Phone: 916-555-5384, Main E-mail: gifts@abc.com, Fax: 916-555-4835, 125 Oak Street, Sacramento, CA 95814, Payment Terms: Net 30, Credit Limit: $1,500), Sales Description: Gift Ware, Sales Price: 0.00, Tax Code: Tax, Income Account: Supplies Sales, Asset Account: Inventory Asset, Reorder Point: 15, Quantity on Hand: 0, Value: 0.00, as of 01/07/2013

▶ When you add an inventory item after finishing the QuickBooks Setup, you may get a duplicate Cost of Goods Sold account, which will be shown as *Cost of Goods Sold. Check each inventory item to make sure it is not used. Once the Cost of Goods Sold account is verified, if you have the *Cost of Goods Sold account, delete it.

▶ Order 15 gift ware items at $5.00 each from the Gifts Galore.

January 8:

▶ Katie typed a 15-page report at $5.00 per page and sold ten reams of paper at $5.99 per ream on account to Helen Newman.

▶ Use Pay Bills to pay Textbook Co. the full amount owed on account of $1,000. This is the opening balance for the vendor. Print Check 1 using Standard Checks. (Remember, no discounts are available for opening balances.)

▶ Received a telephone order for eight additional computer textbooks on account to Sacramento Schools at $110 each

January 10:

▶ Sold three pens at $14.95 each, two sets of stationery at $14.99 each, and three paperback books at $6.99 each to a cash customer using cash as the payment method.

▶ Sacramento Schools picked up the merchandise on sales order. (Use January 10, 2013 for the invoice date.)

▶ Received Check 825 as payment from Sacramento Schools for the 01/02/13 transaction for $274.87, the full amount due, less discount. (Did you use Sales Discounts as the Discount Account?)

▶ Received Check 10525 from Complete Training, Inc., $1,000 as partial payment on account.

▶ Deposit all cash, checks, and credit card receipts.

▶ Prepare Inventory Stock Status by Item Report for January 1-10, 2013. Order any items indicated. (If an item is marked to order but a purchase order has already been prepared, do not order any more of the item. Since Stationery was ordered 01/05/13 and Gift Ware was ordered on 01/07/13 neither of those items need to be ordered.)

▶ Check bills for discount eligibility. Pay any bills that qualify for a discount between January 10-14. (Remember opening balances do not qualify for a discount.)

▶ Backup the company file.

January 11:

▶ Sold fifteen paperback books at $8.99 each and two pens at $35.99 each to a customer using a Visa.

▶ Sold ten reams of paper at $5.99 each, one pen at $8.99, and one box of stationery at $12.99 to a cash customer. Received Check 8106.

January 12:

▶ Katie typed a one-page letter with an envelope on account for Charlie Yu, $8.00. (Qty 1.)

▶ Received gift ware ordered from Gifts Galore. A bill was not included with the order.

January 13:

▶ Received Check 1265 from Helen Newman in payment for full amount due for Invoice 3 after discounts, $58.15. (Since the invoice has a return, subtract the amount of the Credit from the Amount Due; and, then, recalculate the discount.)

▶ Received the textbooks and the bill from Textbook Co. for Purchase Order 5. Date the bill January 13, 2013.

▶ Received a notice from the bank that Check 915 for $350.00 from Charlie Yu was marked NSF and returned. Record the NSF check and charge Charlie the bank's $25 fee for the bad check plus Your Name's Capitol Books' fee of $15. Payment is due on receipt. Add any necessary items and/or accounts. The income account used to record the charges for bad checks is Returned Check Service Charges.

January 14:
► Received Check 10-283 for $270.00 from Hector Gomez in payment of Invoice 4.
► Received Charlie Yu's new Check 304 for payment in full payment of his account including both invoices and all NSF charges.
► Received all but three boxes of stationery ordered. The bill was included with the stationery and the three missing boxes are on back order. (Was your Purchase Order 3 to Supplies Co. for 10 boxes of stationery?)

January 15:
► Received Check 1278 from Helen Newman in payment for full amount due for Invoice 7 after discounts $136.90.
► Deposit all cash, checks, and credit card receipts.
► Check to see if any bills qualify for a discount between January 15 and 19. If any qualify, take the discount and pay them. (Remember, no discounts are available for opening balances.) (Did you use Merchandise Discounts for the Discount Account?)
► Prepare and print an Inventory Stock Status by Item Report for January 1-15 in Landscape orientation. Prepare Purchase Orders for all items marked Order on the Inventory Stock Status by Item Report. Place all orders with preferred vendors. (Refer back to the Enter Transactions information shown before January 1 transactions to find to cost for giftware and paperback books.)
► Backup the company file.

January 17:
► Sold eight textbooks on account at $125 each to State Schools, which is a nonprofit organization.
► Hector Gomez returned one textbook he had purchased for $125. Prepare a refund, then print the credit memo. Finally, print the check.
► Received Credit Memo No. 721 from Supplies Co. for the return of five boxes of stationery at 7.50 each. (Apply the credit to the bill dated 01/14/13 when you pay the bill.)
► Received the bill from Gifts Galore for the gift ware ordered January 7 and received January 12. Date the bill January 17.

January 20:
► A cash customer purchased four textbooks at $109.99 each, one textbook for $89.95, and one gift ware item at $15.90 using Check 289.
► Received Check 891 from Sacramento Schools for $931.39 for payment in full of Invoice 8—not the beginning balance.
► Change the reorder point for Textbooks to 1,500 and Pens to 45.
► Prepare Inventory Stock Status by Item Report. Prepare Purchase Orders for marked items. (If nothing is marked, do not print the report.)

► Check to see if any bills qualify for a discount between January 20 and 24. If any qualify, pay them. If there is a credit shown, apply it; and then, recalculate the discount after subtracting the credit. (Remember, no discounts are available for opening balances.)

► Record the bank deposit on January 20. Deposit all cash, checks, and credit card receipts.

► Backup the company file.

January 21:

► Katie typed an eight-page exam for at $5 per page for Hector Gomez on account. He also purchased 2 pens at 12.99 each and one box of stationery for $14.99.

January 22:

► Sold five gift ware items at $19.99 each, three paperback books at $8.99 each, and three pens at $8.99 each to Helen Newman on account.

January 25:

► Received Check 127 for $162.88 as payment in full from Helen Newman

► Increase the Credit Limit for Complete Training, Inc. to $20,000.00.

► Received a telephone order for 60 textbooks for $99.95 each and 45 textbooks for 119.95 each on account to Complete Training, Inc.

► Prepare Inventory Stock Status by Item Report. Print only if something needs to be ordered.

► Check to see if any bills qualify for a discount between January 25 and 29. If any qualify, accept the discount offered by QuickBooks, and pay them. If there are any credits to apply to any bill payments, apply them and recalculate the discount. (Remember, no discounts are available for opening balances.)

► Deposit all cash, checks, and credit card receipts.

► Backup the company file.

January 29:

► Received Check 4325 for $84.25 from Hector Gomez as payment on his account.

► Received Check 11325 for $2,078.00 from Complete Training.

► Received the back order of three boxes of stationery and the bill from Supplies Co. Date the bill January 29, 2013.

► Received bills and the paperback books ordered from Textbook Co. and the gift ware ordered from Gifts Galore. Date the bills January 29, 2013.

► Complete Training, Inc. picked up the merchandise ordered by telephone. (Did you prepare an invoice from the sales order?)

January 30:

► Prepare Inventory Stock Status by Item Report. If nothing is marked to order, do not print the report.

► Deposit all checks, cash, and credit card receipts.

► Pay both bills due to Supplies Co. (Be sure to discounts if eligible.) Also, pay bills eligible for a discount between January 30 and February 4. Print using a standard style check.

▶ Pay $1,200 rent to the Sacramento Rental Agency, Main Phone: 916-555-1234, Fax: 916-555-4321, 1234 Front Street, Sacramento, CA 95814, Payment Terms Net 30, Account Setting: Rent Expense.
▶ Pay the utility bill of $257 and the telephone bill of $189 to State Utilities & Telephone, Main Phone: 916-555-8523, 8905 Richmond, Sacramento, CA 95814, Payment Terms Net 30. (Did you write just one check?)
▶ Backup the company file.

January 31:
▶ Pay the payroll: The pay period is 01/01/13 through 01/31/13. The check date is 01/31/13. Use the information in the following table to prepare the checks.

PAYROLL TABLE: JANUARY 31, 2013

	Katie Gonzalez	Andrea Nahid	Cassie Egkan
HOURS			
Regular	80	158	144
Overtime (x1.5)			3
Sick			16
Vacation		2	
DEDUCTIONS OTHER PAYROLL ITEMS: EMPLOYEE			
Dental Ins.		30.00	20.00
Medical Ins.		30.00	20.00
DEDUCTIONS: COMPANY			
CA Employment Training Tax	.64	1.27	1.65
Social Security	39.68	78.53	101.99
Medicare	9.28	31.42	23.85
Federal Unemployment	3.84	7.60	9.87
CA-Unemployment	21.76	43.07	55.93
DEDUCTIONS: EMPLOYEE			
Federal Withholding	46.10	126.90	65.53
Social Security	26.88	53.20	69.09
Medicare	9.28	31.42	23.85
CA-Withholding	7.39	56.06	22.50
CA-Disability	6.40	12.67	16.45

▶ Print the paychecks using a voucher-style check. (If the voucher prints two times, it is fine.) Be sure to remove the Intuit logo from the Payroll Printing Preferences.
▶ Before distributing paychecks, you realize that the Social Security Employee Deductions for each employee are incorrect. Go to the checks, unlock them and change the amount

of Social Security Employee Deductions for Katie to 39.68, for Andrea to 78.53, and for Cassie to 101.99. Reprint the checks using Voucher style.

▶ Prepare and print the Payroll Summary Report for January in Landscape orientation. (Adjust column widths and fit the report to print on one page.)

▶ Prepare and print the Payroll Liabilities Balances Report for January in Portrait orientation.

▶ Pay all the payroll liabilities for January 1-31, 2013. Print the standard checks.

▶ Prepare Sales Tax Liability Report for January 1-31, 2013. Print in Landscape orientation. Adjust column widths so the report fits on one page, maintains the same font, and has column headings shown in full.

▶ Pay Sales Tax for January 31, 2013 and print the check.

▶ Print a Sales by Item Summary Report for January 1-31 in Landscape orientation. Adjust column widths so report fits on one-page wide.

▶ Print a Trial Balance for January 1-31 in Portrait orientation.

▶ Enter adjusting entries: Depreciation—Store Equipment & Fixtures $266.66. Supplies used—$400.00. Insurance used a total of $100—$50 fire Insurance, $50 Liability Insurance. (Use a compound entry to record insurance adjustment.)

▶ Record the owner withdrawal for the month $2,000.00.

▶ Prepare a bank reconciliation and record any adjustments. Be sure to use the date of 01/31/13 for the bank statement date, service charges, and interest earned.

SACRAMENTO STATE BANK
102 8th Street
Sacramento, CA 95814
(916) 555-9889

BANK STATEMENT FOR:

Your Name's Capitol Books
1055 Front Street
Sacramento, CA 95814   Acct. # 97-1132-07922   January 2013

Beginning Balance, January 1, 2013			$130,870.25
1/5/2013, Deposit	2,616.85		133,487.10
1/10/2013, Check 1		1,000.00	132,487.10
1/10/2013, Deposit	1,378.33		133,865.43
1/13/2013, NSF Check		350.00	133,515.43
1/15/2013, Deposit	1,174.86		134,690.29
1/17/2013, Check 2		102.90	134,587.39
1/17/2013, Check 3		2,254.00	132,333.39
1/20/2013, Deposit	1,520.86		133,854.25
1/21/2013, Check 4		135.00	133,719.25
1/23/2013, Check 5		14.70	133,704.55
1/23/2013, Check 6		1,960.00	131,744.55
1/25/2013, Deposit	162.88		131,907.43
1/31/2013, Service Charge, $15, and NSF Charge, $25		40.00	131,867.43
1/31/2013, Store Equipment & Fixtures Loan Pmt.: $124.71 Interest, $22.65 Principal		147.36	131,720.07
1/31/2013, Interest	1,976.10		133,696.17
Ending Balance, 1/31/2013			$133,696.17

▶ Print the Detail Reconciliation Report.
▶ Close the Drawing account
▶ Transfer the Net Income/Retained Earnings into the capital account. (Did you, change the name of the account Owners Equity to Retained Earnings.)
▶ Adjust the Merchandise Item of Gift Ware for 1 Gift Set that was damaged. (Use the expense account Merchandise Adjustments.)
▶ Correct the Amount of Net Income to reflect the merchandise adjustment
▶ Print a Statement of Cash Flows for January 1-31, 2013
▶ Print a Standard Profit & Loss Statement for January 1-31, 2013
▶ Print a Standard Balance Sheet As of January 31, 2013
▶ Close the period with a closing date of 01/31/13 (Do not use passwords.)
▶ Print the Journal, expand the columns, use the dates from 12/31/2012 to 01/31/2013, adjust columns, and print in Landscape orientation. (Display as much of the names,

items, and accounts as you can and still print the report on one-page wide.)The order in which your transactions appear may be different from any answer keys provided. As long as all of the transactions have been entered, the order of entry does not matter.

► Backup the company file.

NAME_____

TRANSMITTAL

COMPREHENSIVE PRACTICE SET: YOUR NAME'S CAPITOL BOOKS

Attach the following documents and reports:

Employee Summary for Cassie Egkan
Employee Summary for Andrea Nahid
Account Listing
Item Listing
Transaction List by Customer
Transaction List by Vendor
Standard Balance Sheet, January 1, 2013
Sales Receipt 1: Cash Customer
Invoice 1: Complete Training, Inc.
Payment Receipt: Helen Newman
Sales Order 1: Sacramento Schools
Sales Receipt 2: Cash Customer
Inventory Stock Status by Item,
    January 2, 2013
Purchase Order 1: Exotic Pens
Purchase Order 2: Textbook Co.
Invoice 2: Sacramento Schools
Payment Receipt: Charlie Yu
Invoice 3: Helen Newman
Payment Receipt, Complete Training, Inc.
Invoice 4: Hector Gomez
Bill: Exotic Pens
Inventory Stock Status by Item,
    January 1-5, 2013
Purchase Order 3: Supplies Co.
Deposit Summary, January 5, 2013
Credit Memo No. 5: Helen Newman
Bill: Textbook Co.
Invoice 6: State Schools
Purchase Order 4: Gifts Galore
Invoice 7: Helen Newman
Check 1: Textbook Co.
Sales Order 2: Sacramento Schools
Sales Receipt 3: Cash Customer

Invoice 8: Sacramento Schools
Payment Receipt: Sacramento Schools
Payment Receipt: Complete Training, Inc.
Deposit Summary, January 10, 2013
Inventory Stock Status by Item,
    January 1-10, 2013
Purchase Order 5: Textbook Co.
Sales Receipt 4: Cash Customer
Sales Receipt 5: Cash Customer
Invoice 9: Charlie Yu
Payment Receipt: Helen Newman
Bill: Textbook Co.
Invoice 10: Charlie Yu
Payment Receipt: Hector Gomez
Payment Receipt: Charlie Yu
Bill: Supplies Co.
Payment Receipt: Helen Newman
Deposit Summary, January 15, 2013
Check 2: Exotic Pens
Check 3: Textbook Co.
Inventory Stock Status by Item,
    January 1-15, 2013
Purchase Order 6: Gifts Galore
Purchase Order 7: Textbook Co.
Invoice 11: State Schools
Credit Memo No. 12: Hector Gomez
Check 4: Hector Gomez
Bill Credit: Supplies Co.
Bill: Gifts Galore
Sales Receipt 6: Cash Customer
Payment Receipt: Sacramento Schools
Check 5: Supplies Co.
Check 6: Textbook Co.
Deposit Summary, January 20, 2013

Invoice 13: Hector Gomez
Invoice 14: Helen Newman
Payment Receipt: Helen Newman
Sales Order 3: Complete Training, Inc.
Deposit Summary, January 25, 2013
Payment Receipt: Hector Gomez
Payment Receipt: Complete Training, Inc.
Bill: Supplies Co.
Bill: Textbook Co.
Bill: Gifts Galore
Invoice 15: Complete Training, Inc.
Deposit Summary, January 30, 2013
Check 7: Supplies Co.
Check 8: Sacramento Rental Agency
Check 9: State Utilities & Telephone
Check 10: Katie Gonzalez (Note: Checks
     may print in a different order)
Check 11: Andrea Nahid
Check 12: Cassie Egkan
Check 10: Katie Gonzalez (Corrected)
Check 11: Andrea Nahid (Corrected)
Check 12: Cassie Egkan (Corrected)
Payroll Summary, January 2013
Payroll Liability Balances,
     January 30, 2013
Check 13: Employment Development
     Department
Check 14: Medical Ins., Inc.
Check 15: United States Treasury
Sales Tax Liability Report, January 2013
Check 16: State Board of Equalization
Sales by Item Summary, January 2013
Trial Balance, January 31, 2013
Check 17: Your First & Last Name
Bank Reconciliation Detail Report
Statement of Cash Flows, January 2013
Standard Profit and Loss, January 2013
Balance Sheet, January 31, 2013
Journal, December 31, 2012 –
     January 31, 2013

QUICKBOOKS® PROGRAM INTEGRATION

QuickBooks is integrated to work in conjunction with Microsoft Word and Excel to prepare many different types of letters or send QuickBooks reports directly to an Excel workbook. In order to use the integration features of the program, you must have Microsoft© Word 2000 (or higher) and Microsoft© Excel 2000 (or higher) installed on your computer.

This appendix will use the sample company, Larry's Landscaping & Garden Supply, to provide information regarding program integration with QuickBooks. Since saving the demonstration transactions will make permanent changes to the sample company, you will not need to do the demonstration transactions unless they are assigned by your instructor. Since the material presented in the appendix is for illustration purposes only, memo text boxes and detailed data for entry are not included.

QUICKBOOKS LETTERS

There are many times in business when you need to write a letter of one type or another to your customers. This is an important feature because QuickBooks will insert information, from your customer files directly into a letter.

To prepare a letter to Active Customers, Click **Open a sample file**, and the click the type of sample company you wish to explore—**Sample service-based business**
- If you get an Update Company File message, click **Yes**

A notification regarding QuickBooks Information appears

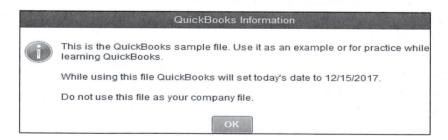

Click **OK** on the QuickBooks Information screen
Click the **Customers** icon to access the Customer Center
Click the **Word** button
Click **Prepare Customer Letters**
- If you get a screen regarding the lack of available templates, click **Copy**

In "Include names that are:" click **Active**
In "Create a letter for each:" click **Customer**

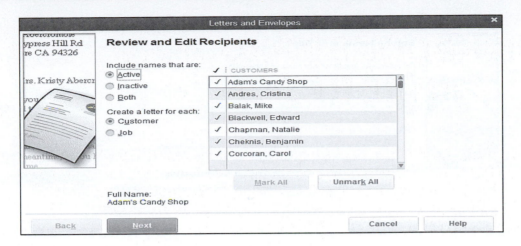

Click **Next**
Scroll through the list of letters
Click **Thanks for business (service)**

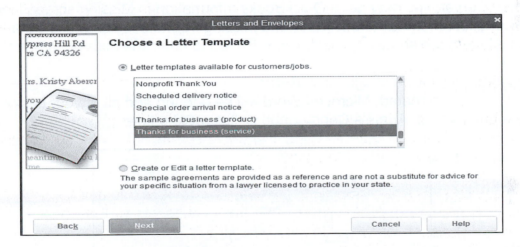

- If you do not find a template that is appropriate or you wish to make permanent changes to one of the existing letter templates, you may do so by clicking Create or Edit a letter template.

Click **Next**
Enter **Your First and Last Name** (your actual name not the words your name) for the name at the end of the letter
Enter your title as **President**

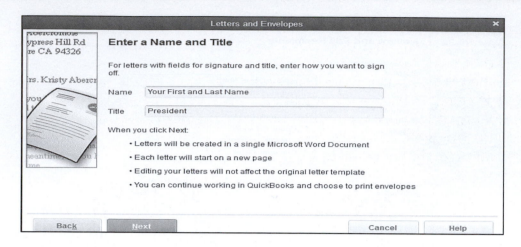

Click **Next**.

Click **OK** on the QuickBooks Information Is Missing screen

- Since many of your customers do not have titles or some other information stored in the Customer Center, you may get a QuickBooks Information Is Missing screen indicating that information to complete this letter was missing from the QuickBooks Data File. Once the letters are shown in Word, you will need to enter the missing information for each letter.

If you get a Server Busy message, click **Retry**

- When the letter is created, Microsoft Word will be opened and all of your customers will have a letter created. Adam's Candy Shop is illustrated below:

- The letters are not technically correct with formats and spacing so may need some adjustment on your part. However, it is much easier to edit letters prepared for you than it is to create a letter for each customer.

To make the short letter appear more balanced:

Press **Ctrl+A** to select the entire document

Click the **Page Layout** tab, click **Margins**, and click the words **Custom Margins**

Change the Top and Bottom margins to **1"**

Change the Left and Right margins to **2"**

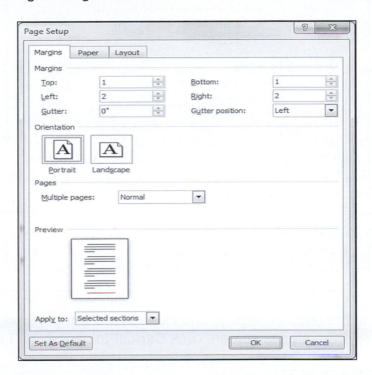

Click **OK**

Position the cursor between the date and the letter address

Press the **Enter** until there are 8 blank lines between the date and the letter address

Delete one of the blank lines between the letter address and the salutation (Dear Mr. Adam Bradley,)

Since the appropriate salutation is: Dear Mr. Bradley:, you should delete his first name.

Click the **View** tab; and then, click **One Page**

- Your letter should look like the following. Notice how much more balanced the letter appears.
- Notice that Adam's Candy Shop address information was automatically inserted in the letter.

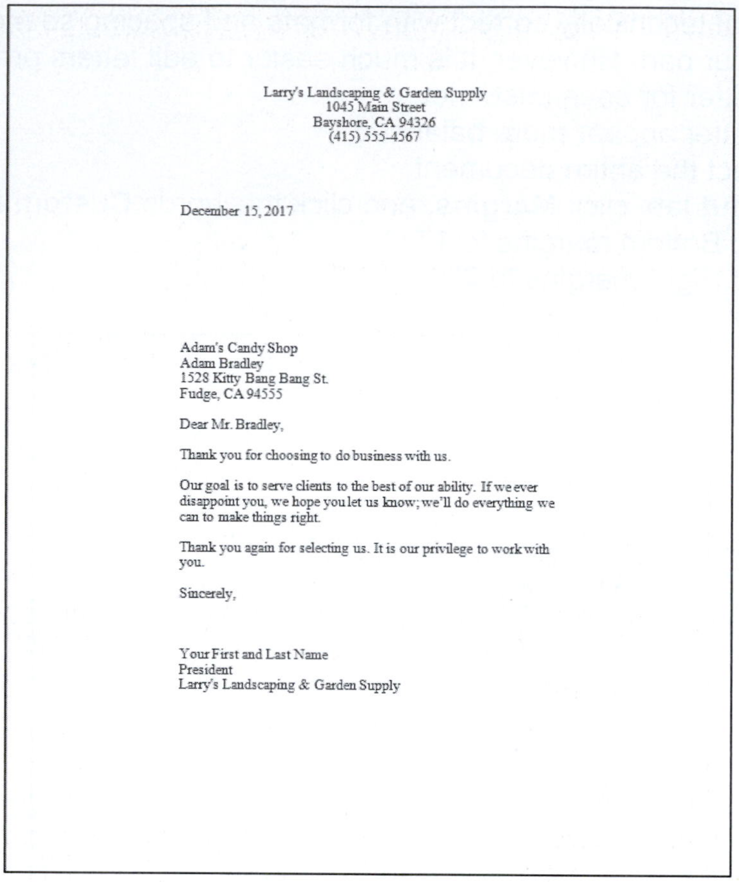

Larry's Landscaping & Garden Supply
1045 Main Street
Bayshore, CA 94326
(415) 555-4567

December 15, 2017

Adam's Candy Shop
Adam Bradley
1528 Kitty Bang Bang St.
Fudge, CA 94555

Dear Mr. Bradley,

Thank you for choosing to do business with us.

Our goal is to serve clients to the best of our ability. If we ever disappoint you, we hope you let us know; we'll do everything we can to make things right.

Thank you again for selecting us. It is our privilege to work with you.

Sincerely,

Your First and Last Name
President
Larry's Landscaping & Garden Supply

Click **Draft** to return to the original display, and close **Word** without saving the letter
On the Print Letters and Envelopes screen, click **Cancel** to cancel the Letters to Customers

EXPORTING INFORMATION TO EXCEL

Many of the reports prepared in QuickBooks can be exported to Microsoft® Excel. This allows you to take advantage of extensive filtering options available in Excel, hide detail for some but not all groups of data, combine information from two different reports, change titles of columns, add comments, change the order of columns, and experiment with *what if* scenarios. Exporting reports to Excel from within a report was demonstrated within the chapters. Information may also be exported from the Customer, Vendor, and Employee Centers.

To export a Customer List to Excel, click the **Excel** button in the **Customer Center**, and click **Export Customer List**
On the Export dialog box click **Create new worksheet** and **in new workbook**
Click the **Export** button

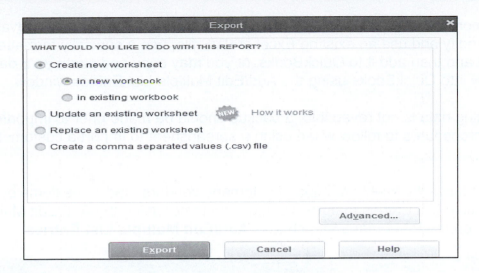

- A detailed Customer List will be displayed in Excel

	A	B	C	D	E	F	G	H	I	J	K	L
1	Active Status	Customer		Balance	Balance Total	Company	Mr./Ms./...	First Name	M.I.	Last Name	Primary Contact	Main Phone
2	Active	Adam's Candy Shop		40.00	40.00	Adam's Candy Shop	Mr.	Adam		Bradley	Adam Bradley	707 555 5734
3	Active	Andres, Cristina		0.00	0.00			Cristina		Andres	Cristina Andres	415-555-2174
4	Active	Balak, Mike		0.00	180.00			Mike		Balak	Mike Balak	415-555-6453
5	Active	Balak, Mike:330 Main St		180.00	180.00	Hair, Nails and Supply		Mike		Balak	Mike Balak	415-555-6453
6	Active	Balak, Mike:Residential		0.00	0.00			Mike		Balak	Mike Balak	415-555-6453
7	Active	Blackwell, Edward		1,125.00	1,125.00	Wild Garden Restaurant		Edward		Blackwell	Edward Blackwell	415-555-3221
8	Active	Chapman, Natalie		0.00	0.00			Natalie		Chapman	Natalie Chapman	415-555-3232
9	Active	Cheknis, Benjamin		0.00	0.00			Benjamin		Cheknis	Benjamin Cheknis	415-555-4356
10	Active	Corcoran, Carol		0.00	0.00			Carol		Corcoran	Carol Corcoran	415-555-8825
11	Active	Crenshaw, Bob		1,591.03	1,591.03	Scrounger's Auto		Bob		Crenshaw	Bob or Carol	415-555-2248
12	Active	Crider, Craig		0.00	0.00	Crider's Critters		Craig		Crider	Craig Crider	415-555-8900

Partial Report

Click the **Close** button in the upper right corner of the Excel title bar to close **Excel**
Click **Don't Save** to close **Book2** without saving
Close the **Customer Center**

IMPORTING DATA FROM EXCEL

Another feature of QuickBooks is the ability to import data from Excel into QuickBooks. You may have Excel or .csv (comma separated value) files that contain important business information about customers, vendors, sales items, and other lists that are not contained in your QuickBooks Company File. That information can be imported directly into QuickBooks and customized as desired. An import file must conform to a specific structure for QuickBooks to interpret the data in the file correctly.

You may import your data from Excel in three ways. First, you may use an advanced import method to modify and use an existing Excel or CVS file, use a specially formatted spreadsheet and then add it to QuickBooks, or you may copy and paste your data from Excel directly into QuickBooks using the Add/Edit Multiple List Entries window.

Since importing data is not reversible, a backup should be made prior to importing data. An example of procedures to follow when using a spreadsheet to import a customer is shown below:

QuickBooks makes it possible to import customers, vendors, and sales items by using the Add/Edit Multiple List Entries feature. To add a customer using the Add/Edit Multiple List Entries, click on the **Lists** menu and choose **Add/Edit Multiple List Entries**

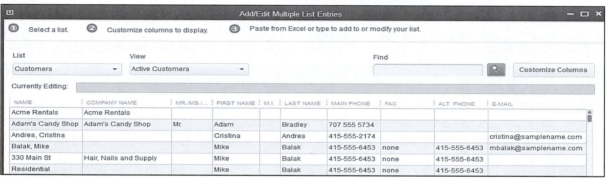

Partial List

To import and export customer information between QuickBooks and Excel, you will need to make sure the column headings and the order in which the columns are listed in QuickBooks matches your Excel spreadsheet
Click **Adam's Candy Shop** in the Name column
• If you get a Time Saving Tip regarding Copy Down, click **OK**.
Right-click **Adam's Candy Shop**, and then click **Insert line**

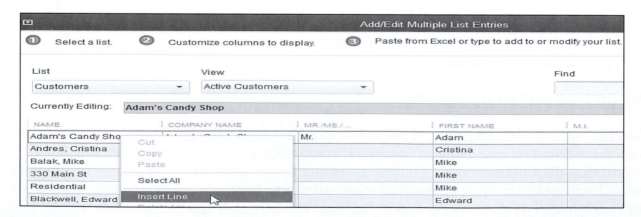

Enter the customer information for **Acme Rentals** on the blank line (or copy and paste from an existing Excel spreadsheet)

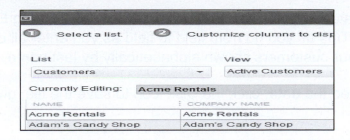

    Click the **Save Changes** button

Click **OK** on the Record(s) Saved screen; and then, click **Close** on the Add/Edit Multiple
    List Entries Screen

An alternate method of adding customers is shown below:

In the Customer Center, click the drop-down list arrow for the Excel menu, and click Import
    from Excel.
Click **No** on the Add/Edit Multiple List Entries
Complete the **Wizard**

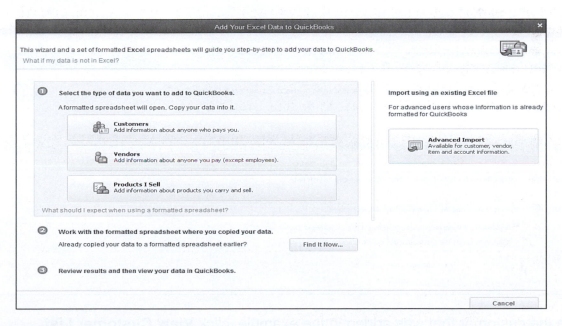

Click **Customers**
Click **Yes** on the Import textbox.
You are taken to a pre-formatted spreadsheet that is ready for data entry.
Click in the Company Name column in Row 8 on the QuickBooks screen

Enter the customer data for **Able, Sandra** (or copy it from an existing Excel document)

- Notice the Coach Tips as you go from field to field as you enter all of the customer data
- Since you want your customers shown alphabetically by last name, Display should be Able, Sandra

When you have entered the data, click the Disk icon to save the file, give the file a name and a location

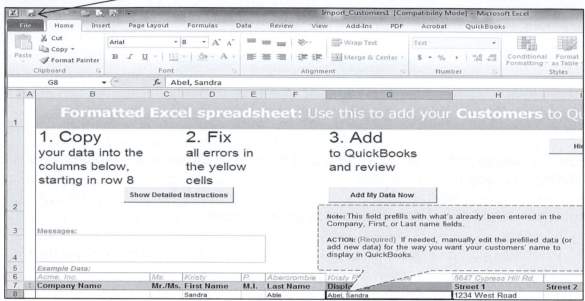

Partial Screen

Click the **Add My Data Now** button

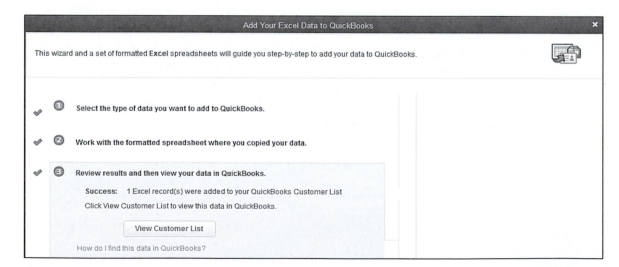

To see the customer that was added in the example, click **View Customer List**

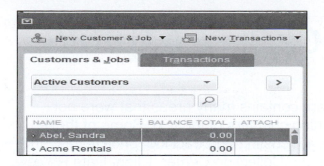

Close the **Customer Center**

MICROSOFT OUTLOOK (Information Only)

After downloading and installing QuickBooks Contact Sync for Outlook (available for no charge), you may use Microsoft Outlook to manage contact information and synchronize your contact data with QuickBooks. Synchronization simultaneously updates data in both your contact manager and QuickBooks. For example, a customer's telephone number changes and you enter the new number in your contact manager but not in QuickBooks. In addition, you enter an address change for a vendor in QuickBooks but not your contact manager. When you synchronize, the telephone number gets updated in QuickBooks and the address gets updated in your contact manager. This brings QuickBooks and your contact manager up to date with each other.

APPS (Information Only)

There are Apps available that connect directly with QuickBooks. Some of these Apps are free while others are available for a fee. When you open the App Center, you will see several Apps displayed. You will also see key categories; such as, Just Added, Mobile, Billing/Invoicing, Customer Management, Expense Management, and eCommerce. You may click on any of these categories to see the available Apps displayed. You may also click Intuit's App Center to see all of the Apps available. At the time of writing, there are tabs for Popular, New, For QuickBooks, For QuickBooks Online, Apps by Intuit, and More Apps. Once an App is downloaded and installed, it is ready for use.

If you opened the Sample Company to view the information presented in this appendix, close it.

QUICKBOOKS® FEATURES

The QuickBooks Program contains many areas that were not explored during the training chapters of the text. Some of these areas are time tracking, job costing and tracking, price levels, and notes. Features such as the Collection Center, Client Data Review, batch invoicing, the Document Center, attaching documents, and customizing the icon bar are also addressed in this appendix.

When possible, the Sample Product-Based Business, Rock Castle Construction, will be used to explore these features.

Since saving the demonstration transactions will make permanent changes to the sample company, you will <u>not</u> need to do the demonstration transactions unless they are assigned by your instructor. Since the material presented in the appendix is for illustration purposes only, memo text boxes and detailed data for entry are not included.

<u>QUICKBOOKS CALENDAR</u>

QuickBooks Calendar is an easy way to view transactions that have been entered, transactions that are due, and tasks listed on the To Do list. You may view the calendar for an entire month, a week, or a day. You may choose which types of transactions appear on the calendar. You may decide whether to show or hide detail and may double-click a transaction to view or edit it.

<u>Open the Calendar</u>

Click the **Calendar** icon to open the Calendar or click Calendar on the drop-down menu for Company

The Monthly Calendar for December, 2017 is shown

The "current" date of **15** is highlighted with the note of **Entered (40)**

- This tells you the number of transactions entered that day.

On the right-side of the Calendar is a list of **Upcoming: Next 7 days** and **Due: Past 60 days**

- This lets you know about transactions that need to be completed.

Beneath the Calendar is a list of **Transactions Entered**

- This shows you exactly what transactions were entered on December 15 (the current date).

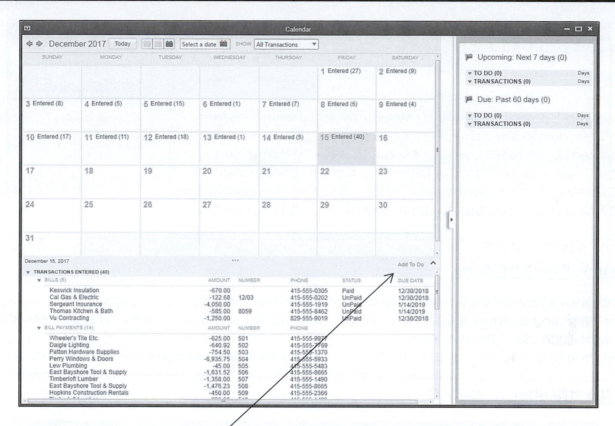

Add a To Do Note:

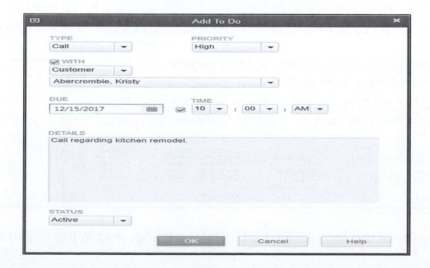

Add a To Do by clicking [Add To Do] beneath the calendar

Create a To Do Note by seletcing the **Type** and **Priority**; if appropriate, **With** and the
Name; **Due date**, and **Time**. Once the information is selected, type the note in the **Details**
section.

Click **OK** and the To Do is added to the Calendar, in the listing for Upcoming Next 7 days,
    and below the calendar

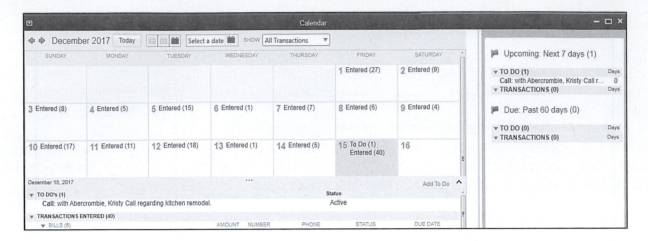

Change Calendar Views

To change the view click one of the icons at the top of the calendar

The first icon will show a daily view, which contains the same information that was shown below the monthly calendar

The middle icon will show you the five-day weekly view and will still have the information list for December 15 shown below and the Upcoming and Past Due information shown on the right side

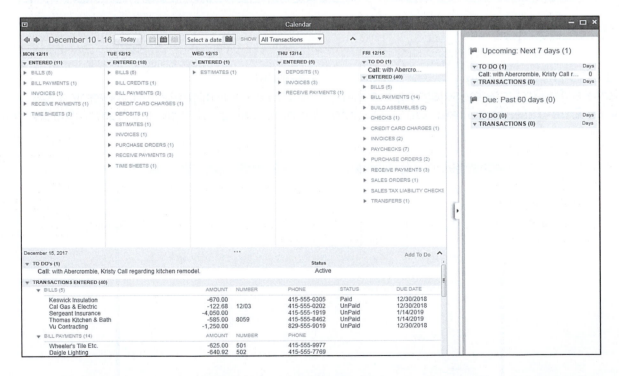

- Notice the To Do at the top of FRI 12/15, in Upcoming, and in the listing below the Calendar.

Close the Calendar

QUICKBOOKS NOTES

QuickBooks allows you to use several types of notes. These are To Do List, Customer notes, Vendor notes, Employee notes, and Time Tracking notes.

To Do List

To Do List contains notes regarding things to do. To Dos are accessed by clicking To Do List on the Company menu. The To Do List is QuickBooks version of a tickler file, which is used to remind you to do something on a particular date.

Steps to Create a To Do Note:

Click **To Do List** on the Company menu
- You will see the current To Do List and will have the opportunity to add, edit, and delete To Dos.

Click the drop-down list arrow for **To Do** and click **New To Do**

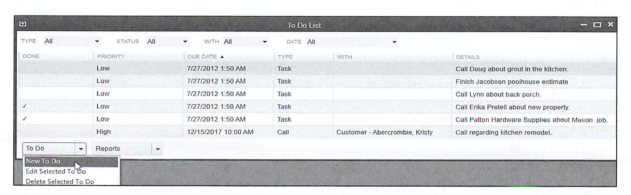

Click the **drop**-down arrow for **Type**, click the appropriate selection (in the example, Meeting is selected)
Click the drop-down arrow for **Priority**, click High, Medium, or Low (in the example, Medium is selected)
Click **With**, and click Lead, Customer, or Vendor (in the Customer is selected)
Enter the **Due date**, **Time**, and the **text** of the note

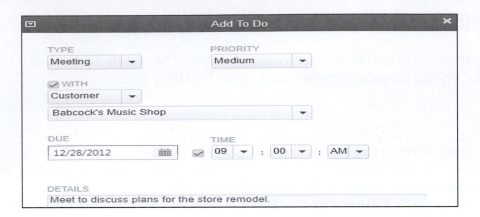

Click **OK**

- The note will be added to the list of To Do notes. Notice the note created in the Calendar earlier in the appendix.

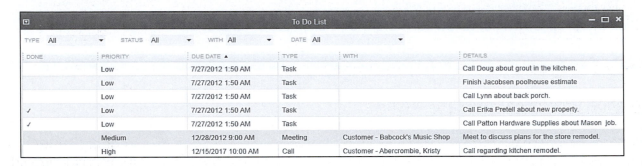

Close the **To Do List**

Customer Notes

In the Customer Center, QuickBooks provides a notepad for recording notes about each customer or job. Approximately ten windows worth of text can be displayed on each customer's notepad. You can also write on the customer notepad when viewing a customer's record or when entering a transaction. When using the customer notepad, an entry may be date stamped, To Do notes may be accessed, and the note may be printed.

Steps to Create Customer or Job Notes

Open the **Customer Center**
Click on the Customer you wish to view or add notes (Kristy Abercrombie)
To access the Customer Notepad, click the **Notes** tab
Click the **Manage Notes** button at the bottom of the list of notes, click **Add New**
Click the **Date/Time Stamp** button and QuickBooks will enter the date and time of the note (the current date and time of your computer), then type the note

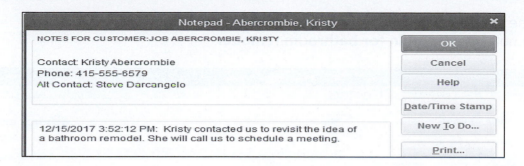

Click **OK** to save
The note will be added to her other notes and displayed in full on the right side of the notes

Exit the notepad, close the **Customer Center**

Vendor, Employee, and Other Names Notes

Vendor notes are recorded on the notepad for individual vendors in the Vendor Center. As with customer notes, this is where important conversations and product information would be recorded. The vendor notepad can be accessed from the Vendor Center. When using the vendor notepad, an entry may be date stamped, To Do notes may be accessed, and the note may be printed. Each entry on your Vendor, Employee, and Other Names lists has its own notepad where you can keep miscellaneous notes to yourself about that vendor, employee, or name. The procedures followed for vendors, employees, or other names are the same as illustrated for customers.

Notes for Time Tracking

The Timer is a separate program that is installed and works in conjunction with QuickBooks. Time Tracking will be discussed separately later in this appendix. Notes regarding the time spent working on a task are entered when using the stopwatch.

Steps to Create Notes for Time Tracking

Click the **Employees** menu and click **Enter Time**
Click **Time/Enter Single Activity**
Click the drop-down list arrow for **Name** and select the employee (Elizabeth N. Mason)
Click the drop-down list arrow for **Customer:Job** and select the customer (Kristy Abercrombie: Kitchen)
Click the drop-down list arrow for **Service Item**, click the item (Blueprint Changes)

Click in the **Notes** section of the window
Enter the note: **Revise plan for bathroom remodel**

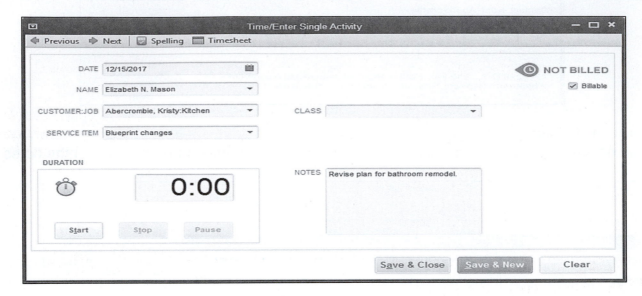

Do <u>not</u> close the Time/Enter Single Activity screen

TRACKING TIME

Many businesses bill their customers or clients for the actual amount of time they spend working for them. In this case you would be tracking billable time. When you complete the invoice to the customer, you can add the billable time to the invoice with a few clicks. In other situations, you may not want to bill for the time; but you may want to track it. For example, you may want to find out how much time you spend working on a job that was negotiated at a fixed price. This will help you determine whether or not you estimated the hours for the job correctly. Also, you may want to track the amount of time employees spend on various jobs, whether or not you bill for the time.

QuickBooks comes with a separate Timer program. You have a choice between tracking time via the Timer and then transferring the time data to QuickBooks, using the Stopwatch on the Time/Enter Single Activity window, or entering time directly into QuickBooks manually on the Weekly Timesheet window or the Time/Enter Single Activity window.

Steps to Track Time as a Single Activity

With the **Time/Enter Single Activity** screen showing the time for Elizabeth N. Mason and the blueprint changes for Kristy Abercrombie, indicate whether or not the time recorded is billable
- A check in the billable box means that this is recorded as billable time. No check means that the time is being tracked but not billed.

Click **Start** on the timer, and when finished with the work, click **Stop** on the timer

- If work is stopped at any time, you may click Pause when stopping and click Start when resuming work.

When finished, click **Stop** and **Save & Close**

Steps to Track Time on a Timesheet

Click **Employees** menu, point to **Enter Time**, and click **Use Weekly Timesheet**
Click the drop-down list arrow for **Name**, and click the name of the employee doing the work (Elizabeth N. Mason)
- Accept the date the computer provides
  - If you want to change the date of the time sheet, click the calendar button, and click the date for the time sheet.
- Any work completed as a Single Activity will appear on the time sheet
If you need to enter the information for the time period, in the Customer column, click the drop-down list arrow for **Customer:Job**
Click the name of the customer for whom work is being performed
Click the drop-down list arrow for **Service Item**, click the name of the service item
Enter any notes regarding the work
Enter the number of hours worked in the appropriate columns for the days of the week
- If the information is the same as the previous timesheet, click Copy Last Sheet
  - The information for the previous timesheet will be entered for this time period.
Indicate whether or not the hours are billable
- QuickBooks Timer records all hours as billable unless otherwise indicated.

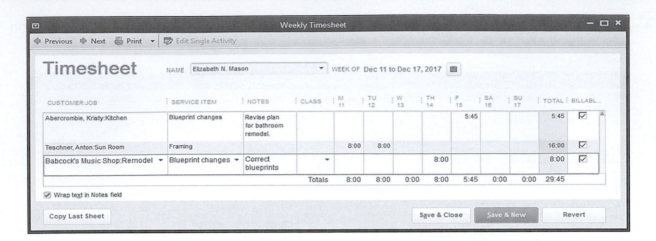

- Notice the Blueprint changes for Kristy Abercrombie:Kitchen were recorded when using the Timer and the information for Babcock's Music Shop:Remodel were added manually. The information for Teschner, Anton: Sun Room was previously added.

When the timesheet is complete, click **Save & Close**

Prepare an Invoice Using Billable Hours

Click the **Create Invoices** icon on the Home Page
Enter the name of the **Customer:Job: (Abercrombie, Kristy: Kitchen)**
The Billable Time/Costs screen appears
"**Select the outstanding billable time and costs to add to this invoice?**" should be selected, click **OK**.

- If the Billable Time/Costs screen does not appear, click the Add Time/Costs button on the Invoice Icon Bar.

Scroll through the list of Time and Costs for the customer
Click the time you wish to bill

Click **OK**

- The time will be entered on the invoice.

The invoice would be completed as previously instructed

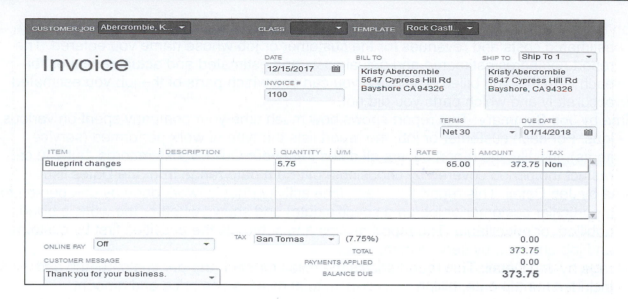

- The time clock keeps time in minutes but enters time on the invoice in tenths of an hour. For example, the 5 hours, 45 minutes billed for blueprint changes is shown as 5.75

Click **Save & Close**

JOB COSTING AND TRACKING

Many companies complete work based on a job for a customer rather than just the customer. In QuickBooks, a job is a project done for a particular customer; for example, a kitchen remodel. You must always associate a job with a customer. However, if you are only doing one job for the customer, you do not have to add a new job to the Customer:Job list. Instead, you can use the Job Info tab to track the status of the job. When you have not set up any jobs for the customer, the Job Info tab is available in the New Customer (or Edit Customer) window. You may also track several jobs for one customer.

When tracking jobs, there are several reports that may be prepared. These are listed in the Jobs, Time & Mileage section of the Report Center. These reports use the information provided when tracking the jobs to display data that may help you answer questions about how well you estimate jobs, how much time you spend on jobs, how profitable jobs are, and mileage costs for the jobs. Some, but not all, of the reports available are:

Job Profitability Summary: This report summarizes how much money your company has made or lost on each job for each customer

Job Profitability Detail: This report shows how much money your company has made to date on the customer or job whose name you entered. The report lists costs and revenues for each item you billed to the customer so you can see which parts of the job were profitable and which parts were not.

Profit & Loss by Job: Show how much money you are making or losing on each job.

Job Estimates vs. Actuals Summary: This report summarizes how accurately your company estimated job-related costs and revenues. The report compares estimated cost to actual cost and estimated revenue to actual revenue for all customers.

Job Estimates vs. Actuals Detail: This report shows how accurately your company estimated costs and revenues for the customer or job whose name you entered. The report compares estimated and actual costs and estimated and actual revenues for each item that you billed. That way, you can see which parts of the job you estimated accurately and which parts you did not.

Time by Job Summary: This report shows how much time your company spent on various jobs. For each customer or job, the report lists the type of work performed (service items). Initially, the report covers all dates from your QuickBooks records, but you can restrict the period covered by choosing a different date range from the Dates list.

Time by Job Detail: This report lists each time activity (that is, work done by one person for a particular customer or job on a specific date) and shows whether the work is billed, unbilled, or not billable. The report groups and subtotals the activities first by customer and job and then by service item.

Mileage by Job Detail: This report shows the miles for each trip per customer:job and includes the trip date, billing status, item, total miles, sales price and amount.

Steps to Create a Job for a Customer

Open the **Customer Center**
Select the customer for whom you want to add a job
- In this example, it is **Abercrombie, Kristy**
Click the **New Customer & Job** button, click **Add Job**

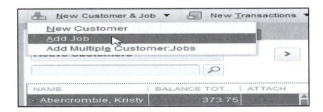

In the New Job window, enter a name for this job
Complete the New Job information:
    On the **Job Info** tab:
    - (Optional) Enter a **Job Description** and a **Job Type**
    Select a **Job Status** (Pending, Awarded, In progress, etc.) from the drop-down list.
    (Optional) Enter a **Start Date**, a **Projected End** date, and/or an **End Date** for the job

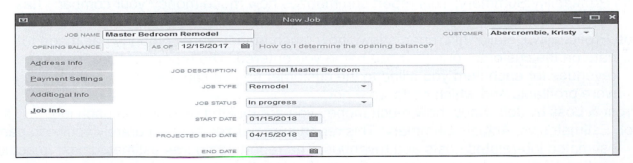

Click **OK** to record the new job.
The job is added to the customer or the Customer List

NAME	BALANCE ...	ATTACH
⋄ Abercrombie, Kristy	373.75	
⋄ Master Bedroom Remodel	0.00	
⋄ Family Room	0.00	
⋄ Kitchen	373.75	
⋄ Remodel Bathroom	0.00	

Close the **Customer Center**

Steps to Create a Bill Received for Expenses Incurred on a Job and Items Purchased for a Job

Enter the bill information as instructed in Chapter 6
Enter the date and amount of the bill
Enter the expense on the Expenses tab
- In example, the expense account **54520: Freight & Delivery** is used.
Click the drop-down list arrow for Customer:Job in the Customer:Job column on the Expenses tab
Click the appropriate Customer:Job
- In the example, the Customer:Job is **Abercrombie, Kristy: Kitchen**

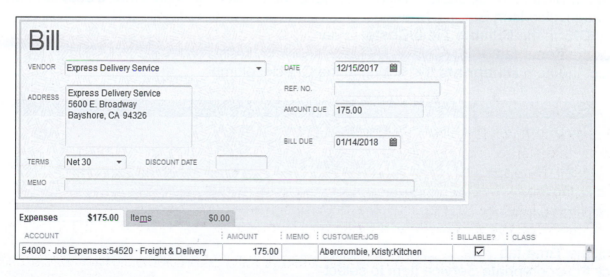

To complete a bill for both expenses and items, click the Items tab and enter the appropriate information.

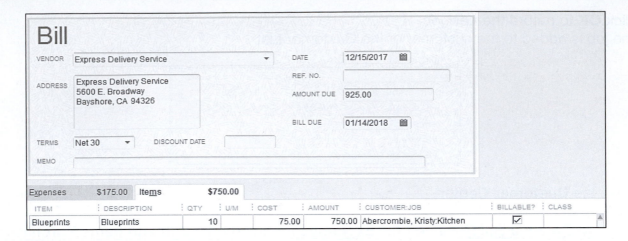

Click **Save & Close**

Steps to Create an Invoice for Items and Time Billed for a Job

Open an Invoice, select the Customer:Job
- In the example, the Customer:Job is **Abercrombie, Kristy: Kitchen**

The Billable Time/Costs screen appears

"**Select the outstanding billable time and costs to add to this invoice?**" should be selected, click **OK**.

- If the Billable Time/Costs screen does not appear, click the **Add Time/Costs** icon on the Invoice Icon Bar.

Click **OK** on the **Billable Time/Costs** screen

Click the **Items** tab

Select the Item **Blueprints** by clicking in the Check column

Click the **Time** tab

Click the appropriate Service Item to select

Click the **Expenses** tab to add the cost of the Delivery to the invoice

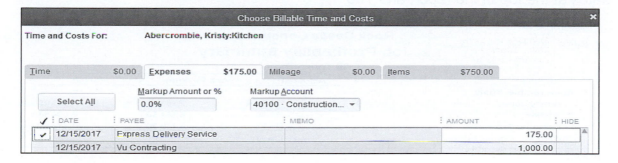

Click **OK**
Enter the Rate of **85.00** for the Blueprints
- Note this is the rate Rock Castle Construction charges customers for the time spent preparing the blueprints. The $750 was the cost of the Blueprints from Express Delivery in the earlier example.

Add the Description **Delivery** to the $175 charge for Express Delivery Service
Complete the Invoice

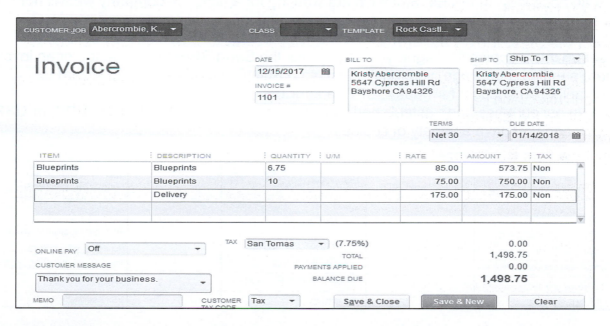

Notice that the Balance Due includes the amount for the delivery, the blueprints, and time billed for blueprints
Click **Save & Close**

Creating Reports Using Jobs and Time

Use **Report Center** or the Reports Menu
Click **Jobs, Time & Mileage**
Click the report you wish to prepare (The example shown is the Job Profitability Summary.)

If preparing the report from the menu, enter the Dates as a range or enter the **From** and **To** dates at the top of the report and Tab

Rock Castle Construction			
Job Profitability Summary			
All Transactions			
	Act. Cost	Act. Revenue	($) Diff.
Abercrombie, Kristy			
Family Room	2,150.00	2,961.05	811.05
Kitchen	3,570.00	6,664.50	3,094.50
Remodel Bathroom	5,416.23	6,749.50	1,333.27
Total Abercrombie, Kristy	11,136.23	16,375.05	5,238.82

Scroll through the report to evaluate the information
Close the report

SENDING MERCHANDISE USING QUICKBOOKS SHIPPING MANAGER

QuickBooks has a shipping manager that works in conjunction with FedEx, UPS, or USPS. In order to send merchandise to a customer, you must set up the shipping manager and have an account with FedEx. Since we are working for a fictitious company we will not do this.

To set up the Shipping Manager, you would click the **Send/Ship** tab at the top of an invoice
Before sending a package, you must complete a Shipping Manager setup wizard to establish an account for FedEx, UPS, and/or USPS.
Once an account has been established, click the down arrow on the **FedEx**, **UPS**, or **USPS** icon and you have a variety of choices:

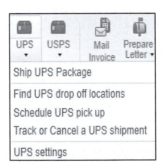

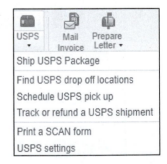

PRICE LEVELS

Price levels are created to increase or decrease inventory, non-inventory, and service item prices. For each price level you create, you assign a name and percentage of increase or decrease. You can use price levels on invoices, sales receipts, or credit memos. When you apply a price level to an item on a sales form, the adjusted price appears in the Rate column. You can assign price levels to customers and jobs. Then, whenever you use that customer and job on a sales form, the associated price level is automatically used to calculate the item price.

Create a Price Level List

From the Lists menu, choose **Price Level List**
Click the **Price Level** button, choose **New**
In the New Price Level window, enter the name of the new price level (Valued Customer in the example below)
In the area for **This price level will**, select either **increase** or **decrease** for **item prices by**
In the Percentage % field, enter the percent number by which the item price will be increased or reduced.
Indicate whether QuickBooks should round numbers.

Click **OK** to go back to the Price Levels list, and close the **Price Level List**

Apply a Price Level on an Invoice

Fill out the invoice as previously instructed (shown below)
In the Rate column, click the drop-down button

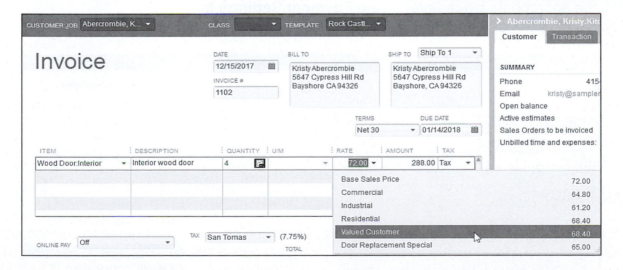

Click the drop-down list arrow for **Rate**, and click a price level to apply to the item (Valued Customer in this example)
- The amount shown next to each price level is the adjusted amount of the item
Save & Close the invoice

Associate a Price Level with a Customer/Job

Access the Customer Center, select the **Customer**
Click the **Edit Customer** icon or double-click the Customer
Click the **Payment Settings** tab
From the Price Level drop-down list, select the price level you want to associate with the
   customer

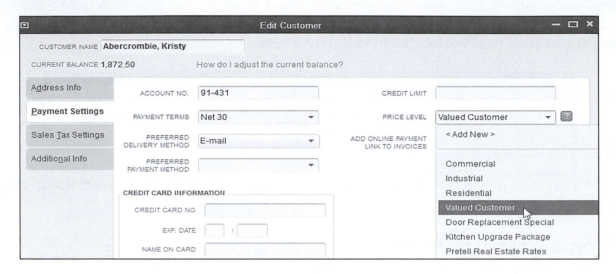

Click **OK**
To apply a Price Level to a Job, click the **Job** listed beneath the customer in the Customer
   Center
Click the **Edit Job** icon or double-click the Job
Click the appropriate **price level** on the **Payment Settings** tab
Click **Residential** as the Price Level, click **OK**

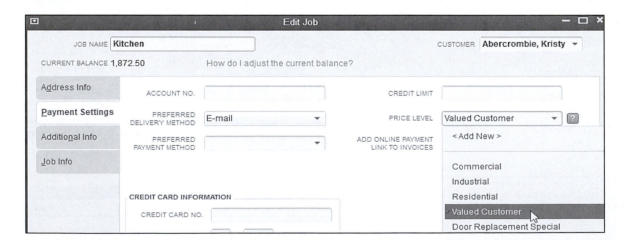

When preparing an invoice, items will automatically appear at the price level selected for
   the customer or job
To verify this, create a new invoice, and then click the drop-down list arrow for Rate

- Notice that the price for the interior wood door in the example below has been entered at the price level selected for the customer (Valued Customer).

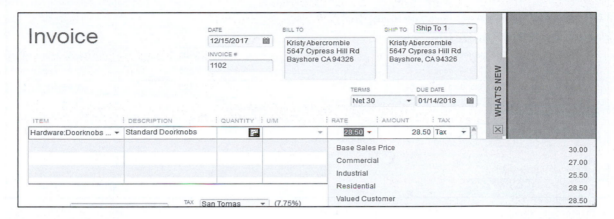

BATCH INVOICING

If you have an invoice that you want to send to multiple customers, you may create a single batch of invoices rather than an invoice for each individual customer.

Click the **Customers** menu and click **Create Batch Invoices**
Click **OK** on the "Is your customer info set up correctly?" message box
- You may add customers to the batch individually or you use a billing group you have already created.
To add customers to the batch, click the customers you want to include, then click the **Add** button

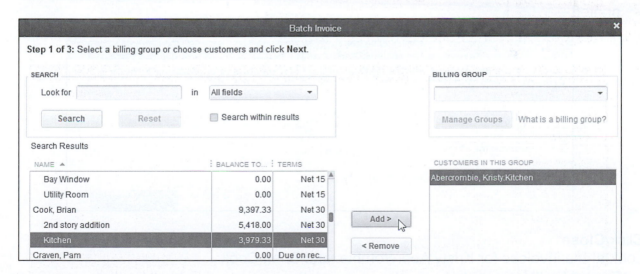

- If you were adding a group, you would click the drop-down list arrow for **Billing Group**, and click the group name.
Click **Next**, select the Items used in the invoices, enter the quantity, select the message

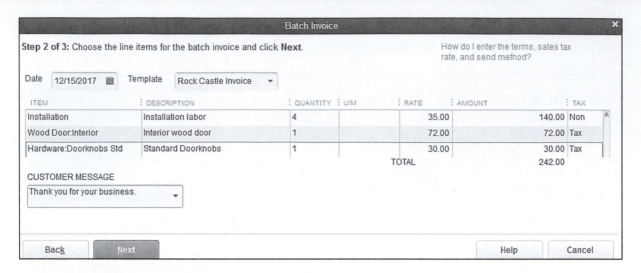

Click **Next** , review the list

Click **Create Invoices**
On the Batch Invoices Summary you will see how many invoices are being emailed or printed

Click **Close**
Look at the invoices for Kristy Abercrombie, and Brian Cook
- Except for the amount of sales tax charged, the invoices should all be the same (Brian Cook's invoice is shown below)

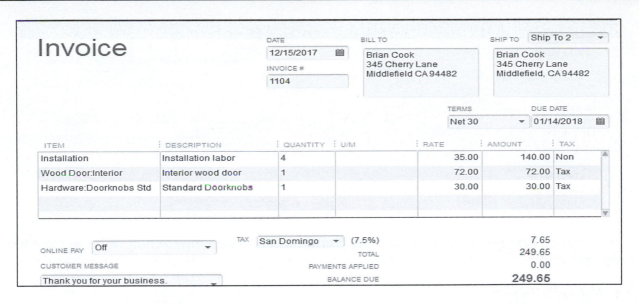

COLLECTIONS CENTER

The Customer Center contains the Collections Center that helps you manage collecting payments from your customers. The Collections Center lists overdue and almost due invoices in a single place. It enables you to send email reminders to one or several customers and tracks customer notes about your collection efforts.

Click the **Collections Center** button in the Customer Center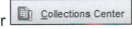
- You will see Overdue and Almost Due tabs.
- The procedures are the same for Overdue and Almost Due invoices so only the Overdue Invoice is illustrated.
- The Overdue and Almost Due information is based on the date of the transaction and the date of your computer.

Information displayed includes the Customer Name, Balance, Days Overdue, Phone, and Notes/Warnings

You may select customers and send batch email to overdue and or almost overdue customers

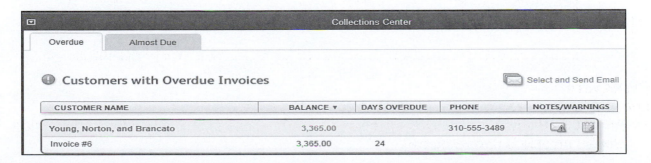

To send an email to the customers with Overdue Invoices, click the **Select and Send Email** icon

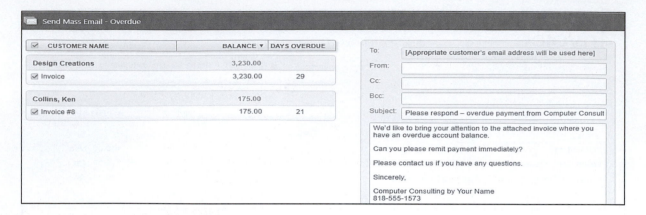

In an actual company, you would click the **Send** button to send the email with the overdue invoice attached.

DOCUMENT CENTER

The Doc Center keeps track of documents you use with QuickBooks. You may add a document from your computer, scan a document, or drag and drop a document from Outlook or Explorer to the Doc Center. The documents may then be attached to QuickBooks records such as invoices, customers, etc.

Click the **Docs** icon to open the Doc Center

To add a document from your computer, click the **Add a Document Folder** icon, find the document, click it to select, click **Open**

The document is added to the Doc Center

To scan a document, click the **Scanner** icon; place the document on your scanner; click **Scan**; on the "What do you want to scan?" screen; select the option for the type of picture or document; click **Scan**; when finished, click **Done Scanning**; give the document a name; click **OK**

To drag and drop a document on the desktop, point to the document icon, hold down the primary mouse button, drag the document to the section that says Drop documents from Outlook, your desktop, or folders here, release the mouse button

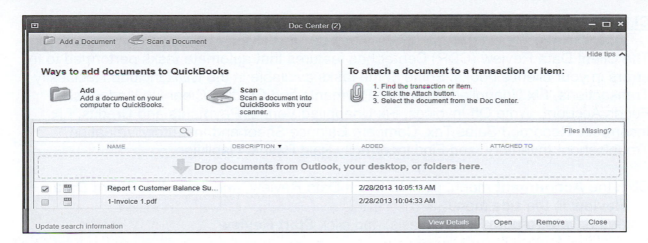

You may view the document by clicking the document, clicking the **Open** button at the bottom of the Doc Center

ATTACHED DOCUMENTS

QuickBooks allows you to attach documents to any record with a Paperclip Attach button. An attached document is a copy of your original source document. Documents may be attached when they are stored on the computer, scanned to the computer, copied by drag and drop, or in the Doc Center.

To attach a document from the Doc Center to a transaction, open and complete the business form
- In the example, a Bill from Thomas Kitchen & Bath was selected.

Click the icon for [Attach File]
Select the **Doc Center** for the document location
Click the document to select, click the **Attach** button
- In the example, a Purchase Order was selected.
The document is attached to the business document

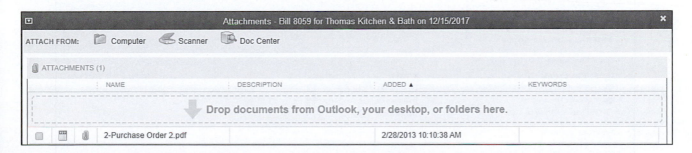

To view the attached document, simply click the **Open** button
When finished attaching documents, click **Done**

CLIENT DATA REVIEW

The Client Data Review (CDR) Center has features that automate tasks performed to fix errors in your client's books. Some of the tasks available in the CDR include Reclassify Transactions, Fix Unapplied Customer Payments and Credits, Clear Up Undeposited Funds Account, Write Off Invoices, Fix Unapplied Vendor Payments and Credits, Fix Incorrectly Recorded Sales Tax, Compare Balance Sheet and Inventory Valuation, Troubleshoot Inventory, and Find Incorrectly Paid Payroll Liabilities.

Click the **Accountant** menu, point to Client Data Review, and then click **Client Data Review** in the side menu

Enter the Date Range, Review Basis, and click **Start Review**

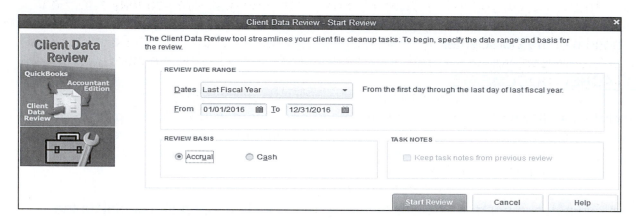

The Client Data chart appears with the tasks listed. As you work on the different review areas, you can indicate the Status of the review, add Task Notes, and add Review Notes

The Review may be printed or saved as a PDF file. You may get an Audit Trail of Review, and when finished, mark the review as complete

Close the Client Data Review when finished

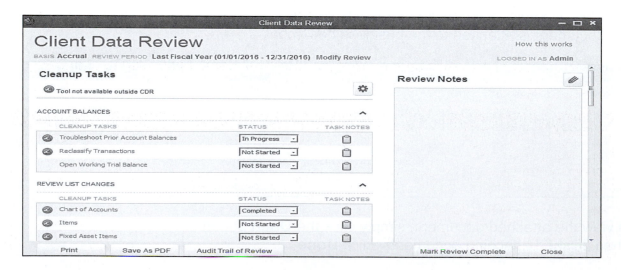

CUSTOMIZE THE ICON BAR(S)

As previously demonstrated within the text, you may use the default Left Icon Bar. If you use this, you may customize it. Both the Left and Top Icon Bars may be customized to display Centers and Commands you use frequently. If you do not use an icon or shortcut shown or wish to add an icon or shortcut that is not shown, you must customize the Icon Bar.

If you are using the Left Icon Bar, right-click anywhere on it to get Customize Shortcuts; and then click **Customize Shortcuts**

If you are using the Top Icon Bar, right-click anywhere on it to get Customize Icon Bar; and then, click the **Customize Icon Bar** button

Either method takes you to the Customize Icon Bar screen, where you may Add, Edit, Delete, or Add Separator to the Icon Bar Content. You may also choose to display icons and text or icons only. The final selection is whether to Show Search Box in Icon Bar.

To delete an icon, you would click the icon and then click the Delete button

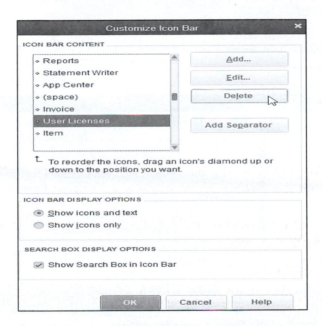

To add an icon, click the **Add** button, click the **Icon Bar Item**; if you wish to change the associated icon, click the icon you wish to use, click **OK**

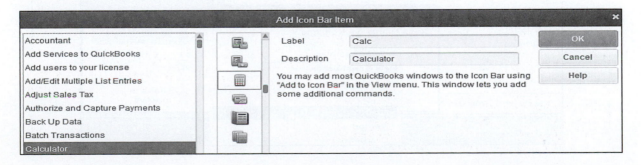

The Icon Bar no longer shows an icon for **User Licenses** but it does show the one for **Calc**

Top Icon Bar

Left Icon Bar

CLASSES

QuickBooks allows you to create classes that you assign to transactions. This lets you track account balances in various segments of your business. Reports may be prepared for the different classes you track. For example, in a construction company like Rock Castle Construction, you may want reports that itemize account balances for each construction division on your jobs. This lets you know how well you managed income and expenses. You may want to track your subcontractors by setting up a subset of the construction divisions; i.e. Rough Electrical and Finish Electrical to distinguish one segment of construction from the other.

To use class tracking, you must select the feature on the Company Preferences tab for Accounting Preferences.

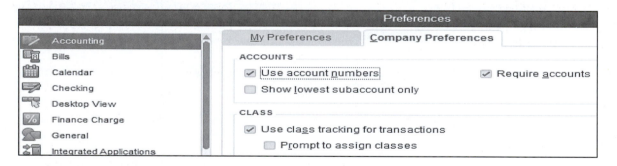

Click **Class List** on the List menu
Click the **Class** button, and then click **New Class**; or use the Ctrl + N shortcut
To complete the following example, enter **Advertising** as the Class Name
Click **Subclass of**, and then click **New Construction**

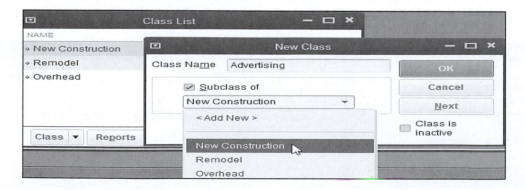

Click **OK** to save the New Class, close the Class List
To use class tracking, every income and expense transaction should have a class assigned. Do this by clicking the **Class** drop-down list and choose a class for every item. For example, work on Kristy Abercrombie's Kitchen should be assigned a class of Remodel for each transaction.

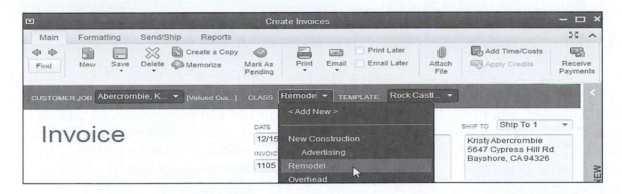

Several reports, such as, a Balance Sheet by Class and a Profit & Loss by Class, etc. are available when working with classes. The example below shows the Construction income section of Rock Castle Construction's Profit & Loss by Class report. This report shows the income earned, the cost of goods sold, and expenses incurred for each account categorized by class; i.e. New Construction, Remodel, Overhead, and Unclassified. The report includes a Totals column so you can see the total amounts for each account and each section of the report.

	New Construction	Remodel	Overhead	Unclassified	TOTAL
12:21 PM					
12/15/17					
Accrual Basis					
Rock Castle Construction					
Profit & Loss by Class					
January 1 through December 15, 2017					
▼ Ordinary Income/Expense					
▼ Income					
▼ 40100 · Construction Income					
40110 · Design Income	3,152.74	33,576.51	0.00	947.50	37,676.75
40130 · Labor Income	52,696.44	156,835.23	0.00	280.00	209,811.67
40140 · Materials Income	68,401.16	51,519.51	0.00	232.50	120,153.17
40150 · Subcontracted Labor Income	58,492.30	24,218.05	0.00	0.00	82,710.35
40199 · Less Discounts given	0.00	−48.35	0.00	0.00	−48.35
40100 · Construction Income - Other	0.00	0.00	0.00	0.00	0.00
Total 40100 · Construction Income	182,742.64	266,100.95	0.00	1,460.00	450,303.59

QUICKBOOKS STATEMENT WRITER

The QuickBooks Statement Writer (QSW) allows you to create customized financial reports from a QuickBooks company file. The QuickBooks Statement Writer contains a library of templates that may be used for statements and supporting documents or you may create your own template. The QSW uses data directly from the QuickBooks company file. You can set preferences, formats, and styles for all of your reports. You may combine accounts and subaccounts automatically or by specification. Supporting documents may also be prepared using the same look as the one used in statements.

To use this feature, click **Statement Writer** in the icon bar

- There may be a fairly lengthy and detailed install update required in order to use the Statement Writer.

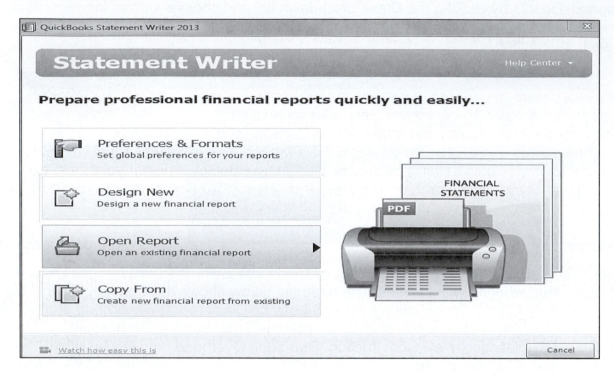

When QuickBooks Statement Writer is on the screen, you click the different buttons to access and design your reports.

QUICKBOOKS®
ONLINE FEATURES

QuickBooks uses the Internet as an integral part of the program. Subscribers to the Payroll Services can receive online updates to tax tables and forms. Online banking and vendor payments can be performed within the program. You can order supplies, obtain product support, access training resources, find a QuickBooks expert in your area, get suggestions for resources for your business, and access Live Community (where you may post questions, give advice, and participate in Webinars).

In addition to the included online items, there are several online subscription programs that may be used in conjunction with QuickBooks. These include Payroll Services; Intuit PaymentNetwork; QuickBooks Connect for online and mobile access; Website activities, such as, domain names, web hosting, web site design, e-commerce, and online marketing; Online data protect and backup services; Merchant Services for processing credit card payments, mobile payments, and point of sale systems; Payment Solutions for e-check processing, e-mail marketing, Web mail; QuickBooks credit card; bill pay, and others.

Use QuickBooks' App Center to access free and for fee Apps that work with QuickBooks and bring together over 135 applications that companies have created to integrate their software products with QuickBooks Premier and QuickBooks Enterprise Solutions.

Intuit makes frequent changes to the applications, programs, and services that are available to work with or through QuickBooks. This appendix explores some of those features that were available at the time of writing.

Since many of the features listed above, may not be completed unless you have an active Intuit Account and subscribe to the services, they cannot be illustrated. Thus, this Appendix will explore only some of the online options listed above. And, as with the other appendices, you should just read the information presented and not try to complete what is illustrated.

INTUIT AND THE INTERNET

At Intuit's Web site you may get up-to-date information about QuickBooks and other products by Intuit. You can access the Intuit Web site at www.Intuit.com through your browser.

CONNECTING TO INTUIT INTERNET IN QUICKBOOKS®

Before connecting to Intuit's Web Site using QuickBooks, you must have the QuickBooks program and a company open. In addition, you must have a modem for your computer, and the modem must be connected to a telephone line or cable. Once the modem is connected and QuickBooks and a company are open, you may establish your Internet connection. QuickBooks has a step-by-step tutorial that will help you do this. Clicking Internet Connection Setup on the Help menu allows you to identify an internet connection and complete the setup. The first screen you see informs QuickBooks of your choice for your Internet connection. You may tell QuickBooks that you have an Internet connection that you identify; that you plan to use your computer's Internet connection; or that you want to sign up for an Internet account with limited access.

To Use Other Internet Connection

Click the **Help** menu, click **Internet Connection Setup**
Click **Use the following connection**, click **Other Internet connection**, and click the **Next**
   button at the bottom of the screen

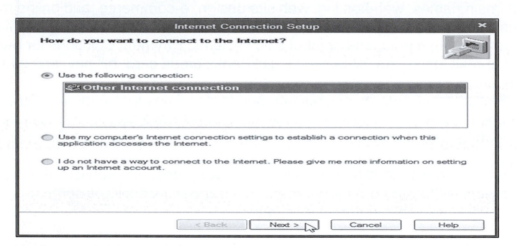

Verify the information provided, click the **Done** button at the bottom of the screen

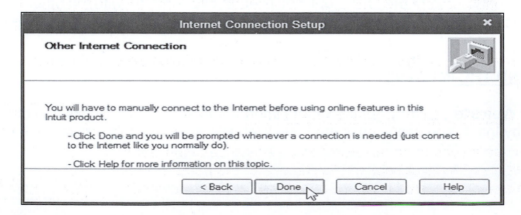

To Use a Computer's Internet Connection

If you have a direct Internet connection, select **Use my computer's Internet connection settings to establish a connection when this application accesses the Internet**, click the **Next** button at the bottom of the screen

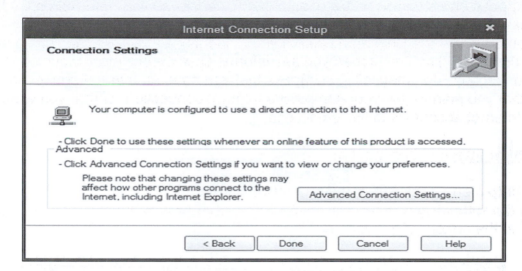

Verify the information; click the **Done** button at the bottom of the screen

To Establish an Internet Provider and Connection

If you do not have an Internet provider, click **I do not have a way to connect to the Internet. Please give me more information on setting up an Internet account** Click **Next**

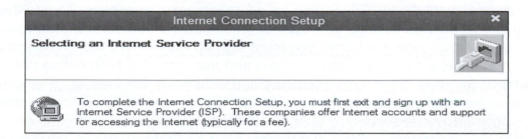

The screen will tell you that you must sign up with an Internet Service Provider. Click **Done**

ACCESS QUICKBOOKS' ONLINE FEATURES

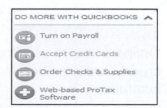

When you see a section on the Home Page or the Left Icon Bar that says "Do More with QuickBooks," clicking one of the items will take you to the areas requested if you have a direct Internet connection.

For example, Order Checks & Supplies in the Do More with QuickBooks section of the Home Page was clicked, QuickBooks connected to the Web and brought up a screen describing QuickBooks Checks and Supplies designed to work with QuickBooks that may be ordered.

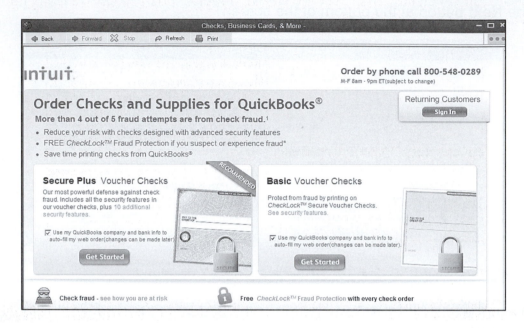

Apps are another example of online access through QuickBooks and were discussed in Appendix A.

ONLINE BANKING AND PAYMENTS

Online banking and payment services are offered through QuickBooks in conjunction with a variety of financial institutions. This is also called online account access. To use this, you must apply for this service through your financial institution. If you bank with or make payments to more than one institution, you must sign up with each institution separately. Most banks will charge a fee for online services and may not offer both online banking and online payment services. Some institutions provide enhanced services, such as allowing QuickBooks to transfer money between two online accounts. With the online banking service, you can download electronic statements from your financial institution or credit card provider into QuickBooks. Once statements have been downloaded, you can see what transactions have cleared your account, find out your current balance, and add transactions that have been processed but have not been entered in QuickBooks.

Online Banking

Online account access allows you to download transactions from your financial institution or credit card provider. You can also transfer money online and send e-mail to your financial institution.

To use the online banking services for account access or payment, you need access to the Internet and an account at a participating financial institution. You must also apply for the service through QuickBooks or through a participating financial service. To see a list of participating financial institutions, click the Banking menu, point to Online Banking, and click **Participating Financial Institutions**

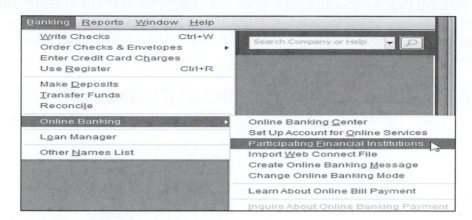

QuickBooks connects to the Internet and a list of banks appears

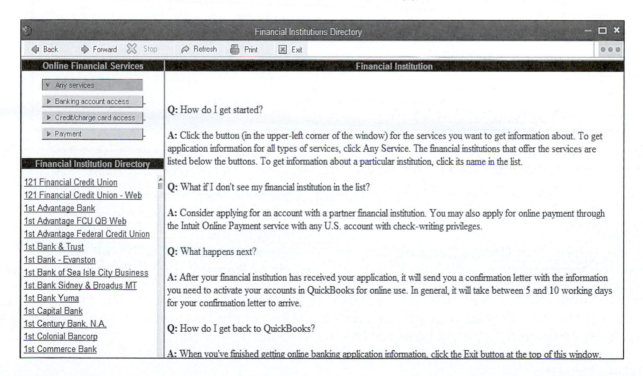

In order to provide security and confidentiality in online services, QuickBooks uses state-of-the-art encryption and authentication security features. All of your online communications with your financial institution require a Personal Identification Number (PIN) or password, which only you possess. You may also use passwords within QuickBooks.

Set Up Online Banking

Since we do not have an actual company, we are unable to setup an online banking account. However, to create an online banking account for your own business, click the **Banking** menu, point to **Online Banking**, and click **Set Up Account for Online Services**. Or edit the Checking (bank) account, and click the button for **Set Up Online Services**. Complete the Online Setup Interview. Once you have setup online banking, the Checking and any other bank accounts that are setup for online banking will have a second screen for Online Services that is accessible when you edit the account.

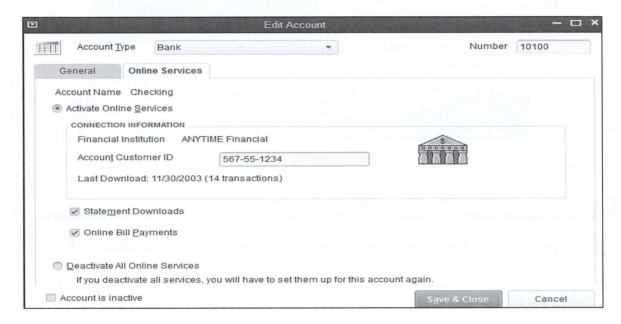

Using Online Banking

Online banking allows you to download current information from and send messages to your financial institution. This can include transactions, balances, online messages, and transfer of funds. To use online banking, click **Banking** on the menu bar, point to Online Banking, and click **Online Banking Center**. You may view and work with your online banking transactions in either the Side-by-Side mode or Register mode. The screen below shows the Side-by-Side Mode.

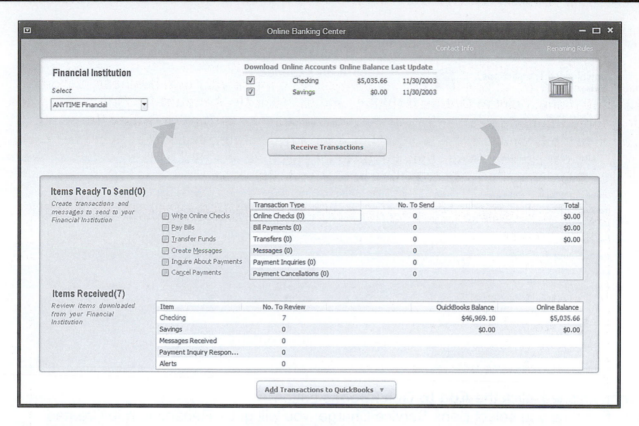

In the section for **Items Received**, Checking is marked with 7 items to Review. Click **Checking**. Once the download is complete, QuickBooks will match downloaded transactions to those in your register and note any unmatched transactions so that they may be entered into your register.

The downloaded transactions shown lists the transactions that occurred since your last download and any transactions that were not matched from previous downloads.
To record the transactions, click each individual item, and mark it accordingly.
For example, click the **11/30/03** transaction labeled as a **Bank Service Charge**
- *Note: Even though the year for the sample company is 2016, many of the transactions have the year 2003. In the example, the word Service is misspelled Severervice.*
Click the drop-down list arrow and select **Great Statewide Bank** as the payee
Click the drop-down list arrow and select **60600 Bank Service Charges** for the account

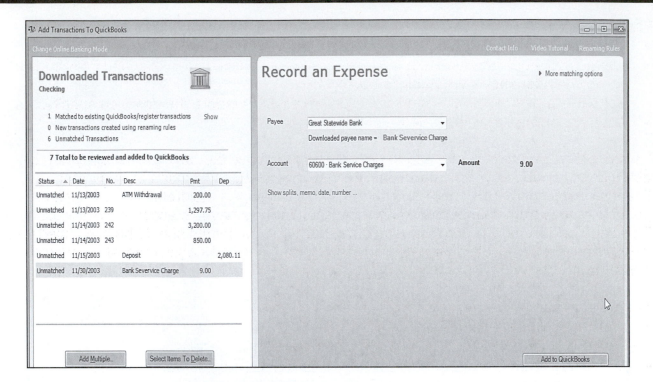

When finished, click the **Add to QuickBooks** button

The first time you select Bank Service Charge, you will get a Renaming rule Created message box notifying you that future Bank Service Charges will automatically be renamed to Great Statewide Bank.

The transaction is no longer shown on the Downloaded Transactions list

Click the **Finish Later** button to exit and, if shown, click **Yes** on the Save and Close screen confirming that all matched transactions will be in your register.

Verify that the service charge was deducted from the checking account by opening the checking account register.

Online Payments

If your financial institution provides this service, you may use the online payment services to create online payment instructions for one or more payments and then send it electronically. You may schedule a payment to arrive on a certain date, inquire about online payments, and cancel them if need be. You can record and pay your bills at the same time, all from within QuickBooks. Online banking through QuickBooks uses state-of-the-art encryption technology and requires a PIN to send transactions. You can use online payment with any U.S. bank account with check-writing privileges.

With online payment you can:

- Pay bills without writing checks or going to the post office.
- Attach additional information to the payment (such as invoice number and invoice date) so your vendor knows which bill to apply it to.
- Schedule a payment in advance, to be delivered on or before the date you specify.
- Apply for online payment services online.

To use online payments, you need to set up a payee. Once the payee is set up, you may either send an electronic funds transfer (EFT) to the payee's institution or have your financial institution print a check and send it to the payee. An electronic funds transfer deducts money from your account and transfers it into the payee's account electronically. This usually takes one or two business days; however, payments should be scheduled four days before they are due. This is called lead time and must be considered when sending online payments.

You may prepare an online payment by

- Writing a check in Write Checks
- Paying a bill in Pay Bills
- Or clicking Write Checks or Pay Bills in the Online Banking Center
- Prepare the check or bill using these methods the same way you always do, except that you designate the transaction as an online transaction and send the payment instructions to your financial institution.

For a check, click **Online Payment** and record the check as usual.

When using Pay Bills to pay your bill, click the drop-down list arrow for **Method**, click **Online Bank Pmt**

The both the Online Check and the Bill Payment will now show in the Online Banking Center Send List

Items Ready To Send (2)		Transaction Type	No. To Send	Total
Create transactions and messages to send to your Financial Institution	Write Online Checks	Online Checks (1)	1	$75.00
	Pay Bills	Bill Payments (1)	1	$250.00

QUICKBOOKS BILLING SOLUTIONS

QuickBooks offers an invoice e-mail service that will instantly e-mail easy-to-read PDF files of invoices, statements, estimates, and payment reminders from QuickBooks. It also has a mailing service that will print, fold, and mail invoices to customers. In addition, payment reminders, e-mail tracking, and customer online payment options are also included. Customers can pay invoices and statements online by entering their credit card information in the Customer Account Center, which is a secure Web site hosted by Intuit. Customers may view their account information online. Charges are processed through the QuickBooks Merchant Services. This requires signing up for the optional QuickBooks Billing Solutions and QuickBooks Merchant Service.

QUICKBOOKS MERCHANT SERVICES AND INTUIT PAYMENT SOLUTIONS

QuickBooks Merchant Services allows your business to accept credit cards from customers. As a subscriber to QuickBooks Merchant Services, credit card charges are processed and deposited into your designated bank account. Everything needed to process credit cards is built right into QuickBooks. This enables you to offer customers more payment options, process credit cards in QuickBooks or remotely. Credit card payments may be entered manually into QuickBooks or by swiping the credit card by using a card reader purchased separately. You can also process recurring charges and bill customers online.

You may set up automatic recurring charges and integrate with Billing Solutions so customers can also pay online. QuickBooks credit card processing also enables credit card fees to be included on the Make Deposits window.

E-Checks may be scanned or accepted by telephone if you have a subscription to Intuit Payment Solutions. A subscription to Check Solution for QuickBooks allows you to deposit checks directly from QuickBooks.

Enter credit card transactions

When you are enrolled in QuickBooks Merchant Services and a transaction is processed for a credit card payment, sales receipt, or customer payment, it is recorded as usual. The checkbox for "Process payment when saving" should be checked.

> ☐ Process VISA payment when saving

When receiving payments by credit card, enter the payment information as usual. Pmt. Method should be Master Card, Visa, or another credit card. Click the checkbox for Process Master Card or Visa payment when saving

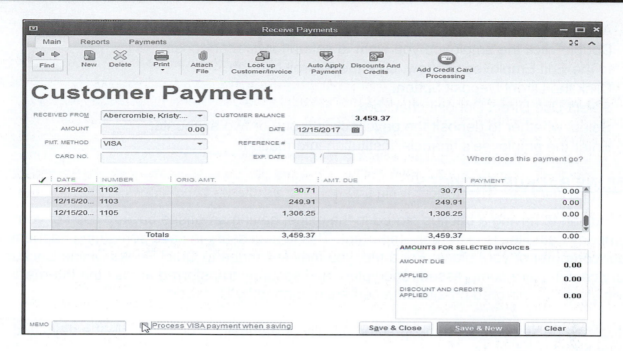

You may also sign up for and attach a credit card reader that will enable you to swipe a card and have the transaction entered directly into QuickBooks.

Once a credit card transaction has been entered, you will get a notice of approval.

In addition, you may download transaction information directly into QuickBooks using an internet-accessible mobile device.

Automatic Credit Card Billing

QuickBooks Merchant Account Services also has an Automatic Credit Card Billing feature that allows you to bill a customer's credit card a fixed amount at regular intervals for recurring services, such as membership fees, insurance premiums, or subscriptions. Prior to setting up a recurring charge, you must have written authorization from your customer.

DIRECT DEPOSIT

Rather than mail or give paychecks to your employees, you may sign up for Direct Deposit if you have a subscription to QuickBooks Payroll. You will go to the Employees menu and click My Payroll Service and Activate Direct Deposit. Some of the information you need to do this is your federal employer identification number, the company's legal name and address, your financial institution routing and account numbers, and your QuickBooks registration number.

You also need to set up those employees who wish to receive their checks by direct deposit. This is done by:

- Accessing the Employee Center.
- Double-click the employee you want to set up for direct deposit.
- In the Edit Employee window, click the Payroll Info tab.
- Click the Direct Deposit button.
- Select Use Direct Deposit checkbox.
- Select whether to deposit the paycheck into one or two accounts.
- Enter the employee's financial institution information.

ONLINE BACKUP SERVICES

In addition to having a backup stored in the office, having an offsite backup copy of your company data files is extremely important. This is necessary in case something happens to your computer or your office. For a fee, you may subscribe to QuickBooks Online Backup Service. Files are compressed, encrypted, and securely transferred across the Internet then stored at mirrored off-site data centers managed by IT experts.

Files may be selected for backup automatically or manually. You schedule the days and times for your backups.

When backing up data files online, the same procedure is followed as instructed in Chapter 1. The only change is that you click Online backup rather than Local backup.

OTHER INTUIT MARKETING TOOLS

Intuit provides several marketing tools. Some of which are:

Intuit Websites: Create your own Website by customizing a professionally-designed website or have a Website designed for you, create a personalized domain name, use email addresses that work with your domain name, website hosting, site traffic reports, and other web services that are provided depending upon the plan selected.

WebListings allows you to enter your business information; then, WebListings will submit it to online business directories.

Web Advertising enables you to promote your business with an ad that appears next to search results related to your business.

Index